LAW, LEGISLATIO

This is Hayek's major statement o\. ,
Marx, Freud, logical positivism and political egalitarianism, ⊓ayₑₖ
shows that the naive application of scientific methods to culture
and education has been harmful and misleading, creating superstition and error rather than an age of reason and culture.

Law, Legislation and Liberty combines all three volumes of
Hayek's comprehensive study on the basic principles of the
political order of a free society. *Rules and Order* deals with the
basic conceptions necessary for a critical analysis of prevailing
theories of justice and of conditions which a constitution securing
personal liberty would have to satisfy. *The Mirage of Social Justice*
presents a critical analysis of the theories of utilitarianism, legal
positivism and 'social justice'. *The Political Order of a Free People*
demonstrates that the democratic ideal is in danger of miscarrying
due to confusions of egalitarianism and democracy, erroneous
assumptions that there can be moral standards without moral discipline, and that tradition can be ignored in proposals for restructuring society.

F.A. Hayek became both a Doctor of Law and a Doctor of Political Science at the University of Vienna. He was made the first
Director of the Austrian Institute of Economic Research and in
1931 was appointed to a chair at the London School of Economics. In 1950 he went to the University of Chicago as Professor
of Social and Moral Sciences and then became Professor of Economics at the Albert-Ludwigs-Universität of Frieburg and Professor
Emeritus in 1967. He was also a Fellow of the British Academy
and was awarded a Nobel Memorial Prize in Economics in 1974.
Hayek died in 1992.

LAW, LEGISLATION AND LIBERTY

*A new statement of the liberal principles
of justice and political economy*

Volume 1
RULES AND ORDER

Volume 2
THE MIRAGE OF SOCIAL JUSTICE

Volume 3
THE POLITICAL ORDER
OF A FREE PEOPLE

F. A. Hayek

 Routledge
Taylor & Francis Group

LONDON AND NEW YORK

Vol. 1 *Rules and Order* first published 1973
Vol. 2 *The Mirage of Social Justice* first published 1976
Vol. 3 *The Political Order of a Free People* first published 1979

First published in one volume with corrections and revised preface
in 1982 by Routledge & Kegan Paul Ltd.

Reprinted 1993, 1998
by Routledge
2 Park Square, Milton Park, Abingdon, Oxon, OX14 4RN

Routledge is an imprint of the Taylor & Francis Group

© F. A. Hayek 1973, 1976, 1979, 1982

Transferred to Digital Printing 2003

Printed and bound by Antony Rowe Ltd, Eastbourne

British Library Cataloguing in Publication Data
A catalogue record for this book is available from the British
Library

ISBN 0-415-09868-8

CONTENTS

Volume 1
RULES AND ORDER

v

CONTENTS

CONTENTS

CONTENTS

Volume 2
THE MIRAGE OF SOCIAL JUSTICE

CONTENTS

CONTENTS

CONTENTS

Volume 3
THE POLITICAL ORDER OF A
FREE PEOPLE

CONTENTS

CONTENTS

CONTENTS

CONSOLIDATED PREFACE
TO ONE-VOLUME EDITION

At last this work can appear in the form it was intended to take when I started on it nearly twenty years ago. Half way through this period, when a first draft was nearly completed, a weakening of my powers, which fortunately proved to be temporary, made me doubt whether I should ever be able to complete it and led me to publish in 1973 a fully completed part of what were to become three separate volumes. When a year later I found my powers returning I discovered that various circumstances made substantial revisions necessary of even those further parts of the draft which I had thought to be in fairly finished state. As I explained in the preface to the second volume, which appeared in 1976, the chief reason was my dissatisfaction with that central chapter which gave that volume its sub-title *The Mirage of Social Justice*. This account I had better repeat here:

> I had devoted to this subject an enormous chapter in which I had tried to show for a large number of instances that what was claimed as demanded by 'social justice' could not be justice because the underlying consideration (one could hardly call it a principle) was not capable of general application. The point I was then mainly anxious to demonstrate was that people would never be able to agree on what 'social justice' required, and that any attempt to determine remunerations according to what it was thought was demanded by justice would make the market unworkable. I have now become convinced, however, that the people who habitually employ the phrase simply do not know themselves what they mean by it and just use it as an assertion that a claim is justified without giving a reason for it.
>
> In my earlier efforts to criticize the concept I had all the time the feeling that I was hitting into a void and I finally attempted, what in such cases one ought to do in the first

instance, to construct as good a case in support of the ideal of 'social justice' as was in my power. It was only then that I perceived that the Emperor had no clothes on, that is, that the term 'social justice' was entirely empty and meaningless. As the boy in Hans Christian Andersen's story, I 'could not see anything, because there was nothing to be seen.' The more I tried to give it a definite meaning the more it fell apart—the intuitive feeling of indignation which we undeniably often experience in particular instances proved incapable of being justified by a general rule such as the conception of justice demands. But to demonstrate that a universally used expression which to many people embodies a quasi-religious belief has no content whatever and serves merely to insinuate that we ought to consent to a demand of some particular group is much more difficult than to show that a conception is wrong.

In these circumstances I could not content myself to show that particular attempts to achieve 'social justice' would not work, but had to explain that the phrase meant nothing at all, and that to employ it was either thoughtless or fraudulent. It is not pleasant to have to argue against a superstition which is held most strongly by men and women who are often regarded as the best in our society, and against a belief that has become almost the new religion of our time (and in which many of the ministers of old religion have found their refuge), and which has become the recognized mark of the good man. But the present universality of that belief proves no more the reality of its object than did the universal belief in witches or the philosopher's stone. Nor does the long history of the conception of distributive justice understood as an attribute of individual conduct (and now often treated as synonymous with 'social justice') prove that it has any relevance to the positions arising from the market process. I believe indeed that the greatest service I can still render to my fellow men would be if it were in my power to make them ashamed of ever again using that hollow incantation. I felt it my duty at least to try and free them of that incubus which today makes fine sentiments the instruments for the destruction of all values of a free civilization—and to try this at the risk of gravely offending many the strength of whose moral feelings I respect.

The present version of the central chapter of this volume has in consequence of this history in some respects a slightly different character from the rest of the volume which in all essentials was completed six or seven years earlier. There was, on the one hand, nothing I could positively demonstrate but my task was to put the burden of proof squarely on those who employ the term. On the other hand, in re-writing that chapter I no longer had that easy access to adequate library facilities which I had when I prepared the first draft of this volume. I have in consequence not been able in that chapter systematically to take account of the more recent literature on the topics I discussed as I had endeavoured to do in the rest of this volume. In one instance the feeling that I ought to justify my position *vis-à-vis* a major recent work has also contributed to delay the completion of this volume. But after careful consideration I have come to the conclusion that what I might have to say about John Rawls' *A Theory of Justice* (1972) would not assist in the pursuit of my immediate object because the differences between us seemed more verbal than substantial. Though the first impression of readers may be different, Rawls' statement which I quote later in this volume (p. 100) seems to me to show that we agree on what is to me the essential point. Indeed, as I indicate in a note to that passage, it appears to me that Rawls has been widely misunderstood on this central issue.

The preface to the third volume, which ultimately appeared in 1979, gives a similar account of the further development that also had better be repeated here:

Except for what are now the last two chapters, most of it was in fairly finished form as long ago as the end of 1969 when indifferent health forced me to suspend the efforts to complete it. It was then, indeed, doubt whether I would ever succeed in doing so which made me decide to publish separately as volume 1 the first third of what had been intended to form a single volume, because it was in completely finished form. When I was able to return to systematic work I discovered, as I have explained in the preface to volume 2, that at least one chapter of the original draft of that part required complete re-writing.

Of the last third of the original draft only what was

intended to be the last chapter (chapter 18) had not been completed at the time when I had discontinued work. But while I believe I have now more or less carried out the original intention, over the long period which has elapsed my ideas have developed further and I was reluctant to send out what inevitably must be my last systematic work without at least indicating in what direction my ideas have been moving. This has had the effect that not only what was meant to be the concluding chapter contains a good deal of, I hope, improved re-statements of arguments I have developed earlier, but that I found it necessary to add an Epilogue which expresses more directly the general view of moral and political evolution which has guided me in the whole enterprise. I have also inserted as chapter 16 a brief recapitulation of the earlier argument.

There were also other causes which have contributed to delay completion. As I had hesitated whether I ought to publish volume 2 without taking full account of the important work of John Rawls, *A Theory of Justice* (Oxford, 1972), two new important books in the field have since appeared which, if I were younger, I should feel I must fully digest before completing my own survey of the same kind of problems: Robert Nozik, *Anarchy, State and Utopia* (New York, 1974) and Michael Oakeshott, *On Human Conduct* (Oxford, 1975). Rightly or wrongly I finally decided that if I made an effort fully to absorb their argument before concluding my own exposition, I would probably never do this. But I regard it as my duty to tell the younger readers that they cannot fully comprehend the present state of thought on these issues unless they make that effort which I must postpone until I have completed the statement of the conclusions at which I had arrived before I became acquainted with these works.

The long period over which the present work has been growing also had the effect that I came to regard it as expedient to change my terminology on some points on which I should warn the reader. It was largely the growth of cybernetics and the related subjects of information and system theory which persuaded me that expression other than those which I habitually used may be more readily comprehensible to the contemporary reader. Though I still like and occasionally use the term 'spontaneous order', I agree that 'self-generating order' or 'self-organizing structures' are sometimes more precise and unambiguous and therefore frequently use them instead of the former term. Similarly, instead of 'order', in conformity with today's predominant usage, I occasionally now use 'system'. Also 'information' is clearly often preferable to where I usually spoke of 'knowledge', since the former clearly refers to the knowledge of particular facts rather than theoretical knowledge to which plain 'knowledge' might be thought to refer. Finally, since 'constructivist' appears to some people still to carry the commendatory connotation derived from the adjective 'constructive', I felt it advisable, in order clearly to bring out the deprecatory sense in which I use that term (significantly of Russian origin) to employ instead the, I am afraid, still more ugly term 'constructivistic'. I should perhaps add that I feel some regret that I have not had the courage consistently to employ certain other neologisms I had suggested, such as 'cosmos', 'taxis', 'nomos', 'thesis', 'catallaxy' and 'demarchy'. But what the exposition has thereby lost in precision it will probably have gained in ready intelligibility.

Perhaps I should also again remind the reader that the present work was never intended to give an exhaustive or comprehensive exposition of the basic principles on which a society of free man could be maintained, but was rather meant to fill the gaps which I discovered after I had made an attempt to restate, in *The Constitution of Liberty*, for the contemporary reader the traditional doctrines of classical liberalism in a form suited to contemporary problems and thinking. It is for this reason a much less complete, much more difficult and personal but, I hope, also more original work than the former. But it is definitely supplementary to and not a substitute for it. To the non-specialist reader I would therefore recommend reading *The Constitution of Liberty* before he proceeds to the more detailed discussion or particular examination of problems to which I have attempted solutions in these volumes. But they are intended to explain why I still regard what have now long been treated as antiquated beliefs as greatly superior to any alternative doctrines which have recently found more favour with the public.

The reader will probably gather that the whole work has

been inspired by a growing apprehension about the direction
in which the political order of what used to be regarded as the
most advanced countries is tending. The growing conviction,
for which the book gives the reasons, that this threatening
development towards a totalitarian state is made inevitable by
certain deeply entrenched defects of construction of the
generally accepted type of 'democratic' government has
forced me to think through alternative arrangements. I
would like to repeat here that, though I profoundly believe
in the basic principles of democracy as the only effective
method which we have yet discovered of making peaceful
change possible, and am therefore much alarmed by the
evident growing disillusionment about it as a desirable *method*
of government—much assisted by the increasing abuse
of the word to indicate supposed *aims* of government—
I am becoming more and more convinced that we
are moving towards an impasse from which political
leaders will offer to extricate us by desperate means.

When the present volume leads up to a proposal of basic
alteration of the structure of democratic government, which at
this time most people will regard as wholly impractical, this is
meant to provide a sort of intellectual stand-by equipment for
the time, which may not be far away, when the breakdown of
the existing institutions becomes unmistakable and when I
hope it may show a way out. It should enable us to preserve
what is truly valuable in democracy and at the same time free
us of its objectionable features which most people still accept
only because they regard them as inevitable. Together with the
similar stand-by scheme I have proposed for depriving
government of the monopolistic powers of control of the
supply of money, equally necessary if we are to escape the
nightmare of increasingly totalitarian powers, which I have
recently outlined in another publication (*Denationalisation of
Money*, 2nd edn, Institute of Economic Affairs, London,
1978), it proposes what is a possible escape from the fate
which threatens us. I shall be content if I have persuaded
some people that if the first experiment of freedom we have
tried in modern times should prove a failure, it is not because
freedom is an impracticable ideal, but because we have tried it
the wrong way.

I trust the reader will forgive a certain lack of system and some unnecessary repetitions in an exposition which has been written and re-written over a period of fifteen years, broken by a long period of indifferent health. I am very much aware of this, but if I tried in my eightieth year to recast it all, I shall probably never complete the task.

The Epilogue I added to that volume before publication indicates that even during the period of restricted activity my ideas have continued to develop imperceptibly more than I was aware before I attempted to sketch my present general view of the whole position in a public lecture. As I said in the concluding words of the present text, it became clear to me that what I said in that Epilogue should not be an Epilogue but a new beginning. I am glad to be able to say now that it has turned out to be such and that that Epilogue has become the outline of a new book of which I have now completed a first draft.

There are a few acknowledgments that I ought to repeat here. Some ten years ago Professor Edwin McClellan of the University of Chicago had again, as on earlier occasions, taken great trouble to make my exposition more readable than I myself could have done. I am deeply grateful for his sympathetic efforts but should add, that since even in the early parts the draft on which he has worked has since undergone further change, he must not be held responsible for whatever defects the present version still has. I have however incurred further obligations to Professor Arthur Shenfield of London who has gone through the final text of the third volume and corrected there a variety of substantial as well as stylistic points, and to Mrs Charlotte Cubitt who, in preparing the final copy of that volume, has further polished the text. I am also much indebted to Mrs Cornelia Crawford of Irvington-on-Hudson, New York, who has again applied her proven skill and understanding in preparing the subject index giving references to all three still separately paginated volumes.

LAW, LEGISLATION AND LIBERTY

Volume 1
RULES AND ORDER

Intelligent beings may have laws of their own making; but they also have some which they never made.

(Montesquieu, De l'Esprit des lois, I, p. i)

INTRODUCTION

There seems to be only one solution to the problem: that the
élite of mankind acquire a consciousness of the limitation of
the human mind, at once simple and profound enough, humble
and sublime enough, so that Western civilisation will resign
itself to its inevitable disadvantages.

G. Ferrero*

When Montesquieu and the framers of the American Constitution
articulated the conception of a limiting constitution[1] that had
grown up in England, they set a pattern which liberal constitutionalism has followed ever since. Their chief aim was to provide
institutional safeguards of individual freedom; and the device in
which they placed their faith was the separation of powers. In the
form in which we know this division of power between the legislature, the judiciary, and the administration, it has not achieved
what it was meant to achieve. Governments everywhere have obtained by constitutional means powers which those men had meant
to deny them. The first attempt to secure individual liberty by
constitutions has evidently failed.

Constitutionalism means limited government.[2] But the interpretation given to the traditional formulae of constitutionalism has
made it possible to reconcile these with a conception of democracy
according to which this is a form of government where the will of
the majority on any particular matter is unlimited.[3] As a result it
has already been seriously suggested that constitutions are an antiquated survival which have no place in the modern conception of
government.[4] And, indeed, what function is served by a constitution which makes omnipotent government possible? Is its function
to be merely that governments work smoothly and efficiently,
whatever their aims?

In these circumstances it seems important to ask what those
founders of liberal constitutionalism would do today if, pursuing

the aims they did, they could command all the experience we have gained in the meantime. There is much we ought to have learned from the history of the last two hundred years that those men with all their wisdom could not have known. To me their aims seem to be as valid as ever. But as their means have proved inadequate, new institutional invention is needed.

In another book I have attempted to restate, and hope to have in some measure succeeded in clarifying, the traditional doctrine of liberal constitutionalism.[5] But it was only after I had completed that work that I came to see clearly why those ideals had failed to retain the support of the idealists to whom all the great political movements are due, and to understand what are the governing beliefs of our time which have proved irreconcilable with them. It seems to me now that the reasons for this development were chiefly: the loss of the belief in a justice independent of personal interest; a consequent use of legislation to authorize coercion, not merely to prevent unjust action but to achieve particular results for specific persons or groups; and the fusion in the same representative assemblies of the task of articulating the rules of just conduct with that of directing government.

What led me to write another book on the same general theme as the earlier one was the recognition that the preservation of a society of free men depends on three fundamental insights which have never been adequately expounded and to which the three main parts of this book are devoted. The first of these is that a self-generating or spontaneous order and an organization are distinct, and that their distinctiveness is related to the two different kinds of rules or laws which prevail in them. The second is that what today is generally regarded as 'social' or distributive justice has meaning only within the second of these kinds of order, the organization; but that it is meaningless in, and wholly incompatible with, that spontaneous order which Adam Smith called 'the Great Society', and Sir Karl Popper called 'the Open Society'. The third is that the predominant model of liberal democratic institutions, in which the same representative body lays down the rules of just conduct and directs government, necessarily leads to a gradual transformation of the spontaneous order of a free society into a totalitarian system conducted in the service of some coalition of organized interests.

This development, as I hope to show, is not a necessary consequence of democracy, but an effect only of that particular form of unlimited government with which democracy has come to be identified. If I am right, it would indeed seem that the particular form of representative government which now prevails in the Western world, and which many feel they must defend because they mistakenly regard it as the only possible form of democracy, has an inherent tendency to lead away from the ideals it was intended to serve. It can hardly be denied that, since this type of democracy has come to be accepted, we have been moving away from that ideal of individual liberty of which it had been regarded as the surest safeguard, and are now drifting towards a system which nobody wanted.

Signs are not wanting, however, that unlimited democracy is riding for a fall and that it will go down, not with a bang, but with a whimper. It is already becoming clear that many of the expectations that have been raised can be met only by taking the powers of decision out of the hands of democratic assemblies and entrusting them to the established coalitions of organized interests and their hired experts. Indeed, we are already told that the function of representative bodies has become to 'mobilize consent', [6] that is, not to express but to manipulate the opinion of those whom they represent. Sooner or later the people will discover that not only are they at the mercy of new vested interests, but that the political machinery of para-government, which has grown up as a necessary consequence of the provision-state, is producing an impasse by preventing society from making those adaptations which in a changing world are required to maintain an existing standard of living, let alone to achieve a rising one. It will probably be some time before people will admit that the institutions they have created have led them into such an impasse. But it is probably not too early to begin thinking about a way out. And the conviction that this will demand some drastic revision of beliefs now generally accepted is what makes me venture here on some institutional invention.

If I had known when I published *The Constitution of Liberty* that I should proceed to the task attempted in the present work, I should have reserved that title for it. I then used the term 'constitution' in the wide sense in which we use it also to describe the state of fitness of a person. It is only in the present book that I address myself to the question of what constitutional arrangements, in the legal sense, might be most conducive to the preservation of individual freedom. Except for a bare hint which few readers will have noticed, [7] I confined myself in the earlier book to stating the principles which the existing types of government would have to follow if they wished to preserve freedom. Increasing awareness that the prevailing institutions make this impossible has led me to concentrate more and more on what at first seemed merely an attractive but impracticable idea, until the utopia lost its strangeness and came to appear to me as the only solution of the problem in which the founders of liberal constitutionalism failed.

Yet to this problem of constitutional design I turn only in volume 3 of this work. To make a suggestion for a radical departure from established tradition at all plausible required a critical re-examination not only of current beliefs but of the real meaning of some fundamental conceptions to which we still pay lip-service. In fact, I soon discovered that to carry out what I had undertaken would require little less than doing for the twentieth century what Montesquieu had done for the eighteenth. The reader will believe me when I say that in the course of the work I more than once despaired of my ability to come even near the aim I had set myself. I am not speaking here of the fact that Montesquieu was also a great literary genius whom no mere scholar can hope to emulate. I refer rather to the purely intellectual difficulty which is a result of the circumstance that, while for Montesquieu the field which such an undertaking must cover had not yet split into numerous specialisms, it has since become impossible for any man to master even the most important relevant works. Yet, although the problem of an appropriate social order is today studied from the different angles of economics, jurisprudence, political science, sociology, and ethics, the problem is one which can be approached successfully only as a whole. This means that whoever undertakes such a task today cannot claim professional competence in all the fields with which he has to deal, or be acquainted with the specialized literature available on all the questions that arise.

Nowhere is the baneful effect of the division into specialisms more evident than in the two oldest of these disciplines, economics and law. Those eighteenth-century thinkers to whom we owe the basic conceptions of liberal constitutionalism, David Hume and Adam Smith, no less than Montesquieu, were still concerned with what some of them called the 'science of legislation', or with principles of policy in the widest sense of this term. One of the main themes of this book will be that the rules of just conduct which the lawyer studies serve a kind of order of the character of which the lawyer is largely ignorant; and that this order is studied chiefly by the economist who in turn is similarly ignorant of the character of the rules of conduct on which the order that he studies rests.

The most serious effect of the splitting up among several specialisms of what was once a common field of inquiry, however, is that it has left a no-man's-land, a vague subject sometimes called 'social philosophy'. Some of the chief disputes within those special disciplines turn, in fact, on differences about questions which are not peculiar to, and are therefore also not systematically examined by, any one of them, and which are for this reason regarded as 'philosophical'. This serves often as an excuse for taking tacitly a position which is supposed either not to require or not to be capable of rational justification. Yet these crucial issues on which not only factual interpretations but also political positions wholly depend, are questions which can and must be answered on the basis of fact and logic. They are 'philosophical' only in the sense that certain widely but erroneously held beliefs are due to the influence of a philosophical tradition which postulates a false answer to questions capable of a definite scientific treatment.

In the first chapter of this book I attempt to show that certain widely held scientific as well as political views are dependent on a particular conception of the formation of social institutions, which I shall call 'constructivist rationalism'—a conception which assumes that all social institutions are, and ought to be, the product of deliberate design. This intellectual tradition can be shown to be false both in its factual and in its normative conclusions, because the existing institutions are not all the product of design, neither would it be possible to make the social order wholly dependent on design without at the same time greatly restricting the utilization of available knowledge. That erroneous view is closely connected with the equally false conception of the human mind as an entity standing outside the cosmos of nature and society, rather than being itself the product of the same process of evolution to which the institutions of society are due.

I have indeed been led to the conviction that not only some of the scientific but also the most important political (or 'ideological') differences of our time rest ultimately on certain basic philosophical differences between two schools of thought, of which one can be shown to be mistaken. They are both commonly referred to as rationalism, but I shall have to distinguish between them as the evolutionary (or, as Sir Karl Popper calls it, 'critical') rationalism on the one hand, and the erroneous constructivist (Popper's 'naïve') rationalism on the other. If the constructivist rationalism can be shown to be based on factually false assumptions, a whole family of schools of scientific as well as political thought will also be proved erroneous.

In the theoretical fields it is particularly legal positivism and the connected belief in the necessity of an unlimited 'sovereign' power which stand or fall with this error. The same is true of utilitarianism, at least in its particularistic or 'act' variety; also, I am afraid that a not inconsiderable part of what is called 'sociology' is a direct child of constructivism when it presents its aims as 'to create the future of mankind' [8] or, as one writer put it, claims 'that socialism is the logical and inevitable outcome of sociology'. [9] All the totalitarian doctrines, of which socialism is merely the noblest and most influential, indeed belong here. They are false, not because of the values on which they are based, but because of a misconception of the forces which have made the Great Society and civilization possible. The demonstration that the differences between socialists and non-socialists ultimately rest on purely intellectual issues capable of a scientific resolution and not on different judgments of value appears to me one of the most important outcomes of the train of thought pursued in this book.

It appears to me also that the same factual error has long appeared to make insoluble the most crucial problem of political organization, namely how to limit the 'popular will' without placing another 'will' above it. As soon as we recognize that the basic order of the Great Society cannot rest entirely on design, and can therefore also not aim at particular foreseeable results, we see that the requirement, as legitimation of all authority, of a commitment to general principles approved by general opinion, may well place effective restrictions on the particular will of all authority, including that of the majority of the moment.

On these issues which will be my main concern, thought seems to have made little advance since David Hume and Immanuel Kant, and in several respects it will be at the point at which they left off that our analysis will have to resume. It was they who came nearer than anybody has done since to a clear recognition of the status of values as independent and guiding conditions of all rational construction. What I am ultimately concerned with here, although I can deal only with a small aspect of it, is that destruction of values by scientific error which has increasingly come to seem to me the great tragedy of our time—a tragedy, because the values which scientific error tends to dethrone are the indispensable foundation of all our civilization, including the very scientific efforts which have turned against them. The tendency of constructivism to represent those values which it cannot explain as determined by arbitrary human decisions, or acts of will, or mere emotions, rather than as the necessary conditions of facts which are taken for granted by its expounders, has done much to shake the foundations of civilization, and of science itself, which also rests on a system of values which cannot be scientifically proved.

ONE

REASON AND EVOLUTION

To relate by whom, and in what connection, the true law of
the formation of free states was recognized, and how this
discovery, closely akin to those which, under the names of
development, evolution, and continuity, have given a new and
deeper method to other sciences, solved the ancient problem
between stability and change, and determined the authority of
tradition on the progress of thought.

Lord Acton*

Construction and evolution

There are two ways of looking at the pattern of human activities
which lead to very different conclusions concerning both its explanation and the possibilities of deliberately altering it. Of these, one
is based on conceptions which are demonstrably false, yet are so
pleasing to human vanity that they have gained great influence and
are constantly employed even by people who know that they rest
on a fiction, but believe that fiction to be innocuous. The other,
although few people will question its basic contentions if they are
stated abstractly, leads in some respects to conclusions so unwelcome that few are willing to follow it through to the end.

The first gives us a sense of unlimited power to realize our
wishes, while the second leads to the insight that there are limitations to what we can deliberately bring about, and to the recognition that some of our present hopes are delusions. Yet the effect of
allowing ourselves to be deluded by the first view has always been
that man has actually limited the scope of what he can achieve. For
it has always been the recognition of the limits of the possible which
has enabled man to make full use of his powers. [1]

The first view holds that human institutions will serve human
purposes only if they have been deliberately designed for these
purposes, often also that the fact that an institution exists is evidence of its having been created for a purpose, and always that we

8

should so re-design society and its institutions that all our actions will be wholly guided by known purposes. To most people these propositions seem almost self-evident and to constitute an attitude alone worthy of a thinking being. Yet the belief underlying them, that we owe all beneficial institutions to design, and that only such design has made or can make them useful for our purposes, is largely false.

This view is rooted originally in a deeply ingrained propensity of primitive thought to interpret all regularity to be found in phenomena anthropomorphically, as the result of the design of a thinking mind. But just when man was well on the way to emancipating himself from this naïve conception, it was revived by the support of a powerful philosophy with which the aim of freeing the human mind from false prejudices has become closely associated, and which became the dominant conception of the Age of Reason.

The other view, which has slowly and gradually advanced since antiquity but for a time was almost entirely overwhelmed by the more glamorous constructivist view, was that that orderliness of society which greatly increased the effectiveness of individual action was not due solely to institutions and practices which had been invented or designed for that purpose, but was largely due to a process described at first as 'growth' and later as 'evolution', a process in which practices which had first been adopted for other reasons, or even purely accidentally, were preserved because they enabled the group in which they had arisen to prevail over others. Since its first systematic development in the eighteenth century this view had to struggle not only against the anthropomorphism of primitive thinking but even more against the reinforcement these naïve views had received from the new rationalist philosophy. It was indeed the challenge which this philosophy provided that led to the explicit formulation of the evolutionary view. [2]

The tenets of Cartesian rationalism

The great thinker from whom the basic ideas of what we shall call constructivist rationalism received their most complete expression was René Descartes. But while he refrained from drawing the conclusions from them for social and moral arguments, [3] these were mainly elaborated by his slightly older (but much more long-lived) contemporary, Thomas Hobbes. Although Descartes' immediate concern was to establish criteria for the truth of propositions, these were inevitably also applied by his followers to judge the appropriateness and justification of actions. The 'radical doubt' which made him refuse to accept anything as true which could not be logically derived from explicit premises that were 'clear and distinct', and therefore beyond possible doubt, deprived of validity all those rules of conduct which could not be justified in this manner. Although Descartes himself could escape the consequences by ascribing such rules of conduct to the design of an omniscient deity, for those among his followers to whom this no longer seemed an adequate explanation the acceptance of anything which was based merely on tradition and could not be fully justified on rational grounds appeared as an irrational superstition. The rejection as 'mere opinion' of all that could not be demonstrated to be true by his criteria became the dominant characteristic of the movement which he started.

Since for Descartes reason was defined as logical deduction from explicit premises, rational action also came to mean only such action as was determined entirely by known and demonstrable truth. It is almost an inevitable step from this to the conclusion that only what is true in this sense can lead to successful action, and that therefore everything to which man owes his achievements is a product of his reasoning thus conceived. Institutions and practices which have not been designed in this manner can be beneficial only by accident. Such became the characteristic attitude of Cartesian constructivism with its contempt for tradition, custom, and history in general. Man's reason alone should enable him to construct society anew. [4]

This 'rationalist' approach, however, meant in effect a relapse into earlier, anthropomorphic modes of thinking. It produced a renewed propensity to ascribe the origin of all institutions of culture to invention or design. Morals, religion and law, language and writing, money and the market, were thought of as having been deliberately constructed by somebody, or at least as owing whatever perfection they possessed to such design. This intentionalist or pragmatic[5] account of history found its fullest expression in the conception of the formation of society by a social contract, first in Hobbes and then in Rousseau, who in many respects was a direct follower of Descartes.[6] Even though their theory was not always meant as a historical account of what actually happened, it was always meant to provide a guideline for deciding whether or not existing institutions were to be approved as rational.

It is to this philosophical conception that we owe the preference which prevails to the present day for everything that is done 'consciously' or 'deliberately', and from it the terms 'irrational' or 'non-rational' derive the derogatory meaning they now have. Because of this the earlier presumption in favour of traditional or established institutions and usages became a presumption against them, and 'opinion' came to be thought of as 'mere' opinion—something not demonstrable or decidable by reason and therefore not to be accepted as a valid ground for decision.

Yet the basic assumption underlying the belief that man has achieved mastery of his surroundings mainly through his capacity for logical deduction from explicit premises is factually false, and any attempt to confine his actions to what could thus be justified would deprive him of many of the most effective means to success that have been available to him. It is simply not true that our actions owe their effectiveness solely or chiefly to knowledge which we can state in words and which can therefore constitute the explicit premises of a syllogism. Many of the institutions of society which are indispensable conditions for the successful pursuit of our conscious aims are in fact the result of customs, habits or practices which have been neither invented nor are observed with any such purpose in view. We live in a society in which we can successfully orientate ourselves, and in which our actions have a good chance of achieving their aims, not only because our fellows are governed by known aims or known connections between means and ends, but because they are also confined by rules whose purpose or origin we often do not know and of whose very existence we are often not aware.

Man is as much a rule-following animal as a purpose-seeking one.[7] And he is successful not because he knows why he ought to observe the rules which he does observe, or is even capable of stating all these rules in words, but because his thinking and acting are governed by rules which have by a process of selection been evolved in the society in which he lives, and which are thus the product of the experience of generations.

The permanent limitations of our factual knowledge

The constructivist approach leads to false conclusions because man's actions are largely successful, not merely in the primitive stage but perhaps even more so in civilization, because they are adapted both to the particular facts which he knows and to a great many other facts he does not and cannot know. And this adaptation to the general circumstances that surround him is brought about by his observance of rules which he has not designed and often does not even know explicitly, although he is able to honour them in action. Or, to put this differently, our adaptation to our environment does not consist only, and perhaps not even chiefly, in an insight into the relations between cause and effect, but also in our actions being governed by rules adapted to the kind of world in which we live, that is, to circumstances which we are not aware of and which yet determine the pattern of our successful actions.

Complete rationality of action in the Cartesian sense demands complete knowledge of all the relevant facts. A designer or engineer needs all the data and full power to control or manipulate them if he is to organize the material objects to produce the intended result. But the success of action in society depends on more particular facts than anyone can possibly know. And our whole civilization in consequence rests, and must rest, on our *believing* much that we cannot *know* to be true in the Cartesian sense.

What we must ask the reader to keep constantly in mind throughout this book, then, is the fact of the necessary and irremediable ignorance on everyone's part of most of the particular facts which determine the actions of all the several members of human society. This may at first seem to be a fact so obvious and incontestable as hardly to deserve mention, and still less to require proof. Yet the result of not constantly stressing it is that it is only too readily forgotten. This is so mainly because it is a very inconvenient fact which makes both our attempts to explain and our attempts to influence intelligently the processes of society very much more difficult, and which places severe limits on what we can say or do about them. There exists therefore a great temptation, as a first approximation, to begin with the assumption that we know everything needed for full explanation or control. This provisional assumption is often treated as something of little consequence which can later be dropped without much effect on the conclusions. Yet this necessary ignorance of most of the particulars which enter the order of a Great Society is the source of the central problem of all social order and the false assumption by which it is provisionally put aside is mostly never explicitly abandoned but merely conveniently forgotten. The argument then proceeds as if that ignorance did not matter.

The fact of our irremediable ignorance of most of the particular facts which determine the processes of society is, however, the reason why most social institutions have taken the form they actually have. To talk about a society about which either the observer or any of its members knows all the particular facts is to talk about something wholly different from anything which has ever existed— a society in which most of what we find in our society would not and could not exist and which, if it ever occurred, would possess properties we cannot even imagine.

I have discussed the importance of our necessary ignorance of the concrete facts at some length in an earlier book[8] and will emphasize its central importance here mainly by stating it at the head of the whole exposition. But there are several points which require re-statement or elaboration. In the first instance, the incurable ignorance of everyone which I am speaking is the ignorance of particular facts which are or will become known to somebody and thereby affect the whole structure of society. This structure of human activities constantly adapts itself, and functions through adapting itself, to millions of facts which in their entirety are not known to anybody. The significance of this process is most obvious and was at first stressed in the economic field. As it has been said, 'the economic life of a non-socialist society consists of millions of relations or flows between individual firms and households. We can establish certain theorems about them, but we can never observe all.'[9] The insight into the significance of our institutional ignorance in the economic sphere, and into the methods by which we have learnt to overcome this obstacle, was in fact the starting point[10] for those ideas which in the present book are systematically applied to a much wider field. It will be one of our chief contentions that most of the rules of conduct which govern our actions, and most of the institutions which arise out of this regularity, are adaptations to the impossibility of anyone taking conscious account of all the particular facts which enter into the order of society. We shall see, in particular, that the possibility of justice rests on this necessary limitation of our factual knowledge, and that insight into the nature of justice is therefore denied to all those constructivists who habitually argue on the assumption of omniscience.

Another consequence of this basic fact which must be stressed here is that only in the small groups of primitive society can collaboration between the members rest largely on the circumstance that at any one moment they will know more or less the same particular circumstances. Some wise men may be better at interpreting the immediately perceived circumstances or at remembering things in remote places unknown to the others. But the concrete events which the individuals encounter in their daily pursuits will be very much the same for all, and they will act together because the events they know and the objectives at which they aim are more or less the same.

The situation is wholly different in the Great[11] or Open Society where millions of men interact and where civilization as we know it has developed. Economics has long stressed the 'division of *labour*' which such a situation involves. But it has laid much less stress on the fragmentation of *knowledge*, on the fact that each member of society can have only a small fraction of the knowledge possessed by all, and that each is therefore ignorant of most of the facts on which the working of society rests. Yet it is the utilization of much more knowledge than anyone can possess, and therefore the fact that each moves within a coherent structure most of whose determinants are unknown to him, that constitutes the distinctive feature of all advanced civilizations.

In civilized society it is indeed not so much the greater knowledge that the individual can acquire, as the greater benefit he receives from the knowledge possessed by others, which is the cause of his ability to pursue an infinitely wider range of ends than merely the satisfaction of his most pressing physical needs. Indeed, a 'civilized' individual may be very ignorant, more ignorant than many a savage, and yet greatly benefit from the civilization in which he lives.

The characteristic error of the constructivist rationalists in this respect is that they tend to base their argument on what has been called the *synoptic delusion*, that is, on the fiction that all the relevant facts are known to some one mind, and that it is possible to construct from this knowledge of the particulars a desirable social order. Sometimes the delusion is expressed with a touching naïveté by the enthusiasts for a deliberately planned society, as when one of them dreams of the development of 'the art of simultaneous thinking: the ability to deal with a multitude of related phenomena at the same time, and of composing in a single picture both the qualitative and the quantitative attributes of these phenomena.'[12] They seem completely unaware that this dream simply assumes away the central problem which any effort towards the understanding or shaping of the order of society raises: our incapacity to assemble as a surveyable whole all the data which enter into the social order. Yet all those who are fascinated by the beautiful plans which result from such an approach because they are 'so orderly, so visible, so easy to understand',[13] are the victims of the synoptic delusion and forget that these plans owe their seeming clarity to the planner's disregard of all the facts he does not know.

Factual knowledge and science

The chief reason why modern man has become so unwilling to admit that the constitutional limitations on his knowledge form a permanent barrier to the possibility of a rational construction of the whole of society is his unbounded confidence in the powers of science. We hear so much about the rapid advance of scientific knowledge that we have come to feel that all mere limitations of knowledge are soon bound to disappear. This confidence rests, however, on a misconception of the tasks and powers of science, that is, on the erroneous belief that science is a method of ascertaining particular facts and that the progress of its techniques will enable us to ascertain and manipulate all the particular facts we might want.

In one sense the saying that our civilization rests on the conquest of ignorance is of course a mere platitude. Yet our very familiarity with it tends to conceal from us what is most important in it: namely that civilization rests on the fact that we all benefit from knowledge which we do *not* possess. And one of the ways in which civilization helps us to overcome that limitation on the extent of individual knowledge is by conquering ignorance, not by the acquisition of more knowledge, but by the utilization of knowledge which is and remains widely dispersed among individuals. The limitation of knowledge with which we are concerned is therefore not a limitation which science can overcome. Contrary to a widely held belief, science consists not of the knowledge of particular facts; and in the case of very complex phenomena the powers of science are also limited by the practical impossibility of ascertaining all the particular facts which we would have to know if its theories were to give us the power of predicting specific events. The study of the relatively simple phenomena of the physical world, where it has proved possible to state the determining relations as functions of a few variables that can be easily ascertained in particular instances, and where as a consequence the astounding progress of disciplines concerned with them has become possible, has created the illusion that soon the same will also be true with regard to the more complex phenomena. But neither science nor any known technique [14] enables us to overcome the fact that no mind, and therefore also no deliberately directed action, can take account of all the particular facts which are known to some men but not as a whole to any particular person.

Indeed, in its endeavour to explain and predict particular events, which it does so successfully in the case of relatively simple phenomena (or where it can at least approximately isolate 'closed systems' that are relatively simple), science encounters the same barrier of factual ignorance when it comes to apply its theories to very complex phenomena. In some fields it has developed important theories which give us much insight into the general character of some phenomena, but will never produce predictions of particular events, or a full explanation—simply because we can never know all the particular facts which according to these theories we would have to know in order to arrive at such concrete conclusions. The best example of this is the Darwinian (or Neo-Darwinian) theory of the evolution of biological organisms. If it were possible to ascertain the particular facts of the past which operated on the selection of the particular forms that emerged, it would provide a complete explanation of the structure of the existing organisms; and similarly, if it were possible to ascertain all the particular facts which will operate on them during some future period, it ought to enable us to predict future development. But, of course, we will never be able to do either, because science has no means of ascertaining all the particular facts that it would have to possess to perform such a feat.

There is another related misconception about the aim and power of science which it will be useful also to mention at this point. This is the belief that science is concerned exclusively with what exists and not with what could be. But the value of science consists largely in telling us what would happen if some facts were different from what they are. All the statements of theoretical science have the form of 'if . . . , then . . .' statements, and they are interesting mainly in so far as the conditions we insert in the 'if' clause are different from those that actually exist.

Perhaps this misconception has nowhere else been so important as in political science where it seems to have become a bar to serious consideration of the really important problems. Here the mistaken idea that science is simply a collection of observed facts has led to a confinement of research to the ascertainment of what *is*, while the chief value of *all* science is to tell us what the consequences would be if conditions were in some respects made different from what they are.

The fact that an increasing number of social scientists confine themselves to the study of what exists in some part of the social system does not make their results more realistic, but makes them largely irrelevant for most decisions about the future. Fruitful social science must be very largely a study of what is *not*: a construction of hypothetical models of possible worlds which might exist if some of the alterable conditions were made different. We need a scientific theory chiefly to tell us what would be the effects if some conditions were as they have never been before. All scientific knowledge is knowledge not of particular facts but of hypotheses which have so far withstood systematic attempts at refuting them.

The concurrent evolution of mind and society: the role of rules

The errors of constructivist rationalism are closely connected with Cartesian dualism, that is with the conception of an independently existing mind substance which stands outside the cosmos of nature and which enabled man, endowed with such a mind from the beginning, to design the institutions of society and culture among which he lives. The fact is, of course, that this mind is an adaptation to the natural and social surroundings in which man lives and that it has developed in constant interaction with the institutions which determine the structure of society. Mind is as much the product of the social environment in which it has grown up and which it has not made as something that has in turn acted upon and altered these institutions. It is the result of man having developed in society and having acquired those habits and practices that increased the chances of persistence of the group in which he lived. The conception of an already fully developed mind designing the institutions which made life in society possible is contrary to all we know about the evolution of man.

The cultural heritage into which man is born consists of a complex of practices or rules of conduct which have prevailed because they made a group of men successful but which were not adopted because it was known that they would bring about desired effects.

Man acted before he thought and did not understand before he acted. What we call understanding is in the last resort simply his capacity to respond to his environment with a pattern of actions that helps him to persist. Such is the modicum of truth in behaviourism and pragmatism, doctrines which, however, have so crudely oversimplified the determining relationships as to become more obstacles than helps to their appreciation.

'Learning from experience', among men no less than among animals, is a process not primarily of reasoning but of the observance, spreading, transmission and development of practices which have prevailed because they were successful—often not because they conferred any recognizable benefit on the acting individual but because they increased the chances of survival of the group to which he belonged. [15] The result of this development will in the first instance not be articulated knowledge but a knowledge which, although it can be described in terms of rules, the individual cannot state in words but is merely able to honour in practice. The mind does not so much make rules as consist of rules of action, a complex of rules that is, which it has not made, but which have come to govern the actions of the individuals because actions in accordance with them have proved more successful than those of competing individuals or groups. [16]

There is in the beginning no distinction between the practices one must observe in order to achieve a particular result and the practices one ought to observe. There is just one established manner of doing things, and knowledge of cause and effect and knowledge of the appropriate or permissible form of action are not distinct. Knowledge of the world is knowledge of what one must do or not do in certain kinds of circumstances. And in avoiding danger it is as important to know what one must never do as to know what one must do to achieve a particular result.

These rules of conduct have thus not developed as the recognized conditions for the achievement of a known purpose, but have evolved because the groups who practised them were more successful and displaced others. They were rules which, given the kind of environment in which man lived, secured that a greater number of the groups or individuals practising them would survive. The problem of conducting himself successfully in a world only partially known to man was thus solved by adhering to rules which had served him well but which he did not and could not *know* to be true in the Cartesian sense.

There are thus two attributes of these rules that govern human conduct and make it appear intelligent which we shall have to stress throughout, because the constructivist approach denies implicitly that it can be rational to observe such rules. Of course in advanced society only some rules will be of this kind; what we want to emphasize is merely that even such advanced societies will in part owe their order to some such rules.

The first of these attributes which most rules of conduct originally possessed is that they are observed in action without being known to the acting person in articulated ('verbalized' or explicit) form. They will manifest themselves in a regularity of action which can be explicitly described, but this regularity of action is not the result of the acting persons being capable of thus stating them. The second is that such rules come to be observed because in fact they give the group in which they are practised superior strength, and not because this effect is known to those who are guided by them. Although such rules come to be generally accepted because their observation produces certain consequences, they are not observed with the intention of producing those consequences—consequences which the acting person need not know.

We cannot consider here the difficult question of how men can learn from each other such, often highly abstract, rules of conduct by example and imitation (or 'by analogy'), although neither those who set the examples nor those who learn from them may be consciously aware of the existence of the rules which they nevertheless strictly observe. This is a problem most familiar to us in the learning of language by children who are able to produce correctly most complicated expressions they have never heard before;[17] but it occurs also in such fields as manners, morals and law, and in most skills where we are guided by rules which we know how to follow but are unable to state.

The important point is that every man growing up in a given culture will find in himself rules, or may discover that he acts in accordance with rules—and will similarly recognize the actions of others as conforming or not conforming to various rules. This is, of course, not proof that they are a permanent or unalterable part of 'human nature', or that they are innate, but proof only that they are part of a cultural heritage which is likely to be fairly constant, especially so long as they are not articulated in words and therefore also are not discussed or consciously examined.

The false dichotomy of 'natural' and 'artificial'

The discussion of the problems with which we are concerned was long hampered by the universal acceptance of a misleading distinction which was introduced by the ancient Greeks and from whose confusing effect we have not yet wholly freed ourselves. This is the division of phenomena between those which in modern terms are 'natural' and those which are 'artificial'. The original Greek terms, which seem to have been introduced by the Sophists of the fifth century B.C., were *physei*, which means 'by nature' and, in contrast to it, either *nomō*, best rendered as 'by convention', or *thesei*, which means roughly 'by deliberate decision'.[18] The use of two terms with somewhat different meanings to express the second part of the division indicates the confusion which has beset the discussion ever since. The distinction intended may be either between objects which existed independently and objects which were the results of human *action*, or between objects which arose independently of, and objects which arose as the result of, human *design*. The failure to distinguish between these two meanings led to the situation where one author could argue with regard to a given phenomenon that it was artificial because it was the result of human action, while another might describe the same phenomenon as natural because it was evidently not the result of human design. Not until the eighteenth century did thinkers like Bernard Mandeville and David Hume make it clear that there existed a category of phenomena which, depending on which of the two definitions one adhered to, would fall into either the one or the other of the two categories and therefore ought to be assigned to a distinct third class of phenomena, later described by Adam Ferguson as 'the result of human action but not of human design'.[19] These were the phenomena which required for their explanation a distinct body of theory and which came to provide the object of the theoretical social sciences.

But in the more than two thousand years during which the distinction introduced by the ancient Greeks has ruled thought almost unchallenged, it has become deeply engrained in concepts and language. In the second century A.D. a Latin grammarian, Aulus Gellius, rendered the Greek terms *physei* and *thesei* by *naturalis* and *positivus*, from which most European languages derived the words to describe two kinds of law.[20]

There occurred later one promising development in the discussion of these questions by the medieval schoolmen, which led close to a recognition of the intermediate category of phenomena that were 'the result of human action but not of human design'. In the twelfth century some of those writers had begun to include under *naturalis* all that was not the result of human invention or a deliberate creation;[21] and in the course of time it came to be increasingly recognized that many social phenomena fell into this category. Indeed, in the discussion of the problems of society by the last of the schoolmen, the Spanish Jesuits of the sixteenth century, *naturalis* became a technical term for such social phenomena as were not deliberately shaped by human will. In the work of one of them, Luis Molina, it is, for example, explained that the 'natural price' is so called because 'it results from the thing itself without regard to laws and decrees, but is dependent on many circumstances which alter it, such as the sentiments of men, their estimation of different uses, often even in consequence of whims and pleasures'.[22] Indeed, these ancestors of ours thought and 'acted under a strong impression of the ignorance and fallibility of mankind',[23] and, for instance, argued that the precise 'mathematical price' at which a commodity could be justly sold was only known to God, because it depended on more circumstances than any man could know, and that therefore the determination of the 'just price' must be left to the market.[24]

These beginnings of an evolutionary approach were submerged, however, in the sixteenth and seventeenth centuries by the rise of constructivist rationalism, with the result that both the term 'reason' and the term 'natural law' completely changed their meaning. 'Reason', which had included the capacity of the mind to distinguish between good and evil, that is between what was and what was not in accordance with established rules,[25] came to mean a capacity to construct such rules by deduction from explicit premises. The conception of natural law was thereby turned into that of a 'law of reason' and thus almost into the opposite of what it had meant. This new rationalist law of nature of Grotius and his successors,[26] indeed, shared with its positivist antagonists the conception that all law was made by reason or could at least be fully justified by it, and differed from it only in the assumption that law could be logically derived from *a priori* premises, while positivism regarded it as a deliberate construction based on empirical knowledge of the effects it would have on the achievement of desirable human purposes.

The rise of the evolutionary approach

After the Cartesian relapse into anthropomorphic thinking on these matters a new start was made by Bernard Mandeville and David Hume. They were probably inspired more by the tradition of the English common law, especially as expounded by Matthew Hale, than by the the law of nature.[27] It came increasingly to be seen that the formation of regular patterns in human relations that were not the conscious aim of human actions raised a problem which required the development of a systematic social theory. This need was met during the second half of the eighteenth century in the field of economics by the Scottish moral philosophers, led by Adam Smith and Adam Ferguson, while the consequences to be drawn for political theory received their magnificent formulations from the great seer Edmund Burke, in whose work we shall, however, seek in vain for a systematic theory. But while in England the development suffered a new setback from the intrusion of constructivism in the form of Benthamite utilitarianism,[28] it gained a new vitality on the continent from the 'historical schools' of linguistics and law.[29] After the beginnings made by the Scottish philosophers, the systematic development of the evolutionary aproach to social phenomena took place mainly in Germany through Wilhelm von Humboldt and F. C. von Savigny. We cannot consider here that development in linguistics, although for a long time it was the only field outside of economics where a coherent theory was achieved, and the extent to which since Roman times the theory of law has been fertilized by conceptions borrowed from the grammarians deserves to be better understood than it is.[30] In the social sciences it was through Savigny's follower Sir Henry Maine[31] that the evolutionary approach re-entered the English tradition. And in the great survey of 1883 of the methods of the social sciences by the founder of the Austrian school of economics, Carl Menger, the central position for all social sciences of the problem of the spontaneous formation of institutions and its genetic character was most fully restated on the continent. In recent times the tradition has been most fruitfully developed by cultural anthropology, at least some of whose leading figures are fully aware of this ancestry.[32]

As the conception of evolution will play a central role throughout our discussion, it is important to clear up some misunderstandings which in recent times have made students of society reluctant to employ it. The first is the erroneous belief that it is a conception which the social sciences have borrowed from biology. It was in fact the other way round, and if Charles Darwin was able successfully to apply to biology a concept which he had largely learned from the social sciences, this does not make it less important in the field in which it originated. It was in the discussion of such social formations as language and morals, law and money, that in the eighteenth century the twin conceptions of evolution and the spontaneous formation of an order were at last clearly formulated, and provided the intellectual tools which Darwin and his contemporaries were able to apply to biological evolution. Those eighteenth-century moral philosophers and the historical schools of law and language might well be described, as some of the theorists of language of the nineteenth century indeed described themselves, as Darwinians before Darwin. [33]

A nineteenth-century social theorist who needed Darwin to teach him the idea of evolution was not worth his salt. Unfortunately some did, and produced views which under the name of 'Social Darwinism' have since been responsible for the distrust with which the concept of evolution has been regarded by social scientists. There are, of course, important differences between the manner in which the process of selection operates in the cultural transmission that leads to the formation of social institutions, and the manner in which it operates in the selection of innate biological characteristics and their transmission by physiological inheritance. The error of 'Social Darwinism' was that it concentrated on the selection of individuals rather than on that of institutions and practices, and on the selection of innate rather than on culturally transmitted capacities of the individuals. But although the scheme of Darwinian theory has only limited application to the latter and its literal use leads to grave distortions, the basic conception of evolution is still the same in both fields.

The other great misunderstanding which has led to a discrediting of the theory of social evolution, is the belief that the theory of evolution consists of 'laws of evolution'. This is true at most in a special sense of the word 'law', and is certainly not true, as it is often thought, in the sense of a statement of a necessary sequence of particular stages or phases through which the process of evolution must pass and which by extrapolation leads to predictions of the future course of evolution. The theory of evolution proper provides no more than an account of a process the outcome of which will depend on a very large number of particular facts, far too numerous for us to know in their entirety, and therefore does not lead to predictions about the future. We are in consequence confined to 'explanations of the principle' or to predictions merely of the abstract pattern the process will follow.[34]

The pretended laws of overall evolution supposedly derived from observation have in fact nothing to do with the legitimate theory of evolution which accounts for the process. They derive from the altogether different conceptions of the historicism of Comte, Hegel and Marx, and their holistic approach, and assert a purely mystical necessity that evolution must run a certain predetermined course. Although it must be admitted that the original meaning of the term 'evolution' refers to such an 'unwinding' of potentialities already contained in the germ, the process by which the biological and social theory of evolution accounts for the appearence of different complex structures does not imply such a succession of particular steps. Those to whom the concept of evolution implies necessary sequences of predetermined 'stages', or 'phases', through which the development of an organism or a social institution must pass, are therefore justified in rejecting such a conception of evolution, for which there is no scientific warrant.

We will mention at this point only briefly that the frequent attempts made to use the conception of evolution, not merely as an explanation of the rise of rules of conduct, but as the basis of a prescriptive science of ethics, also have no foundation in the legitimate theory of evolution, but belong to those extrapolations of observed tendencies as 'laws of evolution' for which there is no justification. This needs saying here as some distinguished biologists who certainly understand the theory of evolution proper have been tempted into such assertions.[35] It is our concern here, however, only to show that such abuses of the concept of evolution in subjects like anthropology, ethics, and also law, which have discredited it for a time, were based on a misconception of the nature of the theory of evolution; and that, if it is taken in its correct meaning, it still remains true that the complex, spontaneously formed structures with which social theory has to deal, can be understood only as the result of a process of evolution and that, therefore, here 'the genetic element is inseparable from the idea of theoretical sciences'.[36]

The persistence of constructivism in current thought

It is difficult to appreciate fully the extent to which the constructivist fallacy has during the last three hundred years determined the attitudes of many of the most independent and courageous thinkers. The rejection of the accounts which religion gave of the source and grounds of validity of the traditional rules of morals and law led to the rejection of these rules themselves so far as they could not be rationally justified. It was to their achievement in thus 'freeing' the human mind that many of the celebrated thinkers of the period owe their fame. We can here illustrate this only by picking out almost at random a few characteristic instances. [37]

One of the best known is, of course, Voltaire, whose views on the problem with which we shall be mainly concerned found expression in the exhortation, 'if you want good laws, burn those you have and make new ones'. [38] Even greater influence was exercised by Rousseau; of him it has been well said that: [39]

> There was even no law except law willed by living men—this was his greatest heresy from many points of view, including the Christian; it was also his greatest affirmation in political theory. . . . What he did, and it was revolutionary enough, was to undermine the faith of many people in the justice of the society in which they lived.

And he did so by demanding that 'society' should be just as if it were a thinking being.

The refusal to recognize as binding any rules of conduct whose justification had not been rationally demonstrated or 'made clear and demonstrative to every individual' [40] becomes in the nineteenth century an ever recurring theme. Two examples will indicate the attitude. Early in that century we find Alexander Herzen arguing: 'You want a book of rules, while I think that when one reaches a certain age one ought to be ashamed of having to use one [because] the truly free man creates his own morality.' [41] And quite in the same manner a distinguished contemporary positivist philosopher contends that 'the power of reason must be sought not in rules that reason dictates to our imagination, but in the ability to free ourselves from any kind of rules to which we have been conditioned through experience and traditions'. [42]

The best description of this state of mind by a representative thinker of our time is found in the account given by Lord Keynes in a talk entitled 'My early beliefs'. [43] Speaking in 1938 about the time thirty-five years before, when he himself was twenty, he says of himself and his friends:

We entirely repudiated a personal liability on us to obey general rules. We claimed the right to judge every individual case on its merits, and the wisdom, experience, and self-control to do so successfully. This was a very important part of our faith, violently and aggressively held, and for the outer world it was our most obvious and dangerous characteristic. We repudiated entirely customary morals, conventions, and traditional wisdom. We were, that is to say, in the strict sense of the term, immoralists . . . we recognized no moral obligation, no inner sanction, to conform or obey. Before heaven we claimed to be our own judge in our own case.

To which he added: 'So far as I am concerned, it is too late to change. I remain, and always will remain, an immoralist.'

To anyone who has himself grown up before the First World War, it is obvious that this was then not an attitude peculiar to the Bloomsbury Group, but a very widespread one, shared by many of the most active and independent spirits of the time.

Our anthropomorphic language

How deeply the erroneous constructivist or intentionalist interpretation pervades our thinking about the phenomena of society is seen when we consider the meaning of many of the terms which we have to use in referring to them. Indeed, most of the errors against which we shall have to argue throughout this book are so deeply built into our language that the use of established terms will lead the unwary almost necessarily to wrong conclusions. The language which we have to use has developed in the course of millennia when man could conceive of an order only as the product of design, and when he regarded as evidence of the action of a personal designer whatever order he discovered in the phenomena. In consequence, practically all the terms that are available to us to describe such orderly structures or their functioning are charged with the suggestion that a personal agent has created them. Because of this they regularly lead to false conclusions.

To some extent this is true of all scientific vocabulary. The physical sciences no less than biology or social theory had to make use of terms of anthropomorphic origin. But the physicist who speaks of 'force' or 'inertia' or of a body 'acting' on another employs these terms in a generally understood technical sense not likely to mislead. But to speak of society as 'acting' at once conjures up associations which are very misleading.

We shall in general refer to this propensity as 'anthropomorphism', although the term is not wholly accurate. To be more exact we ought to distinguish between the even more primitive attitude which *personifies* such entities as society by ascribing to them possession of a mind and which is properly described as *anthropomorphism* or *animism*, and the slightly more sophisticated interpretation which ascribes their order and functioning to the *design* of some distinct agency, and which is better described as *intentionalism*, *artificialism*,[44] or, as we do here, *constructivism*. However, these two propensities shade into each other more or less imperceptibly, and for our purposes we shall generally use 'anthropomorphism' without making the finer distinction.

Since practically the whole vocabulary available for the discussion of the spontaneous orders with which we shall be concerned possesses such misleading connotations, we must in some degree be arbitrary in deciding which words we shall use in a strictly non-anthropomorphic sense and which we shall use only if we want to imply intention or design. To preserve clarity, however, it is essential that with respect to many words we use them either for the results of deliberate constructions only, or for the results of spontaneous formation only, but not for both. Sometimes, however, as in the case of the term 'order', it will be necessary to use it in a neutral sense comprising both spontaneous orders and 'organizations' or 'arrangements'. The last two terms, which we shall use only for results of design, illustrate the fact that it is often as difficult to find terms which always imply design as it is to find those which do not suggest it. The biologist will generally without hesitation speak of 'organization' without implying design, but it would sound odd if he said that an organism not only had but was an organization or that it had been organized. The role that the term 'organization' has played in the development of modern political thought, and the meaning which modern 'organization theory' attaches to it, seem to justify in the present context a restriction of its meaning to results of design only.

Since the distinction between a made order and one which forms itself as a result of regularities of the actions of its elements will be the chief topic of the next chapter, we need not dwell upon it here any further. And in volume 2 we shall have to consider at some length the almost invariably confusing character of the little word 'social' which, because of its particularly elusive character, carries confusion into almost any statement in which it is used.

We shall find too that such current notions as that society 'acts' or that it 'treats', 'rewards', or 'remunerates' persons, or that it 'values' or 'owns' or 'controls' objects or services, or is 'responsible for' or 'guilty of' something, or that it has a 'will' or 'purpose', can be 'just' or 'unjust', or that the economy 'distributes' or 'allocates' resources, all suggest a false intentionalist or constructivist interpretation of words which might have been used without such a connotation, but which almost inevitably lead the user to illegitimate conclusions. We shall see that such confusions are at the root of the basic conceptions of highly influential schools of thought which have wholly succumbed to the belief that all rules or laws must have been invented or explicitly agreed upon by somebody. Only when it is wrongly assumed that all rules of just conduct have deliberately been made by somebody do such sophisms become plausible as that all power of making laws must be arbitrary, or that there must always exist an ultimate 'sovereign' source of power from which all law derives. Many of the age-old puzzles of political theory and many of the conceptions which have profoundly affected the evolution of political institutions are the product of this confusion. This is especially true of that tradition in legal theory which more than any other is proud of having fully escaped from anthropomorphic conceptions, namely legal positivism; for it proves on examination to be entirely based on what we have called the constructivist fallacy. It is actually one of the main offshoots of that rationalist constructivism which, in taking literally the expression that man has 'made' all his culture and institutions, has been driven to the fiction that all law is the product of somebody's will.

One more term whose ambiguity had a similar confusing effect on social theory, and particularly on some positivist theories of law, and which therefore ought to be briefly mentioned here, is the term 'function'. It is an almost indispensable term for the discussion of those self-maintaining structures which we find alike in biological organisms and in spontaneous social orders. Such a function may be performed without the acting part knowing what purpose its action serves. But the characteristic anthropomorphism of the positivist tradition has led to a curious perversion: from the discovery that an institution served a function the conclusion was drawn that the persons performing the function must be directed to do so by another human will. Thus the true insight that the institution of private property served a function necessary for the maintenance of the spontaneous order of society led to the belief that for this purpose a power of direction of some authority was required—an opinion even expressly laid down in the constitutions of some countries which were drawn up under positivist inspiration.

Reason and abstraction

The aspects of the Cartesian tradition which we have described as constructivism are often also referred to simply as rationalism, and this is apt to give rise to a misunderstanding. It has, for instance, become customary to speak of its early critics, especially Bernard Mandeville and David Hume, as 'anti-rationalists' [45] and this has conveyed the impression that these 'anti-rationalists' were less concerned to achieve the most effective use of reason than those who specially claimed the name of rationalists. The fact is, however, that the so-called anti-rationalists insist that to make reason as effective as possible requires an insight into the limitations of the powers of conscious reason and into the assistance we obtain from processes of which we are not aware, an insight which constructivist rationalism lacks. Thus, if the desire to make reason as effective as possible is what is meant by rationalism, I am myself a rationalist. If, however, the term means that conscious reason ought to determine every particular action, I am not a rationalist, and such rationalism seems to me to be very unreasonable. Surely, one of the tasks of reason is to decide how far it is to extend its control or how far it ought to rely on other forces which it cannot wholly control. It is therefore better in this connection not to distinguish between 'rationalism' and 'anti-rationalism' but to distinguish between a constructivist and an evolutionary, or, in Karl Popper's terms, a naïve and a critical rationalism.

Connected with the uncertain meaning of the term 'rationalism' are the opinions generally held about the attitude to 'abstraction' characteristic of 'rationalism'. The name is often even used to describe an undue addiction to abstraction. The characteristic property of constructivist rationalism, however, is rather that it is not content with abstraction—that it does not recognize that abstract concepts are a means to cope with the complexity of the concrete which our mind is not capable of fully mastering. Evolutionary rationalism, on the other hand, recognizes abstractions as the indispensable means of the mind which enable it to deal with a reality it cannot fully comprehend. This is connected with the fact that in the constructivist view 'abstractness' is conceived as a property confined to conscious thought or concepts, while actually it is a characteristic possessed by all the processes which determine action long before they appear in conscious thought or are expressed in language. Whenever a *type* of situation evokes in an individual a *disposition* towards a certain *pattern* of response, that basic relation which is described as 'abstract' is present. There can be little doubt that the peculiar capacities of a central nervous system consist precisely in the fact that particular stimuli do not directly evoke particular responses, but make it possible for certain classes or configurations of stimuli to set up certain dispositions towards classes of actions, and that only the superimposition of many such dispositions specify the particular action that will result. This 'primacy of the abstract', as I have called it elsewhere, [46] will be assumed throughout this book.

Abstractness will here be regarded, therefore, not only as a property possessed to a greater or lesser degree by all (conscious or unconscious) mental processes, but as the basis of man's capacity to move successfully in a world very imperfectly known to him— an adaptation to his ignorance of most of the particular facts of his surroundings. The main purpose of our stress on the rules which govern our actions is to bring out the central importance of the abstract character of all mental processes.

Thus considered, abstraction is not something which the mind produces by processes of logic from its perception of reality, but rather a property of the categories with which it operates—not a product of the mind but rather what constitutes the mind. We never act, and could never act, in full consideration of all the facts of a particular situation, but always by singling out as relevant only some aspects of it; not by conscious choice or deliberate selection, but by a mechanism over which we do not exercise deliberate control.

It will perhaps be clear now that our constant stress on the non-rational character of much of our actions is meant not to belittle or criticize this manner of acting, but, on the contrary, to bring out one of the reasons why it is successful; and not to suggest that we ought to try fully to understand why we do what we do, but to point out that this is impossible; and that we can make use of so much experience, not because we possess that experience, but because, without our knowing it, it has become incorporated in the schemata of thought which guide us.

There are two possible misconceptions of the position taken which we must try to prevent. One derives from the fact that action which is guided by rules we are not aware of is often described as 'instinctive' or 'intuitive'. There is not much harm in these words except that both, and specially 'intuitive', usually refer to the perception of the particular and relatively concrete, while what we are here concerned with are capacities determining very general or abstract properties of the actions taken. As commonly used, the term 'intuitive' suggests an attribute not possessed by abstract rules which we follow in our actions, and for this reason it had better be avoided.

The other possible misunderstanding of our position is the impression that the emphasis we place on the non-conscious character of many of the rules which govern our action is connected with the conception of an unconscious or subconscious mind underlying the theories of psychoanalysis or 'depth-psychology'. But although to some extent the two views may aim at an explanation of the same phenomena, they are in fact wholly different. We shall not use, and in fact regard as unwarranted and false, the whole conception of an unconscious mind which differs from the conscious mind only by being unconscious, but in all other respects operates in the same, rational, goal-seeking manner as the conscious mind. Nothing is gained by postulating such a mystical entity, or by ascribing to the various propensities or rules which together produce the complex order we call mind any of the properties which the resulting order possesses. Psychoanalysis seems in this respect merely to have created another ghost which in turn is held to govern the 'ghost in the machine' [47] of Cartesian dualism.

Why the extreme forms of constructivist rationalism regularly lead to a revolt against reason

In conclusion of this introductory chapter some observations are in place on a phenomenon which transcends the scope of this book but which is of considerable importance for the understanding of its immediate concerns. We refer to the fact that the constructivist rationalism which knows no bounds to the applications of conscious reason has historically again and again given birth to a revolt against reason. Indeed, this development, in which an over-estimation of the powers of reason leads through disillusionment to a violent reaction against the guidance by abstract reason, and to an extolling of the powers of the particular will, is not in the least paradoxical, but almost inevitable.

The illusion that leads constructivist rationalists regularly to an enthronement of the will consists in the belief that reason can transcend the realm of the abstract and by itself is able to determine the desirability of particular actions. Yet it is always only in combination with particular, non-rational impulses that reason can determine what to do, and its function is essentially to act as a restraint on emotion, or to steer action impelled by other factors. The illusion that reason alone can tell us what we ought to do, and that therefore all reasonable men ought to be able to join in the endeavour to pursue common ends as members of an organization, is quickly dispelled when we attempt to put it into practice. But the desire to use our reason to turn the whole of society into one rationally directed engine persists, and in order to realize it common ends are imposed upon all that cannot be justified by reason and cannot be more than the decisions of particular wills.

The rationalist revolt against reason, if we may so call it, is usually directed against the abstractness of thought. It will not recognize that all thought must remain abstract to various degrees and that therefore it can never by itself fully determine particular actions. Reason is merely a discipline, an insight into the limitations of the possibilities of successful action, which often will tell us only what not to do. This discipline is necessary precisely because our intellect is not capable of grasping reality in all its complexity. Although the use of abstraction extends the scope of phenomena which we can master intellectually, it does so by limiting the degree to which we can foresee the effects of our actions, and therefore also by limiting to certain general features the degree to which we can shape the world to our liking. Liberalism for this reason restricts deliberate control of the overall order of society to the enforcement of such general rules as are necessary for the formation of a spontaneous order, the details of which we cannot foresee.

Perhaps nobody has seen this connection between liberalism and the insight into the limited powers of abstract thinking more clearly than that ultra-rationalist who has become the fountain head of most modern irrationalism and totalitarianism, G. W. F. Hegel. When he wrote that 'the view which clings to abstraction is

32

liberalism, over which the concrete always prevails and which always founders in the struggle against it', [48] he truly described the fact that we are not yet mature enough to submit for any length of time to strict discipline of reason and allow our emotions constantly to break through its restraints.

The reliance on the abstract is thus not a result of an over-estimation but rather of an insight into the limited powers of our reason. It is the over-estimation of the powers of reason which leads to the revolt against the submission to abstract rules. Constructivist rationalism rejects the demand for this discipline of reason because it deceives itself that reason can directly master all the particulars; and it is thereby led to a preference for the concrete over the abstract, the particular over the general, because its adherents do not realize how much they thereby limit the span of true control by reason. The *hubris* of reason manifests itself in those who believe that they can dispense with abstraction and achieve a full mastery of the concrete and thus positively master the social process. The desire to remodel society after the image of individual man, which since Hobbes has governed rationalist political theory, and which attributes to the Great Society properties which only individuals or deliberately created organizations can possess, leads to a striving not merely to be, but to make everything rational. Although we must endeavour to make society good in the sense that we shall like to live in it, we cannot make it good in the sense that it will behave morally. It does not make sense to apply the standards of conscious conduct to those unintended consequences of individual action which all the truly social represents, except by eliminating the unintended—which would mean eliminating all that we call culture.

The Great Society and the civilization it has made possible is the product of man's growing capacity to communicate abstract thought; and when we say that what all men have in common is their reason we mean their common capacity for abstract thought. That man uses this capacity largely without explicitly knowing the abstract principles which guide him, and does not understand all the reasons for allowing himself to be thus guided, has produced a situation in which the very over-estimation of those powers of reason of which man is conscious has led him to hold in contempt what has made reason as powerful as it is: its abstract character. It was the failure to recognize that abstractions help our reason go further than it could if it tried to master all the particulars which produced a host of schools of philosophy inimical to abstract reason —philosophies of the concrete, of 'life' and of 'existence' which extol emotion, the particular and the instinctive, and which are only too ready to support such emotions as those of race, nation, and class.

Thus constructivist rationalism, in its endeavour to make everything subject to rational control, in its preference for the concrete and its refusal to submit to the discipline of abstract rules, comes to join hands with irrationalism. Construction is possible only in the service of particular ends which in the last resort must be non-rational, and on which no rational argument can produce agreement if it is not already present at the outset.

TWO

COSMOS AND TAXIS

The man of system . . . seems to imagine that he can arrange
the different members of a great society with as much ease
as the hand arranges the different pieces upon a chessboard.
He does not consider that the pieces upon the chessboard have
no other principle of motion besides that which the hand
impresses upon them; but that, in the great chessboard of human
society, every single piece has a principle of motion of its own,
altogether different from that which the legislature might choose
to impress upon it. If those two principles coincide and act in the
same direction, the game of human society will go on easily and
harmoniously, and is very likely to be happy and successful. If
they are opposite or different, the game will go on miserably and
human society must be at all times in the highest degree of disorder.
Adam Smith*

The concept of order

The central concept around which the discussion of this book will
turn is that of order, and particularly the distinction between two
kinds of order which we will provisionally call 'made' and 'grown'
orders. Order is an indispensable concept for the discussion of all
complex phenomena, in which it must largely play the role the
concept of law plays in the analysis of simpler phenomena.[1] There
is no adequate term other than 'order' by which we can describe it,
although 'system', 'structure' or 'pattern' may occasionally serve
instead. The term 'order' has, of course, a long history in the social
sciences,[2] but in recent times it has generally been avoided, largely
because of the ambiguity of its meaning and its frequent association
with authoritarian views. We cannot do without it, however, and
shall have to guard against misinterpretation by sharply defining
the general sense in which we shall employ it and then clearly
distinguishing between the two different ways in which such order
can originate.

By 'order' we shall throughout describe *a state of affairs in which a multiplicity of elements of various kinds are so related to each other that we may learn from our acquaintance with some spatial or temporal part of the whole to form correct expectations concerning the rest, or at least expectations which have a good chance of proving correct.*[3] It is clear that every society must in this sense possess an order and that such an order will often exist without having been deliberately created. As has been said by a distinguished social anthropologist, 'that there is some order, consistency and constancy in social life, is obvious. If there were not, none of us would be able to go about our affairs or satisfy our most elementary needs.'[4]

Living as members of society and dependent for the satisfaction of most of our needs on various forms of co-operation with others, we depend for the effective pursuit of our aims clearly on the correspondence of the expectations concerning the actions of others on which our plans are based with what they will really do. This matching of the intentions and expectations that determine the actions of different individuals is the form in which order manifests itself in social life; and it will be the question of how such an order does come about that will be our immediate concern. The first answer to which our anthropomorphic habits of thought almost inevitably lead us is that it must be due to the design of some thinking mind.[5] And because order has been generally interpreted as such a deliberate *arrangement* by somebody, the concept has become unpopular among most friends of liberty and has been favoured mainly by authoritarians. According to this interpretation order in society must rest on a relation of command and obedience, or a hierarchical structure of the whole of society in which the will of superiors, and ultimately of some single supreme authority, determines what each individual must do.

This authoritarian connotation of the concept of order derives, however, entirely from the belief that order can be created only by forces outside the system (or 'exogenously'). It does not apply to an equilibrium set up from within[6] (or 'endogenously') such as that which the general theory of the market endeavours to explain. A spontaneous order of this kind has in many respects properties different from those of a made order.

The two sources of order

The study of spontaneous orders has long been the peculiar task of economic theory, although, of course, biology has from its beginning been concerned with that special kind of spontaneous order which we call an organism. Only recently has there arisen within the physical sciences under the name of cybernetics a special discipline which is also concerned with what are called self-organizing or self-generating systems. [7]

The distinction of this kind of order from one which has been made by somebody putting the elements of a set in their places or directing their movements is indispensable for any understanding of the processes of society as well as for all social policy. There are several terms available for describing each kind of order. The made order which we have already referred to as an exogenous order or an arrangement may again be described as a construction, an artificial order or, especially where we have to deal with a directed social order, as an *organization*. The grown order, on the other hand, which we have referred to as a self-generating or endogenous order, is in English most conveniently described as a *spontaneous order*. Classical Greek was more fortunate in possessing distinct single words for the two kinds of order, namely *taxis* for a made order, such as, for example, an order of battle, [8] and *kosmos* for a grown order, meaning originally 'a right order in a state or a community'. [9] We shall occasionally avail ourselves of these Greek words as technical terms to describe the two kinds of order.

It would be no exaggeration to say that social theory begins with—and has an object only because of—the discovery that there exist orderly structures which are the product of the action of many men but are not the result of human design. In some fields this is now universally accepted. Although there was a time when men believed that even language and morals had been 'invented' by some genius of the past, everybody recognizes now that they are the outcome of a process of evolution whose results nobody foresaw or designed. But in other fields many people still treat with suspicion the claim that the patterns of interaction of many men can show an order that is of nobody's deliberate making; in the economic sphere, in particular, critics still pour uncomprehending ridicule on Adam Smith's expression of the 'invisible hand' by which, in the language of his time, he described how man is led 'to promote an end which was no part of his intentions'. [10] If indignant reformers still complain of the chaos of economic affairs, insinuating a complete absence of order, this is partly because they cannot conceive of an order which is not deliberately made, and partly because to them an order means something aiming at concrete purposes which is, as we shall see, what a spontaneous order cannot do.

We shall examine later (see volume 2, chapter 10) how that coincidence of expectations and plans is produced which characterizes the market order and the nature of the benefits we derive from it. For the moment we are concerned only with the fact that an order not made by man does exist and with the reasons why this is not more readily recognized. The main reason is that such orders as that of the market do not obtrude themselves on our senses but have to be traced by our intellect. We cannot see, or otherwise intuitively perceive, this order of meaningful actions, but are only able mentally to reconstruct it by tracing the relations that exist between the elements. We shall describe this feature by saying that it is an abstract and not a concrete order.

The distinguishing properties of spontaneous orders

One effect of our habitually identifying order with a made order or *taxis* is indeed that we tend to ascribe to all order certain properties which deliberate arrangements regularly, and with respect to some of these properties necessarily, possess. Such orders are relatively *simple* or at least necessarily confined to such moderate degrees of complexity as the maker can still survey; they are usually *concrete* in the sense just mentioned that their existence can be intuitively perceived by inspection; and, finally, having been made deliberately, they invariably do (or at one time did) *serve a purpose* of the maker. None of these characteristics necessarily belong to a spontaneous order or *kosmos*. Its degree of complexity is not limited to what a human mind can master. Its existence need not manifest itself to our senses but may be based on purely *abstract* relations which we can only mentally reconstruct. And not having been made it *cannot* legitimately be said to *have a particular purpose*, although our awareness of its existence may be extremely important for our successful pursuit of a great variety of different purposes.

Spontaneous orders are not necessarily complex, but unlike deliberate human arrangements, they may achieve any degree of complexity. One of our main contentions will be that very complex orders, comprising more particular facts than any brain could ascertain or manipulate, can be brought about only through forces inducing the formation of spontaneous orders.

Spontaneous orders need not be what we have called abstract, but they will often consist of a system of abstract relations between elements which are also defined only by abstract properties, and for this reason will not be intuitively perceivable and not recognizable except on the basis of a theory accounting for their character. The significance of the abstract character of such orders rests on the fact that they may persist while all the particular elements they comprise, and even the number of such elements, change. All that is necessary to preserve such an abstract order is that a certain structure of relationships be maintained, or that elements of a certain kind (but variable in number) continue to be related in a certain manner.

Most important, however, is the relation of a spontaneous order to the conception of purpose. Since such an order has not been created by an outside agency, the order as such also can have no purpose, although its existence may be very serviceable to the individuals which move within such order. But in a different sense it may well be said that the order rests on purposive action of its elements, when 'purpose' would, of course, mean nothing more than that their actions tend to secure the preservation or restoration of that order. The use of 'purposive' in this sense as a sort of 'teleological shorthand', as it has been called by biologists, is unobjectionable so long as we do not imply an awareness of purpose of the part of the elements, but mean merely that the elements have acquired regularities of conduct conducive to the maintenance of the order—presumably because those who did act in certain ways had within the resulting order a better chance of survival than those who did not. In general, however, it is preferable to avoid in this connection the term 'purpose' and to speak instead of 'function'.

Spontaneous orders in nature

It will be instructive to consider briefly the character of some spontaneous orders which we find in nature, since here some of their characteristic properties stand out most clearly. There are in the physical world many instances of complex orders which we could bring about only by availing ourselves of the known forces which tend to lead to their formation, and never by deliberately placing each element in the appropriate position. We can never produce a crystal or a complex organic compound by placing the individual atoms in such a position that they will form the lattice of a crystal or the system based on benzol rings which make up an

39

organic compound. But we can create the conditions in which they will arrange themselves in such a manner.

What does in these instances determine not only the general character of the crystal or compound that will be formed but also the particular position of any one element in them? The important point is that the regularity of the conduct of the elements will determine the general character of the resulting order but not all the detail of its particular manifestation. The particular manner in which the resulting abstract order will manifest itself will depend, in addition to the rules which govern the actions of the elements, on their initial position and on all the particular circumstances of the immediate environment to which each of them will react in the course of the formation of that order. The order, in other words, will always be an adaptation to a large number of particular facts which will not be known in their totality to anyone.

We should note that a regular pattern will thus form itself not only if the elements all obey the same rules and their different actions are determined only by the different positions of the several individuals relatively to each other, but also, as is true in the case of the chemical compound, if there are different kinds of elements which act in part according to different rules. Whichever is the case, we shall be able to predict only the general character of the order that will form itself, and not the particular position which any particular element will occupy relatively to any other element.

Another example from physics is in some respects even more instructive. In the familiar school experiment in which iron filings on a sheet of paper are made to arrange themselves along some of the lines of force of a magnet placed below, we can predict the general shape of the chains that will be formed by the filings hooking themselves together; but we cannot predict along which ones of the family of an infinite number of such curves that define the magnetic field these chains will place themselves. This will depend on the position, direction, weight, roughness or smoothness of each of the iron filings and on all the irregularities of the surface of the paper. The forces emanating from the magnet and from each of the iron filings will thus interact with the environment to produce a unique instance of a general pattern, the general character of which will be determined by known laws, but the concrete appearance of which will depend on particular circumstances we cannot fully ascertain.

In society, reliance on spontaneous order both extends and limits our powers of control

Since a spontaneous order results from the individual elements adapting themselves to circumstances which directly affect only some of them, and which in their totality need not be known to anyone, it may extend to circumstances so complex that no mind can comprehend them all. Consequently, the concept becomes particularly important when we turn from mechanical to such 'more highly organized' or essentially complex phenomena as we encounter in the realms of life, mind and society. Here we have to deal with 'grown' structures with a degree of complexity which they have assumed and could assume only because they were produced by spontaneous ordering forces. They in consequence present us with peculiar difficulties in our effort to explain them as well as in any attempt to influence their character. Since we can know at most the rules observed by the elements of various kinds of which the structures are made up, but not all the individual elements and never all the particular circumstances in which each of them is placed, our knowledge will be restricted to the general character of the order which will form itself. And even where, as is true of a society of human beings, we may be in a position to alter at least some of the rules of conduct which the elements obey, we shall thereby be able to influence only the general character and not the detail of the resulting order.

This means that, though the use of spontaneous ordering forces enables us to induce the formation of an order of such a degree of complexity (namely comprising elements of such numbers, diversity and variety of conditions) as we could never master intellectually, or deliberately arrange, we will have less power over the details of such an order than we would of one which we produce by arrangement. In the case of spontaenous orders we may, by determining some of the factors which shape them, determine their abstract features, but we will have to leave the particulars to circumstances which we do not know. Thus, by relying on the spontaneously ordering forces, we can extend the scope or range of the order which we may induce to form, precisely because its particular manifestation will depend on many more circumstances than can be known to us—and in the case of a social order, because such an order will utilize the separate knowledge of all its several members, without this knowledge ever being concentrated in a single mind, or being subject to those processes of deliberate coordination and adaptation which a mind performs.

In consequence, the degree of power of control over the extended and more complex order will be much smaller than that which we could exercise over a made order or *taxis*. There will be many aspects of it over which we will possess no control at all, or which at least we shall not be able to alter without interfering with—and to that extent impeding—the forces producing the spontaneous order. Any desire we may have concerning the particular position of individual elements, or the relation between particular individuals or groups, could not be satisfied without upsetting the overall order. The kind of power which in this respect we would possess over a concrete arrangement or *taxis* we would not have over a spontaneous order where we would know, and be able to influence, only the abstract aspects.

It is important to note here that there are two different respects in which order may be a matter of degree. How well ordered a set of objects or events is depends on how many of the attributes of (or the relations between) the elements we can learn to predict. Different orders may in this respect differ from each other in either or both of two ways: the orderliness may concern only very few relations between the elements, or a great many; and, second, the regularity thus defined may be great in the sense that it will be confirmed by all or nearly all instances, or it may be found to prevail only in a majority of the instances and thus allow us to predict its occurrence only with a certain degree of probability. In the first instance we may predict only a few of the features of the resulting structure, but do so with great confidence; such an order would be limited but may still be perfect. In the second instance we shall be able to predict much more, but with only a fair degree of certainty. The knowledge of the existence of an order will however still be useful even if this order is restricted in either or both these respects; and the reliance on spontaneously ordering forces may be preferable or even indispensable, although the order towards which a system tends will in fact be only more or less imperfectly approached. The market order in particular will regularly secure only a certain probability that the expected relations will prevail, but it is, nevertheless, the only way in which so many activities depending on dispersed knowledge can be effectively integrated into a single order.

Spontaneous orders result from their elements obeying certain rules of conduct

We have already indicated that the formation of spontaneous orders is the result of their elements following certain rules in their responses to their immediate environment. The nature of these rules still needs fuller examination, partly because the word 'rule' is apt to suggest some erroneous ideas, and partly because the rules which determine a spontaneous order differ in important respects from another kind of rules which are needed in regulating an organization or *taxis*.

On the first point, the instances of spontaneous orders which we have given from physics are instructive because they clearly show that the rules which govern the actions of the elements of such spontaneous orders need not be rules which are 'known' to these elements; it is sufficient that the elements actually behave in a manner which can be described by such rules. The concept of rules as we use it in this context therefore does not imply that such rules exist in articulated ('verbalized') forms, but only that it is possible to discover rules which the actions of the individuals in fact follow. To emphasize this we have occasionally spoken of 'regularity' rather than of rules, but regularity, of course, means simply that the elements behave according to rules.

That rules in this sense exist and operate without being explicitly known to those who obey them applies also to many of the rules which govern the actions of men and thereby determine a spontaneous social order. Man certainly does not know all the rules which guide his actions in the sense that he is able to state them in words. At least in primitive human society, scarcely less than in animal societies, the structure of social life is determined by rules of conduct which manifest themselves only by being in fact observed. Only when individual intellects begin to differ to a significant degree will it become necessary to express these rules in a form in which they can be communicated and explicitly taught, deviant behaviour corrected, and differences of opinion about appropriate behaviour decided. Although man never existed without laws that he obeyed, he did, of course, exist for hundreds of thousands of years without laws he 'knew' in the sense that he was able to articulate them.

What is of still greater importance in this connection, however, is that not every regularity in the behaviour of the elements does

43

secure an overall order. Some rules governing individual behaviour might clearly make altogether impossible the formation of an overall order. Our problem is what kind of rules of conduct will produce an order of society and what kind of order particular rules will produce.

The classical instance of rules of the behaviour of the elements which will not produce order comes from the physical sciences: it is the second law of thermodynamics or the law of enthropy, according to which the tendency of the molecules of a gas to move at constant speeds in straight lines produces a state for which the term 'perfect disorder' has been coined. Similarly, it is evident that in society some perfectly regular behaviour of the individuals could produce only disorder: if the rule were that any individual should try to kill any other he encountered, or flee as soon as he saw another, the result would clearly be the complete impossibility of an order in which the activities of the individuals were based on collaboration with others.

Society can thus exist only if by a process of selection rules have evolved which lead individuals to behave in a manner which makes social life possible. It should be remembered that for this purpose selection will operate as between societies of different types, that is, be guided by the properties of their respective orders, but that the properties supporting this order will be properties of the individuals, namely their propensity to obey certain rules of conduct on which the order of action of the group as a whole rests.

To put this differently: in a social order the particular circumstances to which each individual will react will be those known to him. But the individual responses to particular circumstances will result in an overall order only if the individuals obey such rules as will produce an order. Even a very limited similarity in their behaviour may be sufficient if the rules which they all obey are such as to produce an order. Such an order will always constitute an adaptation to the multitude of circumstances which are known to all the members of that society taken together but which are not known as a whole to any one person. This need not mean that the different persons will in similar circumstances do precisely the same thing; but merely that for the formation of such an overall order it is necessary that in some respects all individuals follow definite rules, or that their actions are limited to a certain range. In other words, the responses of the individuals to the events in their environment need be similar only in certain abstract aspects to ensure that a determinate overall order will result.

The question which is of central importance as much for social theory as for social policy is thus what properties the rules must possess so that the separate actions of the individuals will produce an overall order. Some such rules all individuals of a society will obey because of the similar manner in which their environment represents itself to their minds. Others they will follow spontaneously because they will be part of their common cultural tradition. But there will be still others which they may have to be made to obey, since, although it would be in the interest of each to disregard them, the overall order on which the success of their actions depends will arise only if these rules are generally followed.

In a modern society based on exchange, one of the chief regularities in individual behaviour will result from the similarity of situations in which most individuals find themselves in working to earn an income; which means that they will normally prefer a larger return from their efforts to a smaller one, and often that they will increase their efforts in a particular direction if the prospects of return improve. This is a rule that will be followed at least with sufficient frequency to impress upon such a society an order of a certain kind. But the fact that most people will follow this rule will still leave the character of the resulting order very indeterminate, and by itself certainly would not be sufficient to give it a beneficial character. For the resulting order to be beneficial people must also observe some conventional rules, that is, rules which do not simply follow from their desires and their insight into relations of cause and effect, but which are normative and tell them what they ought to or ought not to do.

We shall later have to consider more fully the precise relation between the various kinds of rules which the people in fact obey and the resulting order of actions. Our main interest will then be those rules which, because we can deliberately alter them, become the chief instrument whereby we can affect the resulting order, namely the rules of law. At the moment our concern must be to make clear that while the rules on which a spontaneous order rests, may also be of spontaneous origin, this need not always be the case. Although undoubtedly an order originally formed itself spontaneously because the individuals followed rules which had not been deliberately made but had arisen spontaneously, people gradually learned to improve those rules; and it is at least conceivable that the formation of a spontaneous order relies entirely on rules that were deliberately made. The spontaneous character of the resulting order must therefore be distinguished from the spontaneous origin of the rules on which it rests, and it is possible that an order which would still have to be described as spontaneous rests on rules which are entirely the result of deliberate design. In the kind of society with which we are familiar, of course, only some of the rules which people in fact observe, namely some of the rules of law (but never all, even of these) will be the product of deliberate design, while most of the rules of morals and custom will be spontaneous growths.

That even an order which rests on made rules may be spontaneous in character is shown by the fact that its particular manifestation will always depend on many circumstances which the designer of these rules did not and could not know. The particular content of the order will depend on the concrete circumstances known only to the individuals who obey the rules and apply them to facts known only to them. It will be through the knowledge of these individuals both of the rules and of the particular facts that both will determine the resulting order.

The spontaneous order of society is made up of individuals and organizations

In any group of men of more than the smallest size, collaboration will always rest both on spontaneous order as well as on deliberate organization. There is no doubt that for many limited tasks organization is the most powerful method of effective co-ordination because it enables us to adapt the resulting order much more fully to our wishes, while where, because of the complexity of the circumstances to be taken into account, we must rely on the forces making for a spontaneous order, our power over the particular contents of this order is necessarily restricted.

That the two kinds of order will regularly coexist in every society of any degree of complexity does not mean, however, that we can combine them in any manner we like. What in fact we find in all free societies is that, although groups of men will join in organizations for the achievement of some particular ends, the co-ordination of the activities of all these separate organizations, as well as of the separate individuals, is brought about by the forces making for a spontaneous order. The family, the farm, the plant, the firm, the corporation and the various associations, and all the public institutions including government, are organizations which in turn are integrated into a more comprehensive spontaneous order. It is advisable to reserve the term 'society' for this spontaneous overall order so that we may distinguish it from all the organized smaller groups which will exist within it, as well as from such smaller and more or less isolated groups as the horde, the tribe, or the clan, whose members will at least in some respects act under a central direction for common purposes. In some instances it will be the same group which at times, as when engaged in most of its daily routine, will operate as a spontaneous order maintained by the observation of conventional rules without the necessity of commands, while at other times, as when hunting, migrating, or fighting, it will be acting as an organization under the directing will of a chief.

The spontaneous order which we call a society also need not have such sharp boundaries as an organization will usually possess. There will often be a nucleus, or several nuclei, of more closely related individuals occupying a central position in a more loosely connected but more extensive order. Such particular societies within the Great Society may arise as the result of spatial proximity, or of some other special circumstances which produce closer relations among their members. And different partial societies of this sort will often overlap and every individual may, in addition to being a member of the Great Society, be a member of numerous other spontaneous sub-orders or partial societies of this sort as well as of various organizations existing within the comprehensive Great Society.

Of the organizations existing within the Great Society one which regularly occupies a very special position will be that which we call government. Although it is conceivable that the spontaneous order which we call society may exist without government, if the minimum of rules required for the formation of such an order is observed without an organized apparatus for their enforcement, in most circumstances the organization which we call government becomes indispensable in order to assure that those rules are obeyed.

This particular function of government is somewhat like that of a maintenance squad of a factory, its object being not to produce any particular services or products to be consumed by the citizens, but rather to see that the mechanism which regulates the production of those goods and services is kept in working order. The purposes for which this machinery is currently being used will be determined by those who operate its parts and in the last resort by those who buy its products.

The same organization that is charged with keeping in order an operating structure which the individuals will use for their own purposes, will, however, in addition to the task of enforcing the rules on which that order rests, usually be expected also to render other services which the spontaneous order cannot produce adequately. These two distinct functions of government are usually not clearly separated; yet, as we shall see, the distinction between the coercive functions in which government enforces rules of conduct, and its service functions in which it need merely administer resources placed at its disposal, is of fundamental importance. In the second it is one organization among many and like the others part of a spontaneous overall order, while in the first it provides an essential condition for the preservation of that overall order.

In English it is possible, and has long been usual, to discuss these two types of order in terms of the distinction between 'society' and 'government'. There is no need in the discussion of these problems, so long as only one country is concerned, to bring in the metaphysically charged term 'state'. It is largely under the influence of continental and particularly Hegelian thought that in the course of the last hundred years the practice of speaking of the 'state' (preferably with a capital 'S'), where 'government' is more appropriate and precise, has come to be widely adopted. That which acts, or pursues a policy, is however always the organization of government; and it does not make for clarity to drag in the term 'state' where 'government' is quite sufficient. It becomes particularly misleading when 'the state' rather than 'government' is contrasted with 'society' to indicate that the first is an organization and the second a spontaneous order.

The rules of spontaneous orders and the rules of organization

One of our chief contentions will be that, though spontaneous order and organization will always coexist, it is still not possible to mix these two principles of order in any manner we like. If this is not more generally understood it is due to the fact that for the determination of both kinds of order we have to rely on rules, and that the important differences between the kinds of rules which the two different kinds of order require are generally not recognized.

To some extent every organization must rely also on rules and not only on specific commands. The reason here is the same as that which makes it necessary for a spontaneous order to rely solely on rules: namely that by guiding the actions of individuals by rules rather than specific commands it is possible to make use of knowledge which nobody possesses as a whole. Every organization in which the members are not mere tools of the organizer will determine by commands only the function to be performed by each member, the purposes to be achieved, and certain general aspects of the methods to be employed, and will leave the detail to be decided by the individuals on the basis of their respective knowledge and skills.

Organization encounters here the problem which any attempt to bring order into complex human activities meets: the organizer must wish the individuals who are to co-operate to make use of knowledge that he himself does not possess. In none but the most simple kind of organization is it conceivable that all the details of all activities are governed by a single mind. Certainly nobody has yet succeeded in deliberately arranging all the activities that go on in a complex society. If anyone did ever succeed in fully organizing such a society, it would no longer make use of many minds but would be altogether dependent on one mind; it would certainly not be very complex but extremely primitive—and so would soon be the mind whose knowledge and will determined everything. The facts which could enter into the design of such an order could be only those which were known and digested by this mind; and as only he could decide on action and thus gain experience, there would be none of that interplay of many minds in which alone mind can grow.

What distinguishes the rules which will govern action within an organization is that they must be rules for the performance of assigned tasks. They presuppose that the place of each individual in a fixed structure is determined by command and that the rules each individual must obey depend on the place which he has been assigned and on the particular ends which have been indicated for him by the commanding authority. The rules will thus regulate merely the detail of the action of appointed functionaries or agencies of government.

Rules of organization are thus necessarily subsidiary to commands, filling in the gaps left by the commands. Such rules will be different for the different members of the organization according to the different roles which have been assigned to them, and they will have to be interpreted in the light of the purposes determined by the commands. Without the assignment of a function and the determination of the ends to be pursued by particular commands, the bare abstract rule would not be sufficient to tell each individual what he must do.

By contrast, the rules governing a spontaneous order must be independent of purpose and be the same, if not necessarily for all members, at least for whole classes of members not individually designated by name. They must, as we shall see, be rules applicable to an unknown and indeterminable number of persons and instances. They will have to be applied by the individuals in the light of their respective knowledge and purposes; and their application will be independent of any common purpose, which the individual need not even know.

In the terms we have adopted this means that the general rules of law that a spontaneous order rests on aim at an abstract order, the particular or concrete content of which is not known or foreseen by anyone; while the commands as well as the rules which govern an organization serve particular results aimed at by those who are in command of the organization. The more complex the order aimed at, the greater will be that part of the separate actions which will have to be determined by circumstances not known to those who direct the whole, and the more dependent control will be on rules rather than on specific commands. In the most complex types of organizations, indeed, little more than the assignment of particular functions and the general aim will be determined by command of the supreme authority, while the performance of these functions will be regulated only by rules—yet by rules which at least to some degree are specific to the functions assigned to particular persons. Only when we pass from the biggest kind of organization, government, which as organization must still be dedicated to a circumscribed and determined set of specific purposes, to the overall order of the whole of society, do we find an order which relies solely on rules and is entirely spontaneous in character.

It is because it was not dependent on organization but grew up as a spontaneous order that the structure of modern society has attained that degree of complexity which it possesses and which far exceeds any that could have been achieved by deliberate organization. In fact, of course, the rules which made the growth of this complex order possible were initially not designed in expectation of that result; but those people who happened to adopt suitable rules developed a complex civilization which then often spread to others. To maintain that we must deliberately plan modern society because it has become so complex is therefore paradoxical, and the result of a complete misunderstanding of these circumstances. The fact is, rather, that we can preserve an order of such complexity not by the method of directing the members, but only indirectly by enforcing and improving the rules conducive to the formation of a spontaneous order.

We shall see that it is impossible, not only to replace the spontaneous order by organization and at the same time to utilize as much of the dispersed knowledge of all its members as possible, but also to improve or correct this order by interfering in it by direct commands. Such a combination of spontaneous order and organization it can never be rational to adopt. While it is sensible to supplement the commands determining an organization by subsidiary rules, and to use organizations as elements of a spontaneous order, it can never be advantageous to supplement the rules governing a spontaneous order by isolated and subsidiary commands concerning those activities where the actions are guided by the general rules of conduct. This is the gist of the argument against 'interference' or 'intervention' in the market order. The reason why such isolated commands requiring specific actions by members of the spontaneous order can never improve but must disrupt that order is that they will refer to a part of a system of interdependent actions determined by information and guided by purposes known only to the several acting persons but not to the directing authority. The spontaneous order arises from each element balancing all the various factors operating on it and by adjusting all its various actions to each other, a balance which will be destroyed if some of the actions are determined by another agency on the basis of different knowledge and in the service of different ends.

What the general argument against 'interference' thus amounts to is that, although we can endeavour to improve a spontaneous order by revising the general rules on which it rests, and can supplement its results by the efforts of various organizations, we cannot improve the results by specific commands that deprive its members of the possibility of using their knowledge for their purposes.

We will have to consider throughout this book how these two kinds of rules have provided the model for two altogether different conceptions of law and how this has brought it about that authors using the same word 'law' have in fact been speaking about different things. This comes out most clearly in the contrast we find throughout history between those to whom law and liberty were inseparable[11] and those to whom the two were irreconcilable. We find one great tradition extending from the ancient Greeks and Cicero[12] through the Middle Ages[13] to the classical liberals like John Locke, David Hume, Immanuel Kant[14] and the Scottish moral philosophers, down to various American statesmen[15] of the nineteenth and twentieth centuries, for whom law and liberty could not exist apart from each other; while to Thomas Hobbes, Jeremy Bentham[16] and many French thinkers[17] and the modern legal positivists law of necessity means an encroachment on freedom. This apparent conflict between long lines of great thinkers does not mean that they arrived at opposite conclusions, but merely that they were using the word 'law' in different senses.

The terms 'organism' and 'organization'

A few comments should be added on the terms in which the distinction examined in this chapter has most commonly been discussed in the past. Since the beginning of the nineteenth century the terms 'organism' and 'organization' have been frequently used to contrast the two types of order. As we have found it advisable to avoid the former term and to adopt the latter in a specific sense, some comments on their history may be appropriate.

It was natural that the organismal analogy should have been used since ancient times to describe the spontaneous order of society, since organisms were the only kinds of spontaneous order with which everybody was familiar. Organisms are indeed a kind of spontaneous order and as such show many of the characteristics of other spontaneous orders. It was therefore tempting to borrow such terms as 'growth', 'adaptation', and 'function' from them. They are, however, spontaneous orders of a very special kind, possessing also properties which by no means necessarily belong to all spontaneous orders; the analogy in consequence soon becomes more misleading than helpful.[18]

The chief peculiarity of organisms which distinguishes them from the spontaneous orders of society is that in an organism most of the individual elements occupy fixed places which, at least once the organism is mature, they retain once and for all. They also, as a rule, are more or less constant systems consisting of a fixed number of elements which, although some may be replaced by equivalent new ones, retain an order in space readily perceivable with the senses. They are, in consequence, in the terms we have used, orders of a more concrete kind than the spontaneous orders of society, which may be preserved although the total number of elements changes and the individual elements change their places. This relatively concrete character of the order of organisms shows itself in the fact that their existence as distinct wholes can be perceived intuitively by the senses, while the abstract spontaneous order of social structures usually can only be reconstructed by the mind.

The interpretation of society as an organism has almost invariably been used in support of hierarchic and authoritarian views to which the more general conception of the spontaneous order gives no support. Indeed, since Menenius Agrippa, on the occasion of the first secession of the Roman plebs, used the organismal metaphor to justify the privileges of a particular group, it must have been used innumerable times for similar purposes. The suggestion of fixed places assigned to particular elements according to their distinct 'functions', and the much more concrete determination of the biological structures as compared with the abstract character of the spontaneous structures of society, have indeed made the organismal conception of very questionable value for social theory. It has been abused even more than the term 'order' itself when interpreted as a made order or *taxis*, and has frequently been used to defend a hierarchical order, the necessity of 'degree', the relation of command and obedience, or the preservation of established positions of particular individuals, and for this reason has rightly become suspect.

The term 'organization', on the other hand, which in the nineteenth century was frequently used in contrast to 'organism' to express the distinction we have discussed,[19] and which we shall retain to describe a made order or *taxis*, is of comparatively recent origin. It seems to have come into general use at the time of the French Revolution, with reference to which Kant once observed that 'in a recently undertaken reconstruction of a great people into a great state the word *organization* has been frequently and appropriately used for the institution of the magistracies and even the whole state.'[20] The word became characteristic of the spirit of the Napoleonic period[21] and became the central conception in the plans for the 'reconstruction of society' of the chief founders of modern socialism, the Saint Simonians, and of Auguste Comte.[22] Until the term 'socialism' came into general use 'the organization of society as a whole' was in fact the accepted way of referring to what we now describe as socialism.[23] Its central role, particularly for French thinking during the early part of the nineteenth century, was clearly seen by the young Ernest Renan, who in 1849 could speak of the ideal of a 'scientific organization of mankind as the last word of modern science and its daring but legitimate ambition'.[24]

In English, the word appears to have come into general use around 1790 as a technical term for a 'systematic arrangement for a definite purpose'.[25] But it was the Germans who adopted it with particular enthusiasm and to whom it soon appeared to express a peculiar capacity in which they believed themselves to excel other people. This even led to a curious rivalry between French and German scholars, who during the First World War conducted a slightly comic literary dispute across the fighting lines as to which of the two nations had the stronger claim to possessing the secret of organization.[26]

In confining the term here to a made order or *taxis* we follow what seems to have become the general use in sociology and especially in what is known as 'organization theory'.[27] The idea of organization in this sense is a natural consequence of the discovery of the powers of the human intellect and especially of the general attitude of constructivist rationalism. It appeared for a long time as the only procedure by which an order serviceable to human purposes could be deliberately achieved, and it is indeed the intelligent and powerful method of achieving certain known and forseeable results. But as its development is one of the great achievements of constructivism, so is the disregard of its limits one of its most serious defects. What it overlooks is that the growth of that mind which can direct an organization, and of the more comprehensive order within which organizations function, rests on adaptations to the unforeseeable, and that the only possibility of transcending the capacity of individual minds is to rely on those super-personal 'self-organizing' forces which create spontaneous orders.

THREE

PRINCIPLES AND EXPEDIENCY

The frequent recurrence to fundamental principles is
absolutely necessary to preserve the blessings of liberty.
                              Constitution of North Carolina*

Individual aims and collective benefits

The thesis of this book is that a condition of liberty in which all
are allowed to use their knowledge for their purposes, restrained
only by rules of just conduct of universal application, is likely to
produce for them the best conditions for achieving their aims; and
that such a system is likely to be achieved and maintained only if
all authority, including that of the majority of the people, is limited
in the exercise of coercive power by general principles to which the
community has committed itself. Individual freedom, wherever
it has existed, has been largely the product of a prevailing respect
for such principles which, however, have never been fully articulated in constitutional documents. Freedom has been preserved for
prolonged periods because such principles, vaguely and dimly perceived, have governed public opinion. The institutions by which the
countries of the Western world have attempted to protect individual
freedom against progressive encroachment by government have
always proved inadequate when transferred to countries where such
traditions did not prevail. And they have not provided sufficient
protection against the effects of new desires which even among the
peoples of the West now often loom larger than the older conceptions—conceptions that made possible the periods of freedom when
these peoples gained their present position.

I will not undertake here a fuller definition of the term 'freedom' or enlarge upon why we regard individual freedom as so important. That I have attempted in another book.[1] But a few words
should be said about why I prefer the short formula by which I
have repeatedly described the condition of freedom, namely a state

in which each can use his knowledge for his purposes, to the classic phrase of Adam Smith, 'every man, so long as he does not violate the laws of justice [being] left perfectly free to pursue his own interests in his own way.'[2] The reason for my preference is that the latter formula unnecessarily and unfortunately suggests, without intending to, a connection of the argument for individual freedom with egotism or selfishness. The freedom to pursue his own aims is, however, at least as important for the complete altruist as for the most selfish. Altruism, to be a virtue, certainly does not presuppose that one has to follow another person's will. But it is true that much pretended altruism manifests itself in a desire to make others serve the ends which the 'altruist' regards as important.

We need not return here to the undeniable fact that the beneficial effects on others of one's efforts will often become visible to one only if one acts as part of a concerted effort of many in accordance with a coherent plan, and that it may often be difficult for the isolated individual to do much about the evils that deeply concern him. But it is, of course, part of his freedom that for such purposes he can join (or create) organizations which will enable him to take part in concerted action. And though some of the ends of the altruist will be achievable only by collective action, purely selfish ends too will as often be achieved through it. There is no necessary connection between altruism and collective action, or between egotism and individual action.

Freedom can be preserved only by following principles and is destroyed by following expediency

From the insight that the benefits of civilization rest on the use of more knowledge than can be used in any deliberately concerted effort, it follows that it is not in our power to build a desirable society by simply putting together the particular elements that by themselves appear desirable. Although probably all beneficial improvement must be piecemeal, if the separate steps are not guided by a body of coherent principles, the outcome is likely to be a suppression of individual freedom.

The reason for this is very simple, although not generally understood. Since the value of freedom rests on the opportunities it provides for unforeseen and unpredictable actions, we will rarely know what we lose through a particular restriction of freedom. Any such restriction, any coercion other than the enforcement of general rules, will aim at the achievement of some foreseeable particular result, but what is prevented by it will usually not be known. The direct effects of any interference with the market order will be near and clearly visible in most cases, while the more indirect and remote effects will mostly be unknown and will therefore be disregarded. [3] We shall never be aware of all the costs of achieving particular results by such interference.

And so, when we decide each issue solely on what appear to be its individual merits, we always over-estimate the advantages of central direction. Our choice will regularly appear to be one between a certain known and tangible gain and the mere probability of the prevention of some unknown beneficial action by unknown persons. If the choice between freedom and coercion is thus treated as a matter of expediency, [4] freedom is bound to be sacrificed in almost every instance. As in the particular instance we shall hardly ever know what would be the consequence of allowing people to make their own choice, to make the decision in each instance depend only on the foreseeable particular results must lead to the progressive destruction of freedom. There are probably few restrictions on freedom which could not be justified on the grounds that we do not know the particular loss they will cause.

That freedom can be preserved only if it is treated as a supreme principle which must not be sacrificed for particular advantages was fully understood by the leading liberal thinkers of the nineteenth century, one of whom even described liberalism as 'the system of principles'. [5] Such is the chief burden of their warnings concerning 'What is seen and what is not seen in political economy' [6] and about the 'pragmatism that contrary to the intentions of its representatives inexorably leads to socialism'. [7]

All these warnings were, however, thrown to the wind, and the progressive discarding of principles and the increasing determination during the last hundred years to proceed pragmatically [8] is one of the most important innovations in social and economic policy. That we should foreswear all principles or 'isms' in order to achieve greater mastery over our fate is even now proclaimed as the new wisdom of our age. Applying to each task the 'social techniques' most appropriate to its solution, unfettered by any dogmatic belief, seems to some the only manner of proceeding worthy of a rational and scientific age. [9] 'Ideologies', that is sets of principles, have become generally as unpopular as they have always been with aspiring dictators such as Napoleon I or Karl Marx, the two men

57

who gave the word its modern derogatory meaning.

If I am not mistaken, this fashionable contempt for 'ideology', or for all general principles or 'isms', is a characteristic attitude of disillusioned socialists who, because they have been forced by the inherent contradictions of their own ideology to discard it, have concluded that all ideologies must be erroneous and that in order to be rational one must do without one. But to be guided only, as they imagine it to be possible, by explicit particular purposes which one consciously accepts, and to reject all general values whose conduciveness to particular desirable results cannot be demonstrated (or to be guided only by what Max Weber calls 'purposive rationality') is an impossibility. Although, admittedly, an ideology is something which cannot be 'proved' (or demonstrated to be true), it may well be something whose widespread acceptance is the indispensable condition for most of the particular things we strive for.

Those self-styled modern 'realists' have only contempt for the old-fashioned reminder that if one starts unsystematically to interfere with the spontaneous order there is no practicable halting point and that it is therefore necessary to choose between alternative systems. They are pleased to think that by proceeding experimentally and therefore 'scientifically' they will succeed in fitting together in piecemeal fashion a desirable order by choosing for each particular desired result what science shows them to be the most appropriate means of achieving it.

Since warnings against this sort of procedure have often been misunderstood, as one of my earlier books has, a few more words about their intentions may be appropriate. What I meant to argue in *The Road to Serfdom*[10] was certainly not that whenever we depart, however slightly, from what I regard as the principles of a free society, we shall ineluctably be driven to go the whole way to a totalitarian system. It was rather what in more homely language is expressed when we say: 'If you do not mend your principles you will go to the devil.' That this has often been understood to describe a necessary process over which we have no power once we have embarked on it, is merely an indication of how little the importance of principles for the determination of policy is understood, and particularly how completely overlooked is the fundamental fact that by our political actions we unintentionally produce the acceptance of principles which will make further action necessary.

What is overlooked by those unrealistic modern 'realists' who pride themselves on the modernity of their view is that they are advocating something which most of the Western world has indeed been doing for the past two or three generations, and which is responsible for the conditions of present politics. The end of the liberal era of principles might well be dated at the time when, more than eighty years ago, W. S. Jevons pronounced that in economic and social policy 'we can lay down no hard and fast rules, but must treat every case in detail upon its merits.'[11] Ten years later Herbert Spencer could already speak of 'the reigning school of politics' by whom 'nothing less than scorn is shown for every doctrine which implies restraints on the doings of immediate expediency' or which relies on 'abstract principles'.[12]

This 'realistic' view which has now dominated politics for so long has hardly produced the results which its advocates desired. Instead of having achieved greater mastery over our fate we find ourselves in fact more frequently committed to a path which we have not deliberately chosen, and faced with 'inevitable necessities' of further action which, though never intended, are the result of what we have done.

The 'necessities' of policy are generally the consequences of earlier measures

The contention often advanced that certain political measures were inevitable has a curious double aspect. With regard to developments that are approved by those who employ this argument, it is readily accepted and used in justification of the actions. But when developments take an undesirable turn, the suggestion that this is not the effect of circumstances beyond our control, but the necessary consequence of our earlier decisions, is rejected with scorn. The idea that we are not fully free to pick and choose whatever combination of features we wish our society to possess, or to fit them together into a viable whole, that is, that we cannot build a desirable social order like a mosaic by selecting whatever particular parts we like best, and that many well-intentioned measures may have a long train of unforeseeable and undesirable consequences, seems to be intolerable to modern man. He has been taught that what he has made he can also alter at will to suit his wishes, and conversely, that what he can alter he must also have made in the first instance. He has not yet learnt that this naïve belief derives from that ambiguity of the word 'made' which we discussed earlier.

In fact, of course, the chief circumstance which will make

certain measures seem unavoidable is usually the result of our past actions and of the opinions which are now held. Most of the 'necessities' of policy are of our own creation. I am myself now old enough to have been told more than once by my elders that certain consequences of their policy which I foresaw would never occur, and later, when they did appear, to have been told by younger men that these had been inevitable and quite independent of what in fact was done.

The reason why we cannot achieve a coherent whole by just fitting together any elements we like is that the appropriateness of any particular arrangement within a spontaneous order will depend on all the rest of it, and that any particular change we make in it will tell us little about how it would operate in a different setting. An experiment can tell us only whether any innovation does or does not fit into a given framework. But to hope that we can build a coherent order by random experimentation with particular solutions of individual problems and without following guiding principles is an illusion. Experience tells us much about the effectiveness of different social and economic systems as a whole. But an order of the complexity of modern society can be designed neither as a whole, nor by shaping each part separately without regard to the rest, but only by consistently adhering to certain principles throughout a process of evolution.

This is not to say that these 'principles' must necessarily take the form of articulated rules. Principles are often more effective guides for action when they appear as no more than an unreasoned prejudice, a general feeling that certain things simply 'are not done'; while as soon as they are explicitly stated speculation begins about their correctness and their validity. It is probably true that in the eighteenth century the English, little given to speculation about general principles, were for this reason much more firmly guided by strong opinions about what kinds of political actions were permissible, than the French who tried so hard to discover and adopt such principles. Once the instinctive certainty is lost, perhaps as a result of unsuccessful attempts to put into words principles that had been observed 'intuitively', there is no way of regaining such guidance other than to search for a correct statement of what before was known implicitly.

The impression that the English in the seventeenth and eighteenth centuries, through their gift of 'muddling through' and their 'genius for compromise', succeeded in building up a viable system without talking much about principles, while the French, with all their concern about explicit assumptions and clear formulations, never did so, may thus be misleading. The truth seems to be that while they talked little about principles, the English were much more surely guided by principles, while in France the very speculation about basic principles prevented any one set of principles from taking a firm hold.

The danger of attaching greater importance to the predictable rather than to the merely possible consequences of our actions

The preservation of a free system is so difficult precisely because it requires a constant rejection of measures which appear to be required to secure particular results, on no stronger grounds than that they conflict with a general rule, and frequently without our knowing what will be the costs of not observing the rule in the particular instance. A successful defence of freedom must therefore be dogmatic and make no concessions to expediency, even where it is not possible to show that, besides the known beneficial effects, some particular harmful result would also follow from its infringement. Freedom will prevail only if it is accepted as a general principle whose application to particular instances requires no justification. It is thus a misunderstanding to blame classical liberalism for having been too doctrinaire. Its defect was not that it adhered too stubbornly to principles, but rather that it lacked principles sufficiently definite to provide clear guidance, and that it often appeared simply to accept the traditional functions of government and to oppose all new ones. Consistency is possible only if definite principles are accepted. But the concept of liberty with which the liberals of the nineteenth century operated was in many respects so vague that it did not provide clear guidance.

People will not refrain from those restrictions on individual liberty that appear to them the simplest and most direct remedy of a recognized evil, if there does not prevail a strong belief in definite principles. The loss of such belief and the preference for expediency is in part a result of the fact that we no longer have any principles which can be rationally defended. The rules of thumb which at one time were accepted were not adequate to decide what is and what is not permissible in a free system. We have no longer even a generally understood name for what the term 'free system' only vaguely describes. Certainly neither 'capitalism' nor *laissez-*

faire properly describe it; and both terms are understandably more popular with the enemies than with the defenders of a free system. 'Capitalism' is an appropriate name at most for the partial realization of such a system in a certain historical phase, but always misleading because it suggests a system which mainly benefits the capitalists, while in fact it is a system which imposes upon enterprise a discipline under which the managers chafe and which each endeavours to escape. *Laissez-faire* was never more than a rule of thumb. It indeed expressed protest against abuses of governmental power, but never provided a criterion by which one could decide what were the proper functions of government. Much the same applies to the terms 'free enterprise' or 'market economy' which, without a definition of the free sphere of the individual, say little. The expression 'liberty under the law', which at one time perhaps conveyed the essential point better than any other, has become almost meaningless because both 'liberty' and 'law' no longer have a clear meaning. And the only term that in the past was widely and correctly understood, namely 'liberalism', has 'as a supreme but unintended compliment been appropriated by the opponents of this ideal'.[13]

The lay reader may not be fully aware how much we have already moved away from the ideal expressed by those terms. While the lawyer or political scientist will at once see that what I shall be espousing is an ideal that has largely vanished and has never been fully realized, it is probably true that the majority of people believe that something like it still governs public affairs. It is because we have departed from the ideal so much further than most people realize, and because, unless this development is soon checked, it will by its own momentum transform society from a free into a totalitarian one, that we must reconsider the general principles guiding our political actions. We are still as free as we are because certain traditional but rapidly vanishing prejudices have impeded the process by which the inherent logic of the changes we have already made tends to assert itself in an ever widening field. In the present state of opinion the ultimate victory of totalitarianism would indeed be no more than the final victory of the ideas already dominant in the intellectual sphere over a merely traditionalist resistance.

Spurious realism and the required courage to consider utopia

With respect to policy, the methodological insight that in the case

62

of complex spontaneous orders we will never be able to determine more than the general principles on which they operate or to predict the particular changes that any event in the environment will bring about, has far-reaching consequences. It means that where we rely on spontaneous ordering forces we shall often not be able to foresee the particular changes by which the necessary adaptation to altered external circumstances will be brought about, and sometimes perhaps not even be able to conceive in what manner the restoration of a disturbed 'equilibrium' or 'balance' can be accomplished. This ignorance of how the mechanism of the spontaneous order will solve such a 'problem' which we know must be solved somehow if the overall order is not to disintegrate, often produces a panic-like alarm and the demand for government action for the restoration of the disturbed balance.

Often it is even the acquisition of a partial insight into the character of the spontaneous overall order that becomes the cause of the demands for deliberate control. So long as the balance of trade, or the correspondence of supply and demand of any particular commodity, adjusted itself spontaneously after any disturbance, men rarely asked themselves how this happened. But, once they became aware of the necessity of such constant readjustments, they felt that somebody must be made responsible for deliberately bringing them about. The economist, from the very nature of his schematic picture of the spontaneous order, could counter such apprehension only by the confident assertion that the required new balance would establish itself somehow if we did not interfere with the spontaneous forces; but, as he is usually unable to predict precisely how this would happen, his assertions were not very convincing.

Yet when it is possible to foresee how the spontaneous forces are likely to restore the disturbed balance, the situation becomes even worse. The necessity of adaptation to unforeseen events will always mean that someone is going to be hurt, that someone's expectations will be disappointed or his efforts frustrated. This leads to the demand that the required adjustment be brought about by deliberate guidance, which in practice must mean that authority is to decide who is to be hurt. The effect of this is often that necessary adjustments will be prevented whenever they can be foreseen.

What helpful insight science can provide for the guidance of policy consists in an understanding of the general nature of the spontaneous order, and not in any knowledge of the particulars of a concrete situation, which it does not and cannot possess. The true appreciation of what science has to contribute to the solution of our political tasks, which in the nineteenth century was fairly general, has been obscured by the new tendency derived from a now fashionable misconception of the nature of scientific method: the belief that science consists of a collection of particular observed facts, which is erroneous so far as science in general is concerned, but doubly misleading where we have to deal with the parts of a complex spontaneous order. Since all the events in any part of such an order are interdependent, and an abstract order of this sort has no recurrent concrete parts which can be identified by individual attributes, it is necessarily vain to try to discover by observation regularities in any of its parts. The only theory which in this field can lay claim to scientific status is the theory of the order as a whole; and such a theory (although it has, of course, to be tested on the facts) can never be achieved inductively by observation but only through constructing mental models made up from the observable elements.

The myopic view of science that concentrates on the study of particular facts because they alone are empirically observable, and whose advocates even pride themselves on not being guided by such a conception of the overall order as can be obtained only by what they call 'abstract speculation', by no means increases our power of shaping a desirable order, but in fact deprives us of all effective guidance for successful action. The spurious 'realism' which deceives itself in believing that it can dispense with any guiding conception of the nature of the overall order, and confines itself to an examination of particular 'techniques' for achieving particular results, is in reality highly unrealistic. Especially when this attitude leads, as it frequently does, to a judgment of the advisability of particular measures by consideration of the 'practicability' in the given political climate of opinion, it often tends merely to drive us further into an impasse. Such must be the ultimate results of successive measures which all tend to destroy the overall order that their advocates at the same time tacitly assume to exist.

It is not to be denied that to some extent the guiding model of the overall order will always be an utopia, something to which the existing situation will be only a distant approximation and which many people will regard as wholly impractical. Yet it is only by constantly holding up the guiding conception of an internally consistent model which could be realized by the consistent application of the same principles, that anything like an effective framework for a functioning spontaneous order will be achieved. Adam Smith thought that 'to expect, indeed, that freedom of trade should ever be entirely restored in Great Britain is as absurd as to expect an Oceana or Utopia should ever be established in it.'[14] Yet seventy year later, largely as a result of his work, it was achieved.

Utopia, like ideology, is a bad word today; and it is true that most utopias aim at radically redesigning society and suffer from internal contradictions which make their realization impossible. But an ideal picture of a society which may not be wholly achievable, or a guiding conception of the overall order to be aimed at, is nevertheless not only the indispensable precondition of any rational policy, but also the chief contribution that science can make to the solution of the problems of practical policy.

The role of the lawyer in political evolution

The chief instrument of deliberate change in modern society is legislation. But however carefully we may think out beforehand every single act of law-making, we are never free to redesign completely the legal system as a whole, or to remake it out of the whole cloth according to a coherent design. Law-making is necessarily a continuous process in which every step produces hitherto unforeseen consequences for what we can or must do next. The parts of a legal system are not so much adjusted to each other according to a comprehensive overall view, as gradually adapted to each other by the successive application of general principles to particular problems—principles, that is, which are often not even explicitly known but merely implicit in the particular measures that are taken. For those who imagine it possible to arrange deliberately all the particular activities of a Great Society according to a coherent plan, it should indeed be a sobering reflection that this has not proved possible even for such a part of the whole as the system of law. Few facts show more clearly how prevailing conceptions will bring about a continuous change, producing measures that in the beginning nobody had desired or foreseen but which appear inevitable in due course, than the process of the change of law. Every single step in this process is determined by problems that arise when the principles laid down by (or implicit in) earlier decisions are applied to circumstances which were then not foreseen. There is nothing specially mysterious about these 'inner dynamics of the law' which produce change not willed as a whole by anybody.

In this process the individual lawyer is necessarily more an unwitting tool, a link in a chain of events that he does not see as a whole, than a conscious initiator. Whether he acts as a judge or as the drafter of a statute, the framework of general conceptions into which we must fit his decision is given to him, and his task is to apply these general principles of the law, not to question them. However much he may be concerned about the future implications of his decisions, he can judge them only in the context of all the other recognized principles of the law that are given to him. This is, of course, as it ought to be; it is of the essence of legal thinking and of just decisions that the lawyer strives to make the whole system consistent.

It is often said that the professional bias of the lawyer is conservative.[15] In certain conditions, namely when some basic principles of the law have been accepted for a long time, they will indeed govern the whole system of law, its general spirit as well as every single rule and application within it. At such times it will possess great inherent stability. Every lawyer will, when he has to interpret or apply a rule which is not in accord with the rest of the system, endeavour so to bend it as to make it conform with the others. The legal profession as a whole may thus occasionally in effect even nullify the intention of the legislator, not out of disrespect for the law, but, on the contrary, because their technique leads them to give preference to what is still the predominant part of the law and to fit an alien element into it by so transforming it as to make it harmonize with the whole.

The situation is entirely different, however, when a general philosophy of the law which is not in accord with the greater part of the existing law has recently gained ascendancy. The same lawyers will, through the same habits and techniques, and generally as unwittingly, become a revolutionary force, as effective in transforming the law down to every detail as they were before in preserving it. The same forces which in the first condition make for lack of movement, will in the second tend to accelerate change until it has transformed the whole body of law much beyond the point that anyone foresaw or desired. Whether this process will lead to a new equilibrium or to a disintegration of the whole body of law in the sense in which we still chiefly understand the word, will depend on the character of the new philosophy.

We live in such a period of transformation of the law by inner forces and it is submitted that, if the principles which at present guide that process are allowed to work themselves out to their logical consequences, law as we know it as the chief protection of the freedom of the individual is bound to disappear. Already the lawyers in many fields have, as the instrument of a general conception which they have not made, become the tools, not of principles of justice, but of an apparatus in which the individual is made to serve the ends of his rulers. Legal thinking appears already to be governed to such an extent by new conceptions of the functions of law that, if these conceptions were consistently applied, the whole system of rules of individual conduct would be transformed into a system of rules of organization.

These developments have indeed been noticed with apprehension by many professional lawyers whose chief concern is still with what is sometimes described as 'lawyer's law', that is, those rules of just conduct which at one time were regarded as *the* law. But the leadership in jurisprudence, in the course of the process we have described, has shifted from the practitioners of private law to the public lawyer, with the result that today the philosophical preconceptions which govern the development of all law, including the private law, are almost entirely fashioned by men whose main concern is the public law or the rules of organization of government.

The modern development of law has been guided largely by false economics

It would, however, be unjust to blame the lawyers for this state of affairs more than the economists. The practising lawyer will indeed in general best perform his task if he just applies the general principles of the law which he has learned and which it is his duty consistently to apply. It is only in the theory of law, in the formulation and elaboration of those general principles, that the basic problem of their relation to a viable order of actions arises. For such a formulation and elaboration, an understanding of this order is absolutely essential if any intelligent choice between alternative principles is to be made. During the last two or three generations, however, a misunderstanding rather than an understanding of the character of this order has guided legal philosophy.

The economists in their turn, at least after the time of David Hume and Adam Smith, who were also philosophers of law, certainly showed no more appreciation of the significance of the system of legal rules, the existence of which was tacitly presupposed by their argument. They rarely put their account of the determination of a spontaneous order in a form which could be of much use to the legal theorist. But they have probably contributed unknowingly as much to the transformation of the whole social order as the lawyers have done.

This becomes evident when we examine the reason regularly given by the lawyers for the great changes that the character of law has undergone during the last hundred years. Everywhere, whether it be in English or American, French or German legal literature, we find alleged economic necessities given as the reasons for these changes. To the economist, reading the account by which the lawyers explain that transformation of the law, is a somewhat melancholy experience: he finds all the sins of his predecessors visited upon him. Accounts of the modern development of law are full of references to 'irreversible compelling forces' and 'inevitable tendencies' which are alleged to have imperatively called for the particular changes. The fact that 'all modern democracies' did this or that is adduced as proof of the wisdom or necessity of such changes.

These accounts invariably speak of a past *laissez-faire* period, as if there had been a time when no efforts were made to improve the legal framework so as to make the market operate more beneficially or to supplement its results. Almost without exception they base their argument on the *fable convenue* that free enterprise has operated to the disadvantage of the manual workers, and allege that 'early capitalism' or 'liberalism' had brought about a decline in the material standard of the working class. The legend, although wholly untrue,[16] has become part of the folklore of our time. The fact is, of course, that as the result of the growth of free markets, the reward of manual labour has during the past hundred and fifty years experienced an increase unknown in any earlier period of history. Most contemporary works on legal philosophy are full also of outdated clichés about the alleged self-destructive tendency of competition, or the need for 'planning' created by the increased complexity of the modern world, clichés deriving from the high tide of enthusiasm for 'planning' of thirty or forty years ago, when it was widely accepted and its totalitarian implications not yet clearly understood.

It is indeed doubtful whether as much false economics has been spread during the last hundred years by any other means as by the teaching of the young lawyers by their elders that 'it was necessary' this or that should have been done, or that such and such circumstances 'made it inevitable' that certain measures should be taken. It seems almost to be a habit of thought of the lawyer to regard the fact that the legislature has decided on something as evidence of the wisdom of that decision. This means, however, that his efforts will be beneficial or pernicious according to the wisdom or foolishness of the precedents by which he is guided, and that he is as likely to become the perpetuator of the errors as of the wisdom of the past. If he accepts as mandatory for him the observable trend of development, he is as likely to become simply the instrument through which changes he does not understand work themselves out as the conscious creator of a new order. In such a condition it will be necessary to seek for criteria of the desirability of developments elsewhere than within the science of law.

This is not to say that economics alone provides the principles that ought to guide legislation—although considering the influence that economic conceptions inevitably exercise, one must wish that such influence would come from good economics and not from that collection of myths and fables about economic development which seem today to govern legal thinking. Our contention is rather that the principles and preconceptions which guide the development of law inevitably come in part from outside the law and can be beneficial only if they are based on a true conception about how the activities in a Great Society can be effectively ordered.

The role of the lawyer in social evolution and the manner in which his actions are determined are indeed the best illustration of a truth of fundamental importance: namely that, whether we want it or not, the decisive factors which will determine that evolution will always be highly abstract and often unconsciously held ideas about what is right and proper, and not particular purposes or concrete desires. It is not so much what men consciously aim at, as their opinions about permissible methods, which determine not only what will be done but also whether anyone will have the power of doing it. This is the message reiterated by the greatest students of social affairs and always disregarded, namely that 'though men be much more governed by interest yet even interest itself, and all human affairs, are entirely governed by *opinion*.'[17]

Few contentions meet with such disbelief from most practical men, and are so much disregarded by the dominant school of political thought, as that, what is contemptuously dubbed as an ideology, has dominant power over those who believe themselves to be free from it even more than over those who consciously embrace it. Yet there are few things which must impress themselves more strongly on the student of the evolution of social institutions than the fact that what decisively determines them are not good or bad intentions concerning their immediate consequences, but the general preconceptions in terms of which particular issues are decided.

The power of abstract ideas rests largely on the very fact that they are not consciously held as theories but are treated by most people as self-evident truths which act as tacit presuppositions. That this dominant power of ideas is so rarely admitted is largely due to the oversimplified manner in which it is often asserted, suggesting that some great mind had the power of impressing on succeeding generations their particular conceptions. But which ideas will dominate, mostly without people ever being aware of them, is, of course, determined by a slow and immensely intricate process which we can rarely reconstruct in outline even in retrospect. It is certainly humbling to have to admit that our present decisions are determined by what happened long ago in a remote specialty without the general public ever knowing about it, and without those who first formulated the new conception being aware of what would be its consequences, particularly when it was not a discovery of new facts but a general philosophical conception which later affected particular decisions. These opinions not only the 'men in the street', but also the experts in the particular fields, accept unreflectingly and in general simply because they happen to be 'modern'.

It is necessary to realize that the sources of many of the most harmful agents in this world are often not evil men but highminded idealists, and that in particular the foundations of totalitarian barbarism have been laid by honourable and well-meaning scholars who never recognized the offspring they produced.[18] The fact is that, especially in the legal field, certain guiding philosophical preconceptions have brought about a situation where well-meaning theorists, highly admired to the present day even in free countries, have already worked out all the basic conceptions of a totalitarian order. Indeed, the communists, no less than the fascists or national socialists, had merely to use conceptions provided by generations of legal theorists in order to arrive at their doctrines.

What concerns us here is, however, not so much the past as the present. In spite of the collapse of the totalitarian regimes in the western world, their basic ideas have in the theoretical sphere continued to gain ground, so much so that to transform completely the legal system into a totalitarian one all that is needed now is to allow the ideas already reigning in the abstract sphere to be translated into practice.

Nowhere can this situation be more clearly seen than in Germany, which not only has largely provided the rest of the world with the philosophical conceptions that have produced the totalitarian regimes, but which also has been one of the first to succumb to this product of conceptions nurtured in the abstract sphere. Although the average German has by his experience probably been thoroughly purged of any conscious leaning towards the recognizable manifestations of totalitarianism, the basic philosophical conceptions have merely retreated into the abstract sphere, and now lurk in the hearts of grave and highly respected scholars, ready, unless discredited in time, again to take control of developments.

There is indeed no better illustration or more explicit statement of the manner in which philosophical conceptions about the nature of the social order affect the development of law than the theories of Carl Schmitt who, long before Hitler came to power, directed all his formidable intellectual energies to a fight against liberalism in all its forms; [19] who then became one of Hitler's chief legal apologists and still enjoys great influence among German legal philosophers and public lawyers; and whose characteristic terminology is as readily employed by German socialists as by conservative philosophers. His central belief, as he finally formulated it, is that from the 'normative' thinking of the liberal tradition law has gradually advanced through a 'decisionist' phase in which the will of the legislative authorities decided on particular matters, to the conception of a 'concrete order formation', a development which involves 'a re-interpretation of the ideal of the *nomos* as a total conception of law importing a concrete order and community'. [20] In other words, law is not to consist of abstract rules which make possible the formation of a spontaneous order by the free action of individuals through limiting the range of their actions, but is to be the instrument of arrangement or organization by which the individual is made to serve concrete purposes. This is the inevitable outcome of an intellectual development in which the self-ordering forces of society and the role of law in an ordering mechanism are no longer understood.

FOUR

THE CHANGING CONCEPT OF LAW

Non ex regula ius sumatur, sed ex iure quod est regula fiat.

Julius Paulus*

Law is older than legislation

Legislation, the deliberate making of law, has justly been described as among all inventions of man the one fraught with the gravest consequences, more far-reaching in its effects even than fire and gun-powder.[1] Unlike law itself, which has never been 'invented' in the same sense, the invention of legislation came relatively late in the history of mankind. It gave into the hands of men an instrument of great power which they needed to achieve some good, but which they have not yet learned so to control that it may not produce great evil. It opened to man wholly new possibilities and gave him a new sense of power over his fate. The discussion about who should possess this power has, however, unduly overshadowed the much more fundamental question of how far this power should extend. It will certainly remain an exceedingly dangerous power so long as we believe that it will do harm only if wielded by bad men.[2]

Law in the sense of enforced rules of conduct is undoubtedly coeval with society; only the observance of common rules makes the peaceful existence of individuals in society possible.[3] Long before man had developed language to the point where it enabled him to issue general commands, an individual would be accepted as a member of a group only so long as he conformed to its rules. Such rules might in a sense not be known and still have to be discovered, because from 'knowing how' to act,[4] or from being able to recognize that the acts of another did or did not conform to accepted practices, it is still a long way to being able to state such rules in words. But while it might be generally recognized that the discovery and statement of what the accepted rules were (or the articulation of rules that would be approved when acted upon) was a task requiring special wisdom, nobody yet conceived of law as something which men could make at will.

It is no accident that we still use the same word 'law' for the invariable rules which govern nature and for the rules which govern men's conduct. They were both conceived at first as something existing independently of human will. Though the anthropomorphic tendencies of all primitive thinking made men often ascribe both kinds of law to the creation of some supernatural being, they were regarded as eternal truths that man could try to discover but which he could not alter.

To modern man, on the other hand, the belief that all law governing human action is the product of legislation appears so obvious that the contention that law is older than law-making has almost the character of a paradox. Yet there can be no doubt that law existed for ages before it occurred to man that he could make or alter it. The belief that he could do so appeared hardly earlier than in classical Greece and even then only to be submerged again and to reappear and gradually gain wider acceptance in the later Middle Ages.[5] In the form in which it is now widely held, however, namely that all law is, can be, and ought to be, the product of the free invention of a legislator, it is factually false, an erroneous product of that constructivist rationalism which we described earlier.

We shall later see that the whole conception of legal positivism which derives all law from the will of a legislator is a product of the intentionalist fallacy characteristic of constructivism, a relapse into those design theories of human institutions which stand in irreconcilable conflict with all we know about the evolution of law and most other human institutions.

What we know about pre-human and primitive human societies suggests a different origin and determination of law from that assumed by the theories which trace it to the will of a legislator. And although the positivist doctrine stands also in flagrant conflict with what we know about the history of our law, legal history proper begins at too late a stage of evolution to bring out clearly the origins. If we wish to free ourselves from the all-pervasive influence of the intellectual presumption that man in his wisdom has designed, or ever could have designed, the whole system of legal or moral rules, we should begin with a look at the primitive and even pre-human beginnings of social life.

Social theory has here much to learn from the two young sciences of ethology and cultural anthropology which in many respects have built on the foundation of social theory initially laid in the eighteenth century by the Scottish moral philosophers. In the field of law, indeed, these young disciplines go far to confirm the evolutionary teaching of Edward Coke, Matthew Hale, David Hume and Edmund Burke, F. C. von Savigny, H. S. Maine and J. C. Carter, and are wholly contrary to the rationalist constructivism of Francis Bacon or Thomas Hobbes, Jeremy Bentham or John Austin, or of the German positivists from Paul Laband to Hans Kelsen.

The lessons of ethology and cultural anthropology

The chief points on which the comparative study of behaviour has thrown such important light on the evolution of law are, first, that it has made clear that individuals had learned to observe (and enforce) rules of conduct long before such rules could be expressed in words; and second, that these rules had evolved because they led to the formation of an order of the activities of the group as a whole which, although they are the results of the regularities of the actions of the individuals, must be clearly distinguished from them, since it is the efficiency of the resulting order of actions which will determine whether groups whose members observe certain rules of conduct will prevail. [6]

In view of the fact that man became man and developed reason and language while living for something like a million years in groups held together by common rules of conduct, and that one of the first uses of reason and language must have been to teach and enforce these established rules, it will be useful first to consider the evolution of rules which were merely in fact obeyed, before we turn to the problem of their gradual articulation in words. Social orders resting on most complex systems of such rules of conduct we find even among animals very low on the evolutionary scale. For our present purposes it does not matter that on these lower evolutionary levels the rules are probably mostly innate (or transmitted genetically) and few learned (or transmitted 'culturally'). It is now well established that among the higher vertebrates learning plays an important role in transmitting such rules, so that new rules may rapidly spread among large groups and, in the case of isolated groups, produce distinct 'cultural' traditions. [7] There is little question, on the other hand, that man is also still guided not only by learned but by some innate rules. We are here chiefly interested in the learned rules and the manner of their transmission;

but in considering the problem of the interrelation of rules of conduct and the resulting overall order of actions, it does not matter with which kind of rules we have to deal, or whether, as will usually be the case, both kinds of rules interact.

The study of comparative behaviour has shown that in many animal societies the process of selective evolution has produced highly ritualized forms of behaviour governed by rules of conduct which have the effect of reducing violence and other wasteful methods of adaptation and thus secure an order of peace. This order is often based on the delimitation of territorial ranges or 'property', which serves not only to eliminate unnecessary fighting but even substitutes 'preventive' for 'repressive' checks on the growth of population, for example, through the male who has not established a territory being unable to mate and breed. Frequently we find complex orders of rank which secure that only the strongest males will propagate. Nobody who has studied the literature on animal societies will regard it as only a metaphorical expression when for instance one author speaks of 'the elaborate system of property tenure' of crayfish and the ceremonial displays through which it is maintained,[8] or when another concludes a description of the rivalry between robins by saying that 'victory does not go to the strong but to the righteous—the righteous of course being the owners of property'.[9]

We cannot give here more than these few examples of the fascinating worlds which through these studies are gradually revealed to us,[10] but must turn to the problems that arise as man, living in such groups governed by a multiplicity of rules, gradually develops reason and language and uses them to teach and enforce the rules. At this stage it is sufficient to see that rules did exist, served a function essential to the preservation of the group, and were effectively transmitted and enforced, although they had never been 'invented', expressed in words, or possessed a 'purpose' known to anyone.

Rule in this context means simply a propensity or disposition to act or not to act in a certain manner, which will manifest itself in what we call a *practice*[11] or custom. As such it will be one of the determinants of action which, however, need not show itself in every single action but may only prevail in most instances. Any such rule will always operate in combination and often in competition with other rules or dispositions and with particular impulses; and whether a rule will prevail in a particular case will depend on the strength of the propensity it describes and of the other dispositions or impulses operating at the same time. The conflict which will often arise between immediate desires and the built-in rules or inhibitions is well attested by the observation of animals.[12]

It must be particularly emphasized that these propensities or dispositions possessed by higher animals will often be of a highly general or abstract character, that is, they will be directed towards a very wide class of actions which may differ a great deal among themselves in their detail. They will in this sense certainly be much more abstract than anything incipient language can express. For the understanding of the process of gradual articulation of rules which have long been obeyed, it is important to remember that abstractions, far from being a product of language, were acquired by the mind long before it developed language.[13] The problem of the origin and function of these rules which govern both action and thought is therefore a problem wholly distinct from the problem of how they came to be articulated in verbal form. There is little doubt that even today the rules which have been thus articulated and can be communicated by language are only a part of the whole complex of rules that guide man's actions as a social being. I doubt whether anyone has yet succeeded in articulating all the rules which constitute 'fair play', for example.

The process of articulation of practices

Even the earliest deliberate efforts of headmen or chiefs of a tribe to maintain order must thus be seen as taking place inside a given framework of rules, although they were rules which existed only as a 'knowledge how' to act and not as a 'knowledge that' they could be expressed in such and such terms. Language would certainly have been used early to teach them, but only as a means of indicating the particular actions that were required or prohibited in particular situations. As in the acquisition of language itself, the individual would have to learn to act in accordance with rules by imitating particular actions corresponding to them. So long as language is not sufficiently developed to express general rules there is no other way in which rules can be taught. But although at this stage they do not exist in articulated form, they nevertheless do exist in the sense that they govern action. And those who first attempted to express them in words did not invent new rules but were endeavouring to express what they were already acquainted with.[14]

Although still an unfamiliar conception, the fact that language is often insufficient to express what the mind is fully capable of taking into account in determining action, or that we will often not be able to communicate in words what we well know how to practise, has been clearly established in many fields. [15] It is closely connected with the fact that the rules that govern action will often be much more general and abstract than anything language can yet express. Such abstract rules are learnt by imitating particular actions, from which the individual acquires 'by analogy' the capacity to act in other cases on the same principles which, however, he could never state as principles.

For our purposes this means that, not merely in the primitive tribe but also in more advanced communities, the chief or ruler will use his authority for two quite different purposes: he will do so to teach or enforce rules of conduct which he regards as established, though he may have little idea why they are important or what depends on their observance; he will also give commands for actions which seem to him necessary for the achievement of particular purposes. There will always be ranges of activities with which he will not interfere so long as the individuals observe the recognized rules, but on certain occasions, such as hunting expeditions, migrations, or warfare, his commands will have to direct the individuals to particular actions.

The different character of these two ways in which authority can be exercised would show itself even in relatively primitive conditions in the fact that in the first instance its legitimacy could be questioned while in the second it could not: the right of the chief to require particular behaviour would depend on the general recognition of a corresponding rule, while his directions to the participants of a joint enterprise would be determined by his plan for action and the particular circumstances known to him but not necessarily to the others. It would be the necessity to justify commands of the first sort which would lead to attempts to articulate the rules which they were meant to enforce. Such a necessity to express the rules in words would arise also in the case of disputes which the chief was called upon to settle. The explicit statement of the established practice or custom as a verbal rule would aim at obtaining consent about its existence and not at making a new rule; and it would rarely achieve more than an inadequate and partial expression of what was well known in practice.

The process of a gradual articulation in words of what had long been an established practice must have been a slow and complex one. [16] The first fumbling attempts to express in words what most obeyed in practice would usually not succeed in expressing only, or exhausting all of, what the individuals did in fact take into account in the determination of their actions. The unarticulated rules will therefore usually contain both more and less than what the verbal formula succeeds in expressing. On the other hand, articulation will often become necessary because the 'intuitive' knowledge may not give a clear answer to a particular question. The process of articulation will thus sometimes in effect, though not in intention, produce new rules. But the articulated rules will thereby not wholly replace the unarticulated ones, but will operate, and be intelligible, only within a framework of yet unarticulated rules.

While the process of articulation of pre-existing rules will thus often lead to alterations in the body of such rules, this will have little effect on the belief that those formulating the rules do no more, and have no power to do more, than to find and express already existing rules, a task in which fallible humans will often go wrong, but in the performance of which they have no free choice. The task will be regarded as one of discovering something which exists, not as one of creating something new, even though the result of such efforts may be the creation of something that has not existed before.

This remains true even where, as is undoubtedly often the case, those called upon to decide are driven to formulate rules on which nobody has acted before. They are concerned not only with a body of rules but also with an order of the actions resulting from the observance of these rules, which men find in an ongoing process and the preservation of which may require particular rules. The preservation of the existing order of actions towards which all the recognized rules are directed may well be seen to require some other rule for the decision of disputes for which the recognized rules supply no answer. In this sense a rule not yet existing in any sense may yet appear to be 'implicit' in the body of the existing rules, not in the sense that it is logically derivable from them, but in the sense that if the other rules are to achieve their aim, an additional rule is required.

Factual and normative rules

It is of some importance to recognize that, where we have to deal with non-articulated rules, a distinction that seems very clear and obvious with respect to articulated rules becomes much less clear and perhaps sometimes even impossible to draw. This is the distinction between descriptive rules which assert the regular recurrence of certain sequences of events (including human actions) and the normative rules which state that such sequences 'ought' to take place. It is difficult to say at what particular stage of the gradual transition from a wholly unconscious observance of such rules to their expression in articulated form this distinction becomes meaningful. Is an innate inhibition which prevents a man or animal from taking a certain action, but of which he is wholly unaware, a 'norm'? Does it become a 'norm' when an observer can see how a desire and an inhibition are in conflict, as in the case of Konrad Lorenz's wolf, whose attitude he describes by saying that 'you could see that he would like to bite his opponent's offered throat, but he just cannot'?[17] Or when it leads to a conscious conflict between a particular impulse and a feeling that 'one ought not to do it'? Or when this feeling is expressed in words ('I ought not to'), but still applied only to oneself? Or when, although not yet articulated as a verbal rule, the feeling is shared by all members of the group and leads to expressions of disapproval or even attempts at prevention and punishment when infringed? Or only when it is enforced by a recognized authority or laid down in articulated form?

It seems that the specific character usually ascribed to 'norms' which makes them belong to a different realm of discourse from statements of facts, belongs only to articulated rules, and even there only once the question is raised as to whether we ought to obey them or not. So long as such rules are merely obeyed in fact (either always or at least in most instances), and their observance is ascertainable only from actual behaviour, they do not differ from descriptive rules; they are significant as one of the determinants of action, a disposition or inhibition whose operation we infer from what we observe. If such a disposition or inhibition is produced by the teaching of an articulated rule, its effect on actual behaviour still remains a fact. To the observer the norms guiding the actions of the individuals in a group are part of the determinants of the events which he perceives and which enable him to explain the overall order of actions as he finds it.

This, of course, does not alter the circumstance that our language is so made that no valid inference can lead from a statement containing only a description of facts to a statement of what ought to be. But not all conclusions often drawn from this are compelling. It says no more than that from a statement of fact alone no statements about appropriate, desirable or expedient action, nor any decision about whether to act at all, can be derived. One can follow from the other only if at the same time some end is accepted as desirable and the argument takes the form of 'if you want this, you must do that'. But once such an assumption about the desired end is included in the premises, all sorts of normative rules may be derived from them.

To the primitive mind no clear distinction exists between the only way in which a particular result can be achieved and the way in which it ought to be achieved. Knowledge of cause and effect and knowledge of rules of conduct are still indistinguishable: there is but knowledge of *the* manner in which one must act in order to achieve any result. To the child who learns to add or multiply figures, the way in which this ought to be done is also the only way to obtain the intended result. Only when he discovers that there are other ways than those taught to him, which also will lead him to what he desires, can there arise a conflict between knowledge of fact and the rules of conduct established in the group.

A difference between all purposive action and norm-guided action exists only in so far as in the case of what we usually regard as purposive action we assume that the purpose is known to the acting person, while in the case of norm-guided action the reasons why he regards one way of acting as a possible way of achieving a desired result and another as not possible will often be unknown to him. Yet to regard one kind of action as appropriate and another as inappropriate is as much the result of a process of selection of what is effective, whether it is the consequence of the particular action producing the results desired by the individual or the consequence of action of that kind being conducive or not being conducive to the functioning of the group as a whole. The reason why all the individual members of a group do particular things in a particular way will thus often not be that only in this way they will achieve what they intend, but that only if they act in this manner will that order of the group be preserved within which their individual actions are likely to be successful. The group may have persisted only because its members have developed and transmitted ways of doing things which made the group as a whole more effective than others; but the reason why certain things are done in certain ways no member of the group needs to know.

It has, of course, never been denied that the existence of norms in a given group of men is a fact. What has been questioned is that from the circumstance that the norms are in fact obeyed the conclusion could be drawn that they ought to be obeyed. The conclusion is of course possible only if it is tacitly assumed that the continued existence of the group is desired. But if such continued existence is regarded as desirable, or even the further existence of the group as an entity with a certain order is presupposed as a fact, then it follows that certain rules of conduct (not necessarily all those which are now observed) will have to be followed by its members. [18]

Early law

It should now be easier to see why in all early civilization we find a law like that 'of the Medes and the Persians that changeth not', and why all early 'law-giving' consisted in efforts to record and make known a law that was conceived as unalterably given. A 'legislator' might endeavour to purge the law of supposed corruptions, or to restore it to its pristine purity, but it was not thought that he could make new law. The historians of law are agreed that in this respect all the famous early 'law-givers', from Ur-Nammu [19] and Hammurabi to Solon, Lykurgus and the authors of the Roman Twelve Tables, did not intend to create new law but merely to state what law was and had always been. [20]

But if nobody had the power or the intention to change the law, and only old law was regarded as good law, this does not mean that law did not continue to develop. What it means is merely that the changes which did occur were not the result of intention or design of a law-maker. To a ruler whose power rested largely on the expectation that he would enforce a law presumed to be given independently of him, this law often must have seemed more an obstacle to his efforts at deliberate organization of government than a means for his conscious purposes. It was in those activities of their subjects which they could not directly control, often mainly in the relations of these subjects with outsiders, that new rules developed outside the law enforced by the rulers, while the latter tended to become rigid precisely to the extent to which it had been articulated.

The growth of the purpose-independent rules of conduct which can produce a spontaneous order will thus often have taken place in conflict with the aims of the rulers who tended to try to turn their domain into an organization proper. It is in the *ius gentium*, the law merchant, and the practices of the ports and fairs that we must chiefly seek the steps in the evolution of law which ultimately made an open society possible. Perhaps one might even say that the development of universal rules of conduct did not begin within the organized community of the tribe but rather with the first instance of silent barter when a savage placed some offerings at the boundary of the territory of his tribe in the expectation that a return gift would be made in a similar manner, thus beginning a new custom. At any rate, it was not through direction by rulers, but through the development of customs on which expectations of the individuals could be based, that general rules of conduct came to be accepted.

The classical and the medieval tradition

Although the conception that law was the product of a deliberate human will was first fully developed in ancient Greece, its influence over the actual practice of politics remained limited. Of classical Athens at the height of its democracy we are told that 'at no time was it legal to alter the law by a simple decree of the assembly. The mover of such a decree was liable to the famous "indictment for illegal proceedings" which, if upheld by the courts, quashed the decree, and also, brought within the year, exposed the mover to heavy penalties.'[21] A change in the basic rules of just conduct, the *nomoi*, could be brought about only through a complicated procedure in which a specially elected body, the *nomothetae*, was involved. Nevertheless, we find in the Athenian democracy already the first clashes between the unfettered will of the 'sovereign' people and the tradition of the rule of law;[22] and it was chiefly because the assembly often refused to be bound by the law that Aristotle turned against this form of democracy, to which he even denied the right to be called a constitution.[23] It is in the discussions of this period that we find the first persistent efforts to draw a clear distinction between the law and the particular will of the ruler.

The law of Rome, which has influenced all Western law so profoundly, was even less the product of deliberate law-making. As all other early law it was formed at a time when 'law and the institutions of social life were considered to have always existed and nobody asked for their origin. The idea that law might be created by men is alien to the thinking of early people.'[24] It was only 'the naïve belief of later more advanced ages that all law must rest on legislation.'[25] In fact, the classical Roman civil law, on which the final compilation of Justinian was based, is almost entirely the product of law-finding by jurists and only to a very small extent the product of legislation.[26] By a process very similar to that by which later the English common law developed, and differing from it mainly in that the decisive role was played by the opinions of legal scholars (the *jurisconsults*) rather than the decisions of judges, a body of law grew up through the gradual articulation of prevailing conceptions of justice rather than by legislation.[27] It was only at the end of this development, at Byzantium rather than at Rome and under the influence of Hellenistic thinking, that the results of this process were codified under the Emperor Justinian, whose work was later falsely regarded as the model of a law created by a ruler and expressing his 'will'.

Until the rediscovery of Aristotle's *Politics* in the thirteenth century and the reception of Justinian's code in the fifteenth, however, Western Europe passed through another epoch of nearly a thousand years when law was again regarded as something given independently of human will, something to be discovered, not made, and when the conception that law could be deliberately made or altered seemed almost sacrilegious. This attitude, noticed by many earlier scholars,[28] has been given a classical description by Fritz Kern, and we can do no better than quote his main conclusions:[29]

When a case arises for which no valid law can be adduced, then the lawful men or doomsmen will make new law in the belief that what they are making is good old law, not indeed expressly handed-down, but tacitly existent. They do not, therefore, create the law: they 'discover' it. Any particular judgement in court, which we regard as a particular inference from a general established legal rule, was to the medieval mind in no way distinguishable from the legislative activity of the community; in both cases a law hidden but already existing is discovered, not created. There is, in the Middle Ages, no such thing as the 'first application of a legal rule'. Law is old; new law is a contradiction in terms; for either new law is derived explicitly or implicitly from the old, or it conflicts with the old, in which case it is not lawful. The fundamental idea remains the same;

the old law is the true law, and the true law is the old law. According to medieval ideas, therefore, the enactment of new law is not possible at all; and all legislation and legal reform is conceived of as the restoration of the good old law which has been violated.

The history of the intellectual development by which, from the thirteenth century onwards, and mainly on the European continent, law-making slowly and gradually came to be regarded as an act of the deliberate and unfettered will of the ruler, is too long and complex to be described here. From the detailed studies of this process it appears to be closely connected with the rise of absolute monarchy when the conceptions which later governed the aspirations of democracy were formed.[30] This development was accompanied by a progressive absorption of this new power of laying down new rules of just conduct into the much older power which rulers had always exercised, their power of organizing and directing the apparatus of government, until both powers became inextricably mixed up in what came to be regarded as the single power of 'legislation'.

The main resistance to this development came from the tradition of the 'law of nature'. As we have seen, the late Spanish schoolmen used the term 'natural' as a technical term to describe what had never been 'invented' or deliberately designed but had evolved in response to the necessity of the situation. But even this tradition lost its power when in the seventeenth century 'natural law' came to be understood as the design of 'natural reason'.

The only country that succeeded in preserving the tradition of the Middle Ages and built on the medieval 'liberties' the modern conception of liberty under the law was England. This was partly due to the fact that England escaped a wholesale reception of the late Roman law and with it the conception of law as the creation of some ruler; but it was probably due more to the circumstance that the common law jurists there had developed conceptions somewhat similar to those of the natural law tradition but not couched in the misleading terminology of that school. Nevertheless, 'in the sixteenth and early seventeenth century the political structure of England was not yet fundamentally different from that of the continental countries and it might still have seemed uncertain whether she would develop a highly centralized absolute monarchy as did the countries of the continent.'[31] What prevented such development was the deeply entrenched tradition of a common law that was not conceived as the product of anyone's will but rather as a barrier to all power, including that of the king—a tradition which Edward Coke was to defend against King James I and Francis Bacon, and which Matthew Hale at the end of the seventeenth century masterly restated in opposition to Thomas Hobbes. [32]

The freedom of the British which in the eighteenth century the rest of Europe came so much to admire was thus not, as the British themselves were among the first to believe and as Montesquieu later taught the world, originally a product of the separation of powers between legislature and executive, but rather a result of the fact that the law that governed the decisions of the courts was the common law, a law existing independently of anyone's will and at the same time binding upon and developed by the independent courts; a law with which parliament only rarely interfered and, when it did, mainly only to clear up doubtful points within a given body of law. One might even say that a sort of separation of powers had grown up in England, not because the 'legislature' alone made law, but because it did *not*: because the law was determined by courts independent of the power which organized and directed government, the power namely of what was misleadingly called the 'legislature'.

The distinctive attributes of law arising from custom and precedent

The important insight to which an understanding of the process of evolution of law leads is that the rules which will emerge from it will of necessity possess certain attributes which laws invented or designed by a ruler may but need not possess, and are likely to possess only if they are modelled after the kind of rules which spring from the articulation of previously existing practices. We shall only in the next chapter be able to describe fully all the characteristic properties of the law which is thus formed, and to show that it has provided the standard for what political philosophers long regarded as *the law* in the proper meaning of the word, as contained in such expressions as the 'rule' or 'reign of law', a 'government under the law', or the 'separation of powers'. At this point we want to stress only one of the peculiar properties of this *nomos*, and will merely briefly mention the others in anticipation of later discussion. The law will consist of purpose-independent rules which govern the conduct of individuals towards each other, are intended to apply to an unknown number of further instances, and by defining a protected domain of each, enable an order of actions to form itself wherein the individuals can make feasible plans. It is usual to refer to these rules as abstract rules of conduct, and although this description is inadequate, we shall provisionally employ it for the purpose in hand. The particular point which we want to bring out here is that such law which, like the common law, emerges from the judicial process is necessarily abstract in the sense that the law created by the commands of the ruler need not be so.

The contention that a law based on precedent is more rather than less abstract than one expressed in verbal rules is so contrary to a view widely held, perhaps more among continental than among Anglo-Saxon lawyers, that it needs fuller justification. The central point can probably not be better expressed than in a famous statement by the great eighteenth-century judge Lord Mansfield, who stressed that the common law 'does not consist of particular cases, but of general principles, which are illustrated and explained by those cases'. [33] What this means is that it is part of the technique of the common law judge that from the precedents which guide him he must be able to derive rules of universal significance which can be applied to new cases.

The chief concern of a common law judge must be the expectations which the parties in a transaction would have reasonably formed on the basis of the general practices that the ongoing order of actions rests on. In deciding what expectations were reasonable in this sense he can take account only of such practices (customs or rules) as in fact could determine the expectations of the parties and such facts as may be presumed to have been known to them. And these parties would have been able to form common expectations, in a situation which in some respects must have been unique, only because they interpreted the situation in terms of what was thought to be appropriate conduct and which need not have been known to them in the form of an articulated rule.

Such rules, presumed to have guided expectations in many similar situations in the past, must be abstract in the sense of referring to a limited number of relevant circumstances and of being applicable irrespective of the particular consequences now appearing to follow from their application. By the time the judge is called upon to decide a case, the parties in the dispute will already have acted in the pursuit of their own ends and mostly in particular circumstances unknown to any authority; and the expectations which have guided their actions and in which one of them has been disappointed will have been based on what they regarded as established practices. The task of the judge will be to tell them what ought to have guided their expectations, not because anyone had told them before that this was the rule, but because this was the established custom which they ought to have known. The question for the judge here can never be whether the action in fact taken was expedient from some higher point of view, or served a particular result desired by authority, but only whether the conduct under dispute conformed to recognized rules. The only public good with which he can be concerned is the observance of those rules that the individuals could reasonably count on. He is not concerned with any ulterior purpose which somebody may have intended the rules to serve and of which he must be largely ignorant; and he will have to apply the rules even if in the particular instance the known consequences will appear to him wholly undesirable.[34] In this task he must pay no attention, as has often been emphasized by common law judges, to any wishes of a ruler or any 'reasons of state'. What must guide his decision is not any knowledge of what the whole of society requires at the particular moment, but solely what is demanded by general principles on which the going order of society is based.

It seems that the constant necessity of articulating rules in order to distinguish between the relevant and the accidental in the precedents which guide him, produces in the common law judge a capacity for discovering general principles rarely acquired by a judge who operates with a supposedly complete catalogue of applicable rules before him. When the generalizations are not supplied ready made, a capacity for formulating abstractions is apparently kept alive, which the mechanical use of verbal formulae tends to kill. The common law judge is bound to be very much aware that words are always but an imperfect expression of what his predecessors struggled to articulate.

If today the commands of a legislator often take the form of those abstract rules which have emerged from the judicial process, it is because they have been shaped after that model. But it is highly unlikely that any ruler aiming at organizing the activities of his subjects for the achievement of definite foreseeable results could ever have achieved his purpose by laying down universal rules intended to govern equally the actions of everybody. To restrain himself, as the judge does, so as to enforce only such rules, would require a degree of self-denial not to be expected from one used to issuing specific commands and to being guided in his decisions by the needs of the moment. Abstract rules are not likely to be invented by somebody concerned with obtaining particular results. It was the need to preserve an order of action which nobody had created but which was disturbed by certain kinds of behaviour that made it necessary to define those kinds of behaviour which had to be repressed.

Why grown law requires correction by legislation

The fact that all law arising out of the endeavour to articulate rules of conduct will of necessity possess some desirable properties not necessarily possessed by the commands of a legislator does not mean that in other respects such law may not develop in very undesirable directions, and that when this happens correction by deliberate legislation may not be the only practicable way out. For a variety of reasons the spontaneous process of growth may lead into an impasse from which it cannot extricate itself by its own forces or which it will at least not correct quickly enough. The development of case-law is in some respects a sort of one-way street: when it has already moved a considerable distance in one direction, it often cannot retrace its steps when some implications of earlier decisions are seen to be clearly undesirable. The fact that law that has evolved in this way has certain desirable properties does not prove that it will always be good law or even that some of its rules may not be very bad. It therefore does not mean that we can altogether dispense with legislation.[35]

There are several other reasons for this. One is that the process of judicial development of law is of necessity gradual and may prove too slow to bring about the desirable rapid adaptation of the law to wholly new circumstances. Perhaps the most important, however, is that it is not only difficult but also undesirable for judicial decisions to reverse a development, which has already taken place and is then seen to have undesirable consequences or to be downright wrong. The judge is not performing his function if he disappoints reasonable expectations created by earlier decisions. Although the judge can develop the law by deciding issues which are genuinely doubtful, he cannot really alter it, or can do so at most only very gradually where a rule has become firmly established; although he may clearly recognize that another rule would be better, or more

88

just, it would evidently be unjust to apply it to transactions which had taken place when a different rule was regarded as valid. In such situations it is desirable that the new rule should become known before it is enforced; and this can be effected only by promulgating a new rule which is to be applied only in the future. Where a real change in the law is required, the new law can properly fulfil the proper function of all law, namely that of guiding expectations, only if it becomes known before it is applied.

The necessity of such radical changes of particular rules may be due to various causes. It may be due simply to the recognition that some past development was based on error or that it produced consequences later recognized as unjust. But the most frequent cause is probably that the development of the law has lain in the hands of members of a particular class whose traditional views made them regard as just what could not meet the more general requirements of justice. There can be do doubt that in such fields as the law on the relations between master and servant,[36] landlord and tenant, creditor and debtor, and in modern times between organized business and its customers, the rules have been shaped largely by the views of one of the parties and their particular interests—especially where, as used to be true in the first two of the instances given, it was one of the groups concerned which almost exclusively supplied the judges. This, as we shall see, does not mean that, as has been asserted, 'justice is an irrational ideal' and that 'from the point of rational cognition there are only interests of human beings and hence conflicts of interests',[37] at least when by interests we do not mean only particular aims but long-term chances which different rules offer to the different members of society. It is even less true that, as would follow from those assertions, a recognized bias of some rule in favour of a particular group can be corrected only by biasing it instead in favour of another. But such occasions when it is recognized that some hereto accepted rules are unjust in the light of more general principles of justice may well require the revision not only of single rules but of whole sections of the established system of case law. This is more than can be accomplished by decisions of particular cases in the light of existing precedents.

The origin of legislative bodies

There is no determinable point in history when the power of

deliberately changing the law in the sense in which we have been considering it was explicitly conferred on any authority. But there always existed of necessity an authority which had power to make law of a different kind, namely the rules of the organization of government, and it was to these existing makers of public law that there gradually accrued the power of changing also the rules of just conduct as the necessity of such changes became recognized. Since those rules of conduct had to be enforced by the organization of government, it seemed natural that those who determined that organization should also determine the rules it was to enforce.

A legislative power in the sense of a power of determining the rules of government existed, therefore, long before the need for a power to change the universal rules of just conduct was even recognized. Rulers faced with the task of enforcing a given law and of organizing defence and various services, had long experienced the necessity of laying down rules for their officers or subordinates, and they would have made no distinction as to whether these rules were of a purely administrative character or subsidiary to the task of enforcing justice. Yet a ruler would find it to his advantage to claim for the organizational rules the same dignity as was generally conceded to the universal rules of just conduct.

But if the laying down of such rules for the organization of government was long regarded as the 'prerogative' of its head, the need for an approval of, or a consent to, his measure by representative or constituted bodies would often arise precisely because the ruler was himself supposed to be bound by the established law. And when, as in levying contributions in money or services for the purposes of government, he had to use coercion in a form not clearly prescribed by the established rules, he would have to assure himself of the support at least of his more powerful subjects. It would then often be difficult to decide whether they were merely called in to testify that this or that was established law or to approve of a particular imposition or measure thought necessary for a particular end.

It is thus misleading to conceive of early representative bodies as 'legislatures' in the sense in which the term was later employed by theorists. They were not primarily concerned with the rules of just conduct or the *nomos*. As F. W. Maitland explains:[38]

> The further back we trace our history the more impossible it is for us to draw strict lines of demarcation between the

various functions of the state: the same institution is a legislative assembly, a governmental council, and a court of law . . . For a long time past political theorists have insisted on the distinction between legislation and the other functions of government, and of course the distinction is important though it is not always easy to draw the line with perfect accuracy. But it seems necessary to notice that the power of a statute is by no means confined to what a jurist or political philosopher would consider the domain of legislation. A vast number of statutes he would class rather as *privilegia* than as *leges*; the statute lays down no general rules but deals only with a particular case.

It was in connection with rules of the organization of government that the deliberate making of 'laws' became a familiar and everyday procedure; every new undertaking of a government or every change in the structure of government required some new rules for its organization. The laying down of such new rules thus became an accepted procedure long before anyone contemplated using it for altering the established rules of just conduct. But when the wish to do so arose it was almost inevitable that the task was entrusted to the body which had always made laws in another sense and often had also been asked to testify as to what the established rules of just conduct were.

Allegiance and sovereignty

From the conception that legislation is the sole source of law derive two ideas which in modern times have come to be accepted as almost self-evident and have exercised great influence on political developments, although they are wholly derived from that erroneous constructivism in which earlier anthropomorphic fallacies survive. The first of these is the belief that there must be a supreme legislator whose power cannot be limited, because this would require a still higher legislator, and so on in an infinite regress. The other is that anything laid down by that supreme legislator is law and only that which expresses his will is law.

The conception of the necessarily unlimited will of a supreme legislator, which since Bacon, Hobbes and Austin has served as the supposedly irrefutable justification of absolute power, first of monarchs and later of democratic assemblies, appears self-evident only if the term law is restricted to the rules guiding the deliberate and concerted actions of an organization. Thus interpreted, law, which in the earlier sense of *nomos* was meant to be a barrier to all power, becomes instead an instrument for the use of power.

The negative answer which legal positivism gives to the question of whether there can be effective limits to the power of the supreme legislature would be convincing only if it were true that all law is always the product of the deliberate 'will' of a legislator, and that nothing could effectively limit that power except another 'will' of the same sort. The authority of a legislator always rests, however, on something which must be clearly distinguished from an act of will on a particular matter in hand, and can therefore also be limited by the source from which it derives its authority. This source is a prevailing opinion that the legislator is authorized only to prescribe what is right, where this opinion refers not to the particular content of the rule but to the general attributes which any rule of just conduct must possess. The power of the legislator thus rests on a common opinion about certain attributes which the laws he produces ought to possess, and his will can obtain the support of opinion only if its expression possesses those attributes. We shall later have to consider more fully this distinction between will and opinion. Here it must suffice to say that we shall use the term 'opinion', as distinct from an act of will on a particular matter, to describe a common tendency to approve of some particular acts of will and to disapprove of others, according to whether they do or do not possess certain attributes which those who hold a given opinion usually will not be able to specify. So long as the legislator satisfies the expectation that what he resolves will possess those attributes, he will be free so far as the particular contents of its resolutions are concerned, and will in this sense be 'sovereign'. But the allegiance on which this sovereignty rests depends on the sovereign's satisfying certain expectations concerning the general character of those rules, and will vanish when this expectation is disappointed. In this sense all power rests on, and is limited by, opinion, as was most clearly seen by David Hume. [39]

That all power rests on opinion in this sense is no less true of the powers of an absolute dictator than of those of any other authority. As dictators themselves have known best at all times, even the most powerful dictatorship crumbles if the support of opinion is withdrawn. This is the reason why dictators are so concerned to manipulate opinion through that control of information which is in their power.

The effective limitation of the powers of a legislature does therefore not require another organized authority capable of concerted action above it; it may be produced by a state of opinion which brings it about that only certain kinds of commands which the legislature issues are accepted as laws. Such opinion will be concerned not with the particular content of the decisions of the legislature but only with the general attributes of the kind of rules which the legislator is meant to proclaim and to which alone the people are willing to give support. This power of opinion does not rest on the capacity of the holders to take any course of concerted action, but is merely a negative power of withholding that support on which the power of the legislator ultimately rests.

There is no contradiction in the existence of a state of opinion which commands implicit obedience to the legislator so long as he commits himself to a general rule, but refuses obedience when he orders particular actions. And whether a particular decision of the legislator is readily recognizable as valid law need not depend solely on whether the decision has been arrived at in a prescribed manner, but may also depend on whether it consists of a universal rule of just conduct.

There is thus no logical necessity that an ultimate power must be omnipotent. In fact, what everywhere is the ultimate power, namely that opinion which produces allegiance, will be a limited power, although it in turn limits the power of all legislators. This ultimate power is thus a negative power, but as a power of withholding allegiance it limits all positive power. And in a free society in which all power rests on opinion, this ultimate power will be a power which determines nothing directly yet controls all positive power by tolerating only certain kinds of exercise of that power.

These restraints on all organized power and particularly the power of the legislator could, of course, be made more effective and more promptly operative if the criteria were explicitly stated by which it can be determined whether or not a particular decision can be a law. But the restraints which in fact have long operated on the legislatures have hardly ever been adequately expressed in words. To attempt to do so will be one of our tasks.

FIVE

NOMOS: THE LAW OF LIBERTY

As for the constitution of Crete which is described by
Ephorus, it might suffice to tell its most important provisions.
The lawgiver, he says, seems to take it for granted that liberty
is a state's highest good and for this reason alone makes
property belong specifically to those who acquire it, whereas in
condition of slavery everything belongs to the rulers and
not to the ruled.

Strabo*

The functions of the judge

We must now attempt to describe more fully the distinctive character of those rules of just conduct which emerge from the efforts
of judges to decide disputes and which have long provided the
model which legislators have tried to emulate. It has already been
pointed out that the ideal of individual liberty seems to have flour-
ished chiefly among people where, at least for long periods, judge-
made law predominated. This we have ascribed to the circumstance
that judge-made law will of necessity possess certain attributes
which the decrees of the legislator need not possess and are likely
to possess only if the legislator takes judge-made law for his model.
In this chapter we will examine the distinct attributes of what political theorists have long regarded simply as *the law*, the lawyer's law,
or the *nomos* of the ancient Greeks and the *ius* of the Romans[1]
(and what in other European languages is distinguished as *droit*,
Recht, or *diritto* from the *loi*, *Gesetz*,[2] or *legge*), and contrast with
it in the next chapter those rules of organization of government
with which legislatures have been chiefly concerned.

The distinct character of the rules which the judge will have to
apply, and must endeavour to articulate and improve, is best
understood if we remember that he is called in to correct disturbances of an order that has not been made by anyone and does

not rest on the individuals having been told what they must do. In most instances no authority will even have known at the time the disputed action took place what the individuals did or why they did it. The judge is in this sense an institution of a spontaneous order. He will always find such an order in existence as an attribute of an ongoing process in which the individuals are able successfully to pursue their plans because they can form expectations about the actions of their fellows which have a good chance of being met.

To appreciate the significance of this it is necessary to free ourselves wholly from the erroneous conception that there can be first a society which then gives itself laws.[3] This erroneous conception is basic to the constructivist rationalism which from Descartes and Hobbes through Rousseau and Bentham down to contemporary legal positivism has blinded students to the true relationship between law and government. It is only as a result of individuals observing certain common rules that a group of men can live together in those orderly relations which we call a society. It would therefore probably be nearer the truth if we inverted the plausible and widely held idea that law derives from authority and rather thought of all authority as deriving from law—not in the sense that the law appoints authority, but in the sense that authority commands obedience because (and so long as) it enforces a law presumed to exist independently of it and resting on a diffused opinion of what is right. Not all law can therefore be the product of legislation; but power to legislate presupposes the recognition of some common rules; and such rules which underlie the power to legislate may also limit that power. No group is likely to agree on articulated rules unless its members already hold opinions that coincide in some degree. Such coincidence of opinion will thus have to precede explicit agreement on articulated rules of just conduct, although not agreement on particular ends of action. Persons differing in their general values may occasionally agree on, and effectively collaborate for, the achievement of particular concrete purposes. But such agreement on particular ends will never suffice for forming that lasting order which we call a society.

The character of grown law stands out most clearly if we look at the condition among groups of men possessing common conceptions of justice but no common government. Groups held together by common rules, but without a deliberately created organization for the enforcement of these rules, have certainly often existed. Such a state of affairs may never have prevailed in what we would recognize as a territorial state, but it undoubtedly often existed among such groups as merchants or persons connected by the rules of chivalry or hospitality.

Whether we ought to call 'law' the kind of rules that in these groups may be effectively enforced by opinion and by the exclusion from the group of those who break them, is a matter of terminology and therefore of convenience. [4] For our present purposes we are interested in any rules which are honoured in action and not only in rules enforced by an organization created for that purpose. It is the factual observance of the rules which is the condition for the formation of an order of actions; whether they need to be enforced or how they are enforced is of secondary interest. Factual observance of some rules no doubt preceded any deliberate enforcement. The reasons why the rules arose must therefore not be confused with the reasons which made it necessary to enforce them. Those who decided to do so may never have fully comprehended what function the rules served. But if society is to persist it will have to develop some methods of effectively teaching and often also (although this may be the same thing) of enforcing them. Yet whether they need to be enforced depends also on circumstances other than the consequences of their non-observance. So long as we are interested in the effect of the observance of the rules, it is irrelevant whether they are obeyed by the individuals because they describe the only way the individuals know of achieving certain ends, or whether some sort of pressure, or a fear of sanctions, prevents them from acting differently. The mere feeling that some action would be so outrageous that one's fellows would not tolerate it is in this context quite as significant as the enforcement by that regular procedure which we find in advanced legal systems. What is important for us at this stage is that it will always be in an effort to secure and improve a system of rules which are already observed that what we know as the apparatus of law is developed.

Such law may be gradually articulated by the endeavours of arbitrators or similar persons called in to settle disputes but who have no power of command over the actions on which they have to adjudicate. The questions which they will have to decide will not be whether the parties have obeyed anybody's will, but whether their actions have conformed to expectations which the other parties had reasonably formed because they corresponded to the practices on which the everyday conduct of the members of the group was based. The significance of customs here is that they give rise to expectations that guide people's actions, and what will be regarded as binding will therefore be those practices that everybody counts on being observed and which have thereby become the condition for the success of most activities.[5] The fulfilment of expectations which these customs secure will not be, and will not appear to be, the result of any human will, or dependent on anyone's wishes or on the particular identities of the persons involved. If a need arises to call in an impartial judge, it will be because such a person will be expected to decide the case as one of a kind which might occur anywhere and at any time, and therefore in a manner which will satisfy the expectations of any person placed in a similar position among persons not known to him individually.

How the task of the judge differs from that of the head of an organization

Even where the judge has to find rules which have never been stated and perhaps never been acted upon before, his task will thus be wholly different from that of the leader of an organization who has to decide what action ought to be taken in order to achieve particular results. It would probably never have occurred to one used to organizing men for particular actions to give his commands the form of rules equally applicable to all members of the group irrespective of their allotted tasks, if he had not already had before him the example of the judge. It therefore seems unlikely that any authority with power of command would ever have developed law in the sense in which the judges developed it, that is as rules applicable to anyone who finds himself in a position definable in abstract terms. That human intention should concern itself with laying down rules for an unknown number of future instances presupposes a feat of conscious abstraction of which primitive people are hardly capable. Abstract rules independent of any particular result aimed at were something which had to be found to prevail, not something the mind could deliberately create. If we are today so familiar with the conception of law in the sense of abstract rules that it appears obvious to us that we must also be able deliberately to make it, this is the effect of the efforts of countless generations of judges to express in words what people had learnt to observe in action. In their efforts they had to create the very language in which such rules could be expressed.

The distinctive attitude of the judge thus arises from the circumstance that he is not concerned with what any authority wants done in a particular instance, but with what private persons have 'legitimate' reasons to expect, where 'legitimate' refers to the kind of expectations on which generally his actions in that society have been based. The aim of the rules must be to facilitate that matching or tallying of the expectations on which the plans of the individuals depend for their success.

A ruler sending a judge to preserve the peace will normally not do so for the purpose of preserving an order he has created, or to see whether his commands have been carried out, but to restore an order the character of which he may not even know. Unlike a supervisor or inspector, a judge has not to see whether commands have been carried out or whether everybody has performed his assigned duties. Although he may be appointed by a higher authority, his duty will not be to enforce the will of that authority but to settle disputes that might upset an existing order; he will be concerned with particular events about which the authority knows nothing and with the actions of men who on their part had no knowledge of any particular commands of authority as to what they ought to do.

Thus, 'in its beginnings law (in the lawyer's sense) had for its end, and its sole end, to keep the peace'. [6] The rules which the judge enforces are of interest to the ruler who has sent him only so far as they preserve peace and assure that the flow of efforts of the people will continue undisturbed. They have nothing to do with what the individuals have been told to do by anybody but merely with their refraining from certain kinds of action which no one is allowed to take. They refer to certain presuppositions of an ongoing order which no one has made but which nevertheless is seen to exist.

The aim of jurisdiction is the maintenance of an ongoing order of actions

The contention that the rules which the judge finds and applies serve the maintenance of an existing order of actions implies that it is possible to distinguish between those rules and the resulting order. That they are distinct follows from the fact that only some rules of individual conduct will produce an overall order while others would make such an order impossible. What is required if the separate actions of the individuals are to result in an overall order is that they not only do not unnecessarily interfere with one another, but also that in those respects in which the success of the action of the individuals depends on some matching action by others, there will be at least a good chance that this correspondence will actually occur. But all rules can achieve in this respect is to make it easier for people to find together and to form that match; abstract rules cannot actually secure that this will always happen.

The reason why such rules will tend to develop is that the groups which happen to have adopted rules conducive to a more effective order of actions will tend to prevail over other groups with a less effective order.[7] The rules that will spread will be those governing the practice or customs existing in different groups which make some groups stronger than others. And certain rules will predominate by more successfully guiding expectations in relation to other persons who act independently. Indeed, the superiority of certain rules will become evident largely in the fact that they will create an effective order not only within a closed group but also between people who meet accidentally and do not know each other personally. They will thus, unlike commands, create an order even among people who do not pursue a common purpose. The observance of the rules by all will be important for each because the achievement of his purposes depends on it, but the respective purposes of different persons may be wholly different.

So long as the individuals act in accordance with the rules it is not necessary that they be consciously aware of the rules. It is enough that they *know how* to act in accordance with the rules without *knowing that* the rules are such and such in articulated terms. But their 'know how' will provide sure guidance only in frequently occurring situations, while in more unusual situations this intuitive certainty about what expectations are legitimate will be absent. It will be in the latter situations that there will be the necessity to appeal to men who are supposed to know more about the established rules if peace is to be preserved and quarrels to be prevented. Such a person called in to adjudicate will often find it necessary to articulate and thereby make more precise those rules about which there exist differences of opinion, and sometimes even to supply new rules where no generally recognized rules exist.

The purpose of thus articulating rules in words will in the first instance be to obtain consent to their application in a particular case. In this it will often be impossible to distinguish between the mere articulation of rules which have so far existed only as practices and the statement of rules which have never been acted upon before but which, once stated, will be accepted as reasonable by most. But in neither case will the judge be free to pronounce any rule he likes. The rules which he pronounces will have to fill a definite gap in the body of already recognized rules in a manner that will serve to maintain and improve that order of actions which the already existing rules make possible. [8]

For the understanding of the process by which such a system of rules is developed by jurisdiction it will be most instructive if we consider the situations in which a judge has not merely to apply and articulate already firmly established practices, but where there exists genuine doubt about what is required by established custom, and where in consequence the litigants may differ in good faith. In such cases where there exists a real gap in the recognized law a new rule will be likely to establish itself only if somebody is charged with the task of finding a rule which after being stated is recognized as appropriate.

Thus, although rules of just conduct, like the order of actions they make possible, will in the first instance be the product of spontaneous growth, their gradual perfection will require the deliberate efforts of judges (or others learned in the law) who will improve the existing system by laying down new rules. Indeed, law as we know it could never have fully developed without such efforts of judges, or even the occasional intervention of a legislator to extricate it from the dead ends into which the gradual evolution may lead it, or to deal with altogether new problems. Yet it remains still true that the system of rules as a whole does not owe its structure to the design of either judges or legislators. It is the outcome of a process of evolution in the course of which spontaneous growth of customs and deliberate improvements of the particulars of an existing system have constantly interacted. Each of these two factors has had to operate, within the conditions the other has contributed, to assist in the formation of a factual order of actions, the particular content of which will always depend also on circumstances other than the rules of law. No system of law has ever been designed as a whole, and even the various attempts at codification could do no more than systematize an existing body of law and in doing so supplement it or eliminate inconsistencies.

The judge will thus often have to solve a puzzle to which there may indeed be more than one solution, but in most instances it will be difficult enough to find even one solution which fits all the conditions it must satisfy. The judge's task will thus be an intellectual task, not one in which his emotions or personal preferences, his sympathy with the plight of one of the contestants or his opinion of the importance of the particular objective, may affect his decision. There will be given to him a definite aim, although not a particular concrete end, namely the aim of improving a given order of actions by laying down a rule that would prevent the recurrence of such conflicts as have occurred. In endeavouring to perform this task he will always have to move in a given cosmos of rules which he must accept and will have to fit into this cosmos a piece required by the aim which the system as a whole serves.

'*Actions towards others*' *and the protection of expectations*

Since for a case to come before a judge a dispute must have arisen, and since judges are not normally concerned with relations of command and obedience, only such actions of individuals as affect other persons, or, as they are traditionally described, actions towards other persons (*operationes quae sunt ad alterum*[9]) will give rise to the formulation of legal rules. We shall presently have to examine the difficult question of how such 'actions towards others' are to be defined. At the moment we want merely to point out that actions which are clearly not of this kind, such as what a person does alone within his four walls, or even the voluntary collaboration of several persons, in a manner which clearly cannot affect or harm others, can never become the subject of rules of conduct that will concern a judge. This is important because it answers a problem that has often worried students of these matters, namely that even rules which are perfectly general and abstract might still be serious and unnecessary restrictions of individual liberty.[10] Indeed, such general rules as those requiring religious conformity may well be felt to be the most severe infringement of personal liberty. Yet the fact is simply that such rules are not rules limiting conduct towards others or, as we shall define these, rules delimiting a protected domain of individuals. At least where it is not believed that the whole group may be punished by a supernatural power for the sins of individuals, there can arise no such rules from the limitation of conduct towards others, and therefore from the settlements of disputes.[11]

But what are 'actions towards others', and to what extent can conflict between them be prevented by rules of conduct? The law evidently cannot prohibit all actions which may harm others, not only because no one can foresee all the effects of any action, but also because most changes of plans which new circumstances suggest to some are likely to be to the disadvantage of some others. The protection against disappointment of expectations which the law can give in an ever changing society will always be only the protection of some expectations but not of all. And some harm knowingly caused to others is even essential for the preservation of a spontaneous order: the law does not prohibit the setting up of a new business even if this is done in the expectation that it will lead to the failure of another. The task of rules of just conduct can thus only be to tell people which expectations they can count on and which not.

The development of such rules will evidently involve a continuous interaction between the rules of law and expectations: while new rules will be laid down to protect existing expectations, every new rule will also tend to create new expectation. [12] As some of the prevailing expectations will always conflict with each other, the judge will constantly have to decide which is to be treated as legitimate and in doing so will provide the basis for new expectations. This will in some measure always be an experimental process, since the judge (and the same applies to the law-maker) will never be able to foresee all the consequences of the rule he lays down, and will often fail in his endeavour to reduce the sources of conflicts of expectations. Any new rule intended to settle one conflict may well prove to give rise to new conflicts at another point, because the establishment of a new rule always acts on an order of actions that the law alone does not wholly determine. Yet it is only by their effects on that order of actions, effects which will be discovered only by trial and error, that the adequacy or inadequacy of the rules can be judged.

In a dynamic order of actions only some expectations can be protected

In the course of this process it will be found not only that not all expectations can be protected by general rules, but even that the chance of as many expectations as possible being fulfilled will be most enhanced if some expectations are systematically disappointed. This means also that it is not possible or desirable to prevent all actions which will harm others but only certain kinds of actions. It is regarded as fully legitimate to switch patronage and thereby disappoint the confident expectations of those with whom one used to deal. The harm that one does to another which the law aims to prevent is thus not all harm but only the disappointment of such expectations as the law designates as legitimate. Only in this way can 'do not harm others' be made a rule with meaningful content for a group of men who are allowed to pursue their own aims on the basis of their own knowledge. What can be secured to each is not that no other person will interfere with the pursuit of his aims, but only that he will not be interfered with in the use of certain means.

In an external environment which constantly changes and in which consequently some individuals will always be discovering new facts, and where we want them to make use of this new knowledge, it is clearly impossible to protect all expectations. It would decrease rather than increase certainty if the individuals were prevented from adjusting their plans of action to new facts whenever they became known to them. In fact, many of our expectations can be fulfilled only because others constantly alter their plans in the light of new knowledge. If all our expectations concerning the actions of particular other persons were protected, all those adjustments to which we owe it that in constantly changing circumstances somebody can provide for us what we expect would be prevented. Which expectations ought to be protected must therefore depend on how we can maximize the fulfilment of expectations as a whole.

Such maximization would certainly not be achieved by requiring the individuals to go on doing what they have been doing before. In a world in which some of the facts are unavoidably uncertain, we can achieve some degree of stability and therefore predictability of the overall result of the activities of all only if we allow each to adapt himself to what he learns in a manner which must be unforeseeable to others. It will be through such constant change in the particulars that an abstract overall order will be maintained in which we are able from what we see to draw fairly reliable inferences as to what to expect.

We have merely for a moment to consider the consequences that would follow if each person were required to continue to do what the others had learned to expect from him in order to see that this would rapidly lead to a breakdown of the whole order. If the individuals endeavoured to obey such instructions, some would at once find it physically impossible to do so because some of the circumstances had changed. But the effects of their failing to meet expectations would in turn place others in a similar position, and these effects would extend to an ever increasing circle of persons. (This, incidentally, is one of the reasons why a completely planned system is apt to break down.) Maintaining the overall flow of results in a complex system of production requires great elasticity of the actions of the elements of that system, and it will only be through unforeseeable changes in the particulars that a high degree of predictability of the overall results can be achieved.

We shall later (in volume 2, chapter 10) have to consider more fully the apparent paradox that in the market it is through the systematic disappointment of some expectations that on the whole expectations are as effectively met as they are. This is the manner in which the principle of 'negative feedback' operates. At the moment it should merely be added, to prevent a possible misunderstanding, that the fact that the overall order shows greater regularity than the individual facts has nothing to do with those probabilities which may result from the random movement of elements with which statistics deals, for the individual actions are the product of a systematic mutual adjustment.

Our immediate concern is to bring out that this order of actions based on certain expectations will to some extent always have existed as a fact before people would endeavour to ensure that their expectations would be fulfilled. The existing order of actions will in the first instance simply be a fact which men count on and will become a value which they are anxious to preserve only as they discover how dependent they are on it for the successful pursuit of their aims. We prefer to call it a value rather than an end because it will be a condition which all will want to preserve although no one has aimed at deliberately producing it. Indeed, although all will be aware that their chances depend on the preservation of an order, none would probably be able to describe the character of that order. This will be so because the order cannot be defined in terms of any particular observable facts but only in terms of a system of abstract relationships that will be preserved through the changes of the particulars. It will be, as we have said before, not something visible or otherwise perceptible but something which can only be mentally reconstructed.

Yet, although the order may appear to consist simply in the obedience to rules, and it is true that the obedience to rules is needed to secure order, we have also seen that not all rules will secure order. Whether the established rules will lead to the formation of an overall order in any given set of circumstances will rather depend on their particular content. The obedience to unsuitable rules may well become the cause of disorder, and there are some conceivable rules of individual conduct which clearly would make impossible the integration of individual actions into an overall order.

The 'values' which the rules of just conduct serve will thus not be particulars but abstract features of an existing factual order which men will wish to enhance because they have found them to be conditions of the effective pursuit of a multiplicity of various, divergent, and unpredictable purposes. The rules aim at securing certain abstract characteristics of the overall order of our society that we would like it to possess to a higher degree. We endeavour to make it prevail by improving the rules which we first find underlying current actions. These rules, in other words, are first the property of a factual state of affairs which no one has deliberately created and which therefore has had no purpose, but which, after we begin to understand its importance for the successful pursuit of all our actions, we may try to improve.

While it is, of course, true that norms cannot be derived from premises that contain only facts, this does not mean that the acceptance of some norms aiming at certain kinds of results may not in certain factual circumstances oblige us to accept other norms, simply because in these circumstances the accepted norms will serve the ends which are their justification only if certain other norms are also obeyed. Thus, if we accept a given system of norms without question and discover that in a certain factual situation it does not achieve the result it aims at without some complementary rules, these complementary rules will be required by those already established, although they are not logically entailed by them. And since the existence of such other rules is usually tacitly presumed, it is at least not wholly false, though not quite exact, to contend that the appearance of some new facts may make certain new norms necessary.

An important consequence of this relation between the system of rules of conduct and the factual order of actions is that there can never be a science of law that is purely a science of norms and takes no account of the factual order at which it aims. Whether a new norm fits into an existing system of norms will not be a problem solely of logic, but will usually be a problem of whether, in the existing factual circumstances, the new norm will lead to an order of compatible actions. This follows from the fact that abstract rules of conduct determine particular actions only together with particular circumstances. The test of whether a new norm fits into the existing system may thus be a factual one; and a new norm that logically may seem to be wholly consistent with the already recognized ones may yet prove to be in conflict with them if in some set of circumstances it allows actions which will clash with others permitted by the existing norms. This is the reason why the Cartesian or 'geometric' treatment of law as a pure 'science of norms', where all rules of law are deduced from explicit premises, is so misleading. We shall see that it must fail even in its immediate aim of making judicial decisions more predictable. Norms cannot be judged according to whether they fit with other norms in isolation from facts, because whether the actions which they permit are mutually compatible or not depends on facts.

This is the basic insight which through the history of jurisprudence has constantly appeared in the form of a reference to the 'nature of things' (the *natura rerum* or *Natur der Sache*), [13] which we find in the often quoted statement of O. W. Holmes, that 'the life of law has not been logic, it has been experience', [14] or in such various expressions as 'the exigencies of social life', [15] the 'compatibility' [16] or the 'reconcilability' [17] of the actions to which the law refers.

The maximal coincidence of expectations is achieved by the delimitation of protected domains

The main reason why it is so difficult to see that rules of conduct serve to enhance the certainty of expectations is that they do so not by determining a particular concrete state of things, but by determining only an abstract order which enables its members to derive from the particulars known to them expectations that have a good chance of being correct. This is all that can be achieved in a world where some of the facts change in an unpredictable manner and where order is achieved by the individuals adjusting themselves to new facts whenever they become aware of them. What can remain constant in such an overall order which continually adjusts itself to external changes, and provides the basis of predictions, can only be a system of abstract relationships and not its particular elements. This means that every change must disappoint some expectations, but that this very change which disappoints some expectations creates a situation in which again the chance to form correct expectations is as great as possible.

Such a condition can evidently be achieved only by protecting some and not all expectations, and the central problem is which expectations must be assured in order to maximize the possibility of expectations in general being fulfilled. This implies a distinction between such 'legitimate' expectations which the law must protect and others which it must allow to be disappointed. And the only method yet discovered of defining a range of expectations which will be thus protected, and thereby reducing the mutual interference of people's actions with each other's intentions, is to demarcate for every individual a range of permitted actions by designating (or rather making recognizable by the application of rules to the concrete facts) ranges of objects over which only particular individuals are allowed to dispose and from the control of which all others are excluded. The range of actions in which each will be secured against the interference of others can be determined by rules equally applicable to all only if these rules make it possible to ascertain which particular objects each may command for his purposes. In other words, rules are required which make it possible at each moment to ascertain the boundary of the protected domain of each and thus to distinguish between the *meum* and the *tuum*.

The understanding that 'good fences make good neighbours',[18] that is, that men can use their own knowledge in the pursuit of their own ends without colliding with each other only if clear boundaries can be drawn between their respective domains of free action, is the basis on which all known civilization has grown. Property, in the wide sense in which it is used to include not only material things, but (as John Locke defined it) the 'life, liberty and estates' of every individual, is the only solution men have yet discovered to the problem of reconciling individual freedom with the absence of conflict. Law, liberty, and property are an inseparable trinity. There can be no law in the sense of universal rules of conduct which does not determine boundaries of the domains of freedom by laying down rules that enable each to ascertain where he is free to act.

This was long regarded as self-evident and needing no proof. It was, as the quotation placed at the head of this chapter shows, as clearly understood by the ancient Greeks as by all founders of liberal political thought, from Milton[19] and Hobbes[20] through Montesquieu[21] to Bentham[22] and re-emphasized more recently by H. S. Maine[23] and Lord Acton.[24] It has been challenged only in comparatively recent times by the constructivist approach of socialism and under the influence of the erroneous idea that property had at some late stage been 'invented' and that before that there had existed an earlier state of primitive communism. This myth has been completely refuted by anthropological research.[25] There can be no question now that the recognition of property preceded the rise of even the most primitive cultures, and that certainly all that we call civilization has grown up on the basis of that spontaneous order of actions which is made possible by the delimitation of protected domains of individuals or groups. Although the socialist thinking of our time has succeeded in bringing this insight under the suspicion of being ideologically inspired, it is as well demonstrated a scientific truth as any we have attained in this field.

Before we proceed further it is necessary to guard ourselves against a common misunderstanding about the relations of the rules of law and the property of particular individuals. The classical formula that the aim of rules of just conduct is to assign to each his due (*suum cuique tribuere*) is often interpreted to mean that the law by itself assigns to particular individuals particular things. It does nothing of the kind, of course. It merely provides rules by which it is possible to ascertain from particular facts to whom particular things belong. The concern of the law is not who the particular persons shall be to whom particular things belong, but merely to make it possible to ascertain boundaries which have been determined by the actions of individuals within the limits drawn by those rules, but determined in their particular contents by many other circumstances. Nor must the classical formula be interpreted, as it sometimes is, as referring to what is called 'distributive justice', or as aiming at a state or a distribution of things which, apart from the question of how it has been brought about, can be described as just or unjust. The aim of the rules of law is merely to prevent as much as possible, by drawing boundaries, the actions of different individuals from interfering with each other; they cannot alone determine, and also therefore cannot be concerned with, what the result for different individuals will be.

It is only through thus defining the protected sphere of each that the law determines what are those 'actions towards others' which it regulates, and that its general prohibition of actions 'harming others' is given a determinable meaning. The maximal certainty of expectations which can be achieved in a society in which individuals are allowed to use their knowledge of constantly changing circumstances for their equally changing purposes is secured by rules which tell everyone which of these circumstances must not be altered by others and which he himself must not alter.

Precisely where those boundaries are most effectively drawn is a very difficult question to which we certainly have not yet found all the final answers. The conception of property certainly did not fall ready made from heaven. Nor have we yet succeeded everywhere in so delimiting the individual domain as to constrain the owner in his decisions to take account of all those effects (and only of those effects) we could wish. In our efforts to improve the principles of demarcation we cannot but build on an established system of rules which serves as the basis of the going order maintained by the institution of property. Because the drawing of boundaries serves a function which we are beginning to understand, it is meaningful to ask whether in particular instances the boundary has been drawn in the right place, or whether in view of changed conditions an established rule is still adequate. Where the boundary ought to be drawn, however, will usually not be a decision which can be made arbitrarily. If new problems arise as a result of changes in circumstances and raise, for example, problems of demarcation, where in the past the question as to who had a certain right was irrelevant, and the right in consequence was neither claimed nor assigned, the task will be to find a solution which serves the same general aim as the other rules which we take for granted. The rationale of the existing system may for instance clearly require that electric power be included in the concept of property, though established rules may confine it to tangible objects. Sometimes, as in the case of electro-magnetic waves, no sort of spatial boundaries will provide a working solution and altogether new conceptions of how to allocate control over such things may have to be found. Only where, as in the case of moveable objects (the 'chattels' of the law), it was approximately true that the effects of what the owner did with his property in general affected only him and nobody else, could ownership include the right to use or abuse the object in any manner he liked. But only where both the benefit and the harm caused by the particular use were confined to the domain in which the owner was interested did the conception of exclusive control provide a sufficient answer to the problem. The situation is very different as soon as we turn from chattels to real estate, where the 'neighbourhood effects' and the like make the problem of drawing appropriate 'boundaries' much more difficult.

We shall in a later context have to consider certain further consequences which follow from these considerations, such as that the rules of just conduct are essentially negative in that they aim only at preventing injustice, and that they will be developed by the consistent application to the inherited body of law of the equally negative test of compatibility; and that by the persistent application of this test we can hope to approach justice without ever finally realizing it. We shall then have to return to this complex of questions not from the angle of the properties which judge-made law necessarily possesses, but from the angle of the properties which the law of liberty ought to possess and which therefore should be observed in the process of deliberate law-making.

We must also leave to a later chapter the demonstration that what is called the maximization of the available aggregate of goods and services is an incidental though highly desirable by-product of that matching of expectations which is all the law can aim to facilitate. We shall then see that only by aiming at a state in which a mutual correspondence of expectations is likely to come about can the law help to produce that order resting on an extensive and spontaneous division of labour to which we owe our material wealth.

The general problem of the effects of values on facts

We have repeatedly emphasized that the importance of the rules of just conduct is due to the fact that the observance of these values leads to the formation of certain complex factual structures, and that in this sense important facts are dependent on the prevalence of values which are not held because of an awareness of these factual consequences. Since this relationship is rarely appreciated, some further remarks about its significance will be in place.

What is frequently overlooked is that the facts which result from certain values being held are not those to which the values which guide the actions of the several individuals are attached, but a pattern comprising the actions of many individuals, a pattern of which the acting individuals may not even be aware of and which was certainly not the aim of their actions. But the preservation of this emerging order or pattern which nobody has aimed at but whose existence will come to be recognized as the condition for the successful pursuit of many other aims will in turn also be regarded as a value. This order will be defined not by the rules governing individual conduct but by the matching of expectations which the observance of the rules will produce. But if such a factual state comes to be regarded as a value, it will mean that this value can be achieved only if people are guided in their actions by other values (the rules of conduct) which to them, since they are not aware of their functions, must appear as ultimate values. The resulting order is thus a value which is the unintended and unknown result of the observance of other values.

One consequence of this is that different prevailing values may sometimes be in conflict with each other, or that an accepted value may require the acceptance of another value, not because of any logical relation between them, but through facts which are not their object but the unintended consequences of their being honoured in action. We shall thus often find several different values which become interdependent through the factual conditions that they produce, although the acting persons may not be aware of such an interdependence in the sense that we can obtain the one only if we observe the other. Thus, what we regard as civilization may depend on the factual condition that the several plans of action of different individuals become so adjusted to each other that they can be carried out in most cases; and this condition in turn will be achieved only if the individuals accept private property as a value. Connections of this kind are not likely to be understood until we have learned to distinguish clearly between the regularities of individual conduct which are defined by rules and the overall order which will result from the observance of certain kinds of rules.

The understanding of the role which values play here is often prevented by substituting for 'values' factual terms like 'habits' or 'practices'. It is, however, not possible in the account of the formation of an overall order to replace adequately the conception of values which guide individual action with a statement of the observed regularities in the behaviour of individuals, because we are not in fact able to reduce exhaustively the values that guide action to a list of observable actions. Conduct guided by a value is recognizable by us only because we are acquainted with that value. 'The habit of respecting another's property', for example, can be observed only if we know the rules of property, and though we may reconstruct the latter from the observed behaviour, the reconstruction will always contain more than a description of particular behaviour.

The complex relationship between values and facts creates certain familiar difficulties for the social scientist who studies complex social structures that exist only because the individuals composing them hold certain values. In so far as he takes for granted the overall structure which he studies, he also implicitly presupposes that the values on which it is based will continue to be held. This may be without significance when he studies a society other than his own, as is the case with the social anthropologist who neither wishes to influence the members of the society he studies nor expects that they will take notice of what he says. But the situation is different for the social scientist who is asked for advice on how to reach particular goals within a given society. In any suggestion for modification or improvement of such an order he will have to accept the values which are indispensable for its existence, as it would clearly be inconsistent to try to improve some particular aspect of the order and at the same time propose means that would destroy the values on which the whole order rests. He will have to argue on premises which contain values, and there is no logical flaw if in arguing from such premises he arrives at conclusions which also contain values.

The 'purpose' of law

The insight that the law serves, or is the necessary condition for, the formation of a spontaneous order of actions, though vaguely present in much of legal philosophy, is thus a conception which has been difficult to formulate precisely without the explanation of that order provided by social theory, particularly economics. The idea that the law 'aimed' at some sort of factual circumstance, or that some state of facts would emerge only if some rules of conduct were generally obeyed, we find expressed early, especially in the late schoolmen's conception of law as being determined by the 'nature of things'. It is, as we have already mentioned, at the bottom of the insistence on the law being an 'empirical' or 'experimental' science. But to conceive as a goal an abstract order, the particular manifestation of which no one could predict, and which was determined by properties no one could precisely define, was too much at variance with what most people regarded as an appropriate goal of rational action. The preservation of an enduring system of abstract relationships, or of the order of a cosmos with constantly changing content, did not fit into what men ordinarily understood by a purpose, goal or end of deliberate action.

We have already seen that in the usual sense of purpose, namely the anticipation of a particular, foreseeable event, the law indeed does not serve any purpose but countless different purposes of different individuals. It provides only the means for a large number of different purposes that as a whole are not known to anybody. In the ordinary sense of purpose law is therefore not a means to any purpose, but merely a condition for the successful pursuit of most purposes. Of all multi-purpose instruments it is probably the one after language which assists the greatest variety of human purposes. It certainly has not been made for any one known purpose but rather has developed because it made people who operated under it more effective in the pursuit of their purposes.

Although people are usually well enough aware that in some sense the rules of law are required to preserve 'order', they tend to identify this order with obedience to the rules and will not be aware that the rules serve an order in a different way, namely to effect a certain correspondence between the action of different persons.

These two different conceptions of the 'purpose' of law show themselves clearly in the history of legal philosophy. From Immanuel Kant's emphasis on the 'purposeless' character of the rules of just conduct, [26] to the Utilitarians from Bentham to Ihering who regard purpose as the central feature of law, the ambiguity of the concept of purpose has been a constant source of confusion. If 'purpose' refers to concrete foreseeable results of particular actions, the particularistic utilitarianism of Bentham is certainly wrong. But if we include in 'purpose' the aiming at conditions which will assist the formation of an abstract order, the particular contents of which are unpredictable, Kant's denial of purpose is justified only so far as the application of a rule to a particular instance is concerned, but certainly not for the system of rules as a whole. From such confusion David Hume's stress on the function of the system of law as a whole irrespective of the particular effects ought to have protected later writers. The central insight is wholly contained in Hume's emphasis on the fact that 'the benefit . . . arises from the whole scheme or system . . . only from the observance of the general rule . . . without taking into consideration . . . any particular consequences which may result from the determination of these laws, in any particular case which offers.' [27]

Only when it is clearly recognized that the order of actions is a factual state of affairs distinct from the rules which contribute to its formation can it be understood that such *an abstract order can be the aim of the rules of conduct.* The understanding of this relationship is therefore a necessary condition for the understanding of law. But the task of explaining this causal relationship has in modern times been left to a discipline that had become wholly separate from the study of law and was generally as little understood by the lawyers as the law was understood by the students of economic theory. The demonstration by the economists that the market produced a spontaneous order was regarded by most lawyers with distrust or even as a myth. Although its existence is today recognized by socialist economists as well as by all others, the resistance of most constructivist rationalists to admitting the existence of such an order still blinds most persons who are not professional economists to the insight which is fundamental to all understanding of the relation between law and the order of human actions. Without such an insight into what the scoffers still deride as the 'invisible hand', the function of rules of just conduct is indeed unintelligible, and lawyers rarely possess it. Fortunately it is not necessary for the performance of their everyday task. Only in the philosophy of law, in so far as it guides jurisdiction and legislation, has the lack of such a comprehension of the function of law become significant. It has resulted in a frequent interpretation of law as an instrument of organization for particular purposes, an interpretation which is of course true enough of one kind of law, namely public law, but wholly inappropriate with regard to the *nomos* or lawyer's law. And the predominance of this interpretation has become one of the chief causes of the progressive transformation of the spontaneous order of a free society into the organization of a totalitarian order.

This unfortunate situation has in no way been remedied by the modern alliance of law with sociology which, unlike economics, has become very popular with some lawyers. For the effect of the alliance has been to direct the attention of the lawyer to the specific effects of particular measures rather than to the connection between the rules of law and the overall order. It is not in the descriptive branches of sociology but only in the theory of the overall order of society that an understanding of the relations between law and social order can be found. And because science seems to have been understood by the lawyers to mean the ascertainment of particular facts rather then an understanding of the overall order of society, the ever repeated pleas for co-operation between law and the social sciences have so far not borne much fruit. While it is easy enough to pick from descriptive sociological studies knowledge of some particular facts, the comprehension of that overall order which the rules of just conduct serve requires the mastery of a complex theory which cannot be acquired in a day. Social science conceived as a body of inductive generalizations drawn from the observation of limited groups, such as most empirical sociology undertakes, has indeed little to contribute to an understanding of the function of law.

This is not to suggest that the overall order of society which the rules of just conduct serve is exclusively a matter of economics. But so far only economics has developed a theoretical technique suitable for dealing with such spontaneous abstract orders, which is only now slowly and gradually being applied to orders other than the market. The market order is probably also the only comprehensive order extending over the whole field of human society. It must at any rate be the only one we can fully consider in this book.

The articulation of the law and the predictability of judicial decisions

The order that the judge is expected to maintain is thus not a particular state of things but the regularity of a process which rests on some of the expectations of the acting persons being protected from interference by others. He will be expected to decide in a manner which in general will correspond to what the people regard as just, but he may sometimes have to decide that what *prima facie* appears to be just may not be so because it disappoints legitimate expectations. Here he will have to draw his conclusions not exclusively from articulated premises but from a sort of 'situational logic', based on the requirements of an existing order of actions which is at the same time the undesigned result and the rationale of all those rules which he must take for granted. While the judge's starting point will be the expectations based on already established rules, he will often have to decide which of conflicting expectations held in equally good faith and equally sanctioned by recognized rules is to be regarded as legitimate. Experience will often prove that in new situations rules which have come to be accepted lead to conflicting expectations. Yet although in such situations there will be no known rule to guide him, the judge will still not be free to decide in any manner he likes. If the decision cannot be logically deduced from recognized rules, it still must be consistent with the existing body of such rules in the sense that it serves the same order of actions as these rules. If the judge finds that a rule counted on by a litigant in forming his expectations is false even though it may be widely accepted and might even be universally approved if stated, this will be because he discovers that in some circumstances it clashes with expectations based on other rules. 'We all thought this to be a just rule, but now it proves to be unjust' is a meaningful statement, describing an experience in which it becomes apparent that our conception of the justice or injustice of a particular rule is not simply a matter of 'opinion' or 'feeling', but depends on the requirements of an existing order to which we are committed— an order which in new situations can be maintained only if one of the old rules is modified or a new rule is added. The reason why in such a situation either or even both of the rules counted on by the litigants will have to be modified will not be that their application in the particular case would cause hardship, or that any other consequence in the particular instance would be undesirable, but that the rules have proved insufficient to prevent conflicts.

If the judge here were confined to decisions which could be logically deduced from the body of already articulated rules, he would often not be able to decide a case in a manner appropriate to the function which the whole system of rules serves. This throws important light on a much discussed issue, the supposed greater certainly of the law under a system in which all rules of law have been laid down in written or codified form, and in which the judge is restricted to applying such rules as have become written law. The whole movement for codification has been guided by the belief that it increases the predictability of judicial decisions. In my own case even the experience of thirty odd years in the common law world was not enough to correct this deeply rooted prejudice, and only my return to a civil law atmosphere has led me seriously to question it. Although legislation can certainly increase the certainty of the law on particular points, I am now persuaded that this advantage is more than offset if its recognition leads to the requirement that *only* what has thus been expressed in statutes should have the force of law. It seems to me that judicial decisions may in fact be more predictable if the judge is also bound by generally held views of what is just, even when they are not supported by the letter of the law, than when he is restricted to deriving his decisions only from those among accepted beliefs which have found expression in the written law.

That the judge can, or ought to, arrive at his decisions exclusively by a process of logical inference from explicit premises always has been and must be a fiction. For in fact the judge never proceeds in this way. As has been truly said, 'the trained intuition of the judge continuously leads him to right results for which he is puzzled to give unimpeachable legal reasons'. [28] The other view is a characteristic product of the constructivist rationalism which regards all rules as deliberately made and therefore capable of exhaustive statement. It appears, significantly, only in the eighteenth century and in connection with criminal law [29] where the legitimate desire to restrict the power of the judge to the application of what was unquestionably stated as law was dominant. But even the formula *nulla poena sine lege*, in which C. Beccaria expressed this idea, is not necessarily part of the rule of law if by 'law' is meant only written rules promulgated by the legislator, and not any rules whose binding character would at once be generally recognized if they were expressed in words. Characteristically English common law has never recognized the principle in the first sense, [30] even though it always accepted it in the second. Here the old conviction that a rule may exist which everybody is assumed to be capable of observing, although it has never been articulated as a verbal statement, has persisted to the present day as part of the law.

Whatever one may feel, however, about the desirability of tying the judge to the application of the written law in criminal matters, where the aim is essentially to protect the accused and let the guilty escape rather than punish the innocent, there is little case for it where the judge must aim at equal justice between litigants. Here the requirement that he must derive his decision exclusively from the written law and at most fill in obvious gaps by resort to unwritten principles would seem to make the certainty of the law rather less than greater. It seems to me that in most instances in which judicial decisions have shocked public opinion and have run counter to general expectations, this was because the judge felt that he had to stick to the letter of the written law and dared not depart from the result of the syllogism in which only explicit statements of that law could serve as premises. Logical deduction from a limited number of articulated premises always means following the 'letter' rather than the 'spirit' of the law. But the belief that everyone must be able to foresee the consequences that will follow in an unforeseen factual situation from an application of those statements of the already articulated basic principles is clearly an illusion. It is now probably universally admitted that no code of law can be without gaps. The conclusion to be derived from this would seem to be not merely that the judge must fill in such gaps by appeal to yet unarticulated principles, but also that, even when those rules which have been articulated seem to give an unambiguous answer, if they are in conflict with the general sense of justice he should be free to modify his conclusions when he can find some unwritten rule which justifies such modification and which, when articulated, is likely to receive general assent.

In this connection even John Locke's contention that in a free society all law must be 'promulgated' or 'announced' beforehand would seem to be a product of the constructivist idea of all law as being deliberately made. It is erroneous in the implication that by confining the judge to the application of already articulated rules we will increase the predictability of his decisions. What has been promulgated or announced beforehand will often be only a very imperfect formulation of principles which people can better honour in action than express in words. Only if one believes that all law is an expression of the will of a legislator and has been invented by him, rather than an expression of the principles required by the exigencies of a going order, does it seem that previous announcement is an indispensable condition of knowledge of the law. Indeed it is likely that few endeavours by judges to improve the law have come to be accepted by others unless they found expressed in them what in a sense they 'knew' already.

The function of the judge is confined to a spontaneous order

The contention that the judges by their decisions of particular cases gradually approach a system of rules of conduct which is most conducive to producing an efficient order of actions becomes more plausible when it is realized that this is in fact merely the same kind of process as that by which all intellectual evolution proceeds. As in all other fields advance is here achieved by our moving within an existing system of thought and endeavouring by a process of piecemeal tinkering, or 'immanent criticism', to make the whole more consistent both internally as well as with the facts to which the rules are applied. Such 'immanent criticism' is the main instrument of the evolution of thought, and an understanding of this process the characteristic aim of an evolutionary (or critical) as distinguished from the constructivist (or naïve) rationalism.

The judge, in other words, serves, or tries to maintain and improve, a going order which nobody has designed, an order that has formed itself without the knowledge and often against the will of authority, that extends beyond the range of deliberate organization on the part of anybody, and that is not based on the individuals doing anybody's will, but on their expectations becoming mutually adjusted. The reason why the judge will be asked to intervene will be that the rules which secure such a matching of expectations are not always observed, or clear enough, or adequate to prevent conflicts even if observed. Since new situations in which the established rules are not adequate will constantly arise, the task of preventing conflict and enhancing the compatibility of actions by appropriately delimiting the range of permitted actions is of necessity a never-ending one, requiring not only the application of already established rules but also the formulation of new rules necessary for the preservation of the order of actions. In their endeavour to cope with new problems by the application of 'principles' which they have to distil from the *ratio decidendi* of earlier decisions, and so to develop these inchoate rules (which is what 'principles' are) that they will produce the desired effect in new situations, neither the judges nor the parties involved need to know anything about the nature of the resulting overall order, or about any 'interest of society' which they serve, beyond the fact that the rules are meant to assist the individuals in successfully forming expectations in a wide range of circumstances.

The efforts of the judge are thus part of that process of adaptation of society to circumstances by which the spontaneous order grows. He assists in the process of selection by upholding those rules which, like those which have worked well in the past, make it more likely that expectations will match and not conflict. He thus becomes an organ of that order. But even when in the performance of this function he creates new rules, he is not a creator of a new order but a servant endeavouring to maintain and improve the functioning of an existing order. And the outcome of his efforts will be a characteristic instance of those 'products of human action but not of human design' in which the experience gained by the experimentation of generations embodies more knowledge than was possessed by anyone.

The judge may err, he may not succeed in discovering what is required by the rationale of the existing order, or he may be misled by his preference for a particular outcome of the case in hand; but all this does not alter the fact that he has a problem to solve for which in most instances there will be only one right solution and that this is a task in which his 'will' or his emotional response has no place. If often his 'intuition' rather than ratiocination will lead him to the right solution, this does not mean that the decisive factors in determining the result are emotional rather than rational, any more than in the case of the scientist who also is normally led intuitively to the right hypothesis which he can only afterwards try to test. Like most other intellectual tasks, that of the judge is not one of logical deduction from a limited number of premises, but one of testing hypotheses at which he has arrived by processes only in part conscious. But although he may not know what led him in the first instance to think that a particular decision was right, he must stand by his decision only if he can rationally defend it against all objections that can be raised against it.

If the judge is committed to maintaining and improving a going order of action, and must take his standards from that order, this does not mean, however, that his aim is to preserve any *status quo* in the relations between particular men. It is, on the contrary, an essential attribute of the order which he serves that it can be maintained only by constant changes in the particulars; and the judge is concerned only with the abstract relations which must be preserved while the particulars change. Such a system of abstract relationships is not a constant network connecting particular elements but a network with an ever-changing particular content. Although to the judge an existing position will often provide a presumption of right, his task is as much to assist change as to preserve existing positions. He is concerned with a dynamic order which will be maintained only by continuous changes in the positions of particular people.

But although the judge is not committed to upholding a particular *status quo*, he is committed to upholding the principles on which the existing order is based. His task is indeed one which has meaning only within a spontaneous and abstract order of actions such as the market produces. He must thus be conservative in the sense only that he cannot serve any order that is determined not by rules of individual conduct but by the particular ends of authority. A judge cannot be concerned with the needs of particular persons or groups, or with 'reasons of state' or 'the will of government', or with any particular purposes which an order of actions may be expected to serve. Within any organization in which the individual actions must be judged by their serviceability to the particular ends at which it aims, there is no room for the judge. In an order like that of socialism in which whatever rules may govern individual actions are not independent of particular results, such rules will not be 'justiciable' because they will require a balancing of the particular interests affected in the light of their importance. Socialism is indeed largely a revolt against the impartial justice which considers only the conformity of individual actions to end-independent rules and which is not concerned with the effects of their application in particular instances. Thus a socialist judge would really be a contradiction in terms; for his persuasion must prevent him from applying only those general principles which underlie a spontaneous order of actions, and lead him to take into account considerations which have nothing to do with the justice of individual conduct. He may, of course, be a socialist privately, and keep his socialism out of the considerations which determine his decisions. But he could not act as a judge on socialist principles. We shall later see that this has long been concealed by the belief that instead of acting on principles of just individual conduct he might be guided by what is called 'social justice', a phrase which describes precisely that aiming at particular results for particular persons or groups which is impossible within a spontaneous order.

The socialist attacks on the system of private property have created a widespread belief that the order the judges are required to uphold under that system is an order which serves particular interests. But the justification of the system of several property is not the interest of the property holders. It serves as much the interest of those who at the moment own no property as that of those who do, since the development of the whole order of actions on which modern civilization depends was made possible only by the institution of property.

The difficulty many people feel about conceiving of the judge as serving an existing but always imperfect abstract order which is not intended to serve particular interests is resolved when we remember that it is only these abstract features of the order which can serve as the basis of the decisions of individuals in unforeseeable future conditions, and which therefore alone can determine an enduring order; and that they alone for this reason can constitute a true *common* interest of the members of a Great Society, who do not pursue any particular common purposes but merely desire appropriate means for the pursuit of their respective individual purposes. What the judge can be concerned with in creating law is therefore only improvement of those abstract and lasting features of an order of action which is given to him and which maintains itself through changes in the relation between the particulars, while certain relations between these relations (or relations of a still higher order) are preserved. 'Abstract' and 'lasting' mean in this context more or less the same, as in the long term view which the judge must take he can consider only the effect of the rules he lays down in an unknown number of future instances which may occur at some future time.

Conclusions

We may sum up the results of this chapter with the following description of the properties which will of necessity belong to the law as it emerges from the judicial process: it will consist of rules regulating the conduct of persons towards others, applicable to an unknown number of future instances and containing prohibitions delimiting the boundary of the protected domain of each person (or organized group of persons). Every rule of this kind will in intention be perpetual, though subject to revision in the light of better insight into its interaction with other rules; and it will be valid only as part of a system of mutually modifying rules. These rules will achieve their intended effect of securing the formation of an abstract order of actions only through their universal application, while their application in the particular instance cannot be said to have a specific purpose distinct from the purpose of the system of rules as a whole.

The manner in which this system of rules of just conduct is developed by the systematic application of a negative test of justice and the elimination or modification of such rules as do not satisfy this test we will have to consider further in Volume 2, chapter 8. Our next task, however, will be to consider what such rules of just conduct *cannot* achieve and in what respect the rules required for the purposes or organization differ from them. We shall see that those rules of the latter kind which must be deliberately laid down by a legislature for the organization of government and which constitute the chief occupation of the existing legislatures, can in their nature not be restricted by those considerations which guide and restrict the law-making power of the judge.

In the last resort the difference between the rules of just conduct which emerge from the judicial process, the *nomos* or law of liberty considered in this chapter, and the rules of organization laid down by authority which we shall have to consider in the next chapter, lies in the fact that the former are derived from the conditions of a spontaneous order which man has not made, while the latter serve the deliberate building of an organization serving specific purposes. The former are *discovered* either in the sense that they merely articulate already observed practices or in the sense that they are found to be required complements of the already established rules if the order which rests on them is to operate smoothly and efficiently. They would never have been discovered if the existence of a spontaneous order of actions had not set the judges their peculiar task, and they are therefore rightly considered as something existing independently of a particular human will; while the rules of organization aiming at particular results will be free inventions of the designing mind of the organizer.

SIX

THESIS: THE LAW OF LEGISLATION

The judge addresses himself to standards of consistency,
equivalence, predictability, the legislator to fair shares, social
utility and equitable distribution.

Paul A. Freund*

*Legislation originates from the necessity of establishing rules
of organization*

While in political theory the making of law has traditionally been
represented as the chief function of legislative bodies, their origin
and main concern had little to do with *the law* in the narrow sense in
which we have considered it in the last chapter. This is especially
true of the Mother of Parliaments: the English legislature arose in a
country where longer than elsewhere the rules of just conduct, the
common law, were supposed to exist independently of political
authority. As late as the seventeenth century, it could still be
questioned whether parliament could make law inconsistent with
the common law.[1] The chief concern of what we call legislatures has
always been the control and regulation of government,[2] that is the
direction of an organization—and of an organization only one of
whose aims was to see that the rules of just conduct were obeyed.

As we have seen, rules of just conduct did not need to be deliberately made, though men gradually learned to improve or change
them deliberately. Government, by contrast, is a deliberate contri-
vance which, however, beyond its simplest and most primitive
forms, also cannot be conducted exclusively by *ad hoc* commands of
the ruler. As the organization which a ruler builds up to preserve
peace and to keep out external enemies, and gradually to provide
an increasing number of other services, becomes more and more
distinct from the more comprehensive society comprising all the
private activities of the citizens, it will require distinct rules of its
own which determine its structure, aims, and functions. Yet these

124

rules governing the apparatus of government will necessarily possess a character different from that of the universal rules of just conduct which form the basis of the spontaneous order of society at large. They will be rules of organization designed to achieve particular ends, to supplement positive orders that something should be done or that particular results should be achieved, and to set up for these purposes the various agencies through which government operates. They will be subsidiary to particular commands that indicate the ends to be pursued and the tasks of the different agencies. Their application to a particular case will depend on the particular task assigned to the particular agency and on the momentary ends of government. And they will have to establish a hierarchy of command determining the responsibilities and the range of discretion of the different agents.

This would be true even of an organization which had no task other than the enforcement of the rules of just conduct. Even in such an organization in which the rules of just conduct to be enforced by it were regarded as given, a different set of rules would have to govern its operation. The laws of procedure and the laws setting up the organization of the courts consist in this sense of rules of organization and not of rules of just conduct. Though these rules also aim at securing justice, and in early stages of development at a justice to be 'found', and therefore perhaps in earlier stages of development were more important for the achievement of justice than the rules of just conduct already explicitly formulated, they are yet logically distinct from the latter.

But if, with regard to the organization set up to enforce justice, the distinction between the rules defining just conduct and the rules regulating the enforcement of such conduct is often difficult to draw—and if indeed, the rules of just conduct may be defined only as those which would be found through a certain procedure—with regard to the other services which were gradually assumed by the apparatus of government it is clear that these will be governed by rules of another kind, rules which regulate the powers of the agents of government over the material and personal resources entrusted to them, but which need not give them power over the private citizen.

Even an absolute ruler could not do without laying down some general rules to take care of details. The extent of the powers of a ruler were, however, normally not unlimited but depended on a prevailing opinion of what were his rights. Since the law which it was his duty to enforce was regarded as given once and for all, it was chiefly with regard to the extent and exercise of his other powers that he often found it necessary to seek the consent and support of bodies representing the citizens.

Thus even when the *nomos* was regarded as given and more or less unchangeable, the ruler would often need authorization for special *measures* for which he wanted the collaboration of his subjects. The most important of such measures would be taxation, and it was from the need to obtain consent to taxes that parliamentary institutions arose.[3] The representative bodies called in for this purpose were thus from the beginning concerned primarily with governmental matters rather than with giving law in the narrow sense; though they might also be asked to testify as to what the recognized rules of just conduct were. But since the enforcement of the law was regarded as the primary task of government, it was natural that all the rules which governed its activities came to be called by the same name. This tendency was probably assisted by a desire of governments to confer on its rules of organization the same dignity and respect which *the law* commanded.

Law and statute: the enforcement of law and the execution of commands

There is no single term in English which clearly and unambiguously distinguishes any prescription which has been made, or 'set' or 'posited' by authority from one which is generally accepted without awareness of its source. Sometimes we can speak of an 'enactment', while the more familiar term 'statute' is usually confined to enactments which contain more or less general rules.[4] When we need a precise single term we shall occasionally employ the Greek word *thesis* to describe such 'set' law.

Because the chief activity of all legislatures has always been the direction of government, it was generally true that 'for lawyer's law Parliament has neither time nor taste'.[5] It would not have mattered if this had led only to lawyer's law being neglected by the legislatures and its development left to the courts. But it often led to the lawyer's law being changed incidentally and even inadvertently in the course of decisions on governmental measures and therefore in the service of particular purposes. Any decision of the legislature which touches on matters regulated by the *nomos* will, at least for the case in hand, alter and supersede that law. As a governing body the legislature is not bound by any law, and what it says concerning particular matters has the same force as a general rule and will supersede any such existing rule.

The great majority of the resolutions passed by representative assemblies do not of course lay down rules of just conduct but direct measures of government. This was probably so at all times. [6] Of British legislation it could be said in 1901: 'nine-tenths of each annual volume of statutes are concerned with what may be called administrative law; and an analysis of the content of the General Acts during the last four centuries would probably show a similar proportion.' [7]

The difference in meaning between 'law' as it is applied to the *nomos* and 'law' as it is used for all the other *theseis* which emerge from legislation, comes out most clearly if we consider how differently the 'law' relates to its application in the two cases. A rule of conduct cannot be 'carried out' or 'executed' as one carries out an instruction. One can obey the former or enforce obedience to it; but a rule of conduct merely limits the range of permitted action and usually does not determine a particular action; and what it prescribes is never accomplished but remains a standing obligation on all. Whenever we speak of 'carrying out a law' we mean by the term 'law' not a *nomos* but a *thesis* instructing somebody to do particular things. It follows that the 'law-giver' whose laws are to be 'executed' stands in a wholly different relation to those who are to execute them from the relation in which a 'law-giver' who prescribes rules of just conduct stands to those who have to observe them. The first kind of rules will be binding only on the members of the organization which we call government, while the latter will restrict the range of permitted actions for any member of the society. The judge who applies the law and directs its enforcement does not 'execute' it in the sense in which an administrator carries out a measure, or in which the 'executive' has to carry out the decision of the judge.

A statute (*thesis*) passed by a legislature *may* have all the attributes of a *nomos*, and is likely to have them if deliberately modelled after the *nomos*. But it *need* not, and in most of the cases where legislation is wanted it cannot have this character. In this chapter we shall consider further only those contents of enactments or *theseis* which are not rules of just conduct. There is, as the legal positivists have always emphasized, indeed no limit to what can be put into a statute. But though such 'law' has to be executed by those to whom it is addressed, it does not thereby become law in the sense of rules of just conduct.

Legislation and the theory of the separation of powers

The confusion resulting from this ambiguity of the word 'law' is to be seen already in the earliest discussion of the principle of the separation of powers. When in these discussions 'legislation' is referred to, it seems at first to mean exclusively the laying down of universal rules of just conduct. But such rules of just conduct are of course not 'carried out' by the executive but are applied by the courts to particular litigations as they come before them; what the executive will have to carry out will be the decisions of the court. Only with regard to law in the second sense, namely enactments that do not establish universal rules of conduct but give instructions to government, will the 'executive' have to carry out what the legislature has resolved. Here, then, 'execution' is not execution of a rule (which makes no sense) but the execution of an instruction emanating from the 'legislature'.

The term 'legislature' is historically closely associated with the theory of the separation of powers and indeed became current only at about the time when this theory was first conceived. The belief which one still often encounters that the theory arose from a misinterpretation by Montesquieu of the British constitution of his time is certainly not correct. Although it is true that the actual constitution of Britain then did not conform to that principle, there can be no question that it did then govern political opinion in England [8] and had gradually been gaining acceptance in the great debates of the preceding century. What is important for our purposes is that even in those seventeenth-century discussions it was clearly realized that to conceive of legislation as a distinct activity presupposes an independent definition of what was meant by law, and that the term legislation would become vacuous if everything the legislature prescribed were to be called law. The idea that came to be more and more clearly expressed was that 'not only was law to be couched in general terms, but also the legislature must be restricted to the making of law, and not itself meddle with particular cases'. [9] In the *First Agreement of the People* of 1647 it was explicitly provided 'that in all laws made or to be made every person may be bound alike and that no tenure, estate, character, degree, birth, or place do confer any exemption from the ordinary course of procedure whereunto others are subjected'.[10] And in an 'official defence' of the *Instrument of Government* of 1653 the separation of powers is represented as 'the grand secret of liberty and good government'.[11] Although none of the seventeenth-century endeavours to embody this conception in a constitutional government succeeded, it gained increasing acceptance and John Locke's view clearly was that 'legislative authority is to act *in a particular way* . . . [and] those who wield this authority should make only general rules. They are to govern by promulgated established laws, not to be varied in particular cases.'[12] This became accepted British opinion in the eighteenth century and from it Montesquieu derived his account of the British constitution. The belief was shaken only when in the nineteenth century the conceptions of the Philosophical Radicals and particularly Bentham's demand for an omnicompetent legislature[13] led James Mill to substitute for the ideal of a government under the law the ideal of a government controlled by a popular assembly, free to take any particular action which that assembly approved.[14]

The governmental functions of representative assemblies

If we are not to be misled by the word 'legislature', therefore, we shall have to remember that it is no more than a sort of courtesy title conferred on assemblies which had primarily arisen as instruments of representative *government*. Modern legislatures clearly derive from bodies which existed before the deliberate making of rules of just conduct was even considered possible, and the latter task was only later entrusted to institutions habitually concerned with very different tasks. The noun 'legislature' does not in fact appear before the middle of the seventeenth century and it seems doubtful whether it was then applied to the existing 'constituted bodies' (to use R. A. Palmer's useful term[15]) as a result of a dimly perceived conception of a separation of powers, or, rather, in a futile attempt to restrict bodies claiming control over government to the making of general laws. However that may be, they were in fact never so confined, and 'legislature' has become simply a name for representative assemblies occupied chiefly with directing or controlling government.

The few attempts that were made to restrict those 'legislatures' to law-making in the narrow sense were bound to fail since they constituted an attempt to limit the only existing representative bodies to the laying down of general rules, and to deprive them of control over most of the activities of government. A good illustration of such an attempt is provided by a statement ascribed to Napoleon I, who is reported to have argued that:[16]

> Nobody can have greater respect for the independence of the legislative power than I: but legislation does not mean finance, criticism of the administration, or ninety-nine of the hundred things which in England the Parliament occupies itself with. The legislature should *legislate*, i.e., construct good laws on scientific principles of jurisprudence, but it must respect the independence of the executive as it desires its own independence to be respected.

This is of course the view of the function of legislatures which corresponds to Montesquieu's conception of the separation of powers; and it would have suited Napoleon's book because it would have confined the powers of the only existing representatives of the people to laying down general rules of just conduct and have deprived them of all powers over government. For the same reason it has appealed to others such as G. W. F. Hegel[17] and, more recently, W. Hasbach.[18] But the same reason made it unacceptable to all advocates of popular or democratic government. At the same time, however, the use of the name 'legislature' seems to have appeared attractive to them for another reason: it enabled them to claim for a predominantly governmental body that unlimited or 'sovereign' power which, according to traditional opinion, belonged only to the maker of law in the narrow sense of the term. Thus it came about that governmental assemblies, whose chief activities were of the kind which ought to be limited by law, became able to command whatever they pleased simply by calling their commands 'laws'.

It must be recognized, however, that, if popular or representative government was wanted, the only representative bodies which existed could not have submitted to the limitation which the ideal of separation of powers imposed upon legislatures proper. Such limitation need not have meant that the representative body exercising governmental powers must be exempt from law other than that of its own making. It might have meant that in performing its purely governmental function it was confined by general laws laid down by another body, equally representative or democratic, which derived its supreme authority from its commitment to universal rules of conduct. On the lower echelons of government we have in fact numerous kinds of regional or local representative bodies which in their actions are thus subject to general rules which they cannot alter; and there is no reason why this should not apply also to the highest of all representative bodies directing government. Indeed, only thus could the ideal of government under the law be realized.

It will be useful at this point briefly to interrupt our main argument to consider a certain ambiguity of the concept of 'government'. Although the term covers a wide range of activities which in any orderly society are necessary or desirable, it also carries certain overtones that are inimical to the ideal of freedom under the law. There are, as we have seen, two distinct tasks included under it which must be distinguished: the enforcement of the universal rules of just conduct on the one hand, and, on the other, the direction of the organization built up to provide various services for the citizens at large.

It is in connection with the second group of activities that the term 'government' (and still more the verb 'governing') carries misleading connotations. The unquestioned need for a government that enforces the law and directs an organization providing many other services does not mean, in ordinary times, that the private citizen need be governed in the sense in which the government directs the personal and material resources entrusted to it for rendering services. It is usual today to speak of a government 'running a country' as if the whole society were an organization managed by it. Yet what really depends on it are chiefly certain conditions for the smooth running of those services that the countless individuals and organizations render to each other. These spontaneously ordered activities of the members of society certainly could and would go on even if all the activities peculiar to government temporarily ceased. Of course, in modern times government has in many countries taken over the direction of so many essential services, especially in the field of transport and communication, that the economic life would soon be paralysed if all government-directed services ceased. But this is so not because these services *can* be provided only by government, but because government has assumed the exclusive right to provide them.

Private law and public law

The distinction between universal rules of just conduct and the rules of organization of government is closely related to, and sometimes explicitly equated with, the distinction between private and public law. [19] What we have said so far, then, might be summed up by the statement that the law of legislation consists predominantly of public law. There does not exist, however, general agreement on exactly where the line of distinction between private and public law is to be drawn. The tendency of modern developments has been increasingly to blur this distinction by, on the one hand, exempting governmental agencies from the general rules of just conduct and, on the other, subjecting the conduct of private individuals and organizations to special purpose-directed rules, or even to special commands or permissions by administrative agencies. During the last hundred years it has been chiefly in the service of so-called 'social' aims that the distinction between rules of just conduct and rules for the organization of the services of government has been progressively obliterated.

For our purpose we shall henceforth regard the distinction between private and public law as being equivalent to the distinction between rules of just conduct and rules of organization (and in doing so, in conformity with predominant Anglo-Saxon but contrary to continental-European practice, place criminal law under private rather than public law). It must, however, be pointed out that the familiar terms 'private' and 'public' law can be misleading. Their similarity to the terms private and public welfare is apt to suggest wrongly that private law serves only the welfare of particular individuals and only the public law the general welfare. Even the classical Roman definition, according to which private law aims at the utility of individuals and public law at the condition of the Roman nation, [20] lends itself to such an interpretation. The suggestion that only public law aims at the public welfare is, however, correct only if 'public' is interpreted in a special narrow sense, namely as what concerns the organization of government, and if the term 'public welfare' is therefore not understood to be synonymous with general welfare, but is applied only to those particular aims with which the organization of government is directly concerned.

To regard only the public law as serving general welfare and the private law as protecting only the selfish interests of the individuals would be a complete inversion of the truth: it is an error to believe that only actions which deliberately aim at common purposes serve common needs. The fact is rather that what the spontaneous order of society provides for us is more important for everyone, and therefore for the general welfare, than most of the particular services which the organization of government can provide, excepting only the security provided by the enforcement of the rules of just conduct. A very prosperous and peaceful society is conceivable in which government confines itself to the last task; and for a long time, especially during the Middle Ages, the phrase *utilitas publica* indeed meant no more than that peace and justice which the enforcement of rules of just conduct secures. What is true is merely that the public law as the law of the organization of government requires those to whom it applies to serve deliberately the public interest, while the private law allows the individuals to pursue their respective individual ends and merely aims at so confining individual actions that they will in the result serve the general interest.

The law of organization of government is not law in the sense of rules defining what kind of conduct is generally right, but consists of directions concerning what particular officers or agencies of government are required to do. They would more appropriately be described as the regulations or by-laws of government. Their aim is to authorize particular agencies to take particular actions for specified purposes, for which they are assigned particular means. But in a free society, these means do not include the private citizen. If these regulations of the organization of government are widely regarded as being rules of the same sort as the rules of just conduct, this is due to the circumstance that they emanate from the same authority which possesses also the power to prescribe rules of just conduct. They are called 'laws' as a result of an attempt to claim for them the same dignity and respect which is attached to the universal rules of just conduct. Thus governmental agencies were able to claim the obedience of the private citizen to particular commands aimed at the achievement of specific purposes.

The task of organizing particular services necessarily produces an entirely different conception of the nature of the rules to be laid down from that produced by the task of providing rules as the foundation of a spontaneous order. Yet it is the attitude fostered by the former which has come to dominate the conception of the aims of legislation. Since the deliberate construction of rules is concerned mainly with rules or organization, the thinking about the general principles of legislation has also fallen almost entirely into the hands of public lawyers, that is of the specialists in organization who often have so little sympathy with lawyer's law that one hesitates to describe them as lawyers. It is they who in modern times have almost wholly dominated the philosophy of law and who, through providing the conceptual framwork of all legal thinking and through their influence on judicial decisions, have profoundly affected also the private law. The fact that jurisprudence (especially on the European continent) has been almost entirely in the hands of public lawyers, who think of law primarily as public law, and of order entirely as organization, is chiefly responsible for the sway not only of legal positivism (which in the field of private law just does not make sense) but also of the socialist and totalitarian ideologies implicit in it.

Constitutional law

To the rules which we are in the habit of calling 'law' but which are rules of organization and not rules of just conduct belong in the first instance all those rules of the allocation and limitation of the powers of government comprised in the law of the constitution. They are commonly regarded as the 'highest' kind of law to which a special dignity attaches, or to which more reverence is due than to other law. But, although there are historical reasons which explain this, it would be more appropriate to regard them as a superstructure erected to secure the maintenance of *the law*, rather than, as they are usually represented, as the source of all other law.

The reason why a particular dignity and fundamental character is attributed to the laws of the constitution is that, just because they had to be formally agreed upon, a special effort was required to confer on them the authority and respect which *the law* had long enjoyed. Usually the outcome of a long struggle, they were known to have been achieved at a high price in the comparatively recent past. They were seen as the result of conscious agreement that ended long strife and was often ceremoniously sworn to, consisting of principles whose infringement would revive sectional conflict or even civil war. Frequently they were also documents which for the first time conceded equal rights as full citizens to a numerous and hitherto oppressed class.

Nothing of this, however, alters the fact that a constitution is essentially a superstructure erected over a pre-existing system of law to organize the enforcement of that law. Although, once established, it may seem 'primary' [21] in the logical sense that now the other rules derive their authority from it, it is still intended to support these pre-existing rules. It creates an instrument to secure law and order and to provide the apparatus for the provision of other services, but it does not define what law and justice are. It is also true, as has been well said, that 'public law passes but private law persists'. [22] Even when as a result of revolution or conquest the whole structure of government changes, most of the rules of just conduct, the civil and criminal law, will remain in force—even in cases where the desire to change some of them may have been the main cause of the revolution. This is so because only by satisfying general expectations can a new government obtain the allegiance of its subjects and thereby become 'legitimate'.

Even when a constitution, in determining the power of the different organs of government, limits the power of the law-making assembly proper, as I believe every constitution should and early constitutions intended to do, and when for this purpose it defines the formal properties which a law must possess in order to be valid, such a definition of rules of just conduct would itself not be a rule of just conduct. It would provide what H. L. A. Hart has called a 'rule of recognition', [23] enabling the courts to ascertain whether particular rules possess those properties or not; but it would not itself be a rule of just conduct. Nor would such definition by the rules of recognition alone confer on the pre-existing law its validity. It would provide a guide for the judge, but, like all attempts to articulate conceptions underlying an existing system of norms, it might prove inadequate, and the judge might still have to go beyond (or restrict) the literal meaning of the words employed.

In no other part of public law is there greater resistance to the denying to it the attributes of rules of just conduct than in constitutional law. It seems that to most students of the subject the contention that the law of the constitution is not law in the sense in which we describe the rules of just conduct as law has appeared to be just outrageous and not to be deserving of consideration. Indeed for this reason the most prolonged and searching attempts to arrive at a clear distinction between the two kinds of law, those made in Germany during the later part of the last century concerning what was then called law in the 'material' (or 'substantive') and law in the merely 'formal' sense, could not lead to any result; for none of the participating writers could bring themselves to accept what they saw as the inevitable but, as they thought, absurd conclusion, namely that constitutional law would, on any sensible principle of distinction, have to be classed with the law in the merely formal and not with law in the material sense. [24]

Financial legislation

The field in which the difference between rules of just conduct and other products of legislation stands out most clearly, and where in consequence it was recognized early that the 'political laws' concerning it were something different from the 'juridical laws', was the field in which 'legislation' by representative bodies had first appeared—that is, finance. There is in this field indeed a difficult and important distinction to be made between the authorization of expenditure and the determination of the manner in which the burden is to be apportioned between the different individuals and groups. But that, taken as a whole, a government budget is a plan of action for an organization, conferring authority on particular agencies to do particular things, and not a statement of rules of just conduct, is fairly obvious. In fact, most of a budget, so far as it concerns expenditure, will not contain any rules at all, [25] but will consist of instructions concerning the purposes and the manner in which the means at the disposal of government are to be used. Even the German scholars of the last century who tried so hard to claim for public law the character of what they called 'law in the material sense' had to stop here and to admit that the budget could in no way be brought under that heading. A representative assembly approving such a plan of operation of government clearly acts not as a legislature in the sense in which this term is understood, for example in the conception of the separation of powers, but as the highest organ of government, giving instructions which the executive has to carry out.

This is not to say that in all those actions governed by 'legislative' instructions government ought not also, in the same manner as any other person or agency, to be subject to general rules of just conduct, and in particular be required to respect the private domains defined by those rules. Indeed, the belief that these instructions to government, because they are also called laws, supersede or modify the general rules applicable to everybody, is the chief danger against which we ought to guard ourselves by clearly distinguishing between the two kinds of 'laws'. This becomes evident if we turn from the expenditure side to the revenue side of the budget. The determination of the total revenue to be raised by taxation in a particular year is still a particular decision to be guided by particular circumstances—though whether a burden that a majority is willing to bear may also be imposed on a minority unwilling to do so, or how a given total burden is to be apportioned between the different persons and groups, does raise questions of justice. Here too, then, the obligations of the individuals ought to be governed by general rules, applicable irrespective of the particular size of the expenditure decided upon—indeed by rules which ought to be unalterably given to those who have to decide on expenditure. We are so used to a system under which expenditure is decided upon first and the question of who is to bear the burden considered afterwards, that it is rarely recognized how much this conflicts with the basic principle of limiting all coercion to the enforcement of rules of just conduct.

Administrative law and the police power

Much the greatest part of what is called public law, however, consists of administrative law, that is the rules regulating the activities of the various governmental agencies. So far as these rules determine the manner in which these agencies are to use the personal and material resources placed at their disposal, they are obviously rules of organization similar to those which any large organization will need. They are of special interest only because of the public accountability of those to whom they are applied. The term 'administrative law' is, however, used also with two other meanings.

It is used to describe the regulations laid down by administrative agencies and which are binding not only for the officers of these agencies but also for private citizens dealing with these agencies. Such regulations will clearly be required to determine the use of the various services or facilities provided by government for the citizens, but they often extend beyond this and supplement the general rules delimiting private domains. In the latter case they constitute delegated legislation. There may be good reasons for leaving the determination of some such rules to regional or local bodies. The question whether such rule-making powers should be delegated only to representative bodies or may also be entrusted to bureaucratic agencies, although important, does not concern us here. All that is relevant in the present context is that in this capacity 'administrative legislation' ought to be subject to the same limitations as the true law-making power of the general legislature.

The term 'administrative law' is further used to describe 'administrative powers over persons and property', not consisting of universal rules of just conduct but aiming at particular foreseeable results, and therefore necessarily involving discrimination and discretion. It is in connection with administrative law in this sense that a conflict with the concept of freedom under the law arises. In the legal tradition of the English-speaking world it used to be assumed that in their relation to the private citizens the administrative authorities were under the same rules of general (common or statute) law and subject to the same jurisdiction of the ordinary courts as any private citizen. It was only with respect to administrative law in the sense last mentioned, that is, different law applying to the relations between government agencies and citizens, that A. V. Dicey could maintain, as late as the beginning of this century, that it did not exist in Great Britain[26]—twenty years after foreign authors had written long treatises on British administrative law in the sense discussed before.[27]

As the services which government renders to the citizens develop, a need for regulations of the use of these services obviously arises. The conduct on roads and other public places provided for general use cannot be regulated by the assignment of individual domains but requires rules determined by consideration of expediency. Though such rules for the use of institutions provided for the public will be subject to requirements of justice (mainly in the sense that they ought to be the same for all) they do not aim at justice. The government in laying down such rules will have to be just, but not the persons who are to obey the rules. The 'rule of the road', requiring that we drive on the left or on the right, etc., which is often quoted as an illustration of a general rule, is therefore not really an example of a true rule of just conduct.[28] Like other rules for the use of public institutions, it ought to be the same for all, or at least aim at securing the same benefits for all users, but it does not define just conduct.

Such regulations for the use of public places or institutions are rules aiming at particular results, although they ought not, if intended to serve the 'general welfare', to aim at benefiting particular groups. Yet they may well, as is obvious in the case of traffic regulations, require that agents of government be given power of specific direction. When the police are given authority to do what is necessary to maintain public order, this refers essentially to securing orderly conduct in public places where the individual cannot have as much freedom as is assured to him in his private domain; special measures may here be needed to secure, for example the unimpeded flow of traffic. Government, mostly local government, is given the task of maintaining facilities in working order in such a way that the public can use them most efficiently for its purposes.

There has been a tendency, however, to interpret 'public places' not merely as facilities provided by government for the public, but as any place where the public congregates, even if they are provided commercially, such as department stores, factories, theatres, sports grounds, etc. While there is undoubtedly need for general rules which assure the safety and health of users of such places, it is not obvious that for this purpose a discretionary 'police power' is required. It is significant that so long as the basic ideal of the rule of law was still respected 'British factory legislation', for instance, 'found it possible to rely practically altogether on general rules (although to a large extent framed by administrative regulations)'. [29]

The 'measures' of policy

Where government is concerned with providing particular services, most of them of the kind which have recently come to be described as the 'infrastructure' of the economic system, the fact that such services will often aim at particular effects raises difficult problems. Particular actions of this sort are usually described as 'measures' of policy (especially on the continent by the corresponding terms *mesures* or *Massnahmen*) and it will be convenient to consider some of those problems under this heading. The crucial point has been well expressed by the statement that there can be no 'equality before a measure' as there is equality before the law. [30] What is meant by this is that most measures of this sort will be 'aimed', in the sense that, although their effects cannot be confined to those who are prepared to pay for the services provided by them, they will yet benefit only some more or less clearly discernible group and not all citizens equally. Probably most of the services rendered by government, other than the enforcement of just conduct, are of this sort. The problems which arise can be solved only partially by leaving such services largely to local government or special regional governmental agencies created for a specific purpose, such as water-boards and the like.

The defraying out of a common purse of the costs of services which will benefit only some of those who have contributed to it will usually be agreed upon by the rest only on the understanding that other requirements of theirs will be met in the same manner, so that a rough correspondence of burdens to benefits will result. In the discussion of the organization of such services with approximately determinable beneficiaries, particular interests will regularly be in conflict and a reconciliation will only be attainable by a compromise—which is quite different from what happens in a discussion of general rules of conduct that aim at an abstract order with largely unpredictable benefits. Thus it is so important that the authorities who will be in charge of such matters, even if they are democratic or representative bodies, should, in determining particular services, be subject to general rules of conduct and not be in a position themselves 'to rewrite the rules of the game as they go along'.[31]

When we speak of administrative measures, we generally mean the direction of particular resources towards the rendering of certain services to determinable groups of people. The establishment of a system of schools or health services, financial or other assistance to particular trades or professions, or the use of such instruments as government possesses through its monopoly of the issue of money, are in this sense measures of policy. It is evident that in connection with such measures the distinction between providing facilities to be used by unknown persons for unknown purposes, and providing facilities in the expectation that they will help particular groups, becomes a matter of degree, with many intermediate positions between the two extreme types. No doubt if government became the exclusive provider of many essential services, it could, by determining the character of these services and the conditions on which they are rendered, exercise great influence on the material content of the order of the market. For this reason it is important that the size of this 'public sector' be limited and the government do *not* so co-ordinate its various services that their effects on particular people become predictable. We shall later see that it is also important for this reason that government have no *exclusive* right to the rendering of any service other than the enforcement of rules of just conduct, and thus should not be in a position to prevent other agencies from offering services of the same kind when possibilities appear of providing through the market what perhaps in the past has been impossible thus to provide.

The transformation of private law into public law by 'social'
legislation

If in the course of the last hundred years the principle that in a
free society coercion is permissible only to secure obedience to
universal rules of just conduct has been abandoned, this was done
mainly in the service of what were called 'social' aims. 'Social' as
used here, however, covers various kinds of concepts which must
be carefully distinguished.

In the first instance it meant chiefly the removal of discrimina-
tions by law which had crept in as a result of the greater influence
that certain groups like landlords, employers, creditors, etc., had
wielded on the formation of the law. This does not mean, however,
that the only alternative is instead to favour the class treated un-
fairly in the past, and that there is not a 'mean' position in which
the law treats both parties alike according to the same principles.
Equal treatment in this sense has nothing to do with the question
whether the application of such general rules in a particular situation may lead to *results* which are more favourable to one group than
to the others: justice is not concerned with the results of the various
transactions but only with whether the transactions themselves are
fair. Rules of just conduct cannot alter the fact that, with perfectly
just behaviour on both sides, the low productivity of labour in some
countries will bring about a situation where the wages at which all
can get employment will be very low—and at the same time the
return on capital will be very high—and where higher wages could
be secured to some only by means which would prevent others from
finding employment at all.

We shall see later that justice in this connection can mean only
such wages or prices as have been determined in a free market
without deception, fraud or violence; and that, in this one sense in
which we can talk meaningfully about just wages or just prices, the
result of a wholly just transaction may indeed be that one side gets
very little out of it and the other a great deal. Classical liberalism
rested on the belief that there existed discoverable principles of
just conduct of universal applicability which could be recognized as
just irrespective of the effects of their application on particular
groups.

'Social legislation', second, may refer to the provision by government of certain services which are of special importance to some
unfortunate minorities, the weak or those unable to provide for

themselves. Such service functions of government a wealthy community may decide to provide for a minority—either on moral grounds or as an insurance against contingencies which may affect anybody. Although the provision of such services increases the necessity of levying taxes, these can be raised according to uniform principles; and the duty to contribute to the costs of such agreed common aims could be brought under the conception of general rules of conduct. It would not make the private citizen in any way the object of administration; he would still be free to use his knowledge for his purposes and not have to serve the purposes of an organization.

There is, however, a third kind of 'social' legislation. The aim of it is to direct private activity towards particular ends and to the benefit of particular groups. It was as the result of such endeavours, inspired by the will-o-the-wisp of 'social justice', that the gradual transformation of the purpose-independent rules of just conduct (or the rules of private law) into purpose-dependent rules of organization (or rules of public law) has taken place. This pursuit of 'social justice' made it necessary for governments to treat the citizen and his property as an object of administration with the aim of securing particular results for particular groups. When the aim of legislation is higher wages for particular groups of workers, or higher incomes for small farmers, or better housing for the urban poor, it cannot be achieved by improving the general rules of conduct.

Such endeavours towards a 'socialization' of the law have been taking place in most Western countries for several generations and have already gone far to destroy the characteristic attribute of universal rules of conduct, the equality of all under the same rules. The history of such legislation which began in Germany in the last century under the name *Sozialpolitik* and spread first to the continent and England, and in this century also to the United States, cannot be sketched here. Some of the landmarks in this development which led to the creation of special rules for particular classes are the English Trade Disputes Act of 1906 which conferred on the labour unions unique privileges, [32] and the decisions of the U.S. Supreme Court during the earlier period of the New Deal which conceded to legislatures unlimited powers to 'safeguard the vital interests of the people', [33] saying in effect that for any end a legislature regarded as beneficial it might pass any law it liked.

The country in which this development went further and its

consequences were most fully accepted and explicitly recognized remained, however, the country in which it started. In Germany it had come to be widely understood that the pursuit of these social aims involved the progressive replacement of private law by public law. Indeed, the leaders of socialist thought in the field of law openly pronounced the doctrine that the private law aiming at the co-ordination of individual activities would progressively be replaced by a public law of subordination, and that 'for a social order of law private law was to be regarded only as a provisional and constantly decreasing range of private initiative, temporarily spared within the all-comprehensive sphere of public law'. [34] In Germany this development was much facilitated by a surviving tradition of a fundamentally unlimited power of government, based on a mystique of *Hoheit* and *Herrschaft*, which found its expression in conceptions, then still largely unintelligible in the Western world, such as that the citizen is the subject of the administration, and that administrative law is 'the law peculiar to the relations between the administering state and the subjects it encounters in its activities'. [35]

The mental bias of a legislature preoccupied with government

All this raises questions which will be our main concern in the second volume of this work. Here we can touch on them only briefly to indicate the reasons why the confounding of the making of rules of just conduct with the direction of the government apparatus tends to produce a progressive transformation of the spontaneous order of society into an organization. Only a few preliminary remarks need be added on the altogether different mental attitude which the occupation with questions of organization will produce among the members of an assembly so occupied from that which would prevail in an assembly mainly occupied with law-giving in the classical sense of the term.

Increasingly and inevitably an assembly occupied in the former way tends to think of itself as a body that not merely provides some services for an independently functioning order but 'runs the country' as one runs a factory or any other organization. Since it possesses authority to arrange everything, it cannot refuse responsibility for anything. There will be no particular grievance which it will not be regarded as capable of removing; and since in every one particular instance taken by itself it will generally be capable of remedying such a grievance, it will be assumed that it can remove all grievances at the same time. However, it is a fact that most of the grievances of particular individuals or groups can be removed only by measures which create new grievances elsewhere.

An experienced British Labour parliamentarian has described the duty of the politician as the removal of all sources of discontent.[36] This, of course, requires an arrangement of all particular matters in a manner no set of general rules of conduct can determine. But dissatisfaction does not necessarily mean legitimate dissatisfaction, nor does the existence of dissatisfaction prove that its source can be removed for all. Indeed, it is most likely to be due to circumstances which nobody could prevent or alter in accordance with generally accepted principles. The idea that the aim of government is the satisfaction of all particular wishes held by a sufficiently large number, without any limitation on the means which the representative body may use for this purpose, must lead to a condition of society in which all the particular actions are commanded in accordance with a detailed plan agreed upon through bargaining within a majority and then imposed on all as the 'common aim' to be realized.

NOTES

INTRODUCTION

* Guglielmo Ferrero, *The Principles of Power* (New York, 1942), p. 318. The paragraph from which the quotation is taken begins: 'Order is the exhausting Sisyphean labour of mankind against which mankind is always in a potential state of conflict . . .'

1 The time-honoured phrase widely used in the eighteenth and nineteenth centuries is 'limited constitution', but the expression 'limiting constitution' also occurs occasionally in the earlier literature.

2 See K. C. Wheare, *Modern Constitutions*, revised edition (Oxford, 1960), p. 202: 'the original idea behind [constitutions] is that of limiting government and of requiring those who govern to conform to laws and rules'; see also C. H. McIlwain, *Constitutionalism: Ancient and Modern*, revised edition (Ithaca, N.Y., 1958) p. 21: 'All constitutional government is by definition limited government . . . constitutionalism has one essential quality: it is a legal limitation of government; it is the antithesis of arbitrary rule; its opposite is despotic government, the government of will'; C. J. Friedrich, *Constitutional Government and Democracy* (Boston, 1941), especially p. 131, where a constitution is defined as 'the process by which governmental action is effectively restrained'.

3 See Richard Wollheim, 'A paradox in the theory of democracy', in Peter Laslett and W. G. Runciman (eds); *Philosophy, Politics and Society*, second series (Oxford, 1962), p. 72: 'the modern conception of Democracy is of a form of government in which no restriction is placed upon the governing body.'

4 See George Burdeau, 'Une Survivance: la notion de constitution', in *L'Evolution du droit public, études offertes à Achille Mestre* (Paris, 1956).

5 See F. A. Hayek, *The Constitution of Liberty* (London and Chicago, 1960).

6 See Samuel H. Beer, 'The British legislature and the problem of mobilizing consent,' in Elke Frank (ed), *Lawmakers in a Changing World* (Englewood Cliffs, N.J., 1966), and reprinted in B. Crick (ed), *Essays on Reform* (Oxford, 1967).

7 See F. A. Hayek, op. cit., p. 207 and note 12.
8 Torgny T. Segerstedt, 'Wandel der Gesellschaft', *Bild der Wissenschaft*, vol. vi, May 1969, p. 441.
9 Enrico Ferri, *Annales de l'Institut Internationale de Sociologie*, vol. 1., 1895, p. 166: 'Le socialisme est le point d'arrivée logique et inévitable de la sociologie.'

CHAPTER ONE   REASON AND EVOLUTION

* Lord Acton, *The History of Freedom and Other Essays* (London, 1907), p. 58. Most of the problems to be discussed in this introductory chapter have been examined at somewhat greater length in a series of preliminary studies most of which have been reprinted in F. A. Hayek, *Studies in Philosophy, Politics and Economics* (London and Chicago, 1967) (henceforth referred to as *S.P.P.E.*): see, in particular, chapters 2–6 in that book as well as my lecture (1966) on Dr Bernard Mandeville, in *Proceedings of the British Academy*, lii (London, 1967), and *The Confusion of Language in Political Theory* (London, 1968).

1 It is the fashion today to sneer at any assertion that something is impossible and to point at the numerous instances in which what even scientists represented as impossible has later proved to be possible. Nevertheless, it is true that all advance of scientific knowledge consists in the last resort in the insight into the impossibility of certain events. Sir Edmund Whittaker, a mathematical physicist, has described this as the 'impotence principle' and Sir Karl Popper has systematically developed the idea that all scientific laws consist essentially of prohibitions, that is, of assertions that something cannot happen; see especially Karl Popper, *The Logic of Scientific Discovery* (London, 1954).

2 On the role played by Bernard Mandeville in this connection see my lecture on him quoted in the asterisked note at the beginning of this chapter.

3 The implications of at least the most widely held interpretation of the Cartesian approach for all moral and political problems are clearly brought out in Alfred Espinas, *Descartes et la morale*, 2 vols (Paris, 1925), especially at the beginning of vol 2. On the domination of the whole French Enlightenment by the Cartesian brand of rationalism, see G. de Rugiero, *History of European Liberalism*, trans. R. G. Collingwood (London, 1927), p. 21 *et seq.*:

> To the Cartesian school belong almost all the exponents of the higher and middle culture of the eighteenth century: the scientists, . . . the social reformers, drawing up their indictment against history as a museum of irrational uses and abuses, and endeavouring to reconstruct the whole social system; the jurists,

in whose eyes law is and must be a system deducible from a few
universal and self-evident principles.

See also H. J. Laski, *Studies in Law and Politics* (London and New
Haven, 1922), p. 20:

> What does rationalism [with regard to Voltaire, Montesquieu,
> etc.] mean? It is, essentially, an attempt to apply the principles of
> Cartesianism to human affairs. Take as postulates the inescapable
> evidence of stout common sense, and reason logically from them
> to the conclusions they imply. That common sense, all the
> philosophers believed, will give everywhere the same results:
> what it is to the sage of Ferney it will be in Peking or the woods of
> America.

4 Descartes himself gave expression to this attitude when he wrote in
his *Discours de la méthode* (beginning of part 2) that 'the greatness of
Sparta was due not to the pre-eminence of each of its laws in particular, . . . but to the circumstances that, originated by a single individual, they all tended to a single end.' For a characteristic application
of this idea by an eighteenth-century ruler see the statement by Frederick II of Prussia quoted in G. Küntzel, *Die politischen Testamente
der Hohenzollern* (Leipzig, 1920), vol 2, p. 64, where he maintains
that, as little as Newton could have designed his system of universal
attraction if he had had to collaborate with Leibniz and Descartes,
could a political system originate and maintain itself if it were not the
product of a single mind.

5 'Pragmatic' is the older expression used in this connection chiefly by
Carl Menger, *Untersuchungen über die Methoden der Socialwissen-
schaften* (Leipzig, 1882), translated as *Problems of Economics and
Sociology* by F. J. Nock, with an introduction by Louis Schneider
(Urbana, Ill., 1963), which contains still the best earlier treatment of
these problems.

6 On the decisive influence of Descartes on Rousseau see H. Michel,
L'Idée de l'état (Paris, 1896), p. 66 (with references to earlier authors);
A. Schatz, *L'Individualisme économique et social* (Paris, 1907), p. 40
et seq.; R. Derathé, *Le Rationalisme de Jean-Jacques Rousseau* (Paris,
1948); and the perceptive observation of R. A. Palmer, *The Age of
Democratic Revolution* (Princeton, 1959 and 1964), vol 1, p. 114, that
for Rousseau 'there was even no law except law willed by living men—
this was his greatest heresy from many points of view, including the
Christian: it was also his greatest affirmation in political theory.'

7 See R. S. Peters, *The Concept of Motivation* (London, 1959), p. 5:

> *Man is a rule-following animal.* His actions are not simply directed
> towards ends; they also conform to social standards and conven-
> tions, and unlike a calculating machine he acts because of his

knowledge of rules and objectives. For instance, we ascribe to
. people *traits* of character like honesty, punctuality, considerateness and meanness. Such terms do not, like ambition, or hunger, or social desire, indicate the sort of goals that a man tends to pursue; rather they indicate the type of regulations that he imposes on his conduct whatever his goals may be.

8 See F. A. Hayek, *The Constitution of Liberty* (London and Chicago, 1960), especially ch. 2.

9 J. A. Schumpeter, *History of Economic Analysis* (New York, 1954), p. 241.

10 See my lectures on 'Economics and knowledge' (1936) and 'The use of knowledge in society' (1945), both reprinted in F. A. Hayek, *Individualism and Economic Order* (London and Chicago, 1948).

11 The expression 'the Great Society', which we shall frequently use in the same sense in which we shall use Sir Karl Popper's term 'the Open Society', was, of course, already familiar in the eighteenth century (see for example Richard Cumberland, *A Treatise on the Law of Nature* (London, 1727), ch. 8 section 9, as well as Adam Smith and Rousseau) and in modern times was revived by Graham Wallas when he used it as the title for one of his books (*The Great Society* (London and New York, 1920)). It has probably not lost its suitability by its use as a political slogan by a recent American administration.

12 Lewis Mumford in his introduction to F. Mackenzie (ed), *Planned Society* (New York, 1937), p. vii: 'We have still to develop what Patrick Geddes used sometimes to call the art of simultaneous thinking: the ability to deal with a multitude of related phenomena at the same time, and of composing, in a single picture, both the qualitative and the quantitative attributes of these phenomena.'

13 Jane Jacobs, *The Death and Life of Great American Cities* (New York, 1961).

14 Perhaps the current uncritical enthusiasm about computers makes it advisable to mention that, however great their power of digesting facts fed into them, they do not help us in ascertaining these facts.

15 See A. M. Carr-Saunders, *The Population Problem: A Study in Human Evolution* (Oxford, 1922), p. 223:

> Men and groups of men are naturally selected on account of the customs they practise just as they are selected on account of their mental and physical characters. Those groups practising the most advantageous customs will have an advantage in the constant struggle between adjacent groups over those that practise less advantageous customs. Few customs can be more advantageous than those which limit the numbers of a group to the desirable number, and there is no difficulty in understanding how—once any of these three customs [abortion, infanticide, abstention from

intercourse] had originated it would, by a process of natural selection, come to be so practised that it would produce an approximation to the desirable number.

A very remarkable exposition of the basic idea is to be found in two essays by W. K. Clifford: 'On the scientific basis of morals' (1873) and 'Right and wrong: the scientific ground of their distinction' (1875), both reprinted in W. K. Clifford, *Lectures and Essays* (London, 1879), vol. 2, especially pp. 112–21 and 169–72, of which only some of the most relevant passages can be quoted here:

> Adaptation of means to an end may be produced in two ways that we at present know of: by process of natural selection, and by the agency of an intelligence in which an image or idea of the end preceded the use of the means. In both cases the existence of adaptation is accounted for by the necessity or utility of the end. It seems to me convenient to use the word *purpose* as meaning generally the end to which certain means are adapted, both in these two cases, and in any others that may hereafter become known, provided only that the adaptation is accounted for by the necessity of the end. And there seems to be no objection to the use of the phrase 'final cause' in this wider sense if it is to be kept at all. The word 'design' might then be kept for the special case of adaptation by intelligence. And we may then say that since the process of natural selection has been understood, *purpose* has ceased to suggest *design* to instructed people except in cases where the agency of men is independently probably [p. 117]. Those tribes have on the whole survived in which conscience approved of such actions as tended to the improvement of men's character as citizens and therefore to the survival of the tribe. Hence it is that the moral conscience of the individual, though founded upon the experience of the tribe, is purely intuitive: conscience gives no reasons [p. 119]. *Our sense of right and wrong is derived from such order as we can observe* [p. 121: my italics].

16 See A. M. Carr-Saunders, op. cit., p. 302: 'Mental characters are adapted to the whole of the traditional [as distinguished from the physical] environment. Men come to be selected in accordance with the needs of social organization, and as traditions grow in amount also in accordance with the capability of absorbing tradition.'; See also Peter Farb, *Man's Rise to Civilization* (New York, 1968), p. 13:

> In arriving at their varying ways of life, societies do not make conscious choices. Rather they make unconscious adaptations. Not all societies are presented with the same set of environmental conditions, nor are all societies at the same stage when these choices are presented. For various reasons, some societies adapt

to conditions in a certain way, some in a different way, and others not at all. Adaptation is not a conscious choice, and the people who make up a society do not quite understand what they are doing; they know only that a particular choice works, even though it may appear bizarre to outsiders.

See further, Alexander Alland, Jr, *Evolution and Human Behavior* (New York, 1967).

17 The decisive observation, in modern times first emphasized by Otto Jespersen in *Language, Its Nature, Development and Origin* (London, 1922), p. 130, was already mentioned by Adam Ferguson in *Principles of Moral and Political Science* (Edinburgh, 1792), vol. 1, p. 7: 'The beautiful analogy of expression, on which the rules of grammar are established, is agreeable to the genius of man. Children are frequently misled by it, by following analogy where the practice actually deviates from it. Thus, a little boy, asked how he came by his plaything, said *Father buyed it for him.*'

18 See F. Heinimann, *Nomos and Physis* (Basel, 1945); John Burnet, 'Law and nature in Greek ethics', *International Journal of Ethics*, vii, 1893, and *Early Greek Philosophy*, fourth edition (London, 1930), p. 9; and particularly Karl R. Popper, *The Open Society and Its Enemies* (London and Princeton, 1945 and later), especially ch. 5.

19 Adam Ferguson, *An Essay on the History of Civil Society* (London, 1767), p. 187: 'Nations stumble upon establishments, which are indeed the result of human action, but not the execution of any human design.' In the introduction to his recent edition of this work (Edinburgh, 1966), p. xxiv, Duncan Forbes points out that:

> Ferguson, like Smith, Millar, and others (but not Hume [?]), has dispensed with the 'Legislators and Founders of states', a superstition that Durkheim thought has hindered the development of social science more than anything else, and which is to be found even in Montesquieu. . . . The Legislator myth flourished in the eighteenth century, for a variety of reasons, and its destruction was perhaps the most original and daring *coup* of the social science of the Scottish Enlightenment.

20 See Sten Gagnèr, *Studien zur Ideengeschichte der Gesetzgebung* (Uppsala, 1960), pp. 208 and 242. It would thus seem that the whole confusion involved in the dispute between legal positivism and the theories of the law of nature trace back directly to the false dichotomy here discussed.

21 See ibid., p. 231, on Guillaume de Conches and particularly his statement: 'Et est positiva que est ab hominibus inventa ut suspensio latronis. Naturalis vero que non est homine inventa.'

22 Luis Molina, *De iustitia et iure* (Cologne, 1596–1600), tom. ll, disp.

347, no. 3: 'naturale dicitur, quoniam et ipsis rebus, seclusa quacum-
que humana lege et decreto consurgit, dependetur tamen ab multiis
circumstantiis, quibus variatur, atque ab hominum affectu, ac aesti-
matione, comparatione diversum usum, interdum pro solo hominum
beneplacito et arbitrio.' On Molina see Wilhelm Weber, *Wirtschaftsethik am Vorabend des Liberalismus* (Münster, 1959); and W. S. Joyce,
'The economics of Louis Molina' (1948), unpublished Ph.D. thesis,
Harvard University.

23 Edmund Burke, *Reflections on the Revolution in France*, in *Works*
(London, 1808) vol. 5, p. 437.

24 Johannes de Lugo, *Disputationum de iustitia et iure tomus secundus*
(Lyon, 1642), disp. 26, section 4, No. 40: 'incertitudo ergo nostra
circa pretium iustum Mathematicum . . . provenit ex Deo, quod non
sciamus determinare'; see also Joseph Höffner, *Wirtschaftsethik und
Monopole im fünfzehnten und sechzehnten Jahrhundert* (Jena, 1941), pp.
114-15.

25 As John Locke understood. See his *Essays on the Law of Nature* (1676),
ed W. von Leyden (Oxford, 1954),

> By reason . . . I do not think is meant here that faculty of the
> understanding which forms trains of thought and deduces proofs,
> but certain definite principles of action from which spring all
> virtues and whatever is necessary for the proper moulding of
> morals . . . reason does not so much establish and pronounce
> this law of nature as search for it and discover it. . . . Neither is
> reason so much the maker of that law as its interpreter.

26 See Joseph Kohler, 'Die spanische Naturrechtslehre des 16. und 17.
Jahrhunderts,' *Archiv für Rechts- und Wirtschaftsphilosophie*, x,
1916-17, especially p. 235; and in particular A. P. D'Entreves,
Natural Law (London, 1951), pp. 51 *et seq.*, and the observation on
p. 56 about 'how all of a sudden we are faced with a doctrine which
purposely sets out to construe civil society as the result of a deliberate
act of will on the part of its components.' See also John C. H. Wu,
'Natural law and our common law'. *Fordham Law Review*, xxiii, 1954,
21-2: 'The modern speculative, rationalistic philosophies of Natural
Law are aberrations from the high road of scholastic tradition . . . .
They proceed *more geometrico*'.

27 On Matthew Hale see in particular J. G. A. Pocock, *The Ancient
Constitution and the Feudal Law* (Cambridge, 1957), Ch. 7.

28 See the significant observation by J. M. Guyau, *La Morale anglaise
contemporaine* (Paris, 1879), p. 5:

> Les disciples de Bentham comparent leur maître à Descartes.
> 'Donnez-moi le matière et le mouvement', disait Descartes, 'et je
> ferai le monde'; mais Descartes ne parlait que du monde physique,

oeuvre inerte et insensible. . . . 'Donnez-moi', peut dire à
son tour Bentham, 'donnez-moi les affections humaines, la joie
et la douleur, la peine et le plaisir, et je créerai un monde moral.
Je produirai non seulement la justice, mais encore la generosité,
le patriotisme, la philanthropie, et toutes le vertues aimables
où sublimes dans leur pureté et leur exaltation.'

29 On the indirect influence of Edmund Burke on the German historical
school through the Hannoverian scholars Ernst Brandes and A. W.
Rehberg see H. Ahrens, *Die Rechtsphilosophie oder das Naturrecht*,
fourth edition (Vienna, 1852), p. 64, first French edition (Paris, 1838),
p. 54; and more recently Gunnar Rexius, 'Studien zur Staatslehre der
historischen Schule', *Historische Zeitschrift*, cvii, 1911, Frieda Braun;
Edmund Burke in Deutschland (Heidelberg, 1917); and Klaus Epstein,
The Genesis of German Conservatism (Princeton, 1966).
30 See Peter Stein, *Regulae Iuris* (Edinburgh, 1966), ch. 3.
31 See Paul Vinogradoff, *The Teaching of Sir Henry Maine* (London,
1904), p. 8: 'He [Maine] approached the study of law mainly under
the guidance of the German school of historical jurisprudence which
had formed itself around Savigny and Eichhorn. The special dis-
quisitions of *Ancient Law* on testament, contract, possession, etc.,
leave no doubt as to his close dependence on Savigny's and Puchta's
writings.'
32 On the derivation of social anthropology from the eighteenth- and
nineteenth-century social and legal philosophers see E. E. Evans-
Pritchard, *Social Anthropology* (London, 1915), p. 23; and Max
Gluckman, *Politics, Law and Ritual in Tribal Society* (New York,
1965), p. 17.
33 In addition to such recent studies as J. W. Burrow, *Evolution and
Society: A Study in Victorian Social Theory* (Cambridge, 1966);
Bentley Glass (ed), *Forerunners of Darwin* (Baltimore, 1959); M.
Banton (ed), *Darwinism and the Study of Society* (London, 1961);
Betty J. Meggers (editor for the Anthropological Society of Washing-
ton), *Evolution and Anthropology: A Centennial Appraisal* (Washing-
ton, 1959); and C. C. Gillispie, *Genesis and Geology* (Cambridge,
Mass., 1951), see in particular on David Hume's influence on Charles
Darwin's grandfather, Erasmus Darwin, H. F. Osborn, *From the
Greeks to Darwin*, second edition (New York, 1929), p. 217; F. C.
Haber in Bentley Glass (ed), op. cit., p. 251; on the fact that all three
of the independent discoverers of the theory of evolution, Charles
Darwin, Alfred Russell Wallace and Herbert Spencer, owed the
suggestion to social theory see J. Arthur Thompson, 'Darwin's
predecessors' in A. C. Seward (ed) *Darwin and Modern Science*
(Cambridge, 1909), p. 19; and on Darwin in particular see E. Radl,
Geschichte der biologischen Theorien, II (Leipzig, 1909), p. 121.

See also C. S. Peirce, 'Evolutionary love' (1893), reprinted in his *Collected Papers*, edited by C. Hartshorn and P. Weiss (Cambridge, Mass., 1935), vol 6, p. 293: '*The Origin of Species* of Darwin merely extends politico-economic views of progress to the entire realm of animal and vegetable life.' The whole position has been well summed up by Simon N. Patten, *The Development of English Thought* (New York, 1899), p. xxiii: 'Just as Adam Smith was the last of the moralists and the first of the economists, so Darwin was the last of the economists and the first of the biologists.' Two well-known passages by Sir Frederick Pollock will also bear repetition, the first from *Oxford Lectures and Other Discourses* (London, 1890), p. 41:

> The doctrine of evolution is nothing else than the historical method applied to the facts of nature, the historical method is nothing else than the doctrine of evolution applied to human societies and institutions. When Charles Darwin created the philosophy of natural history (for no less title is due to the idea which transformed the knowledge of organic nature from a multitude of particulars into a continuous whole) he was working in the same spirit and towards the same end as the great publicists who, heeding his field as little as he heeded theirs, had laid in the patient study of historical fact the basis of a solid and rational philosophy of politics and law. Savigny, whom we do not yet know or honour enough, or our own Burke, whom we know and honour, but cannot honour enough, were Darwinians before Darwin. In some measure the same may be said of the great Frenchman Montesquieu, whose unequal but illuminating genius was lost in a generation of formalists.

The second passage is from *Essays in the Law* (London, 1922), p. 11: '*Ancient Law* and *The Origin of Species* were really the outcome, in different branches, of one and the same intellectual movement—that which we associate with the word Evolution.'

The claim to have been Darwinians before Darwin had been made in these words by the linguists August Schleicher, *Die Darwinsche Theorie und die Sprachwissenschaft* (Weimar, 1867), and Max Müller, 'Darwin's Philosophy of Language', *Fraser's Magazine*, vii, 1873, 662.

34 It is indeed to be feared that in social anthropology some of the most enthusiastic advocates of evolutionism, such as the disciples of Leslie A. White, by combining the legitimate 'specific' evolution with what they call 'general' evolution of the sort described above may once more discredit the revived evolutionary approach: see in particular M. D. Sahlins and E. R. Service, *Evolution and Culture* (Ann Arbor, Mich., 1960).

35 See C. H. Waddington, *The Ethical Animal* (London, 1960); T. H. Huxley and Julian Huxley, *Evolution and Ethics 1893-1943* (London,

1947); J. Needham, *Time: The Refreshing River* (London, 1943); and A. G. N. Flew, *Evolutionary Ethics* (London, 1967).

36 Carl Menger, *Problems of Economics and Sociology*, edited by Louis Schneider (Urbana, Ill., 1963), p. 94.

37 At the head of this tradition one should probably mention B. de Spinoza and his often quoted statement in *Ethics* (Everyman edition, p. 187) that, 'He is a free man who lives according to the dictates of reason alone.'

38 Voltaire, *Dictionnaire Philosophique*, s.v. 'Loi', in *Oeuvres complètes de Voltaire*, edited by Hachette, tom. xviii, p. 432: 'Voulez-vous avoir de bonnes lois? Brulez les vôtres et faites nouvelles.'

39 R. A. Palmer, *The Age of Democratic Revolution*, vol. 1 (Princeton, 1959), p. 114.

40 Edmund Burke, 'A vindication of natural society', Preface in *Works* (London, 1808), p. 7.

41 Alexander Herzen, *From the Other Shore*, edited by I. Berlin (London, 1956), pp. 28 and 141.

42 Hans Reichenbach, *The Rise of Scientific Philosophy* (Berkeley, Calif., 1951), p. 141.

43 Quoted in John Maynard Keynes, *Two Memoirs* (London, 1949), p. 97.

44 See J. Piaget, *The Child's Conception of the World* (London, 1929), p. 359: 'The child begins by seeking purpose everywhere and it is only secondarily that it is concerned with classing them as purposes of the things themselves (animism) and purposes of the makers of the things (artificialism).'

45 As, following earlier writers, I have myself done in the past. For the reasons why this expression now appears to me misleading see my lecture on 'Kinds of rationalism' in *S.P.P.E.*

46 See my paper on 'The primacy of the abstract' in A. Koestler and J. R. Smithies (eds), *Beyond Reductionism* (London, 1969).

47 See Gilbert Ryle, *The Concept of Mind* (London, 1949).

48 See G. W. F. Hegel, *Philosophie der Weltgeschichte*, ed G. Lasson, third edition (Leipzig, 1930), and reprinted in *Gesellschaft, Staat, Geschichte*, edited by F. Bülow (Leipzig, no date), p. 317: 'Die Richtung, die an der Abstraktion festhält, ist der *Liberalismus*, über den das Konkrete immer siegt, und gegen das er überall Bankrott macht.' The passage is not contained in the corresponding places of the *Vorlesungen über die Philosophie der Geschichte* in *Werke* (Berlin, 1837), vol 9 or in the *Jubiläumsausgabe* (Stuttgart, 1928), vol. 11, pp. 556-7.

CHAPTER TWO   COSMOS AND TAXIS

* Adam Smith, *The Theory of Moral Sentiments* (London, 1759), Part 6, ch. 2, penultimate paragraph. It deserves to be noted that this

passage contains some of the basic concepts and terms we shall have to use throughout this book: the conception of a spontaneous order of the *Great Society* as contrasted with a deliberate *arrangement* of the elements; the distinction between *coincidence* and *opposition* between the rules (*principles of motion*) inherent in the elements and those imposed upon them by legislation; and the interpretation of the social process as a *game* which will go on smoothly if the two kinds of rules are in concord but will produce *disorder* if they are in conflict.

1 See my essay on 'The theory of complex phenomena', in F. A. Hayek, *Studies in Philosophy, Politics and Economics* (London and Chicago, 1967, henceforth referred to as *S.P.P.E.*). It was in fact at first entirely the result of methodological considerations that led me to resume the use of the unpopular concept of 'order': see also F. A. Hayek, *The Counter-Revolution of Science* (Chicago, 1952), p. 39: 'If social phenomena showed no order except in so far as they were consciously designed, there would indeed be no room for a theoretical science of society and there would be, as is often maintained, only problems of psychology.' In recent discussion the term 'system' is often used in much the same sense in which I use here 'order', which still seems to me preferable.

2 It would seem that the currency of the concept of order in political theory goes back to St Augustine. See in particular his dialogue *Ordo* in J. P. Migne (ed) *Patrologiae cursus completus sec. lat.* 32/47 (Paris, 1861-2), and in a German version *Die Ordnung*, trans. C. J. Peel, fourth edition (Paderborn, 1966).

3 See L. S. Stebbing, *A Modern Introduction to Logic* (London, 1933), p. 228: 'When we know how a set of elements is ordered, we have a basis for inference.' See also Immanuel Kant, *Werke* (Akademie Ausgabe), *Nachlass*, vol 6, p. 669: 'Ordnung ist die Zusammenfügung nach Regeln.'

4 See E. E. Evans-Pritchard, *Social Anthropology* (London, 1951), p. 49; see also ibid., p. 19:

It is evident that there must be uniformities and regularities in social life, that society must have some sort of order, or its members could not live together. It is only because people know the kind of behaviour expected of them, and what kind of behaviour to expect from others, in the various situations of life, and coordinate their activities in submission to rules and under the guidance of values that each and all are able to go about their affairs. They can make predictions, anticipate events, and lead their lives in harmony with their fellows because every society has a form or pattern which allows us to speak of it as a system, or structure, within which, and in accordance with which, its members live their lives.

5 See L. S. Stebbing, op. cit., p. 229: 'Order is most *apparent* where man has been at work.'

6 See J. Ortega y Gasset, *Mirabeau o el politico* (1927), in *Obras Completas* (Madrid, 1947), vol. 3, p. 603: 'Orden no es una presión que desde fuera se ejerce sobra la sociedad, sin un equilibrio que se suscita en su interior.'

7 See H. von Foerster and G. W. Zopf, Jr (eds) *Principles of Self-Organization* (New York, 1962) and, on the anticipation of the main conceptions of cybernetics by Adam Smith, cf. G. Hardin, *Nature and Man's Fate* (New York, 1961), p. 54; and Dorothy Emmet, *Function, Purpose and Powers* (London, 1958), p. 90.

8 See H. Kuhn, 'Ordnung im Werden und Zerfall', in H. Kuhn and F. Wiedmann (eds), *Das Problem der Ordnung* (Sechster Deutscher Kongress für Philosophie, Munich, 1960, publ. Meisenheim am Glan, 1962), especially p. 17.

9 See Werner Jaeger, *Paideia: The Ideals of Greek Culture*, trans. G. Highet, vol. 1, second edition (New York, 1945), p. 110, about 'Anaximander of Miletus transferring the concept of *diké* from the social life of the city-state to the realm of nature. . . . This is the original of the philosophical idea of cosmos: for the word originally signified the *right order* in a state or in a community'; and ibid., p. 179: 'So the physicist's cosmos became by a curious retrogression in thought, the pattern of eunomia in human society.' See also the same author's 'Praise of law' in P. Sayre (ed), *Interpretations of Modern Legal Philosophies: Essays in Honor of Roscoe Pound* (New York, 1947), especially p. 358:

> A world thus 'justified' could be called rightly by another term taken over from the social order, a cosmos. That word occurs for the first time in the language of the Ionian philosophers; by taking this step and extending the rule of *diké* to reality as a whole they clearly revealed the nature of Greek legal thought and showed that it was based on the relationship of justice to being.

And ibid., p. 361: 'The law on which it [the *polis*] was founded was not a mere decree but the *nomos*, which originally meant the sum total of that which was respected by all living custom with regard to what is right and wrong'; and ibid., p. 365 on the fact that even during the period of the dissolution of the old Greek faith in law: 'the strict relationship of the *nomos* to the nature of the cosmos was not universally questioned.'

For Aristotle, who connects *nomos* with *taxis* rather than *kosmos* (see *Politics*, 1287a, 18, and especially 1326a, 30: *ho te gar nomos taxis tis esti*), it is characteristically inconceivable that the order resulting from the *nomos* should exceed what the orderer can survey, 'for who will command its over-swollen multitude in war? or who will serve as

its herald, unless he had the lungs of Stentor?' The creation of order
in such a multitude is for him a task only the gods can achieve. Elsewhere (*Ethics*, IX, x, §3) he even argues that a state, i.e. an ordered
society, of a hundred thousand people is impossible.

10 Adam Smith, *Wealth of Nations*, edited by E. Cannan, vol. 1, p. 421.

11 See G. Sartori, *Democratic Theory* (Detroit, 1962), p. 306:

> Western man for two and a half millennia has sought liberty in the
> law. . . . [Yet] the widespread scepticism about the value of the
> juridical protection of liberty is not unjustified. The reason for
> this is that our conception of law has changed; and that, as a
> consequence, law can no longer give us the protection that it
> did give us in the past.

12 See Philo of Alexandria, *Quod omnis probus liber sit*, 452, 45, Loeb
edition, vol. IX, p. 36: '*hosoi de meta nomou zosin, eleuteroi*'. On free-
dom in ancient Greece see in particular Max Pohlenz, *The Idea of
Freedom in Greek Life and Thought* (Dordrecht, 1962). On Cicero and
the Roman concept of liberty generally see U. von Lübtow, *Blüte und
Verfall der römischen Freiheit* (Berlin, 1953); Theo Mayer-Maly,
'Rechtsgeschichte der Freiheitsidee in Antike und Mittelalter',
Österreichische Zeitschrift für öffentliches Recht, N.F. VI, 1956; and
G. Crifo, 'Su alcuni aspetti della libertà in Roma', *Archivio Giuridico
'Filippo Serafini'*, sesta serie, xxiii, 1958.

13 See R. W. Southern, *The Making of the Middle Ages* (New Haven,
1953), p. 107 *et seq.*:

> The hatred of that which was governed, not by rule, but by will,
> went very deep in the Middle Ages. . . . The higher one rose
> towards liberty, the more the area of action was covered by law, the
> less it was subject by will. . . . Law was not the enemy of free-
> dom; on the contrary, the outline of liberty was traced by the
> bewildering variety of law which was slowly evolved during
> our period. . . . High and low alike sought liberty by insisting
> on enlarging the number of rules under which they lived. . . . It
> was only when the quality of freedom was articulated by being
> attached to the status of knight, burgess or baron that it could be
> observed, analysed and measured. . . . Liberty is a creation
> of law, and law is reason in action; it is reason which makes men,
> as we should say, ends in themselves. Tyranny, whether of
> King John or of the Devil, is a manifestation of the absence of law.

14 Most emphatically, perhaps, Adam Ferguson, *Principles of Moral and
Political Science* (Edinburgh, 1792), vol. 2, p. 258 *et seq.*:

> Liberty or freedom is not, as the origin of the name may seem to
> imply, an exemption from all restraint, but rather the most

effectual application of every just restraint to all the members of a free state, whether they be magistrates or subjects.

It is under just restraints only that every person is safe, and cannot be invaded, either in the freedom of his person, his property, or innocent action. . . . The establishment of a just and effectual government is of all circumstances in civil society the most essential to freedom: that everyone is justly said to be free in proportion as the government under which he resides is sufficiently powerful to protect him, at the same time that it is sufficiently restrained and limited to prevent the abuse of this power.

15 Daniel Webster is credited with the statement that 'Liberty is the creature of law, essentially different from the authorized licentiousness that trespasses on right'; and Charles Evans Hughes with that 'Liberty and Law are one and inseparable'. There are many similar statements by continental legal scholars of the last century, e.g. Charles Beudant, *Le Droit individuel et l'état* (Paris, 1891), p. 5: 'Le Droit, au sens le plus général du mot, est la science de la liberté'; and Karl Binding who argued somewhere that 'Das Recht ist eine Ordnung menschlicher Freiheit.'

16 See J. Bentham, 'Principles of the civil code', in *Theory of Legislation*, edited by C. K. Ogden (London, 1931), p. 98: 'Laws cannot be made except at the expense of liberty.' Also in *Deontology* (London and Edinburgh, 1834), vol. 2, p. 59:

There are few words which, with its derivations, have been more mischievous than this word liberty. When it means anything beyond mere caprice and dogmatism, it means good government; and if good government had had the good fortune to occupy the same place in the public mind which has been occupied by liberty, the crimes and follies which have disgraced and retarded the progress of political improvement would hardly have been committed. The usual definition of liberty—that it is the right to do everything that the law does not forbid—shows with what carelessness words are used in ordinary discourse or composition; for if the laws are bad, what becomes of liberty? and if the laws are good, where is its value? Good laws have a definite intelligible meaning; they pursue an evidently useful end by obviously appropriate means.

17 See for example, Jean Salvaire, *Autorité et liberté* (Montpellier, 1932), p. 65 *et seq.*, who argues that 'the complete realization of liberty is, in fact, nothing else but the complete abolition of law. . . . Law and liberty are mutually exclusive'.

18 Edmund Burke, 'Letter to W. Elliot' (1795), in *Works* (London, 1808), vol. 7, p. 366:

These analogies between bodies natural and politick, though they may sometimes illustrate arguments, furnish no arguments for themselves. They are but too often used under the colour of a specious philosophy, to find apologies for the despair of laziness and pusillanimity, and to excuse the want of all manly efforts, when the exigencies of our country call for them the more loudly.

19 For a characteristic use of the contrast between 'organism' and 'organization' see Adolf Wagner, *Grundlegung der politischen Ökonomie, I. Grundlagen der Volkswirtschaft* (Leipzig, 1876), § § 149 and 299.

20 See Immanuel Kant, *Kritik der Urteilskraft* (Berlin, 1790), Part 2, section 1, § 65n.: 'So hat man sich bei einer neuerlich unternommenen gänzlichen Umbildung eines grossen Volkes zu einem Staat des Wortes *Organisation* häufig für Einrichtung der Magistraturen usw. und selbst des ganzen Staatskörpers sehr schicklich bedient.'

21 See H. Balzac, *Autre étude de femme*, in *La Comédie Humaine*, Pleiade edition, vol. 3, p. 226: 'Organiser, par example, est un mot de l'Empire et qui contient Napoléon tout entier.'

22 See, for example, the journal edited by H. de Saint Simon and Auguste Comte called *Organisateur*, reprinted in *Oeuvres de Saint Simon et d'Enfantin* (Paris, 1865–78), vol. 20, especially p. 220, where the aim of the work is described as 'D'imprimer au XIX siècle le caractère organisateur'.

23 See in particular Louis Blanc, *Organisation du travail* (Paris, 1839), and H. Ahrens, *Rechtsphilosophie*, fourth edition (Vienna, 1852) on 'organization' as the magic word of the communists and socialists; see also Francis Lieber, 'Anglican and Gallican liberty' (1848), in *Miscellaneous Writings* (Philadelphia, 1881), vol 2, p. 385:

> The fact that Gallican liberty expects everything from *organization*, while Anglican liberty inclines to development, explains why we see in France so little improvement and expansion of institutions; but when improvements are attempted, a total abolition of the preceding state of things—a beginning *ab ovo*—a rediscussion of the first elementary principles.

24 See Ernest Renan, *L'Avenir de la Science* (1890), in *Oeuvres complètes* (Paris, 1949), vol. 3, p. 757: 'ORGANISER SCIENTIFIQUEMENT L'HUMAN-ITÉ, tel est donc le dernier mot de la science moderne, telle est son audacieuse mais légitime prétention.'

25 See *Shorter Oxford Dictionary*, s.v. 'organization', which shows, however, that the term was already used by John Locke.

26 Jean Labadie (ed), *L'Allemagne, a-t-elle le secret de l'organisation?* (Paris, 1916).

27 See Dwight Waldo, 'Organization theory: an elephantine problem', *Public Administration Review*, xxx, 1961, and reprinted in *General*

Systems, Yearbook of the Society for General System Research, VII 1962, the preceding volume of which contains a useful collection of, articles on the theory of organization.

CHAPTER THREE PRINCIPLES AND EXPEDIENCY

* The Constitution of the State of North Carolina. The idea is probably derived from David Humes's, *Essays*, in *Works* III, p. 482: 'A government, says Machiavelli, must often be brought back to its original principles.' An earlier version of this chapter appeared in *Towards Liberty, Essays in Honor of Ludwig von Mises* (Menlo Park, Calif., 1971), vol. 1.

1 See F. A. Hayek, *The Constitution of Liberty* (London and Chicago, 1960).

2 Adam Smith, *Wealth of Nations*, edited by E. Cannan (London, 1930), vol. 2, p. 184; see also John Locke, *Second Treatise on Government*, edited by P. Laslett (Cambridge, 1960), section 22: 'a liberty to follow my own will in all things, where the rules prescribe not.'

3 See A. V. Dicey, *Lectures on the Relation between Law and Public Opinion during the Nineteenth Century* (London, 1914), p. 257:

> The beneficial effect of State intervention, especially in the form of legislation, is direct, immediate, and so to speak visible, whilst its evil effects are gradual and indirect, and lie outside our sight. . . . Hence the majority of mankind must almost of necessity look with undue favour upon government intervention. This natural bias can be counteracted only by the existence, in a given society, . . . of a presumption or prejudice in favour of individual liberty, that is of *laissez-faire.*

Similarly, E. Küng, *Der Interventionismus* (Bern, 1941), p. 360: 'Die günstigen und gewollten Nachwirkungen der meisten wirtschafts-politischen Massnahmen treten kurz nach ihrer Inkraftsetzung auf, die manchmal schwerer wirkenden Fernwirkungen erst später.'

4 As has been preached with such far-reaching effect on the American intellectuals by John Dewey: see for example, his essay 'Force and coercion', *International Journal of Ethics*, xvi, 1916, especially p. 362. 'Whether the use of force is justified or not . . . is, in substance, a question of efficiency (including economy) of means in the accomplishment of ends.'

5 Benjamin Constant, 'De l'arbitraire', in *Oeuvres politiques*, edited by C. Louandre (Paris, 1874), pp. 71–2.

6 Frederic Bastiat, *Ce qu'on voit et ce qu'on ne voit pas en economie politique* (Paris, 1850), English translation in his *Selected Essays in Political Economy*, edited by G. B. de Huszar (Princeton, 1964), his last and most brilliant essay.

7 Carl Menger, *Problems of Economics and Sociology*, edited by L. Schneider (Urbana, Ill., 1963).

8 See W. Y. Elliott, *The Pragmatic Revolt in Politics* (New York, 1928).

9 On these lines particularly R. A. Dahl and Charles Lindblom, *Politics, Economics, and Welfare* (New York, 1953), pp. 3-18, e.g. p. 16: 'Techniques and not "isms" are the kernel of rational action in the Western world. Both socialism and capitalism are dead.' This is precisely the cause of our drift.

10 London and Chicago, 1944.

11 See Preface to W. S. Jevons, *The State in Relation to Labour* (London, 1882).

12 Herbert Spencer, *Justice: Being Part IV of the Principles of Ethics* (London, 1891), p. 44.

13 J. A. Schumpeter, *History of Economic Analysis* (New York, 1954), p. 394.

14 Adam Smith, *op. cit.* vol. 1, p. 435.

15 See for example, Max Weber, *On Law in Economy and Society*, edited by Max Rheinstein (Cambridge, Mass., 1954), p. 298.

16 See the essays on *Capitalism and the Historians*, by various authors, edited by the present writer (London and Chicago, 1953).

17 David Hume, *Essays*, in *Works* III, p. 125, and compare the passages by J. S. Mill and Lord Keynes quoted on p. 113 and in note 14 to ch. 6 of my book, *The Constitution of Liberty*, to which may now be added a similar statement by G. Mazzini which I have seen quoted without source: 'Ideas rule the world and its events. A revolution is the passage of an idea from theory to practice. Whatever men say, material interests never have caused, and never will cause a revolution.'

18 It was therefore also not, as J. A. Schumpeter kindly suggested in a review of *The Road to Serfdom* in *Journal of Political Economy*, xiv, 1946, 'politeness to a fault' but profound conviction about what are the decisive factors if that book 'hardly ever attributes to opponents anything beyond intellectual error'.

19 As one of Carl Schmitt's followers, George Dahm, reviewing Schmitt's *Drei Arten des rechtswissenschaftlichen Denkens* (Hamburg, 1934), in *Zeitschrift für die gesamte Staatswissenschaft*, xcv, 1935, p. 181, wrote, all Schmitt's works 'sind von Anfang an auf ein bestimmtes Ziel gerichtet gewesen: die Entlarvung und Zerstörung des liberalen Rechtsstaates und die Überwindung des Gesetzgebungsstaates'. The most appropriate comment on Schmitt came from Johannes Huizinga, *Homo Ludens* (1944), English translation (London, 1947), p. 209:

> I know of no sadder and deeper fall from human reason than Schmitt's barbarous and pathetic delusion about the friend-foe principle. His inhuman cerebrations do not even hold water as a piece of formal logic. For it is not war that is serious but peace.

. . . Only by transcending this pitiable friend-foe relationship will mankind enter into the dignity of man's estate. Schmitt's brand of 'seriousness' merely takes us back to the savage level.

20 See Carl Schmitt, op. cit., p. 11 *et seq.*

CHAPTER FOUR   THE CHANGING CONCEPT OF LAW

* Julius Paulus, Roman jurist of the third century A.D., in *Digests* 50.17.1: 'What is right is not derived from the rule but the rule arises from our knowledge of what is right.' See also the observation by the twelfth-century glossator Franciscus Accursius, gloss to *Digests*, I.1.1. pr. 9: 'est autem ius a iustitia, sicut a matre sua, ergo prius fuit iustitia quam ius.' On the whole complex of problems to be discussed in this chapter see Peter Stein, *Regulae Iuris* (Edinburgh, 1966), especially p. 20: 'in origin *lex* was declaratory of *ius*.'

1 Bernhard Rehfeld, *Die Wurzeln des Rechts* (Berlin, 1951), p. 67:

> Das Auftauchen des Phänomens der Gesetzgebung . . .
> bedeutet in der Menschheitsgeschichte die Erfindung der Kunst,
> Recht und Unrecht zu *machen*. Bis dahin hatte man geglaubt,
> Recht nicht setzen, sondern nur anwenden zu können als etwas,
> das seit jeher war. An dieser Vorstellung gemessen ist die
> Erfindung der Gesetzgebung vielleicht die folgenschwerste
> gewesen, die je gemacht wurde—folgenschwerer als die des
> Feuers oder des Schiesspulvers—denn am stärksten von allen
> hat sie das Schicksal des Menschen in seine Hand gelegt.

2 This illusion, characteristic of many thinkers of our time, was expressed by Lord Keynes in a letter to me on 28 June 1944, quoted in R. F. Harrod, *The Life of John Maynard Keynes* (London, 1951), p. 436, in which, commenting on my book *The Road to Serfdom*, he remarked that 'dangerous acts can be done safely in a community which thinks and feels rightly, which would be the way to hell if they were executed by those who think and feel wrongly'.

3 David Hume, *Treatise* II, p. 306:

> But, though it be possible for men to maintain a small unculti-
> vated society without government, it is impossible they should
> maintain a society of any kind without justice, and the observance
> of the three fundamental laws concerning the stability of
> possession, translation by consent, and the performance of promises.
> They are therefore antecedent to government.

See also Adam Ferguson, *Principles of Moral and Political Science* (Edinburgh, 1792), vol. 1, p. 262:

The first object of concert and convention, on the part of man, is not to give society existence, but to perfect the society in which he finds himself already by nature placed; not to establish subordination, but to correct the abuse of subordination already established: And that material, on which the political genius of men is to work, is not, as poets have figured, a scattered race, in a state of individuality to be collected together into troops, by the charms of music or the lessons of philosophy. But a material much nearer to the point to which the political act would carry it, a troop of men by mere instinct assembled together; placed in the subordinate relation of parent and child, of noble and plebeian, if not of rich and poor, or other adventitious, if not original distinction, which constitutes, in fact, a relation of power and dependence, by which a few are in condition to govern the many, and a part has an ascendance over the whole;

and Carl Menger, *Problems of Economics and Sociology* (Urbana, Ill., 1963), especially p. 227:

National law in its most original form is thus, to be sure, not the result of a contract or of reflection aiming at the assurance of common welfare. Nor is it, indeed, given with the nation, as the historical school asserts. Rather, it is older than the appearance of the latter. Indeed, it is one of the strongest ties by which the population of a territory becomes a nation and achieves state organization.

4 See Gilbert Ryle, 'Knowing how and knowing that', *Proceedings of the Aristotelian Society*, 1945–6, and *The Concept of Mind* (London, 1949), ch. 2; see also my essay 'Rules, perception and intelligibility', *Proceedings of the British Academy*, xlviii, 1962, reprinted in my *Studies in Philosophy, Politics and Economics* (London and Chicago, 1967) (*S.P.P.E.*).

5 See Sten Gagnèr, *Studien zur Ideengeschichte der Gesetzgebung* (Uppsala, 1960); Alan Gewirt, *Marsilius of Padua, Defender of Peace* (New York, 1951 and 1956); and T. F. T. Plucknett, *Statutes and their Interpretation in the First Half of the Fourteenth Century* (Cambridge, 1922).

6 See my essay on 'Notes on the evolution of rules of conduct', in *S.P.P.E.*

7 The best documented and most fully studied instance of the development of distinct 'cultural' traditions among separated groups of animals of the same species is that of the Japanese macaque monkeys which in comparatively recent times were split by the extension of human cultivation into distinct groups which appear in a short time to have acquired clearly distinguishable cultural traits. See also on this

J. E. Frisch, 'Research on primate behaviour in Japan', *American Anthropologist*, lxi, 1959; F. Imanishi, 'Social behavior in Japanese monkeys: "Macaca fuscata",' *Psychologia*, I. 1957; and S. Kawamura, 'The process of sub-cultural propagation among Japanese macaques,' in C. H. Southwick (ed), *Primate Social Behavior* (Princeton, 1963).

8 V. C. Wynne-Edwards, *Animal Dispersion in Relation to Social Behaviour* (Edinburgh, 1966), p. 456; see also ibid., p. 12:

> The substitution of a parcel of ground as the object of competition in place of the actual food it contains so that each individual or family unit has a separate holding of the resource to exploit, is the simplest and most direct kind of limiting convention it is possible to have. . . . Much space is devoted in later chapters to studying the almost endless variety of density limiting factors . . . The food territory just considered is concrete enough. . . . We shall find that abstract goals are especially characteristic of gregarious species.

And ibid., p. 190:

> 'There is little new in this situation so far as mankind is concerned, except in degree of complexity; all conventional behaviour is inherently social and moral in character; and so far from being an exclusively human attribute, we find that the primary code of conventions evolved to prevent population density from exceeding the optimum, stems not only from the lowest vertebrate classes, but appears well established among the invertebrate phyla as well.

9 David Lack, *The Life of the Robin*, revised edition (London, 1946), p. 35.

10 Apart from the well-known works of Konrad Z. Lorenz and N. Tinbergen see I. Eibl-Eibesfeldt, *Grundlagen der vergleichenden Verhaltensforschung—Ethologie* (Munich, 1967); and Robert Ardrey, *The Territorial Imperative* (New York, 1966).

11 See J. Rawls, 'Justice as fairness', *Philosophical Review*, lxvii, 195.

12 See for example, the description in Konrad Z. Lorenz, *King Solomon's Ring* (London and New York, 1952), p. 188, quoted later in this chapter.

13 See my essay on 'The primacy of the abstract', in A. Koestler and J. R. Smithies (eds) *Beyond Reductionism: New Perspectives in the Life Sciences* (London, 1969).

14 See the works of Noam Chomsky, especially *Current Issues in Linguistic Theory* (The Hague, 1966); and Kenneth L. Pike, *Language in Relation to a Unified Theory of the Structure of Human Behaviour* (The Hague, 1967).

15 See Michael Polanyi, *Personal Knowledge* (London and Chicago, 1958), especially chs. 5 and 6 on 'Skills' and 'Articulation' and my essay on 'Rules, perception and intelligibility' in *S.P.P.E.*

16 Perhaps it should be explicitly pointed out that the distinction between articulated and not-articulated rules is not the same as the more
familiar one between written and unwritten law—neither in the literal
sense of these terms nor in the sense in which statute law is sometimes
described as written law in contrast to the common law. Unwritten
law that is orally handed down may be fully articulated and often was.
Yet a system like that of the common law permits a taking into account of yet unarticulated rules which will often be stated in words for
the first time by a judge expressing what he rightly regards as existing
law.

17 Konrad Z. Lorenz, op. cit., p. 188.

18 See my lecture on *Die Irrtümer des Konstruktivismus und die Grundlagen legitimer Kritik gesellschaftlicher Gebilde* (Munich and Salzburg,
1970), pp. 24 *et seq.*

19 See S. N. Kramer, *History Begins at Sumer* (New York, 1952), p. 52.

20 This did not of course, prevent these men coming later to be regarded as the makers of that law because they had codified it. See
John Burnet, 'Law and nature in Greek ethics', *International Journal
of Ethics*, vii, 1897, p. 332:

> But a code of law framed by a known law-giver, a Zalenkos or a
> Charondas, a Lykurgus or a Solon, could not be accepted in this
> way as part of the everlasting order of things. It was clearly
> 'made', and, therefore, from the point of view of φυσις, artificial
> and arbitrary. It seemed as if it might just as well have been made
> otherwise or not at all. A generation which had seen laws in the
> making could hardly help asking whether all morality had not
> been 'made' in the same way.

21 A. H. M. Jones, *Athenian Democracy* (Oxford, 1957), p. 52.

22 See Lord Acton, *History of Freedom* (London, 1907), p. 12:

> On a memorable occasion the assembled Athenians declared it
> monstrous that they should be prevented from doing whatever
> they chose; no force that existed could restrain them, and they
> resolved that no duty should restrain them, and that they would
> be bound by no laws that were not of their own making. In this
> way the emancipated people of Athens became a tyrant.

23 Aristotle, *Politics*, IV, iv, 4, 1292a, Loeb edition, p. 305:

> And it would seem a reasonable criticism to say that such a
> democracy is not a constitution at all; for where the laws do not
> govern there is no constitution, as the law ought to govern all
> things while the magistrates control particulars, and we ought to
> judge this constitutional government; if then democracy really is
> one of the forms of constitution, it is manifest that an organization

of this kind, in which all things are administered by resolutions of the assembly, is not even a democracy in the proper sense, for it is impossible for a voted resolution to be a universal rule.

24 Max Kaser, *Römische Rechtsgeschichte* (Göttingen, 1950), p. 54.
25 Ibid. See also Max Rheinstein, 'Process and change in the cultural spectrum coincident with expansion: government and law', in C. H. Kraeling and R. M. Adams (eds), *City Invincible* (Chicago, 1960), p. 117:

> The notion that valid norms of conduct might be established by way of legislation was peculiar to later states of Greek and Roman history; in Western Europe it was dormant until the discovery of Roman law and the rise of absolute monarchy. The proposition that all law is the command of a sovereign is a postulate engendered by the democratic ideology of the French Revolution that all law had to emanate from the duly elected representatives of the people. It is not, however, a true description of reality, least of all in the countries of the Anglo-Saxon Common Law.

On Rome in particular see Theodor Mommsen, *Abriss des römischen Staatsrechts* (Leipzig, 1893), p. 319: 'Aber auch mit Hinzuziehung der Bürgerschaft hat der Magistrat der bestehenden Rechtsordnung gegenüber keineswegs freie Hand. Im Gegenteil gilt diese, als nicht durch die Comitien geschaffen, auch nicht als von ihrem Belieben abhängig, vielmehr als ewig und unveränderlich.'
26 Peter Stein, op. cit., p. 20: 'The Romans did not resort readily to legislation in matters of private law.'
27 See W. W. Buckland and A. D. McNair, *Roman Law and Common Law* (Cambridge, 1936).
28 In addition to the authors quoted in F. A. Hayek, *The Constitution of Liberty*, (London and Chicago, 1960), p. 163 and notes 5 and 6, see R. Sohm, *Fränkische Reichs- und Gerichtsverfassung* (Weimar, 1871), p. 102: 'Das Volksrecht ist *das* Recht des deutschen Rechts. Das Volksrecht ist das Stammesgewohnheitsrecht. Die gesetzgebende Gewalt ist in der Staatsgewalt nicht enthalten. Die capitula sind nicht Rechtsnormen, sondern Norm für die Ausübung der königlichen Gewalt'; J. E. A. Jolliffe, *The Constitutional History of Medieval England from the English Settlement to 1485*, second edition (London, 1947), p. 334:

> Until well into the thirteenth century the primitive conception of a society living within the frame of an inherited law had deprived the king of the quality of law-maker and restricted the *commune consilium* to recognition of custom, and participation in adjustments of right and procedure by way of assize. Vital changes

were, no doubt, made, but they were made in such a way as to obscure their real nature as legislative change.

A footnote to this passage points out that Bracton regarded as permissible only *legem in melius convertire* but not *legem mutare*. A similar conclusion may be found in F. Fichtenau, *Arenga, Spätantike und Mittelalter im Spiegel von Urkundenformeln* (Graz and Cologne, 1957), p. 178: 'Früher war dem Herrscher allein das leges custodire aufgegeben gewesen. Recht und Gesetz standen ja über ihm und das Neue musste stets im Alten seine Begründung finden.'

29 Fritz Kern, *Kingship and Law in the Middle Ages*, trans. S. B. Chrimes (London, 1939), p. 151; G. Barraclough, *Law Quarterly Review*, lvi, 1940, p. 76, describes this work as 'two remarkable essays whose conclusions, though they may be modified or limited, will assuredly never be challenged.'

30 See in particular Sten Gagnèr, op. cit.

31 I believe this passage, for which I have lost the reference, is by F. W. Maitland. See also A. V. Dicey, *Law of the Constitution*, ninth edition (London, 1939), p. 370:

> A lawyer, who regards the matter from an exclusively legal point of view, is tempted to assert that the real subject in dispute between statesmen such as Bacon and Wentworth on the one hand, and Coke or Eliot on the other, was whether a strong administration of the Continental type should, or should not, be permanently established in England.

32 See W. S. Holdsworth, *A History of English Law*, vol. 5 (London, 1924), p. 439:

> It was in Coke's writings that this [conception of the supremacy of the common law] and other mediaeval conceptions were given their modern form; and therefore it is largely owing to the influence of his writings that these mediaeval conceptions have become part of our modern law. If their influence upon some parts of our modern law has not been wholly satisfactory, let us remember that they saved Englishmen from a criminal procedure allowed to use torture, and that they preserve for England and the world the constitutional doctrine of the rule of law.

33 Quoted by W. S. Holdsworth, *Some Lessons from Legal History* (London, 1928), p. 18.

34 See David Hume, *Essays* (London, 1875), vol. 2, p. 274:

> All the laws of nature, which regulate property, as well as civil laws, are general, and regard only some essential circumstances of the case, without taking into consideration the characters,

situations, and connexions of the persons concerned, or any particular consequences which may result from the determination of these laws, in any particular case which offers. They deprive, without scruple, a beneficent man of all his possessions, if acquired by mistake, without a good title; in order to bestow them on a selfish miser who has already heaped up immense stores of superfluous riches. Public utility requires that property should be regulated by general inflexible rules; and though such rules are adopted as best serve the same end of public utility, it is impossible for them to prevent all particular hardships, or make beneficial consequences result from every individual case. It is sufficient if the whole plan or scheme be necessary to the support of civil society, and if the balance of good, in the main, do thereby preponderate much above that of evil.

35 The case for relying even in modern times for the development of law on the gradual process of judicial precedent and scholarly interpretation has been persuasively argued by the late Bruno Leoni, *Liberty and the Law* (Princeton, 1961). But although his argument is an effective antidote to the prevailing orthodoxy which believes that only legislation can or ought to alter the law, it has not convinced me that we can dispense with legislation even in the field of private law with which he is chiefly concerned.

36 See W. S. Jevons, *The State in Relation to Labour* (London, 1882), p. 33: 'The great lesson we learn [from 650 years of legislation of English Parliaments] is that legislation with regard to labour has almost always been class-legislation. It is the effort of some dominant body to keep down a lower class, which had begun to show inconvenient aspirations.'

37 H. Kelsen, *What is Justice?* (Berkeley, Calif., 1957), p. 21.

38 F. W. Maitland, *Constitutional History of England* (Cambridge, 1908), p. 382.

39 See David Hume, op. cit., vol. 1., p. 125: 'Though men be much governed by interest, yet even interest itself, and all human affairs, are entirely governed by opinion.'

CHAPTER FIVE   NOMOS: THE LAW OF LIBERTY

* Strabo, *Geography*, 10,4,16, in the Loeb edition by H. L. Jones vol. 5, p. 145. While Strabo lived at the beginning of our era, Ephorus of Kyme whom he quotes and of whose works only fragments are preserved lived from about 400–330 B.C.

1 See for example, the statement by the grammarian Servius of the fourth century A.D. (quoted by P. Stein, *Regulae Iuris*, (Edinburgh, 1966), p. 109): 'ius generale est, sed lex est species, ius ad non scrip-

tum pertinet, leges ad ius scriptum.' It has been suggested with some justification (by Alvaro d'Ors, *De la Guerra, de la Paz* (Madrid, 1954), p. 160, quoted by Carl Schmitt. *Verfassungsrechtliche Aufsätze* (Berlin, 1958), p. 427), that it was a major misfortune that Cicero translated the Greek term *nomos* with *lex* instead of with *ius*. For Cicero's use of the term *lex* see in particular *De legibus*, II, v–vi, Loeb edition by C. W. Keyes (London, 1929), pp. 384-6: 'Est lex iustorum iniustorumque distinctio . . . nec vero iam aliam esse ullam legem puto non modo habendam, sed ne appellandum quidem.'

2 See the often quoted statement by H. Triepel in *Festgabe der Berliner juristischen Fakultät für W. Kahl* (Tübingen, 1923), p. 93: 'Heilig ist nicht das Gesetz, heilig ist nur das Recht, und das Recht steht über dem Gesetz.'

3 See the passages from David Hume, Adam Ferguson and Carl Menger quoted in chapter 4, note 3, of this book.

4 See H. L. A. Hart, *The Concept of Law* (Oxford, 1961).

5 See James Coolidge Carter, *Law, Its Origin, Growth and Function* (New York and London, 1907), p. 59: 'All complaints by one man against another, whether of a civil or criminal nature, arose from the fact that something had been done *contrary to the complainant's expectations of what should have been done.*' See also ibid., p. 331:

> The great general rule governing human action at the beginning, namely that it must conform to fair expectations, is still the scientific rule. All the forms of conduct complying with this rule are consistent with each other and become the recognized customs. All those inconsistent with it are stigmatized as bad practices. The body of custom therefore tends to become a harmonious system.

On this important work which is not as well known as it deserves see M. J. Gronson, 'The juridical evolutionism of James Coolidge Carter', *University of Toronto Law Journal*, 1953.

6 Roscoe Pound, *Jurisprudence*, vol. 1 (New York, 1959), p. 371.

7 As we frequently have to speak of 'a group prevailing over others' it should perhaps be stressed that this does not necessarily mean victory in a clash of forces, or even that the members of such a group will displace the individual members of other groups. It is much more likely that the success of a group will attract members of others which thus become incorporated in the first. Sometimes the successful group will become an aristocracy within a given society and as a result the rest will model their conduct after that of the former. But in all these instances the members of the more successful group will often not know to which peculiarity they owe their success, nor cultivate that trait because they know what depends on it.

8 Many of the earlier theorists of natural law had come close to an

insight into this relation between the rules of law and the order of actions which it serves. See Roscoe Pound, *Interpretations of Legal History* (New York, 1923), p. 5:

> In fact jurist or text-writer or judge or legislator, working under the theory of natural law, measured all situations and sought to solve all difficulties by referring them to an idealized picture of the social order of the time and place and a conception of the aims of law in terms of that order. . . . Accordingly the ideal of the social order was taken to be the ultimate reality of which legal institutions and rules and doctrines were but reflections or declarations.

The medieval conception of a social order was, however, still largely one of the particular status of the different individuals or classes and only some of the late Spanish schoolmen approached the conception of an abstract order based on a uniform law for all.

9 For the use of this term by the late Spanish schoolmen see C. von Kaltenborn, *Die Vorläufer des Hugo Grotius* (Leipzig, 1848), p. 146. The conception of justice being confined to action towards others however, goes back at least to Aristotle, *Nicomachean Ethics*, V, i, 15–20, Loeb edition, pp. 256–9.

10 This is a legitimate objection to the manner in which I have treated the subject in *The Constitution of Liberty* (London and Chicago, 1960) and I hope that the present statement will satisfy the critics who have pointed out this defect, such as Lord Robbins (*Economica*, February, 1961), J. C. Rees (*Philosophy*, 38, 1963) and R. Hamowy (*The New Individualist Review*, 1 (1), 1961).

11 This is, of course, implied in Immanuel Kant's (and Herbert Spencer's) formula about the 'equal liberty of others' being the only legitimate ground for a restriction of liberty by law. On the whole subject see John Rawls, *A Theory of Justice* (Oxford, 1972).

12 See P. A. Freund, 'Social justice and the law', in R. B. Brandt (ed), *Social Justice* (New York, 1962), p. 96: 'Reasonable expectations are more generally the ground rather than the product of law'.

13 Heinrich Dernburg, *Pandekten*, second edition (Berlin, 1888), p. 85: 'Die Lebensverhältnisse tragen, wenn auch mehr oder weniger entwickelt, ihr Mass und ihre Ordnung in sich. Diese den *Dingen innewohnende Ordnung* nennt man Natur der Sache. Auf sie muss der denkende Jurist zurückgehen, wo es an einer positiven Norm fehlt oder wenn dieselbe unvollständig oder unklar ist.'

14 See O. W. Holmes, Jr, *The Common Law* (New York, 1963), p. 7:

> The life of law has not been logic, it has been experience. The felt necessities of the time, the prevalent moral and political theories, institutions of public policy, avowed or unconscious, even the

prejudices which judges share with their fellow-men, have a good deal more to do than syllogisms in determining the rules by which men should be governed. The law embodies the story of a nation's development through many centuries, and it cannot be dealt with as if it contained only the axioms and corollaries of a book of mathematics.

See also Roscoe Pound, *Law and Morals* (Chapel Hill, N.C., 1926), p. 97: 'The problem of law is to keep conscious free-willing beings from interference with each other. It is so to order them that each shall exercise his freedom in a way consistent with the freedom of all others, since all others are to be regarded equally as ends in themselves.'

15 Paul Van der Eycken, *Méthode positive de l'interprétation juridique* (Brussels and Paris, 1907), p. 401:

> On regardait précédemment le droit comme le produit de la volonté consciente du législateur. Aujourd'hui on voit en lui une force naturelle. Mais si l'on peut attribuer au droit l'épithète de naturel, c'est, nous l'avons dit, dans un sens bien différent de celui qu'avait autrefois l'expression de 'droit naturel'. Elle signifiait alors que la nature avait imprimé en nous, comme un élément même de la raison, certains principes dont la foule des articles des codes n'étaient que les applications. La même expression doit signifier actuellement que le droit résulte des relations de fait entre les choses. Comme ces relations elles-mêmes, le droit naturel est en travail perpetuel. . . . Le législateur n'a de ce droit qu'une conscience fragmentaire; il la traduit par les prescriptions qu'il édicte. Lorsqu'il s'agira de fixer le sens de celle-ci, où faudra-t-il le chercher? Manifestement à leur source: c'est-à-dire dans les exigences de la vie sociale. La probabilité la plus forte de découvrir le sens de la loi se trouve là. De même lorsqu'il s'agira de combler les lacunes de la loi, ce n'est pas aux déductions logiques, c'est aux nécessités qu'on demandera la solution.

16 C. Perelman and L. Olbrechts-Tyteca, *La Nouvelle Rhétorique— traité de l'argumentation* (Paris, 1958), vol. 1, pp. 264–70, especially §46: *Contradiction et Incompatibilité* and §47: *Procédés permettant d'éviter un incompatibilité*, of which only a few significant passages can be quoted here. p. 263:

> L'incompatibilité dépend soit de la nature des choses, soit d'une décision humaine.' (p. 264.) 'Des incompatibilités peuvent résulter de l'application à des situations determinés de plusieurs règles morales ou juridiques, de textes legaux ou sacrés. Alors que la contradiction entre deux propositions suppose un formalisme où du moins une systeme des notions univoques, l'incompatibilité est toujours

rclativc à dcs circonstances contingentes, que celles-ci soient constituées par des lois naturelles, des événements particuliers où des décisions humaines.

Similarly see also Charles P. Curtis, 'A better theory of legal interpretation', *Vanderbilt Law Review*, iii, 1949, p. 423: 'The most important criterion is simply consistency with all the rest of the law. This contract or that will is a very small part of our total law, just as truly as this or that statute is a larger piece; and, though Justice has larger aims, the virtue on which the Law stakes its hopes is consistency.'

17 See Jürgen von Kempski, 'Bemerkungen zum Begriff der Gerechtigkeit', *Studium Generale*, xii, 1959, and reprinted in the same author's *Recht und Politik* (Stuttgart, 1965), p. 51: 'Wir wollen davon sprechen, dass den Privatrechtsordnungen ein Verträglichkeitsprinzip für Handlungen zu Grunde liegt'; and the same author's *Grundlagen zu einer Strukturtheorie des Rechts*, in *Abhandlungen der Geistes—und Sozialwissenschaftlichen Klasse der Akademie der Wissenschaften und Literatur in Mainz*, 1961, No. 2, p. 90: 'Wir fragen, welchen strukturellen Erfordernissen Handlungen entsprechen müssen, wenn sie miteinander verträglich sein sollen; mit andern Worten, wir betrachten eine Welt, in der die Handelnden nicht miteinander kollidieren.'

18 Robert Frost in the poem 'Mending wall'.

19 John Milton, *The Tenure of Kings and Magistrates*, in *Works*, edited by R. Fletcher (London, 1838), p. 27: 'The power which is at the root of all liberty to dispose and economise in the land which God has given them, as masters of family in their own inheritance.'

20 Thomas Hobbes, *The Leviathan* (London, 1651), p. 91.

21 Montesquieu, *The Spirit of the Laws*, XVI, chapter 15.

22 J. Bentham, *The Theory of Legislation*, edited by C. K. Ogden (London, 1931), p. 113: 'Property and law are born together and must die together.'

23 Sir Henry Maine, *Village Communities* (London, 1880), p. 230: 'Nobody is at liberty to attack several property and to say at the same time that he values civilization. The history of the two cannot be disentangled.'

24 Lord Acton, *The History of Freedom* (London, 1907), p. 297: 'A people averse to the institution of private property is without the first elements of freedom.'

25 See A. I. Hallowell, 'Nature and function of property as a social institution', *Journal of Legal and Political Sociology*, i, 1943, p. 134:

> From the standpoint of our contention that property rights of some kind are in fact not only universal but that they are a basic factor in the structuralization of the role of individuals in relation to basic economic processes, it is significant that eighteenth-century thinkers sensed the fundamental importance of

property rights, even though their reasoning was on different lines from ours.

See also H. I. Hogbin, *Law and Order in Polynesia* (London, 1934), p. 77 *et seq.* and the introduction to this work by B. Malinowski, p. xli as well as the latter's *Freedom and Civilization* (London, 1944), pp. 132–3.

26 See in particular Immanuel Kant, *Metaphysik der Sitten*, in *Werke* (Akademie Ausgabe) vol. 6, pp. 382 and 396; and Mary J. Gregor, *Laws of Freedom* (Oxford, 1963).

27 David Hume, *Enquiry Concerning the Principles of Morals*, in *Essays* (London, 1875), vol. 2, p. 273.

28 Roscoe Pound, 'The theory of judicial decision', *Harvard Law Review*, ix, 1936, p. 52.

29 The most influential statement of this view is probably that by C. Beccaria, *On Crimes and Punishment* (1764), trans H. Paolucci (New York, 1963), p. 15: 'A judge is required to complete a perfect syllogism in which the major premise must be the general law, the minor the action that does or does not conform to the law; and the conclusion the acquittal or punishment.'

30 See Sir Alfred Denning, *Freedom under the Law* (London, 1949).

CHAPTER SIX THESIS: THE LAW OF LEGISLATION

* Paul A. Freund, 'Social justice and the law', in R. Brandt (ed), *Social Justice* (Englewood Cliffs, N.J., 1962), p. 94, and in the author's collection of essays *On Law and Justice* (Cambridge, Mass., 1968), p. 83. Compare with this J. W. Hurst, *Law and Social Process in U.S. History* (Ann Arbor, Mich., 1960), p. 5: 'Despite much contrary rhetoric our main operating philosophy has always been to use law to allocate resources positively to affect conditions of life where we saw something useful to be accomplished by doing so. . . . Law has meant organization for making and implementing choices among scarce resources of human satisfaction.'

On the Greek term *thesis* used in the title of this chapter (which corresponds to the German term *Satzung*) see John Burnet, 'Law and nature in Greek Ethics', *International Journal of Ethics*, vii, 1897, p. 332, where he shows that in contrast to *nomos*, which originally meant 'use', *thesis* 'may mean either the giving of law or the adoption of laws so given, and it thus contains the germ not only of the theory of the original legislator, but also that known as the Social Contract.'

1 See the famous statement by Edward Coke in 'Dr. Bonham's case', 8 Rep. 118a (1610): 'And it appears in our books, that in many cases, the Common Law will controul Acts of Parliament, and sometimes adjudge them to be utterly void: for when an Act of Parliament is

against common right and reason, or repugnant, or impossible to be performed, the Common Law will controul it, and adjudge such Act to be void.' For discussion of the significance of this case see C. H. McIlwain, *The High Court of Parliament* (New Haven, 1910); T. F. T. Plucknett, 'Bonham's case and judicial review', *Harvard Law Review*, xl, 1926-7; and S. E. Thorne, 'Bonham's case', *Law Quarterly Review*, liv, 1938. Even as late as 1766 William Pitt could still argue in the House of Commons (*Parliamentary History of England* (London, 1813), vol. 6, col. 195) that 'There are many things a parliament cannot do. It cannot make itself executive, nor dispose of offices which belong to the crown. It cannot take any man's property, even that of the meanest cottager, as in the case of enclosures, without his being heard.'

2 See J. C. Carter, *Law, Its Origin, Growth, and Function* (New York and London, 1907), p. 115: 'At the first appearance of legislation its province and the province of Public Law were nearly coterminous. The province of Private Law is scarcely touched.'

3 See Courtenay Ilbert, *Legislative Methods and Forms* (Oxford, 1901), p. 208: 'The English Legislature was originally constituted, not for legislative, but for financial purposes. Its primary function was, not to make laws, but to grant supplies.'

4 See J. C. Gray, *Nature and Sources of Law*, second edition (New York, 1921), p. 161: 'A statute is a general rule. A resolution by the legislature that a town shall pay one hundred dollars to Timothy Coggan is not a statute.'

5 Courtenay Ilbert, op. cit., p. 213.

6 See J. C. Carter, op. cit., p. 116:

> We find in the numerous volumes of statute books vast masses of matter which, though in the form of laws, are not laws in the proper sense. These consist in the making of provisions for the maintenance of public works of the State, for the building of asylums, hospitals, school-houses, and a great variety of similar matters. This is but the record of the actions of the State in relation to the *business* in which it is engaged. The State is a great public corporation which conducts a vast mass of business, and the written provisions for this, though in the form of laws, are not essentially different from the minutes or ordinary corporate bodies recording their actions . . . it is substantially true that the whole vast body of legislation is confined to Public Law and that its operation on Private Law is remote and indirect and aimed only to make the unwritten law of custom more easily and certainly enforced.

See also Walter Bagehot, *The English Constitution* (1967), World's Classics edition (Oxford, 1928), p. 10: 'The legislature chosen, in name, to make laws, in fact finds its principal business in making and keeping an executive'; and ibid., p. 119:

> An immense mass, indeed, of the legislation is not, in the proper language of jurisprudence, legislation at all. A law is a general command applicable to many cases. The 'special acts' which crowd the statute book and weary parliamentary committees are applicable to one case only. They do not lay down rules according to which railways shall be made, but enact that such and such a railway shall be made from this place to that place, and they have no bearing on any other transaction.

7 Courtenay Ilbert, op. cit., p. 6. See also ibid., p. 209 *et seq.*:

> When the authors of books on jurisprudence write about law, when professional lawyers talk about law, the kind of law about which they are mainly thinking is that which is found in Justinian's *Institutes*, or in the Napoleonic Codes, or in the New Civil Code of the German Empire, that is to say, the legal rules which relate to contracts and torts, to property, to family relations and inheritance, or else to law of crimes as is to be found in a Penal Code. They would also include the law of procedure, or 'adjective' law, to use a Benthamic term, in accordance with which substantive rules of law are administered by the courts. These branches of law make up what may perhaps be called 'lawyers' law.

8 See M. J. C. Vile, *Constitutionalism and the Separation of Powers* (Oxford, 1967); and W. B. Gwyn, *The Meaning of the Separation of Powers, Tulane Studies in Political Science*, IX (New Orleans, 1965). Gwyn shows that the idea of the separation of powers was inspired by three altogether different considerations which he labels the rule of law, and the accountability and the efficiency arguments. The rule of law argument would require that the legislature could pass only rules of just conduct equally binding on all private persons and on government. The accountability argument aims at making the small number of men who necessarily in fact conduct government responsible to the representative assembly, while the efficiency argument requires the delegation of the power of action to government because an assembly cannot efficiently conduct operations. It is obvious that on the second and on the third ground the assembly would be concerned also with government, but only in a supervisory or controlling capacity.

9 M. J. C. Vile, op. cit., p. 44.

10 *The First Agreement of the People of 28 October 1647*, in S. R. Gardiner, *History of the Great Civil War*, new edition (London, 1898), vol 3, p. 392.

11 [Marchamont Needham?], *A True Case of the Common Wealth* (London, 1654) quoted by M. J. C. Vile, op. cit., p. 10, where the book is

described as an 'official defence' of the *Instrument of Government of 1653*.

12 M. J. C. Vile, op. cit., p. 63: 'The power of legislation is itself limited to the exercise of its own proper functioning. John Locke's view was that the legislative authority is *to act in a particular way* . . . those who wield this authority should make *only* general rules. They are to govern by promulgated established Laws, not to be varied in particular cases.' See also ibid., pp. 214 and 217.

13 J. Bentham, *Constitutional Code*, in *Works*, IX, p. 119:

> Why render the legislation omnicompetent? . . . Because it will better enable it to give effects to the will of the supreme constitutive, and advancement to the interest and security of the members of the state. . . . Because the practice upon which it puts an exclusion is, in a constitution such as the present, pregnant with evil in all imaginable shapes. Any limitation is in contradiction to the general happiness principle.

14 On the role of James Mill in this connection see M. J. C. Vile, op. cit., p. 217.

15 Robert A. Palmer, *The Age of Democratic Revolution*, vol 1, (Princeton, 1959).

16 The statement is quoted by J. Seeley, *Introduction to Political Science* (London, 1896), p. 216, but I have not been able to trace it in Napoleon's published correspondence.

17 G. W. F. Hegel, *Philosophie der Weltgeschichte* (quoted from the extracts in *Gesellschaft, Staat, Geschichte*, edited by F. Bülow, (Leipzig, 1931), p. 321):

> Die erste Verfassung in Frankreich enthielt die absoluten Rechtsprinzipien in sich. Sie war die Konstituierung des Königtums; an der Spitze des Staates sollte der Monarch stehen, dem mit seinen Ministern die Ausübung zustehen sollte; der gesetzgebende Körper hingegen sollte die Gesetze machen. Aber diese Verfassung war sogleich ein innerer Widerspruch; denn die ganze Macht der Administration war in die gesetzgebende Gewalt verlegt: das Budget, Krieg und Frieden, die Aushebung der bewaffneten Macht kam der gesetzgebenden Körperschaft zu. Das Budget aber ist seinem Begriffe nach kein Gesetz, denn es wiederholt sich alle Jahre, und die Gewalt, die es zu machen hat, ist Regierungsgewalt. . . . Die Regierung wurde also in die Kammern verlegt wie in England in das Parlament.

18 W. Hasbach, *Die moderne Demokratie* (Jena, 1912), pp. 17 and 167.

19 See J. C. Carter, op. cit., p. 234: 'Legislative commands thus made, requiring special things to be done, are part of the machinery of government, but a part very different from that relating to the rules

which govern ordinary conduct of men in relation to each other. It is properly described as *public law*, by way of distinction from private law.' See also J. Walter Jones, *Historical Introduction to the Theory of Law* (Oxford, 1956), p. 146:

> There is e.g., the view that the essence of the State is the possession of supreme force. Public law, owing to its connection with the State, appears so strongly marked by the characteristic of force that the feature of order or regularity, which is so pronounced in the rules with which the lawyer is for the most part concerned, seems altogether overshadowed. In the result, the difference between public and private law becomes one of kind rather than of degree—a difference between force and rule. Public law ceases to be law at all, or at least to be law in the same sense as private law.
>
> At the opposite pole are found those lawyers who are primarily occupied with an independent science of public law. They have to recognize that it is too late in the day to deny that the rules grouped together as private law are entitled to the name of law, but far from regarding the association of the rules, forming the public law, with force, as a proof of their inferiority in comparison with private law, they see in it rather the mark of an inherent superiority. . . . The distinction therefore becomes one between relations of subordination and of co-ordination.

The clearest distinction between constitutional law as consisting of rules of organization and private law as of rules of conduct has been drawn by W. Burkhardt, *Einführung in die Rechtswissenschaft*, second edition (Zürich, 1948), especially p. 137:

> Der *erste* [der doppelten Gegensätze auf die die Gegenüberstellung von öffentlichen und privaten Recht zielt] beruht auf einer grundlegenden Verschiedenheit der Rechtsnormen: die *materiellen oder Verhaltensnormen* schreiben den Rechtsgenossen vor, was sie tun oder lassen sollen: die *formellen oder organisatorischen Normen* bestimmen, wie, d.h. durch wen und in welchem Verfahren, diese Regeln des Verhaltens gesetzt, angewendet und (zwangsweise) durchgesetzt werden. Die ersten kann man Verhaltensnormen, die zweiten Verfahrensnormen oder (i.w.S.) Verfassungsnormen nennen. Man nennt die ersten auch materielle, die zweiten formelle Normen. . . . Die ersten geben den Inhalt des Rechts, das rechtlich geforderte Verhalten, die zweiten entscheiden über seine Gültigkeit.

Burkhardt's distinction appears to have been accepted chiefly by other Swiss lawyers; see in particular Hans Nawiaski, *Allgemeine Rechtslehre als System der rechtlichen Grundbegriffe* (Zürich, 1948),

p. 265, and C. Du Pasquier, *Introduction à la théorie générale et la philosophie du droit*, third edition (Neuchatel, 1948), p. 49.

See, however, H. L. A. Hart, *The Concept of Law* (Oxford, 1961), p. 78:

> Under rules of one type, which may well be considered the basic or primary type, human beings are required to do or abstain from certain actions, whether they wish or not. Rules of the other type are in a sense parasitic or secondary on the first; for they provide that human beings may by doing or saying certain things introduce new rules of the primary type, extinguish or modify old ones, or in various ways determine their incidence or control their operations.

See also Lon L. Fuller, *The Morality of Law* (New Haven, 1964), p. 63: 'Today there is a strong tendency to identify law, not with rules of conduct but with a hierarchy of power or command'; and ibid. p. 169, where he speaks of 'a confusion between law in the usual sense of rule of conduct directed toward the citizen, and government action generally'.

20 Ulpian, *Digests*. I,1,1,2, defines private law as *ius quod ad singulorum utilitatem spectat* and public law as *ius quod ad statum rei Romanae spectat*.

21 See Ernest Barker, *Principles of Social and Political Theory* (Oxford, 1951), p. 9: 'Some of it is primary or constitutional and some secondary or ordinary law.'

22 See J. E. M. Portalis, *Discours préliminaire du premier projet de code civil* (1801) in *Conference du Code Civil* (Paris, 1805), vol. 1, p. xiv: 'L'experience prouve que les hommes changent plus facilement le domination que de lois,'; See also H. Huber, *Recht, Staat und Gesellschaft* (Bern, 1954), p. 5: 'Staatsrecht vergeht, Privatrecht besteht.' Unfortunately, however, as Alexis de Tocqueville pointed out long ago, it is also true that constitutions pass, but administrative law persists.

23 H. L. A. Hart, op. cit.

24 Characteristic and most influential in the German literature in this respect is the criticism by A. Haenel, *Studien zum deutschen Staatsrecht, II. Das Gesetz im formellen und materiellen Sinn* (Leipzig, 1888), pp. 225–6, of E. Seligmann's definition of a *Rechtssatz* in *Der Begriff des Gesetzes im materiellen und formellen Sinn* (Berlin, 1886), p. 63, as a rule that 'abstrakt ist und eine nicht vorauszusehende Anzahl von Fällen ordnet', on the ground that this would exclude the fundamental rules of constitutional law. Indeed, it does, and the fathers of the American Constitution would probably have been horrified if it had been suggested that their handiwork was intended to be superior to the rules of just conduct as embodied in the common law.

25 See in particular Johannes Heckel, 'Einrichtung und rechtliche Be-deutung des Reichshaushaltgesetzes', *Handbuch des deutschen Staats-rechtes* (Tübingen, 1932), vol. 2, p. 390.
26 A. V. Dicey, *Lectures on the Relation between Law and Public Opinion in England during the Nineteenth Century* (London, 1903).
27 Rudolf Gneist, *Das englische Verwaltungsrecht der Gegenwart* (Berlin, 1883).
28 See in particular Walter Lippmann, *An Inquiry into the Principles of a Good Society* (Boston, 1937).
29 See E. Freund, *Administrative Powers over Persons and Property* (Chicago, 1928), p. 98.
30 Carl Schmitt, 'Legalität und Legitimität' (1932), reprinted in *Verfassungsrechtliche Aufsätze* (Berlin, 1958), p. 16.
31 Hans J. Morgenthau, *The Purpose of American Politics* (New York, 1960), p. 281: 'In our age, aside from still being the umpire, the state has also become the most powerful player, who, in order to make sure of the outcome, rewrites the rules of the game as he goes along.'
32 See Paul Vinogradoff, *Custom and Right* (Oslo, 1925), p. 10:

> The Trade Disputes Act of 1906 conferred on the unions an immunity from prosecution on the ground of tortious acts of their agents; this immunity stands in flagrant disagreement with the law of agency and the law as to companies represented by their officers in accordance with the Statutory Orders of 1883. The reason for this discordant state of the law is to be found in the resolve of legislation to secure for the unions a favourable position in their struggle with the employers.

> See also the comments by A. V. Dicey, J. A. Schumpeter and Lord MacDermott quoted in F. A. Hayek, *The Constitution of Liberty* (London and Chicago, 1960), p. 504, note 3.

33 *Home Building and Loan Ass. v. Blaisdell*, 290 U.S. 398, 434, 444, 1934, according to which the state has 'authority to safeguard the vital interests of its people' and for this purpose to prevent 'the perversion of the [contract] clause through its use as an instrument to throttle the capacity of the States to protect their fundamental interests'.
34 Gustav Radbruch, 'Vom individualistischen Recht zum sozialen Recht' (1930), reprinted in *Der Mensch im Recht* (Göttingen, 1957), p. 40:

> Für eine individualistische Rechtsordnung ist das öffentliche Recht, ist der Staat nur der schmale schützende Rahmen, der sich um das Privatrecht und das Privateigentum dreht, für eine soziale Rechtsordnung ist umgekehrt das Privatrecht nur ein vorläufig ausgesparter und sich immer verkleinernder Spielraum

für die Privatinitiative innerhalb des all umfassenden öffentlichen Rechts.

35 Otto Mayer, *Deutsches Verwaltungsrecht*, vol 1. second edition (Munich and Leipzig, 1924), p. 14: 'Verwaltungsrecht ist das dem Verhaltniss zwischen dem verwaltenden Staate und den ihm dabei begegnenden Untertanen eigentumliche Recht.'

36 C. A. R. Crosland, *The Future of Socialism* (London, 1956), p. 205.

LAW, LEGISLATION AND LIBERTY

Volume 2
THE MIRAGE OF SOCIAL JUSTICE

In a free society the state does not administer the affairs of men. It administers justice among men who conduct their own affairs.

(Walter Lippmann, *An Inquiry into the Principles of a Good Society* (Boston, 1937), p. 267)

SEVEN

GENERAL WELFARE AND PARTICULAR PURPOSES

It is evident, that if men were to regulate their conduct . . . , by the view of a peculiar *interest*, either public or private, they would involve themselves in endless confusion, and would render all government, in a great measure, ineffectual. The private interest of every one is different; and though the public interest in itself be always one and the same, yet it becomes the source of great dissentions, by reason of the different opinions of particular persons concerning it. . . . Were we to follow the same advantage, in assigning particular possessions to particular persons, we should disappoint our end, and perpetuate the confusion, which that rule is intended to prevent. We must, therefore, proceed by general rules, and regulate ourselves by general interests, in modifying the law of nature concerning the stability of possessions.

David Hume*

In a free society the general good consists principally in the facilitation of the pursuit of unknown individual purposes

It is one of the axioms of the tradition of freedom that coercion of individuals is permissible only where it is necessary in the service of the general welfare or the public good. Yet though it is clear that the stress on the general or common or public character[1] of the legitimate objects of governmental power is directed against its use in the service of particular interests, the vagueness of the different terms which have been employed has made it possible to declare almost any interest a general interest and to make large numbers serve purposes in which they are not in the least interested. The common welfare or the public good has to the present time remained a concept most recalcitrant to any precise definition and therefore capable of being given almost any content suggested by the interests of the ruling group.[2]

I

The chief reason for this has probably been that it seemed natural to assume that the public interest must in some sense be a sum of all the private interests,[3] and that the problem of aggregating all those private interests seemed insoluble. The fact, however, is that in a Great Society in which the individuals are to be free to use their own knowledge for their own purposes, the general welfare at which a government ought to aim cannot consist of the sum of particular satisfactions of the several individuals for the simple reason that neither those nor all the circumstances determining them can be known to government or anybody else. Even in the modern welfare societies the great majority and the most important of the daily needs of the great masses are met as a result of processes whose particulars government does not and cannot know. The most important of the public goods for which government is required is thus not the direct satisfaction of any particular needs, but the securing of conditions in which the individuals and smaller groups will have favourable opportunities of mutually providing for their respective needs.

That the prime public concern must be directed not towards particular known needs but towards the conditions for the preservation of a spontaneous order which enables the individuals to provide for their needs in manners not known to authority was well understood through most of history. For those ancient authors whose ideas chiefly provide the foundations of the modern ideal of freedom, the Stoics and Cicero, public utility and justice were the same. And on the frequent occasions when *utilitas publica* was invoked during the Middle Ages, what was generally meant was simply the preservation of peace and justice. Even to seventeenth century writers like James Harrington the 'public interest . . . was no other than the common right and justice excluding all partiality or private interest' and therefore identical with 'the empire of laws and not of men'.[4]

Our concern at this stage is solely whether those rules of individual conduct which serve the general welfare can aim at some aggregate of known particular results or merely at creating conditions likely to improve the chances of all in the pursuit of their aims. Apart from the fact that the particular aims pursued by the different individuals must be mostly unknown to those who lay down or enforce the rules, it is also not part of the general interest that every private desire be met. The order of the Great Society does rest and must rest on constant undesigned frustrations of some efforts—efforts which ought not to have been made but in free men can be discouraged only by failure. The interest of some individuals will always be that some changes in the structure of society made necessary by changes in circumstances to which in the general interest that structure ought to adapt itself, should not be allowed to take place. In the process of exploration in which each individual examines the facts known to him for their suitability for his own uses, the necessity of abandoning false leads is as important as the adoption of more successful means when they become generally known. Nor can the choice of the appropriate set of rules be guided by balancing for each of the alternative set of rules considered the particular predictable favourable effects against the particular predictable unfavourable effects, and then selecting the set of rules for which the positive net result is greatest; for most of the effects on particular persons of adopting one set of rules rather than another are not predictable. It will not be the interests of particular people but kinds of interests which we shall alone be able to balance against each other; and the classification for this purpose of interests into different kinds possessing different degrees of importance will not be based on the importance of these interests to those directly concerned, but will be made according to the importance to the successful pursuit of certain kinds of interests for the preservation of the overall order.

Moreover, while agreement is not possible on most of the particular ends which will not be known except to those who pursue them (and would be even less possible if the ultimate effects of the decision on particular interests were known), agreement on means can to a great extent be achieved precisely because it is not known which particular ends they will serve. Among the members of a Great Society who mostly do not know each other, there will exist no agreement on the relative importance of their respective ends. There would exist not harmony but open conflict of interests if agreement were necessary as to which particular interests should be given preference over others. What makes agreement and peace in such a society possible is that the individuals are not required to agree on ends but only on means which are capable of serving a great variety of purposes and which each hopes will assist him in the pursuit of his own purposes. Indeed, the possibility of extending an order of peace, beyond the small group which could agree on particular ends, to the members of the Great Society who could not agree on them, is due to the discovery of a method of collaboration which requires agreement only on means and not on ends.

3

It was the discovery that an order definable only by certain abstract characteristic would assist in the pursuit of a great multiplicity of different ends which persuaded people pursuing wholly different ends to agree on certain multi-purpose instruments which were likely to assist everybody. Such agreement became possible not only in spite of but also because of the fact that the particular results it would produce could not be foreseen. It is only because we cannot predict the actual result of the adaptation of a particular rule, that we can assume it to increase everyone's chances equally. That it is thus ignorance of the future outcome which makes possible agreement on rules which serve as common means for a variety of purposes is recognized by the practice in many instances of deliberately making the outcome unpredictable in order to make agreement on the procedure possible: whenever we agree on drawing lots we deliberately substitute equal chances for the different parties for the certainty as to which of them will benefit from the outcome.[5] Mothers who could never agree whose desperately ill child the doctor should attend first, will readily agree before the event that it would be in the interest of all if he attend the children in some regular order which increased his efficiency. When in agreeing on such a rule, we say that 'it is better for all of us if . . .' we mean not that we are certain that it will in the end benefit all of us, but that, on the basis of our present knowledge, it gives us all a better chance, though some will certainly in the end be worse off than they would have been if a different rule had been adopted.

The rules of conduct which prevail in a Great Society are thus not designed to produce particular foreseen benefits for particular people, but are multi-purpose instruments developed as adaptations to certain *kinds* of environment because they help to deal with certain *kinds* of situations. And this adaptation to a kind of environment takes place through a process very different from that in which we might decide on a procedure designed to achieve particular foreseen results. It is based not on anticipation of particular needs, but on the past experience that certain kinds of situations are likely to occur with various degrees of probability. And the result of such past experience gained through trial and error is preserved not as a recollection of particular events, or as explicit knowledge of the kind of situation likely to occur, but as a sense of the importance of observing certain rules. The reason why one rule rather than another was adopted and passed on will be that the group that had adopted it did in fact prove the more efficient, not that its members foresaw the effects the adoption of the rule would have. What would be preserved would be only the effects of past experiences on the selection of rules, not the experiences themselves.

Just as a man, setting out on a walking tour, will take his pocket knife with him, not for a particular foreseen use but in order to be equipped for various possible contingencies, or to be able to cope with kinds of situations likely to occur, so the rules of conduct developed by a group are not means for known particular purposes but adaptations to kinds of situations which past experience has shown to recur in the kind of world we live in. Like the knowledge that induces one to take his pocket knife with him the knowledge embodied in the rules is knowledge of certain general features of the environment, not knowledge of particular facts. In other words, appropriate rules of conduct are not derived from explicit knowledge of the concrete events we will encounter; rather, they are an adaptation to our environment, an adaptation which consists of rules we have developed and for the observance of which we will usually not be able to give adequate reasons. In so far as such rules have prevailed because the group that had adopted them was more successful, nobody need ever have known why that group was successful and why in consequence its rules became generally adopted. In fact, the reason why these were adopted in the first instance, and the reason why they have proved to make this group strong, may be quite different. And although we can endeavour to find out what function a particular rule performs within a given system of rules, and to judge how well it has performed that function, and may as a result try to improve it, we can do so always only against the background of the whole system of other rules which together determine the order of action in that society. But we can never rationally reconstruct in the same manner the whole system of rules, because we lack the knowledge of all the experiences that entered into its formation. The whole system of rules can therefore never be reduced to a purposive construction for known purposes, but must remain to us the inherited system of values guiding that society.

In this sense the general welfare which the rules of individual conduct serve consists of what we have already seen to be the purpose of the rules of law, namely that abstract order of the whole which does not aim at the achievement of known particular results but is preserved as a means for assisting in the pursuit of a great variety of individual purposes.

5

The general interest and collective goods

Though the maintenance of a spontaneous order of society is the prime condition of the general welfare of its members, and the significance of these rules of just conduct with which we are chiefly concerned, we must, before we further examine these relations between rules of individual conduct and welfare, briefly consider another element of the general welfare which must be distinguished from the one in which we shall be mainly interested. There are many kinds of services which men desire but which, because if they are provided they cannot be confined to those prepared to pay for them, can be supplied only if the means are raised by compulsion. Once an apparatus for coercion exists, and particularly if this apparatus is given the monopoly of coercion, it is obvious that it will also be entrusted with supplying the means for the provision of such 'collective goods', as the economists call those services which can be rendered only to all the members of various groups.

But though the existence of an apparatus capable of providing for such collective needs is clearly in the general interest, this does not mean that it is in the interest of society as a whole that all collective interests should be satisfied. A collective interest will become a general interest only in so far as all find that the satisfaction of collective interests of particular groups on the basis of some principle of reciprocity will mean for them a gain in excess of the burden they will have to bear. Though the desire for a particular collective good will be a common desire of those who benefit from it, it will rarely be general for the whole of the society which determines the law, and it becomes a general interest only in so far as the mutual and reciprocal advantages of the individuals balance. But as soon as government is expected to satisfy such particular collective, though not truly general, interests, the danger arises that this method will be used in the service of particular interests. It is often erroneously suggested that all collective interests are general interests of the society; but in many instances the satisfaction of collective interests of certain groups may be decidedly contrary to the general interests of society.

The whole history of the development of popular institutions is a history of continuous struggle to prevent particular groups from abusing the governmental apparatus for the benefit of the collective interest of these groups. This struggle has certainly not ended with the present tendency to define as the general interest anything that a majority formed by a coalition of organized interests decides upon.

That this service-part of governmental activities which aims at the needs of particular groups has in modern times achieved such prominence is a result of the fact that it is with such particular aimed services that politicians and civil servants are mainly concerned, and that it is through providing them that the former can earn the support of their constituents. It is a sad fact that a service aimed at the truly general welfare will gain little credit because nobody feels that he specially benefits by it, and few even know how it will affect them. For the elected representative a specific gift in his hands is much more interesting and a more effective key to power than any benefits he can procure indiscriminately for all.

The provision of collective goods for particular groups is, however, frequently not in the general interest of society. A restriction of output, or some other limitation, will often be a collective good to all members of a particular trade, but it will certainly not be in the general interest that this collective good be provided.

While the comprehensive spontaneous order which the law serves is a precondition for the success of most private activity, the services which the government can render beyond the enforcement of rules of just conduct are not only supplementary or subsidiary[6] to the basic needs which the spontaneous order provides for. They are services which will grow in volume as wealth and the density of population increase, but they are services which must be fitted into that more comprehensive order of private efforts which government neither does nor can determine, and which ought to be rendered under the restrictions of the same rules of law to which the private efforts are subject.

Government, in administering a pool of material resources entrusted to it for the purpose of providing collective goods, is of course itself under the obligation to act justly in doing so, and cannot limit itself to ensuring that the individuals do not act unjustly. In the case of services aimed at particular groups, the justification for financing them through taxation is that only thus can we make those who benefit pay for what they receive; similarly justice clearly requires that what each group receives out of the common pool should be roughly proportional to what it is made to contribute. A majority is here evidently under an obligation to be just; and if we entrust decisions of this kind to democratic or majority government, we do so because we hope that such government is more likely to serve the public interest in this sense. But it would obviously be a

7

perversion of that ideal if we were to define the general interest as whatever the majority desires.

So far as it is possible within the framework of this book, where for reasons of space most of the problems of public finance must be left out, we shall later have to consider the relations between what are usually described as the private and the public sector of the economy (in volume 3). Here we shall consider further only those aspects of general welfare which the rules of just individual conduct serve. We return thus to the question of the aim, not of the rules of organization of government (the public law), but of those rules of individual conduct which are required for the formation of spontaneous order.

Rules and ignorance

To proceed with this task we must recall once more the fundamental fact stressed at the beginning of this study: the impossibility for anyone of knowing all the particular facts on which the overall order of the activities in a Great Society is based. It is one of the curiosities of intellectual history that, in the discussions of rules of conduct, this crucial fact has been so little considered although it alone makes the significance of these rules intelligible. Rules are a device for coping with our constitutional ignorance. There would be no need for rules among omniscient people who were in agreement on the relative importance of all the different ends. Any examination of the moral or legal order which leaves this fact out of account misses the central problem.

The function of rules of conduct as a means for overcoming the obstacle presented by our ignorance of the particular facts which must determine the overall order is best shown by examining the relation between two expressions which we have regularly employed together to describe the conditions of freedom. We have described these conditions as a state in which the individuals are allowed to use their own knowledge for their own purposes.[7] The utilization of factual knowledge widely dispersed among millions of individuals is clearly possible only if these individuals can decide on their actions on the basis of whatever knowledge they possess. What still needs to be shown is that they can do so only if they are also allowed to decide for which purposes they will use their knowledge.

For in an uncertain world the individuals must mostly aim not at some ultimate ends but at procuring means which they think will help them to satisfy those ultimate ends; and their selection of the immediate ends which are merely means for their ultimate ends, but which are all that they can definitely decide upon at a particular moment, will be determined by the opportunities known to them. The immediate purpose of a man's efforts will most often be to procure means to be used for unknown future needs—in an advanced society most frequently that generalized means, money, which will serve for the procurement of most of his particular ends. What he will need in order to choose successfully from among the opportunities known to him are signals in the form of known prices he can get for the alternative services or goods he can produce. Given this information, he will be able to use his knowledge of the circumstances of his environment to select his immediate aim, or the role from which he can hope for the best results. It will be through this choice of immediate aims, for him merely a generalized means for achieving his ultimate ends, that the individual will use his particular knowledge of facts in the service of the needs of his fellows; and it is thus due to the freedom of choosing the ends of one's activities that the utilization of the knowledge dispersed through society is achieved.

Such utilization of dispersed knowledge is thus also made possible by the fact that the opportunities for the different individuals are different. It is because the circumstances in which the different individuals find themselves at a given moment are different, and because many of these particular circumstances are known only to them, that there arises the opportunity for the utilization of so much diverse knowledge—a function which the spontaneous order of the market performs. The idea that government can determine the opportunities for all, and especially that it can ensure that they are the same for all, is therefore in conflict with the whole *rationale* of a free society.

That at any given moment the position of each individual in society is the result of a past process of tentative exploration, in the course of which he or his ancestors have with varying fortunes pushed into every nook and corner of their (physical and social) environment, and that in consequence opportunities which any change in conditions creates are likely to be acted upon by someone, is the basis of that utilization of widely dispersed factual knowledge on which the affluence and adaptability of a Great Society rests. But it is at the same time the cause of undesigned and unavoidable inequalities of opportunity which the decisions of one generation

9

create for their descendants. That parents in their choice of a place to live or of their occupation usually consider the effects their decisions will have on the prospects of their children is an important factor in the adaptation of the use of human resources to foreseeable future developments. But so long as the individual is free to make such decisions, these considerations will be taken into account only if the risk is borne not only by those who decide but also by their descendants. If they were assured that wherever they moved or whatever occupations they chose, government would have to guarantee that the chances for their children would be the same, and that these children would be sure of the same facilities whatever their parents decided, an important factor would be left out of account in those decisions which in the general interest ought to guide them.

That the opportunities of the different members of a large and widely distributed population, resulting from circumstances which from the point of view of the present must appear as accidental, will of necessity be different, is thus inevitably connected with the effectiveness of that discovery procedure, which the market order constitutes. We need merely to consider the effects that would be produced if government succeeded in making equal the substantive chances of all in order to see that it would thereby deprive the whole system of its rationale. To succeed therein, government would have to do more than merely ensure that the conditions affecting the positions of the individuals were the same for all which necessarily depend on its actions. It would have to control effectively all the external conditions influencing the success of an individual's efforts. And, conversely, freedom of choice would lose all importance if somebody had power to determine, and therefore would know, the opportunities of the different individuals. In order to make the chances of different individuals substantively equal, it would be necessary to compensate for those differences in individual circumstances which government cannot directly control. As in some games which are played for the pleasure of the game and not for the result, government would have to handicap the different individuals so as to compensate for individual advantages or disadvantages. But the result would be to make it not worthwhile for the individual to act in accordance with what is the rationale of the whole system, that is, to take advantage of those peculiar opportunities which chance has thrown in his way but not in that of others.

Once we see that, in the absence of a unified body of knowledge of all the particulars to be taken into account, the overall order depends on the use of knowledge possessed by the individuals and used for their purposes, it becomes clear that the role of government in that process cannot be to determine particular results for particular individuals or groups, but only to provide certain generic conditions whose effects on the several individuals will be unpredictable. It can enhance the chances that the efforts of unknown individuals towards equally unknown aims will be successful by enforcing the observance of such abstract rules of conduct as in the light of past experience appear to be most conducive to the formation of a spontaneous order.

The significance of abstract rules as guides in a world in which most of the particulars are unknown

We are in general little aware of the degree to which we are guided in most of our plans for action by the knowledge not of concrete particular facts but by knowledge of what kinds of conduct are 'appropriate' in certain kinds of circumstances—not because they are means to a particular desired result, but because they are a restriction on what we may do without upsetting an order on whose existence we all count in deciding on our actions. The extent to which all that is truly social is of necessity general and abstract in a Great Society, and as such will limit but not fully determine our decisions, is easily overlooked. We are accustomed to think of the familiar and well-known as the concrete and tangible, and it requires some effort to appreciate that what we have in common with our fellows is not so much a knowledge of the same particulars as a knowledge of some general and often very abstract features of a kind of environment.

That this is so is most vividly brought home to us only on rare occasions such as when we visit a part of our native country which we had not known before. Though we have never before seen the people who live in that part, their *manner* of speech, and their *type* of physiognomy, their *style* of building and their *ways* of cultivating the land, their *modes of conduct* and their moral and aesthetic *values* will be familiar to us. We will usually not be able to define what it is that we recognize, and since we recognize it 'intuitively' we will be rarely aware that what we thus recognize are abstract features of the objects or events. In one sense it is of course obvious that what can be common to the views and opinions of men who are members of a Great Society must be general and abstract. Only in the small 'face-to-face-society', in which every member knows every other, will it be mainly particular things. But the greater the society the greater the likelihood that the knowledge which its members will have in common will be abstract features of things or actions; and in the Great or Open Society the common element in the thinking of all will be almost entirely abstract. It is not attachment to particular things but attachment to the abstract rules prevailing in that society which will guide its members in their actions and will be the distinguishing attribute of its peculiar civilization. What we call the *tradition* or the national *character* of a people, and even the characteristic man-made features of the landscape of a country, are not particulars but manifestations of rules governing both the actions and the perceptions[8] of the people. Even where such traditions come to be represented by concrete symbols—a historical site, a national flag, a symbolic shrine, or the person of a monarch or leader—these symbols 'stand for' general conceptions which can be stated only as abstract rules defining what is and what is not done in that society.

What makes men members of the same civilization and enables them to live and work together in peace is that in the pursuit of their individual ends the particular monetary impulses which impel their efforts towards concrete results are guided and restrained by the same abstract rules. If emotion or impulse tells them what they want, the conventional rules tell them how they will be able and be allowed to achieve it. The action, or the act of will, is always a particular, concrete, and individual event, while the common rules which guide it are social, general, and abstract. Though individual men will have similar desires in the sense that they aim at similar objects, the objects in themselves will in general be different particulars. What reconciles the individuals and knits them into a common and enduring pattern of a society is that to these different particular situations they respond in accordance with the same abstract rules.

Will and opinion, ends and values, commands and rules, and other terminological issues

As the range of persons extends among whom some agreement is necessary to prevent conflict, there will necessarily be less and less agreement on the particular ends to be achieved; agreement will increasingly be possible only on certain abstract aspects of the kind of society in which they wish to live. This is a consequence of the fact that the more extensive society becomes, the fewer will be the particular facts known to (or the particular interests shared by) all members of that society. People living in the great urban centres and reading metropolitan newspapers often have the illusion that the facts of the world which they currently learn are largely the same as those that become known to most of their fellow-citizens; but for the greater part of the population of the world, or even of the different sections of a big country, it is probably true that there are very few common elements in the assortment of particular concrete events which become known to them. And what is true of the particular facts known to them is equally true of the particular aims of their activities and of their desires.

But though for this reason there can exist little agreement between them on concrete and particular acts, there may still exist, if they belong to the same culture or tradition, a far-reaching similarity in their *opinions*—an agreement which concerns not particular concrete events but certain abstract features of social life which may prevail at different places and at different times. But to bring this out clearly is made difficult by the vagueness of the expressions at our disposal.

Ordinary language in this field is so imprecise with respect to some of the key terms that it seems necessary to adopt certain conventions in our use of them. Though I believe that the sense in which I shall use them is close to their central meaning, they are certainly not always used in this sense and have a somewhat blurred range of connotations some of which we must exclude. We shall consider the main terms in question in pairs, of which the first will always be used here to refer to a particular or unique event, while the second will describe general or abstract features.

The first of these pairs of terms to be so distinguished, and perhaps the most important, or at least the one which through disregard of the distinction has caused the greatest confusion in political theory, is *will* and *opinion*. [9] We shall call *will* only the aiming at a particular concrete result which, together with the known particular circumstances of the moment, will suffice to determine a particular action. In contrast, we shall call *opinion* the view about the desirability or undesirability of different forms of actions, or actions of certain kinds, which leads to the approval or disapproval of the conduct of particular persons according as they do or do not conform to that view. Such opinions, referring only to the manner of acting, would therefore not be sufficient fully to determine a particular action except in combination with concrete ends. An act of will determines what shall be done at a particular moment, while an opinion will tell us merely what rules to observe when the occasion arises. The distinction is related to that between a particular *impulse* evoking action and a mere *disposition* to act in a certain manner. Aiming at a particular result, the will ceases when the 'end' is achieved, while an opinion, constituting a lasting disposition,[10] will guide many particular acts of will. And while a will always aims at a purpose, we would rightly suspect the genuineness of an opinion if we knew that it was determined by a purpose.

We shall similarly distinguish between particular *ends*, i.e. particular expected effects which motivate particular actions, and *values*, which term we shall understand to refer to generic classes of events, defined by certain attributes and generally regarded as desirable. By 'desirable' in this connection we thus mean more than that a particular action is in fact desired by somebody on a particular occasion; it is used to describe a lasting attitude of one or more persons towards a *kind* of event. We shall accordingly say that, e.g., the law or the rules of just conduct serve not (concrete or particular) ends but (abstract and generic) values, namely the preservation of a kind of order.

There exists a close relationship between the distinction within each of these pairs of terms and the distinction which we have discussed earlier between a *command* and a *rule*. A command regularly aims at a particular result or particular foreseen results, and together with the particular circumstances known to him who issues or receives the command will determine a particular action. By contrast, a rule refers to an unknown number of future instances and to the acts of an unknown number of persons, and merely states certain attributes which any such action ought to possess.

Finally, the observance of rules, or the holding of common values, may secure, as we have seen, that a pattern or order of actions will emerge which will possess certain abstract attributes; but it will not be sufficient to determine the particular manifestation of the pattern or any one particular event or result.

It may be useful, before leaving these terminological questions, to mention here briefly a few other terms which are currently employed in connection with the problems we are considering. There is in the first instance the widely used description of a free society as *pluralistic*. This, of course, is intended to express that it is governed by a multiplicity of individual ends which are not ordered in a particular hierarchy binding on the members.

The multiplicity of independent ends implies also a multiplicity of independent centres of decision, and different types of society are accordingly sometimes distinguished as monocentric and poly-centric.[11] This distinction coincides with the distinction we have introduced earlier between an organization (*taxis*) and a spontane-ous order (*kosmos*), but seems to stress only one particular aspect of the differences between the two kinds of order.

Finally, I understand that Professor Michael Oakeshott, in his oral teaching, has long used the terms *teleocratic* (and *teleocracy*) and *nomocratic* (and *nomocracy*) to bring out the same distinction. A teleocratic order, in which the same hierarchy of ends is binding on all members, is necessarily a made order or organization, while a nomocratic society will form a spontaneous order. We shall occasionally make use of these terms when we want to stress the end-governed character of the organization or the rule-governed character of the spontaneous order.

Abstract rules operate as ultimate values because they serve unknown particular ends

Rules of just conduct assist the settlement of disputes about particu-lars in so far as agreement exists about the rule applicable to the case in hand, even though there may exist no agreement about the importance of the particular aims pursued by the disputing parties. When in a dispute a rule is pointed out which has invariably been observed in past instances that had some abstract features in com-mon with the present issue, the only recourse open to the other party is to point to another rule, also recognized as valid as soon as stated and equally applicable to the present instance, which would require a modification of the conclusions derived from the first rule. Only if we can discover such another rule, or can show that our opponent would himself not accept the first rule in all instances to which it applies, can we demonstrate that a decision based only on the first rule would be wrong. Our whole conception of justice rests on the belief that different views about particulars are capable of being settled by the discovery of rules that, once they are stated, command general assent. If it were not for the fact that we often can discover that we do agree on general principles which are applicable, even though we at first disagree on the merits of the particular case, the very idea of justice would lose its meaning.

The applicable rules define the features which are relevant for the decision as to whether an act was just or unjust. All features of the particular case must be disregarded which cannot be brought under a rule that once it is stated is accepted as defining just conduct. The important point here is not that the rule has been explicitly stated before, but that when articulated it is accepted as corresponding to general usage. The first formulation of what has already guided the sense of justice and, when first stated, is recognized as expressing what men have long felt, is as much a discovery as any discovery of science—even though, like the latter, it will often be only a better approximation to what it aims at than anything that had been stated before.

It is of little significance for our present purpose whether such general rules came to govern opinion because the advantages to be gained from observing them were recognized, or because groups who happened to accept rules which made them more efficient came to prevail over others obeying less effective rules. A more important point is that the rules which have been adopted because of their beneficial effects in the majority of cases will have these beneficial effects only if they are applied to all cases to which they refer, irrespective of whether it is known, or even true, that they will have a beneficial effect in the particular case. As David Hume put it in his classical exposition of the rationale of rules of justice:[12]

> a single act of justice is frequently contrary to *public interest*; and were it to stand alone, without being followed by other acts, may, in itself, be very prejudicial to society . . . Nor is every single act of justice, considered apart, more conducive to private interest, than to public; . . . But however single acts of justice may be contrary, either to public or private interest, it is certain, that the whole plan or scheme is highly conducive, or indeed absolutely requisite, both to the support of society, and to the well-being of every individual.

The resolution of this apparent paradox is, of course, that the enforcement of those abstract rules serves the preservation of an equally abstract order whose particular manifestations are largely unpredictable, and that this order will be preserved only if it is generally expected that those rules will be enforced in all cases, irrespective of the particular consequences some may foresee. This means that, though these rules ultimately serve particular (though mostly unknown) ends, they will do so only if they are treated not as means but as ultimate values, indeed as the only values common to all and distinct from the particular ends of the individuals. This is what is meant by the principle that the ends do not justify the means, and by such adages as *fiat justitia, pereat mundus* (let justice prevail even if the world perish). Only if applied universally, without regard to particular effects, will they serve the permanent preservation of the abstract order, a timeless purpose which will continue to assist the individuals in the pursuit of their temporary and still unknown aims. Those rules which are common values serve the maintenance of an order of whose existence those who apply them are often not even aware. And however much we may often dislike the unforeseeable consequences of applying the rules in a particular case, we can usually not see even all the immediate consequences, and still less the more remote effects that will be produced if the rule were not expected to be applied in all future instances.

The rules of just conduct are thus not concerned with the protection of particular interests, and all pursuit of particular interests must be subject to them. This applies as much to the tasks of government in its capacity as administrator of common means destined for the satisfaction of particular purpose, as to the actions of private persons. And this is the reason why government, when it is concerned with the temporary and particular, should be under a law which is concerned with the permanent and general; and why those whose task it is to formulate rules of just conduct should not be concerned with the temporary and particular ends of government.

The constructivist fallacy of utilitarianism

The constructivist interpretation of rules of conduct is generally known as 'utilitarianism'. In a wider sense the term is, however, also applied to any critical examination of such rules and of institutions with respect to the function they perform in the structure of society. In this wide sense every one who does not regard all existing values as unquestionable but is prepared to ask why they should be held would have to be described as a utilitarian. Thus Aristotle, Thomas Aquinas,[13] and David Hume,[14] would have to be described as utilitarians, and the present discussion of the function of rules of conduct might also be so called. No doubt utilitarianism owes much of its appeal to sensible people to the fact that thus interpreted it includes all rational examination of the appropriateness of existing rules.

Since the late eighteenth century 'utilitarianism' has, however, been used in moral and legal theory in a narrower sense, and that is how we shall here employ the term. This special meaning is partly the result of a gradual change of meaning of the term utility itself. Originally 'utility', as the term 'usefulness' still clearly does, expressed an attribute of *means*—the attribute of being capable of potential uses. That something was useful indicated it was capable of uses in situations likely to occur, and the degree of usefulness depended on the likelihood of the occurrence of those situations in which the thing might prove helpful and the importance of the needs it was likely to satisfy.

It was only comparatively late that the term utility denoting an attribute of means came to be used to describe a supposedly common attribute of the different ends which they served. Since the means were seen in some measure to reflect the importance of the ends, utility came to mean some such common attribute of the ends as the pleasure or satisfaction which were connected with them. Though it had in earlier times been fully understood that most of our efforts must be directed to providing means for unforeseen particular purposes, the rationalist desire explicitly to derive the usefulness of means from known ultimate ends led to the attribution to these ends of a measurable common attribute for which either the term pleasure or the term utility was employed.

The distinction which it is necessary to make for our purposes is one between the usefulness of something for known particular ends and its usefulness for various kinds of needs expected to occur in a kind of environment or in kinds of likely situations. Only in the former instance would the usefulness of an object or practice be derived from the importance of particular foreseen future uses, and would constitute a reflection of the importance of particular ends. In the latter instance the property of usefulness would be judged on the basis of past experience as an instrumental property not depending on particular known ends but as a means of dealing with a variety of situations likely to occur.

The strict utilitarianism of Jeremy Bentham and his school[15] undertakes to judge the appropriateness of conduct by an explicit calculation of the balance of the pleasure and the pain that it will cause. Its inadequacy was long concealed by the utilitarians relying in the defence of their position on two different and irreconcilable contentions which have only recently been clearly distinguished,[16] neither of which by itself provides an adequate account of the determination of moral or legal rules. Of these two positions between which the utilitarians constantly shifted the first is incapable of accounting for the existence of *rules* and therefore for the phenomena which we normally describe as morals and law, while the other is bound to assume the existence of rules not accountable for by utilitarian considerations and thus must abandon the claim that the whole system of moral rules can be derived from their known utility.

Bentham's conception of a calculus of pleasure and pain by which the greatest happiness of the greatest number is to be determined presupposes that all the particular individual effects of any one action can be known by the acting person. Pursued to its logical conclusion it leads to a particularistic or 'act' utilitarianism which dispenses with rules altogether and judges each individual action according to the utility of its known effects. Bentham, it is true, safeguarded himself against such an interpretation by a constant recourse to such statements as that every action (now interpreted as any action of a certain *kind*) should have the *tendency* to produce *on the whole* a maximum balance of pleasure. But at least some of his followers clearly saw that the logic of the argument demanded that each individual action should be decided upon in the light of a full knowledge of its particular consequences. Thus we find Henry Sidgwick maintained that 'we have in each case to compare all the pleasures and pains that can be foreseen as probable results of the different alternatives of conduct, and adopt the alternative which seems likely to lead to the greatest happiness of the whole';[17] and G. E. Moore that 'it must always be the duty of every agent to do that one among all actions which he *can* do on any given occasion, whose *total consequences* will have the greatest intrinsic value.'[18]

The alternative interpretation as a generic or, as it is now usually called, 'rule' utilitarianism was expressed most clearly by William Paley when he demanded that a *kind* of action, to be morally approved, 'must be expedient on the whole, at the long run, in all its effects collateral and remote, as well as in those which are immediate and direct; as it is obvious, that, in computing consequences, it makes no difference in what way or what distance they ensue'.[19]

The extensive discussion of recent years of the respective merits of particularistic ('act-') and generic ('rule-') utilitarianism has made it clear that only the former can claim to be consistent in basing the approval or disapproval of actions exclusively on their foreseen effects of 'utility', but that at the same time, in order to do so, it must proceed on a factual assumption of omniscience which is never satisfied in real life and which, if it were ever true, would make the existence of those bodies of rules which we call morals and law not only superfluous but unaccountable and contrary to the assumption; while, on the other hand, no system of generic or rule utilitarianism could treat all rules as fully determined by utilities known to the acting person, because the effects of any rule will depend not only on its being always observed but also on the other rules observed by the acting persons and on the rules being followed by all the other members of the society. To judge the utility of any one rule would therefore always presuppose that some other rules were taken as given and generally observed and not determined by any known utility, so that among the determinants of the utility of any one rule there would always be other rules which could not be justified by their utility. Rule-utilitarianism consistently pursued could therefore never give an adequate justification of the whole system of rules and must always include determinants other than the known utility of particular rules.

The trouble with the whole utilitarian approach is that, as a theory professing to account for a phenomenon which consists of a body of rules, it completely eliminates the factor which makes rules necessary, namely our ignorance. It has indeed always amazed me how serious and intelligent men, as the utilitarians undoubtedly were, could have failed to take seriously this crucial fact of our necessary ignorance of most of the particular facts, and could have proposed a theory which presupposes a knowledge of the particular effects of our individual actions when in fact the whole existence of the phenomenon they set out to explain, namely of a system of rules of conduct, was due to the impossibility of such knowledge. It would seem that they never grasped the significance of rules as an adaptation to this inescapable ignorance of most of the particular circumstances which determine the effects of our actions, and thus disregarded the whole rationale of the phenomenon of rule-guided action.[20]

Man has developed rules of conduct not because he knows but because he does not know what all the consequences of a particular action will be. And the most characteristic feature of morals and law as we know them is therefore that they consist of rules to be obeyed irrespective of the known effects of the particular action. How we should wish men to behave who were omniscient and could foresee all the consequences of their actions is without interest to us. Indeed there would be no need for rules if men knew everything—and strict act-utilitarianism of course must lead to the rejection of all rules.

Like all general purpose tools, rules serve because they have become adapted to the solution of recurring problem situations and thereby help to make the members of the society in which they prevail more effective in the pursuit of their aims. Like a knife or a hammer they have been shaped not with a particular purpose in view but because in this form rather than in some other form they have proved serviceable in a great variety of situations. They have not been constructed to meet foreseen particular needs but have been selected in a process of evolution. The knowledge which has given them their shape is not knowledge of particular future effects but knowledge of the recurrence of certain problem situations or tasks, of intermediate results regularly to be achieved in the service of a great variety of ultimate aims; and much of this knowledge exists not as an awareness of an enumerable list of situations for which one has to be prepared, or of the importance of the kind of problems to be solved, or of the probability that they will arise, but as a propensity to act in certain types of situations in a certain manner.

Most rules of conduct are thus not derived by an intellectual process from the knowledge of the facts of the environment, but constitute the only adaptation of man to these facts which we have achieved, a 'knowledge' of them of which we are not aware and which does not appear in our conceptual thought, but which manifests itself in the rules which we obey in our actions. Neither the groups who first practised these rules, nor those who imitated them, need ever have known why their conduct was more successful than that of others, or helped the group to persist.

It must be stressed that the importance we attach to the observation of particular rules does not simply reflect the importance of particular ends which may depend on their observance; the importance attached to a rule is rather a compound result of two distinct factors which we shall rarely be able to assess separately: the importance of particular effects and the frequency of their occurrence. Just as in biological evolution it may matter less for the preservation of the species if no provision is made to avoid certain lethal but rare effects than if a frequently occurring kind of event doing only slight damage to the individual is avoided, so the rules of conduct that have emerged from the process of social evolution may often be adequate to prevent frequent causes of minor disturbances of the social order but not rare causes of its total disruption.

The only 'utility' which can be said to have determined the rules of conduct is thus not a utility known to the acting persons, or to any one person, but only a hypostatized 'utility' to society as a whole. The consistent utilitarian is therefore frequently driven to interpret the products of evolution anthropomorphically as the product of design and to postulate a personified society as the author of these rules. Though this is rarely admitted as naively as by a recent author who explicitly maintained that to the utilitarian society must appear 'as a sort of single great person',[21] such anthropomorphism is characteristic of all constructivist conceptions of which utilitarianism is but a particular form. This basic error of utilitarianism has been most concisely expressed by Hastings Rashdall in the contention that 'all moral judgements are ultimately judgements as to the value of ends.'[22] This is precisely what they are not; if agreement on particular ends were really the ground for moral judgments, moral rules as we know them would be unnecessary.[23]

The essence of all rules of conduct is that they label *kinds* of actions, not in terms of their largely unknown effects in particular instances, but in terms of their probable effect which need not be foreseeable by the individuals. It is not because of those effects of our actions which we knowingly bring about, but because of the effects our actions have on the continuous maintenance of an order of actions, that particular rules have come to be regarded as important. Like the order which they serve, but at one further remove, they assist only indirectly the satisfaction of particular needs by helping to avoid kinds of conflicts which past experience has shown to occur in the normal pursuit of a great variety of aims. They serve not to make any particular plan of action successful, but to reconcile many different plans of actions. It is the interpretation of rules of conduct as part of a plan of action of 'society' towards the achievement of some single set of ends which gives all utilitarian theories their anthropomorphic character.

Utilitarianism, to succeed in its aims, would have to attempt a sort of reductionism which traces all rules to the deliberate choice of means for known ends. As such it is about as likely to be successful as an attempt to account for the particular features of a language by tracing the effects of successive efforts at communication through a few thousand generations. Rules of conduct as well as rules of speech are the product not of direct adaptation to particular known facts, but of a cumulative process in which at any moment the chief factor is the existence of a factual order determined by already established rules. It will always be within such an order, functioning more or less adequately, that new rules will develop; and it will at every stage be only as part of such a working system that the expediency of any one rule can be judged. Rules in this sense have a function within an operating system but not a purpose—a function which cannot be derived from known particular effects on particular needs, but only from an understanding of the whole structure. But in fact nobody has yet achieved such a full understanding or succeeded in reconstructing an altogether new system of moral or legal rules from the knowledge of the needs and the effects of known means. [24]

Like most tools, rules are not part of a plan of action but rather equipment for certain unknown contingencies. Indeed, a great part of all our activities is also guided not by a knowledge of the particular ultimate needs which they serve, but by a desire to accumulate a stock of tools and of knowledge, or to manoeuvre for positions, in short to accumulate 'capital' in the widest sense of the term, which we think will come in useful in the kind of world in which we live. And this sort of activity seems indeed to become more prevalent the more intelligent we become. We adapt more and more, not to the particular circumstances, but so as to increase our adaptability to kinds of circumstances which may occur. The horizon of our sight consists mostly of means, not of particular ultimate ends.

We may of course aim at the 'greatest happiness of the greatest number' if we do not delude ourselves that we can determine the sum of this happiness by some calculation, or that there is a known aggregate of results at any one time. What the rules, and the order they serve, can do is no more than to increase the opportunities for unknown people. If we do the best we can to increase the opportunities for any unknown person picked at random, we will achieve the most we can, but certainly not because we have any idea of the sum of utility of pleasure which we have produced.

All valid criticism or improvement of rules of conduct must proceed within a given system of such rules

Since any established system of rules of conduct will be based on experiences which we only partly know, and will serve an order of action in a manner which we only partly understand, we cannot hope to improve it by reconstructing anew the whole of it. If we are to make full use of all the experience which has been transmitted only in the form of traditional rules, all criticism and efforts at improvement of particular rules must proceed within a framework of given values which for the purpose in hand must be accepted as not requiring justification. We shall call 'immanent criticism' this sort of criticism that moves within a given system of rules and judges particular rules in terms of their consistency or compatibility with all other recognized rules in inducing the formation of a certain kind of order of actions. This is the only basis for a critical examination of moral or legal rules once we recognize the irreducibility of the whole existing system of such rules to known specific effects that it will produce.

The consistency or compatibility of the different rules which make up a system is not primarily logical consistency. Consistency in this connection means that the rules serve the same abstract order of actions and prevent conflict between persons obeying these rules in the kind of circumstances to which they have been adapted. Whether any two or more rules are consistent or not will therefore depend in part on the factual conditions of the environment; and the same rules may therefore be sufficient to prevent conflict in one kind of environment but not in another. On the other hand, rules which are logically inconsistent in the sense that they may lead in any given situation to requirements or prohibitions of acts of any one person which are mutually contradictory, may yet be made compatible if they stand in a relation of superiority or inferiority to each other, so that the system of rules itself determines which of the rules is to 'overrule' the other.

All real moral problems are created by conflicts of rules, and most frequently are problems caused by uncertainty about the relative importance of different rules. No system of rules of conduct is complete in the sense that it gives an unambiguous answer to all moral questions; and the most frequent cause of uncertainty is probably that the order of rank of the different rules belonging to a system is only vaguely determined. It is through the constant necessity of dealing with such questions to which the established system of rules gives no definite answer that the whole system evolves and gradually becomes more determinate, or better adapted to the kind of circumstances in which the society exists.

When we say that all criticism of rules must be immanent criticism, we mean that the test by which we can judge the appropriateness of a particular rule will always be some other rule which for the purpose in hand we regard as unquestioned. The great body of rules which in this sense is tacitly accepted determines the aim which the rules being questioned must also support; and this aim, as we have seen, is not any particular event but the maintenance or restoration of an order of actions which the rules tend to bring about more or less successfully. The ultimate test is thus not consistency of the rules but compatibility of the actions of different persons which they permit or require.

It may at first seem puzzling that something that is the product of tradition should be capable of both being the object and the standard of criticism. But we do not maintain that all tradition as such is sacred and exempt from criticism, but merely that the basis of criticism of any one product of tradition must always be other products of tradition which we either cannot or do not want to question; in other words, that particular aspects of a culture can be critically examined only within the context of that culture. We can never reduce a system of rules or all values as a whole to a purposive construction, but must always stop with our criticism at something that has no better ground for existence than that it is the accepted basis of the particular tradition. Thus we can always examine a part of the whole only in terms of that whole which we cannot entirely reconstruct and the greater part of which we must accept unexamined. As it might also be expressed: we can always only tinker with parts of a given whole but never entirely redesign it. [25]

This is so mainly because the system of rules into which the rules guiding the action of any one person must be fitted does not merely comprise all the rules governing his actions but also the rules which govern the actions of the other members of the society. There is little significance in being able to show that if everybody adopted some proposed new rule a better overall result would follow, so long as it is not in one's power to bring this about. But one may well adopt a rule which within the existing system of rules leads to less disappointment of expectations than the established rules, and thus by introducing a new rule increase the likelihood that the expectations of others will not be disappointed. This apparently paradoxical result, that a change of the rules introduced by one may lead to less disappointment of expectations on the part of others, and may in consequence ultimately prevail, is closely connected with the fact that the expectations which guide us refer less to the actions which other persons will take than to the effects of these actions, and that the rules on which we count are mostly not rules prescribing particular actions but rules restraining actions —not positive but negative rules. It may well be customary in a particular society to allow the run-off of water or other substances from one's land to damage the land of one's neighbour, and such carelessness may therefore be tolerated although it will again and again upset somebody's expectations. If then anyone, out of consideration for his neighbour, adopts the new rule of preventing such damaging run-off, he will, by acting differently from the common practice, reduce the frequency of disappointments of the expectations on which people base their plans; and such a new rule adopted by one may come to be generally accepted because it fits better into the established system of rules than the practice which had so far prevailed.

The necessity of immanent criticism thus derives in a great measure from the circumstance that the effects of any person's action will depend on the various rules which govern the actions of his fellows. The 'consequences of one's actions' are not simply a physical fact independent of the rules prevailing in a given society, but depend very largely on the rules which the other members of society obey; and even where it is possible for one to discover a new rule which, if generally adopted, might be more beneficial for all, the rules which the others in fact follow must be among the data from which he will have to derive his belief in the more beneficial character of the new rule which he proposes. This may well mean that the rule one ought to follow in a given society and in particular circumstances in order to produce the best consequences, may not be the best rule in another society where the system of generally adopted rules is different. This circumstance greatly restricts the extent to which the private moral judgment of any individual can produce an improvement over the established system of rules; it also accounts for the fact that, if he moves in different kinds of societies, different rules may on different occasions be obligatory for the same individual.

The much discussed question of 'moral relativity' is thus clearly connected with the fact that all moral (and legal) rules serve an existing factual order which no individual has the power to change fundamentally; because such change would require changes in the rules which other members of the society obey, in part unconsciously or out of sheer habit, and which, if a viable society of a different type were to be created, would have to be replaced by other rules which nobody has the power to make effective. There can, therefore, be no absolute system of morals independent of the kind of social order in which a person lives, and the obligation incumbent upon us, to follow certain rules derives from the benefits we owe to the order in which we live.

It would seem to me, for instance, to be clearly morally wrong to revive an already unconscious old Eskimo who, at the beginning of their winter migration,[26] in accordance with the morals of his people and with his approval, had been left behind by his group to die—and to be right only if I regarded it as right, and in my power, to transfer him into a wholly different society in which I was able and willing to provide for his survival.

That our moral obligations derive from our benefiting from an order which rests on certain rules is simply the reverse of the fact that it is the observance of common rules which integrates the individuals into the order which we call a society, and that such a society can persist only if some sort of pressure exists to make the members conform to such rules. There are, undoubtedly, many forms of tribal or closed societies which rest on very different systems of rules. All that we are here maintaining is that we know only of one kind of such systems of rules, undoubtedly still very imperfect and capable of much improvement, which makes the kind of open or 'humanistic' society possible where each individual counts as an individual and not only as a member of a particular group, and where therefore universal rules of conduct can exist which are equally applicable to all responsible human beings. It is only if we accept such a universal order as an aim, that is, if we want to continue on the path which since the ancient Stoics and Christianity has been characteristic of Western civilization, that we can defend this moral system as superior to others—and at the same time endeavour to improve it further by continued immanent criticism.

'Generalization' and the test of universalizability

Closely connected with the test of internal consistency as a means of developing a system of rules of conduct are the questions commonly discussed under the headings of generalization or universalization. In fact, used as a test of the appropriateness of a rule, the possibility of its generalization or universalization amounts to a test of consistency or compatibility with the rest of the accepted system of rules or values. But before we show why this must be so it is necessary to consider briefly the meaning in which the conception of generalization is properly used in this connection. It is usually interpreted[27] as referring to the question of what would be the consequences if everybody did a certain thing. But most actions, except the most ordinary ones, would become obnoxious if everybody performed them. The necessity of generally forbidding or enjoining a certain *kind* of action, like rules in general, follows from our ignorance of what the consequences of a kind of action have in particular instances. To consider the simplest and most typical case: we frequently know that a certain kind of action will often be harmful, but neither we (or the legislator) nor the acting person will know whether that will be so in any particular instance. When therefore we try to define the kind of action which we wish to be avoided, we will as a rule only succeed in so defining it that it includes most of the instances in which it will have harmful effects, but also many in which it will not. The only way to prevent the harmful effects will then be to prohibit this class of action generally, irrespective of whether in fact it will have a harmful effect on a particular given occasion; and the problem will be whether we should generally prohibit this kind of action or accept the harm that will follow from it in a certain number of instances.

If we now turn to the more interesting question of what is meant when it is asked whether such a generalization is 'possible' or whether something 'can' be made a general rule, it is evident that the 'possibility' referred to is not a physical possibility or impossibility, nor the practical possibility of generally enforcing obedience to such a rule. The appropriate interpretation is suggested by the manner in which Immanuel Kant approached the problem, namely by asking whether we can 'want' or 'will' that such a rule be generally applied. Here the obstacle to generalization which is contemplated is evidently itself a moral one and this must mean a conflict with some other rule or value which we are not prepared to sacrifice. In other words, the test of 'universalizability' applied to any one rule will amount to a test of compatibility with the whole system of accepted rules—a test which, as we have seen, may either lead to a clear 'yes' or 'no' answer or may show that, if the system of rules is to give definite guidance, some of the rules will have to be modified, or so arranged into a hierarchy of greater or lesser importance (or superiority and inferiority), that in case of conflict we know which is to prevail and which is to give.

To perform their functions rules must be applied through the long run

The facts that rules are a device for coping with our ignorance of the effects of particular actions, and that the importance we attach to these rules is based both on the magnitude of the possible harm that they serve to prevent and the degree of probability that will be inflicted if they are disregarded, show that such rules will perform their function only if they are adhered to for long periods. This follows from the circumstance that the rules of conduct contribute to the formation of an order by being obeyed by the individuals and by being used by them for their purposes, mostly unknown to those who may have laid down the rules or are entitled to alter them. Where, as is the case with law, some of the rules of conduct are deliberately laid down by authority, they will thus perform their function only if they become the basis of the planning of the individuals. The maintenance of a spontaneous order through the enforcement of rules of conduct must therefore always aim at results in the long run, in contrast to the rules of organization serving known particular purposes which must essentially aim at predictable short run results. Hence the conspicuous difference in outlook between the administrator, necessarily concerned with particular known effects, and the judge or law-giver, who ought to be concerned with the maintenance of an abstract order in disregard of the particular foreseen results. A concentration on particular results necessarily leads to a short run view, since only in the short run will the particular results be foreseeable, and raises in consequence conflicts between particular interests that can be decided only by an authoritative decision in favour of one or the other. Predominant concern with the visible short run effects thus progressively leads to a dirigist organization of the whole society. Indeed, what will certainly be dead in the long run if we concentrate on immediate results is freedom. A nomocratic society must confine coercion wholly to the enforcement of rules serving a long run order.

The idea that a structure whose surveyable parts are not

comprehended as meaningful, or show no recognizable design, and where we do *not* know why particular things happen, should be a more effective foundation for the successful pursuit of our ends than a deliberately constructed organization, and that it may even be to our advantage that changes occur for which nobody knows the reason (because they register facts which as a whole are not known to anybody), is so contrary to the ideas of constructivist rationalism which have governed European thought since the seventeenth century, that it will become generally accepted only with the spreading of an evolutionary or critical rationalism that is aware not only of the powers but also of the limits of reason, and recognizes that this reason itself is a product of social evolution. The demand for that kind of pellucid order which would satisfy the standards of the constructivists, on the other hand, must lead to a destruction of an order much more comprehensive than any we can deliberately construct. Freedom means that in some measure we entrust our fate to forces which we do not control; and this seems intolerable to those constructivists who believe that man can master his fate—as if civilization and reason itself were of his making.

EIGHT

THE QUEST FOR JUSTICE

Every single legal rule may be thought of as one of the bulwarks or boundaries erected by society in order that its members shall not collide with each other in their actions.

P. Vinogradoff*

Justice is an attribute of human conduct

We have chosen the term 'rules of just conduct' to describe those end-independent rules which serve the formation of a spontaneous order, in contrast to the end-dependent rules of organization. The former are the *nomos* which is at the basis of a 'private law society'[1] and makes an Open Society possible; the latter, so far as they are law, are the public law which determines the organization of government. We did not contend, however, that all rules of just conduct which may in fact be obeyed should be regarded as law, nor that every single rule which forms part of a system of rules of just conduct is by itself a rule defining just conduct. We have still to examine the vexing question of the relation between justice and law. This question has been confused as much by the belief that all that can be decided by legislative decision must be a question of justice, as by the belief that it is the will of the legislature which determines what is just. We shall first consider some often disregarded limitations of the applicability of the term justice.

Strictly speaking, only human conduct can be called just or unjust. If we apply the terms to a state of affairs, they have meaning only in so far as we hold someone responsible for bringing it about or allowing it to come about. A bare fact, or a state of affairs which nobody can change, may be good or bad, but not just or unjust.[2] To apply the term 'just' to circumstances other than human actions or the rules governing them is a category mistake. Only if we mean to blame a personal creator does it make sense to describe it as unjust that somebody has been born with a physical defect, or

31

been stricken with a disease, or has suffered the loss of a loved one. Nature can be neither just nor unjust. Though our inveterate habit of interpreting the physical world animistically or anthropomorphically often leads us to such a misuse of words, and makes us seek a responsible agent for all that concerns us, unless we believe that somebody could and should have arranged things differently, it is meaningless to describe a factual situation as just or unjust.

But if nothing that is not subject to human control can be just (or moral), the desire to make something capable of being just is not necessarily a valid argument for our making it subject to human control; because to do so may itself be unjust or immoral, at least when the actions of another human being are concerned.

In certain circumstances it may be a legal or moral duty to bring about a certain state of affairs which then can often be described as just. That in such instances the term 'just' refers in fact to the actions and not to the results becomes clear when we consider that it can apply only to such consequences of a person's actions as it has been in his power to determine. It presupposes not only that those whose duty it is thought to be to bring about that state can actually do so, but that the means by which they can do so are also just or moral.

The rules by which men try to define kinds of actions as just or unjust may be correct or incorrect; and it is established usage to describe as unjust a rule which describes as just a kind of action which is unjust. But though this is a usage that is so general that it must be accepted as legitimate, it is not without danger. What we really mean when we say, e.g., that a rule which we all thought to be just proves to be unjust when applied to a particular case, is that it is a wrong rule which does not adequately define what we regard as just, or that the verbal formulation of the rule does not adequately express the rule which guides our judgment.

Evidently, not only the actions of individuals but also the concerted actions of many individuals, or the actions of organizations, may be just or unjust. Government is such an organization, but society is not. And, though the order of society will be affected by actions of government, so long as it remains a spontaneous order, the particular results of the social process cannot be just or unjust. This means that the justice or injustice of the demands which government makes on the individual must be decided in the light of rules of just conduct and not by the particular results which will follow from their application to an individual case. Government certainly ought to be just in all it does; and the pressure of public opinion is likely to drive it to extend any discernible principles on which it acts to their possible limits, whether it intends to do so or not. But how far its duty in justice extends must depend on its power to affect the position of the different individuals in accordance with uniform rules.

Only those aspects of the order of human actions which can be determined by rules of just conduct do therefore raise problems of justice. To speak of justice always implies that some person or persons ought, or ought not, to have performed some action; and this 'ought' in turn presupposes the recognition of rules which define a set of circumstances wherein a certain kind of conduct is prohibited or required. We know by now that the 'existence' of a recognized rule does not in this context necessarily mean that the rule has been stated in words. It requires only that a rule can be found which distinguishes between different kinds of conduct on lines which people in fact recognize as just or unjust.

Rules of just conduct refer to such actions of individuals as affect others. In a spontaneous order the position of each individual is the resultant of the actions of many other individuals, and nobody has the responsibility or the power to assure that these separate actions of many will produce a particular result for a certain person. Though his position may be affected by the conduct of some other person or of the concerted actions of several, it will rarely be dependent on them alone. There can, therefore, in a spontaneous order, be no rules which will determine what anyone's position ought to be. Rules of individual conduct, as we have seen, determine only certain abstract properties of the resulting order, but not its particular, concrete content.

It is, of course, tempting to call 'just' a state of affairs that comes about because all contributing to it behave justly (or not unjustly); but this is misleading where, as in the case of a spontaneous order, the resulting state was not the intended aim of the individual actions. Since only situations which have been created by human will can be called just or unjust, the particulars of a spontaneous order cannot be just or unjust: if it is not the intended or foreseen result of somebody's action that A should have much and B little, this cannot be called just or unjust. We shall see that what is called 'social' or 'distributive' justice is indeed meaningless within a spontaneous order and has meaning only within an organization.

33

Justice and the law

We are not contending that all rules of just conduct which are in fact observed in a society are law, nor that all that is commonly called law consists of rules of just conduct. Our contention is rather that the law which consists of rules of just conduct has a very special standing which not only makes it desirable that it have a distinct name (such as *nomos*), but also makes it exceedingly important that it be clearly distinguished from other commands called law, so that in developing this sort of law its characteristic properties are clearly seen. The reason for this is that, if we want to preserve a free society, only that part of the law which consists of rules of just conduct (i.e. essentially the private and criminal law) must be binding for, and be enforced on, the private citizen—whatever else may also be law binding those who are members of the organization of government. We shall see that the loss of the belief in a law which serves justice and not particular interests (or particular ends of government) is largely responsible for the progressive undermining of individual freedom.

We need not dwell here on the much discussed question of what is required for a recognized rule of just conduct to be entitled to the name of law. Though most people would hesitate to give this name to a rule of just conduct which, though usually obeyed, was in no way enforced, it seems difficult to deny it to rules which are enforced by a largely effective though unorganized social pressure, or the exclusion of the breaker of a rule from the group.[3] There is evidently a gradual transition from such a state to what we regard as a mature legal system in which deliberately created organizations are charged with the enforcement and modification of this primary law. The rules governing these organizations are of course part of the public law and, like government itself, are superimposed upon the primary rules, for the purpose of making these more effective.

But if, in contrast to the public law, the private and criminal law aims at establishing and enforcing rules of just conduct, this does not mean that every one of the separate rules in which they are stated, taken by itself, is a rule of just conduct, but only that the system as a whole[4] serves to determine such rules. All rules of just conduct must refer to certain states of affairs; and it is often more convenient to define by separate rules these states of affairs to which particular rules of conduct refer than to repeat these definitions in every rule which refers to such a state. The individual domains which the rules of just conduct protect will have to be referred to again and again, and the manner in which such domains are acquired, transferred, lost, and delimited will usefully be stated once and for all in rules whose function will be solely to serve as points of reference for rules of just conduct. All the rules which state the conditions under which property can be acquired and transferred, valid contracts or wills made, or other 'rights' or 'powers' acquired and lost, serve merely to define the conditions on which the law will grant the protection of enforceable rules of just conduct. Their aim is to make the relevant states of affairs recognizable, and to ensure that the parties will understand each other in entering obligations. If a form is omitted which the law prescribes for a transaction, this does not mean that a rule of just conduct has been infringed, but that the protection of certain rules of just conduct will not be granted which would have been granted had the form been observed. Such states as 'ownership' have no significance except through the rules of conduct which refer to them; leave out those rules of just conduct which refer to ownership, and nothing remains of it.

Rules of just conduct are generally prohibitions of unjust conduct

We have seen earlier (chapter 5) how from the process of gradual extension of rules of just conduct to circles of persons who neither share, nor are aware of, the same particular ends, a type of rule has developed which is usually described as 'abstract'. This term is appropriate, however, only if it is not used in the strict sense in which it is employed in logic. A rule applying only to persons whose finger-prints show a particular pattern, definable by an algebraic formula, would in the sense in which this term is used in logic certainly be an abstract rule. But since experience has taught us that every individual is uniquely identified by his finger-prints, such a rule would in fact apply only to an ascertainable individual. What is meant by the term abstract is expressed in a classical juridical formula that states that the rule must apply to an unknown number of future instances.[5] Here legal theory has found it necessary explicitly to acknowledge our inevitable ignorance of the particular circumstances which we wish those to use who learn of them.

We have already indicated earlier that such reference to an unknown number of future instances is closely connected with certain other properties of those rules which have passed through the process of generalization, namely that these rules are almost all negative in the sense that they prohibit rather than enjoin particular kinds of actions, [6] that they do so in order to protect ascertainable domains within which each individual is free to act as he chooses, [7] and that the possession of this character by a particular rule can be ascertained by applying to it a test of generalization or universalization. We shall try to show that these are all necessary characteristics of those rules of just conduct which form the foundation of a spontaneous order, but do not apply to those rules of organization which make up the public law. [8]

That practically all rules of just conduct are negative in the sense that they normally impose no positive duties on any one, unless he has incurred such duties by his own actions, is a feature that has again and again, as though it were a new discovery, been pointed out, but scarcely ever systematically investigated. [9] It applies to most rules of conduct but not without exception. Some parts of family law impose duties which do not result from a deliberate action (such as duties of children towards parents) but from a position in which the individual has been placed by circumstances beyond his control. And there are a few other rather exceptional instances in which a person is deemed by the rules of just conduct to have been placed by circumstances in a particular close community with some other persons and in consequence to incur a specific duty towards them. It is significant that the English common law appears to know only one such case, namely the case of assistance in danger on the high seas. [10] Modern legislation tends to go further and in some countries has imposed positive duties of action to preserve life where this is in the power of a particular person. [11] It may be that in the future there will be further developments in this direction; but they will probably remain limited because of the great difficulty of specifying by a general rule on whom such a duty rests. At present, at any rate, rules of just conduct which require positive action remain rare exceptions, confined to instances where accident has temporarily placed persons in a close community with others. We shall not go far wrong if for our purposes we treat all rules of just conduct as negative in character.

That they had to become so is a necessary effect of the process of extension of rules beyond the community which can share, or even know of, the same purposes. [12] Rules which are end-independent, in the sense that they are not confined to those following particular designated purposes, can also never fully determine a particular action but only limit the range of permitted kinds of action and leave the decision on the particular action to be taken by the actor in the light of his ends. We have seen already that this leads to the confinement of rules to prohibitions of actions towards others which are likely to harm them, and that this can be achieved only by rules which define a domain of the individuals (or organized groups) with which others are not allowed to interfere.

We have also seen that rules of conduct cannot simply prohibit all actions that cause harm to others. To buy or not to buy from, and to serve or not to serve, a particular person, is an essential part of our freedom; but if we decide not to buy from one or not to serve another, this may cause great harm if those affected have counted on our custom or our services; and in disposing of what is ours, a tree in our garden, or the façade of our house, we may deprive our neighbour of what to him has great sentimental value. Rules of just conduct cannot protect all interests, not even all interests which to somebody are of great importance, but only what are called 'legitimate' expectations, that is expectations which the rules define and which the rules of law may sometimes have created in the first instance.[13]

The chief function of rules of just conduct is thus to tell each what he can count upon, what material objects or services he can use for his purposes, and what is the range of actions open to him. They cannot, if they are to secure to all the same freedom of decision, give similar assurance of what others will do, unless these others have voluntarily and for their own purposes consented to act in a particular manner.

The rules of just conduct thus delimit protected domains not by directly assigning particular things to particular persons, but by making it possible to derive from ascertainable facts to whom particular things belong. Though this ought to have been made clear for all time by David Hume and Immanuel Kant,[14] whole books have been based on the erroneous assumption that 'the law confers on each person a wholly unique set of liberties with regard to the use of material goods and imposes on each person a unique set of restrictions with regard thereto. . . . In regard to acts which involve the use of those things I own, the law favours me above everyone else.'[15] Such an interpretation misses completely the aim of abstract rules of just conduct.

What rules of just conduct in fact do is to say under what

conditions this or that action will be within the range of the permissible; but they leave it to the individuals under these rules to create their own protected domain. Or, in legal terms, the rules do not confer rights on particular persons, but lay down the conditions under which such rights can be acquired. What will be the domain of each will depend partly on his actions and partly on facts beyond his control. The rules serve merely to enable each to deduce from facts which he can ascertain the boundaries of the protected domain which he and others have succeeded in cutting out for themselves.[16]

Since the consequences of applying rules of just conduct will always depend on factual circumstances which are not determined by these rules, we cannot measure the justice of the application of a rule by the result it will produce in a particular case. In this respect what has been correctly said of John Locke's view on the justice of competition, namely that 'it is the way in which competition is carried on, not its result, that counts',[17] is generally true of the liberal conception of justice, and of what justice can achieve in a spontaneous order. That it is possible for one through a single just transaction to gain much and for another through an equally just transaction to lose all,[18] in no way disproves the justice of these transactions. Justice is not concerned with those unintended consequences of a spontaneous order which have not been deliberately brought about by anybody.[19]

The rules of just conduct thus merely serve to prevent conflict and to facilitate co-operation by eliminating some sources of uncertainty. But since they aim at enabling each individual to act according to his own plans and decisions, they cannot wholly eliminate uncertainty. They can create certainty only to the extent that they protect means against the interference by others, and thus enable the individual to treat those means as being at his disposal. But they cannot assure him success in the use of these means, neither in so far as it depends only on material facts, nor in so far as it depends on the actions of others which he expects. They can, for instance, not assure him that he will be able at the expected price to sell what he has to offer or to buy what he wants.

Not only the rules of just conduct, but also the test of their justice, are negative

As in the extension of rules from the end-connected tribal society (or teleocracy) to the rule-connected open society (or nomocracy) these rules must progressively shed their dependence on concrete ends, and by passing this test become gradually abstract and negative, so the legislator who undertakes to lay down rules for a Great Society must subject to the test of universalization what he wants to apply to such a society. The conception of justice as we understand it, that is, the principle of treating all under the same rules, did only gradually emerge in the course of this process; it then became the guide in the progressive approach to an Open Society of free individuals equal before the law. To judge actions by rules, not by particular results, is the step which has made the Open Society possible. It is the device man has tumbled upon to overcome the ignorance of every individual of most of the particular facts which must determine the concrete order of a Great Society.

Justice is thus emphatically not a balancing of particular interests at stake in a concrete case, or even of the interests of determinable classes of persons, nor does it aim at bringing about a particular state of affairs which is regarded as just. It is not concerned with the results that a particular action will in fact bring about. The observation of a rule of just conduct will often have unintended consequences which, if they were deliberately brought about, would be regarded as unjust. And the preservation of a spontaneous order often requires changes which would be unjust if they were determined by human will.

It should perhaps be pointed out here that in a society of omniscient persons there would be no room for a conception of justice: every action would have to be judged as a means of bringing about known effects, and omniscience would presumably include knowledge of the relative importance of the different effects. Like all abstractions, justice is an adaptation to our ignorance—to our permanent ignorance of particular facts which no scientific advance can wholly remove. It is as much because we lack the knowledge of a common hierarchy of the importance of the particular ends of different individuals as because we lack the knowledge of particular facts, that the order of the Great Society must be brought about by the observance of abstract and end-independent rules.

The test which the rules of just conduct have passed in the process of their evolution to become general (and usually negative) is itself a negative test which makes necessary a gradual reformulation of these rules so as to eliminate all references to particular facts or effects that cannot be known to those who are to obey the

39

rules. Only those rules can pass this test which are end-independent and refer only to facts which those who are to obey them can know or readily ascertain.

Rules of just conduct are thus determined not by 'will' or 'interest', or any similar aim at particular results, but develop through a persistent effort (Ulpian's 'constans et perpetua voluntas') [20] to bring consistency into a system of rules inherited by each generation. The legislator who wishes deliberately to fit into the existing system new rules of the same sort as those that have made possible the Open Society, must subject these rules to such a negative test. Operating upon and within such a system, and faced with the task of improving the function of an existing order of actions, he will generally have little choice which rule to lay down.

The persistent application of the negative test of universalizability, or the necessity of commitment to the universal application of the rules laid down, and the endeavour to modify and supplement the existing rules so as to eliminate all conflict between them (or with yet unarticulated but generally acceptable principles of justice), may in the course of time bring about a complete transformation of the whole system. But while the negative test will assist us in selecting from, or modifying, a given body of rules, it will never provide us with a positive reason for the whole. It is irrelevant (and, of course, normally unknown) from which initial system of rules this evolution started; and it is quite possible that one kind of system of such rules is so much more effective than all others in producing a comprehensive order for a Great Society that, as a result of the advantages derived from all changes in the direction towards it, there may occur in systems with very different beginnings a process corresponding to what biologists call 'convergent evolution'. 'The necessities of human society' [21] may bring about an independent emergence, at many different times and places, of the same sort of system, such as that based on private property and contract. It would indeed seem that wherever a Great Society has arisen, it has been made possible by a system of rules of just conduct which included what David Hume called 'the three fundamental laws of nature, *that of stability of possession, of its transference by consent*, and *of the performance of promises*', [22] or, as a modern author sums up the essential content of all contemporary systems of private law, 'freedom of contract, the inviolability of property, and the duty to compensate another for damage due to his fault.' [23]

Those who are entrusted with the task of articulating, interpreting, and developing the existing body of rules of just conduct will thus always have to find answers to definite problems, and not to impose their unfettered will. They may originally have been chosen because they were believed to be most likely to formulate rules that would satisfy the general sense of justice and fit into the whole system of existing rules. Though the naive constructivist interpretation of the origin of social institutions tends to assume that the rules of law must be the product of somebody's will, this is in fact contrary to actual development and just as mythical as the origin of society from a social contract. Those who were trusted to formulate the rules were not given unlimited power to invent whatever rules they thought fit. They were chosen because they had shown skill in finding formulations which satisfied the rest and which proved workable. It is true that their success often placed them in a position which enabled them to keep the trust when they no longer deserved it, or to preserve their power without the trust. This does not alter the fact that they derived their authority from their presumed capacity to put into effect what was required by an accepted kind of order, and to discover what would be regarded as just. In short, theirs was an authority derived from their presumed capacity to find justice, not to create it.

The task of developing a system of law is thus an intellectual task of great difficulty which cannot be performed without taking certain rules as given and moving within the system determined by them. It is a task which can be performed more or less successfully, but which will not normally leave those entrusted with it free to follow their own will. It is more like the search for truth than to the construction of some new edifice. In the effort to disentangle and reconcile a complex of unarticulated rules and to transform it into a system of explicit rules, conflicts among what are accepted values will often be encountered. It will occasionally be necessary to reject some accepted rules in the light of more general principles. The guiding principle will always be that justice, i.e. the generally applicable rule, must prevail over the particular (though perhaps also generally felt) desire.

Though our sense of justice will generally provide the starting point, what it tells us about the particular case is not an infallible or ultimate test. It may be and can be proved to be wrong. Though the justification of our subjective feeling that some rule is just must be that we are prepared to commit ourselves to apply it universally, this does not exclude the possibility that we may later discover cases to which, if we had not committed ourselves, we should wish not to apply the rule, and where we discover that what we had thought to be quite just is in fact not so; in which event we may be forced to alter the rule for the future. Such a demonstration of a conflict between the intuitive feeling of justice and rules we wish also to preserve may often force us to review our opinion.

We shall later have to consider further the changes in the recognized rules which will be necessary for the preservation of the overall order if the rules of just conduct are to be the same for all. We shall then see that often effects which seem unjust to us may still be just in the sense that they are necessary consequences of the just actions of all concerned. In the abstract order in which we live and to which we owe most of the advantages of civilization, it must thus in the last resort be our intellect and not intuitive perception of what is good which must guide us. Our present moral views undoubtedly still contain layers or strata deriving from earlier phases of the evolution of human societies—the small horde to the organized tribe, the still larger groups of clans and the other successive steps towards the Great Society. And though some of the rules or opinions emerging in later stages may actually presuppose the continued acceptance of earlier ones, other new elements may be in conflict with some of those earlier origins which still persist.

The significance of the negative character of the test of injustice

The fact that, though we have no positive criteria of justice, we do have negative criteria which show us what is unjust, is very important in several respects. It means, in the first instance, that, though the striving to eliminate the unjust will not be a sufficient foundation for building up a wholly new system of law, it can be an adequate guide for developing an existing body of law with the aim of making it more just. In such an effort towards the development of a body of rules, most of which are accepted by the members of society, there will therefore also exist an 'objective' (in the sense of being inter-personally valid, but not of universal—because it will be valid only for those other members of the society who accept most of its other rules) test of what is unjust. Such a test of injustice may be sufficient to tell us in what direction we must develop an established system of law, though it would be insufficient to enable us to construct a wholly new system of law.

It should be mentioned here that it was solely in the sense of such a negative test, to be applied in the development of an established system of law, that in his philosophy of law Immanuel Kant employed the principle of the categorical imperative. This has often been overlooked because in his theory of morals he used the principle as if it were an adequate premise from which the whole system of moral rules could be deductively derived. So far as his philosophy of law is concerned, Kant was fully aware that the categorical imperative provided only a necessary but not a sufficient condition of justice, or only what we have called a negative test which enables us progressively to eliminate what is unjust, namely the test of universalizability. He also saw more clearly than most later philosophers of law that as a result of passing this test, 'juridical laws [must] abstract altogether from our ends, they are essentially negative and limiting principles which merely restrict our exercise of freedom.'[24]

It is significant that there exists a close parallel between this treatment of rules of justice as prohibitions and as subject to a negative test and the modern development in the philosophy of science, especially by Karl Popper,[25] which treats the laws of nature as prohibitions and regards as their test the failure of persistent efforts of falsification, a test which, in the last resort, also proves to be a test of internal consistency of the whole system. The positions in the two fields are analogous also in that we can always only endeavour to approach truth, or justice, by persistently eliminating the false or unjust, but can never be sure that we have achieved final truth or justice.

Indeed it would seem that as little as we can believe what we will, or hold to be true what we will, can we regard as just what we will. Though our desire that something should be regarded as just may long overrule our reason, there are necessities of thought against which such desire is powerless. While I may possibly convince myself by spurious reasoning that something I would wish to be just was really just, whether it is so clearly is not a matter of will but of reason. It will not merely be the contrary view of others which will prevent me from regarding as just what is in fact not so, nor some strong sentiment which the particular question at issue arouses in me, but the necessity of consistency without which thought would become impossible. This will drive me to test my belief in the justice of the particular act by the compatibility of the rule by which I judge it with all the other rules in which I also believe.

The contrary belief, that objective criteria of justice must be positive criteria, has historically been of great influence. Classical liberalism depended on a belief in objective justice. Legal positivism, however, did succeed in demonstrating that there are no positive criteria of justice; and it drew from this the false conclusion that there could be no objective criteria of justice whatsoever. Indeed legal positivism is largely the product of such a despair of finding any objective criteria of justice.[26] From the seeming impossibility of doing so it concluded that all questions of justice were solely a matter of will, or interests, or emotions. If this were true, the whole basis of classical liberalism would collapse.[27]

The positivist conclusion was, however, reached only through the tacit but erroneous assumption that objective criteria of justice must be positive criteria, i.e. premises from which the whole system of rules of just conduct could be logically deduced. But if we do not insist that the test of justice must enable us to build up a whole system of new rules of just conduct, but are content persistently to apply the negative test of injustice to the parts of an inherited system, the greater part of whose rules are universally accepted, we may accept the contention of positivism that there are no positive criteria of justice; yet we can still maintain that the further development of the rules of just conduct is not a matter of arbitrary will but of inner necessity, and that solutions to open problems of justice are discovered, not arbitrarily decreed. The fact that there are no positive criteria of justice does not leave unfettered will as the only alternative. We may still be bound by justice to develop the existing system in a particular way, and be able to demonstrate that we must alter particular rules in a certain way to eliminate injustice.

Legal positivism has become one of the main forces which have destroyed classical liberalism because the latter presupposes a conception of justice which is independent of the expediency for achieving particular results. Legal positivism, like the other forms of constructivists pragmatism of a William James[28] or John Dewey[29] or Vilfredo Pareto,[30] are therefore profoundly antiliberal in the original meaning of the word, though their views have become the foundations of that pseudo-liberalism which in the course of the last generation has arrogated the name.

The ideology of legal positivism

Since there exists some uncertainty about the precise meaning of the term 'legal positivism', and as the term is currently used in several different senses,[31] it will be useful to start the examination of this doctrine with a discussion of the original meaning of the term 'positive law'. We shall see that the suggestion contained in this term that only deliberately made law is real law still provides the essential core of the positivist doctrine on which all its other assertions depend.

As we have seen earlier,[32] the use of the term 'positive' with respect to law derives from the Latin rendering as *positus* (that is 'set down') or *positivus* of the Greek expression *thesei* which described that which was deliberate creation of a human will, in contrast to what had not been so invented but had arisen *physei*, by nature. We find this stress on the deliberate creation of all law by human will clearly at the beginning of the modern history of legal positivism, in Thomas Hobbes' 'non veritas sed auctoritas facit legem'[33] and his definition of law as 'the command of him that have the legislative power'.[34] It has rarely been expressed more crudely than by Jeremy Bentham, who maintained that 'the whole body of law . . . is distinguished into two branches—the arrangements of one of which are arrangements which have really been made— made by hands universally acknowledged as duly authorized, and competent to the making of such arrangements. . . . This branch of law may stand distinguished . . . by the name of *real* law, really existing law, legislator-made law; under the English Government it stands already distinguished by the name of *statute* law. . . . The arrangements supposed to be made by the other branch . . . may stand distinguished by the appellation of unreal, not really existing, imaginary, fictitious, spurious, judge-made law. Under the English Government the division is actually distinguished by the unexpressive, uncharacteristic, and inappropriate names of *common* law and *unwritten* law.'[35] It is from Bentham that John Austin derived his conception of 'all law being laid down by an intelligent being' and that 'there can be no law without a legislative act.'[36] This central contention of positivism is equally essential to its most highly developed modern form, the version of Hans Kelsen, which maintains that 'norms prescribing human behaviour can emanate only from human will, not from human reason.'[37]

So far as this is intended to assert that the *content* of all rules of law has been deliberately made by an act of will it is simply a naive expression of the constructivist fallacy and as such factually false. There is, however, a fundamental ambiguity in the contention

that the legislator 'determines' what is to be the law, an
ambiguity which assists the positivists to escape some conclusions
which would too evidently show the fictitious character of their
basic assumption.[38] The contention that the legislator determines
what is to be law may mean merely that he instructs the agents
which enforce the law how they have to proceed in order to find
what the law is. In a mature legal system, where there is a single
organization which has the monopoly of enforcing the law, the head
of this organization, (and that is today the legislator) must clearly
give such instructions to the agencies of the organization which he
has set up. But this does not necessarily imply that the legislator
determines the *content* of that law, or need even know what that
content is. The legislator may instruct the courts to maintain the
common law and have little idea what the content of that law is.
He may instruct the courts to enforce customary rules, native law,
or the observation of good faith or equity—all instances where the
content of the law that is to be enforced is certainly not created by
the legislator. It is an abuse of words to assert that in such instances
the law expresses the will of the legislator. If the legislator merely
tells the courts how to proceed in order to find out what the law is,
this by itself tells us nothing about how the content of this law is
determined. Positivists, however, seem to believe that when they
have established that the former is true in all mature legal systems,
they have shown that it is the will of the legislator which determines
the content of the law. From this conclusion follow almost all the
characteristic tenets of positivism.

It is evident that so far as legal rules of just conduct, and particularly the private law, are concerned, the assertion of legal positivism
that their content is always an expression of the will of the legislator
is simply false. This, of course, has been shown again and again by
the historians of private law and especially of the common law.[39]
It is necessarily true only of those rules of organization which
constitute the public law; and it is significant that nearly all the
leading modern legal positivists have been public lawyers and in
addition usually socialists—organization men, that is, who can
think of order only as organization, and on whom the whole
demonstration of the eighteenth century thinkers that rules of just
conduct can lead to the formation of a spontaneous order seems to
have been lost.

Positivism has for this reason tried to obliterate the distinction
between rules of just conduct and the rules of organization, and

has insisted that all that is currently termed law is of the same character, and, particularly, that the conception of justice has nothing to do with determining what the law is. From the insight that there are no positive criteria of justice they erroneously conclude that there can be no objective test of justice whatever (and, in addition, think of justice not as a matter of just conduct but as a problem of distributive justice); and that, as Gustav Radbruch revealingly expressed it, 'if nobody can ascertain what is just, somebody must determine what shall be legal.'[40]

After demonstrating without difficulty that the part of law in which they are chiefly interested, namely the law of the organization of government or the public law, has nothing to do with justice, they proceed to assert that this must be true of all that is commonly called law, including the law which serves the maintenance of a spontaneous order. Here they completely disregard the fact that the rules which are required to maintain an operating spontaneous order and the rules which govern an organization have altogether different functions. The existence of a private law appears to them, however, rather as an anomaly which is bound to disappear. To Radbruch it is explicitly a 'temporarily reserved and constantly diminishing sphere of free initiative within the all-comprehensive public law';[41] and to Hans Kelsen 'all genuine laws' are conditional orders to officials to apply sanctions.[42] Under the influence of the positivists we are in fact approaching such a state: theirs is becoming a sort of self-fulfilling prophecy.

The positivist insistence that all that as a result of a particular historical development is today *called* 'law' must have the same character, leads to the claim that the theorist must give the word a single definition which covers all the instances to which the word 'law' is applied, and that all that satisfies this definition must be accepted as law for all purposes. But after men have fought for centuries for what they regarded as an 'order of law', meaning thereby not any order enforced by authority but an order formed as a result of the individuals obeying universal rules of just conduct; after the term 'law' has for nearly as long determined the meaning of such political ideals as that of the Rule of Law, the *Rechtsstaat*, the Separation of Powers and the much older conception of law as the protection of individual freedom, and served in constitutional documents to limit the manner in which fundamental rights may be restricted; we cannot, if we are not to make nonsense of one of the determinants of Western civilization, like

47

Humpty Dumpty or Professor Glanville Williams,[43] insist that 'when I use a word it means just what I want it to mean,—neither more nor less!'[44] We must at least recognize that in certain contexts, including legal contexts, the word 'law' has a very specific meaning, different from that in which it is used in other contexts, and that what is called law in that specific sense may differ in origin, attributes, functions and possible content from some of the other statements also called 'law'.

Yet the definition of law as the product of the will of the legislator leads not only to the inclusion in 'law' of all the expressions of the will of the legislator, whatever its content ('Law may have any content whatever'[45]) but also to the view that content constitutes no significant distinction between different statements called law, and, in particular, that justice can in no sense be a determinant of what in fact is law but that it is rather the law which determines what is just. Contrary to the older tradition which had regarded justice as prior to law,[46] and at least certain parts of law as limited by conceptions of justice, the contention that the lawgiver was the creator of justice became the most characteristic tenet of legal positivism. From Thomas Hobbes' 'no law can be unjust'[47] to Hans Kelsen's 'just is only another word for legal or legitimate'[48] the efforts of the positivists have invariably been directed towards discrediting the conception of justice as a guide for determining what the law is.

The 'pure theory of law'

This central contention of legal positivism clearly implies the claim not merely that the legislator who sets up courts must indicate how these courts are to ascertain the law, but that the legislator creates the *content* of that law and in doing so has a completely free hand. In its most highly developed form, the 'pure theory of law' of Hans Kelsen, this result is made to appear plausible by a persistent but highly misleading use of words in an unusual special sense which evidently has become so habitual with the adherents of that school that they are no longer aware of it.

In the first instance, and most important, in order to serve the connection between 'law' and 'rule', Kelsen substitutes for 'rule' the term 'norm', and then, doing violence to language,[49] uses the latter term to include what he calls 'individual norms', i.e., every imperative and every ought-statement. In the second instance, he uses the term 'order' not for a factual state of affairs, but for the 'norms' prescribing a particular arrangement,[50] thus denying himself the insight that some, but only some, rules of conduct will in certain circumstances induce the formation of an order which for this reason must be distinguished from other rules.[51] Third, the term 'existence' is used of a norm as being synonymous with 'validity', and 'validity' is defined as being logically derivable from some act of will of the ultimate authority, or the 'basic norm'.[52] Fourth and finally, he uses the terms 'creating', 'setting' or 'positing' (*erzeugen* or *setzen*) to include everything that is 'constituted by human acts',[53] so that not only the products of human design but also such spontaneous growths as the rules of language or morals or etiquette must be regarded as 'set, that is, positive norms'.[54]

These last two usages produce together a *double* ambiguity. The assertion that a norm has arisen in a particular manner may not only mean *either* that the content of the rule has been formed in the particular way specified *or* that validity has been conferred in a particular manner on such an existing rule; it may also mean *either* that this content has been deliberately invented by a rational process, *or* that it is the 'result of human action but not of human design' (that is 'natural' in one of the senses in which the word has been used in the past).

It would exceed the scope of this book to examine the curious claim that the 'pure theory of law' is a 'normative science', or what this term means.[55] It is admittedly not an empirical science of fact and could claim at most to be a science in the sense in which logic or mathematics are sciences. What it in fact does is merely to elaborate the consequences of its definition of 'law', from which it follows that the 'existence' of a norm is the same as its 'validity', and that this validity is determined by its logical derivability from a hypothetical 'basic norm'—though the factual element of the 'efficacy' of the whole system of norms to which it belongs also enters in a manner never satisfactorily explained. This definition of the concept of law is postulated as the only possible and significant definition, and by representing as 'cognition' what are simply the consequences of the definition adopted, the 'pure theory' claims to be entitled to deny (or represent as meaningless) statements in which the term 'law' is used in a different and narrower sense. This is particularly true of the important assertion that no distinction can be drawn between a legal system in which the rule of law (or government under the law, or the *Rechtsstaat*) prevails and where this is not the case, and that therefore every legal order, even one where the powers of authority are wholly unlimited, is an instance of the rule of law.[56]

Conclusions drawn from a definition can never tell us anything about what is true of particular objects observable in the world of facts. The insistence that the term 'law' must be used only in that particular sense, and that no further distinctions between different kinds of law are relevant for a legal 'science' has, however, a definite purpose: this purpose is to discredit a certain conception which has for long guided legislation and the decisions of courts, and to whose influence we owe the growth of the spontaneous order of a free society. This is the conception that coercion is legitimate only if it is applied in the enforcement of universal rules of just conduct equally applicable to all citizens. The aim of legal positivism is to make coercion in the service of particular purposes or any special interests as legitimate as its use in preserving the foundations of a spontaneous order.

How little legal positivism in fact helps us to ascertain what is the law we see most clearly where this matters most, i.e. in the case of the judge who has to ascertain what rule he is to apply to a particular case. Whenever no specific prescription of the legislator tells him what to do (and often he is in effect told no more than that he ought to be just!), the fact that the authorization of the legislator confers on his decision 'the force of law' does not tell him what the law is which he ought to enforce. The judge is bound not merely by the designation by the legislator of some particular rules as valid, but by the internal requirements of a system which no one has deliberately designed as a whole, some parts of which may never yet have been articulated, and which, though tending to become consistent, is never in fact wholly so. There clearly does exist, independent of the will and even of the knowledge of the legislator, such a system of rules which is generally obeyed and to which the legislator often refers the judge. This is the wholly legitimate meaning of the contention that the judge may be bound by a law to which neither the legislator nor he himself has given its particular content, which thus exists independently of either, and which the judge may or may not be successful in finding, since it exists only implicitly in the whole system of rules and its relation to the factual order of actions. It is also clear that the judge may make a false decision which, though it may become valid (acquire 'the force of law'), will remain nevertheless in a meaningful sense contrary to the law. Evidently where a judicial decision has obtained the 'force of law' but is also 'contrary to the law', the term law is used in two different senses which must be distinguished but which are confused when the 'individual norm' set by the judge is treated as the same kind of thing as the rule which he infringes. For the judge the question whether a certain rule is valid cannot be answered by any logical derivation from the act which conferred upon him power to order enforcement of the rule, but only by reference of the implications of a system of rules which factually exists independently of either his will or that of a legislator.

The constant use, by Kelsen and his followers, of terms like 'creating' to describe a process by which validity is conferred upon rules and commands, even whole systems of rules which exist in the ordinary meaning of the word (i.e. are known and acted upon), and may have existed long before and independently of the legislator (and even be unknown to him), leads them constantly to assertions which do not follow from their premises. The fact that a system of rules on which a legislator confers validity may in its content not be a product of his design but may exist independently of his will, and that he neither contemplates, nor regards himself as capable of, replacing this existing system of recognized rules by a wholly new one, but accepts some of the established rules as beyond question, has an important consequence. It means that in many instances in which he would like to restate the law he will not be able to make whatever rules he likes, but will be bound by the requirements of the part of the system which is given to him. Or, to put this differently: *it will be the whole complex of rules which in fact are observed in a given society that will determine what particular rule it will be rational to enforce or which ought to be enforced.* Though those two sets of rules may in part be the same, yet the first set of rules may include some which need not be enforced because they are universally obeyed, while the second set of rules will contain some which would not voluntarily be obeyed but whose observance is important for the same reasons as the observance of the first, so that those who observe the first have good reasons for demanding that the second be also obeyed.

Of course, until validity is conferred upon such rules, they are according to the definition of the positivists not yet 'norms' or law, and do not 'exist' as legal norms. By this sleight of hand it is proved that they are 'created' by the arbitrary will of the legislator. But this assertion, which the unwary reader is apt to apply to the content of the rules, of which it would not be true, has been turned into a tautology which cannot be contradicted under the definitions adopted. It is nevertheless used to support such assertions as that the rules of positive law 'are derived from the arbitrary will of a human authority,'[57] that 'norms prescribing human behaviour can emanate only from human will, not from human reason',[58] or that ' "positive" law means a law created by acts of human beings which take place in time and space.'[59]

The constant use of such expressions produces the *suggestio falsi*, to which apparently their users themselves frequently succumb, that it always is and must be an act of unfettered human will which determines the content of the law. Yet the basic question of what rule ought to be enforced in a particular instance can often not be answered by logical derivation from some expression of will, nor decided by an act of will, but only by a process ratiocination which shows which is the rule whose application in the particular case satisfies the requirement of being capable of universalization without conflicting with other recognized rules. In short, the original assertion that all valid law is set law is made good by re-defining 'set' as 'made valid' and 'made valid' as 'in fact enforced by authority'. This is certainly not what was meant when it was originally asserted that all valid law must be 'posited'; nor does this definition of law relieve the judge of the necessity of deciding what the law is—it may even require him to refer in that effort to a 'natural law' to which the legislator has directed him and which consists of rules existing (in the ordinary sense of this word) independently of the will of the legislator. The existence of a recognized procedure by which it is determined what is to be accepted as just thus does not exclude that this procedure may depend for its conclusions on a prevailing conception of justice— even if for most problems likely to arise such references to general principles of justice are precluded by the prescription of a particular answer.

The insistence that the word 'law' must always be used and interpreted in the sense given to it by the legal positivists, and especially that the difference between the functions of the two kinds of rules actually laid down by legislatures are irrelevant for legal science, has thus a definite purpose. It is to remove all limitations on the power of the legislator that would result from the assumption that he is entitled to make law only in a sense which substantively limits the content of what he can make into law. It is, in other words, directed against the doctrine, most explicitly expounded by John Locke, that 'the legislative authority is an authority to act *in a particular* way . . . those who wield this authority should make only general rules.' [60]

Legal positivism is in this respect simply the ideology of socialism —if we may use the name of the most influential and respectable form of constructivism to stand for all its various forms—and of the omnipotence of the legislative power. It is an ideology born out of the desire to achieve complete control over the social order, and the belief that it is in our power to determine deliberately in any manner we like, every aspect of this social order.

In the case of the pure theory of law this ideological character becomes most apparent in the fervour with which it is used by its adherents to represent as invalid and ideologically inspired certain important conclusions which others have drawn concerning the significance of law. Law, in the specific sense in which this term has, constantly if not always consistently, been used since antiquity, has been understood by a long line of modern writers from Grotius through Locke, Hume and Bentham down to Emil Brunner, as being inseparable from private property and at the same time the indispensable condition of individual freedom. But while such understanding is true of those generic rules of just conduct which are necessary for the formation of a spontaneous order, it is of course not true of the specific commands which the direction of an organization requires. For those, on the other hand, who make the power of the legislator necessarily unlimited, individual freedom becomes a matter 'beyond salvation' [61] and freedom comes to mean exclusively the collective freedom of the community, i.e. democracy. [62] Legal positivism has thereby also become the chief ideological support of the unlimited powers of democracy.

But if the will of the majority is to be unlimited, it will of course be only the particular aims of that majority which can determine what is the law. 'Hence', as Kelsen maintains, 'from the point of view of rational cognition, there are only interests of human beings and hence conflicts of interests. The solution of these can be brought about either by satisfying one interest at the expense of the other, or by a compromise between the conflicting interests. It is not possible to prove that the one or the other solution is just.' [63]

The demonstration that there is no *positive* test of justice is here used to prove that there can be no objective test of justice whatever

53

which could be used to determine whether a rule of law is valid or not.[64] The possibility that there may exist a negative test which enables us to eliminate certain norms as unjust is not even considered.

Historically, however, it was the pursuit of justice that has created the system of generic rules which in turn became the foundation and preserver of the developing spontaneous order. To bring about such an order the ideal of justice need not determine the particular content of the rules which can be regarded as just (or at least not unjust). What is required is merely a negative test that enables us progressively to eliminate rules which prove to be unjust, because they are not universalizable within the system of other rules whose validity is not questioned. It is thus at least conceivable that several different systems of rules of just conduct may satisfy this test. The fact that there exist different ideas of what is just does not preclude the possibility that the negative test of injustice may be an objective test which several different but not all systems of such rules can satisfy. The pursuit of the ideal of justice (like the pursuit of the ideal of truth) does not presuppose that it is known what justice (or truth) is, but only that we know what we regard as unjust (or untrue). Absence of injustice is merely a necessary but not a sufficient determinant of appropriate rules. Whether, at least in a given state of knowledge of a certain physical environment, the persistent application of this negative test will, as we have suggested, produce a process of convergent evolution, so that only one such system will fully satisfy the test, must remain an open question.

The characterization of Kelsen's pure theory of law as an ideology is here not meant as a reproach, though its defenders are bound to regard it as such. Since every social order rests on an ideology, every statement of the criteria by which we can determine what is appropriate law in such an order must also be an ideology. The only reason why it is important to show that this is also true of the pure theory of law is that its author prides himself on being able to 'unmask' all other theories of law as ideologies[65] and to have provided the only theory which is not an ideology. This *Ideologiekritik* is even regarded by some of his disciples as one of Kelsen's greatest achievements.[66] Yet, since every cultural order can be maintained only by an ideology, Kelsen succeeds only in replacing one ideology with another that postulates that all orders maintained by force are orders of the same kind, deserving the description (and

54

dignity) of an order of law, the term which before was used to describe a particular kind of order valued because it secured individual freedom. Though within his system of thought his assertion is tautologically true, he has no right to assert, as he constantly does, that other statements in which, as he knows, [67] the term 'law' is used in a different sense, are not true. What 'law' is to mean we can ascertain only from what those who used the word in shaping our social order intended it to mean, not by attaching to it some meaning which covers all the uses ever made of it. Those men certainly did *not* mean by law, as Kelsen does, any 'social technique' which employs force, but used it in order to distinguish a particular 'social technique', a particular kind of restraint on the use of force, which by the designation of law they tried to distinguish from others. The use of enforceable generic rules in order to induce the formation of a self-maintaining order and the direction of an organization by command towards particular purposes are certainly not the same 'social techniques'. And if, because of accidental historical developments, the term 'law' has come to be used in connection with both these different techniques, it should certainly not be the aim of analysis to add to the confusion by insisting that these different uses of the word must be brought under the same definition.

The fact that man has undesignedly brought about the self-maintaining factual order of the social cosmos by pursuing an ideal which he called justice, and which did not specifically designate as just particular acts, but merely required him to discover such rules as could be consistently applied to all, and persistently to revise the system of traditional rules so as to eliminate all conflicts between the several rules that would emerge as the result of their generalization, means that this system can be understood, interpreted, improved, and even its particular content ascertained, only with reference to this ideal of justice. It is this ideal which men had in mind when they distinguished an order of law from arbitrary government, and which they therefore required their judges to observe.

It is only too true, as not only determined opponents of positivism such as Emil Brunner,[68] but in the end even life-long positivists like Gustav Radbruch [69] have recognized, that it was the prevalence of positivism which made the guardians of the law defenceless against the new advance of arbitrary government. After having been persuaded to accept a definition of law under which every state was a state of law, they had no choice but to act on the view which Kelsen approves retrospectively by maintaining that 'from the point of view of the science of law, the law (*Recht*) under the Nazi-government was law (*Recht*). We may regret it but we cannot deny that it was law.' [70] Yes—it was so regarded because law was so defined by the predominant positivist view.

It must be admitted that in this respect the Communists were at least more frank than socialists like Kelsen who, by insisting that their peculiar definition of law was the only legitimate one, surreptitiously derived what appeared to be statements of fact from what is merely a definition of law different from that presupposed by those whose statements they pretended to refute. The early theorists of communist law at least openly admitted that communism means 'the victory of socialism over any law' and the 'gradual extinction of law as such', because 'in a socialist community . . . all law is transformed into administration, all fixed rules into discretion and considerations of utility.' [71]

Law and morals

While we cannot attempt here to review the whole complex of problems concerning the relation of law and morals which have recently been much discussed, [72] a few points must be considered, in the first instance the connection of this issue with legal positivism. For as a result of the work of Professor H. L. A. Hart, which in most regards appears to me one of the most effective criticisms of legal positivism, this name is now often used to mean 'the simple contention that it is in no sense a necessary truth that laws reproduce or satisfy certain demands of morality'; and Professor Hart himself, who maintains this position, is for this reason represented as a positivist. [73] Yet in spite of my rejection of those theses of positivism which we have considered in the preceding section, I see no reason to reject the statement of Professor Hart quoted above if every term in it is carefully noted. Certainly many rules of law have no relation to moral rules, and others may unquestionably be valid law although they are in conflict with recognized moral rules. His statement also does not exclude the possibility that in some instances the judge may have to refer to the existing moral rules in order to find out what the law is: namely in such cases where the recognized rules of law either explicitly refer to such moral conceptions as 'good faith' etc., or tacitly presuppose the observance of certain other rules of conduct which in the past have not had to be enforced but which must be generally obeyed if the already articulated rules of law are to secure the order which they serve. The law of all countries is full of such references to prevailing moral convictions to which the judge can give content only on the basis of his knowledge of these moral beliefs.

A wholly different question is that of whether the existence of strongly and widely held moral convictions in any matter is by itself a justification for their enforcement. The answer seems to be that within a spontaneous order the use of coercion can be justified only where this is necessary to secure the private domain of the individual against interference by others, but that coercion should not be used to interfere in that private sphere where this is not necessary to protect others. Law serves a social order, i.e. the relations between individuals, and actions which affect nobody but the individuals who perform them ought not to be subject to the control of law, however strongly they may be regulated by custom and morals. The importance of this freedom of the individual within his protected domain, and everywhere where his actions do not conflict with the aims of the actions of others, rests mainly on the fact that the development of custom and morals is an experimental process, in a sense in which the enforcement of uniform rules of law cannot be—a process in which alternative rules compete and the more effective are selected by the success of the group obeying them, and may ultimately provide the model for appropriate legislation. This is not to say that the private conduct of individuals may not in some respects, especially in so far as it affects propagation, be very important for the future of the particular group to which they belong. Yet it must remain questionable whether membership in a community can entitle one to a legitimate interest in the prospects of propagation of other members of the same community, or whether this matter is not better regulated by the different fertility of the groups which will be the consequence of freedom.

Another question of some importance is that of how far prevailing moral standards limit not only the powers of the legislator but even the extent to which the application of recognized principles of the law can and should be carried. This is particularly significant in connection with the ideal underlying the Open Society that the same rules should be applied to all human beings. It is an ideal which I, for one, hope we shall continue gradually to approach because it seems to me the indispensable condition of a universal order of peace. Yet I greatly fear that the achievement of this ideal will be delayed rather than speeded up by all too impatient attempts to press for it. Such attempts to push a principle further than general sentiment is yet ready to support it is apt to produce a reaction which may make impossible for a considerable period even what more modest attempts might have achieved. While I look forward, as an ultimate ideal, to a state of affairs in which national boundaries have ceased to be obstacles to the free movement of men, I believe that within any period with which we can now be concerned, any attempt to realize it would lead to a revival of strong nationalist sentiments and a retreat from positions already achieved. However far modern man accepts in principle the ideal that the same rules should apply to all men, in fact he does concede it only to those whom he regards as similar to himself, and only slowly learns to extend the range of those he does accept as his likes. There is little legislation can do to speed up this process and much it may do to reverse it by re-awakening sentiments that are already on the wane.

The main point, however, which in conclusion should be stressed once more, is that the difference between moral and legal rules is not one between rules which have spontaneously grown and rules which have been deliberately made; for most of the rules of law also have not been deliberately made in the first instance. Rather, it is a distinction between rules to which the recognized procedure of enforcement by appointed authority ought to apply and those to which it should not, and therefore a distinction which would lose all meaning if all recognized rules of conduct, including all the rules which the community regards as moral rules, were to be enforced. But which rules ought to be enforced and are therefore to be regarded as law is determined not only by specific designation of some particular rules as enforceable by authority, but often follows from the interdependence of some groups of rules where the observation of every one of them is required for the achievement of what those already designated as enforceable serve: namely, the preservation of an ongoing overall order of actions. If such rules are enforced because they serve an order on whose existence everybody relies, this provides of course no justification for the enforcement of other recognized rules which do not in the same manner affect the existence of this interpersonal order of actions.

There may, in other words, exist a body of rules the regular observance of which produces a factual order of actions and some of which have already had legal validity conferred upon them by authority, while some may only in fact have been observed, or may only have been implicit in those already validated in the sense that the latter will achieve their purpose only if the former are observed. The validation of certain rules must therefore be deemed to authorize the judge to treat as also valid those which are implicit in them, although they have never before been confirmed specifically by the legislator or through an enforcement by a court.

The 'law of nature'

One of the chief sources of confusion in the field is that all theories which oppose legal positivism are alike labelled and lumped together under the misleading name of 'natural law', though some of them have nothing in common with each other except their opposition to legal positivism. This false dichotomy is now insisted upon mainly by the positivists, because their constructivist approach allows only that the law should be either the product of the design of a human or the product of the design of a super-human intelligence. [74] But, as we have seen, the term 'natural' was used earlier to assert that law was the product not of any rational design but of a process of evolution and natural selection, an unintended product whose function we can learn to understand, but whose present significance may be wholly different from the intention of its creators.

The position maintained in this book is therefore likely also to be represented by the positivists as a natural law theory. But though it is true that it develops an interpretation which in the past has been called 'natural' by some of its defenders, the term as currently used is so misleading that it ought to be avoided. True, even today the terms 'natural' and 'nature' are used in several quite different senses, but this is a further reason for avoiding them in scientific discussion. When we use 'nature' or 'natural' to describe the permanent order of the external or material world, and contrast this with what is supernatural or with what is artificial, we clearly mean something different from what we mean when we use it to say that something is part of the nature of an object. [75] While in the former sense cultural phenomena are clearly not natural, in the latter a particular cultural phenomenon may clearly be part of the nature of, or inseparable from, certain cultural structures.

Though there can be no justification for representing the rules of just conduct as natural in the sense that they are part of an external and eternal order of things, or permanently implanted in an unalterable nature of man, or even in the sense that man's mind is so fashioned once and for all that he must adopt those particular rules of conduct, it does not follow from this that the rules of conduct which in fact guide him must be the product of a deliberate choice on his part; or that he is capable of forming a society by adopting any rules he decides upon; or that these rules may not be given to him independent of any particular person's will and in this sense exist 'objectively'. It is sometimes held that only what is universally true can be regarded as an objective fact and that everything which is specific to a particular society can therefore not be regarded as such.[76] But this certainly does not follow from the ordinary meaning of the term 'objective'. The views and opinions which shape the order of a society, as well as the resulting order of that society itself, are not dependent on any one person's decision and will often not be alterable by any concrete act of will; and in this sense they must be regarded as an objectively existing fact. Those results of human action which are not brought about by human design may therefore well be objectively given to us.

The evolutionary approach to law (and all other social institutions) which is here defended has thus as little to do with the rationalist theories of natural law as with legal positivism. It rejects both the interpretation of law as the construct of a super-natural force and its interpretation as the deliberate construct of any human mind. It does not stand in any sense between legal positivism and most natural law theories, but differs from either in a dimension different from that in which they differ from each other.

We must again refrain here from examining the methodological objection which the adherents of the pure theory of law are likely to raise against this position, namely that it is not a juristic 'science of norms', but what they would describe as a sociology of law.[77] In brief the answer to this contention is that even in order to ascertain what in a given community is in fact the law, not only the scientist but also the judge requires a theory which does not logically derive the validity of law from some fictitious 'basic norm', but which explains the function of this law; because the law which he often will have to find may consist in some yet unarticulated rule which serves the same function as the unquestioningly accepted rules of law—namely to assist the constant re-formation of a factually existing spontaneous order.[78]

Law and sovereignty

There is little we need to add now to what has been said earlier (volume I, chapter IV, pp. 92–3) on the concept of sovereignty which plays such a central role in positivist legal theory. It is of interest here chiefly because its interpretation by positivism as the necessarily unlimited power of some supreme legislative authority has become one of the chief supports of the theory of popular sovereignty or the unlimited powers of a democratic legislature. For a positivist who defines law so as to make its substantive content dependent on an act of will of the legislator, this conception becomes indeed a logical necessity. If the term law is used in this sense, any legal limitation of the power of the supreme legislator is by definition excluded. But if the power of the legislator is not derived from some fictitious basic norm, but from a state of widespread opinion concerning the kind of rules he is authorized to lay down, his power might well be limited without the intervention of a higher authority capable of expressing explicit acts of will.

The logic of the positivist argument would be compelling only if its assertion that all law derives from the will of a legislator did not merely mean, as it does in the system of Kelsen, that its validity is derived from some act of deliberate will, but that its content is so derived. This, however, is factually often not the case. A legislator, in trying to maintain a going spontaneous order, cannot pick and choose any rules he likes to confer validity upon them, if he wants to achieve his aim. His power is not unlimited because it rests on the fact that some of the rules which he makes enforceable are regarded as right by the citizens, and the acceptance by him of these rules necessarily limits his powers of making other rules enforceable.

The concept of sovereignty, like that of the 'state', may be an indispensable tool for international law—though I am not sure that if we accept the concept there as our starting point, we do not thereby make the very idea of an international law meaningless. But for the consideration of the problem of the internal character of a legal order, both concepts seem to be as unnecessary as they are misleading. Indeed the whole history of constitutionalism, at least since John Locke, which is the same as the history of liberalism, is that of a struggle against the positivist conception of sovereignty and the allied conception of the omnipotent state.

NINE

'SOCIAL' OR DISTRIBUTIVE JUSTICE

So great is the uncertainty of merit, both from its natural
obscurity, and from the self-conceit of each individual, that no
determinate rule of conduct could ever follow from it.

David Hume*

Welfare, however, has no principle, neither for him who
receives it, nor for him who distributes it (one will place it here
and another there); because it depends on the material content
of the will, which is dependent upon particular facts and therefore incapable of a general rule.

Immanuel Kant*

The concept of 'social justice'

While in the preceding chapter I had to defend the conception of
justice as the indispensable foundation and limitation of all law, I
must now turn against an abuse of the word which threatens to
destroy the conception of law which made it the safeguard of
individual freedom. It is perhaps not surprising that men should
have applied to the joint effects of the actions of many people, even
where these were never foreseen or intended, the conception of
justice which they had developed with respect to the conduct of
individuals towards each other. 'Social' justice (or sometimes
'economic' justice) came to be regarded as an attribute which the
'actions' of society, or the 'treatment' of individuals and groups by
society, ought to possess. As primitive thinking usually does when
first noticing some regular processes, the results of the spontaneous
ordering of the market were interpreted as if some thinking being
deliberately directed them, or as if the particular benefits or harm
different persons derived from them were determined by deliberate
acts of will, and could therefore be guided by moral rules. This
conception of 'social' justice is thus a direct consequence of that
anthropomorphism or personification by which naive thinking tries

to account for all self-ordering processes. It is a sign of the imma-
turity of our minds that we have not yet outgrown these primitive
concepts and still demand from an impersonal process which
brings about a greater satisfaction of human desires than any
deliberate human organization could achieve, that it conform to the
moral precepts men have evolved for the guidance of their individual actions.[1]

The use of the term 'social justice' in this sense is of comparatively recent date, apparently not much older than a hundred years.
The expression was occasionally used earlier to describe the
organized efforts to enforce the rules of just individual conduct,[2]
and it is to the present day sometimes employed in learned discussion to evaluate the effects of the existing institutions of society.[3]
But the sense in which it is now generally used and constantly
appealed to in public discussion, and in which it will be examined
in this chapter, is essentially the same as that in which the expression 'distributive justice' had long been employed. It seems to have
become generally current in this sense at the time when (and
perhaps partly because) John Stuart Mill explicitly treated the two
terms as equivalent in such statements as that

> society should treat all equally well who have deserved equally
> well of it, that is, who have deserved equally well absolutely.
> This is the highest abstract standard of social and distributive
> justice; towards which all institutions, and the efforts of all
> virtuous citizens should be made in the utmost degree to
> converge[4]

or that

> it is universally considered just that each person should obtain
> that (whether good or evil) which he deserves; and unjust that
> he should obtain a good, or be made to undergo an evil, which
> he does not deserve. This is perhaps the clearest and most
> emphatic form in which the idea of justice is conceived by the
> general mind. As it involves the idea of desert, the question
> arises of what constitutes desert.[5]

It is significant that the first of these two passages occurs in the
description of one of five meanings of justice which Mill distinguishes, of which four refer to rules of just individual conduct
while this one defines a factual state of affairs which may but need

not have been brought about by deliberate human decision. Yet Mill appears to have been wholly unaware of the circumstance that in this meaning it refers to situations entirely different from those to which the four other meanings apply, or that this conception of 'social justice' leads straight to full-fledged socialism.

Such statements which explicitly connect 'social and distributive justice' with the 'treatment' by society of the individuals according to their 'deserts' bring out most clearly its difference from plain justice, and at the same time the cause of the vacuity of the concept: the demand for 'social justice' is addressed not to the individual but to society—yet society, in the strict sense in which it must be distinguished from the apparatus of government, is incapable of acting for a specific purpose, and the demand for 'social justice' therefore becomes a demand that the members of society should organize themselves in a manner which makes it possible to assign particular shares of the product of society to the different individuals or groups. The primary question then becomes whether there exists a moral duty to submit to a power which can co-ordinate the efforts of the members of society with the aim of achieving a particular pattern of distribution regarded as just.

If the existence of such a power is taken for granted, the question of how the available means for the satisfaction of needs ought to be shared out becomes indeed a question of justice—though not a question to which prevailing morals provide an answer. Even the assumption from which most of the modern theorists of 'social justice' start, namely that it would require equal shares for all in so far as special considerations do not demand a departure from this principle, would then appear to be justified. [6] But the prior question is whether it is moral that men be subjected to the powers of direction that would have to be exercised in order that the benefits derived by the individuals could be meaningfully described as just or unjust.

It has of course to be admitted that the manner in which the benefits and burdens are apportioned by the market mechanism would in many instances have to be regarded as very unjust *if* it were the result of a deliberate allocation to particular people. But this is not the case. Those shares are the outcome of a process the effect of which on particular people was neither intended nor foreseen by anyone when the institutions first appeared—institutions which were then permitted to continue because it was found that they improve for all or most the prospects of having their needs

64

satisfied. To demand justice from such a process is clearly absurd, and to single out some people in such a society as entitled to a particular share evidently unjust.

The conquest of public imagination by 'social justice'

The appeal to 'social justice' has nevertheless by now become the most widely used and most effective argument in political discussion. Almost every claim for government action on behalf of particular groups is advanced in its name, and if it can be made to appear that a certain measure is demanded by 'social justice', opposition to it will rapidly weaken. People may dispute whether or not the particular measure is required by 'social justice'. But that this is the standard which ought to guide political action, and that the expression has a definite meaning, is hardly ever questioned. In consequence, there are today probably no political movements or politicians who do not readily appeal to 'social justice' in support of the particular measures which they advocate.

It also can scarcely be denied that the demand for 'social justice' has already in a great measure transformed the social order and is continuing to transform it in a direction which those who called for it never foresaw. Though the phrase has undoubtedly helped occasionally to make the law more equal for all, whether the demand for justice in distribution has in any sense made society juster or reduced discontent must remain doubtful.

The expression of course described from the beginning the aspirations which were at the heart of socialism. Although classical socialism has usually been defined by its demand for the socialization of the means of production, this was for it chiefly a means thought to be essential in order to bring about a 'just' distribution of wealth; and since socialists have later discovered that this redistribution could in a great measure, and against less resistance, be brought about by taxation (and government services financed by it), and have in practice often shelved their earlier demands, the realization of 'social justice' has become their chief promise. It might indeed be said that the main difference between the order of society at which classical liberalism aimed and the sort of society into which it is now being transformed is that the former was governed by principles of just individual conduct while the new society is to satisfy the demands for 'social justice'—or, in other words, that the former demanded just action by the individuals while the latter more and more places the duty of justice on authorities with power to command people what to do.

The phrase could exercise this effect because it has gradually been taken over from the socialist not only by all the other political movements but also by most teachers and preachers of morality. It seems in particular to have been embraced by a large section of the clergy of all Christian denominations, who, while increasingly losing their faith in a supernatural revelation, appear to have sought a refuge and consolation in a new 'social' religion which substitutes a temporal for a celestial promise of justice, and who hope that they can thus continue their striving to do good. The Roman Catholic church especially has made the aim of 'social justice' part of its official doctrine;[7] but the ministers of most Christian denominations appear to vie with each other with such offers of more mundane aims—which also seem to provide the chief foundation for renewed ecumenical efforts.

The various modern authoritarian or dictatorial governments have of course no less proclaimed 'social justice' as their chief aim. We have it on the authority of Mr Andrei Sakharov that millions of men in Russia are the victims of a terror that 'attempts to conceal itself behind the slogan of social justice'.

The commitment to 'social justice' has in fact become the chief outlet for moral emotion, the distinguishing attribute of the good man, and the recognized sign of the possession of a moral conscience. Though people may occasionally be perplexed to say which of the conflicting claims advanced in its name are valid, scarcely anyone doubts that the expression has a definite meaning, describes a high ideal, and points to grave defects of the existing social order which urgently call for correction. Even though until recently one would have vainly sought in the extensive literature for an intelligible definition of the term,[8] there still seems to exist little doubt, either among ordinary people or among the learned, that the expression has a definite and well understood sense.

But the near-universal acceptance of a belief does not prove that it is valid or even meaningful any more than the general belief in witches or ghosts proved the validity of these concepts. What we have to deal with in the case of 'social justice' is simply a quasi-religious superstition of the kind which we should respectfully leave in peace so long as it merely makes those happy who hold it, but which we must fight when it becomes the pretext of coercing other men. And the prevailing belief in 'social justice' is at present probably the gravest threat to most other values of a free civilization.

Whether Edward Gibbon was wrong or not, there can be no doubt that moral and religious beliefs can destroy a civilization and that, where such doctrines prevail, not only the most cherished beliefs but also the most revered moral leaders, sometimes saintly figures whose unselfishness is beyond question, may become grave dangers to the values which the same people regard as unshakeable. Against this threat we can protect ourselves only by subjecting even our dearest dreams of a better world to ruthless rational dissection.

It seems to be widely believed that 'social justice' is just a new moral value which we must add to those that were recognized in the past, and that it can be fitted within the existing framework of moral rules. What is not sufficiently recognized is that in order to give this phrase meaning a complete change of the whole character of the social order will have to be effected, and that some of the values which used to govern it will have to be sacrificed. It is such a transformation of society into one of a fundamentally different type which is currently occurring piecemeal and without awareness of the outcome to which it must lead. It was in the belief that something like 'social justice' could thereby be achieved, that people have placed in the hands of government powers which it can now not refuse to employ in order to satisfy the claims of the ever increasing number of special interests who have learnt to employ the open sesame of 'social justice'.

I believe that 'social justice' will ultimately be recognized as a will-o'-the-wisp which has lured men to abandon many of the values which in the past have inspired the development of civilization—an attempt to satisfy a craving inherited from the traditions of the small group but which is meaningless in the Great Society of free men. Unfortunately, this vague desire which has become one of the strongest bonds spurring people of good will to action, not only is bound to be disappointed. This would be sad enough. But, like most attempts to pursue an unattainable goal, the striving for it will also produce highly undesirable consequences, and in particular lead to the destruction of the indispensible environment in which the traditional moral values alone can flourish, namely personal freedom.

*The inapplicability of the concept of justice to the results of a
spontaneous process*

It is now necessary clearly to distinguish between two wholly different problems which the demand for 'social justice' raises in a market order.

The first is whether within an economic order based on the market the concept of 'social justice' has any meaning or content whatever.

The second is whether it is possible to preserve a market order while imposing upon it (in the name of 'social justice' or any other pretext) some pattern of remuneration based on the assessment of the performance or the needs of different individuals or groups by an authority possessing the power to enforce it.

The answer to each of these questions is a clear no.

Yet it is the general belief in the validity of the concept of 'social justice' which drives all contemporary societies into greater and greater efforts of the second kind and which has a peculiar self-accelerating tendency: the more dependent the position of the individuals or groups is seen to become on the actions of government, the more they will insist that the governments aim at some recognizable scheme of distributive justice; and the more governments try to realize some preconceived pattern of desirable distribution, the more they must subject the position of the different individuals and groups to their control. So long as the belief in 'social justice' governs political action, this process must progressively approach nearer and nearer to a totalitarian system.

We shall at first concentrate on the problem of the meaning, or rather lack of meaning, of the term 'social justice', and only later consider the effects which the efforts to impose *any* preconceived pattern of distribution must have on the structure of the society subjected to them.

The contention that in a society of free men (as distinct from any compulsory organization) the concept of social justice is strictly empty and meaningless will probably appear as quite unbelievable to most people. Are we not all constantly disquieted by watching how unjustly life treats different people and by seeing the deserving suffer and the unworthy prosper? And do we not all have a sense of fitness, and watch it with satisfaction, when we recognize a reward to be appropriate to effort or sacrifice?

The first insight which should shake this certainty is that we experience the same feelings also with respect to differences in human fates for which clearly no human agency is responsible and which it would therefore clearly be absurd to call injustice. Yet we do cry out against the injustice when a succession of calamities befalls one family while another steadily prospers, when a meritorious effort is frustrated by some unforeseeable accident, and particularly if of many people whose endeavours seem equally great, some succeed brilliantly while others utterly fail. It is certainly tragic to see the failure of the most meritorious efforts of parents to bring up their children, of young men to build a career, or of an explorer or scientist pursuing a brilliant idea. And we will protest against such a fate although we do not know anyone who is to blame for it, or any way in which such disappointments can be prevented.

It is no different with regard to the general feeling of injustice about the distribution of material goods in a society of free men. Though we are in this case less ready to admit it, our complaints about the outcome of the market as unjust do not really assert that somebody has been unjust; and there is no answer to the question of *who* has been unjust. Society has simply become the new deity to which we complain and clamour for redress if it does not fulfil the expectations it has created. There is no individual and no co-operating group of people against which the sufferer would have a just complaint, and there are no conceivable rules of just individual conduct which would at the same time secure a functioning order and prevent such disappointments.

The only blame implicit in those complaints is that we tolerate a system in which each is allowed to choose his occupation and therefore nobody can have the power and the duty to see that the results correspond to our wishes. For in such a system in which each is allowed to use his knowledge for his own purposes[9] the concept of 'social justice' is necessarily empty and meaningless, because in it nobody's will can determine the relative incomes of the different people, or prevent that they be partly dependent on accident. 'Social justice' can be given a meaning only in a directed or 'command' economy (such as an army) in which the individuals are ordered what to do; and any particular conception of 'social justice' could be realized only in such a centrally directed system. It presupposes that people are guided by specific directions and not by rules of just individual conduct. Indeed, no system of rules of just individual conduct, and therefore no free action of the individuals, could produce results satisfying any principle of distributive justice.

We are of course not wrong in perceiving that the effects of the processes of a free society on the fates of the different individuals are not distributed according to some recognizable principle of justice. Where we go wrong is in concluding from this that they are unjust and that somebody is to be blamed for this. In a free society in which the position of the different individuals and groups is not the result of anybody's design—or could, within such a society, be altered in accordance with a generally applicable principle—the differences in reward simply cannot meaningfully be described as just or unjust. There are, no doubt, many kinds of individual action which are aimed at affecting particular remunerations and which might be called just or unjust. But there are no principles of individual conduct which would produce a pattern of distribution which as such could be called just, and therefore also no possibility for the individual to know what he would have to do to secure a just remuneration of his fellows.

The rationale of the economic game in which only the conduct of the players but not the result can be just

We have seen earlier that justice is an attribute of human conduct which we have learnt to exact because a certain kind of conduct is required to secure the formation and maintenance of a beneficial order of actions. The attribute of justice may thus be predicated about the intended results of human action but not about circumstances which have not deliberately been brought about by men. Justice requires that in the 'treatment' of another person or persons, i.e. in the intentional actions affecting the well-being of other persons, certain uniform rules of conduct be observed. It clearly has no application to the manner in which the impersonal process of the market allocates command over goods and services to particular people: this can be neither just nor unjust, because the results are not intended or foreseen, and depend on a multitude of circumstances not known in their totality to anybody. The conduct of the individuals in that process may well be just or unjust; but since their wholly just actions will have consequences for others which were neither intended nor foreseen, these effects do not thereby become just or unjust.

The fact is simply that we consent to retain, and agree to enforce, uniform rules for a procedure which has greatly improved the chances of all to have their wants satisfied, but at the price of all individuals and groups incurring the risk of unmerited failure. With the acceptance of this procedure the recompense of different groups and individuals becomes exempt from deliberate control. It is the only procedure yet discovered in which information widely dispersed among millions of men can be effectively utilized for the benefit of all—and used by assuring to all an individual liberty desirable for itself on ethical grounds. It is a procedure which of course has never been 'designed' but which we have learnt gradually to improve after we had discovered how it increased the efficiency of men in the groups who had evolved it.

It is a procedure which, as Adam Smith (and apparently before him the ancient Stoics) understood,[10] in all important respects (except that normally it is not pursued solely as a diversion) is wholly analogous to a game, namely a game partly of skill and partly of chance. We shall later describe it as the game of catallaxy. It proceeds, like all games, according to rules guiding the actions of individual participants whose aims, skills, and knowledge are different, with the consequence that the outcome will be unpredictable and that there will regularly be winners and losers. And while, as in a game, we are right in insisting that it be fair and that nobody cheat, it would be nonsensical to demand that the results for the different players be just. They will of necessity be determined partly by skill and partly by luck. Some of the circumstances which make the services of a person more or less valuable to his fellows, or which may make it desirable that he change the direction of his efforts, are not of human design or foreseeable by men.

We shall in the next chapter have to return to the rationale of the discovery procedure which the game of competition in a market in effect constitutes. Here we must content ourselves with emphasizing that the results for the different individuals and groups of a procedure for utilizing more information than any one person or agency can possess, must themselves be unpredictable, and must often be different from the hopes and intentions which determined the direction and intensity of their striving; and that we can make effective use of that dispersed knowledge only if (as Adam Smith was also one of the first to see clearly)[11] we allow the principle of negative feedback to operate, which means that some must suffer unmerited disappointment.

We shall also see later that the importance for the functioning of the market order of particular prices or wages, and therefore of the incomes of the different groups and individuals, is not due chiefly to the effects of the prices on all of those who receive them, but to the effects of the prices on those for whom they act as signals to change the direction of their efforts. Their function is not so much to reward people for what they *have* done as to tell them what in their own as well as in general interest they *ought* to do. We shall then also see that, to hold out a sufficient incentive for those movements which are required to maintain a market order, it will often be necessary that the return of people's efforts do *not* correspond to recognizable merit, but should show that, in spite of the best efforts of which they were capable, and for reasons they could not have known, their efforts were either more or less successful than they had reason to expect. In a spontaneous order the question of whether or not someone has done the 'right' thing cannot always be a matter of merit, but must be determined independently of whether the persons concerned ought or could have known what was required.

The long and the short of it all is that men can be allowed to decide what work to do only if the remuneration they can expect to get for it corresponds to the value their services have to those of their fellows who receive them; and that *these values which their services will have to their fellows will often have no relations to their individual merits or needs.* Reward for merit earned and indication of what a person should do, both in his own and in his fellows' interest, are different things. It is not good intentions or needs but doing what in fact most benefits others, irrespective of motive, which will secure the best reward. Among those who try to climb Mount Everest or to reach the Moon, we also honour not those who made the greatest efforts, but those who got there first.

The general failure to see that in this connection we cannot meaningfully speak of the justice or injustice of the results is partly due to the misleading use of the term 'distribution' which inevitably suggests a personal distributing agent whose will or choice determines the relative position of the different persons or groups.[12] There is of course no such agent, and we use an impersonal process to determine the allocation of benefits precisely because through its operation we can bring about a structure of relative prices and remunerations that will determine a size and composition of the total output which assures that the real equivalent of each individual's share that accident or skill assigns to him will be as large as we know to make it.

It would serve little purpose to enquire here at greater length into the relative importance of skill and luck in actually determining relative incomes. This will clearly differ a great deal between different trades, localities and times, and in particular between highly

competitive and less enterprising societies. I am on the whole inclined to believe that within any one trade or profession the correspondence between individual ability and industry is higher than
is commonly admitted, but that the relative position of all the
members of a particular trade or profession compared with others
will more often be affected by circumstances beyond their control
and knowledge. (This may also be one reason why what is called
'social' injustice is generally regarded as a graver fault of the existing order than the corresponding misfortunes of individuals.)[13] But
the decisive point is not that the price mechanism does on the
whole bring it about that rewards are proportioned to skill and
effort, but that even where it is clear to us that luck plays a great
part, and we have no idea why some are regularly luckier in guess-
ing than others, it is still in the general interest to proceed on the
presumption that the past success of some people in picking winners makes it probable that they will also do so in the future, and
that it is therefore worthwhile to induce them to continue their
attempts.

The alleged necessity of a belief in the justice of rewards

It has been argued persuasively that people will tolerate major inequalities of the material positions only if they believe that the
different individuals get on the whole what they deserve, that they
did in fact support the market order only because (and so long as)
they thought that the differences of remuneration corresponded
roughly to differences of merit, and that in consequence the maintenance of a free society presupposes the belief that some sort of
'social justice' is being done.[14] The market order, however, does
not in fact owe its origin to such beliefs, nor was originally justified
in this manner. This order could develop, after its earlier beginnings had decayed during the middle ages and to some extent been
destroyed by the restrictions imposed by authority, when a thous-
and years of vain efforts to discover substantively just prices or
wages were abandoned and the late schoolmen recognized them to
be empty formulae and taught instead that the prices determined
by just conduct of the parties in the market, i.e. the competitive
prices arrived at without fraud, monopoly and violence, was all that
justice required.[15] It was from this tradition that John Locke and
his contemporaries derived the classical liberal conception of justice
for which, as has been rightly said, it was only 'the way in which

competition was carried on, not its results',[16] that could be just or unjust.

It is unquestionably true that, particularly among those who were very successful in the market order, a belief in a much stronger moral justification of individual success developed, and that, long after the basic principles of such an order had been fully elaborated and approved by catholic moral philosophers, it had in the Anglo–Saxon world received strong support from Calvinist teaching. It certainly is important in the market order (or free enterprise society, misleadingly called 'capitalism') that the individuals believe that their well-being depends primarily on their own efforts and decisions. Indeed, few circumstances will do more to make a person energetic and efficient than the belief that it depends chiefly on him whether he will reach the goals he has set himself. For this reason this belief is often encouraged by education and governing opinion —it seems to me, generally much to the benefit of most of the members of the society in which it prevails, who will owe many important material and moral improvements to persons guided by it. But it leads no doubt also to an exaggerated confidence in the truth of this generalization which to those who regard themselves (and perhaps are) equally able but have failed must appear as a bitter irony and severe provocation.

It is probably a misfortune that, especially in the USA, popular writers like Samuel Smiles and Horatio Alger, and later the sociologist W. G. Sumner, have defended free enterprise on the ground that it regularly rewards the deserving, and it bodes ill for the future of the market order that this seems to have become the only defence of it which is understood by the general public. That it has largely become the basis of the self-esteem of the businessman often gives him an air of self-righteousness which does not make him more popular.

It is therefore a real dilemma to what extent we ought to encourage in the young the belief that when they really try they will succeed, or should rather emphasize that inevitably some unworthy will succeed and some worthy fail—whether we ought to allow the views of those groups to prevail with whom the over-confidence in the appropriate reward of the able and industrious is strong and who in consequence will do much that benefits the rest, and whether without such partly erroneous beliefs the large numbers will tolerate actual differences in rewards which will be based only partly on achievement and partly on mere chance.

There is no 'value to society'

The futile medieval search for the just price and just wage, finally abandoned when it was recognized that only that 'natural' price could be regarded as just which would be arrived at in a competitive market where it would be determined not by any human laws or decrees but would depend on so many circumstances that it could be known beforehand only by God,[17] was not the end of the search for that philosophers' stone. It was revived in modern times, not only by the general demand for 'social justice', but also by the long and equally abortive efforts to discover criteria of justice in connection with the procedures for reconciliation or arbitration in wage disputes. Nearly a century of endeavours by public spirited men and women in many parts of the world to discover principles by which just wage rates could be determined have, as more and more of them acknowledge, produced not a single rule which would do this.[18] It is somewhat surprising in view of this when we find an experienced arbitrator like Lady Wootton, after admitting that arbitrators are 'engaged in the impossible task of attempting to do justice in an ethical vacuum', because 'nobody knows in this context what justice is', drawing from it the conclusion that the criteria should be determined by legislation, and explicitly demand a political determination of all wages and incomes.[19] One can hardly carry any further the illusion that Parliament can determine what is just, and I don't suppose the writer would really wish to defend the atrocious principle implied that all rewards should be determined by political power.

Another source of the conception that the categories of just and unjust can be meaningfully applied to the remunerations determined by the market is the idea that the different services have a determined and ascertainable 'value to society', and that the actual remuneration frequently differs from the value. But though the conception of a 'value to society' is sometimes carelessly used even by economists, there is strictly no such thing and the expression implies the same sort of anthropomorphism or personification of society as the term 'social justice'. Services can have value only to particular people (or an organization), and any particular service will have very different values for different members of the same society. To regard them differently is to treat society not as a spontaneous order of free men but as an organization whose members are all made to serve a single hierarchy of ends. This would

75

necessarily be a totalitarian system in which personal freedom would be absent.

Although it is tempting to speak of a 'value to society' instead of a man's value to his fellows, it is in fact highly misleading if we say, e.g., that a man who supplies matches to millions and thereby earns $200,000 a year is worth more 'to society' than a man who supplies great wisdom or exquisite pleasure to a few thousand and thereby earns $20,000 a year. Even the performance of a Beethoven sonata, a painting by Leonardo or a play by Shakespeare have no 'value to society' but a value only to those who know and appreciate them. And it has little meaning to assert that a boxer or a crooner is worth more to society than a violin virtuoso or a ballet dancer if the former renders services to millions and the latter to a much smaller group. The point is not that the true values are different, but that the values attached to the different services by different groups of people are incommensurable; all that these expressions mean is merely that one in fact receives a larger aggregate sum from a larger number of people than the other.[20]

Incomes earned in the market by different persons will normally not correspond to the relative values of their services to any one person. Although, in so far as any one of a given group of different commodities is consumed by any one person, he or she will buy so much of each that the relative values to them of the last units bought will correspond to their relative prices, many pairs of commodities will never be consumed by the same person: the relative price of articles consumed only by men and of articles consumed only by women will not correspond to the relative values of these articles to anybody.

The remunerations which the individuals and groups receive in the market are thus determined by what these services are worth to those who receive them (or, strictly speaking, to the last pressing demand for them which can still be satisfied by the available supply) and not by some fictitious 'value to society'.

Another source of the complaint about the alleged injustice of this principle of remuneration is that the remuneration thus determined will often be much higher than would be necessary to induce the recipient to render those services. This is perfectly true but necessary if all who render the same service are to receive the same remuneration, if the kind of service in question is to be increased so long as the price still exceeds costs, and if anyone who wishes to buy or sell it at the current price is to be able to do so.

The consequence must be that all but the marginal sellers make a gain in excess of what was necessary to induce them to render the services in question—just as all but the marginal buyers will get what they buy for less than they were prepared to pay. The remuneration of the market will therefore hardly ever seem just in the sense in which somebody might endeavour justly to compensate others for the efforts and sacrifice incurred for his benefit.

The consideration of the different attitudes which different groups will take to the remuneration of different services incidentally also shows that the large numbers by no means grudge all the incomes higher than theirs, but generally only those earned by activities the functions of which they do not understand or which they even regard as harmful. I have never known ordinary people grudge the very high earnings of the boxer or torero, the football idol or the cinema star or the jazz king—they seem often even to revel vicariously in the display of extreme luxury and waste of such figures compared with which those of industrial magnates or financial tycoons pale. It is where most people do not comprehend the usefulness of an activity, and frequently because they erroneously regard it as harmful (the 'speculator'—often combined with the belief that only dishonest activities can bring so much money), and especially where the large earnings are used to accumulate a fortune (again out of the erroneous belief that it would be desirable that it should be spent rather than invested) that the outcry about the injustice of it arises. Yet the complex structure of the modern Great Society would clearly not work if the remunerations of all the different activities were determined by the opinion which the majority holds of their value—or indeed if they were dependent on any one person's understanding or knowledge of the importance of all the different activities required for the functioning of the system.

The main point is not that the masses have in most instances no idea of the values which a man's activities have to his fellows, and that it is necessarily their prejudices which would determine the use of the government's power. It is that nobody knows except in so far as the market tells him. It is true enough that our esteem of particular activities often differs from the value given to them by the market; and we express this feeling by an outcry about the injustice of it. But when we ask what ought to be the relative remunerations of a nurse and a butcher, of a coal miner and a judge at a high court, of the deep sea diver or the cleaner of sewers, of the organizer of a new industry and a jockey, of the inspector of taxes and the inventor of a life-saving drug, of the jet pilot or the professor of mathematics, the appeal to 'social justice' does not give us the slightest help in deciding—and if we use it it is no more than an insinuation that the others ought to agree with our view without giving any reason for it.

It might be objected that, although we cannot give the term 'social justice' a precise meaning, this need not be a fatal objection because the position may be similar to that which I have earlier contended exists with regard to justice proper: we might not know what is 'socially just' yet know quite well what is 'socially unjust'; and by persistently eliminating 'social injustice' whenever we encounter it, gradually approach 'social justice'. This, however, does not provide a way out of the basic difficulty. There can be no test by which we can discover what is 'socially unjust' because there is no subject by which such an injustice can be committed, and there are no rules of individual conduct the observance of which in the market order would secure to the individuals and groups the position which as such (as distinguished from the procedure by which it is determined) would appear just to us.[21] It does not belong to the category of error but to that of nonsense, like the term 'a moral stone'.

The meaning of 'social'

One might hope to get some help in the search for the meaning of 'social justice' by examining the meaning of the attribute 'social'; but the attempt to do so soon leads into a quagmire of confusion nearly as bad as that which surrounds 'social justice' itself.[22] Originally 'social' had of course a clear meaning (analogous to formations like 'national', 'tribal', or 'organizational'), namely that of pertaining to, or characteristic of the structure and operations of society. In this sense justice clearly is a social phenomenon and the addition of 'social' to the noun a pleonasm[23] such as if we spoke of 'social language'—though in occasional early uses it might have been intended to distinguish the generally prevailing views of justice from that held by particular persons or groups.

But 'social justice' as used today is not 'social' in the sense of 'social norms', i.e. something which has developed as a practice of individual action in the course of social evolution, not a product of society or of a social process, but a conception to be imposed upon society. It was the reference of 'social' to the whole of society, or to the interests of all its members, which led to its gradually acquiring a predominant meaning of moral approbation. When it came into general use during the third quarter of the last century it was meant to convey an appeal to the still ruling classes to concern themselves more with the welfare of the much more numerous poor whose interests had not received adequate consideration.[24] The 'social question' was posed as an appeal to the conscience of the upper classes to recognize their responsibility for the welfare of the neglected sections of society whose voices had till then carried little weight in the councils of government. 'Social policy' (or *Social-politik* in the language of the country then leading in the movement) became the order of the day, the chief concern of all progressive and good people, and 'social' came increasingly to displace such terms as 'ethical' or simply 'good'.

But from such an appeal to the conscience of the public to concern themselves with the unfortunate ones and recognize them as members of the same society, the conception gradually came to mean that 'society' ought to hold itself responsible for the particular material position of all its members, and for assuring that each received what was 'due' to him. It implied that the processes of society should be deliberately directed to particular results and, by personifying society, represented it as a subject endowed with a conscious mind, capable of being guided in its operation by moral principles.[25] 'Social' became more and more the description of the pre-eminent virtue, the attribute in which the good man excelled and the ideal by which communal action was to be guided.

But while this development indefinitely extended the field of application of the term 'social', it did not give it the required new meaning. It even so much deprived it of its original descriptive meaning that American sociologists have found it necessary to coin the new term 'societal' in its place. Indeed, it has produced a situation in which 'social' can be used to describe almost any action as publicly desirable and has at the same time the effect of depriving any terms with which it is combined of clear meaning. Not only 'social justice' but also 'social democracy', 'social market economy'[26] or the 'social state of law' (or rule of law—in German *sozialer Rechtsstaat*) are expressions which, though justice, democracy, the market economy or the *Rechtsstaat* have by themselves perfectly good meanings, the addition of the adjective 'social' makes them capable of meaning almost anything one likes. The word has indeed become one of the chief sources of confusion of political discourse and can probably no longer be reclaimed for a useful purpose.

There is apparently no end to the violence that will be done to language to further some ideal and the example of 'social justice' has recently given rise to the expression 'global justice'! Its negative, 'global injustice', was defined by an ecumenical gathering of American religious leaders as 'characterized by a dimension of sin in the economic, political, social, sexual, and class structures and systems of global society'![27] It would seem as if the conviction that one is arguing in a good cause produced more sloppy thinking and even intellectual dishonesty than perhaps any other cause.

'Social justice' and equality

The most common attempts to give meaning to the concept of 'social justice' resort to egalitarian considerations and argue that every departure from equality of material benefits enjoyed has to be justified by some recognizable common interest which these differences serve.[28] This is based on a specious analogy with the situation in which some human agency has to distribute rewards, in which case indeed justice would require that these rewards be determined in accordance with some recognizable rule of general applicability. But earnings in a market system, though people tend to regard them as rewards, do not serve such a function. Their rationale (if one may use this term for a role which was not designed but developed because it assisted human endeavour without people understanding how), is rather to indicate to people what they ought to do if the order is to be maintained on which they all rely. The prices which must be paid in a market economy for different kinds of labour and other factors of production if individual efforts are to match, although they will be affected by effort, diligence, skill, need, etc., cannot conform to any one of these magnitudes; and considerations of justice just do not make sense[29] with respect to the determination of a magnitude which does not depend on anyone's will or desire, but on circumstances which nobody knows in their totality.

The contention that all differences in earnings must be justified by some corresponding difference in deserts is one which would certainly not have been thought to be obvious in a community of farmers or merchants or artisans, that is, in a society in which success or failure were clearly seen to depend only in part on skill and industry, and in part on pure accident which might hit anyone—although even in such societies individuals were known to complain to God or fortune about the injustice of their fate. But, though people resent that their remuneration should in part depend on pure accident, that is in fact precisely what it must if the market order is to adjust itself promptly to the unavoidable and unforeseen changes in circumstances, and the individual is to be allowed to decide what to do. The now prevalent attitude could arise only in a society in which large numbers worked as members of organizations in which they were remunerated at stipulated rates for time worked. Such communities will not ascribe the different fortunes of its members to the operation of an impersonal mechanism which serves to guide the directions of efforts, but to some human power that ought to allocate shares according to merit.

The postulate of material equality would be a natural starting point only if it were a necessary circumstance that the shares of the different individuals or groups were in such a manner determined by deliberate human decision. In a society in which this were an unquestioned fact, justice would indeed demand that the allocation of the means for the satisfaction of human needs were effected according to some uniform principle such as merit or need (or some combination of these), and that, where the principle adopted did not justify a difference, the shares of the different individuals should be equal. The prevalent demand for material equality is probably often based on the belief that the existing inequalities are the effect of somebody's decision—a belief which would be wholly mistaken in a genuine market order and has still only very limited validity in the highly interventionist 'mixed' economy existing in most countries today. This now prevalent form of economic order has in fact attained its character largely as a result of governmental measures aiming at what was thought to be required by 'social justice'.

When the choice, however, is between a genuine market order, which does not and cannot achieve a distribution corresponding to any standard of material justice, and a system in which government uses its powers to put some such standard into effect, the question is not whether government ought to exercise, justly or unjustly, powers it must exercise in any case, but whether government should possess and exercise additional powers which can be used to determine the shares of the different members of society. The demand for 'social justice', in other words, does not merely require government to observe some principle of action according to uniform rules in those actions which it must perform in any case, but demands that it undertake additional activities, and thereby assume new responsibilities—tasks which are not necessary for maintaining law and order and providing for certain collective needs which the market could not satisfy.

The great problem is whether this new demand for equality does not conflict with the equality of the rules of conduct which government must enforce on all in a free society. There is, of course, a great difference between government treating all citizens according to the same rules in all the activities it undertakes for other purposes, and government doing what is required in order to place the different citizens in equal (or less unequal) material positions. Indeed, there may arise a sharp conflict between these two aims. Since people will differ in many attributes which government cannot alter, to secure for them the same material position would require that government treat them very differently. Indeed, to assure the same material position to people who differ greatly in strength, intelligence, skill, knowledge and perseverance as well as in their physical and social environment, government would clearly have to treat them very differently to compensate for those disadvantages and deficiencies it could not directly alter. Strict equality of those benefits which government could provide for all, on the other hand, would clearly lead to inequality of the material positions.

This, however, is not the only and not even the chief reason why a government aiming to secure for its citizens equal material positions (or any determined pattern of material welfare) would have to treat them very unequally. It would have to do so because under such a system it would have to undertake to tell people what to do. Once the rewards the individual can expect are no longer an appropriate indication of how to direct their efforts to where they are most needed, because these rewards correspond not to the value which their services have for their fellows, but to the moral merit or desert the persons are deemed to have earned, they lose the guiding function they have in the market order and would have to be replaced by the commands of the directing authority. A central planning office would, however, have to decide on the tasks to be allotted to the different groups or individuals wholly on grounds of expediency or efficiency and, in order to achieve its ends, would have to impose upon them very different duties and burdens. The individuals might be treated according to uniform rules so far as their rewards were concerned, but certainly not with respect to the different kinds of work they would have to be made to do. In assigning people to their different tasks, the central planning authority would have to be guided by considerations of efficiency and expediency and not by principles of justice or equality. No less than in the market order would the individuals in the common interest have to submit to great inequality—only these inequalities would be determined not by the interaction of individual skills in an impersonal process, but by the uncontradictable decision of authority.

As is becoming clear in ever increasing fields of welfare policy, an authority instructed to achieve particular results for the individuals must be given essentially arbitrary powers to make the individuals do what seems necessary to achieve the required result. Full equality for most cannot but mean the equal submission of the great masses under the command of some élite who manages their affairs. While an equality of rights under a limited government is possible and an essential condition of individual freedom, a claim for equality of material position can be met only by a government with totalitarian powers.[30]

We are of course not wrong when we perceive that the effects on the different individuals and groups of the economic processes of a free society are not distributed according to some recognizable principle of justice. Where we go wrong is in concluding from this that they are unjust and that somebody is responsible and to be blamed for this. In a free society in which the position of the different individuals and groups is not the result of anybody's design—or could within such a society not be altered in accordance with a principle of general applicability—the differences in rewards cannot meaningfully be described as just or unjust. There are, no doubt, many kinds of individual actions which are aimed at affecting particular remunerations and which might be regarded as unjust. But there are no principles of individual conduct which would produce a pattern of distribution which as such could be called just, and therefore also no possibility for the individual to know what he would have to do to secure a just remuneration of his fellows.

Our whole system of morals is a system of rules of individual conduct, and in a Great Society no conduct guided by such rules, or by decisions of the individuals guided by such rules, could produce for the individuals results which would appear to us as just in the sense in which we regard designed rewards as just or unjust: simply because in such a society nobody has the power or the knowledge which would enable him to ensure that those affected by his actions will get what he thinks right for them to get. Nor could anyone who is assured remuneration according to some principle which is accepted as constituting 'social justice' be allowed to decide what he is to do: remuneration indicating how urgent it was that a certain work should be done could not be just in this sense, because the need for work of a particular kind would often depend on unforeseeable accidents and certainly not on the good intentions or efforts of those able to perform it. And an authority that fixed remunerations with the intention of thereby reducing the kind and number of people thought necessary in each occupation could not make these remunerations 'just', i.e. proportionate to desert, or need, or the merits of any other claim of the persons concerned, but would have to offer what was necessary to attract or retain the number of people wanted in each kind of activity.

'*Equality of opportunity*'

It is of course not to be denied that in the existing market order not only the results but also the initial chances of different individuals are often very different; they are affected by circumstances of their physical and social environment which are beyond their control but in many particular respects might be altered by some governmental action. The demand for equality of opportunity or equal starting conditions (*Startgerechtigkeit*) appeals to, and has been supported by, many who in general favour the free market order. So far as this refers to such facilities and opportunities as are of necessity affected by governmental decisions (such as appointments to public office and the like), the demand was indeed one of the central points of classical liberalism, usually expressed by the French phrase 'la carrière ouverte aux talents'. There is also much to be said in favour of the government providing on an equal basis the means for the schooling of minors who are not yet fully responsible citizens, even though there are grave doubts whether we ought to allow government to administer them.

But all this would still be very far from creating real equality of opportunity, even for persons possessing the same abilities. To achieve this government would have to control the whole physical and human environment of all persons, and have to endeavour to provide at least equivalent chances for each; and the more government succeeded in these endeavours, the stronger would become the legitimate demand that, on the same principle, any still remaining handicaps must be removed—or compensated for by putting extra burden on the still relatively favoured. This would have to go on until government literally controlled every circumstance which could affect any person's well-being. Attractive as the phrase of equality of opportunity at first sounds, once the idea is extended beyond the facilities which for other reasons have to be provided by government, it becomes a wholly illusory ideal, and any attempt concretely to realize it apt to produce a nightmare.

'Social justice' and freedom under the law

The idea that men ought to be rewarded in accordance with the assessed merits or deserts of their services 'to society' presupposes an authority which not only distributes these rewards but also assigns to the individuals the tasks for the performance of which they will be rewarded. In other words, if 'social justice' is to be brought about, the individuals must be required to obey not merely general rules but specific demands directed to them only. The type of social order in which the individuals are directed to serve a single system of ends is the organization and not the spontaneous order of the market, that is, not a system in which the individual is free because bound only by general rules of just conduct, but a system in which all are subject to specific directions by authority.

It appears sometimes to be imagined that a mere alteration of the rules of individual conduct could bring about the realization of 'social justice'. But there can be no set of such rules, no principles by which the individuals could so govern their conduct that in a Great Society the joint effect of their activities would be a distribution of benefits which could be described as materially just, or any other specific and intended allocation of advantages and disadvantages among particular people or groups. In order to achieve *any* particular pattern of distribution through the market process, each producer would have to know, not only whom his efforts will benefit (or harm), but also how well off all the other people (actually or potentially) affected by his activities will be as the result of the services they are receiving from other members of the society. As we have seen earlier, appropriate rules of conduct can determine only the formal character of the order of activities that will form itself, but not the specific advantages particular groups or individuals will derive from it.

This rather obvious fact still needs to be stressed since even eminent jurists have contended that the substitution of 'social' or distributive for individual or commutative justice need not destroy the freedom under the law of the individual. Thus the distinguished German legal philosopher Gustav Radbruch explicitly maintained that 'the socialist community would also be a *Rechtsstaat* [i.e., the Rule of Law would prevail there], although a *Rechtsstaat* governed not by commutative but by distributive justice.'[31] And of France it is reported that 'it has been suggested that some highly placed administrators should be given the permanent task of "pronouncing" on the distribution of national income, as judges pronounce on legal matters.'[32] Such beliefs, however, overlook the fact that no specific pattern of distribution can be achieved by making the individuals obey rules of conduct, but that the achievement of such particular pre-determined results requires deliberate co-ordination of all the different activities in accordance with the concrete circumstances of time and place. It precludes, in other words, that the several individuals act on the basis of their own knowledge and in the service of their own ends, which is the essence of freedom, but requires that they be made to act in the manner which according to the knowledge of the directing authority is required for the realization of the ends chosen by that authority.

The distributive justice at which socialism aims is thus irreconcilable with the rule of law, and with that freedom under the law which the rule of law is intended to secure. The rules of distributive justice cannot be rules for the conduct towards equals, but must be rules for the conduct of superiors towards their subordinates. Yet though some socialists have long ago themselves drawn the inevitable conclusion that 'the fundamental principles of formal law by which every case must be judged according to general rational principles . . . obtains only for the competitive phase of capitalism,'[33] and the communists, so long as they took socialism seriously, had even proclaimed that 'communism means not the victory of socialist law, but the victory of socialism over any law, since with the abolition of classes with antagonistic interests, law will disappear altogether',[34] when, more than thirty years ago, the present author made this the central point of a discussion of the political effects of socialist economic policies,[35] it evoked great

86

indignation and violent protests. But the crucial point is implied even in Radbruch's own emphasis on the fact that the transition from commutative to distributive justice means a progressive displacement of private by public law,[36] since public law consists not of rules of conduct for private citizens but of rules of organization for public officials. It is, as Radbruch himself stresses, a law that subordinates the citizens to authority.[37] Only if one understands by law not the general rules of just conduct only but any command issued by authority (or any authorization of such commands by a legislature), can the measures aimed at distributive justice be represented as compatible with the rule of law. But this concept is thereby made to mean mere legality and ceases to offer the protection of individual freedom which it was originally intended to serve.

There is no reason why in a free society government should not assure to all protection against severe deprivation in the form of an assured minimum income, or a floor below which nobody need to descend. To enter into such an insurance against extreme misfortune may well be in the interest of all; or it may be felt to be a clear moral duty of all to assist, within the organized community, those who cannot help themselves. So long as such a uniform minimum income is provided outside the market to all those who, for any reason, are unable to earn in the market an adequate maintenance, this need not lead to a restriction of freedom, or conflict with the Rule of Law. The problems with which we are here concerned arise only when the remuneration for services rendered is determined by authority, and the impersonal mechanism of the market which guides the direction of individual efforts is thus suspended.

Perhaps the acutest sense of grievance about injustice inflicted on one, not by particular persons but by the 'system', is that about being deprived of opportunities for developing one's abilities which others enjoy. For this any difference of environment, social or physical, may be responsible, and at least some of them may be unavoidable. The most important of these is clearly inseparable from the institution of the family. This not only satisfies a strong psychological need but in general serves as an instrument for the transmission of important cultural values. There can be no doubt that those who are either wholly deprived of this benefit, or grew up in unfavourable conditions, are gravely handicapped; and few will question that it would be desirable that some public institution so far as possible should assist such unfortunate children when relatives and neighbours fail. Yet few will seriously believe (although Plato did) that we can fully make up for such a deficiency, and I trust even fewer that, because this benefit cannot be assured to all, it should, in the interest of equality, be taken from those who now enjoy it. Nor does it seem to me that even material equality could compensate for those differences in the capacity of enjoyment and of experiencing a lively interest in the cultural surroundings which a suitable upbringing confers.

There are of course many other irremediable inequalities which must seem as unreasonable as economic inequalities but which are less resented than the latter only because they do not appear to be man-made or the consequence of institutions which could be altered.

The spatial range of 'social justice'

There can be little doubt that the moral feelings which express themselves in the demand for 'social justice' derive from an attitude which in more primitive conditions the individual developed towards the fellow members of the small group to which he belonged. Towards the personally known member of one's own group it may well have been a recognized duty to assist him and to adjust one's actions to his needs. This is made possible by the knowledge of his person and his circumstances. The situation is wholly different in the Great or Open Society. Here the products and services of each benefit mostly persons he does not know. The greater productivity of such a society rests on a division of labour extending far beyond the range any one person can survey. This extension of the process of exchange beyond relatively small groups, and including large numbers of persons not known to each other, has been made possible by conceding to the stranger and even the foreigner the same protection of rules of just conduct which apply to the relations to the known members of one's own small group.

This application of the same rules of just conduct to the relations to all other men is rightly regarded as one of the great achievements of a liberal society. What is usually not understood is that this extension of the same rules to the relations to all other men (beyond the most intimate group such as the family and personal friends) requires an attenuation at least of some of the rules which are enforced in the relations to other members of the smaller group. If the legal duties towards strangers or foreigners are to be the same as those towards the neighbours or inhabitants of the same village or town, the latter duties will have to be reduced to such as can also be applied to the stranger. No doubt men will always wish to belong also to smaller groups and be willing voluntarily to assume greater obligations towards self-chosen friends or companions. But such moral obligations towards some can never become enforced duties in a system of freedom under the law, because in such a system the selection of those towards whom a man wishes to assume special moral obligations must be left to him and cannot be determined by law. A system of rules intended for an Open Society and, at least in principle, meant to be applicable to all others, must have a somewhat smaller content than one to be applied in a small group.

Especially a common agreement on what is the due status or material position of the different members is likely to develop only in the relatively small group in which the members will be familiar with the character and importance of each other's activities. In such small communities the opinion about appropriate status will also still be associated with a feeling about what one self owes to the other, and not be merely a demand that somebody provide the appropriate reward. Demands for the realization of 'social justice' are usually as a matter of course, though often only tacitly, addressed to national governments as the agencies which possess the necessary powers. But it is doubtful whether in any but the smallest countries standards can be applied nationally which are derived from the condition of the particular locality with which the individual is familiar, and fairly certain that few men would be willing to concede to foreigners the same right to a particular income that they tend to recognize in their fellow citizens.

It is true that in recent years concern about the suffering of large numbers in the poor countries has induced the electorates of the wealthier nations to approve substantial material aid to the former; but it can hardly be said that in this considerations of justice played a significant role. It is indeed doubtful whether any substantial help would have been rendered if competing power groups had not striven to draw as many as possible of the developing countries into their orbit. And it deserves notice that the modern technology which has made such assistance possible could develop only because some countries were able to build up great wealth while most of the world saw little change.

Yet the chief point is that, if we look beyond the limits of our national states, and certainly if we go beyond the limits of what we regard as our civilization, we no longer even deceive ourselves that we know what would be 'socially just', and that those very groups within the existing states which are loudest in their demands for 'social justice', such as the trade unions, are regularly the first to reject such claims raised on behalf of foreigners. Applied to the international sphere, the complete lack of a recognized standard of 'social justice', or of any known principles on which such a standard could be based, becomes at once obvious; while on a national scale most people still think that what on the level of the face-to-face society is to them a familiar idea must also have some validity for national politics or the use of the powers of government. In fact, it becomes on this level a humbug—the effectiveness of which with well-meaning people the agents of organized interests have learnt successfully to exploit.

There is in this respect a fundamental difference between what is possible in the small group and in the Great Society. In the small group the individual can know the effects of his actions on his several fellows, and the rules may effectively forbid him to harm them in any manner and even require him to assist them in specific ways. In the Great Society many of the effects of a person's actions on various fellows must be unknown to him. It can, therefore, not be the specific effects in the particular case, but only rules which define kinds of actions as prohibited or required, which must serve as guides to the individual. In particular, he will often not know who the individual people will be who will benefit by what he does, and therefore not know whether he is satisfying a great need or adding to abundance. He cannot aim at just results if he does not know who will be affected.

Indeed the transition from the small group to the Great or Open Society—and the treatment of every other person as a human being rather than as either a known friend or an enemy—requires a reduction of the range of duties we owe to all others.

If a person's legal duties are to be the same towards all, including the stranger and even the foreigner (and greater only where he has voluntarily entered into obligations, or is connected by physical ties as between parents and children), the legally enforceable duties to neighbour and friend must not be more than those towards the stranger. That is, all those duties which are based on personal acquaintance and familiarity with individual circumstances must cease to be enforceable. The extension of the obligation to obey certain rules of just conduct to wider circles and ultimately to all men must thus lead to an attenuation of the obligation towards fellow members of the same small group. Our inherited or perhaps in part even innate moral emotions are in part inapplicable to Open Society (which is an abstract society), and the kind of 'moral socialism' that is possible in the small group and often satisfies a deeply ingrained instinct may well be impossible in the Great Society. Some altruistic conduct aimed at the benefit of some known friend that in the small group might be highly desirable, need not be so in the Open Society, and may there even be harmful (as e.g. the requirement that members of the same trade refrain from competing with each other).[38]

It may at first seem paradoxical that the advance of morals should lead to a reduction of specific obligations towards others: yet whoever believes that the principle of equal treatment of all men, which is probably the only chance for peace, is more important than special help to visible suffering, must wish it. It admittedly means that we make our rational insight dominate over our inherited instincts. But the great moral adventure on which modern man has embarked when he launched into the Open Society is threatened when he is required to apply to all his fellow-men rules which are appropriate only to the fellow members of a tribal group.

Claims for compensation for distasteful jobs

The reader will probably expect me now to examine in greater detail the particular claims usually justified by the appeal to 'social justice'. But this, as bitter experience has taught me, would be not only an endless but also a bootless task. After what has been said already, it should be obvious that there are no practicable standards of merit, deserts, or needs, on which in a market order the distribution of material benefits could be based, and still less any principle by which these different claims could be reconciled. I shall therefore confine myself to considering two arguments in which the appeal to 'social justice' is very commonly used. The first case is usually quoted in theoretical argument to illustrate the injustice of the distribution by the market process, though little is done about it in practice, while the second is probably the most frequent type of situation in which the appeal to social justice leads to government action.

The circumstance which is usually pointed out to demonstrate

the injustice of the existing market order is that the most unpleasant jobs are commonly also the worst paid. In a just society, it
is contended, those who have to dig coal underground or to clean
chimneys or sewers, or who perform other unclean or menial
tasks, should be remunerated more highly than those whose work
is pleasurable.

It is of course true that it would be unjust if persons, although
equally able as others to perform other tasks, were without special
compensation assigned by a superior to such distasteful duties. If,
e.g., in such an organization as an army, two men of equal capacity
were made to perform different tasks, one of which was attractive
and the other very unpleasant, justice would clearly require that
the one who had regularly to perform the unpleasant duty should
in some way be specially compensated for it.

The situation is entirely different, however, where people earn
their living by selling their services to whoever pays best for them.
Here the sacrifice brought by a particular person in rendering the
service is wholly irrelevant and all that counts is the (marginal)
value the services have to those to whom they are rendered. The
reason for this is not only that the sacrifices different people bring
in rendering the same kind of service will often be very different, or
that it will not be possible to take account of the reason why some
will be capable of rendering only less valuable services than others.
But those whose aptitudes, and therefore also remunerations, will
be small in the more attractive occupations will often find that they
can earn more than they could otherwise by undertaking unpleasant
tasks that are scorned by their more fortunate fellows. The very fact
that the more unpleasant occupations will be avoided by those who
can render services that are valued more highly by the buyers, will
open to those whose skills are little valued opportunities to earn
more than they otherwise could.

That those who have to offer to their fellows little that is valuable
may have to incur more pain and effort to earn even a pittance than
others who perhaps actually enjoy rendering services for which they
are well paid, is a necessary concomitant of any system in which
remuneration is based on the values the services have to the user
and not on an assessment of merit earned. It must therefore prevail
in any social order in which the individual is free to choose whatever
occupation he can find and is not assigned to one by authority.

The only assumption on which it could be represented as just
that the miner working underground, or the scavenger, or slaughter-

house workers, should be paid more highly than those engaged in more pleasant occupations, would thus be that this was necessary to induce a sufficient number of persons to perform these tasks, or that they are by some human agency deliberately assigned to these tasks. But while in a market order it may be a misfortune to have been born and bred in a village where for most the only chance of making a living is fishing (or for the women the cleaning of fish), it does not make sense to describe this as unjust. Who is supposed to have been unjust?—especially when it is considered that, if these local opportunities had not existed, the people in question would probably never have been born at all, as most of the population of such a village will probably owe its existence to the opportunities which enabled their ancestors to produce and rear children.

The resentment of the loss of accustomed positions

The appeal to 'social justice' which in practice has probably had the greatest influence is not one which has been much considered in literary discussion. The considerations of a supposed 'social injustice' which have led to the most far-reaching interference with the functioning of the market order are based on the idea that people are to be protected against an unmerited descent from the material position to which they have become accustomed. No other consideration of 'social justice' has probably exercised as widespread an influence as the 'strong and almost universal belief that it is unjust to disappoint legitimate expectations of wealth. When differences of opinion arise, it is always on the question of what expectations are legitimate.' It is believed, as the same author says, 'that it is legitimate even for the largest classes to expect that no very great and sudden changes will be made to their detriment.'[39]

The opinion that long established positions create a just expectation that they will continue serves often as a substitute for more substantial criteria of 'social justice'. Where expectations are disappointed, and in consequence the rewards of effort often disproportionate to the sacrifice incurred, this will be regarded as an injustice without any attempt to show that those affected had a claim in justice to the particular income which they expected. At least when a large group of people find their income reduced as a result of circumstances which they could not have altered or foreseen, this is commonly regarded as unjust.

The frequent recurrence of such undeserved strokes of misfortune affecting some group is, however, an inseparable part of
the steering mechanism of the market: it is the manner in which the
cybernetic principle of negative feedback operates to maintain the
order of the market. It is only through such changes which indicate
that some activities ought to be reduced, that the efforts of all can be
continuously adjusted to a greater variety of facts than can be known
to any one person or agency, and that that utilization of dispersed
knowledge is achieved on which the well-being of the Great Society
rests. We cannot rely on a system in which the individuals are
induced to respond to events of which they do not and cannot know
without changes of the values of the services of different groups
occurring which are wholly unrelated to the merits of their members. It is a necessary part of that process of constant adaptation to
changing circumstances on which the mere maintenance of the
existing level of wealth depends that some people should have to
discover by bitter experience that they have misdirected their efforts
and are forced to look elsewhere for a remunerative occupation.
And the same applies to the resentment of the corresponding undeserved gains that will accrue to others for whom things have
turned out better than they had reason to expect.

The sense of injury which people feel when an accustomed income is reduced or altogether lost is largely the result of a belief
that they have morally deserved that income and that, therefore, so
long as they work as industriously and honestly as they did before,
they are in justice entitled to the continuance of that income. But
the idea that we have morally deserved what we have honestly
earned in the past is largely an illusion. What is true is only that it
would have been unjust if anybody had taken from us what we have
in fact acquired while observing the rules of the game.

It is precisely because in the cosmos of the market we all constantly receive benefits which we have not deserved in any moral
sense that we are under an obligation also to accept equally undeserved diminutions of our incomes. Our only moral title to what
the market gives us we have earned by submitting to those rules
which makes the formation of the market order possible. These rules
imply that nobody is under an obligation to supply us with a particular income unless he has specifically contracted to do so. If we
were all to be consistently deprived, as the socialists propose to do,
of all 'unearned benefits' which the market confers upon us, we
would have to be deprived of most of the benefits of civilization.

It is clearly meaningless to reply, as is often done, that, since we owe these benefits to 'society', 'society' should also be entitled to allocate these benefits to those who in its opinion deserve them. Society, once more, is not an acting person but an orderly structure of actions resulting from the observation of certain abstract rules by its members. We all owe the benefits we receive from the operation of this structure not to anyone's intention to confer them on us, but to the members of society generally obeying certain rules in the pursuit of their interests, rules which include the rule that nobody is to coerce others in order to secure for himself (or for third persons) a particular income. This imposes upon us the obligation to abide by the results of the market also when it turns against us.

The chance which any individual in our society has of earning an income approximating that which he has now is the consequence of most individuals obeying the rules which secure the formation of that order. And though this order provides for most good prospects for the successful employment of their skills, this success must remain dependent also on what from the point of view of the individual must appear as mere luck. The magnitude of the chances open to him are not of his making but the result of others submitting to the same rules of the game. To ask for protection against being displaced from a position one has long enjoyed, by others who are now favoured by new circumstances, means to deny to them the chances to which one's own present position is due.

Any protection of an accustomed position is thus necessarily a privilege which cannot be granted to all and which, if it had always been recognized, would have prevented those who now claim it from ever reaching the position for which they now demand protection. There can, in particular, be no right to share equally in a general increase of incomes if this increase (or perhaps even their maintenance at the existing level) is dependent on the continuous adjustment of the whole structure of activities to new and unforeseen circumstances that will alter and often reduce the contributions some groups can make to the needs of their fellows. There can thus be in justice no such claims as, e.g., those of the American farmer for 'parity', or of any other group to the preservation of their relative or absolute position.

The satisfaction of such claims by particular groups would thus not be just but eminently unjust, because it would involve the denial to some of the chances to which those who make this claim owe their position. For this reason it has always been conceded only

95

to some powerfully organized groups who were in the position to enforce their demands. Much of what is today done in the name of 'social justice' is thus not only unjust but also highly unsocial in the true sense of the word: it amounts simply to the protection of entrenched interests. Though it has come to be regarded as a 'social problem' when sufficiently large numbers clamour for protection of their accustomed position, it becomes a serious problem chiefly because, camouflaged as a demand for 'social justice', it can engage the sympathy of the public. We shall see in volume 3 why, under the existing type of democratic institutions, it is in practice inevitable that legislatures with unlimited powers yield to such demands when made by sufficiently large groups. This does not alter the fact that to represent such measures as satisfying 'social justice' is little more than a pretext for making the interest of the particular groups prevail over the general interest of all. Though it is now usual to regard every claim of an organized group as a 'social problem', it would be more correct to say that, though the long run interests of the several individuals mostly agree with the general interest, the interests of the organized groups almost invariably are in conflict with it. Yet it is the latter which are commonly represented as 'social'.

Conclusions

The basic contention of this chapter, namely that in a society of free men whose members are allowed to use their own knowledge for their own purposes the term 'social justice' is wholly devoid of meaning or content, is one which by its very nature cannot be *proved*. A negative assertion never can. One may demonstrate for any number of particular instances that the appeal to 'social justice' in no way assists the choices we have to make. But the contention that in a society of free men the term has no meaning whatever can only be issued as a challenge which will make it necessary for others to reflect on the meaning of the words they use, and as an appeal not to use phrases the meaning of which they do not know.

So long as one assumes that a phrase so widely used must have some recognizable meaning one may endeavour to prove that attempts to enforce it in a society of free individuals must make that society unworkable. But such efforts become redundant once it is recognized that such a society lacks the fundamental precondition for the application of the concept of justice to the manner in which material benefits are shared among its members, namely that this is determined by a human will—or that the determination of rewards by human will could produce a viable market order. One does not have to prove that something is impracticable which cannot exist.

What I hope to have made clear is that the phrase 'social justice' is not, as most people probably feel, an innocent expression of good will towards the less fortunate, but that it has become a dishonest insinuation that one ought to agree to a demand of some special interest which can give no real reason for it. If political discussion is to become honest it is necessary that people should recognize that the term is intellectually disreputable, the mark of demagogy or cheap journalism which responsible thinkers ought to be ashamed to use because, once its vacuity is recognized, its use is dishonest. I may, as a result of long endeavours to trace the destructive effect which the invocation of 'social justice' has had on our moral sensitivity, and of again and again finding even eminent thinkers thoughtlessly using the phrase,[40] have become unduly allergic to it, but I have come to feel strongly that the greatest service I can still render to my fellow men would be that I could make the speakers and writers among them thoroughly ashamed ever again to employ the term 'social justice'.

That in the present state of the discussion the continued use of the term is not only dishonest and the source of constant political confusion, but destructive of moral feeling, is shown by the fact that again and again thinkers, including distinguished philosophers,[41] after rightly recognizing that the term justice in its now predominant meaning of distributive (or retributive) justice is meaningless, draw from this the conclusion that the concept of justice itself is empty, and who in consequence jettison one of the basic moral conceptions on which the working of a society of free men rests. But it is justice in this sense which courts of justice administer and which is the original meaning of justice and must govern men's conduct if peaceful coexistence of free men is to be possible. While the appeal to 'social justice' is indeed merely an invitation to give moral approval to demands that have no moral justification, and which are in conflict with that basic rule of a free society that only such rules as can be applied equally to all should be enforced, justice in the sense of rules of just conduct is indispensable for the intercourse of free men.

We are touching here upon a problem which with all its ramifications is much too big to try to be examined here systematically, but which must at least be mentioned briefly. It is that we can't have any morals we like or dream of. Morals, to be viable, must satisfy certain requirements, requirements which we may not be able to specify but may only be able to find out by trial and error. What is required is not merely consistency, or compatibility of the rules as well as the acts demanded by them. A system of morals also must produce a functioning order, capable of maintaining the apparatus of civilization which it presupposes.

We are not familiar with the concept of non-viable systems of morals and certainly cannot observe them anywhere in practice since societies which try them rapidly disappear. But they are being preached, often by widely revered saintly figures, and the societies in decay which we can observe are often societies which have been listening to the teaching of such moral reformers and still revere the destroyers of their society as good men. More often, however, the gospel of 'social justice' aims at much more sordid sentiments: the dislike of people who are better off than oneself, or simply envy, that 'most anti-social and evil of all passions' as John Stuart Mill called it, [42] that animosity towards great wealth which represents it as a 'scandal' that some should enjoy riches while others have basic needs unsatisfied, and camouflages under the name of justice what has nothing to do with justice. At least all those who wish to despoil the rich, not because they expect that some more deserving might enjoy that wealth, but because they regard the very existence of the rich as an outrage, not only cannot claim any moral justification for their demands, but indulge in a wholly irrational passion and in fact harm those to whose rapacious instincts they appeal.

There can be no moral claim to something that would not exist but for the decision of others to risk their resources on its creation. What those who attack great private wealth do not understand is that it is neither by physical effort nor by the mere act of saving and investing, but by directing resources to the most productive uses that wealth is chiefly created. And there can be no doubt that most of those who have built up great fortunes in the form of new industrial plants and the like have thereby benefited more people through creating opportunities for more rewarding employment than if they had given their superfluity away to the poor. The suggestion that in these cases those to whom in fact the workers are most indebted do wrong rather than greatly benefit them is an absurdity. Though there are undoubtedly also other and less meritorious ways of acquiring large fortunes (which we can hope to control by improving the rules of the game), the most effective and important is by directing investment to points where they most enhance the productivity of labour—a task in which governments notoriously fail, for reasons inherent in non-competitive bureaucratic organizations.

But it is not only by encouraging malevolent and harmful prejudices that the cult of 'social justice' tends to destroy genuine moral feelings. It also comes, particularly in its more egalitarian forms, into constant conflict with some of the basic moral principles on which any community of free men must rest. This becomes evident when we reflect that the demand that we should equally esteem all our fellow men is irreconcilable with the fact that our whole moral code rests on the approval or disapproval of the conduct of others; and that similarly the traditional postulate that each capable adult is primarily responsible for his own and his dependants' welfare, meaning that he must not through his own fault become a charge to his friends or fellows, is incompatible with the idea that 'society' or government owes each person an appropriate income.

Though all these moral principles have also been seriously weakened by some pseudo-scientific fashions of our time which tend to destroy all morals—and with them the basis of individual freedom—the ubiquitous dependence on other people's power, which the enforcement of any image of 'social justice' creates, inevitably destroys that freedom of personal decisions on which all morals must rest.[43] In fact, that systematic pursuit of the *ignis fatuus* of 'social justice' which we call socialism is based throughout on the atrocious idea that political power ought to determine the material position of the different individuals and groups—an idea defended by the false assertion that this must always be so and socialism merely wishes to transfer this power from the privileged to the most numerous class. It was the great merit of the market order as it has spread during the last two centuries that it deprived everyone of such power which can be used only in arbitrary fashion. It had indeed brought about the greatest reduction of arbitrary power ever achieved. This greatest triumph of personal freedom the seduction of 'social justice' threatens again to take from us. And it will not be long before the holders of the power to enforce 'social justice' will entrench themselves in their position by awarding the benefits of 'social justice' as the remuneration for the conferment of that power and in order to secure to themselves the support of a praetorian guard which will make it certain that their view of what is 'social justice' will prevail.

Before leaving the subject I want to point out once more that the recognition that in such combinations as 'social', 'economic', 'distributive' or 'retributive' justice the term 'justice' is wholly empty should not lead us to throw the baby out with the bath water. Not only as the basis of the legal rules of just conduct is the justice which the courts of justice administer exceedingly important; there unquestionably also exists a genuine problem of justice in connection with the deliberate design of political institutions, the problem to which Professor John Rawls has recently devoted an important book. The fact which I regret and regard as confusing is merely that in this connection he employs the term 'social justice'. But I have no basic quarrel with an author who, before he proceeds to that problem, acknowledges that the task of selecting specific systems or distributions of desired things as just must be 'abandoned as mistaken in principle, and it is, in any case, not capable of a definite answer. Rather, the principles of justice define the crucial constraints which institutions and joint activities must satisfy if persons engaging in them are to have no complaints against them. If these constraints are satisfied, the resulting distribution, whatever it is, may be accepted as just (or at least not unjust).'[44] This is more or less what I have been trying to argue in this chapter.

APPENDIX TO CHAPTER NINE

JUSTICE AND INDIVIDUAL RIGHTS

The transition from the negative conception of justice as defined by rules of individual conduct to a 'positive' conception which makes it a duty of 'society' to see that individuals have particular things, is often effected by stressing the *rights* of the individual. It seems that among the younger generation the welfare institutions into which they have been born have engendered a feeling that they have a claim in justice on 'society' for the provision of particular things which it is the duty of that society to provide. However strong this feeling may be, its existence does not prove that the claim has anything to do with justice, or that such claims can be satisfied in a free society.

There is a sense of the noun 'right' in which every rule of just individual conduct creates a corresponding right of individuals. So far as rules of conduct delimit individual domains, the individual will have a right to his domain, and in the defence of it will have the sympathy and the support of his fellows. And where men have formed organizations such as government for enforcing rules of conduct, the individual will have a claim in justice on government that his right be protected and infringements made good.

Such claims, however, can be claims in justice, or rights, only in so far as they are directed towards a person or organization (such as government) which can act, and which is bound in its actions by rules of just conduct. They will include claims on people who have voluntarily incurred obligations, or between people who are connected by special circumstances (such as the relations between parents and children). In such circumstances the rules of just conduct will confer on some persons rights and on others corresponding obligations. But rules as such, without the presence of the particular circumstances to which they refer, cannot confer on anyone a right to a particular sort of thing. A child has a right to be fed, clad, and housed because a corresponding duty is placed on the parents or guardians, or perhaps a particular authority. But there

APPENDIX—JUSTICE AND INDIVIDUAL RIGHTS

can be no such right in the abstract determined by a rule of just conduct without the particular circumstances being stated which determine on whom the corresponding obligation rests. Nobody has a right to a particular state of affairs unless it is the duty of someone to secure it. We have no right that our houses do not burn down, nor a right that our products or services find a buyer, nor that any particular goods or services be provided for us. Justice does not impose on our fellows a general duty to provide for us; and a claim to such a provision can exist only to the extent that we are maintaining an organization for that purpose. It is meaningless to speak of a right to a condition which nobody has the duty, or perhaps even the power, to bring about. It is equally meaningless to speak of right in the sense of a claim on a spontaneous order, such as society, unless this is meant to imply that somebody has the duty of transforming that cosmos into an organization and thereby to assume the power of controlling its results.

Since we are all made to support the organization of government, we have by the principles determining that organization certain rights which are commonly called political rights. The existence of the compulsory organization of government and its rules of organization does create a claim in justice to shares in the services of government, and may even justify a claim for an equal share in determining what government shall do. But it does not provide a basis for a claim on what government does not, and perhaps could not, provide for all. We are not, in this sense, members of an organization called society, because the society which produces the means for the satisfaction of most of our needs is not an organization directed by a conscious will, and could not produce what it does if it were.

The time-honoured political and civil rights which have been embodied in formal Bills of Right constitute essentially a demand that so far as the power of government extends it ought to be used justly. As we shall see, they all amount to particular applications of, and might be effectively replaced by, the more comprehensive formula that no coercion must be used except in the enforcement of a generic rule applicable to an unknown number of future instances. It may well be desirable that these rights should become truly universal as a result of all governments submitting to them. But so long as the powers of the several governments are at all limited, these rights cannot produce a duty of the governments to bring about a particular state of affairs. What we can require is that so far as government acts it ought to act justly; but we cannot derive from them any positive powers government ought to have. They leave wholly open the question whether the organization for coercion which we call government can and ought in justice be used to determine the particular material position of the several individuals or groups.

To the negative rights which are merely a complement of the rules protecting individual domains and which have been institutionalized in the charters of organization of governments, and to the positive rights of the citizens to participate in the direction of this organization, there have recently been added new positive 'social and economic' human rights for which an equal or even higher dignity is claimed.[1] These are claims to particular benefits to which every human being as such is presumed to be entitled without any indication as to who is to be under the obligation to provide those benefits or by what process they are to be provided.[2] Such positive rights, however, demand as their counterpart a decision that somebody (a person or organization) should have the duty of providing what the others are to have. It is, of course, meaningless to describe them as claims on 'society' because 'society' cannot think, act, value, or 'treat' anybody in a particular way. If such claims are to be met, the spontaneous order which we call society must be replaced by a deliberately directed organization: the cosmos of the market would have to be replaced by a taxis whose members would have to do what they are instructed to do. They could not be allowed to use their knowledge for their own purposes but would have to carry out the plan which their rulers have designed to meet the needs to be satisfied. From this it follows that the old civil rights and the new social and economic rights cannot be achieved at the same time but are in fact incompatible; the new rights could not be enforced by law without at the same time destroying that liberal order at which the old civil rights aim.

The new trend was given its chief impetus through the proclamation by President Franklin Roosevelt of his 'Four Freedoms' which included 'freedom *from* want' and 'freedom *from* fear' together with the old 'freedom *of* speech' and 'freedom *of* worship'. But it found its definite embodiment only in the *Universal Declaration of Human Rights* adopted by the General Assembly of the United Nations in 1948. This document is admittedly an attempt to fuse the rights of the Western liberal tradition with the altogether different conception deriving from the Marxist Russian Revolution.[3] It adds to the list of the classical civil rights enumerated in its first twenty-one articles seven further guarantees intended to express the new 'social and economic rights'. In these additional clauses 'every one, as a member of society' is assured the satisfaction of positive claims to particular benefits without at the same time placing on anyone the duty or burden of providing them. The document also completely fails to define these rights in such a manner that a court could possibly determine what their contents are in a particular instance. What, for instance, can be the legal meaning of the statement that every one 'is entitled to the realization . . . of the economic, social, and cultural rights indispensible for his dignity and free development of his personality' (Art. 22)? Against whom is 'every one' to have a claim to 'just and favourable conditions of work' (Art. 23 (1)) and to 'just and favourable employment' (Art. 23 (3))? What are the consequences of the requirement that every one should have the right 'freely to participate in the cultural life of the community and to share in the scientific advances and its benefits' (Art. 27 (1))? 'Every one' is even said to be 'entitled to a social and international order in which the rights and freedoms set forth in this Declaration are fully realized' (Art. 28)—on the assumption apparently that not only is this possible but that there exists now a known method by which these claims can be satisfied for all men.

It is evident that all these 'rights' are based on the interpretation of society as a deliberately made organization by which everybody is employed. They could not be made universal within a system of rules of just conduct based on the conception of individual responsibility, and so require that the whole of society be converted into a single organization, that is, made totalitarian in the fullest sense of the word. We have seen that rules of just conduct which apply to everybody alike but subject nobody to the commands of a superior can never determine what particular things any person is to have. They can never take the form of 'everybody must have so and so.' In a free society what the individual will get must always depend in some measure on particular circumstances which nobody can foresee and nobody has the power to determine. Rules of just conduct can therefore never confer on any person as such (as distinct from the members of a particular organization) a claim to particular things; they can bring about only opportunities for the acquiring of such claims.

It apparently never occurred to the authors of the Declaration that not everybody is an employed member of an organization whose right 'to just and favourable remuneration, including reasonable limitations of working hours and periodic holidays with pay' (Art. 24) can be guaranteed. The conception of a 'universal right' which assures to the peasant, to the Eskimo, and presumably to the Abominable Snowman, 'periodic holidays with pay' shows the absurdity of the whole thing. Even the slightest amount of ordinary common sense ought to have told the authors of the document that what they decreed as universal rights were for the present and for any foreseeable future utterly impossible of achievement, and that solemnly to proclaim them as rights was to play an irresponsible game with the concept of 'right' which could result only in destroying the respect for it.

The whole document is indeed couched in that jargon of organization thinking which one has learnt to expect in the pronouncement of trade union officials or the International Labour Organization and which reflects an attitude business employees share with civil servants and the organization men of the big corporations, but which is altogether inconsistent with the principles on which the order of a Great Society rests. If the document were merely the production of an international group of social philosophers (as in origin it is), it would constitute only somewhat disturbing evidence of the degree to which organization thinking has permeated the thinking of these social philosophers and how much they have become total strangers to the basic ideals of a free society. But its acceptance by a body of presumably responsible statesmen, seriously concerned with the creation of a peaceful international order, gives cause for much greater apprehension.

Organization thinking, largely as a result of the sway of the rationalist constructivism of Plato and his followers, has long been the besetting vice of social philosophers; perhaps it should therefore not surprise us that academic philosophers in their sheltered lives as members of organizations should have lost all understanding of the forces which hold the Great Society together and, imagining themselves to be Platonic philosopher-kings, should propose a re-organization of society on totalitarian lines. If it should be true, as we are told, that the social and economic rights of the Universal Declaration of Human Rights would today be 'accepted by the vast majority of American and British moralists,'[4] this would merely indicate a sorry lack of critical acumen on the part of these thinkers.

The spectacle, however, of the General Assembly of the United

Nations solemnly proclaiming that *every* individual (!), 'keeping this Declaration constantly in mind' (!), should strive to insure the universal observation of those human rights, would be merely comic if the illusions which this creates were not so profoundly tragic. To see the most comprehensive authority which man has yet created undermining the respect it ought to command by giving countenance to the naive prejudice that we can create any state of affairs which we think to be desirable by simply decreeing that it ought to exist, and indulging in the self-deception that we can benefit from the spontaneous order of society and at the same time mould it to our own will, is more than merely tragic.[5]

The fundamental fact which these illusions disregard is that the availability of all those benefits which we wish as many people as possible to have depends on these same people using for their production their own best knowledge. To establish enforceable rights to the benefits is not likely to produce them. If we wish everybody to be well off, we shall get closest to our goal, not by commanding by law that this should be achieved, or giving everybody a legal claim to what we think he ought to have, but by providing inducements for all to do as much as they can that will benefit others. To speak of rights where what are in question are merely aspirations which only a voluntary system can fulfil, not only misdirects attention from what are the effective determinants of the wealth which we wish for all, but also debases the word 'right', the strict meaning of which it is very important to preserve if we are to maintain a free society.

TEN

THE MARKET ORDER OR CATALLAXY

The judgement of mankind about what is equitable is liable to change, and . . . one of the forces which cause it to change is mankind's discovery from time to time that what was supposed to be quite just and equitable in some particular matter has become, or perhaps always was, uneconomical.

Edwin Cannan*

The nature of the market order

In chapter 2 we have discussed the general character of all spontaneous orders. It is necessary now to examine more fully the special attributes possessed by the order of the market and the nature of the benefits we owe to it. This order serves our ends not merely, as all order does, by guiding us in our actions and by bringing about a certain correspondence between the expectations of the different persons, but also, in a sense which we must now make more precise, by increasing the prospects or chances of every one of a greater command over the various goods (i.e. commodities and services) than we are able to secure in any other way. We shall see, however, that this manner of co-ordinating individual actions will secure a high degree of coincidence of expectations and an effective utilization of the knowledge and skills of the several members only at the price of a constant disappointment of some expectations.

For a proper understanding of the character of this order it is essential that we free ourselves of the misleading associations suggested by its usual description as an 'economy'. An economy, in the strict sense of the word in which a household, a farm, or an enterprise can be called economies, consists of a complex of activities by which a given set of means is allocated in accordance with a unitary plan among the competing ends according to their relative importance. The market order serves no such single order of ends.

What is commonly called a social or national economy is in this sense not a single economy but a network of many interlaced economies.[1] Its order shares, as we shall see, with the order of an economy proper some formal characteristics but not the most important one: its activities are not governed by a single scale or hierarchy of ends. The belief that the economic activities of the individual members of society are or ought to be part of one economy in the strict sense of this term, and that what is commonly described as the economy of a country or a society ought to be ordered and judged by the same criteria as an economy proper, is a chief source of error in this field. But, whenever we speak of the economy of a country, or of the world, we are employing a term which suggests that these systems ought to be run on socialist lines and directed according to a single plan so as to serve a unitary system of ends.

While an economy proper is an organization in the technical sense in which we have defined that term, that is, a deliberate arrangement of the use of the means which are known to some single agency, the cosmos of the market neither is nor could be governed by such a single scale of ends; it serves the multiplicity of separate and incommensurable ends of all its separate members.

The confusion which has been created by the ambiguity of the word economy is so serious that for our present purposes it seems necessary to confine its use strictly to the original meaning in which it describes a complex of deliberately co-ordinated actions serving a single scale of ends, and to adopt another term to describe the system of numerous interrelated economies which constitute the market order. Since the name 'catallactics' has long ago been suggested for the science which deals with the market order[2] and has more recently been revived,[3] it would seem appropriate to adopt a corresponding term for the market order itself. The term 'catallactics' was derived from the Greek verb *katallattein* (or *katallassein*) which meant, significantly, not only 'to exchange' but also 'to admit into the community' and 'to change from enemy into friend'.[4] From it the adjective 'catallactic' has been derived to serve in the place of 'economic' to describe the kind of phenomena with which the science of catallactics deals. The ancient Greeks knew neither this term nor had a corresponding noun; if they had formed one it would probably have been *katallaxia*. From this we can form an English term *catallaxy* which we shall use to describe the order brought about by the mutual adjustment of many individual economies in a market. A catallaxy is thus the special kind of spontaneous order produced by the market through people acting within the rules of the law of property, tort and contract.

A free society is a pluralistic society without a common hierarchy of particular ends

It is often made a reproach to the Great Society and its market order that it lacks an agreed ranking of ends. This, however, is in fact its great merit which makes individual freedom and all it values possible. The Great Society arose through the discovery that men can live together in peace and mutually benefiting each other without agreeing on the particular aims which they severally pursue. The discovery that by substituting abstract rules of conduct for obligatory concrete ends made it possible to extend the order of peace beyond the small groups pursuing the same ends, because it enabled each individual to gain from the skill and knowledge of others whom he need not even know and whose aims could be wholly different from his own. [5]

The decisive step which made such peaceful collaboration possible in the absence of concrete common purposes was the adoption of barter or exchange. It was the simple recognition that different persons had different uses for the same things, and that often each of two individuals would benefit if he obtained something the other had, in return for his giving the other what he needed. All that was required to bring this about was that rules be recognized which determined what belonged to each, and how such property could be transferred by consent. [6] There was no need for the parties to agree on the purposes which this transaction served. It is indeed characteristic of such acts of exchange that they serve different and independent purposes of each partner in the transaction, and that they thus assist the parties as means for different ends. The parties are in fact the more likely to benefit from exchange the more their needs differ. While within an organization the several members will assist each other to the extent that they are made to aim at the same purposes, in a catallaxy they are induced to contribute to the needs of others without caring or even knowing about them.

In the Great Society we all in fact contribute not only to the satisfaction of needs of which we do not know, but sometimes even to the achievement of ends of which we would disapprove if we knew about them. We cannot help this because we do not know for what purposes the goods or services which we supply to others will be used by them. That we assist in the realization of other people's aims without sharing them or even knowing them, and solely in order to achieve our own aims, is the source of strength of the Great Society. So long as collaboration presupposes common purposes, people with different aims are necessarily enemies who may fight each other for the same means; only the introduction of barter made it possible for the different individuals to be of use to each other without agreeing on the ultimate ends.

When this effect of exchange of making people mutually benefit each other without intending to do so was first clearly recognized,[7] too much stress was laid on the resulting division of labour and on the fact that it was their 'selfish' aims which led the different persons to render services to each other. This is much too narrow a view of the matter. Division of labour is extensively practised also within organizations; and the advantages of the spontaneous order do not depend on people being selfish in the ordinary sense of this word. The important point about the catallaxy is that it reconciles different knowledge and different purposes which, whether the individuals be selfish or not, will greatly differ from one person to another. It is because in the catallaxy men, while following their own interests, whether wholly egotistical or highly altruistic, will further the aims of many others, most of whom they will never know, that it is as an overall order so superior to any deliberate organization: in the Great Society the different members benefit from each other's efforts not only in spite of but often even because of their several aims being different.[8]

Many people regard it as revolting that the Great Society has no common concrete purposes or, as we may say, that it is merely means-connected and not ends-connected. It is indeed true that the chief common purpose of all its members is the purely instrumental one of securing the formation of an abstract order which has no specific purposes but will enhance for all the prospects of achieving their respective purposes. The prevailing moral tradition, much of which still derives from the end-connected tribal society, makes people often regard this circumstance as a moral defect of the Great Society which ought to be remedied. Yet it was the very restriction of coercion to the observance of the negative rules of just conduct that made possible the integration into a peaceful order of individuals and groups which pursued different ends; and it is the absence of prescribed common ends which makes a society of free men all that it has come to mean to us.

Though the conception that a common scale of particular values is a good thing which ought, if necessary, to be enforced, is deeply founded in the history of the human race, its intellectual defence today is based mainly on the erroneous belief that such a common scale of ends is necessary for the integration of the individual activities into an order, and a necessary condition of peace. This error is, however, the greatest obstacle to the achievement of those very ends. A Great Society has nothing to do with, and is in fact irreconcilable with 'solidarity' in the true sense of unitedness in the pursuit of known common goals. [9] If we all occasionally feel that it is a good thing to have a common purpose with our fellows, and enjoy a sense of elation when we can act as members of a group aiming at common ends, this is an instinct which we have inherited from tribal society and which no doubt often still stands us in good stead whenever it is important that in a small group we should act in concert to meet a sudden emergency. It shows itself conspicuously when sometimes even the outbreak of war is felt as satisfying a craving for such a common purpose; and it manifests itself most clearly in modern times in the two greatest threats to a free civilization: nationalism and socialism. [10]

Most of the knowledge on which we rely in the pursuit of our ends is the unintended by-product of others exploring the world in different directions from those we pursue ourselves because they are impelled by different aims; it would never have become available to us if only those ends were pursued which we regarded as desirable. To make it a condition for the membership of a society that one approved of, and deliberately supported, the concrete ends which one's fellow members serve, would eliminate the chief factor which makes for the advancement of such a society. Where agreement on concrete objects is a necessary condition of order and peace, and dissent a danger to the order of the society, where approval and censure depend on the concrete ends which particular actions serve, the forces for intellectual progress would be much confined. However much the existence of agreement on ends may in many respects smooth the course of life, the possibility of disagreement, or at least the lack of compulsion to agree on particular ends, is the basis of the kind of civilization which has grown up since the Greeks developed independent thought of the individual as the most effective method of advancement of the human mind. [11]

Though not a single economy, the Great Society is still held together mainly by what vulgarly are called economic relations

The misconception that the market order is an economy in the strict sense of the term is usually found combined with the denial that the Great Society is held together by what are loosely called economic relations. These two views are frequently held by the same persons because it is certainly true that those deliberate organizations which are properly called economies are based on an agreement on common ends which in turn mostly are non-economic; while it is the great advantage of the spontaneous order of the market that it is merely means-connected and that, therefore, it makes agreement on ends unnecessary and a reconciliation of divergent purposes possible. What are commonly called economic relations are indeed relations determined by the fact that the use of all means is affected by the striving for those many different purposes. It is in this wide sense of the term 'economic' that the interdependence or coherence of the parts of the Great Society is purely economic.[12]

The suggestion that in this wide sense the only ties which hold the whole of a Great Society together are purely 'economic' (more precisely 'catallactic') arouse great emotional resistance. Yet the fact can hardly be denied; nor the fact that, in a society of the dimensions and complexity of a modern country or of the world, it can hardly be otherwise. Most people are still reluctant to accept the fact that it should be the disdained 'cash-nexus' which holds the Great Society together, that the great ideal of the unity of mankind should in the last resort depend on the relations between the parts being governed by the striving for the better satisfaction of their material needs.

It is of course true that within the overall framework of the Great Society there exist numerous networks of other relations that are in no sense economic. But this does not alter the fact that it is the market order which makes peaceful reconciliation of the divergent purposes possible—and possible by a process which redounds to the benefit of all. That interdependence of all men, which is now in everybody's mouth and which tends to make all mankind One World, not only is the effect of the market order but could not have been brought about by any other means. What today connects the life of any European or American with what happens in Australia, Japan or Zaire are repercussions transmitted by the network of market relations. This is clearly seen when we reflect how little, for instance, all the technological possibilities of transportation and communication would matter if the conditions of production were the same in all the different parts of the world.

The benefits from the knowledge which others possess, including all the advances of science, reach us through channels provided and directed by the market mechanism. Even the degree to which we can participate in the aesthetic or moral strivings of men in other parts of the world we owe to the economic nexus. It is true that on the whole this dependence of every man on the actions of so many others is not a physical but what we call an economic fact. It is therefore a misunderstanding, caused by the misleading terms used, if the economists are sometimes accused of 'pan-economism', a tendency to see everything from the economic angle, or, worse, wanting to make 'economic purposes' prevail over all others.[13] The truth is that catallactics is the science which describes the only overall order that comprehends nearly all mankind, and that the economist is therefore entitled to insist that conduciveness to that order be accepted as a standard by which all particular institutions are judged.

It is, however, a misunderstanding to represent this as an effort to make 'economic ends' prevail over others. There are, in the last resort, no economic ends. The economic efforts of the individuals as well as the services which the market order renders to them, consist in an allocation of means for the competing ultimate purposes which are always non-economic. The task of all economic activity is to reconcile the competing ends by deciding for which of them the limited means are to be used. The market order reconciles the claims of the different non-economic ends by the only known process that benefits all—without, however, assuring that the more important comes before the less important, for the simple reason that there can exist in such a system no single ordering of needs. What it tends to bring about is merely a state of affairs in which no need is served at the cost of withdrawing a greater amount of means from the use for other needs than is necessary to satisfy it. The market is the only known method by which this can be achieved without an agreement on the relative importance of the different ultimate ends, and solely on the basis of a principle of reciprocity through which the opportunities of any person are likely to be greater than they would otherwise be.

The aim of policy in a society of free men cannot be a maximum of foreknown results but only an abstract order

The erroneous interpretation of the catallaxy as an economy in the strict sense of this word frequently leads to attempts to evaluate the benefits which we derive from it in terms of the degree of satisfaction of a given order of ends. But, if the importance of the various demands is judged by the price offered, this approach, as has been pointed out innumerable times, by the critics of the market order even more frequently than by its defenders, involves us in a vicious circle: because the relative strength of the demand for the different goods and services to which the market will adjust their production is itself determined by the distribution of incomes which in turn is determined by the market mechanism. Many writers have concluded from this that if this scale of relative demands cannot without circular reasoning be accepted as the common scale of values, another scale of ends must be postulated if we are to judge the effectiveness of this market order.

The belief that there can be no rational policy without a common scale of concrete ends implies, however, an interpretation of the catallaxy as an economy proper and for this reason is misleading. Policy need not be guided by the striving for the achievement of particular results, but may be directed towards securing an abstract overall order of such character that it will secure for the members the best chance of achieving their different and largely unknown particular ends. The aim of policy in such a society would have to be to increase equally the chances for any unknown member of society of pursuing with success his equally unknown purposes, and to restrict the use of coercion (apart from the raising of taxes) to the enforcement of such rules as will, if universally applied, tend in this sense to improve everyone's opportunities.

A policy making use of the spontaneously ordering forces therefore cannot aim at a known maximum of particular results, but must aim at increasing, for any person picked out at random, the prospects that the overall effect of all changes required by that order will be to increase his chances of attaining his ends. We have seen[14] that the common good in this sense is not a particular state of things but consists in an abstract order which in a free society must leave undetermined the degree to which the several particular needs will be met. The aim will have to be an order which will increase everybody's chances as much as possible—

not at every moment, but only 'on the whole' and in the long run.

Because the results of any economic policy must depend on the use made of the operation of the market by unknown persons guided by their own knowledge and their own aims, the goal of such a policy must be to provide a multi-purpose instrument which at no particular moment may be the one best adapted to the particular circumstances, but which will be the best for the great variety of circumstances likely to occur. If we had known those particular circumstances in advance, we could probably have better equipped ourselves to deal with them; but since we do not know them beforehand, we must be content with a less specialized instrument which will allow us to cope even with very unlikely events.

The game of catallaxy

The best way to understand how the operation of the market system leads not only to the creation of an order, but also to a great increase of the return which men receive from their efforts, is to think of it, as suggested in the last chapter, as a game which we may now call the game of catallaxy. It is a wealth-creating game (and not what game theory calls a zero-sum game), that is, one that leads to an increase of the stream of goods and of the prospects of all participants to satisfy their needs, but which retains the character of a game in the sense in which the term is defined by the *Oxford English Dictionary*: 'a contest played according to rules and decided by superior skill, strength or good fortune'. That the outcome of this game for each will, because of its very character, necessarily be determined by a mixture of skill and chance will be one of the main points we must now try to make clear.

The chief cause of the wealth-creating character of the game is that the returns of the efforts of each player act as the signs which enable him to contribute to the satisfaction of needs of which he does not know, and to do so by taking advantage of conditions of which he also learns only indirectly through their being reflected in the prices of the factors of production which they use. It is thus a wealth-producing game because it supplies to each player information which enables him to provide for needs of which he has no direct knowledge and by the use of means of the existence of which without it he would have no cognizance, thus bringing about the satisfaction of a greater range of needs than would otherwise be possible. The manufacturer does not produce shoes because he knows that Jones needs them. He produces because he knows that dozens of traders will buy certain numbers at various prices because they (or rather the retailer they serve) know that thousands of Joneses, whom the manufacturer does not know, want to buy them. Similarly, a manufacturer will release resources for additional production by others by substituting, say, aluminium for magnesium in the production of his output, not because he knows of all the changes in demand and supply which on balance have made aluminium less scarce and magnesium more scarce, but because he learns the one simple fact that the price at which aluminium is offered to him has fallen relatively to the price of magnesium. Indeed, probably the most important instance of the price system bringing about the taking into account of conflicts of desires which otherwise would have been overlooked is the accounting of costs— in the interests of the community at large the most important aspect, i.e. the one most likely to benefit many other persons, and the one at which private enterprise excels but government enterprise notoriously fails.

Thus in the market order each is made by the visible gain to himself to serve needs which to him are invisible, and in order to do so to avail himself of to him unknown particular circumstances which put him in the position to satisfy these needs at as small a cost as possible in terms of other things which it is possible to produce instead. And where only a few know yet of an important new fact, the much maligned speculators will see to it that the relevant information will rapidly be spread by an appropriate change of prices. The important effect of this will of course be that all changes are currently taken account of as they become known to somebody connected with the trade, not that the adaptation to the new facts will ever be perfect.

The current prices, it must be specially noted, serve in this process as indicators of what ought to be done in the present circumstances and have no necessary relation to what has been done in the past in order to bring the current supply of any particular good on the market. For the same reason that the prices which guide the direction of the different efforts reflect events which the producer does not know, the return from his efforts will frequently be different from what he expected, and must be so if they are to guide production appropriately. The remunerations which the market determines are, as it were, not functionally related with what people *have* done, but only with what they *ought* to do. They are incentives which as a rule guide people to success, but will produce a viable order only because they often disappoint the expectations they have caused when relevant circumstances have unexpectedly changed. It is one of the chief tasks of competition to show which plans are false. The facts that full utilization of the limited information which the prices convey is usually rewarded, and that this makes it worth-while to pay the greatest attention to them, are as important as that in the case of unforeseen changes the expectations are disappointed. The element of luck is as inseparable from the operation of the market as the element of skill.

There is no need morally to justify specific distributions (of income or wealth) which have not been brought about deliberately but are the outcome of a game that is played because it improves the chances of all. In such a game nobody 'treats' people differently and it is entirely consistent with respecting all people equally that the outcome of the game for different people is very different. It would also be as much a gamble what the effects of any one man's efforts would be worth if they were directed by a planning authority, only that not his knowledge but that of the authority would be used in determining the success or failure of his efforts.

The sum of information reflected or precipitated in the prices is wholly the product of competition, or at least of the openness of the market to anyone who has relevant information about some source of demand or supply for the good in question. Competition operates as a discovery procedure not only by giving anyone who has the opportunity to exploit special circumstances the possibility to do so profitably, but also by conveying to the other parties the information that there is some such opportunity. It is by this conveying of information in coded form that the competitive efforts of the market game secure the utilization of widely dispersed knowledge.

Even more important, perhaps, than the information about wants that may be satisfied and for whose satisfaction an attractive price is offered, is the information about the possibility of doing so by a smaller outlay than is currently incurred of resources which are needed also elsewhere. And it is not merely, or perhaps even chiefly, the fact that prices will spread the knowledge that some technical possibilities exist to produce a commodity more efficiently, but above all the indication which of the available technical methods is the most economical in the given circumstances, and the changes in the relative scarcities of the different materials and other factors, which alter the relative advantages of the different methods, which is of decisive importance. Almost any product can be produced by a great many different quantitative combinations of the various factors of production, and which of them will be the least costly, i.e. will involve the least sacrifice of other goods that might be produced with them, is indicated by the relative prices of these factors.[15]

By thus endeavouring to produce their outputs as cheaply as possible the producers in a sense will indeed make the total product of the catallaxy as great as possible. The prices at which they can buy the different factors on the market will tell each which quantities of any two of them cost the same because they bring elsewhere the same marginal return; and he will thereby be induced so to adjust the relative amounts of any pair of factors he requires that such quantities of them will make the same marginal contributions to his output (be 'marginal substitutes' for each other) as will cost him the same amount of money. If this is generally done, and the marginal rates of substitution between any two factors have become the same in all their uses, the market has reached the horizon of catallactic possibilities at which the greatest possible quantity of the particular combination of goods is being produced which in the circumstances can be produced.

For the case of only two goods this horizon of catallactic possibilities can be illustrated by a simple diagram known in economic theory as a transformation curve: if the quantities of the two goods are measured along two rectangular co-ordinates, any straight line through the origin will represent the locus of all possible total quantities of two products in a given quantitative proportion, say $a+2b$, $2a+4b$, $3a+6b$, etc., etc., and there will be, for any given supply of factors, an absolute maximum that can be obtained if these two factors are distributed economically between the two uses. The convex curve connecting the points standing for the maxima of the different combinations of the two goods is the 'transformation curve' representing the horizon of catallactic possibilities for these two goods in the existing situation. The important point about this range of potential maxima is that it is not simply a technical fact but is determined by the momentary scarcity or plenty of the different factors, and that the horizon of catallactic possibilities will be reached only if the marginal rates of substitution between the different factors are made the same in all their uses—which, of course, in a catallaxy producing many goods, can be achieved only by all producers adjusting the relative quantities of the different factors which they use according to their uniform market prices.

The horizon of catallactic possibilities (which for a system producing n goods would be represented by an n-dimensional surface) would indicate the range of what are now usually described as Pareto-optima, i.e. all the combinations of different goods which can be produced for which it is impossible so to rearrange production that some consumer gets more of something without in consequence anybody else getting less of anything (which is always possible if the product corresponds to any point inside the horizon).

If there is no accepted order of rank of the different needs, there is no way of deciding which among the different combinations of goods corresponding to this horizon is larger than any other. Yet every one of these combinations is a 'maximum' in a peculiar limited sense which, however, is the only sense in which, for a society which has no agreed hierarchy of ends, we can speak of a maximum at all: it corresponds to the largest amount of the particular combination of goods which can be produced by the known techniques (a sense in which the largest quantity of one good only that could be produced if nothing else were produced would be one of the maxima included in the horizon of possibilities!). The combination in fact produced will be determined by the relative strength of the demand for the different goods—which in turn depends on the distribution of incomes, that is the prices paid for the contributions of the different factors of production, and these again serve merely (or are necessary in order) to secure that the horizon of catallactic possibilities be approached.

The effect of all this is thus that, while the share of each factor of production in the total output is determined by the instrumental necessities of the only known process by which we can secure a steady approach to that horizon, the material equivalent of any given individual share will be as large as it can possibly be made. In other words, while the share of each player in the game of catallaxy will be determined partly by skill and partly by chance, the content of the share which is allocated to him by that mixed game of chance and skill will be a true maximum.

It would, of course, be unreasonable to demand more from the operation of a system in which the several actors do not serve a common hierarchy of ends but co-operate with each other only because they can thereby mutually assist each other in their respective pursuit of their individual ends. Nothing else is indeed possible in an order in which the participants are free in the sense of being allowed to use their own knowledge for their own purposes. So long as the game is played by which alone all this knowledge can be utilized and all these ends taken into account, it would be inconsistent and unjust to divert some part of the stream of goods to some group of players whom some authority thinks deserves it. On the other hand, in a centrally directed system, it would be impossible to reward people in accordance with the value which their voluntary contributions have to their fellows, because, without an effective market, the individuals could neither know, nor be allowed to decide, where to apply their efforts. The responsibility for the use of his gifts and the usefulness of the results would rest entirely with the directing authority.

Men can be allowed to act on their own knowledge and for their own purposes only if the reward they obtain is dependent in part on circumstances which they can neither control nor foresee. And if they are to be allowed to be guided in their actions by their own moral beliefs, it cannot also be morally required that the aggregate effects of their respective actions on the different people should correspond to some ideal of distributive justice. In this sense freedom is inseparable from rewards which often have no connection with merit and are therefore felt to be unjust.

In judging the adaptations to changed circumstances comparisons of the new with the former position are irrelevant

While in the case of bilateral barter the reciprocal advantages to both parties are easy to see, the position may at first seem to be different in the conditions of multilateral or multiangular exchange which are the rule in modern society. Here a person will normally render services to one group of persons, but himself receive services from another group. And as every decision will usually be a question of from whom to buy and to whom to sell, though it is still true that in this case both parties of the new transaction will gain, we must consider also the effects on those with whom the participants in the new transactions have decided not to deal again because their new partners have offered them more favourable terms. The effects of such decisions on third persons will be felt particularly severely when these have come to count on the opportunity to deal with the persons with whom they have done so in the past, and now find their expectations disappointed and their incomes diminished. Must we not in this case count the loss of those from whom demand or supply has turned as an offset against the gain of those who have availed themselves of the new opportunities?

As we have seen in the last chapter, such undeserved diminutions of the material positions of whole groups are the source of a main complaint against the market order. Yet such diminutions of the relative, and often even of the absolute position of some will be a necessary and constantly recurring effect so long as in the several transactions the parties consider only their own advantage and not the effects of their decisions on others. Does this mean that something is disregarded that ought to be taken into account in the formation of a desirable order?

The conditions which prevailed earlier, however, are wholly irrelevant for what is appropriate after the external circumstances have changed. The past position of those who are now forced to descend from it was determined by the operation of the same process as that which now favours others. The action of the market takes account only of the conditions known to exist at present (or expected to prevail in the future); it adapts relative values to them without regard to the past. Those whose services were more valuable in the past were then accordingly paid for them. The new position is not an improvement over the past condition in the sense that it constitutes a better adaptation to the same circumstances; it represents the same kind of adaptation to new circumstances as the former position did with respect to the circumstances which existed then.

In the context of an order the advantage of which is that it continually adapts the use of resources to conditions unforeseen and unknown to most people, bygones are forever bygones[16]—the past conditions tell us nothing about what is appropriate now. Though to some extent past prices will serve as the chief basis for forming expectations about future prices, they will do so only where a large part of the conditions have remained unchanged, but not where extensive changes have occurred.

Any discovery of more favourable opportunities for satisfying their needs by some will thus be a disadvantage to those on whose services they would otherwise have relied. Yet in this respect the effects of new and more favourable opportunities for exchanging which appear for particular individuals are for society as a whole as beneficial as the discovery of new or hitherto unknown material resources. The parties to the new exchange transaction will now be able to satisfy their needs by the expenditure of a smaller part of their resources, and what they thereby save can be used to provide additional services to others. Of course, those who as a result will be deprived of their former customers will incur a loss which it would be in their interest to prevent. But like all others, they will have been profiting all the time from the repercussions of thousands of similar changes elsewhere which release resources for a better supply of the market. And though in the short run the unfavourable effect on them may out-balance the sum of the indirect beneficial effects, in the long run the sum of all those particular effects, although they always will harm some, are likely to improve the chances for all. This result, however, will occur only if the immediate and generally more visible effects are systematically disregarded and policy is governed by the probability that in the long run all will profit by the utilization of every opportunity of the kind.

The known and concentrated harm to those who lose part or all of the customary source of income must, in other words, not be allowed to count against the diffused (and, from the point of view of policy, usually unknown and therefore indiscriminate) benefits to many. We shall see that the universal tendency of politics is to give preferential consideration to few strong and therefore conspicuous effects over the numerous small and therefore neglected ones, and therefore to grant special privileges to groups threatened with the loss of positions they have achieved. But when we reflect that most of the benefits we currently owe to the market are the results of continuous adaptations which are unknown to us, and because of which only some but not all of the consequences of our deliberate decisions can be foreseen, it should be obvious that we will achieve the best results if we abide by a rule which, if consistently applied, is likely to increase everybody's chances. Though the share of each will be unpredictable, because it will depend only in part on his skill and opportunities to learn facts, and in part on accident, this is the condition which alone will make it the interest of all so to conduct themselves as to make as large as possible the aggregate product of which they will get an unpredictable share. Of the resulting distribution it cannot be claimed that it is materially just, but only that it is the result of a process which is known to improve the chances of all and not the consequence of specific directed measures which favour some on principles that could not be generally acted upon.

*Rules of just conduct protect only material domains and not market
values*

The value which any person's products or services will have in the
market, and therefore his share in the aggregate product, will
always depend also on decisions which other persons make in the
light of the changing possibilities known to them. A particular
price or a particular share in the total output can therefore be
assured to any person only by requiring particular other persons to
buy from him at a certain price. This is clearly incompatible with
the principle that coercion is to be limited to the enforcement of
uniform rules of just conduct equally applicable to all. Rules of just
conduct which are end-independent cannot determine what anyone
must do (apart from the discharge of obligations voluntarily
entered into), but only what he must not do. They merely lay down
the principles determining the protected domain of each on which
nobody must encroach.

In other words, rules of just conduct can enable us merely to
determine which particular things belong to particular persons, but
not what these things will be worth, or what benefit they will
confer on those to whom they belong. The rules serve to provide
information for the decision of individuals, and thus help to reduce
uncertainty, but they cannot determine what use the individual can
make of this information and therefore also not eliminate *all* uncertainty. They tell each individual only what are the particular
things he can count on being able to use, but not what the results of
his use will be so far as these depend on the exchange of the product
of their efforts with others.

It is clearly misleading to express this by saying that the rules of
just conduct allocate particular things to particular people. They
state the conditions under which any person can acquire or give up
particular things, but do not by themselves definitely determine the
particular conditions in which he will find himself. His domain
will at any moment depend on how successfully he has used these
conditions, and on the particular opportunities he happens to have
encountered. In a sense it is even true that such a system gives to
those who already have. But this is its merit rather than its defect,
because it is this feature which makes it worth-while for everybody
to direct his efforts not only towards immediate results but also
towards the future increase of his capacity of rendering services to
others. It is the possibility of acquisition for the purpose of

improving the capacity for future acquisition which engenders a continuous overall process in which we do not at every moment have to start from scratch, but can begin with equipment which is the result of past efforts in order to make as large as possible the earnings from the means which we control.

The correspondence of expectations is brought about by a disappointment of some expectations

The abstract rule of conduct can (and, in order to secure the formation of a spontaneous order, should) thus protect only the expectation of command over particular physical things and services, and not the expectations concerning their market value, i.e. the terms on which they can be exchanged for other things. This is a point of central importance which is frequently misunderstood. From it follow several significant corollaries. First, though it is the aim of law to increase certainty, it can eliminate only certain sources of uncertainty and it would be harmful if it attempted to eliminate all uncertainty: it can protect expectations only by prohibiting interference with a man's property (including claims on such future services of others as these others have voluntarily promised) and not by requiring others to take particular actions. It can, therefore, not assure any one that the goods and services which he has to offer will have a particular value, but only that he will be allowed to obtain for them what price he can.

The reason why the law can protect only some but not all expectations, or remove only some but not all sources of uncertainty, is that rules of just conduct can only limit the range of permitted actions in such a manner that the intentions of different persons will not clash, but cannot positively determine what actions those individuals must perform. By restraining the range of actions which any individual may take, the law opens for all the possibility of effective collaboration with others, but does not assure it. Rules of conduct that equally limit the freedom of each so as to assure the same freedom to all can merely make possible agreements for obtaining what is now possessed by others, and thereby channel the efforts for all towards seeking agreement with others. But they cannot secure the success of these efforts, or determine the terms on which such agreements can be concluded.

The correspondence of expectations that makes it possible for all parties to achieve what they are striving for is in fact brought about by a process of learning by trial and error which must involve a constant disappointment of some expectations. The process of adaptation operates, as do the adjustments of any self-organizing system, by what cybernetics has taught us to call negative feedback: responses to the differences between the expected and the actual results of actions so that these differences will be reduced. This will produce an increased correspondence of expectations of the different persons so long as current prices provide some indications of what future prices will be, that is, so long as, in a fairly constant framework of known facts, always only a few of them change; and so long as the price mechanism operates as a medium of communicating knowledge which brings it about that the facts which become known to some, through the effects of their actions on prices, are made to influence the decision of others.

It may at first appear paradoxical that in order to achieve the greatest attainable certainty it should be necessary to leave uncertain so important an object of expectations as the terms at which things can be bought and sold. The paradox disappears, however, when we remember that we can aim only at providing the best basis for judging what of necessity is uncertain and for securing continual adaptation to what has not been known before: we can strive only for the best utilization of partial knowledge that constantly changes, and that is communicated mainly through changes in prices, and not for the best utilization of a given and constant stock of knowledge. The best we can attain in such a situation is not certainty but the elimination of avoidable uncertainty—which cannot be attained by preventing unforeseen changes from spreading their effects, but only by facilitating the adaptation to such changes.

It is often contended that it is unjust to let the burden of such unforeseeable changes fall on people who could not foresee them, and that, if such risks are unavoidable, they ought to be pooled and the losses equally born by all. It can, however, hardly be known whether any particular change was unforeseeable for all. The whole system rests on providing inducements for all to use their skill to find out particular circumstances in order to anticipate impending changes as accurately as possible. This incentive would be removed if each decision did not carry the risk of loss, or if an authority had to decide whether a particular error in anticipation was excusable or not.[17]

Abstract rules of just conduct can determine only chances and not particular results

Rules of just conduct that apply equally to all members of society can refer only to some but not to all of the conditions under which their actions take place. It is a consequence of this that they can secure for all individuals only chances and not the certainty of a particular outcome. Even in a game with equal chances for all players there will be some winners and some losers. By assuring the individual of some of the elements of the situation in which he will have to act, his prospects will be improved, but necessarily many factors left undetermined on which his success depends. The aim of legislation, in laying down rules for an unknown number of future instances, can therefore be only to increase the chances of unknown persons whose opportunities will chiefly depend on their individual knowledge and skill as well as on the particular conditions in which accident will place them. The efforts of the legislator can thus be directed only towards increasing the chances for all, not in the sense that the incidence of the diffused effects of his decision on the various individuals will be known, but only in the sense that he can aim at increasing the opportunities that will become available to some unknown persons.

It is a corollary of this that each individual will have a claim in justice, not to an equal chance in general, but only that the principles guiding all coercive measures of government should be equally likely to benefit anybody's chances; and that these rules be applied in all particular instances irrespective of whether the effect on particular individuals seems desirable or not. So long as the positions of the different individuals are to be left at all dependent on their skill and on the particular circumstances they encounter, nobody can assure that they will all have the same chances.

In such a game in which the results for the individuals depend partly on chance and partly on their skill, there is evidently no sense in calling the outcome either just or unjust. The position is somewhat like that in a competition for a prize in which we shall attempt to make conditions such that we can say who performs best, but will not be able to decide whether the best actual performance is proof of higher merit. We shall not be able to prevent accidents from interfering, and in consequence cannot be sure that the results will be proportionate to the capacity of the competitors or their particular qualities that we desire to encourage. Though we want

THE MARKET ORDER OR CATALLAXY

nobody to cheat, we cannot prevent anyone from stumbling. Although we employ competition to find out who performs best, the result will only show who did best on the particular occasion, but not that the victor will generally do best. Too often we shall find that 'the race is not to the swift, nor the battle to the strong, neither yet bread to the wise, nor yet riches to men of understanding, nor yet favour to men of skill; but time and chance happeneth to them all.'[18] It is our ignorance of the effects of the application of the rules on particular people which makes justice possible in a spontaneous order of free men.[19]

Consistent justice will even often demand that we act as if we were ignorant of circumstances which in fact we do know. Both freedom and justice are values that can prevail only among men with limited knowledge and would have no meaning in a society of omniscient men. Consistent use of the power which we do possess over the structure of the market order will require systematic disregard of the concrete foreseeable effects a judicial decision will have. As the judge can be just only if he follows the principles of the law and disregards all the circumstances not referred to by its abstract rules (but which may be highly relevant for the moral evaluation of the action), so the rules of justice must limit the circumstances which may be taken into account in all instances. If *tout comprendre est tout pardonner*, this is precisely what the judge must not attempt because he never knows all. The need to rely on abstract rules in maintaining a spontaneous order is a consequence of that ignorance and uncertainty; and the enforcement of rules of conduct will achieve its purpose only if we adhere to them consistently and do not treat them merely as a substitute for knowledge which in the particular case we do not possess. It is therefore not the effect of their application in the particular cases but only the effects of their universal application that will lead to the improvement of everybody's chances and will therefore be accepted as just.[20] In particular, all concern with short run effects is bound to increase the preponderance of the visible and predictable effects over the invisible and distant ones, while rules intended to benefit all alike must not allow effects which accident has brought to the knowledge of the judge to outweigh those which he cannot know.

In a spontaneous order undeserved disappointments cannot be avoided. They are bound to cause grievances and a sense of having been treated unjustly, although nobody has acted unjustly. Those affected will usually, in perfectly good faith and as a matter of justice, put forward claims for remedial measures. But if coercion is to be restricted to the enforcement of uniform rules of just conduct, it is essential that government should not possess the power to accede to such demands. The reduction of the relative position of some about which they complain is the consequence of their having submitted to the same chances to which not only some others now owe the rise in their position, but to which they themselves owed their past position. It is only because countless others constantly submit to disappointments of their reasonable expectations that every one has as high an income as he has; and it is therefore only fair that he accept the unfavourable turn of events when they go against him. This is no less true when not a single individual but members of a large group share—and mutually support—that sense of grievance, and the change in consequence comes to be regarded as constituting a 'social problem'.

Specific commands ('interference') in a catallaxy create disorder and can never be just

A rule of just conduct serves the reconciliation of the different purposes of many individuals. A command serves the achievement of particular results. Unlike a rule of just conduct, it does not merely limit the range of choice of the individuals (or require them to satisfy expectations they have deliberately created) but commands them to act in a particular manner not required of other persons.

The term 'interference' (or 'intervention') is properly applied only to such specific orders which, unlike the rules of just conduct, do not serve merely the formation of a spontaneous order but aim at particular results. It was in this sense only that the classical economists used the term. They would not have applied it to the establishment or improvement of those generic rules which are required for the functioning of the market order and which they explicitly presupposed in their analysis.

Even in ordinary language 'interference' implies the operation of a process that proceeds by itself on certain principles because its parts obey certain rules. We would not call it interference if we oiled a clockwork, or in any other way secured the conditions that a going mechanism required for its proper functioning. Only if we changed the position of any particular part in a manner which is not in accord with the general principle of its operation, such as shifting the hands of a clock, can it properly be said that we have interfered. The aim of interference thus is always to bring about a particular result which is different from that which would have been produced if the mechanism had been allowed unaided to follow its inherent principles.[21] If the rules on which such a process proceeds are determined beforehand, the particular results it will produce at any one time will be independent of the momentary wishes of men.

The particular results that will be determined by altering a particular action of the system will always be inconsistent with its overall order: if they were not, they could have been achieved by changing the rules on which the system was henceforth to operate. Interference, if the term is properly used, is therefore by definition an isolated act of coercion,[22] undertaken for the purpose of achieving a particular result, and without committing oneself to do the same in all instances where some circumstances defined by a rule are the same. It is, therefore, always an unjust act in which somebody is coerced (usually in the interest of a third) in circumstances where another would not be coerced, and for purposes which are not his own.

It is, moreover, an act which will always disrupt the overall order and will prevent that mutual adjustment of all its parts on which the spontaneous order rests. It will do this by preventing the persons to whom the specific commands are directed from adapting their actions to circumstances known to them, and by making them serve some particular ends which others are not required to serve, and which will be satisfied at the expense of some other unpredictable effects. Every act of interference thus creates a privilege in the sense that it will secure benefits to some at the expense of others, in a manner which cannot be justified by principles capable of general application. What in this respect the formation of a spontaneous order requires is what is also required by the confinement of all coercion to the enforcement of rules of just conduct: that coercion be used only where it is required by uniform rules equally applicable to all.

The aim of law should be to improve equally the chances of all

Since rules of just conduct can affect only the chances of success of the efforts of men, the aim in altering or developing them should be to improve as much as possible the chances of anyone selected at random. Since in the long run it cannot be predicted when and where the particular conjunction of circumstances will occur to which any rule refers, it must also be unknown who will benefit by such an abstract rule and how much different persons will benefit. Such universal rules intended to apply for an indefinite period can thus aim solely at increasing the *chances* of unknown persons.

We prefer to speak in this context of chances rather than of probabilities because the latter term suggests numerical magnitudes which will not be known. All the law can do is to add to the number of favourable possibilities likely to arise for some unknown person and thus to build up an increasing likelihood that favourable opportunities will come anyone's way. But though the aim ought to be to add to everyone's prospects, it will normally not be known whose prospects will be improved by a particular legislative measure, and how much.

It should be noted that the concept of the chance enters here in two ways. In the first instance the relative position of any given persons can be described only as a range of opportunities which, if precisely known, could be represented as a probability distribution. Second, there is the question of the probability that any one member of the society will occupy any of the positions thus described. The resulting concept of the chances of any member of the society to have a certain range of opportunities is thus a complex one to which it is difficult to give mathematical precision. This would be useful, however, only if the numerical magnitudes were known, which, of course, they are not.[23]

It is obvious that the endeavour to add indiscriminately to anyone's chances will not result in making everybody's chances the same. The chances will always depend not only on future events which the law does not control, but also on the initial position of any individual at the moment the rules in question are adopted. In a continuous process this initial position of any person will always be a result of preceding phases, and therefore be as much an undesigned fact and dependent on chance as the future development. And since a part of most people's efforts will normally be directed to the improvement of their chances for the future, rather than to the satisfaction of their current needs, and more so as they have already succeeded in making provisions for the latter, the initial position of anyone will always be as much the result of a series of past accidents as of his efforts and foresight. It appears, therefore, that it is because the individual is free to decide whether to use the results of his current efforts for current consumption or for increasing his future opportunities that the position he has already achieved will improve his chances of reaching a still better position, or that 'to those who have will be given'. The possibility of distributing the use of one's resources over time will therefore always also tend to increase the discrepancy between the merits of a person's current efforts and the benefits which he currently receives.

To the extent that we rely on the institution of the family for the launching of the individual in life, the chain of events affecting the prospects of anyone will necessarily extend even beyond the period of his individual life. It is therefore inevitable that in the ongoing process of the catallaxy the starting point, and therefore also the prospects, of the different individuals will be different.

This is not to say that there may not be a case in justice for correcting positions which have been determined by earlier unjust acts or institutions. But unless such injustice is clear and recent, it will generally be impracticable to correct it. It will on the whole seem preferable to accept the given position as due to accident and simply from the present onwards to refrain from any measures aiming at benefiting particular individuals or groups. Though it might seem reasonable so to frame laws that they will tend more strongly to improve the opportunities of those whose chances are relatively small, this can rarely be achieved by generic rules. There are, no doubt, instances where the past development of law has introduced a bias in favour or to the disadvantage of particular groups; and such provisions ought clearly to be corrected. But on the whole it would seem that the fact which, contrary to a widely held belief, has contributed most during the last two hundred years to increase not only the absolute but also the relative position of those in the lowest income groups has been the general growth of wealth which has tended to raise the income of the lowest groups more than the relatively higher ones. This, of course, is a consequence of the circumstance that, once the Malthusian devil has been exorcized, the growth of aggregate wealth tends to make labour more scarce than capital. But nothing we can do, short of establishing absolute equality of all incomes, can alter the fact that a certain percentage of the population must find itself in the bottom of the scale; and as a matter of logic the chance of any person picked out at random being among the lowest 10 per cent must be one tenth![24]

The Good Society is one in which the chances of anyone selected at random are likely to be as great as possible

The conclusion to which our considerations lead is thus that we should regard as the most desirable order of society one which we would choose if we knew that our initial position in it would be decided purely by chance (such as the fact of our being born into a particular family). Since the attraction such chance would possess for any particular adult individual would probably be dependent on the particular skills, capacities and tastes he has already acquired, a better way of putting this would be to say that the best society would be that in which we would prefer to place our children if we knew that their position in it would be determined by lot. Very few people would probably in this case prefer a strictly egalitarian order. Yet, while one might, for instance, regard the kind of life lived in the past by the landed aristocracy as the most attractive kind of life, and would choose a society in which such a class existed if he were assured that he or his children would be a member of that class, he would probably decide differently if he knew that that position would be determined by drawing lots and that in consequence it would be much more probable that he would become an agricultural labourer. He would then very likely choose that very type of industrial society which did not offer such delectable plums to a few but offered better prospects to the great majority.[25]

THE DISCIPLINE OF ABSTRACT
RULES AND THE EMOTIONS OF
THE TRIBAL SOCIETY

Liberalism—it is well to recall this today—is the supreme form
of generosity; it is the right which the majority concedes to
minorities and hence it is the noblest cry that has ever resounded
on this planet. It announces the determination to share existence
with the enemy; more than that, with an enemy which is weak.
It was incredible that the human species should have arrived at
so noble an attitude, so paradoxical, so refined, so anti-natural.
Hence it is not to be wondered at that this same humanity
should soon appear anxious to get rid of it. It is a discipline too
difficult and complex to take firm root on earth.

José Ortega y Gasset *

*The pursuit of unattainable goals may prevent the achievement of
the possible*

It is not enough to recognize that 'social justice' is an empty phrase
without determinable content. It has become a powerful incantation which serves to support deep-seated emotions that are threatening to destroy the Great Society. Unfortunately it is not true that
if something cannot be achieved, it can do no harm to strive for it.[1]
Like chasing any mirage it is likely to produce results which one
would have done much to avoid if one had foreseen them. Many
desirable aims will be sacrificed in the vain hope of making
possible what must forever elude our grasp.

We live at present under the governance of two different and
irreconcilable conceptions of what is right; and after a period of
ascendancy of conceptions which have made the vision of an Open
Society possible, we are relapsing rapidly into the conceptions of
the tribal society from which we had been slowly emerging. We
had hoped that with the defeat of the European dictators we had
banished the threat of the totalitarian state; but all we have
achieved was to put down the first flare-up of a reaction which is
slowly spreading everywhere. Socialism is simply a re-assertion of

that tribal ethics whose gradual weakening had made an approach to the Great Society possible. The submergence of classical liberalism under the inseparable forces of socialism and nationalism is the consequence of a revival of those tribal sentiments.

Most people are still unwilling to face the most alarming lesson of modern history: that the greatest crimes of our time have been committed by governments that had the enthusiastic support of millions of people who were guided by moral impulses. It is simply not true that Hitler or Mussolini, Lenin or Stalin, appealed only to the worst instincts of their people: they also appealed to some of the feelings which also dominate contemporary democracies. Whatever disillusionment the more mature supporters of these movements may have experienced as they came to see the effects of the policies they had supported, there can be no doubt that the rank and file of the communist, national-socialist or fascist movements contained many men and women inspired by ideals not very different from those of some of the most influential social philosophers in the Western countries. Some of them certainly believed that they were engaged in the creation of a just society in which the needs of the most deserving or 'socially most valuable' would be better cared for. They were led by a desire for a visible common purpose which is our inheritance from the tribal society and which we still find breaking through everywhere.

The causes of the revival of the organizational thinking of the tribe

One reason why in recent times we have seen a strong revival of organizational thinking and a decline in the understanding of the operation of the market order is that an ever growing proportion of the members of society work as members of large organizations and find their horizon of comprehension limited to what is required by the internal structure of such organizations. While the peasant and the independent craftsman, the merchant and the journeyman, were familiar with the market and, even if they did not understand its operation, had come to accept its dictates as the natural course of things, the growth of big enterprise and of the great administrative bureaucracies has brought it about that an ever increasing part of the people spend their whole working life as members of large organizations, and are led to think wholly in terms of the requirements of the organizational form of life. Even though in the pre-industrial society the great majority also spent most of their lives within the familial organization which was the unit of all economic activity,[2] the heads of the households saw society as a network of family units connected by the markets.

Today organizational thinking increasingly dominates the activities of many of the most powerful and influential figures of modern society, the organizers themselves.[3] The modern improvements in the technique of organization, and the consequent increase of the range of particular tasks which can be performed by means of large-scale organization far beyond what was possible before, have created the belief that there are no limits to what organization can achieve. Most people are no longer aware of the extent to which the more comprehensive order of society on which depends the very success of the organizations within it is due to ordering forces of an altogether different kind.

The other main reason for the growing dominance of organizational thinking is that the success of the deliberate creation of new rules for purposive organizations has in many respects been so great, that men no longer recognize that the more comprehensive order within which the organizations operate rests on a different type of rules which have not been invented with a definite foreseen purpose in mind, but are the product of a process of trial and error in the course of which more experience has been accumulated than any living person is aware of.

The immoral consequences of morally inspired efforts

Though in the long perspective of Western civilization the history of law is a history of a gradual emergence of rules of just conduct capable of universal application, its development during the last hundred years has become increasingly one of the destruction of justice by 'social justice', until even some students of jurisprudence have lost sight of the original meaning of 'justice'. We have seen how the process has mainly taken the form of a replacement of the rules of just conduct by those rules of organization which we call public law (a 'subordinating law'), a distinction which some socialist lawyers are trying hard to obliterate.[4] In substance this has meant that the individual is no longer bound only by rules which confine the scope of his private actions, but has become increasingly subject to the commands of authority. The growing technological possibilities of control, together with the presumed moral superiority of a society whose members serve the same hierarchy of ends, have made this totalitarian trend appear under a moral guise. It is indeed the concept of 'social justice' which has been the Trojan Horse through which totalitarianism has entered.

The values which still survive from the small end-connected groups whose coherence depended upon them, are, however, not only different from, but often incompatible with, the values which make possible the peaceful coexistence of large numbers in the Open Society. The belief that while we pursue the new ideal of this Great Society in which all human beings are regarded as equal, we can also preserve the different ideals of the small closed society, is an illusion. To attempt it leads to the destruction of the Great Society.

The possibility of men living together in peace and to their mutual advantage without having to agree on common concrete aims, and bound only by abstract rules of conduct,[5] was perhaps the greatest discovery mankind ever made. The 'capitalist' system which grew out of this discovery no doubt did not fully satisfy the ideals of liberalism, because it grew up while legislators and governments did not really understand the *modus operandi* of the market, and largely in spite of the policies actually pursued.[6] Capitalism as it exists today in consequence undeniably has many remediable defects that an intelligent policy of freedom ought to correct. A system which relies on the spontaneous ordering forces of the market, once it has reached a certain level of wealth, is also by no means incompatible with government providing, outside the market, some security against severe deprivation. But the attempt to secure to each what he is thought to deserve, by imposing upon all a system of common concrete ends towards which their efforts are directed by authority, as socialism aims to do, would be a retrograde step that would deprive us of the utilization of the knowledge and aspirations of millions, and thereby of the advantages of a free civilization. Socialism is not based merely on a different system of ultimate values from that of liberalism, which one would have to respect even if one disagreed; it is based on an intellectual error which makes its adherents blind to its consequences. This must be plainly said because the emphasis on the alleged difference of the ultimate values has become the common excuse of the socialists for shirking the real intellectual issue. The pretended difference of the underlying value judgments has become a protective cloak used to conceal the faulty reasoning underlying the socialist schemes.

In the Great Society 'social justice' becomes a disruptive force

Not only is it impossible for the Great Society to maintain itself while enforcing rules of 'social' or distributive justice; for its preservation it is also necessary that no particular groups holding common views about what they are entitled to should be allowed to enforce these views by preventing others to offer their services at more favourable terms. Though common interests of those whose position is affected by the same circumstances are likely to produce strong common opinions about what they deserve, and will provide a motive for common action to achieve their ends, any such group action to secure a particular income or position for its members creates an obstacle to the integration of the Great Society and is therefore anti-social in the true sense of this word. It must become a divisive force because it produces not a reconciliation of, but a conflict between, the interests of the different groups. As the active participants in the struggle for 'social justice' well know, it becomes in practice a struggle for power of organized interests in which arguments of justice serve merely as pretexts.

The chief insight we must hold on to is that not always when a group of people have strong views about what they regard as their claims in justice does this mean that there exists (or can be found) a corresponding rule which, if universally applied, would produce a viable order. It is a delusion to believe that whenever a question is represented as one of justice it must be possible to discover a rule capable of universal application which will decide that question.[7] Nor does the fact that a law endeavours to meet somebody's claim for justice prove that it is a rule of just conduct.

All groups whose members pursue the same or parallel aims will develop common views about what is right for members of those groups. Such views, however, will be right only for all those who pursue the same aims, but may be wholly incompatible with any principles by which such a group can be integrated into the overall order of society. The producers of any particular commodity or service who all aim at a good remuneration for their efforts will regard as unjust the action of any fellow producer who tends to reduce the incomes of the others. Yet it will be precisely the kind of actions by some members of the group that the rest regard as harmful which will fit the activities of the members of the group into the overall pattern of the Great Society and thereby benefit all.

It is certainly in itself not unjust if a barber in one city receives

$3 for a haircut while in another city only $2 is paid for the same work. But it would clearly be unjust if the barbers in the first prevented any from the second city from improving their position by offering their services in the first for, say, $2.50 and thus, while improving their position, lowering the income of the first group. Yet it is precisely against such efforts that established groups are today permitted to combine in defence of their established position. The rule 'do nothing which will decrease the income of the members of your own group' will often be regarded as an obligation of justice toward one's fellow members. But it cannot be accepted as a rule of just conduct in a Great Society where it will conflict with the general principles on which the activities of that society are co-ordinated. The other members of that society will have every interest and moral right to prevent the enforcement of such a rule that the members of a special group regard as just, because the principles of integration of the Great Society demand that the action of some of those occupied in a particular manner should often lead to a reduction of the incomes of their fellows. This is precisely the virtue of competition. The conceptions of group justice would often proscribe all effective competition as unjust—and many of the 'fair competition' demands aim in effect at little less.

It is probably true that in any group whose members know that their prospects depend on the same circumstances, views will develop that represent as unjust all conduct of any member which harms the others; and there will in consequence arise a desire to prevent such conduct. But by any outsider it will rightly be regarded as unjust if any member of such a group is prevented by his fellows from offering him more advantageous terms than the rest of the group are willing to offer. And the same is true when some 'interloper' who before was not recognized as a member of the group is made to conform to the standards of the group as soon as his efforts compete with theirs.

The important fact which most people are reluctant to admit, yet which is probably true in most instances, is that, though the pursuit of the selfish aims of the individual will usually lead him to serve the general interest, the collective actions of organized groups are almost invariably contrary to the general interest. What in fact leads to the condemnation as anti-social of that pursuit of individual interests which contributes to the general interest, and to the commendation as 'social' of the subservience to those sectional interests which destroy the overall order, are sentiments which we have inherited from earlier forms of society. The use of coercion in the service of this kind of 'social justice', meaning the interests of the particular group to which the individual belongs, will thus always mean the creation of particular preserves of special groups united against the outsiders—interest groups which exist because they are allowed to use force or pressure on government for the benefit of their members. But, however much the members of such groups may agree among themselves that what they want is just, there exists no principle which could make it appear as just to the outsider. Yet today, if such a group is only large enough, its representation of the demands of its members as just is commonly accepted as one view of justice which must be taken into account in ordering the whole, even though it does not rest on any principle which could be generally applied.

From the care of the most unfortunate to the protection of vested interests

We must not lose sight, however, of the fact that at the beginning of the striving for 'social justice' stood the laudable desire to abolish destitution, and that the Great Society has brilliantly succeeded in abolishing poverty in the absolute sense.[8] Nobody capable of useful work need today lack food and shelter in the advanced countries, and for those incapable of themselves earning enough these necessities are generally provided outside the market. Poverty in the relative sense must of course continue to exist outside of any completely egalitarian society: so long as there exists inequality, somebody must be the bottom of the scale. But the abolition of absolute poverty is not helped by the endeavour to achieve 'social justice'; in fact, in many of the countries in which absolute poverty is still an acute problem, the concern with 'social justice' has become one of the greatest obstacles to the elimination of poverty. In the West the rise of the great masses to tolerable comfort has been the effect of the general growth of wealth and has been merely slowed down by measures interfering with the market mechanism. It has been this market mechanism which has created the increase of aggregate income, which also has made it possible to provide outside the market for the support of those unable to earn enough. But the attempts to 'correct' the results of the market in the direction of 'social justice' have probably produced more injustice in the form of new privileges, obstacles to mobility and frustration of efforts than they have contributed to the alleviation of the lot of the poor.

This development is a consequence of the circumstance that the appeal to 'social justice' that was originally made on behalf of the most unfortunate was taken up by many other groups whose members felt that they did not get as much as they thought that they deserved, and particularly by those groups who felt threatened in their present positions. As a demand that political action should assign to the members of any group the position which in some sense it deserved, 'social justice' is irreconcilable with the ideal that coercion should be used only to enforce the same rules of just conduct which all could take into account in making their plans. Yet when those claims were first admitted in favour of groups with whose misfortune everybody sympathized, the floodgates were opened to the demand by all who found their relative position threatened that their position be protected by government action. Misfortune, however, cannot create a claim for protection against risks which all have had to run in order to attain the position they occupy. The very language in current use which at once labels as a 'social problem' anything which causes dissatisfaction of any group, and suggests that it is the duty of the legislature to do something about such 'social injustice', has turned the conception of 'social justice' into a mere pretext for claims for privileges by special interests.

Those who turn with indignation against a conception of justice which failed, e.g., to prevent 'the rapidly proceeding up-rooting of the peasantry which commenced already after the Napoleonic wars, or the decline of the artisanry after the middle of the century, or the pauperization of the wage labourers'[9] wholly misconceive what can be achieved by enforcement of rules of just conduct in a world of free men who reciprocally serve each other for their own benefit and to whom nobody assigns tasks or allocates benefits. Since today we can probably even feed the numbers to which mankind has grown only thanks to the intensive utilization of dispersed knowledge which is made possible by the market—not to speak of maintaining that level of comfort which the great majority has reached in some parts of the world—it certainly would not be just to exempt some from the necessity of accepting a less favourable position than they had already attained if an unforeseen turn of events diminishes the value of their services to the rest. However sorry we may be for those who, through no fault of their own but as a result of unforeseeable developments, find themselves in a reduced position, this does not mean that we can have both the progressive increase in the level of general wealth on which the future improvement of the conditions of the great masses depends and no such recurrent declines of the position of some groups.

'Social justice' has in practice become simply the slogan used by all groups whose status tends to decline—by the farmer, the independent craftsman, the coalminer, the small shopkeeper, the clerical worker and a considerable part of the old 'middle class', rather than the industrial workers on whose behalf it was first raised but who have in general been the beneficiaries of recent developments. That the appeal to justice by such groups frequently succeeds in mobilizing the sympathy of many who regard the traditional hierarchy of society as a natural one, and who resent the ascent of new types to that middle position to which once the bare capacity to read and write gave access, does not show that such demands have any connection with generally applicable rules of just conduct.

In the existing political order such claims will in fact be met only when such groups are large enough to count politically and especially when it is possible to organize their members for common action. We shall see later that only some but not all such interests can be thus organized, and that in consequence the resulting advantages can be achieved only by some and will harm the rest. Yet the more organizations of interests are used for this purpose, the more necessary does it become for each group to organize for pressure on government, since those who fail to do so will be left out in the cold. Thus the conception of 'social justice' has resulted in the assurance by government of an appropriate income to particular groups, which has made the progressive organization of all such 'interests' inevitable. But the protection of expectations which such assurance involves cannot possibly be granted to all in any but a stationary society. The only just principle is therefore to concede this privilege to none.

At one time this argument would have had to be directed chiefly against the trade unions, since they were the first of such groups who succeeded in clothing their demands with the aura of legitimacy (and in being allowed to use coercion for their enforcement) by representing them as a requirement of 'social justice'. But though it was initially the use in the service of relatively poor and unfortunate groups that made discrimination in their favour appear justifiable, such discrimination served as the thin end of the wedge by which the principle of equality under the law was destroyed. It is now simply those who are numerically strong, or can readily be organized to withhold essential services, who gain in the process of political bargaining which governs legislation in contemporary democracy. But the particular absurdities which arise when a democracy attempts to determine the distribution of incomes by majority vote will occupy us further only in the third volume of the present work.

Attempts to 'correct' the order of the market lead to its destruction

The predominant view today appears to be that we should avail ourselves in the main of the ordering forces of the market, indeed must in a great measure do so, but should 'correct' its results where they are flagrantly unjust. Yet so long as the earnings of particular individuals or groups are not determined by the decision of some agency, no particular distribution of incomes can be meaningfully described as more just than another. If we want to make it substantively just, we can do so only by replacing the whole spontaneous order by an organization in which the share of each is fixed by some central authority. In other words, 'corrections' of the distribution brought about in a spontaneous process by particular acts of interference can never be just in the sense of satisfying a rule equally applicable to all. Every single act of this kind will give rise to demands by others to be treated on the same principle; and these demands can be satisfied only if all incomes are thus allocated.

The current endeavour to rely on a spontaneous order corrected according to principles of justice amounts to an attempt to have the best of two worlds which are mutually incompatible. Perhaps an absolute ruler, wholly independent of public opinion, might confine himself to mitigating the hardships of the more unfortunate ones by isolated acts of intervention and let a spontaneous order determine the positions of the rest. And it is certainly possible to take entirely out of the market process those who cannot adequately maintain themselves on the market and support them by means set aside for the purpose. For a person at the beginning of an uncertain career, and for his children, it might even be perfectly rational to agree that all should insure for a minimum of sustenance in such an eventuality. But a government dependent on public opinion, and particularly a democracy, will not be able to confine such attempts to supplement the market to the mitigation of the lot of the poorest. Whether it intends to let itself be guided by principles or not, it is in fact, if it has the power to do so, certain to be driven on by the principles implicit in the precedents it sets. By the measures it takes it will produce opinions and set standards which will force it to continue on the course on which it has embarked.

It is possible to 'correct' an order only by assuring that the principles on which it rests are consistently applied, but not by applying to some part of the whole principles which do not apply to the rest. As it is the essence of justice that the same principles are universally applied, it requires that government assist particular groups only in conditions in which it is prepared to act on the same principle in all similar instances.

The revolt against the discipline of abstract rules

The rise of the ideal of impersonal justice based on formal rules has been achieved in a continuous struggle against those feelings of personal loyalty which provide the basis of the tribal society but which in the Great Society must not be allowed to influence the use of the coercive powers of government. The gradual extension of a common order of peace from the small group to ever larger communities has involved constant clashes between the demands of sectional justice based on common visible purposes and the requirements of a universal justice equally applicable to the stranger and to the member of the group.[10] This has caused a constant conflict between emotions deeply ingrained in human nature through millennia of tribal existence and the demands of abstract principles whose significance nobody fully grasped. Human emotions are attached to concrete objects, and the emotions of justice in particular are still very much connected with the visible needs of the group to which each person belongs—the needs of the trade or profession, of the clan or the village, the town or the country to which each belongs. Only a mental reconstruction of the overall order of the Great Society enables us to comprehend that the deliberate aim at concrete common purposes, which to most people still appears as more meritorious and superior to blind obedience to abstract rules, would destroy that larger order in which all human beings count alike.

As we have already seen, much that will be truly social in the small end-connected group because it is conducive to the coherence of the working order of that society, will be anti-social from the point of view of the Great Society. The demand for 'social justice' is indeed an expression of revolt of the tribal spirit against the abstract requirements of the coherence of the Great Society with no such visible common purpose. It is only by extending the rules of just conduct to the relations with all other men, and at the same time depriving of their obligatory character those rules which cannot be universally applied, that we can approach a universal order of peace which might integrate all mankind into a single society.

While in the tribal society the condition of internal peace is the devotion of all members to some common visible purposes, and therefore to the will of somebody who can decide what at any moment these purposes are to be and how they are to be achieved, the Open Society of free men becomes possible only when the individuals are constrained only to obey the abstract rules that demarcate the domain of the means that each is allowed to use for his purposes. So long as any particular ends, which in a society of any size must always be the ends of some particular persons or group, are regarded as a justification of coercion, there must always arise conflicts between groups with different interests. Indeed, so long as particular purposes are the foundation of political organization, those whose purposes are different are inevitably enemies; and it is true that in such a society politics necessarily is dominated by the friend-enemy relation.[11] Rules of just conduct can become the same for all only when particular ends are not regarded as justification for coercion (apart from such special passing circumstances as war, rebellion or natural catastrophes).

The morals of the open and of the closed society

The process we are describing is closely associated with, and indeed a necessary consequence of, the circumstance that in an extensive market order the producers are led to serve people without knowing of their individual needs. Such an order which relies on people working with the effect of satisfying the wants of people of whom they do not know presupposes and requires somewhat different moral views, from one in which people serve visible needs. The indirect guidance by an expected monetary return, operating as an indicator of the requirements of others, demanded new moral conceptions which do not prescribe particular aims but rather general rules limiting the range of permitted actions.

It did become part of the ethos of the Open Society that it was better to invest one's fortune in instruments making it possible to produce more at smaller costs than to distribute it among the poor, or to cater for the needs of thousands of unknown people rather than to provide for the needs of a few known neighbours. These views, of course, did not develop because those who first acted upon them understood that they thus conferred greater benefits on their fellows, but because the groups and societies which acted in this way prospered more than others; it became in consequence gradually the recognized moral duty of the 'calling' to do so. In its purest form this ethos regards it as the prime duty to pursue a self-chosen end as effectively as possible without paying attention to the role it plays in the complex network of human activities. It is the view which is now commonly but somewhat misleading described as the Calvinist ethic—misleading because it prevailed already in the mercantile towns of medieval Italy and was taught by the Spanish Jesuits at about the same time as Calvin.[12]

We still esteem doing good only if it is done to benefit specific known needs of known people, and regard it as really better to help one starving man we know than to relieve the acute need of a hundred men we do not know; but in fact we generally are doing most good by pursuing gain. It was somewhat misleading, and did his cause harm, when Adam Smith gave the impression as if the significant difference were that between the egoistic striving for gain and the altruistic endeavour to meet known needs. The aim for which the successful entrepreneur wants to use his profits may well be to provide a hospital or an art gallery for his home town. But quite apart from the question of what he wants to do with his profits after he has earned them, he is led to benefit more people by aiming at the largest gain than he could if he concentrated on the satisfaction of the needs of known persons. He is led by the invisible hand of the market to bring the succour of modern conveniences to the poorest homes he does not even know.[13]

It is true, however, that the moral views underlying the Open Society were long confined to small groups in a few urban localities, and have come generally to govern law and opinion in the Western world so comparatively recently that they are often still felt to be artificial and unnatural in contrast to the intuitive, and in part perhaps even instinctive, sentiments inherited from the older tribal society. The moral sentiments which made the Open Society possible grew up in the towns, the commercial and trading centres, while the feelings of the large numbers were still governed by the parochial sentiments and the xenophobic and fighting attitudes governing the tribal group.[14] The rise of the Great Society is far too recent an event to have given man time to shed the results of a development of hundreds of thousands of years, and not to regard as artificial and inhuman those abstract rules of conduct which often conflict with the deeply ingrained instincts to let himself be guided in action by perceived needs.

The resistance against the new morals of the Open Society was strengthened also by the realization that it not only indefinitely enlarged the circle of other people in relation to whom one had to obey moral rules, but that this extension of the scope of the moral code necessarily brought with itself a reduction of its content. If the enforceable duties towards all are to be the same, the duties towards none can be greater than the duties towards all—except where special natural or contractual relations exist. There can be a general obligation to render assistance in case of need towards a circumscribed group of fellow-men, but not towards men in general. The moral progress by which we have moved towards the Open Society, that is, the extension of the obligation to treat alike, not only the members of our tribe but persons of ever wider circles and ultimately all men, had to be bought at the price of an attenuation of the enforceable duty to aim deliberately at the well-being of the other members of the same group. When we can no longer know the others or the circumstances under which they live, such a duty becomes a psychological and intellectual impossibility. Yet the disappearance of these specific duties leaves an emotional void by depriving men both of satisfying tasks and the assurance of support in case of need.[15]

It would therefore not be really surprising if the first attempt of man to emerge from the tribal into an open society should fail because man is not yet ready to shed moral views developed for the tribal society; or, as Ortega y Gasset wrote of classical liberalism in the passage placed at the head of this chapter, it is not to be wondered that 'humanity should soon appear anxious to get rid of . . . so noble an attitude, so paradoxical, so refined, so anti-natural . . . a discipline too difficult and complex to take firm root on earth.' At a time when the great majority are employed in organizations and have little opportunity to learn the morals of the market, their intuitive craving for a more humane and personal morals corresponding to their inherited instincts is quite likely to destroy the Open Society.

146

It should be realized, however, that the ideals of socialism (or of 'social justice') which in such a position prove so attractive, do not really offer a new moral but merely appeal to instincts inherited from an earlier type of society. They are an atavism, a vain attempt to impose upon the Open Society the morals of the tribal society which, if it prevails, must not only destroy the Great Society but would also greatly threaten the survival of the large numbers to which some three hundred years of a market order have enabled mankind to grow.

Similarly the people who are described as alienated or estranged from a society based on the market order are not the bearers of a new moral but the non-domesticated or un-civilized who have never learnt the rules of conduct on which the Open Society is based, but want to impose upon it their instinctive, 'natural' conceptions derived from the tribal society. What especially most of the members of the New Left do not appear to see is that that equal treatment of all men which they also demand is possible only under a system in which individual actions are restricted merely by formal rules rather than guided by their known effects.

The Rousseauesque nostalgia for a society guided, not by learnt moral rules which can be justified only by a rational insight into the principles on which this order is based, but by the unreflected 'natural' emotions deeply grounded on millennia of life in the small horde, leads thus directly to the demand for a socialist society in which authority ensures that visible 'social justice' is done in a manner which gratifies natural emotions. In this sense, however, of course all culture is unnatural and, though undesigned, still artificial because relying on obedience to learnt rules rather than on natural instincts. This conflict between what men still feel to be natural emotions and the discipline of rules required for the preservation of the Open Society is indeed one of the chief causes of what has been called the 'fragility of liberty': all attempts to model the Great Society on the image of the familiar small group, or to turn it into a community by directing the individuals towards common visible purposes, must produce a totalitarian society.

The old conflict between loyalty and justice

The persistent conflict between tribal morals and universal justice has manifested itself throughout history in a recurrent clash between the sense of loyalty and that of justice. It is still loyalty to such particular groups as those of occupation or class as well as those of clan, nation, race or religion which is the greatest obstacle to a universal application of rules of just conduct. Only slowly and gradually do those general rules of conduct towards all fellow men come to prevail over the special rules which allowed the individual to harm the stranger if it served the interest of his group. Yet while only this process has made possible the rise of the Open Society, and offers the distant hope of a universal order of peace, current morals do not yet wholeheartedly approve this development; indeed, there has in recent times taken place a retreat from positions which had already been largely achieved in the Western world.

If in the distant past perhaps altogether inhuman demands were sometimes made in the name of formal justice, as when in ancient Rome the father was praised who as a magistrate unflinchingly condemned his son to death, we have learned to avoid the gravest of such conflicts, and in general to reduce the requirements of formal justice to what is compatible with our emotions. The advance of justice continued until recent times as a progressive ascendancy of the general rules of just conduct applying to our relations to any fellow member of society over the special rules serving the needs of particular groups. It is true that this development in some measure stopped at national frontiers; but most nations were of such a size that it still brought about a progressive replacement of the rules of the purpose-connected organization by the rules of the spontaneous order of an Open Society.

The main resistance to this development was due to its requiring a predominance of abstract rational principles over those emotions that are evoked by the particular and the concrete, or the predominance of conclusions derived from abstract rules, whose significance was little understood, over the spontaneous response to the perception of concrete effects which touched the lives and conditions of those familiar to us. This does not mean that those rules of conduct which refer to special personal relations have lost their importance for the functioning of the Great Society. It merely means that, since in a society of free men the membership in such special groups will be voluntary, there must also be no power of enforcing the rules of such groups. It is in such a free society that a clear distinction between the moral rules which are not enforced and the rules of law which are enforced becomes so important. If the smaller groups are to be integrated into the more comprehensive order of society at large, it must be through the free movement of individuals between groups into which they may be accepted if they submit to their rules.

The small group in the Open Society

The revolt against the abstractness of the rules we are required to obey in the Great Society, and the predilection for the concrete which we feel to be human, are thus merely a sign that intellectually and morally we have not yet fully matured to the needs of the impersonal comprehensive order of mankind. To submit comprehendingly to those rules which have made the approach to the Open Society possible and which we have obeyed so long as we attributed them to the command of a higher personal authority, and not to blame some imagined personal agent for any misfortune that we encounter, evidently requires a degree of insight into the working of a spontaneous order which few persons have yet attained.

Even moral philosophers often appear simply to wallow in the emotions inherited from the tribal society without examining their compatibility with the aspirations of the universal humanism that they also champion. Most people indeed will watch with regret the decline of the small group in which a limited number of persons were connected by many personal ties, and the disappearance of certain sentiments connected with it. But the price we have to pay for the achievement of the Great Society in which all human beings have the same claims on us is that these claims must be reduced to the avoidance of harmful actions and cannot include positive duties. The individual's free choice of his associates will in general have the effect that for different purposes he will be acting with different companions and that none of these connections will be compulsory. This presupposes that none of these small groups has power to enforce its standards on any unwilling person.

The savage in us still regards as good what was good in the small group but what the Great Society must not only refrain from enforcing but cannot even allow particular groups to enforce. A peaceful Open Society is possible only if it renounces the method of creating solidarity that is most effective in the small group, namely acting on the principle that 'if people are to be in harmony, then let them strive for some common end'. This is the conception of creating coherence which leads straight to the interpretation of all politics as a matter of friend-enemy relations. It is also the device which has been effectively employed by all dictators.

Except when the very existence of a free society is threatened by an enemy, it must deny itself what in many respects is still the strongest force making for cohesion, the common visible purpose. It must bid farewell, so far as the use of coercion is concerned, to the use of some of the strong moral emotions which still stand us in good stead in the small group and which, though still needed within the small groups from which the Great Society is built up, must result in tension and conflict if enforced in the Great Society.

The conception through which the atavistic craving for visible common purposes which so well served the needs of the small group today chiefly expresses itself is that of 'social justice'. It is incompatible with the principles on which the Great Society rests and indeed the opposite of those forces making for its coherence which can truly be called 'social'. Our innate instincts are here in conflict with the rules of reason we have learned, a conflict we can resolve only by limiting coercion to what is required by abstract rules and by abstaining from enforcing what can be justified only by the desire for particular results.

The kind of abstract order on which man has learnt to rely and which has enabled him peacefully to co-ordinate the efforts of millions, unfortunately cannot be based on such feelings as love which constituted the highest virtue in the small group. Love is a sentiment which only the concrete evokes, and the Great Society has become possible through the individual's efforts being guided not by the aim of helping particular other persons, but the confinement of the pursuit of their purposes by abstract rules.

The importance of voluntary associations

It would be a sad misunderstanding of the basic principles of a free society if it were concluded that, because they must deprive the small group of all coercive powers, they do not attach great value to voluntary action in the small groups. In restricting all coercion to the agencies of government and confining its employment to the enforcement of general rules, these principles aim at reducing all coercion as much as possible and leaving as much as possible to voluntary efforts. The mischievous idea that all public needs should be satisfied by compulsory organization and that all the means that the individuals are willing to devote to public purposes should be under the control of government, is wholly alien to the basic principles of a free society. The true liberal must on the contrary desire as many as possible of those 'particular societies within the state', voluntary organizations between the individual and government, which the false individualism of Rousseau and the French Revolution wanted to suppress; but he wants to deprive them of all exclusive and compulsory powers. Liberalism is not individualistic in the 'everybody for himself' sense, though necessarily suspicious of the tendency of organizations to arrogate exclusive rights for their members.

We shall later (in chapter 15) have to consider more fully the problems raised by the consideration that such voluntary organizations, because their power is so much greater than that of any individual, may have to be restricted in their activities by law in ways in which the individual need not be restrained and, in particular, that they may have to be denied some of the rights to discriminate which for the individual are an important part of his freedom. What we wish to stress at this point, however, is not the necessary limits but rather the importance of the existence of numerous voluntary associations, not only for the particular purposes of those who share some common interest, but even for public purposes in the true sense. That government should have the monopoly of coercion is necessary in order to limit coercion; but this must not mean that government should have the exclusive right to pursue public purposes. In a truly free society, public affairs are not confined to the affairs of government (least of all of central government) and public spirit should not exhaust itself in an interest in government.[16]

It is one of the greatest weaknesses of our time that we lack the patience and faith to build up voluntary organizations for purposes which we value highly, and immediately ask the government to bring about by coercion (or with means raised by coercion) anything that appears as desirable to large numbers. Yet nothing can have a more deadening effect on real participation by the citizen than if government, instead of merely providing the essential framework for spontaneous growth, becomes monolithic and takes charge of the provision for all needs which can be provided for only by the common efforts of many. It is the great merit of the spontaneous order concerned only with means that it makes possible the existence of a large number of distinct and voluntary value communities serving such values as science, the arts, sports and the like. And it is a highly desirable development that in the modern world these groups tend to extend beyond national boundaries and that, e.g. a mountain climber in Switzerland may have more in common with a mountain climber in Japan than with the football fan in his own country; and that he may even belong to a common association with the former which is wholly independent of any political organization to which either belongs.

The present tendency of governments to bring all common interests of large groups under their control tends to destroy real public spirit; and as a result an increasing number of men and women are turning away from public life who in the past would have devoted much effort to public purposes. On the European continent the over-solicitude of governments has in the past largely prevented the development of voluntary organizations for public purposes and produced a tradition in which private efforts were often regarded as the gratuitous meddling of busybodies, and modern developments seem progressively to have produced a similar situation even in the Anglo-Saxon countries where at one time private efforts for public purposes were so characteristic a feature of social life.

NOTES

* David Hume, *Treatise, Works*, ed. T. H. Green and T. H. Grose (London, 1890), vol. II, p. 318.

1 On the meaning of the concepts of common or public utility (or interest) in classical antiquity, when their equivalents were extensively used both in Greek and in Latin, see A. Steinwenter, 'Utilitas publica—utilitas singulorum', *Festschrift Paul Koschaker* (Weimar, 1939), vol. I, and J. Gaudemet, 'Utilitas publica', *Revue historique de droit français et étranger*, 4ᵉ série, 29, 1951. The medieval use is discussed in W. Merk, 'Der Gedanke des gemeinen Besten in der deutschen Staats- und Rechtsentwicklung', *Festschrift für A. Schultze* (Weimar, 1934).

2 For the upshots of the extensive but not very fruitful discussion of this subject, mainly in the USA, see *Nomos V, The Public Interest*, ed. C. J. Friedrich (New York, 1962), and the earlier literature mentioned in that work.

3 J. Bentham, *An Introduction to the Principles of Morals and Legislation*, new ed. (London, 1823), vol. I, p. 4: 'The interest of the community then is, what?—the sum of the interests of the several members who compose it.'

4 James Harrington, *The Prerogative of Popular Government* (1658) in *The Oceana and his Other Works*, ed. J. Toland (London, 1771), p. 224: 'the public interest (which is no other than common right and justice) may be called the empire of laws and not of men.'

5 Cf. the Book of Proverbs, 18:18, 'The lot causes contentions to cease, and parteth between the mighty.'

6 In this sense the 'principle of subsidiarity' is much stressed in the social doctrines of the Roman Catholic Church.

7 I ought probably to have explained earlier why I prefer the expression 'each being allowed to use his own knowledge for his own purposes' to the essentially equivalent expression of Adam Smith that every one should be free 'to pursue his own interest in his own way' (*Wealth of Nations*, ed. E. Cannan, London, 1904 and later, vol. II, p. 43 and elsewhere). The reason is that to the modern ear Smith's

phrase suggests a spirit of selfishness which is probably not intended and certainly inessential to the argument.

8 Cf. my essays on 'Rules, Perception, and Intelligibility' in *Proceedings of the British Academy*, XLVIII, 1962 (London, 1963), reprinted in *Studies in Philosophy, Politics, and Economics* (London and Chicago, 1967) and 'The Primacy of the Abstract' in A. Koestler and J. R. Smithies (eds) *Beyond Reductionism* (London, 1969).

9 It would seem that the commendatory use of 'will' rather than opinion came only with the Cartesian tradition and became general only through J.-J. Rousseau. The ancient Greeks were protected against the underlying confusion by the fact that the only word corresponding to 'willing' which their language offered (*boulomai*) clearly referred to aiming at a particular concrete object (Cf. M. Pohlenz, *Der Hellenische Mensch* (Göttingen, 1946), p. 210). When Aristotle (*Politics*, 1287a) demands that 'reason' and not 'will' should govern, this clearly means that abstract rules and not particular ends should govern all acts of coercion. We find the contrast then in ancient Rome as one between *voluntas* and *habitus animi*, the latter a rendering of the Aristotelian *héxis psychēs*. (Cf. esp. the interesting contrast between Cicero's definition of justice: 'iustitia est habitus animi, communi utilitate conservata, suam cuique tribuens dignitatem' in *De inventione*, 2,53,161,—and Ulpian's better known formula: 'iustitia est constans et perpetua voluntas ius suum cuique tribuendi' in *Dig.* 1,1.) Throughout the Middle Ages and early modern times we find *ratio* and *voluntas* constantly contrasted and finally arbitrariness characterized by the brief formula 'stat pro ratione voluntas'. No doubt C. H. McIlwain is right when in *Constitutionalism and the Modern State* (rev. ed., Ithaca, New York, 1947, p. 145) he stressed in the old terms that 'even in a popular state, such as we trust ours is, the problem of law versus will remains the most important of all political problems'. It is perhaps of interest that G. W. F. Hegel (*Grundlinien der Philosophie des Rechts*, para. 258, in Leipzig edn, 1911, p. 196) credits Rousseau to have established the *will* as the principle of the state.

10 Cf. J. Bentham, *Introduction to the Principles of Morals and Legislation* (London, 1789) ch. XI, sect. I, p. 131 of Oxford 1889 edn: 'disposition is a kind of fictitious entity, feigned for the convenience of discourse, in order to express what there is supposed to be *permanent* in a man's frame of mind, where, on such and such an occasion, he has been influenced by such or such a motive, to engage in an act, which, as it appears to him, was of such and such a tendency.' It seems clear that Bentham can conceive of such a disposition only as the result of conscious processes of the mind which recurrently decide upon to act in a certain manner.

11 Cf. M. Polanyi, *The Logic of Liberty* (London, 1951).

12 D. Hume, *A Treatise on Human Nature, Works*, (London, 1890), vol.
II, p. 269. The whole long paragraph from which these sentences are
taken deserves careful reading.
13 Thomas Aquinas, *Summa Theologiae*, Ia IIae, q. 95, art. 3: 'Finis
autem humanae legis est utilitas hominum.'
   It is misleading to represent as utilitarians all authors who account
for the existence of certain institutions by their utility, because
writers like Aristotle or Cicero, Thomas Aquinas or Mandeville,
Adam Smith or Adam Ferguson, when they spoke of utility, appear
to have thought of this utility favouring a sort of natural selection of
institutions, not determining their deliberate choice by men. When
in the passage quoted in note 9 above Cicero speaks of justice as a
'habitus animi, communi utilitate conservata' this is certainly not
meant in the sense of a constructivist but in that of a sort of evolutionary utilitarianism. On the derivation of both traditions in the modern
world from Bernard Mandeville see my lecture 'Dr Bernard Mandeville', *Proceedings of the British Academy*, vol. 52, pp. 134ff.
14 For the use of the conception of utility by David Hume see particularly his discussion of the stability of possession in *Treatise*, vol. II,
pp. 273ff., where he argues that these rules 'are not derived from any
utility or advantage, which either the *particular* person or the public
may reap from his enjoyment of any *particular* goods. . . .
   'It follows, therefore, that the general rules, that *possession must be
stable*, is not applied by particular judgements, but by other general
rules, which must extend to the whole society, and be inflexible
either by spite or favour.' I do not know whether Bentham did ever
explicitly say, as C. W. Everett (*The Education of Jeremy Bentham*
(London, 1931), p. 47) suggests, that Hume's idea of utility 'was a
vague one, as it was used simply as synonymous with conduciveness
to an end, and with no intimation of happiness as connected with the
idea.' If he did so, he had a true sense of the meaning of the word.
15 Bentham himself was well aware of this intellectual ancestry and of
the contrast of his constructivist approach to the evolutionary tradition of the common law; cf. his letter to Voltaire of about 1776
quoted in C. W. Everett, *The Education of Jeremy Bentham* (Columbia,
1931), pp. 110ff., in which he wrote: 'I have taken council of you
much oftener than of our own Ld. Coke and Hale and Blackstone. . . .
I have built solely on the foundation of utility, laid as it is by Helvetius.
Beccaria has been *lucerna pedibus* or if you please *manibus meis*.' Much
information on the influence of the Continental rationalists, especially
Beccaria and Maupertius, is to be found in D. Baumgardt, *Bentham
and the Ethics of Today* (Princeton, 1952), esp. pp. 85, 221–6, and
particularly the revealing passage from a manuscript of Bentham of
about 1782, quoted on p. 557: 'The idea of considering happiness as
resoluble into a number of (individual) pleasures, I took from

Helvetius: before whom it can scarcely be said to have a meaning. (This is directly contrary to the doctrine laid down in Cicero's Tusculan disputation: which book, like most of the philosophical writings of that great master of language is nothing but a heap of nonsense.) The idea of estimating the value of each sensation by analysing it into these four ingredients, I took from Beccaria.'

16 Some of the most important of these studies (by J. O. Urmson, J. Harrison, John Rawls, J. J. C. Smart, H. J. McCloskey, R. B. Brandt, A. Donagan, B. J. Diggs, and T. L. S. Sprigge) have been conveniently brought together in a volume edited by M. D. Bayles, *Contemporary Utilitarianism* (Garden City, New York, 1968). To these ought to be added two articles by J. D. Mabbott, 'Interpretations of Mill's "Utilitarianism"', *Philosophical Quarterly*, vol. VI, 1956, and 'Moral Rules', *Proceedings of the British Academy*, vol. XXXIX, 1953, and the books by R. M. Hare, *Freedom and Reason* (Oxford, 1963), J. Hospers, *Human Conduct* (New York, 1961), M. G. Singer, *Generalisation in Ethics* (London, 1963) and S. E. Toulmin, *An Examination of the Place of Reason in Ethics* (Cambridge, 1950). Two more recent books of considerable importance, which for the time being ought to bring this discussion to a close, are David Lyons, *Forms and Limits of Utilitarianism* (Oxford, 1965), and D. H. Hodgson, *Consequences of Utilitarianism* (Oxford, 1967). A more complete bibliography will be found in N. Rescher, *Distributive Justice* (New York, 1966). Since the present chapter was completed the central issue was discussed in J. J. C. Smart and Bernard Williams, *Utilitarianism: For and Against* (Cambridge, 1973). What in the text is called 'particularistic' utilitarianism and is now most frequently described as 'act utilitarianism' has also been designated 'crude', 'extreme' and 'direct' utilitarianism, while what we call 'generic' and is more usually called 'rule'-utilitarianism has also been named 'modified', 'restricted' and 'indirect' utilitarianism.

17 Henry Sidgwick, *The Methods of Ethics* (London, 1874), p. 425.

18 G. E. Moore, *Ethics* (London, 1912), p. 232, but cf. his *Principia Ethica* (Cambridge, 1903), p. 162.

19 W. Paley, *The Principles of Moral and Political Philosophy* (1785; London, 1824 edn), p. 47, and cf. John Austin, *The Province of Jurisprudence* (1832; ed. H. L. A. Hart, London, 1954), lecture II, p. 38: 'Now the tendency of a human action (as its tendency is thus understood) is the whole of its tendency: the sum of its probable consequences, in so far as they are important and material: the sum of its remote and collateral, as well as of its direct consequences, in so far as any of its consequences may influence the general happiness ... we ... must look at the *class* of actions to which they belong. The probable *specific* consequences of doing that single act, are not the object of inquiry.'

20 The nearest approach to taking ignorance seriously in any discussion of utilitarianism known to me occurs in the article 'Utilitarianism' by J. J. C. Smart in the *Encyclopaedia of Philosophy*, vol. VIII, p. 210.

21 John W. Chapman, 'Justice and Fairness', in *Nomos VI, Justice* (New York, 1964), p. 153: 'Justice as reciprocity makes sense only if society is seen as a plurality of persons and not, as the utilitarian would have it, as a sort of single great person.'

22 Hastings Rashdall, *The Theory of Good and Evil* (London, 1907), vol. I, p. 184.

23 Cf. Gregory Vlastos, 'Justice', *Revue Internationale de la Philosophie*, XI, 1957, p. 338: 'The feature of Benthamism to which all of these would object most strenuously is that what we commonly call "acting on principle" has almost no place on this theory: one is supposed to live by applying the felicific calculus from act to act.' In the same article (p. 333) Vlastos quotes an interesting passage from Bishop Butler's *Dissertation Upon the Nature of Virtue* (an Appendix to *The Analogy of Religion*, 1736, reprinted as Appendix to *Five Sermons by Butler*, ed. S. M. Brown, New York, 1950) in which Butler argues against authors who imagine 'the whole of virtue to consist in simply aiming, according to the best of their judgement, at promoting the happiness of mankind in the present state.'

24 Theodor Geiger, *Vorstudien zu einer Soziologie des Rechts* (Copenhagen, 1947, 2nd edn, Darmstadt, 1964), p. 111: 'Es ist nun in der Tat so, dass die Ursachen für die So-Gestaltung eines gegebenen habituellen Ordnungsgefüges unbekannt sind—und es vorläufig wohl auch bleiben.'

25 This, I believe, is what Karl Popper (*The Open Society and its Enemies*, Princeton, 1963) means by 'piecemeal engineering', an expression which I feel reluctant to adopt because 'engineering' suggests to me too much a technological problem of reconstruction on the basis of the total knowledge of the physical data, while the essential point about the practicable improvement is an experimental attempt to improve the functioning of some part without a full comprehension of the structure of the whole.

26 Cf. E. Westermarck, *The Origin and Development of Moral Ideas*, vol. I (London, 1906), pp. 386ff. and 399ff., summarized in his *Ethical Relativity* (London, 1932), pp. 184ff.

27 Cf. M. G. Singer, *Generalization in Ethics* (New York, 1961).

CHAPTER EIGHT THE QUEST FOR JUSTICE

* Paul Vinogradoff, *Common-Sense in Law* (London and New York, 1914), p. 70. Cf. also *ibid.*, pp. 46f.:

The problem consists in allowing such an exercise of each personal will as is compatible with the exercise of other wills. . . . [A law] is a limitation of one's freedom of action for the sake of avoiding collision with others. . . . In social life, as we know, men have not only to avoid collisions, but to arrange co-operation in all sorts of ways, and the one common feature of all these forms of co-operation is the limitation of individual wills in order to achieve a common purpose.

And pp. 61f.: 'We can hardly define a right better than by saying that it is the *range of action assigned to a particular will within the social order established by law.*' In the third edition by H. G. Hambury (London, 1959) the passages occur on pp. 51, 34f. and 45.

1 See Franz Boehm, 'Privatrechtsgesellschaft und Marktwirtschaft', *Ordo* XVII, 1966, pp. 75–151, and 'Der Rechtsstaat und der soziale Wohlfahrtsstaat' in *Reden und Schriften*, ed. E. S. Mestmäcker (Karlsruhe, 1960), pp. 102f.

2 For interpretations of justice as an attribute of a factual state of affairs rather than of human actions cf. Hans Kelsen, *What is Justice?* (California, 1957) p. 1:

Justice is primarily a possible, but not a necessary, quality of a social order regulating the mutual relations of men. Only secondarily it is a virtue of man, since a man is just, if his behaviour conforms to the norms of a social order supposed to be just. . . . Justice is social happiness. It is happiness guaranteed by a social order.

Similarly A. Brecht, *Political Theory* (Princeton, 1959), p. 146: 'Postulates of justice are generally expressed in terms of some desirable state of affairs, for instance one where equality, or "more" equality, would be established. . . . Even when not expressed in such terms, postulates of justice can be translated into them.'

3 Cf. H. L. A. Hart, *The Concept of Law* (Oxford, 1961), p. 195: 'There are no settled principles forbidding the use of the word "law" of systems where there are no centrally organized sanctions.' Hart draws an important distinction between 'primary rules' under which 'human beings are required to do or abstain from certain actions, whether they wish or not' (p. 78) and 'secondary rules of recognition, change, and adjudication', i.e. the rules of the organization which has been set up to enforce the rules of conduct. Though this is of the greatest importance, I find it difficult to regard the development of this distinction as 'the decisive step from the pre-legal to the legal world' (p. 91) or to characterize law 'as a union of primary rules of obligation with secondary rules' (*ibid.*) as very helpful.

4 It would be possible to argue endlessly whether the law is or is not a

'system of rules', but this is largely a terminological question. If by 'system of rules' is understood a collection of articulated rules, this would certainly not constitute the whole law. Ronald M. Dworkin, who in an essay entitled 'Is Law a System of Rules?' (in R. S. Summers, ed., *Essays in Legal Philosophy*, Oxford and California, 1968) uses the term 'system' as equivalent to 'collection' (p. 52) and seems to accept only articulated rules as rules, shows convincingly that a system of rules so interpreted would be incomplete and requires for its completion what he calls 'principles'. (Cf. also Roscoe Pound, 'Why Law Day', *Harvard Law School Bulletin*, vol. x, no. 3, 1958, p. 4: 'The vital, the enduring part of the law is in principles—starting points for reasoning, not rules. Principles remain relatively constant or develop along constant lines. Rules have relatively short lives. They do not develop; they are repealed and are superseded by other rules.') I prefer to use the term *system* for a body of rules that are mutually adjusted to each other and possess an order of rank, and of course I include in 'rules' not only articulated but also not yet articulated rules which are implicit in the system or have yet to be found to make the several rules consistent. Thus, while I wholly agree with the substance of Professor Dworkin's argument, I should, in my terminology, affirm that the law *is* a system (and not a mere collection) of (articulated and unarticulated) rules.

5 In a general way this idea appears in the English literature at least in the eighteenth century and has been expressed especially by William Paley in his *Principles of Moral and Political Philosophy* (1785, new ed. London, 1824), p. 348: 'general laws are made . . . without forseeing whom they might affect' and recurs in its modern form in C. K. Allen, *Law in the Making* (6th ed., London, 1958), p. 367: 'a legal rule, like every kind of rule, aims at establishing a generalisation for an indefinite number of cases of a certain kind.' It was most systematically developed in that Continental (mainly German) discussion about the distinction between law in the 'material' and law in the merely 'formal' sense to which we have referred earlier (note 24 to chapter VI) and appears to have been established there by Hermann Schulze, *Das Preussische Staatsrecht* (Leipzig, 1877), vol. II, p. 209: 'Dem Merkmal der Allgemeinheit ist genügt, wenn sich nur der Regel überhaupt eine Zahl von nicht vorauszusehenden Fällen logisch unterzuordnen hat.' (See also *ibid.*, p. 205 for references to earlier relevant writings.) Of later works see particularly Ernst Seligmann, *Der Begriff des Gesetzes im materiellen und formellen Sinn* (Berlin, 1886), p. 63: 'In der Tat ist es ein Essentiale des Rechtsgesetzes, dass es abstrakt ist und eine nicht vorauszusehende Anzahl von Fällen ordnet.' M. Planiol, *Traité élémentaire de Droit Civil* (12th ed., Paris, 1937), p. 69: 'la loi est établie en permanence pour un nombre indéterminé d'actes et de faits, . . . un decision obligatoire d'une

manière permanente, pour un nombre de fois indéterminé.' Z. Giacometti, *Die Verfassungsgerichtsbarkeit des schweizerischen Bundesgerichts* (Zürich, 1933), p. 99: 'Generell abstrakt ist jede . . . an eine unbestimmte Vielheit von Personen für eine unbestimmte Vielheit von Fällen gerichtete Anordnung'; and the same author's *Allgemeine Lehre des rechtsstaatlichen Verwaltungsrechts* (Zürich, 1960), p. 5: 'Eine solche Bindung der staatlichen Gewaltenträger an generelle, abstrakte Vorschriften, die für eine unbestimmte Vielheit von Menschen gelten und die eine unbestimmte Vielheit von Tatbeständen regeln ohne Rücksicht auf einen bestimmten Einzelfall oder eine bestimmte Person. . . .' W. Burckhardt, *Einführung in die Rechtswissenschaft* (2nd ed., Zürich, 1948), p. 200: 'Die Pflichten, die das Gesetz den Privaten auferlegt, müssen (im Gegensatz zu den Pflichten der Beamten) zum Voraus für eine unbestimmte Anzahl möglicher Fälle vorgeschrieben sein.' H. Kelsen, *Reine Rechtslehre* (2nd ed., Vienna, 1960), pp. 362–3: 'Generell ist eine Norm, wenn sie . . . in einer von vornherein unbestimmten Zahl von gleichen Fällen gilt. . . . In dieser Beziehung ist sie dem abstrakten Begriff analog.' Donato Donati, 'I caratteri della legge in senso materiale,' *Rivista di Diritto Publico*, 1911 (and reprinted in *Scritti di Diritto Publico*, Padua, 1961, vol. II), p. 11 of the separate offprint: 'Questa generalità deve intendersi, non già nel senso, semplicemente, di *pluralità*, ma in quelle, invece, di universalità. Commando generale, in altre termini, sarebbe, non già quelle che concerne una *pluralità* di persone o di azioni, ma soltanto quello che concerne una universalità di persone o di azioni, vale a dire: non quello che concerne un numero di persone o di azioni *determinato* o *determinabile*, ma quello che concerne un numero di persone o di azioni *indeterminato* e *indeterminabile*.'

6 All these attributes of law in the narrow sense have been brought out in the extensive Continental discussion of the distinction between what was called law in the 'material' and law in the merely 'formal' sense, but were often wrongly treated as alternative or even incompatible criteria of law in the 'material' sense. See P. Laband, *Staatsrecht des deutschen Reiches* (5th ed., Tübingen, 1911–14), II, pp. 54–6; E. Seligmann, *Der Begriff des Gesetzes im materiellen und formellen Sinn* (Berlin, 1886); A. Haenel, *Studien zum deutschen Staatsrecht*, vol. II: *Gesetz im formellen und materiellen Sinne* (Leipzig, 1888); L. Duguit, *Traité de droit constitutionel* (2nd ed., Paris, 1921); R. Carré de Malberg, *La Loi: Expression de la volonté générale* (Paris, 1931); and Donato Donati, 'I caratteri della legge in senso materiale', *Rivista di Diritto Publico*, 1911, reprinted in the author's *Scritti di Diritto Publico* (Padua, 1961). The best known definition of law in the material sense is probably that given by Georg Jellinek, *Gesetz und Verordnung* (Freiburg, 1887), p. 240:

Hat ein Gesetz den nächsten Zweck, die Sphäre der freien
Tätigkeiten von Persönlichkeiten gegeneinander abzugrenzen, ist
es der sozialen Schrankenziehung halber erlassen, so enthält es
Anordnungen eines Rechtssatzes, ist daher auch ein Gesetz im
materiellen Sinn; hat es jedoch einen anderen Zweck, so ist es kein
materielles, sondern nur ein formelles Gesetz, das seinen Inhalt
nach als Anordnung eines Verwaltungsaktes, oder als ein Rechts-
spruch sich charakterisiert.

7 See, apart from the quotation from P. Vinogradoff placed at the head
of this chapter, particularly F. C. von Savigny, *System des heutigen
Römischen Rechts*, vol. i (Berlin, 1840), pp. 331–2:

Sollen nun in solcher Berührung freie Wesen nebeneinander
bestehen, sich gegenseitig fördernd, nicht hemmend, in ihrer
Entwicklung, so ist dieses nur möglich durch Anerkennung einer
unsichtbaren Grenze, innerhalb welcher das Dasein, und die
Wirksamkeit jedes einzelnen einen sichern, freien Raum gewinne.
Die Regel, wodurch jene Grenze und durch die dieser freie Raum
bestimmt wird, ist das Recht.

Also P. Laband, *Das Staatsrecht des Deutschen Reiches* (4th ed.,
Tübingen, 1901), vol. ii, p. 64, where he ascribes to the state the task
of 'die durch das gesellige Zusammenleben der Menschen gebotenen
Schranken und Grenzen der natürlichen Handlungsfreiheit der
Einzelnen zu bestimmen.' J. C. Carter, *Law, Its Origin, Growth, and
Function* (New York and London, 1907), pp. 133–4: 'Custom thus
fostered and enforced became the beginning of law. The direct and
necessary tendency of this restraint was to trace out boundary lines of
individual action within which each person might freely move without exciting the opposition of others. Here we find exhibited in its
earliest and simplest form the function of law.' J. Salmond, *Jurisprudence* (10th ed. by G. Williams, London, 1947), p. 62: 'The rule
of justice determines the sphere of individual liberty within the limits
which are consistent with the general welfare of mankind. Within the
sphere of liberty so delimited for every man by the rule of justice,
he is left free to seek his own interest in accordance with the rule of
wisdom.' H. Lèvy-Ullman, *La Définition du droit* (Paris, 1917), p.
165: 'Nous définirons donc le droit: la délimination de ce que les
hommes et leur groupements ont la liberté de faire et de ne pas faire,
sans encourir une condemnation, une saisie, une mise en jeu particulière de la force.' Donato Donati, 'I caratteri della legge in senso
materiale', *Rivista di Diritto Publico*, 1911 and reprinted in the author's
Scritti di Diritto Publico (Padua, 1961), vol. ii, p. 23 of the separate
offprint of the article:

La funzione del diritto e infatti sorge e si esplica per la deliminazione

NOTES TO PAGE 36

delle diverse sfere spettanti a ciascun consociato. La società
umana si transforma de società anarchica in società ordinata per
questo, che interviene una volontà ordinatrice a determinare la
cerchia dell' attività di ciascuno: dell' attività lecita come dell'
attività doverosa.

8 Adam Smith, *The Theory of Moral Sentiments* (London, 1801), Part
VI, sect. ii, introd. vol. II, p. 58:

> The wisdom of every state or commonwealth endeavours, as well
> as it can, to employ the force of the society to restrain those who
> are subject to its authority, from hurting or disturbing the happi-
> ness of one another. The rules which it establishes for this purpose,
> constitute the civil and criminal law of each particular state or
> country.

9 The emphasis on the primary character of injustice appears already
in Herakleitos (see J. Burnet, *Early Greek Philosophy*, 4th ed., London, 1930, p. 166) and it is clearly stated by Aristotle in the *Nicomachean Ethics*, 1134 a: 'Law exists for men between whom there is
injustice.' In modern times it frequently reappears, e.g. in La Roche-
foucauld, *Maximes* (1665) no. 78: 'L'amour de la justice n'est que la
crainte de souffrir injustice' and becomes prominent with David
Hume, Immanuel Kant and Adam Smith, for whom the rules of just
conduct serve mainly the delimitation and protection of individual
domains. L. Bagolini, *La Simpatia nella morale e nel diritto* (Bologna,
1952), p. 60 even describes the treatment of 'il probleme de diritto e
della giustizia del punto di vista del ingiustizia' as specially characteristic of the thinking of Adam Smith. Cf. the latter's *Theory of Moral
Sentiments* (1759), part II, sect. II, chapter I, vol. I, p. 165 of ed. of
1801: 'Mere justice is, upon most occasions, but a negative virtue, and
only hinders us from hurting our neighbour. The man who barely
abstains from violating either the person, or the estate, or the reputation of his neighbours, has surely little positive merit. He fulfils, however, all the rules of what is peculiarly called justice, and does every
thing which his equals can with propriety force him to do, or which
they can punish him for not doing. We may often fulfil all the rules
of justice by sitting still and doing nothing.' Cf. also Adam Ferguson,
Institutes of Moral Philosophy (Edinburgh, 1785), p. 189: 'The fundamental law of morality, in its first application to the actions of men, is
prohibitory and forbids the commission of wrong'; John Millar, *An
Historical View of the English Government* (London, 1787), quoted in
W. C. Lehmann, *John Millar of Glasgow* (Cambridge, 1960), p. 340:
'Justice requires no more than that I abstain from hurting my
neighbour'; Similarly J.-J. Rousseau, *Émile* (1762) Book II: 'La plus
sublime vertu est negative; elle nous instruit de ne jamais faire de mal

NOTES TO PAGE 36

à personne.' This view seems to have been widespread also among lawyers so that F. C. von Savigny, *System des Heutigen Römischen Rechts*, I (Berlin, 1840), p. 332 could say that 'Viele aber gehen, um den Begriff des Rechts zu finden, von dem entgegengesetzten Standpunkt aus, von dem Begriff des Unrechts. Unrecht ist ihnen Störung der Freiheit durch fremde Freiheit, die der menschlichen Entwicklung hinderlich ist, und daher als ein Übel abgewehrt werden muss.'

In the nineteenth century two outspoken representatives of this view are the philosopher Arthur Schopenhauer and the economist Frédéric Bastiat, who may possibly have been indirectly influenced by the former. See A. Schopenhauer, *Parerga und Paralipomena*, II, 9, 'Zur Rechtslehre und Politik', in *Sämtliche Werke*, ed. A. Hübscher (Leipzig, 1939), vol. VI, p. 257: 'Der Begriff des *Rechts* ist nämlich ebenso wie auch der der *Freiheit* ein *negativer*, sein Inhalt ist eine blosse Negation. Der Begriff des *Unrechts* ist der positive und gleichbedeutend mit Verletzung im weitesten Sinn, also laesio.' F. Bastiat, *La Loi* (1850), in *Oeuvres Complètes* (Paris, 1854), vol. IV, p. 35: 'Cela est si vrai qu'ainsi qu'un des mes amis me le faisait remarquer, dire que le but de la Loi est de faire régner la Justice, c'est de se servir d'une expression qui n'est pas vigoureusement exacte. Il faudrait dire: *Le but de la Loi est d'empêcher l'Injustice de régner.* En effet, ce n'est pas la Justice qui a une existence propre, c'est l'Injustice. L'un résulte de la absence de l'autre.' Cf. also J. S. Mill, *Utilitarianism* (1861, ed. J. Plamenatz, Oxford, 1949), p. 206: 'for justice, like many other moral attributes, is best defined by its opposites.'

More recently, among philosophers, Max Scheler has emphasized the same point. See his *Der Formalismus in der Ethik und die materielle Wertethik* (3rd ed., 1927), p. 212: 'Niemals kann daher (bei genauer Reduktion) die Rechtsordnung sagen, was sein soll (oder was recht ist), sondern immer nur, was nicht sein soll (oder nicht recht ist). Alles, was innerhalb der Rechtsordnung *positiv* gesetzt ist, ist reduziert auf pure Rechtsein- und Unrechtseinverhalte, stets ein *Unrechtseinverhalt*.' Cf. also Leonhard Nelson, *Die Rechtswissenschaft ohne Recht*, (Leipzig, 1917), p. 133, about the 'Auffassung vom Recht . . . wonach das Recht . . . die Bedeutung einer negativen, den Wert möglicher positiver Zwecke einschränkenden Bedingung hat'; and *ibid.*, p. 151, about the 'Einsicht in den negativen (Werte nur beschränkenden) Charakter des Rechts'.

Among contemporary authors cf. further L. C. Robbins, *The Theory of Economic Policy* (London, 1952), p. 193: The classical Liberal 'proposes, as it were, a division of labour: the state shall prescribe what individuals shall not do, if they are not to get into each other's way, while citizens shall be left free to do anything which is not so forbidden. To the one is assigned the task of establishing formal rules, to the other responsibility for the substance of specific action.'

K. E. Boulding, *The Organisational Revolution* (New York, 1953), p. 83: 'The difficulty seems to be that "justice" is a negative concept; that is, it is not justice which leads to action, but injustice or discontent.' McGeorge Bundy, 'A Lay View of Due Process', in A. E. Sutherland (ed.), *Government under Law* (Harvard, 1956), p. 365: 'I suggest, then, that legal process is best understood not as a source of pure and positive justice, but rather as an imperfect remedy for gross wrongs. . . . Or perhaps we can think of the law not as something good in itself, but as an instrument which derives its value less from what it does than what it prevents. . . . What one asks of [the courts] is not that they do justice but that they give some protection against grave injustice.' Bernard Mayo, *Ethics and Moral Life* (London, 1958), p. 204: 'With certain apparent exceptions . . . the function of law is to prevent something.' H. L. A. Hart, *The Concept of Law* (Oxford, 1961), p. 190: 'The common requirement of law and morality consists for the most part not of active services to be rendered but of forbearances, which are usually formulated in negative form as prohibitions.' Lon L. Fuller, *The Morality of the Law* (Yale, 1964), p. 42: 'In what may be called the basic morality of social life, duties that run towards other persons generally . . . normally require only forbearances, or as we say, are negative in nature.' J. R. Lucas, *The Principles of Politics* (Oxford, 1966), p. 130:

> In the face of human imperfection, we articulate the Rule of law partly in terms of procedures designed not to secure that absolute Justice will be done but to be a safeguard against the worst sort of injustice. Injustice rather than Justice 'wears the trousers' in political philosophy, because, being fallible, we cannot say in advance what the just decision will always be, and, living among selfish men, we cannot always secure that it will be carried out, so, for the sake of definiteness, we adopt a negative approach, and lay down procedures to avoid certain likely forms of injustice, rather than aspire to all forms of Justice.

On the whole issue see particularly E. N. Cahn, *The Sense of Injustice* (New York, 1949) who defines 'justice' (pp. 13f.) as 'the active process of remedying or preventing what would arouse a sense of Injustice'. Cf. also the dictum of Lord Atkin, quoted by A. L. Goodhart, *English Law and the Moral Law* (London, 1953), p. 95: 'the rule that you are to love your neighbour becomes in law, you must not injure your neighbour.'

10 See A. L. Goodhart, *op. cit.*, p. 100 and J. B. Ames, 'Law and Morals', *Harvard Law Review*, XXII, 1908/9, p. 112.
11 See para. 330c of the German Penal Code, added in 1935, which provides punishment for 'anybody who in cases of accident, common danger or distress does not render help, although this is needed and

can be reasonably expected from him, especially if he can do so without himself incurring substantial danger or violating other important duties.'

12 That 'general obligation to help and sustain one another' which Max Gluckman (*Politics, Law and Ritual in Tribal Society*, London and Chicago, 1965, p. 54) describes as characteristic of the tribal society and especially the kinship group, and for the lack of which the Great Society is generally blamed, is incompatible with it and its abandonment part of the price we pay for the achievement of a more extensive order of peace. This obligation can exist only towards particular, known people—and though in a Great Society it may well be a moral obligation towards people of one's choice, it cannot be enforced under equal rules for all.

13 Cf. Paul A. Freund, 'Social Justice and the Law', in Richard B. Brandt, ed., *Social Justice* (Englewood Cliffs, New Jersey, 1962), p. 96: 'Reasonable expectations are more generally the ground rather than the product of law, as well as a basis for a critique of positive law and thus a ground of law in the process of becoming.'

14 I. Kant, *Metaphysik der Sitten, Rechtslehre*. I,2, para. 9: 'Bürgerliche Verfassung ist hier allein der rechtliche Zustand, durch welchen jedem das Seine nur gesichert, eigentlich aber nicht ausgemacht oder bestimmt wird.—Alle Garantie setzt also das Seine von jedem (dem es gesichert wird) schon voraus.' In the translation by John Ladd (*The Metaphysical Elements of Justice*, Indianapolis, 1965, p. 65): 'A civil constitution only provides the juridical condition under which each person's property is secured and guaranteed to him, but it does not actually stipulate and determine what that property shall be.'

15 R. L. Hale, *Freedom through Law* (California, 1952), p. 15.

16 Only through this interpretation the famous formula of Ulpian (*Dig.*, I,1.10) 'Iustitia est constans et perpetua voluntas suum cuique tribuere' is preserved from becoming a tautology. It is of some interest that Ulpian in this phrase has evidently substituted *voluntas* for an older term describing an attitude of mind: see Cicero, *De Inventione*, II, 35, 160: 'Iustitia est habitus animi, communi utilitate conservata, suum cuique tribuens dignitatem.'

17 John W. Chapman, 'Justice and Fairness', *Nomos* VI, 1963, p. 153.

18 D. Hume, *An Enquiry concerning the Principles of Morals*, *Works* IV, p. 274:

All the laws of nature, which regulate property, as well as all civil laws, are general, and regard alone some essential circumstances of the case, without taking into consideration the characters, situations, and connexions of the person concerned, or any particular consequences which may result from the determination of these laws, in any particular case which offers. They deprive, without scruple, a beneficient man of all his possessions, if acquired by mistake, without a good title; in order to bestow them on a selfish miser, who has already heaped up immense stores of superfluous riches. Public utility requires, that property should be regulated by general inflexible rules; and though such rules are adopted as best serve the same end of public utility, it is impossible for them to prevent all particular hardships, or make beneficial consequences flow from every individual case. It is sufficient, if the whole plan or scheme be necessary for the support of civil society, and if the balance of good, in the main, do thereby preponderate much above that of evil.

19 Cf. John Rawls, 'Constitutional Liberty and the Concept of Justice', *Nomos* VI, *Justice* (New York. 1963), p. 102:

Put another way, the principles of justice do not select specific distributions of desired things as just, given the wants of particular persons. This task is abandoned as mistaken in principle, and it is, in any case, not capable of a definite answer. Rather, the principles of justice define the constraints which institutions and joint activities must satisfy if persons engaging in them are to have no complaints against them. If these constraints are satisfied, the resulting distribution, whatever it is, may be accepted as just (or at least not unjust).

20 See note 16 above.
21 Cf. D. Hume, *Enquiry Works* IV, p. 195: 'all these institutions arise merely from the necessities of human society.'
22 D. Hume, *Treatise, Works* II, p. 293.
23 Leon Duguit as described by J. Walter Jones, *Historical Introduction to the Theory of Law* (Oxford, 1940), p. 114.
24 See M. J. Gregor, *Laws of Freedom* (London, 1964), p. 81: Cf. also the statement a few paragraphs earlier that 'juridical laws . . . merely forbid us to employ certain means of achieving whatever ends we have', and p. 42 for the description of the character of Kant's negative test for just law as 'merely the limitation of freedom through the formal condition of its thorough-going consistency with itself'.

I owe it to this excellent book that I became aware *how* closely my conclusions agree with Kant's philosophy of law, which, apart from occasional references, I had not seriously examined since my student days. What I had not seen before I read Miss Gregor's book was that in his legal philosophy Kant sticks consistently to the use of the categorical imperative as a negative test and that he does not attempt as he does in his philosophy of morals, to use it as a premise for a process of deduction through which the positive content of the moral rules is to be derived. This suggests to me very strongly, though I have no proof to offer, that Kant probably did not, as is generally assumed, discover the principle of the categorical imperative in morals and afterwards applied it to law, but that he rather found the basic conception in Hume's treatment of the rule of law and then applied it to morals. But while his brilliant treatment of development of the ideal of the rule of law with its stress on the negative and end-independent character of the legal rules seems to me to be one of his permanent achievements, his attempt to turn what in law is a test of justice to be applied to an existing body of rules into a premise from which the system of moral rules can be deductively derived was bound to fail.

25 Karl R. Popper, *The Logic of Scientific Discovery* (London, 1955), *The Open Society and its Enemies* (esp. 4th ed., Princeton, 1963), and *Conjectures and Refutations* (2nd ed., London, 1965).

26 Cf. e.g. G. Radbruch's statement quoted below, note 69.

27 See the full account of this development in John H. Hallowell, *The Decline of Liberalism as an Ideology with Particular Reference to German Politico-Legal Thought* (California, 1943), esp. pp. 77 and 111ff. Hallowell clearly shows how the leading liberal legal theorists in the Germany of the late nineteenth century by their acceptance of a legal positivism which regarded all law as the deliberate creation of a legislator and who were interested only in the constitutionality of an act of legislation and not in the character of the rules laid down, deprived themselves of any possibility of a resistance to the super-session of the 'material' by the merely 'formal' *Rechtsstaat* and at the same time discredited liberalism by this connection with a legal positivism with which it is fundamentally incompatible. A recognition of this fact can also be found in the early writings of Carl Schmitt, especially in his *Die geistesgeschichtliche Lage des deutschen Parlamentarismus* (2nd ed., Munich, 1926) p. 26:

> Konstitutionelles und absolutistisches Denken haben also an dem Gesetzesbegriff ihren Prüfstein, aber natürlich nicht an dem, was man in Deutschland seit Laband Gesetz im formellen Sinn nennt und wonach alles, was unter der Mitwirkung der Volksvertretung zustandekommt, Gesetz heisst, sondern an einem nach logischen Merkmalen bestimmten Satz. Das entscheidende Merkmal bleibt immer, ob das Gesetz ein genereller, rationaler Satz ist, oder Massnahme, konkrete Einzelverfügung, Befehl.

28 William James, *Pragmatism* (new impr., New York, 1940) p. 222: ' "The true", to put it briefly, is only the expedient in the way of our thinking, just as "the right" is only the expedient in the way of our behaving.'

29 John Dewey and James Tuft, *Ethics* (New York, 1908 and later); John

Dewey, *Human Nature and Conduct* (New York, 1922 and later); and *Liberalism and Social Action* (New York, 1963 edn).

30 Vilfredo Pareto, *The Mind and Society* (London and New York, 1935), para. 1210: 'When a person says: "That thing is unjust," what he means is that the thing is offensive to his sentiments as his sentiments stand in the state of social equilibrium to which he is accustomed.'

31 Cf. H. L. A. Hart, *op. cit.*, p. 253.

32 See vol. I, p. 20.

33 Thomas Hobbes, *Leviathan*, ch. 26, Latin ed. (London, 1651), p. 143.

34 Thomas Hobbes, *Dialogue of the Common Laws* (1681), in *Works*, vol. VI, p. 26.

35 Jeremy Bentham, *Constitutional Code* (1827), in *Works*, vol. IX, p. 8 and cf. *The Theory of Legislation*, ed. C. K. Ogden (London, 1931), p. 8: 'The primitive sense of the word *law*, and the ordinary meaning of the word, is . . . the will of command of a legislator.'

36 John Austin, *Lectures on Jurisprudence*, 4th ed. (London, 1879), vol. I, pp. 88 and 555. Cf. also I.c., p. 773: 'The rights and duties of political subordinates, and the rights and duties of private persons, are creatures of a common author, namely, the Sovereign State'; also *The Province of Jurisprudence Determined*, ed. H. L. A. Hart (London, 1954), p. 124: 'Strictly speaking, every law properly so called, is a *positive* law. For it is *put* or set by its individual or collective author, or it exists by the *position* or institution of its individual or collective author.'

37 Hans Kelsen, *What is Justice?* (California, 1967), p. 20. The works of Kelsen to which in the following we shall most frequently refer will be indicated by the year of publication only, namely:

1935, 'The Pure Theory of Law', *Law Quarterly Review*, 51.

1945, *General Theory of Law and State* (Harvard).

1957, *What is Justice?* (California).

1960, *Reine Rechtslehre*, 2nd ed. (Vienna).

38 Kelsen himself repeatedly stresses that 'it is impossible to "will" ' something of which one is ignorant' (1949, p. 34, similarly 1957, p. 273), but then circumvents, as we shall see, the difficulty this would create for less sophisticated forms of positivism by confining the 'will' of the legislator to the conferring of validity on a rule, so that the legislator who had made something into a 'norm' need not know the content of the law he has 'made'.

The first author to have made this shuffle was apparently Thomas Hobbes, See *Leviathan*, ch. XXVI: 'The legislator is he, not by whose authority the law was first made, but by whose authority they now continue to be laws.'

39 The objections of the legal historians at least since H. S. Maine are directed against the conception of law as the command of a sovereign. Cf. e.g., H. Kantorowicz, *The Definition of Law* (Cambridge, 1958),

p. 35: 'The whole history of legal science, particularly the work of the Italian glossators and the German pandectists, would become unintelligible if law were to be considered as a body of commands of the sovereign.'

40 Gustav Radbruch, *Rechtsphilosophie* (6th ed., Stuttgart, 1963), p. 179: 'Vermag niemand festzustellen, was gerecht ist, so muss jemand festsetzen, was rechtens sein soll.' Cf. also A. Brecht, *Political Theory* (Princeton, 1959), p. 147: 'Science . . . is unable to decide which state of affairs *is* really just. Opinions differ and science cannot decide between them in absolute terms.'

41 Gustav Radbruch, 'Vom individualistischen zum sozialen Recht' (1930), reprinted in *Der Mensch im Recht* (Göttingen, 1957), p. 39: 'Für eine soziale Rechtsordnung [ist] das Privatrecht . . . nur ein vorläufig ausgesparter und sich immer verkleinernder Spielraum für die Privatinitiative innerhalb des allumfassenden öffentlichen Rechts.' Cf. also in his *Rechtsphilosophie*, p. 224: 'Der Sozialismus würde ein fast völliges Aufgehen des privaten Rechts im öffentlichen Recht bedeuten.'

42 H. A. L. Hart, *The Concept of Law* (Oxford, 1961), p. 35, with reference to the statement by H. Kelsen, *Central Theory of Law and State* (Harvard, 1945), p. 63: 'One shall not steal; if somebody steals he shall be punished. . . . If at all existent, the first norm is contained in the second norm which is the only genuine norm. . . . Law is the primary norm which stipulates the sanction.' Cf. also Kelsen, 1957, p. 248 where private property is represented as 'a public function *par excellence*', and the conception of 'a specific sphere of "private" interest' as an 'ideological' conception.

43 Glanville Williams, 'The Controversy concerning the Word "Law" ', *British Year Book of International Law*, XXII, 1945, revised version in P. Laslett (ed.), *Philosophy, Politics, and Society* (Oxford, 1956); and 'Language and the Law', *Law Quarterly Review* LXI and LXII, 1945 and 1946.

44 Lewis Carroll, *Through the Looking Glass*, chapter VI.

45 H. Kelsen, 'The Pure Theory of Law', *Harvard Law Review*, LI, 1935, p. 517: 'Any content whatever can be legal; there is no human behaviour which could not function as the content of a legal norm'; also *General Theory of Law and State*, (Harvard, 1945) p. 113: 'Legal norms may have any kind of content.'

46 Cf. the quotations from Paulus and Accursius above, vol. 1, chapter IV, note to quotation at head of chapter.

47 Thomas Hobbes, *Leviathan*, Pt 1, ch. 13.

48 H. Kelsen, 'The Pure Theory of Law', *Law Quarterly Review*, vol. 50, 1934, p. 482.

49 E. Bodenheimer, *Jurisprudence* (Harvard, 1962), p. 169 describes this use with some justification as a *contradictio in adjecto* (a contradiction in terms).

50 This, of course, has long been legal usage and was made popular
among social scientists by Max Weber, whose influential discussion of
the relation between 'Legal Order and Economic Order' (in *Max
Weber of Law in Economy and Society*, ed. Max Rheinstein (Harvard,
1954), ch. I, sec. 5; cf. also ch. II. sec. I) is for our purposes wholly
useless and rather characteristic of a widespread confusion. For
Weber 'order' is throughout something which is 'valid' or 'binding',
which is to be enforced or contained in a maxim of law. In other
words, order exists for him only as organization and the existence of
a spontaneous order never becomes a problem. Like most positivists
or socialists he thinks in this respect anthropomorphically and knows
order only as *taxis* but not as *kosmos* and thereby blocks for himself
the access to the genuine theoretical problems of a science of society.

51 Cf. e.g., Kelsen, 1945, p. 3: 'Law is an order of human behavior
and "order" is a system of rules'; *ibid.*, p. 98: 'an order, a system of
norms. It is this order—or what amounts to the same thing, this
organisation— . . .'; 1960, p. 32: 'Eine "Ordnung" ist ein System
von Normen, deren Einheit dadurch konstituiert wird, dass sie alle
denselben Geltungsgrund haben'; and *Demokratie und Sozialismus*
(Vienna, 1967), p. 100, note: 'So wie ja die Jurisprudenz nicht sanderes
ist als eine Ordnungslehre.'

In one place at least Kelsen gives a quite adequate and defensible
description of a 'natural' order, but evidently believes that with this
description he has already demonstrated its metaphysical and non-
factual character. In the essay on 'Die Idee des Naturrechts' (1928),
reprinted in his *Aufsätze zur Ideologiekritik*, ed. E. Topitsch (Neuwied,
1964), p. 75, he writes:

> Unter einer 'natürlichen' Ordnung ist eine solche gemeint, die
> nicht auf dem menschlichen und darum unzulänglichen Willen
> beruht, die nicht 'willkürlich' geschaffen ist, sondern die sich
> gleichsam 'von selbst', aus einer irgendwie objektiv gegebenen,
> d.h. aber unabhängig vom subjektiv-menschlichen Willen
> existenten, dem Menschen aber doch irgendwie fassbaren, vom
> Menschen erkannten Grundtatsache, aus einem vom menschlichen
> Verstand nicht ursprünglich produzierten, aber von ihm doch
> reproduzierbaren Grundprinzip ergibt. Diese objektive Tatsache,
> dieses Grundprinzip, ist die 'Natur', oder in einem religiös-
> personifikativen Ausdruck 'Gott'.

If 'order' is here interpreted as a factual order of actions, 'objective'
as given independently of the will of *any one* person, and 'not produced by human will' as not the result of human action but of human
design, this (except for the last sentence) becomes not only an
empirically meaningful statement but a statement which is factually
true of spontaneous social orders.

52 Kelsen, 1945, p. 40: 'The existence of a legal norm is its validity.' Cf. also *ibid.*, pp. 30, 155 and 170 as well as 1957, p. 267: 'If we say a norm "exists" we mean that a norm is valid.' Similarly 1960, p. 9: 'Mit dem Worte "Geltung" bezeichnen wir die spezifische Existenz einer Norm.'

53 Kelsen 1945, pp. 115–22.

54 Kelsen 1960, p. 9: 'Da der Tatbestand der Gewohnheit durch Akte menschlichen Verhaltens konstituiert wird, sind auch die durch die Gewohnheit erzeugten Normen durch Akte menschlichen Verhaltens gesetzt, und sohin, wie die Normen, die der subjektive Sinn von Gesetzgebungsakten sind, *gesetzte*, das heisst *positive* Normen.'
I find it difficult to believe that in such phrases as the following the words I have italicized are consistently used to mean either the conferring of validity or the determination of the content of a rule: 1945, p. 113: 'A norm is a valid legal norm by virtue of the fact that it has been created according to a definite rule and by virtue thereof only'; *ibid.*, p. 392: the rules of positive law 'are *derived from* the arbitrary will of human authority'; 1957, p. 138: 'positive law . . . *created* by man'; *ibid.*, p. 25: 'A norm belongs to a certain legal order only if it has *come into being* in a certain way'; *ibid.*, p. 251: 'customary law—law *created* by a specific method'; *ibid.*, p. 289: 'the social order, termed "law", tries to *bring about a certain behavior of men*, considered by the *lawmaker* as desirable', which clearly appears to refer to the determination of the *content* of the law; 'On the Pure Theory of Law', *Israel Law Review*, I, 1966, p. 2: 'In order to be "positive" a legal norm . . . must be "posited", that is to say, stated, established or— as formulated in a figure of speech—"created" by an act of a human being', and *Aufsätze zur Ideologiekritik*, ed. E. Topitsch (Neuwied, 1965), p. 85: 'Die Normen des positiven Rechtes gelten . . . weil sie auf eine bestimmte Art erzeugt, von einem bestimmten Menschen *gesetzt* sind.' And I confess myself completely baffled by the meaning of a statement like that in 'Die Lehre von den drei Gewalten oder Funktionen des Staates', *Kant-Festschrift der Internationalen Vereinigung für Rechts- und Wirtschaftsphilosophie* (Berlin, 1924), p. 220: 'Auch das sogenannte Gewohnheitsrecht wird gesetzt, ist "positiv", ist Produkt einer Rechtserzeugung, Rechtsschöpfung, wenn auch keiner Rechts*satzung*', which literally says that customary law, although 'set', is not the product of a setting of law.

55 Such an examination would show that Kelsen's conception of a 'science' which 'seeks to discover the nature of law itself' (1957, p. 226) rests on what Karl Popper has called 'methodological essentialism, i.e. the theory that it is the aim of science to reveal essences and to describe them by means of definitions' (K. Popper, *The Open Society and its Enemies*, new ed. Princeton, 1963, vol. I, p. 32). The consequence is that Kelsen represents as 'cognition' what are merely

consequences of a definition and regards himself as entitled to represent as false (or meaningless) all statements in which the term 'law' is used in a different and narrower sense than the one he gives it and represents as the only legitimate one. The 'pure theory of law' is thus one of those pseudo-sciences like Marxism and Freudianism which are represented as irrefutable because all their statements are true by definition but tell us nothing about what is the fact. Kelsen has therefore also no business to represent, as he constantly does, as false or meaningless statements in which the term law is used in a different sense.

56 The assertion that every state is a state of law (*Rechtsstaat*) or that the rule of law prevails of necessity in every state is one of the most frequently reiterated throughout Kelsen's work. See e.g. *Hauptprobleme der Staatsrechtslehre* (Tübingen, 1911), p. 249, *Der soziologische und der juristische Staatsbegriff* (Tübingen, 1922), p. 190; 1935, p. 486; 1960, p. 314.

57 Kelsen, 1946, p. 392.

58 Kelsen, 1957, p. 20.

59 Kelsen, 1957, p. 295.

60 M. J. C. Vile, *Constitutionalism and the Separation of Powers* (Oxford, 1967), p. 63, based chiefly on John Locke, *Second Treatise of Government*, XI, para. 142: 'They are to govern by *promulgated established Laws*, not to be varied in particular cases, but to have one Rule for Rich and Poor, for the Favourite at Court, and the Country Man at Plough.'

61 Hans Kelsen, *Vom Wesen und Wert der Demokratie* (Tübingen, 1920), p. 10: 'Die im Grunde genommen unrettbare Freiheit des Individuums', which in the second edition of 1929, p. 13 becomes the 'im Grunde unmögliche Freiheit des Individuums'.

62 Kelsen, 1957, p. 23: 'democracy, by its very nature, means freedom.'

63 Kelsen, 1957, pp. 21f. Almost literally the same statement also in 1945, p. 13.

64 Cf. *ibid.*, p. 295: 'He who denies the justice of such [i.e. any positive] "law" and asserts that the so-called law is not "true" law, has to prove it; and this proof is practically impossible since there is no objective criterion of justice.'

65 E.g. in 'Was ist die Reine Rechtslehre?' in *Demokratie und Rechtsstaat, Festschrift für Z. Giacometti* (Zürich, 1953), p. 155: 'Von den vielen in der traditionellen Jurisprudenz vorgetragenen Doktrinen, die die Reine Rechtslehre als politische Ideologien aufgezeigt hat. . . .'

66 See the editor's Introduction to Hans Kelsen, *Aufsätze zur Ideologiekritik*, ed. E. Topitsch (Neuwied, 1964).

67 E.g. in 'Die Lehre von den drei Gewalten oder Funktionen des Staates' in *Kant-Festschrift zu Kant's 200 Geburtstag*, ed. by the Internationale Vereinigung für Rechts- und Wirtschaftsphilosophie

(Berlin, 1924), p. 219: 'Dagegen muss angenommen werden, dass im Gesetzgebungsbegriff der Gewaltenlehre unter "Gesetz" nur die generelle Norm verstanden sein soll. . . . Bei dem Worte "Gesetz" denkt man eben nur oder doch vornehmlich an generelle oder abstrakte Normen'; and 1945, p. 270: 'By "legislation" as a function we can hardly understand anything other than the creation of general legal norms.'

68 E. Brunner, *Justice and the Social Order* (New York, 1945), p. 7: 'The totalitarian state is simply and solely legal positivism in political practice.'

69 G. Radbruch, *Rechtsphilosophie* (4th ed. by E. Wolf, Stuttgart, 1950), p. 355: 'Diese Auffassung vom Gesetz und seiner Geltung (wir nennen sie die positivistische Lehre) hat die Juristen wie das Volk wehrlos gemacht gegen Gesetze noch so willkürlichen und verbrecherischen Inhalts. Sie setzt letzten Endes das Recht der Macht gleich, nur wo die Macht ist, ist das Recht.' See also in the same work, p. 352:

> Der Positivismus hat in der Tat mit seiner Überzeugung 'Gesetz ist Gesetz' den deutschen Juristenstand wehrlos gemacht gegen Gesetze willkürlichen und verbrecherischen Inhalts. Dabei ist der Positivismus gar nicht in der Lage, aus eigener Kraft die Geltung von Gesetzen zu begründen. Er glaubt die Geltung von Gesetzen schon damit erwiesen zu haben, dass es die Macht besessen hat, sich durchzusetzen.

70 Hans Kelsen in *Das Naturrecht in der politischen Theorie*, ed. F. M. Schmoelz (Salzburg, 1963), p. 148.

According to this view every judge in history who was not legally independent and who obeyed an order of an absolute king to decide in a manner contrary to generally recognized rules of justice would still have to be described as acting in accordance with the law. The judges under the Nazis which obeyed such commands under what they regarded as authoritative compulsion may deserve our commiseration; but only confusion is produced when it is maintained that their action was governed by the law.

Characteristically this conception was taken over (presumably via the British socialist lawyers—cf. *The Constitution of Liberty*, chapter 16, section 5) by H. J. Laski, *The State in Theory and Practice*, London, 1934, p. 177: 'The Hitlerite State, equally with that of Britain or France, is a Rechtsstaat in the sense that dictatorial power has been transferred to the Führer by legal order.'

71 For references and further quotations see my book *The Constitution of Liberty* (London and Chicago, 1960), p. 240 and notes, and for Kelsen's comments his *The Communist Theory of Law* (New York, 1955).

72 Mainly in connection with the British *Report of the Committee on Homosexual Offences and Prostitution* (London, Cmd 247, 1957), generally known as the Wolfenden Report, and its discussion by Lord Devlin in his British Academy Lecture on 'The Enforcement of Morals', *Proceedings of the British Academy*, XLV, 1959 (also separately issued). See particularly H. L. A. Hart, *Law, Liberty, and Morality* (Oxford, 1963), and Lon L. Fuller, *The Morality of Law* (Yale, 1964).

73 R. M. Dworkin, 'The Model of Rules', *University of Chicago Law Review*, vol. 35, 1967, reprinted in Robert S. Summers, *Essays in Legal Philosophy* (Oxford, 1968).

74 The incapacity of the philosophical positivists to conceive of a third possibility in addition to the conception of rules being invented by a human mind and their having been invented by a superhuman intelligence is shown very clearly in Auguste Comte's phrase in his *Système de la Politique Positive* (Paris, 1854), vol. 1, p. 356, about 'La superiorité nécessaire de la moral demontré sur la moral revellée'. It is still the same conception when we find Kelsen, 'On the Pure Theory of Law', *Israel Law Review*, I, 1966, p. 2, note, asserting that 'Natural law is—in the last analysis—divine law, because if nature is supposed to create law it must have a will and the will can only be the will of God which manifests itself in the nature created by Him.' This comes out even more clearly in the essay to which Kelsen refers at this place, namely 'Die Grundlage der Naturrechtslehre', *Österreichische Zeitschrift für öffentliches Recht*, XIII, 1963.

75 Cf. David Hume, *Treatise* Part II, sec. II, *Works* II, p. 258:

> where an invention is obvious and absolutely necessary, it may as properly be said to be natural as anything that proceeds immediately from original principles, without the intervention of thought or reflection. Though the rules of justice be *artificial*, they are not *arbitrary*. Nor is the expression improper to call them *Laws of Nature*; if by natural we understand what is common to any species, or even if we confine it to mean what is inseparable from the species.

Cf. also K. R. Popper, *The Open Society and its Enemies* (4th ed., Princeton, 1963), I, pp. 6off., esp. p. 64: 'Nearly all misunderstandings can be traced back to one fundamental misapprehension, namely, to the belief that "convention" implies "arbitrariness" '.

76 Cf., e.g., E. Westermarck, *Ethical Relativity* (London, 1932), p. 183: 'objectivity implies universality'.

77 On these matters Kelsen's early works *Über Grenzen juristischer und soziologischer Methode* (Tübingen, 1911) and *Der soziologische und der juristische Staatsbegriff* (Tübingen, 1922) have still to be consulted to obtain a picture of his conception of a legal 'science'.

78 Cf. Maffeo Pantaleoni, *Erotemi di Economia* (Bari, 1925), vol. I, p. 112.
'Quella disposizione che crea un *ordine*, è la disposizione giusta; essa
è quella che crea un stato di diritto. Ma, la creazione di un ordine, or
di un ordinamento, è appunto ciò stesso che esclude il caso, l'arbitrio
o il cappricio l'incalcolabile l'insaputo il mutevole senza regola.'
Also Ludwig von Mises. *Theory and History* (Yale 1957) p. 54: 'The
ultimate yardstick of justice is conduciveness to the preservation of
social cooperation'; and Max Rheinstein, 'The Relations of Morals
and Law', *Journal of Public Law*, I, 1952, p. 298: 'The just law is that
which reason shows us as being apt to facilitate, or at least not to
impede, the achievement of and preservation of a peaceful order of
society.'

CHAPTER NINE 'SOCIAL' OR DISTRIBUTIVE JUSTICE

* The first quotation is taken from David Hume, *An Enquiry Concerning the Principles of Morals*, sect. III, part II, *Works* IV, p. 187, and
ought to be given here in its context: the

> most obvious thought would be, to assign the largest possessions
> to the most extensive virtue, and give every one the power of doing
> good proportioned to his inclination.... But were mankind to
> execute such a law; so great is the uncertainty of merit, both from
> its natural obscurity, and from the self-conceit of each individual,
> that no determinate rule of conduct would ever follow from it; and
> the total dissolution of society must be the immediate consequence.

The second quotation is translated from Immanuel Kant (*Der Streit
der Fakultäten* (1798), sect. 2, para. 6, note 2) and reads in the
original: 'Wohlfahrt aber hat kein Prinzip, weder für den der sie
empfängt, noch für den der sie austeilt (der eine setzt sie hierin, der
andere darin); weil es dabei auf das *Materiale* des Willens ankommt,
welches empirisch und so einer allgemeinen Regel unfähig ist.' An
English translation of this essay in which the passage is rendered
somewhat differently will be found in *Kant's Political Writings*, ed.
H. Reiss, trs. H. B. Nisbett (Cambridge, 1970), p. 183, note.

1 Cf. P. H. Wicksteed, *The Common Sense of Political Economy*
(London, 1910), p. 184: 'It is idle to assume that ethically desirable
results will necessarily be produced by an ethically indifferent instrument.'

2 Cf. G. del Vecchio, *Justice* (Edinburgh, 1952), p. 37. In the eighteenth
century the expression 'social justice' was occasionally used to
describe the enforcement of rules of just conduct within a given
society, so e.g. by Edward Gibbon, *Decline and Fall of the Roman
Empire*, chapter 41 (World's Classics edn, vol. IV, p. 367).

3 E.g. by John Rawls, *A Theory of Justice* (Harvard, 1971).

4 John Stuart Mill, *Utilitarianism* (London, 1861), chapter 5, p. 92; in H. Plamenatz, ed., *The English Utilitarians* (Oxford, 1949), p. 225.

5 *Ibid.*, pp. 66 and 208 respectively. Cf. also J. S. Mill's review of F. W. Newman, *Lectures on Political Economy*, originally published in 1851 in the *Westminster Review* and republished in *Collected Works*, vol. v (Toronto and London, 1967), p. 444: 'the distinction between rich and poor, so slightly connected as it is with merit and demerit, or even with exertion and want of exertion, is obviously unjust.' Also *Principles of Political Economy*, book II, ch. 1, §, ed. W. J. Ashley (London, 1909), pp. 211ff.: 'The proportioning of remuneration to work done is really just only in so far as the more or less of the work is a matter of choice: when it depends on natural differences of strength and capacity, this principle of remuneration is itself an injustice, it gives to those who have.'

6 See e.g. A. M. Honoré, 'Social Justice' in *McGill Law Journal*, VIII, 1962 and revised version in R. S. Summers, ed., *Essays in Legal Philosophy* (Oxford, 1968), p. 62 of the reprint: 'The first [of the two propositions of which the principle of social justice consists] is the contention that *all men considered merely as men and apart from their conduct or choice have a claim to an equal share in all those things, here called advantages, which are generally desired and are in fact conducive to well-being.*' Also W. G. Runciman, *Relative Deprivation and Social Justice* (London, 1966), p. 261.

7 Cf. especially the encyclicals *Quadragesimo Anno* (1931) and *Divini Redemptoris* (1937) and Johannes Messner, 'Zum Begriff der sozialen Gerechtigkeit' in the volume *Die soziale Frage und der Katholizismus* (Paderborn, 1931) issued to commemorate the fortieth anniversary of the encyclical *Rerum Novarum.*

8 The term 'social justice' (or rather its Italian equivalent) seems to have been first used in its modern sense by Luigi Taparelli-d'Anzeglio, *Saggio teoretico di diritto naturale* (Palermo, 1840) and to have been made more generally known by Antonio Rosmini-Serbati, *La costituzione secondo la giustizia sociale* (Milan, 1848). For more recent discussions cf. N. W. Willoughby, *Social Justice* (New York, 1909); Stephen Leacock, *The Unsolved Riddle of Social Justice* (London and New York, 1920); John A. Ryan, *Distributive Justice* (New York, 1916); L. T. Hobhouse, *The Elements of Social Justice* (London and New York, 1922); T. N. Carver, *Essays in Social Justice* (Harvard, 1922); W. Shields, *Social Justice, The History and Meaning of the Term* (Notre Dame Ind. 1941); Benevuto Donati 'Che cosa è giustizia sociale?', *Archivio giuridico*, vol. 134, 1947; C. de Pasquier, 'La notion de justice sociale', *Zeitschrift für Schweizerisches Recht*, 1952; P. Antoine, 'Qu-est-ce la justice sociale?', *Archives de Philosophie*, 24, 1961; For a more complete list of this literature see G. del Vecchio, *op. cit.*, pp. 37-9.

In spite of the abundance of writings on the subject, when about ten years ago I wrote the first draft of this chapter, I found it still very difficult to find any serious discussion of what people meant when they were using this term. But almost immediately afterwards a number of serious studies of the subject appeared, particularly the two works quoted in note 6 above as well as R. W. Baldwin, *Social Justice* (Oxford and London, 1966), and R. Rescher, *Distributive Justice* (Indianapolis, 1966). Much the most acute treatment of the subject is to be found in a German work by the Swiss economist Emil Küng, *Wirtschaft und Gerechtigkeit* (Tübingen, 1967) and many sensible comments in H. B. Acton, *The Morals of the Market* (London, 1971), particularly p. 71: 'Poverty and misfortune are evils but not injustices'. Very important is also Bertrand de Jouvenel, *The Ethics of Redistribution* (Cambridge, 1951) as well as certain passages in his *Sovereignty* (London, 1957), two of which may here be quoted. P. 140: 'The justice now recommended is a quality not of a man and a man's actions, but of a certain configuration of things in social geometry, no matter by what means it is brought about. Justice is now something which exists independently of just men.' P. 164: 'No proposition is likelier to scandalise our contemporaries than this one: it is impossible to establish a just social order. Yet it flows logically from the very idea of justice, on which we have, not without difficulty, thrown light. To do justice is to apply, when making a share-out, the relevant serial order. But it is impossible for the human intelligence to establish a relevant serial order for all resources in all respects. Men have needs to satisfy, merits to reward, possibilities to actualize; even if we consider these three aspects only and assume that—what is not the case—there are precise *indicia* which we can apply to these aspects, we still could not weight correctly among themselves the three sets of *indicia* adopted.'

The at one time very famous and influential essay by Gustav Schmoller on 'Die Gerechtigkeit in der Volkswirtschaft' in that author's *Jahrbuch für Volkswirtschaft etc.*, vol. v, 1895 is intellectually most disappointing—a pretentious statement of the characteristic muddle of the do-gooder foreshadowing some unpleasant later developments. We know now what it means if the great decisions are to be left to the 'jeweilige Volksbewusstsein nach der Ordnung der Zwecke, die im Augenblick als die richtige erscheint'!

9 Cf. note 7 to chapter VII above.

10 Cf. Adam Smith, *The Theory of Moral Sentiments* (London, 1801), vol. II, part VII, sect. ii, ch. 1, p. 198: 'Human life the Stoics appear to have considered as a game of great skill, in which, however, there was a mixture of chance or of what is vulgarly understood to be chance.' See also Adam Ferguson *Principles of Moral and Political Science* (Edinburgh 1792) vol. 1 p. 7: 'The Stoics conceived of

human life under the image of a Game, at which the entertainment and merit of the players consisted in playing attentively and well whether the stake was great or small.' In a note Ferguson refers to the *Discourses of Epictetus* preserved by Arrian, book II, ch. 5.

11 Cf. G. Hardin, *Nature and Man's Fate* (New York, 1961), p. 55: 'In a free market, says Smith in effect, prices are regulated by negative feedback.' The much ridiculed 'miracle' that the pursuit of self-interest serves the general interest reduces to the self-evident proposition that an order in which the action of the elements is to be guided by effects of which they cannot know can be achieved only if they are induced to respond to signals reflecting the effects of those events. What was familiar to Adam Smith has belatedly been rediscovered by scientific fashion under the name of 'self-organizing systems'.

12 See L. von Mises, *Human Action* (Yale, 1949), p. 255 note: 'There is in the operation of the market economy nothing which could properly be called distribution. Goods are not first produced and then distributed, as would be the case in a socialist state.' Cf. also M. R. Rothbard, 'Towards a Reconstruction of Utility and Welfare Economics' in M. Sennholz (ed.), *On Freedom and Free Enterprise* (New York, 1965), p. 231.

13 Cf. W. G. Runciman, *op. cit.*, p. 274: 'Claims for social justice are claims on behalf of a group, and the person relatively deprived within an individual category will, if he is the victim of an unjust inequality, be a victim only of individual injustice.'

14 See Irving Kristol, 'When Virtue Loses all Her Loveliness—Some Reflections on Capitalism and "The Free Society"', *The Public Interest*, no. 21 (1970), reprinted in the author's *On the Democratic Idea in America* (New York, 1972), as well as in Daniel Bell and Irving Kristol (eds), *Capitalism Today* (New York, 1970).

15 Cf. J. Höffner, *Wirtschaftsethik und Monopole im 15. und 16. Jahrhundert* (Jena, 1941) und 'Der Wettbewerb in der Scholastik', *Ordo*, V, 1953; also Max Weber, *On Law in Economy and Society*, ed. Max Rheinstein (Harvard, 1954) pp. 295ff., but on the latter also H. M. Robertson, *Aspects on the Rise of Economic Individualism* (Cambridge, 1933) and B. Groethuysen, *Origines de l'esprit bourgeois en France* (Paris, 1927). For the most important expositions of the conception of a just price by the late sixteenth century Spanish Jesuits see particularly L. Molina, *De iustitia et de iure*, vol. 2, *De Contractibus* (Cologne, 1594), disp. 347, no. 3 and especially disp. 348, no. 3, where the just price is defined as that which will form 'quando absque fraude, monopoliis, atque aliis versutiies, communiter res aliqua vendi consuevit pretio in aliqua regione, aut loco, it habendum est pro mensura et regula judicandi pretium iustum rei illius in ea regione.' About man's inability to determine beforehand what a just price would be see also particularly Johannes de Salas, *Commentarii in*

Secundum Secundae D. Thomas de Contractibus (Lyon, 1617), *Tr. de empt. et Vend.* IV, n. 6, p. 9: '. . . quas exacte comprehendere, et ponderare Dei est, not hominum'; and J. de Lugo, *Disputationes de Iustitia et Iure* (Lyon, 1643), vol. II, d. 26, s. 4, n. 40; 'pretium iustum matematicum, licet soli Deo notum.' See also L. Molina, *op. cit.*, disp. 365, no. 9: 'omnesque rei publicae partes ius habent conscendendi ad gradum superiorem, si cuiusque sors id tulerit, neque cuiquam certus quidam gradus debitur, qui descendere et conscendere possit.' It would seem that H. M. Robertson (*op. cit.*, p. 164) hardly exaggerates when he writes 'It would not be difficult to claim that the religion which favoured the spirit of capitalism was Jesuitry, not Calvinism.'

16 John W. Chapman, 'Justice and Fairness', *Nomos VI, Justice* (New York, 1963), p. 153. This Lockean conception has been preserved even by John Rawls, at least in his earlier work, 'Constitutional Liberty and the Concept of Justice', *Nomos VI, Justice* (New York, 1963), p. 117, note: 'If one assumes that law and government effectively act to keep markets competitive, resources fully employed, property and wealth widely distributed over time, and maintains a reasonable social minimum, then, if there is equality of opportunity, the resulting distribution will be just or at least not unjust. It will have resulted from the working of a just system . . . a social minimum is simply a form of rational insurance and prudence.'

17 See passages quoted in note 15 above.

18 See M. Fogarty, *The Just Wage* (London, 1961).

19 Barbara Wootton, *The Social Foundation of Wage Policy* (London, 1962), pp. 120 and 162, and now also her *Incomes Policy, An Inquest and a Proposal* (London, 1974).

20 Surely Samuel Butler (*Hudibras*, II,1) was right when he wrote

For what is worth in any thing
But so much money as 'twill bring.

21 On the general problem of remuneration according to merit, apart from the passages by David Hume and Immanuel Kant placed at the head of this chapter, see chapter VI of my book *The Constitution of Liberty* (London and Chicago, 1960) and cf. also Maffeo Pantaleoni, 'L'atto economico' in *Erotemi di Economia* (2 vols, Padua, 1963), vol. I, p. 101:

E tre sono le proposizioni che conviene comprendere bene:
La prima è che il merito è una parola vuota di senso.
La seconda è che il concetto di giustizia è un polisenso che si presta a quanti paralogismi si vogliono ex amphibologia.
La terza è che la remunerazione non può essere commisurata da una produttività (marginale) capace di determinazione isolamente,

cioè senza la simultanea determinazione della produttività degli altri fattori con i quali entra in una combinazione di complimentarità.

22 On the history of the term 'social' see Karl Wasserrab, *Sozialwissenschaft und soziale Frage* (Leipzig, 1903); Leopold von Wiese, *Der Liberalismus in Vergangenheit und Zukunft* (Berlin, 1917), and *Sozial, Geistig, Kulturell* (Cologne, 1936); Waldemar Zimmermann, 'Das "Soziale" im geschichtlichen Sinn- und Begriffswandel' in *Studien zur Soziologie, Festgabe für L. von Wiese* (Mainz, 1948); L. H. A. Geck, *Über das Eindringen des Wortes 'sozial' in die deutsche Sprache* (Göttingen, 1963); and Ruth Crummenerl, 'Zur Wortgeschichte von "sozial" bis zur englischen Aufklärung', unpublished essay for the State examination in philology (Bonn, 1963). Cf. also my essay 'What is "Social"? What does it Mean?' in a corrected English version in my *Studies in Philosophy, Politics and Economics* (London and Chicago, 1967).

23 Cf. G. del Vecchio, *op. cit.*, p. 37.

24 Very instructive on this is Leopold von Wiese, *Der Liberalismus in Vergangenheit und Zukunft* (Berlin, 1917) pp. 115ff.

25 Characteristic for many discussions of the issue by social philosophers is W. A. Frankena, 'The Concept of Social Justice', in *Social Justice*, ed. R. B. Brandt (New York, 1962), p. 4, whose argument rests on the assumption that 'society' *acts* which is a meaningless term if applied to a spontaneous order. Yet this anthropomorphic interpretation of society seems to be one to which utilitarians are particularly prone, although this is not often as naively admitted as by J. W. Chapman in the statement quoted before in note 21 to chapter VII.

26 I regret this usage though by means of it some of my friends in Germany (and more recently also in England) have apparently succeeded in making palatable to wider circles the sort of social order for which I am pleading.

27 Cf. the 'Statement of Conscience' received by the 'Aspen Consultation on Global Justice', an 'ecumenical gathering of American religious leaders' at Aspen, Colorado, 4–7 June 1974, which recognized that 'global injustice is characterised by a dimension of sin in the economic, political, social, racial, sexual and class structures and systems of global society.' *Aspen Institute Quarterly* (New York), no. 7, third quarter, 1974, p. 4.

28 See particularly A. M. Honoré, *op. cit.* The absurdity of the contention that in a Great Society it needs moral justification if *A* has more than *B*, as if this were the result of some human artifice, becomes obvious when we consider not only the elaborate and complex apparatus of government which would be required to prevent this, but also that this apparatus would have to possess power to direct the

efforts of all citizens and to claim the products of those efforts.

29 One of the few modern philosophers to see this clearly and speak out plainly was R. G. Collingwood. See his essay on 'Economics as a philosophical science,' *Ethics* 36, 1926, esp. p. 74: 'A just price, a just wage, a just rate of interest, is a contradiction in terms. The question of what a person ought to get in return for his goods and labour is a question absolutely devoid of meaning.'

30 If there is any one fact which all serious students of the claims for equality have recognized it is that material equality and liberty are irreconcilable. Cf. A. de Tocqueville, *Democracy in America*, book II, ch. I (New York, edn 1946, vol. II, p. 87): democratic communities 'call for equality in freedom, and if they cannot obtain that, they still call for equality in slavery'; William S. Sorley, *The Moral Life and the Moral Worth* (Cambridge, 1911), p. 110: 'Equality is gained only by constant interference with liberty'; or more recently Gerhard Leibholz, 'Die Bedrohung der Freiheit durch die Macht der Gesetzgeber', in *Freiheit der Persönlichkeit* (Stuttgart, 1958), p. 80: 'Freiheit erzeugt notwendig Ungleichheit und Gleichheit notwendig Unfreiheit', are merely a few instances which I readily find in my notes. Yet people who claim to be enthusiastic supporters of liberty still clamour constantly for material equality.

31 Gustav Radbruch, *Rechtsphilosophie* (Stuttgart, 1956), p. 87: 'Auch das sozialistische Gemeinwesen wird also ein Rechtsstaat sein, ein Rechtsstaat freilich, der statt von der ausgleichenden von der austeilenden Gerechtigkeit beherrscht wird.'

32 See M. Duverger, *The Idea of Politics* (Indianapolis, 1966), p. 201.

33 Karl Mannheim, *Man and Society in an Age of Reconstruction* (London, 1940), p. 180.

34 P. J. Stuchka (President of the Soviet Supreme Court) in *Encyclopedia of State and Law* (in Russian, Moscow, 1927), quoted by V. Gsovski, *Soviet Civil Law* (Ann Arbor, Michigan, 1948), I, p. 70. The work of E. Paschukanis the Soviet author who has most consistently developed the idea of the disappearance of law under socialism, has been described by Karl Korsch in *Archiv sozialistischer Literatur*, III, (Frankfurt, 1966) as the only consistent development of the teaching of Karl Marx.

35 *The Road to Serfdom* (London and Chicago, 1944), chapter IV. For discussions of the central thesis of that book by lawyers see W. Friedmann, *The Planned State and the Rule of Law* (Melbourne, 1948), reprinted in the same author's *Law and Social Change in Contemporary Britain* (London, 1951): Hans Kelsen, 'The Foundations of Democracy', *Ethics* 66, 1955; Roscoe Pound, 'The Rule of Law and the Modern Welfare State', *Vanderbilt Law Review*, 7, 1953; Harry W. Jones, 'The Rule of Law and the Modern Welfare State', *Columbia Law Review*, 58, 1958; A. L. Goodhart, 'The Rule

of Law and Absolute Sovereignty', *University of Pennsylvania Law Review*, 106, 1958.

36 G. Radbruch, *op. cit.*, p. 126.

37 Radbruch's conceptions of these matters are concisely summed up by Roscoe Pound (in his introduction to R. H. Graves, *Status in the Common Law*, London, 1953, p. XI): Radbruch

> starts with a distinction between commutative justice, a correcting justice which gives back to one what has been taken away from him or gives him a substantial substitute, and distributive justice, a distribution of the goods of existence not equally but according to a scheme of values. Thus there is a contrast between co-ordinating law, which secures interests by reparation and the like, treating all individuals as equal, and subordinating law, which prefers some or the interests of some according to its measure of value. Public law, he says, is a law of subordination, subordinating individual to public interests but not the interests of other individuals with those public interests.

38 Cf. Bertrand de Jouvenel, *Sovereignty* (Chicago, 1957), p. 136:

> The small society, as the milieu in which man is first found, retains for him an infinite attraction; he undoubtedly goes to it to renew his strength; but ... any attempt to graft the same features on a large society is utopian and leads to tyranny. With that admitted, it is clear that as social relations become wider and more various, the common good conceived as reciprocal trustfulness cannot be sought in methods which the model of the small, closed society inspires; such a model is, in the contrary, entirely misleading.

39 Edwin Cannan, *The History of Local Rates in England*, 2nd edn (London, 1912), p. 162.

40 While one has become used to find the confused minds of social philosophers talking about 'social justice', it greatly pains me if I find a distinguished thinker like the historian Peter Geyl (*Encounters in History*, London, 1963, p. 358) thoughtlessly using the term. J. M. Keynes (*The Economic Consequences of Mr. Churchill*, London, 1925, *Collected Writings*, vol. IX, p. 223) also writes unhesitatingly that 'on grounds of social justice no case can be made for reducing the wages of the miners.'

41 Cf. e.g. Walter Kaufmann, *Without Guilt and Justice* (New York, 1973) who, after rightly rejecting the concepts of distributive and retributive justice, believes that this must lead him to reject the concept of justice altogether. But this is not surprising after even *The Times* (London) in a thoughtful leading article (1 March 1957) apropos the appearance of an English translation of Josef Pieper's

Justice (London, 1957) had observed that 'roughly, it may be said that in so far as the notion of justice continues to influence political thinking, it has been reduced to the meaning of the phrase "distributive justice" and that the idea of commutative justice has almost entirely ceased to influence our calculations except in so far it is embodied in laws and customs—in the maxims for instance of the Common Law—which are preserved from sheer conservatism.' Some contemporary social philosophers indeed beg the whole issue by so *defining* 'justice' that it includes *only* distributive justice. See e.g. Brian M. Barry, 'Justice and the Common Good', *Analysis*, 19, 1961, p. 80: 'although Hume uses the expression "rules of justice" to cover such things as property rules, *"justice" is now analytically tied to "desert" and "need"*, so that one could quite properly say that some of what Hume calls "rules of justice" were unjust' (italics added). Cf. *ibid.*, p. 89.

42 J. S. Mill, *On Liberty*, ed. McCallum (Oxford, 1946), p. 70.

43 On the destruction of moral values by scientific error see my discussion in my inaugural lecture as Visiting Professor at the University of Salzburg, *Die Irrtümer des Konstruktivismus und die Grundlagen legitimer Kritik gesellschaftlicher Gebilde* (Munich, 1970, now reprinted for the Walter Eucken Institute at Freiburg i.Brg. by J. C. B. Mohr, Tübingen, 1975).

44 John Rawls, 'Constitutional Liberty and the Concept of Justice', *Nomos IV, Justice* (New York, 1963), p. 102, where the passage quoted is preceded by the statement that 'It is the system of institutions which has to be judged and judged from a general point of view.' I am not aware that Professor Rawls' later more widely read work *A Theory of Justice* (Harvard, 1971) contains a comparatively clear statement of the main point, which may explain why this work seems often, but as it appears to me wrongly, to have been interpreted as lending support to socialist demands, e.g. by Daniel Bell, 'On Meritocracy and Equality', *Public Interest*, Autumn 1972, p. 72, who describes Rawls' theory as 'the most comprehensive effort in modern philosophy to justify a socialistic ethic.'

APPENDIX TO CHAPTER NINE

This appendix has been published as an article in the 75th anniversary issue of the Norwegian journal *Farmand* (Oslo, 1966).

1 For discussions of the problem cf. the papers assembled in the *Philosophical Review*, April 1955 and in D. D. Raphael (ed.), *Political Theory and the Rights of Man* (London, 1967).

2 See the *Universal Declaration of Human Rights* adopted by the General Assembly of the United Nations on 10 December 1948. It is reprinted, and the intellectual background of this document can be

found, in the volume entitled *Human Rights, Comments and Interpreta-tions*, a symposium edited by UNESCO (London and New York, 1945). It contains in the Appendix not only a 'Memorandum Circulated by UNESCO on the Theoretical Bases of the Rights of Men' (pp. 251–4), but also a 'Report of the UNESCO Committee on the Theoretical Bases of the Human Rights' (in other places described as the 'UNESCO Committee on the Principles of the Rights of Men'), in which it is explained that their efforts were directed towards reconciling the two different 'complementary' working concepts of human rights, of which one 'started, from the premises of inherent individual rights . . . while the other was based on Marxist principles', and at finding 'some common measure of the two tendencies'. 'This common formulation,' it is explained, 'must by some means reconcile the various divergent or opposing formu-lations now in existence'! (The British representatives on that com-mittee were Professors H. J. Laski and E. H. Carr!).

3 *Ibid.*, p. 22, Professor E. H. Carr, the chairman of the UNESCO Committee of experts, explains that 'If the new declaration of the rights of man is to include provisions for social services, for main-tenance in childhood, in old age, in incapacity or in unemployment, it becomes clear that no society can guarantee the enjoyment of such rights unless it in turn has the right to call upon and direct the productive capacities of the individuals enjoying them'!

4 G. Vlastos, 'Justice', *Revue Internationale de la Philosophie*, 1957, p. 331.

5 On the whole document cf. Maurice Cranston, 'Human Rights, Real and Supposed' in the volume edited by D. D. Raphael quoted in note 1 above, where the author argues that 'a philosophically respectable concept of human rights has been muddied, obscured, and debilitated in recent years by an attempt to incorporate in it specific rights of a different logical category.' See also the same author's *Human Rights Today* (London, 1955).

CHAPTER TEN   THE MARKET ORDER OR CATALLAXY

* Edwin Cannan, *The History of Local Rates in England* (London, 2nd ed., 1912), p. 173. The term 'uneconomical' is used in it in that wide sense in which it refers to what is required by the market order, a sense in which it is somewhat misleading and had better be avoided.

1 Cf. Carl Menger, *Problems of Economics and Sociology* (Illinois, 1963), p. 93:

> The *nation* as such is not a large subject that has needs, that works, practices economy, and consumes; and what is called 'national economy' is therefore not the economy of a nation in the true

sense of the word. 'National economy' is not a phenomenon analogous to the singular economies in the nation to which also the economy of finance belongs. It is not a large singular economy; just as little as it is one opposed to or existing along with the singular economies in the nation. It is in its most general form of phenomena a peculiar complication of singular economies.

Cf. also Appendix I to that work.

2 Richard Whately, *Introductory Lectures on Political Economy* (London, 1855), p. 4.

3 Especially by L. von Mises, *Human Action* (Yale, 1949), *passim*.

4 H. G. Liddell and R. A. Scott, *A Greek-English Dictionary* (London, new ed., 1940), s.v. *katallagden, katallage, katallagma, katallaktikos, katallasso (-tto), katallakterios* and *katallaxis*.

5 In the Greek terms we have used an economy proper is thus a *taxis* and a *teleocracy*, while the katallaxy is a *kosmos* and a *nomocracy*.

6 It was these rules to which David Hume and Adam Smith emphatically referred as 'rules of justice' and which Adam Smith meant when (*The Theory of Moral Sentiments*, part I, sect. ii, chap. iii) he spoke of justice as 'the main pillar of the whole edifice. If it is removed, the great, the immense fabric of human society, the fabric which to raise and support seems in this world, if I may say so, to have been the peculiar and darling care of Nature, must in a moment crumble into atoms.'

7 At the beginning of the eighteenth century, when Bernard Mandeville with his *Fable of the Bees* became its most influential expositor. But it seems to have been more widespread and is to be found, e.g., in the early Whig literature such as in Thomas Gordon, 'Cato's Letter' no. 63, dated 27 January 1721 (in the reprint in *The English Libertarian Heritage*, ed. David L. Jacobson, Indianapolis, 1965, pp. 138–9): 'Every Man's honest Industry and useful Talents, while they are employed for the Publick, will be employed for himself; and while he serves himself, he will serve the Publick; Publick and private Interest will secure each other; all will chearfully give a Part to secure the Whole—and be brave to defend it.' It then found first expression in classical works (in both instances probably under the influence of Mandeville) in C. de S. de Montesquieu, *The Spirit of the Laws*, Book III, sect. 7 (trs. T. Nugent, New York, 1949), p. 35: 'Each individual advances the public good, while he only thinks of promoting his own interest', and in David Hume, *Treatise* in *Works* II, p. 289: 'I learn to do a service to another, without bearing him any real kindness'; and *ibid.*, p. 291: 'advantage to the public, though it not be intended for that purpose'; cf. also *Essays, Works* III, p. 99: 'made it not the interest, even of bad men, to act for the public good.' It occurs later in Josiah Tucker, *Elements of Commerce* (London, 1756), in

NOTES TO PAGES 110-13

Adam Smith, *Theory of Moral Sentiments* (London, 1759), part IV, chapter I, where he speaks of men being 'led by an invisible hand . . . without intending it, without knowing it, [to] advance the interest of society', and of course in its most famous formulation in Smith's *Wealth of Nations* (ed. Cannan, London, 1910), vol. I, p. 421: 'By directing that industry in such a manner as its produce may be of the greatest value, he intends only his own gain, and he is in this, as in many other cases, led by an invisible hand to promote an end which was no part of his intention. Nor is it always the worse for the society that it was no part of it. By pursuing his own interest he frequently promotes that of the society more effectually than when he really intends to promote it.' Cf. also Edmund Burke, *Thoughts and Details of Scarcity* (1795), in *Works* (World's Classics ed.), vol. VI, p. 9: 'The benign and wise disposer of all things, who obliges men whether they will or not, in pursuing their own selfish interest, to connect the general good with their own individual success.'

8 Cf. Adam Smith, *Wealth of Nations*, I, p. 16: 'It is not from the benevolence of the butcher, the brewer, or the baker, that we expect our dinner, but from their regard to their own interest.'

9 It is in the insistence on social 'solidarity' that the constructivist approach to sociology of Auguste Comte, Emile Durkheim and Léon Duguit shows itself most clearly.

10 Both of which were characteristically regarded by John Stuart Mill as the only 'elevated' feelings left in modern man.

11 On the significance of the development of criticism by the ancient Greeks see particularly Karl R. Popper, *The Open Society and Its Enemies* (London and Princeton, 1947 and later), *passim*.

12 Cf. already A. L. C. Destutt de Tracy, *A Treatise on Political Economy* (Georgetown, 1817), pp. 6ff.: 'Society is purely and solely a continual series of exchanges. . . . *Commerce is the whole of society*.' Before the term 'society' came into general use, 'economy' was often used where we would now speak of 'society'. Cf. for instance John Wilkins, *Essay toward a Real Character and a Philosophical Language* (London, 1668) as quoted by H. R. Robbins, *A Short History of Linguistics* (London, 1967), pp. 114-15, who appears to use 'economical' as equivalent to 'interpersonal'. At that time 'economy' seems also to have been used generally to mean what we call here a spontaneous order, as such frequently recurring phrases as the 'economy of creation' and the like show.

13 The chief objections to the 'allocational' approach or the 'economicism' of much of current economic theory from very different angles comes, on the one side, from J. M. Buchanan, most recently restated in the essay 'Is Economics the Science of Choice' in E. Streissler (ed.), *Roads to Freedom* (London, 1969), and G. Myrdal, especially in *The Political Element in the Development of Economic*

Theory (London, 1953) and *Beyond the Welfare State* (Yale, 1960). Cf. also Hans Peter, *Freiheit der Wirtschaft* (Cologne, 1953); Gerhard Weisser, 'Die Überwindung des Ökonomismus in der Wirtschaftswissenschaft' in *Grundfragen der Wirtschaftsordnung* (Berlin, 1954); and Hans Albert, *Ökonomische Theorie und Politische Ideologie* (Göttingen, 1954).

What is often inexactly though perhaps conveniently described as 'economic ends' are the most general and yet undifferentiated means such as money or general purchasing power which in the course of the ordinary process of earning a living are the immediate ends, because the particular purpose for which they will be used is not yet known. On the fact that there are strictly speaking no economic ends and for the clearest statement of economics seen as a theory of choice see L. C. Robbins, *The Nature and Significance of Economic Science* (London, 1930 and later).

14 See also chapter 7 above.

15 It is a point which cannot be too often stressed since it is so frequently misunderstood, especially by socialists, that technological knowledge tells us only which techniques are available, but not which is the most economical or efficient. Contrary to a widely held belief there is not such a thing as a purely technical optimum—a conception usually derived from the false idea that there is only one uniform factor, namely energy, which is really scarce. For this reason what is the most efficient technique of producing something in the USA may be exceedingly uneconomical in, say, India.

16 W. S. Jevons, *The Theory of Political Economy* (London, 1871), p. 159.

17 Much of the knowledge of the individuals which can be so useful in bringing about particular adaptations is not ready knowledge which they could possibly list and file in advance for the use of a central planning authority when the occasion arose; they will have little knowledge beforehand of what advantage they could derive from the fact that, say, magnesium has become much cheaper than aluminium, or nylon than hemp, or one kind of plastic than another; what they possess is a capacity of finding out what is required by a given situation, often an acquaintance with particular circumstances which beforehand they have no idea might become useful.

18 Ecclesiastes 9:11.

19 I suspect it was also this ignorance which Cicero had in mind when he argued that neither nature nor will but intellectual weakness was the mother of justice. See *De Re Publica*, 3, 13: 'iustitiae non natura nec voluntas sed imbecillitas mater est.' This at least seems to be what he means when in many other places he speaks of 'humani generis imbecillitas'.

20 Cf. the passage by David Hume quoted earlier, above, chapter 7, note 12.

21 The distinction introduced by Wilhelm Röpke, *Die Gesellschaftskrise der Gegenwart* (fifth ed., Erlenbach-Zürich, 1948), p. 259, between acts of interference which 'conform' and those which do not 'conform' with the market order (or, as other German authors have expressed it, are or are not *systemgerecht*) aims at the same distinction, but I should prefer not to describe 'conform' measures as 'interference'.

22 Cf. L. von Mises, *Kritik des Interventionismus* (Jena, 1929), pp. 5ff.: 'Nicht unter den Begriff des Eingriffes fallen Handlungen der Obrigkeit, die mit den Mitteln des Marktes arbeiten, d.h.solche, die Nachfrage oder Angebot durch Veränderungen der Marktfaktoren zu beeinflussen suchen. . . . *Der Eingriff ist ein von einer gesellschaftlichen Gewalt ausgehender isolierter Befehl, der die Eigentümer der Produktionsmittel und die Unternehmer zwingt, die Produktionsmittel anders zu verwenden als sie es sonst tun würden.*'

23 The chances of any person picked out at random of earning a particular income would then be represented by a Gaussian hill, i.e. a three-dimensional surface one co-ordinate of which represented the probability of that person belonging to a class with a particular probability distribution of expectations of a certain income (arranged according to the value of the median) while the second co-ordinate represented the distribution of probabilities of the particular incomes for that class. It would show, e.g., that a person whose position gave him a better *chance* of earning a particular income than a certain other person might in fact earn much less than the latter.

24 The chance of all will be increased most if we act on principles which will result in raising the general level of incomes without paying attention to the consequent shifts of particular individuals or groups from one position on the scale to another. (The shifts will necessarily occur in the course of such a process, and must occur to make the rise of the average level possible.) It is not easy to illustrate this by the available statistics of the changes of income distribution during periods of rapid economic progress. But in the one country for which fairly adequate information of this kind is available, the USA, it would seem that a person who in 1940 belonged to the group whose individual incomes were greater than those of 50 per cent of the population but smaller than those of 40 per cent of the population, even if he had by 1960 descended to the 30–40 per cent group, would still have enjoyed a larger absolute income than he did in 1940.

25 It may help the reader if I illustrate the general contention stated in the text by an account of the personal experience which led me to see the problem in this manner. That a person in an established position inevitably takes an attitude different from that which ought to be taken in considering the general problem was vividly brought home to me as an inhabitant of London in the summer of 1940 when it

appeared quite probable that I and all the resources with which I might provide for my family would soon be destroyed by enemy bombing. It was at that time, when we were all prepared for much worse than eventually happened, that I received offers from several neutral countries to place my then small children with some unknown family with whom they would presumably remain if I did not survive the war. I had thus to consider the relative attractiveness of social orders as different as those of the USA, Argentina and Sweden, on the assumption that the conditions in which my children would grow up in that country would be determined more or less by chance. This led me, as abstract speculation perhaps never could have done, to realize that where my children were concerned, rational preferences should be guided by considerations somewhat different from those which would determine a similar choice for myself who occupied already an established position and believed (perhaps wrongly) that this would count for more in a European country than in the USA. Thus, while the choice for myself would have been influenced by the considerations of the relative chances for a man in his early forties with formed skills and tastes, a certain reputation and with affiliations with classes of particular inclinations, the choice for my children would have had to be made in consideration of the particular environment in which chance was likely to place them in one of those countries. For the sake of my children who still had to develop their personalities, then, I felt that the very absence in the USA of the sharp social distinctions which would favour me in the Old World should make me decide for them in favour of the former. (I should perhaps add that this was based on the tacit assumption that my children would there be placed with a white and not with a coloured family.)

CHAPTER ELEVEN THE DISCIPLINE OF ABSTRACT RULES AND
THE EMOTIONS OF THE TRIBAL SOCIETY

* José Ortega y Gasset, *The Revolt of the Masses* (London, 1932), p. 83.
1 This is surprisingly maintained by such an acute thinker as Michael Polanyi with regard to central planning in *The Logic of Liberty* (London, 1951), p. 111: 'How can central economic planning, if it is utterly incapable of achievement, be a danger to liberty as it is widely assumed to be?' It may well be impossible to achieve what the planners intend and yet the attempt to realize their intentions do much harm.
2 Cf. Peter Laslett, *The World we Have Lost* (London and New York, 1965).
3 See W. H. Whyte, *The Organization Man* (New York, 1957).
4 See Martin Bullinger, *Oeffentliches Recht und Privatrecht* (Stuttgart, 1968).

5 In the present connection we revert to the term 'abstract rule' in order to stress that the rules of just conduct do not refer to specific purposes and that the resulting order is what Sir Karl Popper has called an 'abstract society'.

6 Cf. Adam Smith, *Wealth of Nations*, ed. Cannan, vol. II, p. 43:

> The natural effort of every individual to better his own condition, where suffered to exert itself with freedom and security, is so powerful a principle, that it is alone, and without any assistance, not only capable of carrying on the society to wealth and prosperity, but of surmounting a hundred impertinent obstructions with which the folly of human laws too often encumbers its operations; though the effect of these obstructions is always more or less either to encroach upon its freedom, or to diminish its security.

7 C. Perelman, *Justice* (New York, 1967), p. 20: 'A form of behavior or a human judgement can be termed just only if it can be subjected to rules or criteria.'

8 Since it is frequently ignored that this was both the aim and the achievement of classical liberalism, two statements from the middle of the last century deserve to be quoted. N. W. Senior (cited by L. C. Robbins, *The Theory of Economic Policy*, London, 1952, p. 140) wrote in 1848: 'To proclaim that no man, whatever his vices or even his crimes, shall die of hunger or cold, is a promise that in the state of civilization of England, or of France, can be performed not merely with safety but with advantage, because the gift of mere subsistence may be subjected to conditions which no one will voluntarily accept.' In the same year the German constitutional lawyer Moritz Mohl, as representative to the German Constitutional Assembly at Frankfurt, could maintain (*Stenographischer Bericht über die Verhandlungen der Deutschen konstituierenden Nationalversammlung zu Frankfurt a.M.*, ed., Franz Wigard, Leipzig, 1949, vol. 7, p. 5109) that 'es gibt in Deutschland, meines Wissens, nicht einen einzigen Staat, in welchem nicht positive, ganz bestimmte Gesetze beständen, welche verhindern, dass jemand verhungere. In allen deutschen Gesetzgebungen, die mir bekannt sind, ist die Gemeinde gehalten, den, der sich nicht selbst erhalten kann, zu erhalten.'

9 Cf. Franz Beyerle, 'Der andere Zugang zum Naturrecht', *Deutsche Rechtswissenschaft*, 1939, p. 20: 'Zeitlos und unbekümmert um die eigene Umwelt hat sie [die Pandektenlehre] keine einzige soziale Krise ihrer Zeit erkannt und geistig aufgefangen. Weder die rasch fortschreitende Entwurzelung des Bauerntums, die schon nach den napoleonischen Kriegen einsetzte, noch das Absinken der handwerklichen Existenzen nach der Jahrhundertmitte, noch endlich die Verelendung der Lohnarbeiterschaft.' From the number of times this statement by a distinguished teacher of private law has been quoted

in the current German literature it seems to express a widely held view.

10 J.-J. Rousseau has clearly seen that what in his sense of the 'general will' may be just for a particular group, may not be so for a more comprehensive society. Cf. *The Political Writings of J.-J. Rousseau*, ed. E. E. Vaughan (Cambridge, 1915), vol. 1, p. 243: 'Pour les membres de l'association, c'est une volonté générale; pour la grande société, c'est une volonté particulière, qui très souvent se trouve droite au premier égard, et vicieuse au second.' But to the positivist interpretation of justice which identifies it with the commands of some legitimate authority, it comes inevitably to be thought that, as e.g. E. Forsthoff, *Lehrbuch des Verwaltungsrechts* (eighth ed., Munich, 1961, vol. 1, p. 66) maintains, 'any question of a just order is a question of law'. But this 'orientation on the idea of justice', as this view has been curiously called, is certainly not sufficient to turn a command into a rule of just conduct unless by that phrase is meant, not merely that the rule satisfies somebody's claim for just treatment, but that the rule satisfies the Kantian test of universal applicability.

11 This is the main thesis of Carl Schmitt, *Der Begriff des Politischen* (Berlin, 1932). Cf. the comment on it by J. Huizinga quoted on p. 71 of vol. 1 of the present work.

12 See note 15 to chapter 9 above.

13 The constructivist prejudice which still makes so many socialists scoff at the 'miracle' that the unguided pursuit of their own interests by the individuals should produce a beneficial order is of course merely the reverse form of that dogmatism which opposed Darwin on the ground that the existence of order in organic nature was proof of intelligent design.

14 Cf. H. B. Acton, *The Morals of Markets* (London, 1971).

15 Cf. Bertrand de Jouvenel, *Sovereignty* (London and Chicago, 1957), p. 136: 'We are thus driven to three conclusions. The first is that the small society, the milieu in which man is first found, retains for him an infinite attraction; the next, that he undoubtedly goes to it to renew his strength; but, the last, that any attempt to graft the same features on a large society is utopian and leads to tyranny'; to which the author adds in a footnote: 'In this respect Rousseau (*Rousseau Juge de Jean-Jaques*, Third Dialogue) displayed a wisdom which his disciples missed: 'His object could not be to recall populous countries and large states to their primitive simplicity, but only to check, if possible, the progress of those whom smallness and situation had preserved from the same headlong rush to the perfection of society and the deterioration of the species.'

16 Cf. Richard Cornuelle, *Reclaiming the American Dream* (New York, 1965).

LAW, LEGISLATION AND LIBERTY

Volume 3
THE POLITICAL ORDER
OF A FREE PEOPLE

A constitution that achieves the greatest possible freedom
by framing the laws in such a way that the freedom of each can
coexist with the freedom of all.

Immanuel Kant (*Critique of Pure Reason*, II, i. 1)

TWELVE

MAJORITY OPINION AND
CONTEMPORARY DEMOCRACY

But the great number [of the Athenian Assembly] cried out
that it was monstrous if the people were to be prevented from
doing whatever they wished. . . . Then the Prytanes, stricken
with fear, agreed to put the question—all of them except
Socrates, the son of Sophroniscus; and he said that in no case
would he act except in accordance with the law.

Xenophon*

The progressive disillusionment about democracy

When the activities of modern government produce aggregate
results that few people have either wanted or foreseen this is
commonly regarded as an inevitable feature of democracy. It can
hardly be claimed, however, that such developments usually correspond to the desires of any identifiable group of men. It appears
that the particular process which we have chosen to ascertain what
we call the will of the people brings about results which have little to
do with anything deserving the name of the 'common will' of any
substantial part of the population.

We have in fact become so used to regard as democratic only the
particular set of institutions which today prevails in all Western
democracies, and in which a majority of a representative body lays
down the law *and* directs government, that we regard this as the
only possible form of democracy. As a consequence we do not care
to dwell on the fact that this system not only has produced many
results which nobody likes, even in those countries in which on the
whole it has worked well, but also has proved unworkable in most
countries where these democratic institutions were not restrained
by strong traditions about the appropriate tasks of the representative
assemblies. Because we rightly believe in the basic ideal of democracy we feel usually bound to defend the particular institutions

1

which have long been accepted as its embodiment, and hesitate to criticize them because this might weaken the respect for an ideal we wish to preserve.

It is no longer possible, however, to overlook the fact that in recent times in spite of continued lip-service and even demands for its further extension, there has arisen among thoughtful persons an increasing disquiet and serious alarm about the results it often produces.[1] This does not everywhere take the form of that cynical realism which is characteristic of some contemporary political scientists who regard democracy merely as just another form of an inevitable struggle in which it is decided 'who gets what, when, and how'.[2] Yet that there prevails deep disillusionment and doubt about the future of democracy, caused by a belief that those developments of it which hardly anybody approves are inevitable, can scarcely be denied. It found its expression many years ago in Joseph Schumpeter's well known contention that, although a system based on the free market would be better for most, it is doomed beyond hope, while socialism, though it cannot fulfil its promises, is bound to come.[3]

It seems to be the regular course of the development of democracy that after a glorious first period in which it is understood as and actually operates as a safeguard of personal freedom because it accepts the limitations of a higher nomos, sooner or later it comes to claim the right to settle any particular question in whatever manner a majority agrees upon. This is what happened to the Athenian democracy at the end of the fifth century, as shown by the famous occurrence to which the quotation at the head of this chapter refers; and in the next century Demosthenes (and others) were to complain that 'our laws are no better than so many decrees; nay, you will find that the laws which have to be observed in drafting the decrees are later than the decrees themselves.'[4]

In modern times a similar development started when the British Parliament claimed sovereign, that is unlimited, powers and in 1766 explicitly rejected the idea that in its particular decisions it was bound to observe any general rules not of its own making. Though for a time a strong tradition of the rule of law prevented serious abuse of the power that Parliament had arrogated to itself, it proved in the long run the great calamity of modern development that soon after representative government was achieved all those restraints upon the supreme power that had been painfully built up during the evolution of constitutional monarchy were successively dismantled

2

as no longer necessary. That this in effect meant the abandonment of constitutionalism which consists in a limitation of all power by permanent principles of government was already seen by Aristotle when he maintained that 'where the laws are not sovereign . . . since the many are sovereign not as individuals but collectively . . . such a democracy is not a constitution at all';[5] and it was recently pointed out again by a modern author who speaks of 'constitutions which are so democratic that they are properly speaking no longer constitutions'.[6] Indeed, we are now told that the 'modern conception of democracy is a form of government in which no restriction is placed on the governing body'[7] and, as we have seen, some have already drawn the conclusion that constitutions are an antiquated survival which have no place in the modern conception of government.[8]

Unlimited power the fatal defect of the prevailing form of democracy

The tragic illusion was that the adoption of democratic procedures made it possible to dispense with all other limitations on governmental power. It also promoted the belief that the 'control of government' by the democratically elected legislation would adequately replace the traditional limitations,[9] while in fact the necessity of forming organized majorities for supporting a programme of particular actions in favour of special groups introduced a new source of arbitrariness and partiality and produced results inconsistent with the moral principles of the majority. As we shall see, the paradoxical result of the possession of unlimited power makes it impossible for a representative body to make the general principles prevail on which it agrees, because under such a system the majority of the representative assembly, in order to remain a majority, *must* do what it can to buy the support of the several interests by granting them special benefits.

So it came about that with the precious institutions of representative government Britain gave to the world also the pernicious principle of parliamentary sovereignty[10] according to which the representative assembly is not only the highest but also an unlimited authority. The latter is sometimes thought to be a necessary consequence of the former, but this is not so. Its power may be limited, not by another superior 'will' but by the consent of the people on which all power and the coherence of the state rest. If that consent approves only of the laying down and enforcement of general rules of just conduct, and nobody is given power to coerce except for the enforcement of these rules (or temporarily during a violent disruption of order by some cataclysm), even the highest constituted power may be limited. Indeed, the claim of Parliament to sovereignty at first meant only that it recognized no other will above it; it only gradually came to mean that it could do whatever it liked—which does not necessarily follow from the first, because the consent on which the unity of the state and therefore the power of any of its organs are founded may only restrain power but not confer positive power to act. It is allegiance which creates power and the power thus created extends only so far as it has been extended by the consent of the people. It was because this was forgotten that the sovereignty of law became the same thing as the sovereignty of Parliament. And while the conception of the rule (reign, sovereignty or supremacy) of law presupposes a concept of law defined by the attributes of the rules, not by their source, *today legislatures are no longer so called because they make the laws, but laws are so called because they emanate from legislatures*, whatever the form or content of their resolutions.[11]

If it could be justly contended that the existing institutions produce results which have been willed or approved by a majority, the believer in the basic principle of democracy would of course have to accept them. But there are strong reasons to think that what those institutions in fact produce is in a great measure an unintended outcome of the particular kind of machinery we have set up to ascertain what we believe to be the will of the majority, rather than a deliberate decision of the majority or anybody else. It would seem that wherever democratic institutions ceased to be restrained by the tradition of the Rule of Law, they led not only to 'totalitarian democracy' but in due time even to a 'plebiscitary dictatorship'.[12] This should certainly make us understand that what is a precious possession is not a particular set of institutions that are easily enough copied, but some less tangible traditions; and that the degeneration of these institutions may even be a necessary result wherever the inherent logic of the machinery is not checked by the predominance of the prevailing general conceptions of justice. May it not be true, as has been well said, that 'the belief in democracy presupposes belief in things higher than democracy'?[13] And is there really no other way for people to maintain a democratic government than by handing over unlimited power to a group of elected representatives whose decisions must be guided by the exigencies of a bargaining process in which they bribe a sufficient number of

4

voters to support an organized group of themselves numerous enough to outvote the rest?

The true content of the democratic ideal

Though a great deal of nonsense has been and still is being talked about democracy and the benefits its further extension will secure, I am profoundly disturbed by the rapid decline of faith in it. This sharp decrease of the esteem in which democracy is held by critical minds ought to alarm even those who never shared the unmeasured and uncritical enthusiasm it used to inspire until recently, and which made the term describe almost anything that was good in politics. As seems to be the fate of most terms expressing a political ideal, 'democracy' has been used to describe various kinds of things which have little to do with the original meaning of the term, and now is even often used where what is really meant is 'equality'. Strictly speaking it refers to a method or procedure for determining governmental decisions and neither refers to some substantial good or aim of government (such as a sort of material equality), nor is it a method that can be meaningfully applied to non-governmental organizations (such as educational, medical, military or commercial establishments). Both of these abuses deprive the word 'democracy' of any clear meaning.[14]

But even a wholly sober and unsentimental consideration which regards democracy as a mere convention making possible a peaceful change of the holders of power[15] should make us understand that it is an ideal worth fighting for to the utmost, because it is our only protection (even if in its present form not a certain one) against tyranny. Though democracy itself is not freedom (except for that indefinite collective, the majority of 'the people') it is one of the most important safeguards of freedom. As the only method of peaceful change of government yet discovered, it is one of those paramount though negative values, comparable to sanitary precautions against the plague, of which we are hardly aware while they are effective, but the absence of which may be deadly.

The principle that coercion should be allowed only for the purpose of ensuring obedience to rules of just conduct approved by most, or at least by a majority, seems to be the essential condition for the absence of arbitrary power and therefore of freedom. It is this principle which has made possible the peaceful co-existence of men in a Great Society and the peaceful change of the directors of organized power. But that whenever common action is necessary it should be guided by the opinion of the majority, and that no power of coercion is legitimate unless the principle guiding it is approved by at least a majority, does not imply that the power of the majority must be unlimited—or even that there must be a possible way of ascertaining what it called the will of the majority on every conceivable subject. It appears that we have unwittingly created a machinery which makes it possible to claim the sanction of an alleged majority for measures which are in fact not desired by a majority, and which may even be disapproved by a majority of the people; and that this machinery produces an aggregate of measures that not only is not wanted by anybody, but that could not as a whole be approved by any rational mind because it is inherently contradictory.

If all coercive power is to rest on the opinion of the majority, then it should also not extend further than the majority can genuinely agree. This does not mean that there must exist specific approval by the majority of any particular action of the government. Such a demand would clearly be impossible to fulfil in a complex modern society so far as the current direction of the detail of the government machinery is concerned, that is for all the day-to-day decisions about how the resources placed at the disposal of government are to be used. But it does mean that the individual should be bound to obey only such commands as necessarily follow from the general principles approved by the majority, and that the power of the representatives of the majority should be unrestricted only in the administration of the particular means placed at their disposal.

The ultimate justification of the conferment of a power to coerce is that such a power is required if a viable order is to be maintained, and that all have therefore an interest in the existence of such a power. But this justification does not extend further than the need. There is clearly no need that anybody, not even the majority, should have power over all the particular actions or things occurring in society. The step from the belief that only what is approved by the majority should be binding for all, to the belief that all that the majority approves shall have that force, may seem small. Yet it is the transition from one conception of government to an altogether different one: from the conception by which government has definite limited tasks required to bring about the formation of a spontaneous order, to the conception that its powers

6

are unlimited; or a transition from a system in which through recognized procedures we decide how certain common affairs are to be arranged, to a system in which one group of people may declare anything they like as a matter of common concern and on this ground subject it to those procedures. While the first conception refers to necessary common decisions requisite for the maintenance of peace and order, the second allows some organized sections of the people to control everything, and easily becomes the pretext of oppression.

There is, however, no more reason to believe in the case of the majority that because they want a particular thing this desire is an expression of their sense of justice, than there is ground for such a belief in the case of individuals. In the latter we know only too well that their sense of justice will often be swayed by their desire for particular objects. But as individuals we have generally been taught to curb illegitimate desires, though we sometimes have to be restrained by authority. Civilization largely rests on the fact that the individuals have learnt to restrain their desires for particular objects and to submit to generally recognized rules of just conduct. Majorities, however, have not yet been civilized in this manner because they do not have to obey rules. What would we not all do if we were genuinely convinced that our desire for a particular action proves that it is just? The result is not different if people are persuaded that the agreement of the majority on the advantage of a particular measure proves that it is just. When people are taught to believe that what they agree is necessarily just, they will indeed soon cease to ask whether it is so. Yet the belief that all on which a majority can agree is by definition just has for several generations been impressed upon popular opinion. Need we be surprised that in the conviction that what they resolve is necessarily just, the existing representative assemblies have ceased even to consider in the concrete instances whether this is really so?[16]

While the agreement among many people on the justice of a particular *rule* may indeed be a good though not an infallible test of its justice, it makes nonsense of the conception of justice if we define as just whatever particular measure the majority approves— justifiable only by the positivist doctrine that there are no objective tests of justice (or rather injustice—see chapter 8 above). There exists a great difference between what a majority may decide on any particular question and the general principle relevant to the issue which it might be willing to approve if it were

7

put to it, as there will exist among individuals. There is, therefore, also great need that a majority be required to prove its conviction that what it decides is just by *committing* itself to the universal application of the rules on which it acts in the particular case; and its power to coerce should be confined to the enforcement of rules to which it is prepared to commit itself.

The belief that the will of the majority on particular matters determines what is just leads to the view, now widely regarded as self-evident, that the majority cannot be arbitrary. This appears to be a necessary conclusion only if, according to the prevalent interpretation of democracy (and the positivistic jurisprudence as its foundation), the source from which a decision emanates rather than its conformity with a rule on which the people agree, is regarded as the criterion of justice, and 'arbitrary' is arbitrarily defined as not determined by democratic procedure. 'Arbitrary' means, however, action determined by a particular will unrestrained by a general rule—irrespective of whether this will is the will of one or a majority. It is, therefore, not the agreement of a majority on a particular action, nor even its conformity with a constitution, but only the willingness of a representative body to commit itself to the universal application of a rule which requires the particular action, that can be regarded as evidence that its members regard as just what they decide. Today, however, the majority is not even asked whether it regards a particular decision as just; nor could its individual members assure themselves that the principle that is applied in the particular decision will also be applied in all similar instances. Since no resolution of a representative body binds it in its future decisions, it is in its several measures not bound by any general rules.

The weakness of an elective assembly with unlimited powers

The crucial point is that votes on rules applicable to all, and votes on measures which directly affect only some, have a wholly different character. Votes on matters that concern all, such as general rules of just conduct, are based on a lasting strong opinion and thus something quite different from votes on particular measures for the benefit (and often also at the expense) of unknown people— generally in the knowledge that such benefits will be distributed from the common purse in any case, and that all the individual can do is to guide this expenditure in the direction he prefers. Such a system is bound to produce the most paradoxical results in a Great Society, however expedient it may be for arranging local affairs where all are fairly familiar with the problems, because the number and complexity of the tasks of the administration of a Great Society far exceed the range where the ignorance of the individual could be remedied by better information at the disposal of the voters or representatives.[17]

The classical theory of representative government assumed that the deputies

> when they make no laws but what they themselves and their posterity must be subject to; when they can give no money, but what they must pay their share of; when they can do no mischief, but what must fall upon their own heads in common with their countrymen; their principals may expect then good laws, little mischief, and much frugality.[18]

But the electors of a 'legislature' whose members are mainly concerned to secure and retain the votes of particular groups by procuring special benefits for them will care little about what others will get and be concerned only with what they gain in the haggling. They will normally merely agree to something being given to others about whom they know little, and usually at the expense of third groups, as the price for having their own wishes met, without any thought whether these various demands are just. Each group will be prepared to consent even to iniquitous benefits for other groups out of the common purse if this is the condition for the consent of the others to what this group has learnt to regard as its right. The result of this process will correspond to nobody's opinion of what is right, and to no principles; it will not be based on a judgment of merit but on political expediency. Its main object is bound to become the sharing out of funds extorted from a minority. That this is the inevitable outcome of the actions of an unrestrained 'interventionist' legislature was clearly foreseen by the early theorists of representative democracy.[19] Who indeed would pretend that in modern times the democratic legislatures have granted all the special subsidies, privileges and other benefits which so many special interests enjoy because they regard these demands as just? That A be protected against the competition of cheap imports and B against being undercut by a less highly trained operator, C against a reduction in his wages, and D against the loss of his job is not in the general interest, however much the advocates of such a measure pretend

9

that this is so. And it is not chiefly because the voters are convinced that it is in the general interest but because they want the support of those who make these demands that they are in turn prepared to support *their* demands. The creation of the myth of 'social justice' which we have examined in the last volume is indeed largely the product of this particular democratic machinery, which makes it necessary for the representatives to invent a moral justification for the benefits they grant to particular interests.

Indeed people often come genuinely to believe that it must in some sense be just if the majority regularly concedes special benefits to particular groups—as if it had anything to do with justice (or any moral consideration) if every party that wants majority support must promise special benefits to some particular groups (such as the farmers or peasants, or legal privileges to the trade unions) whose votes may shift the balance of power. Under the existing system thus every small interest group can enforce its demands, not by persuading a majority that the demands are just or equitable, but by threatening to withhold that support which the nucleus of agreed individuals will need to become a majority. The pretence that the democratic legislatures have granted all the special subsidies, privileges and other benefits which so many particular interests today enjoy because they thought these to be just would of course be simply ridiculous. Though skilful propaganda may occasionally have moved a few soft-hearted individuals on behalf of special groups, and though it is of course useful to the legislators to claim that they have been moved by considerations of justice, the artefacts of the voting machinery which we call the will of the majority do certainly not correspond to any opinion of the majority about what is right or wrong.

An assembly with power to vote on benefits to particular groups must become one in which bargains or deals among the majority rather than substantive agreement on the merits of the different claims will decide. The fictitious 'will of the majority' emerging from this bargaining process is no more than an agreement to assist its supporters at the expense of the rest. It is to the awareness of this fact that policy is largely determined by a series of deals with special interests that 'politics' owes its bad reputation among ordinary men.

Indeed, to the high-minded who feel that the politician should concern himself exclusively with the common good the reality of constant assuaging of particular groups by throwing them titbits or more substantial gifts must appear as outright corruption. And the

10

fact that majority government does not produce what the majority wants but what each of the groups making up the majority must concede to the others to get their support for what it wants itself amounts to that. That this is so is today accepted as one of the commonplaces of everyday life and that the experienced politician will merely pity the idealist who is naive enough to condemn this and to believe it could be avoided if only people were more honest, is therefore perfectly true so far 'as the existing institutions are concerned, and wrong only in taking it as an inevitable attribute of all representative or democratic government, an inherent corruption which the most virtuous and decent man cannot escape. It is however not a necessary attribute of all representative or democratic government, but a necessary product only of all unlimited or omnipotent government dependent on the support of numerous groups. Only limited government can be decent government, because there does not exist (and cannot exist) general moral rules for the assignments of particular benefits—as Kant put it, because 'welfare has no principle but depends on the material content of the will and therefore is incapable of a general principle'.[20] It is not democracy or representative government as such, but the particular institution, chosen by us, of a single omnipotent 'legislature' that make it necessarily corrupt.

Corrupt at the same time weak: unable to resist pressure from the component groups the governing majority *must do what it can do* to gratify the wishes of the groups from which it needs support, however harmful to the rest such measures may be—at least so long as this is not too easily seen or the groups who have to suffer are not too popular. While immensely and oppressively powerful and able to overwhelm all resistance from a minority, it is wholly incapable of pursuing a consistent course of action, lurching like a steam roller driven by one who is drunk. If no superior judiciary authority can prevent the legislature from granting privileges to particular groups there is no limit to the blackmail to which government will be subject. If government has the power to grant their demands it becomes their slave—as in Britain where they make impossible any policy that might pull the country out of its economic decline.[21] If government is going to be strong enough to maintain order and justice we must deprive the politicians of that cornucopia the possession of which makes them believe that they can and ought 'to remove all sources of discontent.'[22] Unfortunately, every necessary adaptation to changed circumstances is bound to cause widespread

11

discontent, and what will be mainly demanded from politicians is to make these unwelcome changes unnecessary for the individuals.

One curious effect of this condition in which the granting of special benefits is guided not by a general belief of what is just but by 'political necessity' is that it is apt to create erroneous beliefs of the following kind: if a certain group is regularly favoured because it may swing the balance of the votes the myth will arise that it is generally agreed that it deserves this. But it would of course be absurd to conclude if the farmers, the small business men, or the municipal workers got their demands regularly satisfied that they must have a just claim, if in reality this merely happens because without the support of a substantial part of these groups no government would have a majority. Yet there seems to be a paradoxical reversal of what democratic theory assumes to happen: that the majority is not guided by what is generally believed to be right, but what it thinks it is necessary to do in order to maintain its coherence is being regarded as just. It is still believed that consent of the majority is proof of the justice of a measure, although most members of the majority will often consent only as payment of the price for the fulfilment of their own sectional demands. Things come to be regarded as 'socially just' merely because they are regularly done, not because anyone except the beneficiaries regards them as just on their own merits. But the necessity of constantly wooing splinter groups produces in the end purely fortuitous moral standards and often leads people to believe that the favoured social groups are really specially deserving because they are regularly singled out for special benefits. Sometimes we do encounter the argument that 'all modern democracies have found it necessary to do this or that', used as if it were proof of the desirability of a measure rather than merely the blind result of a particular mechanism.

Thus the existing machinery of unlimited democratic government produces a new set of 'democratic' pseudo-morals, an artifact of the machinery which makes people regard as socially just what is regularly done by democracies, or can by clever use of this machinery be extorted from democratic governments. The spreading awareness that more and more incomes are determined by government action will lead to ever new demands by groups whose position is still left to be determined by market forces for similar assurance of what they believe they deserve. Every time the income of some group is increased by government action a legitimate claim for similar treatment is provided for other groups. It is merely the expectations of many which legislatures have created by the boons they have already conferred on certain groups that they will be treated in the same manner that underlies most of the demands for 'social justice'.

Coalitions of organized interests and the apparatus of para-government

So far we have considered the tendency of the prevailing democratic institutions only in so far as it is determined by the necessity to bribe the individual voter with promises of special benefits for his group, without taking into account a factor which greatly accentuates the influence of some particular interests, their ability to organize and to operate as organized pressure groups.[23] This leads to the particular political parties being united not by any principles but merely as coalitions or organized interests in which the concerns of those pressure groups that are capable of effective organization greatly preponderate over those that for one reason or another cannot form effective organizations.[24] This greatly enhanced influence of the organizable groups further distorts the distribution of benefits and makes it increasingly unrelated to the requirements of efficiency or any conceivable principle of equity. The result is a distribution of incomes chiefly determined by political power. The 'incomes policy' nowadays advocated as a supposed means to combat inflation is in fact largely inspired by the monstrous idea that all material benefits should be determined by the holders of such power.[25]

It is part of this tendency that in the course of this century an enormous and exceedingly wasteful apparatus of para-government has grown up, consisting of trade associations, trades unions and professional organizations, designed primarily to divert as much as possible of the stream of governmental favour to their members. It has come to be regarded as obviously necessary and unavoidable, yet has arisen only in response to (or partly as defence against being disadvantaged in) the increasing necessity of an all-mighty majority government maintaining its majority by buying the support of particular small groups.

Political parties in these conditions become in fact little more than coalitions of organized interests whose actions are determined by the inherent logic of their mechanics rather than by any general principles or ideals on which they are agreed. Except for some ideological parties in the West who disapprove of the system now

13

prevailing in their countries and aim at wholly replacing these by some imaginary utopia, it would indeed be difficult to discern in the programmes, and even more in the actions, of any major party a consistent conception of the sort of social order on which its followers agree. They are all driven, even if that is not their agreed aim, to use their power to impose some particular structure upon society i.e. some form of socialism, rather than create the conditions in which society can gradually evolve improved formations.[26]

The inevitability of such developments in a system where the legislature is omnipotent is cleary seen if we ask how a majority united on common action and capable of directing current policy can be formed. The original democratic ideal was based on the conception of a common opinion on what is right being held by most of the people. But community of opinion on basic values is not sufficient to determine a programme for current governmental action. The specific programme that is required to unite a body of supporters of a government, or to hold together such a party, must be based on some aggregation of different interests which can only be achieved by a process of bargaining. It will not be an expression of common desire for the particular results to be achieved; and, as it will be concerned with the use of the concrete resources at the disposal of government for particular purposes, it will generally rest on the consent of the several groups to particular services rendered to some of them in return for other services offered to each of the consenting groups.

It would be mere pretence to describe a programme of action thus decided upon in a bargaining democracy as in any sense an expression of the common opinion of the majority. Indeed, there may exist nobody who desires or even approves of all the things contained in such a programme; for it will often contain elements of such contradictory character that no thinking person could ever desire them all for their own sake. Considering the process by which such programmes for common action are agreed upon, it would indeed be a miracle if the outcome were anything but a conglomerate of the separate and incoherent wishes of many different individuals and groups. On many of the items included in the programme most members of the electorate (or many of the representative assembly) will have no opinion at all because they know nothing of the circumstances involved. Towards many more they will be indifferent or even adversely disposed, but prepared to consent as payment for the realization of their own wishes. For most individuals the choice between party programmes will therefore be mainly a choice between evils, namely between different benefits to be provided for others at their expense.

The purely additive character of such a programme for governmental action stands out most clearly if we consider the problem that will face the leader of the party. He may or he may not have some chief objective for which he deeply cares. But whatever his ultimate objective, what he needs to achieve it is power. For this he needs the support of a majority which he can get only by enlisting people who are little interested in the objectives which guide him. To build up support for his programme he will therefore have to offer effective enticements to a sufficient number of special interests to bring together a majority for the support of his programme as a whole.

The agreement on which such a programme for governmental action is based is something very different from that common opinion of a majority which it was hoped would be the determining force in a democracy. Nor can this kind of bargaining be regarded as the kind of compromise that is inevitable whenever people differ and must be brought to agree on some middle line which does not wholly satisfy anybody. A series of deals by which the wishes of one group are satisfied in return for the satisfaction of the wishes of another (and frequently at the expense of a third who is not consulted) may determine aims for common action of a coalition, but does not signify popular approval of the overall results. The outcome may indeed be wholly contrary to any principles which the several members of the majority would approve if they ever had an opportunity to vote on them.

This domination of government by coalitions of organized interests (when they were first observed they were generally described as 'sinister interests') is usually regarded by the outsider as an abuse, or even a kind of corruption. It is, however, the inescapable result of a system in which government has unlimited powers to take whatever measures are required to satisfy the wishes of those on whose support it relies. A government with such powers cannot refuse to exercise them and still retain the support of a majority. We have no right to blame the politicians for doing what they must do in the position in which we have placed them. We have created conditions in which it is known that the majority has power to give any particular section of the population whatever it demands. But a government that possesses such unlimited powers can stay in office only by satisfying a sufficiently large number of pressure groups to assure itself of the support of a majority.

Government, in the narrow sense of the administration of the special resources set aside for the satisfaction of common needs, will to some extent always have that character. Its task is to hand out particular benefits to different groups, which is altogether distinct from that of legislation proper. But while this weakness is comparatively innocuous as long as government is confined to determining the use of an amount of resources placed at its disposal according to rules it cannot alter (and particularly when, as in local government, people can escape exploitation by voting with their feet), it assumes alarming proportions when government and rule-making come to be confused and the persons who administer the resources of government also determine how much of the total resources it ought to control. To place those who ought to define what is right in a position in which they can maintain themselves only by giving their supporters what they want, is to place at their disposal all the resources of society for whatever purpose they think necessary to keep them in power.

If the elected administrators of a certain share of the resources of a society were under a law which they could not alter, though they would have to use them so as to satisfy their supporters, they could not be driven beyond what can be done without interfering with the freedom of the individual. But if they are at the same time also the makers of those rules of conduct, they will be driven to use their power to organize not only the resources belonging to government, but all the resources of society, including the individual's, to serve the particular wishes of their constituents.

We can prevent government from serving special interests only by depriving it of the power to use coercion in doing so, which means that we can limit the powers of organized interests only by limiting the powers of government. A system in which the politicians believe that it is their duty, and in their power, to remove all dissatisfaction,[27] must lead to a complete manipulation of the people's affairs by the politicians. If that power is unlimited, it will and must be used in the service of particular interests, and it will induce all the organizable interests to combine in order to bring pressure upon government. The only defence that a politician has against such pressure is to point to an established principle which prevents him from complying and which he cannot alter. No system in which those who direct the use of the resources of government are not

16

bound by unalterable rules can escape becoming an instrument of the organized interests.

Agreement on general rules and on particular measures

We have repeatedly stressed that in a Great Society nobody can possess knowledge of, or have any views about, all the particular facts which might become the object of decisions by government. Any member of such a society can know no more than some small part of the comprehensive structure of relationships which makes up the society; but his wishes concerning the shaping of the sector of the overall pattern to which he belongs will inevitably conflict with the wishes of the others.

Thus, while nobody knows all, the separate desires will often clash in their effects and must be reconciled if agreement is to be reached. Democratic *government* (as distinguished from democratic legislation) requires that the consent of the individuals extend much beyond the particular facts of which they can be aware; and they will submit to a disregard of their own wishes only if they have come to accept some general rules which guide all particular measures and by which even the majority will abide. That in such situations conflict can be avoided only by agreement on general rules while, if agreement on the several particulars were required, conflicts would be irreconcilable, seems to be largely forgotten today.

True general agreement, or even true agreement among a majority, will in a Great Society rarely extend beyond some general principles, and can be maintained only on such particular measures as can be known to most of its members.[28] Even more important, such a society will achieve a coherent and self-consistent overall order only if it submits to general rules in its particular decisions, and does not permit even the majority to break these rules unless this majority is prepared to commit itself to a new rule which it undertakes henceforth to apply without exception.

We have seen earlier that commitment to rules is in some degree necessary even to a single individual who endeavours to bring order into a complex of actions he cannot know in detail in advance. It is even more necessary where the successive decisions will be made by different groups of people with reference to different parts of the whole. Successive votes on particular issues

17

would in such conditions not be likely to produce an aggregate result of which anyone would approve, unless they were all guided by the same general rules.

It has in a great measure been an awareness of the unsatisfactory results of the established procedures of democratic decision-making that has led to the demand for an overall plan whereby all government action will be decided upon for a long period ahead. Yet such a plan would not really provide a solution for the crucial difficulty. At least, as it is usually conceived, it would still be the result of a series of particular decision on concrete issues and its determination would therefore raise the same problems. The effect of the adoption of such a plan is usually that it becomes a substitute for real criteria of whether the measures for which it provides are desirable.

The decisive facts are that not only will a true majority view in a Great Society exist only on general principles, but also that a majority can exercise some control over the outcome of the market process only if it confines itself to the laying down of general principles and refrains from interfering with the particulars even if the concrete results are in conflict with its wishes. It is inevitable that, when for the achievement of some of our purposes we avail ourselves of a mechanism that responds in part to circumstances unknown to us, its effects on some particular results should be contrary to our wishes, and that there will therefore often arise a conflict between the general rules we wish to see obeyed and the particular results that we desire.

In collective action this conflict will manifest itself most conspicuously because, while as individuals we have in general learned to abide by rules and are able to do so consistently, as members of a body that decides by majority votes we have no assurance that future majorities will abide by those rules which might forbid us to vote for particulars which we like but which are obtainable only by infringing an established rule. Though as individuals we have learnt to accept that in pursuing our aims we are limited by established rules of just conduct, when we vote as members of a body that has power to alter these rules, we often do not feel similarly restrained. In the latter situation most people will indeed regard it as reasonable to claim for themselves benefits of a kind which they know are being granted to others, but which they also know cannot be granted universally and which they would therefore perhaps prefer not to see granted to anybody at all. In the course of the particular decisions on specific issues the voters or their representatives will therefore often be led to support measures in conflict with principles which they would prefer to see generally observed. So long as there exist no rules that are binding on those who decide on the particular measures, it is thus inevitable that majorities will approve measures of a kind which, if they were asked to vote on the principle, they would probably prohibit once and for all.

The contention that in any society there will usually exist more agreement on general principles than on particular issues will at first perhaps appear contrary to ordinary experience. Daily practice seems to show that it is usually easier to obtain agreement on a particular issue than on a general principle. This, however, is a consequence merely of the fact that we usually do not explicitly know, and have never put into words, those common principles on which we know well how to act and which normally lead different persons to agree in their judgments. The articulation or verbal formulation of these principles will often be very difficult. This lack of conscious awareness of the principles on which we act does not disprove, however, that in fact we usually agree on particular moral issues only because we agree on the rules applicable to them. But we will often learn to express these common rules only by the examination of the various particular instances in which we have agreed, and by a systematic analysis of the points on which we agree.

If people who learn for the first time about the circumstances of a dispute will generally arrive at similar judgements on its merits, this means precisely that, whether they know it or not, they are in fact guided by the same principles, while, when they are unable to agree, this would seem to show that they lack such common principles. This is confirmed when we examine the nature of the arguments likely to produce agreement among parties who first disagreed on the merits of a particular case. Such arguments will always consist of appeals to general principles, or at least to facts which are relevant only in the light of some general principle. It will never be the concrete instance as such, but always its character as one of a class of instances, or as one that falls under a particular rule, that will be regarded as relevant. The discovery of such a rule on which we can agree will be the basis for arriving at an agreement on the particular issue.

THIRTEEN

THE DIVISION OF DEMOCRATIC POWERS

The most urgent problem of our age for those who give most
urgency to the preservation of democratic institutions is that of
restraining the vote-buying process.

W. H. Hutt*

The loss of the original conception of the functions of a legislature

It cannot be our task here to trace the process by which the original
conception of the nature of democratic constitutions gradually was
lost and replaced by that of the unlimited power of the democratically elected assembly. That has been done recently in an
important book by M. J. C. Vile in which it is shown how during the
English Civil War the abuse of its powers by Parliament 'had shown
to men who had previously seen only the royal power as a danger,
that parliament could be as tyrannical as a king' and how this led to
'the realisation that legislatures must also be subjected to restriction
if individual freedom was not to be invaded'.[1] This remained the
doctrine of the old Whigs until far into the eighteenth century. It
found its most famous expression in John Locke who argued in
effect that 'the legislative authority is the authority *to act in a
particular way*'. Furthermore, Locke argued, those who wield this
authority should make only general rules. 'They are to govern by
promulgated established Laws, not to be varied in particular
cases.'[2] One of the most influential statements is met with in *Cato's
Letters* by John Trenchard and Thomas Gordon in which, in a
passage already quoted in part, the former could maintain in 1721
that

> when the deputies thus act for their own interest, by acting for the
> interest of their principals; when they can make no laws but what
> they themselves, and their posterity must be subject to; when

they can give no money, but what they must pay their share of; when they can do no mischief but what fall upon their own heads in common with their countrymen; their principals may then expect good laws, little mischief, and much frugality.[3]

Even towards the end of the century, moral philosophers could still regard this as the basic principle of the British constitution and argue, as William Paley did in 1785, that when the legislative and the judicial character

are united in the same person or assembly, particular laws are made for particlar cases, springing oftentimes from partial motives, and directed to private ends: whilst they are kept separate, general laws are made by one body of men, without foreseeing whom they may affect; and when made must be applied by the other, let them affect whom they will . . . .

When the parties and the interests to be affected by the law were known, the inclinations of the law-makers would inevitably attach on one side or the other . . . .

Which dangers, by the division of the legislative and judicial functions, are effectually provided against. Parliament knows not the individuals upon whom its acts will operate; it has no cases or parties before it, no private designs to serve; consequently its resolutions will be suggested by the consideration of universal effects and tendencies, which always produces impartial and commonly advantageous regulations.[4]

No doubt this theory was an idealization even then and in fact the arrogation of arbitrary powers by Parliament was regarded by the spokesmen of the American colonies as the ultimate cause of the break with the mother country. This was most clearly expressed by one of the profoundest of their political philosophers, James Wilson, who

rejected Blackstone's doctrine of parliamentary sovereignty as outmoded. The British do not understand the idea of a constitution which limits and superintends the operations of the legislature. This was an improvement in the science of government reserved to the Americans.[5]

We shall not further consider here the American attempt to limit in their Constitution the powers of the legislature, and its limited success. It in fact did no more to prevent Congress from becoming primarily a governmental rather than a truly legislative institution

21

and from developing in consequence all the characteristics which this chief preoccupation is apt to impress on an assembly and which must be the chief topic of this chapter.

Existing representative institutions have been shaped by the needs of government, not of legislation

The present structure of democratic governments has been decisively determined by the fact that we have charged the representative assemblies with two altogether different tasks. We call them 'legislatures' but by far the greater part of their work consists not in the articulation and approval of general rules of conduct but in the direction of the measures of government concerning particular matters.[6] We want, and I believe rightly, that both the laying down of general rules of conduct binding upon all and the administration of the resources and machinery placed at the disposal of government be guided by the wishes of the majority of the citizens. This need not mean, however, that these two tasks should be placed into the hands of the same body, nor that every resolution of such a democratically elected body must have the validity and dignity that we attach to the appropriately sanctioned general rules of conduct. Yet by calling 'law' every decision of that assembly, whether it lays down a rule or authorizes particular measures, the very awareness that these are different things has been lost.[7] Because most of the time and energy of the representative assemblies is taken up by the task of organizing and directing government, we have not only forgotten that government is different from legislation but have come to think that an instruction to government to take particular actions is the normal content of an act of law-giving. Probably the most far-reaching effect of this is that the very structure and organization of the representative assemblies has been determined by the needs of their governmental tasks but is unfavourable to wise rule-making.

It is important to remember in this connection that the founders of modern representative government were almost all apprehensive of political parties (or 'factions', as they usually called them), and to understand the reasons for their apprehension. The political theorists were still concerned chiefly with what they conceived to be the main task of a legislature, that is, the laying down of rules of just conduct for the private citizen, and did not attach much importance to its other task, the directing or controlling of government or administration. For the former task clearly a body widely representative of the various shades of opinion but not committed to a particular programme of action would seem desirable.

But, as government rather than legislation became the chief task of the representative assemblies, their effectiveness for this task demanded the existence within them of a majority of members agreed on a programme of action. The character of modern parliamentary institutions has in fact been wholly shaped by these needs of democratic *government* rather than by those of democratic *legislation* in the strict sense of the latter term. The effective direction of the whole apparatus of government, or the control of the use of all the personal and material resources placed under its supervision, demands the continuous support of the executive authority by an organized majority committed to a coherent plan of action. Government proper will have to decide constantly what particular demands of interests it can satisfy; and even when it is limited to the use of those particular resources which are entrusted to its administration, it must continually choose between the requirements of different groups.

All experience has shown that if democratic government is to discharge these tasks effectively it must be organized on party lines. If the electorate is to be able to judge its performance, there must exist an organized group among the representatives that is regarded as responsible for the conduct of government, and an organized opposition that watches and criticizes and offers an alternative government if the people become dissatisfied with the one in power.

It is, however, by no means true that a body organized chiefly for the purpose of directing government is also suited for the task of legislation in the strict sense, i.e. to determine the permanent framework of rules of law under which it has to move its daily tasks.

Let us recall once more how different the task of government proper is from that of laying down the universally applicable rules of just conduct. Government is to act on concrete matters, the allocation of particular means to particular purposes. Even so far as its aim is merely to enforce a set of rules of just conduct given to it, this requires the maintenance of an apparatus of courts, police, penal institutions, etc., and the application of particular means to particular purposes. But in the wider sphere of government, that of rendering to the citizens other services of various kinds, the employment of the resources at its command will require constant choosing of the particular ends to be served, and such decisions

23

must be largely a matter of expediency. Whether to build a road along one route or another one, whether to give a building one design or a different one, how to organize the police or the removal of rubbish, and so on, are all not questions of justice which can be decided by the application of a general rule, but questions of effective organization for satisfying the needs of various groups of people, which can be decided only in the light of the relative importance attached to the competing purposes. If such questions are to be decided democratically, the decisions will be about whose interests are to prevail over those of others.

Administration of common means for public purposes thus requires more than agreement on rules of just conduct. It requires agreement on the relative importance of particular ends. So far as the administration of those resources of society that are set aside for the use of government is concerned, somebody must have power to decide for which ends they are to be used. Yet the difference between a society of free men and a totalitarian one lies in the fact that in the former this applies only to that limited amount of resources that is specifically destined for governmental purposes, while in the latter it applies to all the resources of society including the citizens themselves. The limitation of the powers of government that a free society presupposes requires thus that even the majority should have unrestricted power only over the use of those resources which have been dedicated to common use, and that the private citizen and his property are not subject to specific commands (even of the legislature), but only to such rules of conduct as apply equally to all.

Since the representative assemblies which we call legislatures are predominantly concerned with governmental tasks, these tasks have shaped not only their organization but also the entire manner of thinking of their members. It is today often said that the principle of the separation of powers is threatened by the increasing assumption of legislative function by the administration. It was in fact largely destroyed much earlier, namely when the bodies called legislatures assumed the direction of government (or, perhaps more correctly, legislation was entrusted to existing bodies mainly concerned with government). The separation of powers has been supposed to mean that every coercive act of government required authorization by a universal rule of just conduct approved by a body not concerned with the particularly momentary ends of government. If we now call 'law' also the authorization of particular acts of government by a resolution of the representative assembly, such 'legislation' is not legislation in the sense in which the concept is used in the theory of the separation of powers; it means that the democratic assembly exercises executive powers without being bound by laws in the sense of general rules of conduct it cannot alter.

Bodies with powers of specific direction are unsuited for law-making

Though, if we want democratic government, there is evidently need for a representative body in which the people can express their wishes on all the issues which concern the actions of government, a body concerned chiefly with these problems is little suited for the task of legislation proper. To expect it to do both means asking it to deprive itself of some of the means by which it can most conveniently and expeditiously achieve the immediate goals of government. In its performance of governmental functions it will in fact not be bound by any general rules, for it can at any moment make the rules which enable it to do what the momentary task seems to require. Indeed, any particular decision it would make on a specific issue will automatically abrogate any previously existing rule it infringes. Such a combination of governmental and rule-making power in the hands of one representative body is evidently irreconcilable, not only with the principle of the separation of powers, but also with the ideals of government under the law and the rule of law.

If those who decide on particular issues can make for any purpose whatever law they like, they are clearly not under the rule of law; and it certainly does not correspond to the ideal of the rule of law if, whatever particular group of people, even if they be a majority, decide on such an issue is called a law. We can have a rule of law or a rule of majority, we can even have a rule of laws made by a majority which also governs[8] but only so long as the majority itself, when it decided particular matters, is bound by rules that it cannot change *ad hoc,* will the rule of law be preserved. Government subject to the control of a parliamentary assembly will assure a government under the law only if that assembly merely restrains the powers of the government by general rules but does not itself direct the actions of government, and by doing so make legal anything it orders government to do. The existing situation is such that even the awareness has been lost of the distinction between law in the sense

25

of rules of just conduct and law in the sense of the expression of the majority's will on some particular matter. The conception that law is whatever the so-called legislature decides in the manner prescribed by the constitution is a result of the peculiar institutions of European democracy, because these are based on the erroneous belief that the recognized representatives of the majority of the people must have of necessity unlimited powers. American attempts to meet this difficulty have provided only a limited protection.

An assembly whose chief task is to decide what particular things should be done, and which in a parliamentary democracy supervises its executive committee (called government) in the carrying out of a programme of action approved by it, has no inducement or interest to tie itself by general rules. It can adapt the particular rules it lays down to the needs of the moment, and these rules will in general tend to serve the needs of the organization of government rather than the needs of the self-generating order of the market. Where it concerns itself with rules of just conduct, this will mostly be by-products of government and subservient to the needs of government. Such legislation will tend progressively to increase the discretionary powers of the government machinery and, instead of imposing limitations on government, become a tool to assist in the achievement of its particular ends.

The ideal of a democratic control of government and that of the limitation of government by law are thus different ideals that certainly cannot be both achieved by placing into the hands of the same representative body both rule-making and governmental powers. Though it would be possible to assure the realization of both these ideals, no nation has yet succeeded in doing this effectively by constitutional provisions; peoples have approached this state only temporarily thanks to the prevailing of certain strong political traditions. In recent times the effect of the existing institutional set up has been progressively to destroy what had remained of the tradition of the rule of law.

During the early periods of the representative government members of parliament could still be regarded as representatives of the general and not of the particular interests.[9] Though governments needed the confidence of the majority of parliament, this did not yet mean that an organized majority had to be maintained for the carrying out of a programme of policy. In peace-time at least most of the current activities of government were chiefly of a routine character for which little parliamentary authorization was needed beyond the approval of the annual budget; and this became the chief instrument through which the British House of Commons directly guided the activities of government.

The character of existing 'legislatures' determined by their governmental tasks

Although anyone even remotely familiar with modern politics has long come to take the present character of parliamentary proceedings for granted, when we come to think of it it is really astounding how far the reality of the concerns and practices of modern legislature differs from the image that most reasonable persons would form of an assembly which has to decide on the grave and difficult questions of the improvement of the legal order, or of the framework of rules within which the struggle of divergent interests ought to be conducted. An observer who was not used to the existent arrangements would probably soon come to the conclusion that politics as we know it is a necessary result of the fact that it is in the same arena that those limits are laid down and the struggle is conducted which they ought to restrain, and that the same persons who compete, for votes by offering the special favours are also supposed to lay down the limits of governmental power. There exists clearly an antagonism between these two tasks and it is illusory to expect the delegates to deprive themselves of those powers of bribing their mandatories by which they preserve their position.

It is hardly an exaggeration to say that the character of existing representative bodies has in the course of time been shaped almost entirely by their governmental tasks. From the methods of election of the members, the periods for which they are elected, the division of the assembly into organized parties, its order of business and rules of procedure, and above all the mental attitudes of the members, everything is determined by the concern with governmental measures, not with legislation. At least in the lower houses the budget, which is of course as far from legislation proper as anything can be, is the main event of the year.

All this tends to make the members agents of the interests of their constituents rather than representatives of public opinion. The election of an individual becomes a reward for having delivered the goods rather than an expression of confidence that the good sense, honesty and impartiality which he has shown in his private dealings

27

will still guide him in his service to the public. People who hope to be re-elected on the basis of what their party during the preceding three or four years has conferred in conspicuous special benefits on their voters are not in the sort of position which will make them pass the kind of general laws which would really be most in the public interest.

It is a well-known fact that as a result of his double task the typical representative has neither time nor interest nor the desire or competence to preserve, and still less to improve, those limits to the coercive powers of government which is one of the chief purposes of law (the other being the protection against violence or coercion of people by their fellows)—and therefore, one may hope, of legislation. The governmental task of the popular assemblies, however, not only interferes with but often is in outright conflict with the aims of the law-maker.

We have earlier quoted the comments of one of the closest observers of British Parliament (a former Parliamentary Counsel of the Treasury) that 'For lawyer's law, parliament has neither time nor taste'.[10] It is worth while now to quote Sir Courtenay Ilbert's fuller account of the position in the British Parliament at the beginning of the century:

> The bulk of the members are not really interested in technical questions of law, and would always prefer to let the lawyers develop their rules and procedures in their own way. The substantial business of Parliament as a legislature [!] is to keep the machinery of State in working order. And the laws which are required for this purpose belong to the domain, not of private or of criminal law, but what is called on the Continent administrative law. . . . The bulk of the Statute book of each year will usually consist of administrative regulations, relating to matters which lie outside the ordinary reading and practice of the barrister.[11]

While this was already true of the British Parliament at the beginning of the century, I know of no contemporary democratic legislature of which it is not now equally true. The fact is that the legislators are in general largely ignorant of law proper, the lawyer's law which constitutes the rules of just conduct, and they concern themselves mostly with certain aspects of administrative law which progressively created for them a separate law even in England, where it was once understood that the private law limited the

28

powers of governmental agents as much as those of the ordinary citizens. The result is that the British (who at one time flattered themselves that such a thing as administrative law was unknown in their country) are now subject to hundreds of administrative agencies capable of issuing binding orders.

The almost exclusive concern of the representatives with government rather than legislation is a consequence of the fact that they know that their re-election depends chiefly on the record of their party in government and not on legislation. It is the voters' satisfaction with the immediate effects of governmental measures, not their judgement of the effect of alterations in the law, noticeable only in the long run, which they will express at the polls. Since the individual representative knows that his re-election will depend chiefly on the popularity of his party and the support he will receive from his party, it will be the short run effects of the measures taken by it that will be his chief concern. Considerations about the principles involved may affect his initial choice of party, but since, once he has been elected for one party, a change of party may end his political career, he will in general leave such worries to the leaders of his party and immerse himself in the daily work arising out of the grievances of his constituents, dealing in its course with much routine administration.

His whole bias will thus be towards saying 'yes' to particular demands while the chief task of a true legislator ought to be to say 'no' to all claims for special privileges and to insist that certain kinds of things simply are not done. Whatever may have been the ideal described by Edmund Burke, a party today in general is not agreed on values but united for particular purposes. I do not wish to deny that even present day parties often form around a nucleus united by common principles or ideals. But since they must attract a following by promising other things, they can rarely if ever remain true to their principles and achieve a majority. It certainly is helpful to a party if it has principles by which it can justify the granting of special advantages to a sufficient number of groups to obtain a majority support.

The socialists have in this respect an advantage and, until they have accomplished their first aim and, having achieved control of the means of production, they have to face the task of assigning particular shares of the product to the different groups, are tied together by their belief in a common principle—or at least a form of words like 'social justice', the emptiness of which they have not yet discovered. They can concentrate on creating a new machinery rather than its use, and direct all their hopes to what the new machinery will achieve when completed. But they also are of course from the outset, as we have seen, agreed on the destruction of law in the sense of general rules of just conduct and its replacement by administrative orders. A socialist legislature would therefore be a purely governmental body—probably confined to rubber stamping the work of the planning bureaucracy.

` For the task of laying down the limits of what government may do clearly a type of person is wanted wholly different from those whose main interest is to secure their re-election by getting special benefits for their supporters. One would have to entrust this not to men who have made party politics their life's concern and whose thinking is shaped by their preoccupation with their prospects of re-election, but to persons who have gained respect and authority in the ordinary business of life and who are elected because they are trusted to be more experienced, wise and fair, and who are then enabled to devote all their time to the long run problems of improving the legal framework of all actions, including those of government. They would have ample time to learn their jobs as legislators and not be helpless before (and the object of contempt of) that bureaucracy which makes in fact today the laws because the representative assemblies have not the time to do so.

Nothing indeed is more conspicuous in those assemblies than that what is supposed to be the chief business of a legislature is constantly crowded out, and that more and more of the tasks which the man in the street imagines to be the main occupation of the legislators are in fact performed by civil servants. It is largely because the legislatures are preoccupied by what in effect is discretionary administration that the true work of legislation is increasingly left in the hands of the bureaucracy, which of course has little power of restraining the governmental decision of the 'legislatures' which are too busy to legislate.

No less significant is it that when parliaments have to deal with true legislation concerning problems on which strong moral convictions exist and which many representatives regard as matters of conscience, such as the death penalty, abortion, divorce, euthanasia, the use of drugs (including alcohol and tobacco), pornography and the like, parties find it necessary to relax control over the voting of their members—in effect in all cases where we really want to find out what is dominant *opinion* on major issues rather than the views on particular measures. It shows that there exist in fact no simple lines dividing the citizens into distinct groups of people who agree among themselves on a variety of principles as the party organization suggests. Agreement to obey certain principles is a different thing from agreeing to the manner of distributing various benefits.

An arrangement by which the interest of the highest authority is directed chiefly to government and not to law can only lead to a steady growth of the preponderance of government over law—and the progressive growth of the activities of government is largely a result of this arrangement. It is an illusion to expect from those who owe their positions to their power to hand out gifts that they will tie their own hands by inflexible rules prohibiting all special privileges. To leave the law in the hands of elective governors is like leaving the cat in charge of the cream jug—there soon won't be any, at least no law in the sense in which it limits the discretionary powers of government. Because of this defect in the construction of our sup- posedly constitutional democracies we have in fact again got that unlimited power which the eighteenth-century Whigs represented as 'so wild and monstrous a thing that however natural it be to desire it, it is as natural to oppose it'.[12]

Party legislation leads to the decay of democratic society

A system which may place any small group in the position to hold a society to ransom if it happens to be the balance between opposing groups, and can extort special privileges for its support of a party, has little to do with democracy or 'social justice'. But it is the unavoidable product of the unlimited power of a single elective assembly not precluded from discrimination by a restriction of its powers either to true legislation or to government under a law which it cannot alter.

Not only will such a system produce a government driven by blackmail and corruption, but it will also produce laws which are disapproved by the majority and in their long-run effects may lead to the decline of the society. Who would seriously maintain that the most fateful law in Britain's modern history, the Trade Disputes Act of 1906, was an expression of the will of the majority?[13] With the Conservative opposition wholly opposed, it is more than ques- tionable whether even the majority of the members of the govern- ing Liberal party approved of a bill 'drawn up by the first generation

31

of Labour MPs'.[14] Yet the majority of the Liberal party depended on Labour support, and although the bill shocked the leading representatives of the British constitutional tradition probably more than any other act of modern legislative history,[15] the spectacular legal privileges granted in it to the trades unions has since become the chief cause of the progressive decline of the British economy.

Nor is there, with the present character of the existing Parliament, much hope that they will prove more capable of dealing intelligently with such crucial future tasks of legislation as the limits to the powers of all corporate bodies or the prohibition of restraints on competition. It is to be feared that they will be decided mainly by the popularity or unpopularity of the particular groups that are directly affected rather than by an understanding of the requirements of a functioning market order.

A further peculiar sort of bias of government created by the necessity to gain votes by benefiting particular groups or activities operates indirectly through the need to gain the support of those second-hand dealers of ideas, mainly in what are now called the 'media', who largely determine public opinion. This expresses itself among other manifestations in a support of modern art which the majority of the people certainly does not care for in the least, and certainly also in some of the governmental support to technological advance (the flight to the moon!) for which such support is certainly very questionable but by which a party can secure the sympathy and the support of those intellectuals who run the 'media'.

Democracy, so far as the term is not used simply as a synonym for egalitarianism, is increasingly becoming the name for the very process of vote-buying, for placating and remunerating those special interests which in more naive times were described as the 'sinister interests'. What we are concerned with now is, however, to show that what is responsible for this is not democracy as such but the particular form of democracy which we are practising today. I believe in fact that we should get a more representative sample of the true opinion of the people at large if we picked out by drawing lots some five hundred mature adults and let them for twenty years devote themselves to the task of improving the law, guided only by their conscience and the desire to be respected, than by the present system of auction by which every few years we entrust the power of legislation to those who promise their supporters the greatest special benefits. But, as we shall show later, there are better alternative systems of democracy than that of a single omnipotent assembly with unlimited powers which has produced the blackmail and corruption system of politics.

The constructivistic superstition of sovereignty

The conception that the majority of the people (or their elected representatives) ought to be free to decree whatever they can agree upon, and that in this sense they must be regarded as omnipotent, is closely connected with the conception of popular sovereignty. Its error lies not in the belief that whatever power there is should be in the hands of the people, and that their wishes will have to be expressed by majority decisions, but in the belief that this ultimate source of power must be unlimited, that is, the idea of sovereignty itself. The pretended logical necessity of such an unlimited source of power simply does not exist. As we have already seen, the belief in such a necessity is a product of the false constructivistic interpretation of the formation of human institution which attempts to trace them all to an original designer or some other deliberate act of will. The basic source of social order, however, is not a deliberate decision to adopt certain common rules, but the existence among the people of certain opinions of what is right and wrong. What made the Great Society possible was not a deliberate imposition of rules of conduct, but the growth of such rules among men who had little idea of what would be the consequence of their general observance.

Since all power rests on pre-existing opinions, and will last only so long as those opinions prevail, there is no real personal source of this power and no deliberate will which has created it. The conception of sovereignty rests on a misleading logical construction which starts from the initial assumption that the existing rules and institutions derive from a uniform will aiming at their creation. Yet, far from arising from such a pre-existing will capable of imposing upon the people whatever rules it likes, a society of free men presupposes that all power is limited by the common beliefs which made them join, and that where no agreement is present no power exists.[16]

Except where the political unit is created by conquest, people submit to authority not to enable it to do what it likes, but because they trust somebody to act in conformity with certain common conceptions of what is just. There is not first a society which then gives itself rules, but it is common rules which weld dispersed bands into a society. The terms of submission to the recognized authority become a permanent limit of its powers because they are the condition of the coherence and even existence of the state—and these terms of submission were understood in the liberal age to be that coercion could be used only for the enforcement of recognized general rules of just conduct. The conception that there must be an unlimited will which is the source of all power is the result of a constructivistic hypostasation, a fiction made necessary by the false factual assumptions of legal positivism but unrelated to the actual sources of allegiance.

The first question we should always ask in contemplating the structure of governmental powers is not who possesses such and such a power, but whether the exercise of such a power by any agency is justified by the implicit terms of submission to that agency. The ultimate limit of power is therefore not somebody's will on particular matters, but something quite different: the concurrence of opinions among members of a particular territorial group on rules of just conduct. The famous statement by Francis Bacon which is the ultimate source of legal positivism, that 'a supreme and absolute power cannot conclude itself, neither can that which is in its true nature revocable be fixed'[17] thus wrongly presupposes a derivation of all power from some act of purposive will. But the resolve that 'we will let us by governed by a good man, but if he is unjust we will throw him out' does not mean that we confer on him unlimited powers or powers which we already have! Power does not derive from some single seat but rests on the support by common opinion of certain principles and does not extend further than this support. Though the highest source of deliberate decisions cannot effectively limit its own powers, it is itself limited by the source from which its power derives which is not another act of will but a prevailing state of opinion. There is no reason why allegiance, and therefore the authority of the state, should survive the arrogation of arbitrary powers which has neither the support of the public nor can be effectively enforced by the usurping government.

In the Western world unlimited sovereignty was scarcely ever claimed by anyone since antiquity until the arrival of absolutism in the sixteenth century. It was certainly not conceded to medieval princes and hardly ever claimed by them. And although it was successfully claimed by the absolute monarchs of the European Continent, it was not really accepted as legitimate until after the advent of modern democracy which in this respect has inherited the tradition of absolutism. Till then the conception was still kept alive that legitimacy rested in the last resort on the approval by the people at large of certain fundamental principles underlying and limiting all government, and not on their consent to particular measures. But when this explicit consent that was devised as a check upon power came to be regarded as the sole source of power, the conception of unlimited power was for the first time invested with the aura of legitimacy.

The idea of the omnipotence of some authority as a result of the source of its power is thus essentially a degeneration that, under the influence of the constructivistic approach of legal positivism, appeared wherever democracy had existed for any length of time. It is, however, by no means a necessary consequence of democracy, but a consequence only of the deceptive belief that, once democratic procedures have been adopted, all the results of the machinery of ascertaining the will of the majority in fact correspond to the *opinion* of a majority, and that there is no limit to the range of question on which agreement of the majority can be ascertained by this procedure. It was helped by the naive belief that in this way the people were 'acting together'; and a sort of fairy tale spread that 'the people' are doing things and that this is morally preferable to the separate actions by individuals. In the end this fantasy led to the curious theory that the democratic decision-making process always is directed towards the common good—the common good being defined as the conclusions which the democratic procedures produces. The absurdity of this is shown by the fact that different but equally justifiable procedures for arriving at a democratic decision may produce very different results.

The requisite division of the powers of representative assemblies

The classical theory of representative government assumed that its aim could be achieved by allowing the division between the legislature and the administration to coincide with the division between an elected representative assembly and an executive body appointed by it. It failed to do so because there was of course as strong a case for democratic government as for democratic legislation and the sole democratically elected assembly inevitably claimed the right to direct government as well as the power to legislate. It thus came to combine the powers of legislation with those of government. The result was the revival of the monstrous establishment of an absolute power not restricted by any rules. I trust there will come a time when people will look with the same horror at the idea of a body of men, even one authorized by the majority of the citizens, who possesses power to order whatever it likes, as we feel today about most other forms of authoritarian government. It creates a barbarism, not because we have given barbarians power, but because we have released power from the restraint of rules, producing effects that are inevitable, whoever the people to whom such power is entrusted. It may well be that common people often have a stronger sense of justice than any intellectual élite guided by the lust for new deliberate construction; yet when unrestricted by any rules they are likely to act more arbitrarily than any élite or even a single monarch who is so bound. This is so, not because the faith in the common man is misplaced, but because he is thereby given a task which exceeds human capacities.

Though government proper in the performance of its characteristic tasks cannot be strictly tied to rules, its powers for this very reason ought always to be limited in extent and scope, namely confined to the administration of a sharply circumscribed range of means entrusted to its care. All power, however, that is not thus confined to a particular mass of material things but is unlimited in extent should be confined to the enforcement of general rules; while those who have the rule-making power should be confined to providing for the enforcement of such general rules and have no power of deciding on particular measures. All ultimate power should, in other words, be subject to the test of justice, and be free to do what it desires only in so far as it is prepared to commit itself to a principle that is to be applied in all similar instances.

The aim of constitutions has been to prevent all arbitrary action. But no constitution has yet succeeded in achieving this aim. The belief that they have succeeded in this has however led people to regard the terms 'arbitrary' and 'unconstitutional' as equivalent. Yet the prevention of arbitrariness, though one of the aims, is by no means a necessary effect of obeying a constitution. The confusion on this point is a result of the mistaken conception of legal positivism. The test of whether a constitution achieves what constitutions are meant to do is indeed the effective prevention of arbitrariness; but this does not mean that every constitution provides an adequate test of what is arbitrary, or that something that is permitted by a constitution may not still be arbitrary.

If the supreme power must always prove the justice of its intentions by committing itself to general rules, this requires institutional arrangements which will secure that general rules will always prevail over the particular wishes of the holders of authority— including even the case where a very large majority favours a particular action but another, much smaller majority would be prepared to commit itself to a rule which would preclude that action. (This is not incompatible with the former, since it would be entirely rational to prefer that actions of the kind in question be prohibited altogether, yet so long as they are permitted to favour a particular one.) Or, to put this differently, even the largest majority should in its coercive acts be able to break a previously established rule *only* if it is prepared explicitly to abrogate it and to commit itself to a new one. Legislation in the true sense ought always to be a commitment to act on stated principles rather than a decision how to act in a particular instance. It must, therefore, essentially aim at effects in the long run, and be directed towards a future the particular circumstances of which are not yet known; and the resulting laws must aim at helping unknown people for their equally unknown purposes. This task demands for its successful accomplishment persons not concerned with particular situations or committed to the support of particular interests, but men free to look at their tasks from the point of view of the long run desirability of the rules laid down for the community as a whole.

Though true legislation is thus essentially a task requiring the long view, even more so than that of the designing of a constitution, it differs from the latter in that it must be a continuous task, a persistent effort to improve the law gradually and to adapt it to new conditions—essentially helping where jurisdiction cannot keep pace with a rapid development of facts and opinions. Though it may require formal decisions only at long intervals, it demands constant application and study of the kind for which politicians busy wooing their supporters and fully occupied with pressing matters demanding rapid solution will not really have time.

The task of legislation proper differs from the task of constitution-making also in that it will be concerned with rules of greater generality than those contained in a constitution. A constitution is chiefly concerned with the organization of government and the allocation of the different powers to the various parts of this organization. Though it will often be desirable to include in the formal

37

documents 'constituting' the organization of the state some principles of substantive justice in order to confer upon these special
protection, it is still true that a constitution is essentially a superstructure erected to serve the enforcement of existing conceptions
of justice but not to articulate them: it presupposes the existence of
a system of rules of just conduct and merely provides a machinery
for their regular enforcement.

We need not pursue this point further at this stage since all that we
want to point out here is that the task of true legislation is as
different from that of constitution-making as it is from that of
governing, and that it ought to be as little confused with the former
as with the latter. It follows from this that, if such confusion is to be
avoided, a three-tiered system of representative bodies is needed,
of which one would be concerned with the semi-permanent
framework of the constitution and need act only at long intervals
when changes in that framework are considered necessary, another
with the continuous task of gradual improvement of the general
rules of just conduct, and a third with the current conduct of
government, that is, the administration of the resources entrusted
to it.

Democracy or demarchy?

We cannot consider here further the changes which the meaning of
the concept of democracy has undergone by its increasingly common transfer from the political sphere in which it is appropriate to
other spheres in which it is very doubtful whether it can be meaningfully applied:[18] and whether its persistent and deliberate abuse
by the communists as in such terms as 'people's democracies', which
of course lack even the most basic characteristics of a democracy,
does not make it unsuitable to describe the ideal it was originally
meant to express. These tendencies are mentioned here merely
because they are contributing further to deprive the term 'democracy' of clear meaning and turn it into a word-fetish used to clothe
with an aura of legitimacy any demands of a group that wishes to
shape some feature of society to its special wishes.

The legitimacy of the demands for more democracy becomes
particularly questionable when they are directed to the manner in
which organizations of various kinds are conducted. The problems
which arise here show themselves at once when it is asked who are
to be regarded as the 'members' of such organizations for whom a

share in their direction is claimed. It is by no means obvious that a person who finds it in his interest to sell his services should thereby also acquire a voice in its conduct or in determining the purposes towards which this organization is to be directed. We all know that the conduct of the campaign of an army could not be directed democratically. It is the same with such simple operations as the building of a house or the conduct of an enterprise of the bureaucratic machinery of government.

And who are the 'members' of a hospital, or an hotel, or a club, a teaching institution or a department store? Those who serve these institutions, those whom these institutions serve, or those who provide the material means required to render the services? I ask these questions here simply to make clear that the term democracy, though we all still use it and feel we ought to defend the ideal it describes, has ceased to express a definite conception to which one can commit oneself without much explanation, and which in some of the senses in which it is now frequently used has become a serious threat to the ideals it was once meant to depict. Though I firmly believe that government ought to be conducted according to principles approved by a majority of the people, and must be so run if we are to preserve peace and freedom, I must frankly admit that *if* democracy is taken to mean government by the unrestricted will of the majority I am not a democrat, and even regard such government as pernicious and in the long run unworkable.

A question which has arisen here is whether those who believe in the original ideal of democracy can still usefully avail themselves of that old name to express their ideal. I have come seriously to doubt whether this is still expedient and feel more and more convinced that, if we are to preserve the original ideal, we may have to invent a new name for it. What we need is a word which expresses the fact that the *will* of the greater number is authoritative and binding upon the rest only if the former prove their intention of acting justly by committing themselves to a general rule. This demands a name indicating a system in which what gives a majority legitimate power is not bare might but the proven conviction that it regards as right what it decrees.

It so happens that the Greek word 'democracy' was formed by combining the word for the people (*demos*) with that of the two available terms for power, namely *kratos* (or the verb *kratein*) which had not already been used in such a combination for other purposes. *Kratein*, however, unlike the alternative verb *archein* (used in such compounds as monarchy, oligarchy, anarchy, etc.) seems to stress brute force rather than government by rule. The reason why in ancient Greece the latter root could not be used to form the term *demarchy* to express a rule by the people was that the term *demarch* had (at least in Athens) been preempted by an earlier use for the office of the head of a local group or district (the *deme*), and thus was no longer available as a description of government by the people at large. This need not prevent us today from adopting the term *demarchy* for the ideal for which *democracy* was originally adopted when it gradually supplanted the older expression *isonomy*, describing the ideal of an equal law for all.[19] This would give us the new name we need if we are to preserve the basic ideal in a time when, because of the growing abuse of the term democracy for systems that lead to the creation of new privileges by coalitions or organized interests, more and more people will turn against that prevailing system. If such a justified reaction against abuse of the term is not to discredit the ideal itself, and lead people in their disillusionment to accept much less desirable forms of government, it would seem necessary that we have a new name like demarchy to describe the old ideal by a name that is not tainted by long abuse.

FOURTEEN

THE PUBLIC SECTOR AND THE PRIVATE SECTOR

The distinction between legislation and taxation is essential to liberty.

William Pitt, Earl of Chatham*

The double task of government

Since in this book we are mainly concerned with the limits that a free society must place upon the coercive powers of government, the reader may get the mistaken impression that we regard the enforcement of the law and the defence against external enemies as the only legitimate functions of government. Some theorists in the past have indeed advocated such a 'minimal state'.[1] It may be true that in certain conditions, where an undeveloped government apparatus is scarcely yet adequate to perform this prime function, it would be wise to confine it to it, since an additional burden would exceed its weak powers and the effect of attempting more would be that it did not even provide the indispensable conditions for the functioning of a free society. Such considerations are not relevant, however, to advanced Western societies, and have nothing to do with the aim of securing individual liberty to all, or with making the fullest use of the spontaneous ordering forces of a Great Society.

Far from advocating such a 'minimal state',[2] we find it unquestionable that in an advanced society government ought to use its power of raising funds by taxation to provide a number of services which for various reasons cannot be provided, or cannot be provided adequately, by the market. Indeed, it could be maintained that, even if there were no other need for coercion, because everybody voluntarily obeyed the traditional rules of just conduct, there would still exist an overwhelming case for giving the territorial authorities power to make the inhabitants contribute to a common fund from which such services could be financed. The contention

41

that where the market can be made to supply the services required it is the most effective method of doing so does not imply that we may not resort to other methods where the former is not applicable. Nor can it be seriously questioned that where certain services can be provided only if all beneficiaries are made to contribute to their costs, because they cannot be confined to those to pay for them, only the government should be entitled to use such coercive powers.

Any adequate discussion of the manner in which the service activities of the government should be regulated, or the raising and the administration of the material means placed at the disposal of government for these services controlled, would require another volume of about the same size as the present one. All we can attempt here in a single chapter is to indicate the wide range of such wholly legitimate activities which, as the administrator of common resources, government may legitimately undertake. The purpose of such a sketch can be no more than to prevent the impression that by limiting the *coercive* activities and the monopoly of government to the enforcement of rules of just conduct, defence, and the levying of taxes to finance its activities, we want to restrict government wholly to those functions.

While it is the possession of coercive powers which enables government to obtain the means for rendering services which cannot be rendered commercially, this should not mean that as the supplier or organizer of such services it ought to be able to use the coercive powers. We shall see that the necessity of relying on the coercive powers to raise the finance does not even necessarily mean that those services ought also to be organized by government. That organization by government is sometimes the most expedient way of providing them certainly does not mean that as the provider of the services government need or ought to claim any of those attributes of authority and reverence which it traditionally and rightly enjoys in its authoritative functions (and which particularly in the German tradition have found their most marked expression in the mystique of *Hoheit* and *Herrschaft*). It is indeed most important that we keep clearly apart these altogether different tasks of government and do not confer upon it in its service functions the authority which we concede to it in the enforcement of the law and defence against enemies. There is no reason whatsoever why such authority or exclusive right should be transferred to the purely utilitarian service agencies entrusted to government simply because it alone can finance them. There is nothing reprehensible in treating these agencies as a purely utilitarian device, quite as useful as the butcher and the baker but no more so—and somewhat more suspect, because of the powers of compulsion which they can employ to cover their costs. If modern democracy often fails to show that respect for the law which is due to it, it also tends unduly to extol the role of the state in its service functions and to claim for it in this role privileges which it ought to possess only as the upholder of law and order.

Collective goods

The effectiveness of the market order and of the institution of several property rests on the fact that in most instances the producers of particular goods and services will be able to determine who will benefit from them and who pay for their costs. The conditions that the benefits due to a person's activities can be confined to those willing to pay for them, and withheld from those not willing (and, correspondingly, that all harm done has to be paid for), is largely satisfied so far as material commodities in private possessions are concerned: ownership of a particular movable subject generally confers on the owner control over most of the beneficial or harmful effects of its use. But as soon as we turn from commodities in the narrow sense to land, this is true only to a limited degree. It is often impossible to confine the effects of what one does to one's own land to this particular piece; and hence arise those 'neighbourhood effects' which will not be taken into account so long as the owner has to consider only the effects on his property. Hence also the problems which arise with respect to the pollution of air or water and the like. In these respects calculation by the individuals which takes into account only the effects upon their protected domain will not secure that balancing of costs and benefits which will in general be achieved where we have to do with the use of particular movable things with regard to which the owner alone will experience the effects of their use.

In some instances the conditions which the market requires in order to perform its ordering function will be satisfied only with respect to some of the results of activities of the individuals. These will on the whole still be effectively guided by the price mechanism, even though some of the effects of these activities will spill over on others who either do not pay for the benefits they receive or are not compensated for damage done to them. In these instances the economists speak of (positive or negative) *external* effects. In other instances, however, it is either technically impossible, or would be prohibitively costly, to confine certain services to particular persons, so that these services can be provided only for all (or at least will be provided more cheaply and effectively if they are provided for all). To this category belong not only such obvious instances as the protection against violence, epidemics, or such natural forces as floods or avalanches, but also many of the amenities which make life in modern cities tolerable, most roads (except some long-distance highways where tolls can be charged), the provision of standards of measure, and of many kinds of information ranging from land registers, maps, and statistics to the certification of the quality of some goods or services offered in the market. In many instances the rendering of such services could bring no gain to those who do so, and they will therefore not be provided by the market. These are the collective or public goods proper, for the provision of which it will be necessary to devise some method other than that of sale to the individual users.

It might at first be thought that for such purposes coercion would be unnecessary, because the recognition of a common interest that can be satisfied only by common action would lead a group of reasonable people voluntarily to join in the organizing of such services and pay for them. But, though this is likely to happen in comparatively small groups, it is certainly not true of large groups. Where large numbers are involved, most individuals, however much they may wish that the services in question should be made available, will reasonably believe that it will make no difference to the results whether they themselves agree to contribute to the costs or not. Nor will any individual who consents to contribute have the assurance that the others will also do so and that therefore the object will be attained. Indeed, wholly rational considerations will lead each individual, while wishing that all the others would contribute, to refuse himself to do so.[3] If, on the other hand, he knows that compulsion can be applied only if it is applied to all including himself, it will be rational for him to agree to be compelled, provided this compulsion is also applied to others. This will in many instances be the only way in which collective goods can be provided which are desired by all or at least by a large majority.

The morality of this kind of coercion to positive action is, perhaps, not as obvious as the morality of the rules which merely prevent the individual from infringing the protected domain of others. Particularly where the collective good in question is not wanted by all or at least by a considerable majority, this does raise serious problems. Yet it will clearly be in the interest of the different individuals to agree that the compulsory levying of means to be used also for purposes for which they do not care so long as others are similarly made to contribute to ends which they desire but the others do not. Though this looks as if the individuals were made to serve purposes for which they do not care, a truer way of looking at it is to regard it as a sort of exchange: each agreeing to contribute to a common pool according to the same uniform principles on the understanding that his wishes with regard to the services to be financed from that pool will be satisfied in proportion to his contributions. So long as each may expect to get from this common pool services which are worth more to him than what he is made to contribute, it will be in his interest to submit to the coercion. Since in the case of many collective goods it will not be possible to ascertain with any precision who will benefit from them or to what extent, all we can aim at will be that each should feel that in the aggregate all the collective goods which are supplied to him are worth at least as much as the contribution he is required to make.

With many collective goods which satisfy the needs only of the inhabitants of a particular region or locality, this aim can be more closely approached if not only the administration of the services but also the taxation is placed in the hands of a local rather than a central authority. If in the greater part of this book, for the sake of brevity, we shall as a rule have to speak of government in the singular and must stress that only government ought to possess the power of raising funds by compulsion, this must not be misunderstood to mean that such power should be concentrated in a single central authority. A satisfactory arrangement for the provision of collective goods seems to require that the task be to a great extent delegated to local and regional authorities. Within the scope of this book we shall have little opportunity to consider the whole issue of centralization versus decentralization of government, or of unitary government versus federalism. We can merely emphasize here that our stress on coercion being a monopoly of government by no means necessarily implies that this power of coercion should be concentrated in a single central government. On the contrary, the delegation of all powers that can be exercised locally to agencies whose powers are confined to the locality is probably the best way of securing that the burdens of and the benefits from government action will be approximately proportional.

Two points must chiefly be remembered throughout the following discussion of the public sector. The first is that, contrary to an assumption often tacitly made, the fact that some services must be financed by compulsory levies by no means implies that such services should also be administered by government. Once the problem of finance is solved, it will often be the more effective method to leave the organization and management of such services to competitive enterprise and rely on appropriate methods of apportioning the funds raised by compulsion among the producers in accordance with some expressed preference of the users. Professor Milton Friedman has developed an ingenious scheme of this kind for the financing of education through vouchers to be given to the parents of the children and to be used by them as total or partial payment for the services rendered by schools of their choice, a principle capable of application in many other fields.[4]

The second important point to be remembered throughout is that in the case of collective goods proper, as well as in some instances of these 'external effects' which make part of the effects of individual activities a kind of collective good (or collective nuisance), we are resorting to an *inferior* method of providing these services because the conditions necessary for their being provided by the more efficient method of the market are absent. Where the services in question will be most effectively provided if their production is guided by the spontaneous mechanism of the market, it will still be desirable to rely on it, and to use the coercive method of central determination only for the raising of the funds but leave the organization of the production of these services and the distribution of the available means among the different producers still as far as possible to the forces of the market. And one of the guiding considerations in resorting to the technique of deliberate organization where this is indispensable for the achievement of particular goals, must always be that we do not do so in a manner which impairs the functioning of the spontaneous market order on which we remain dependent for many other and often more important needs.

The delimitation of the public sector

If government has the exclusive right of coercion this will often mean that it is alone able to provide certain services which must be financed by coercive levies. This ought not to mean, however, that the right of providing such services should be reserved to government if other means can be found for providing them. The current distinction between the public sector and the private is sometimes erroneously taken to mean that some services beyond the enforcement of rules of just conduct should be reserved to government by law. There is no justification for this. Even if in given circumstances only government is in fact able to supply particular services, this is no reason for prohibiting private agencies from trying to find methods of providing these services without the use of coercive powers. It is even important that the manner in which government provides such services should not be such that it makes it impossible for others to provide them. New methods may be found for making a service saleable which before could not be restricted to those willing to pay for it, and thus make the market method applicable to areas where before it could not be applied. Wireless broadcasting is an instance: so long as the transmission of any station can be received by anybody, a sale to the particular users of a programme is impossible. But technical advance might well open the possibility of confining reception to those using particular equipment, making the operation of the market possible.

What is generally described as the public sector ought thus not to be interpreted as a set of functions or services reserved to the government; it should rather be regarded as a circumscribed amount of material means placed at the disposal of government for the rendering of services it has been asked to perform. In this connection government needs no other special power than that of compulsory raising means in accordance with some uniform principle, but in administering these means it ought not to enjoy any special privileges and should be subject to the same general rules of conduct and potential competition as any other organization.

The existence of such a public sector[5] comprising all the personal and material resources placed under the control of government, and all the institutions and facilities provided and maintained by it for general use, creates problems of regulation which are determined today by legislation. The 'laws' which are made for this purpose are, however, of a very different character from those universal rules of conduct which we have so far considered as *the law*. They regulate the rendering, and the use by private persons, of such public facilities as roads and the various other public services that are provided by government for general use. The rules required will clearly be in the nature of rules of organization aiming at particular results, rather than rules of just conduct delimiting private spheres; and their content will be determined chiefly by considerations of efficiency or expediency rather than of justice. They are affairs of government, not of legislation proper; and though in establishing such rules for the use of the services it provides, government ought to be bound by certain general requirements of justice, such as the avoidance of arbitrary discrimination, the substantive content of the rules will be determined mainly by considerations of expediency or the efficiency of the services to be rendered.

A good example of such rules for the use of public institutions that is often but misleadingly cited as an instance of rules of just conduct is the Rule of the Road, or the whole system of traffic regulations. Though these rules also have the form of rules of conduct, they differ from the universal rules of just conduct in not delimiting private domains and not applying universally but only to the use of certain facilities provided by government. (The Rule of the Road, for example, does not apply to the traffic in a private park closed to the general public.)

Though such special regulations for the use of facilities provided by government for the public are undoubtedly necessary, we must guard against the prevailing tendency to extend this conception of regulation to other so-called public places which are provided commercially by private enterprise. A privately owned theatre, factory, department store, sports ground or general purpose building does not become a public place in the strict sense because the public at large is invited to use it. There exists unquestionably a strong case for the establishment of uniform rules under which such places may be thrown open to the public: it is evidently desirable that on entering such a place one may presume that certain requirements of safety and health are met. But such rules which must be observed in throwing private institutions open for general use fall into a somewhat different category from those made for the use and conduct of institutions provided and maintained by government. Their content will not be determined by the purpose of the institution, and their aim will merely be to protect the persons using its facilities by informing them what they may count upon in any place they are invited to enter for their own purposes, and what they will be allowed to do there. The particular owner will of course be free to add to these legal requirements for any place open to the general public his own special terms on which he is prepared to admit customers. And most of the special regulations that will be laid down for the use of particular services provided by government are of this kind rather than general laws.

The independent sector

That the 'public sector' should not be conceived of as a range of purposes for the pursuit of which government has a monopoly, but rather as a range of needs that government is asked to meet so long and in so far as they cannot be met better in other ways, is particularly important to remember in connection with another important issue which we can only even more briefly touch upon here. Though government may have to step in where the market fails to supply a needed service, the use of the coercive powers of government for raising the required means is often not the only, or the best, alternative. It may be the most effective means of providing collective goods in those intances where they are wanted by a majority, or at least by a section of the population sufficiently numerous to make its weight felt politically. There will at all times be many services wanted, however, which are needed by many and which have all the characteristics of collective goods, but for which only relatively small numbers care. It is the great merit of the market that it serves minorities as well as majorities. There are some fields, particularly those usually described as 'cultural' concerns, in which it must even appear doubtful whether the views of majorities ought to be allowed to gain a preponderant influence, or those of small groups overlooked—as is likely to happen when the political organization becomes the only channel through which some tastes can express themselves. All new tastes and desires are necessarily at first tastes and desires of a few, and if their satisfaction were dependent on approval by a majority, much of what the majority might learn to like after they have been exposed to it might never become available.

It should be remembered that long before government entered those fields, many of the now generally recognized collective needs were met by the efforts of the public-spirited individuals or groups providing means for public purposes which they regarded as important. Public education and public hospitals, libraries and museums, theatres and parks, were not first created by governments. And although in these fields in which private benefactors have led the way, governments have now largely taken over,[6] there is still need for initiative in many areas whose importance is not yet generally recognized and where it is not possible or desirable that government take over.

In the past it has been initially the churches, but more recently, and especially in the English-speaking world, it has been to a great extent foundations and endowments, private associations and the innumerable private charities and welfare agencies, that have led the way. To some extent these have had their origin in the dedication of large private fortunes for various philanthropic purposes. But many are due to idealists with small means who have devoted their organizational and propagandist talents to a particular cause. There can be no doubt that we owe to such voluntary efforts the recognition of many needs and the discovery of many methods of meeting them which we could never have expected from the government; and that in some fields voluntary effort is more effective and provides outlets for valuable energies and sentiments of individuals that otherwise would remain dormant. No governmental agency has ever thought out or brought into being so effective an organization as Alcoholics Anonymous. It seems to me that local efforts at rehabilitation offer more hope for the solution of the urgent problems of our cities than governmental 'urban renewal'.[7] And there would be many more such developments if the habit of appealing to government, and a short-sighted desire to apply at once and everywhere the now visible remedies, did not so often lead to the whole field being preempted by government whose often clumsy first attempts then block the way for something better.

In this respect the accepted two-fold division of the whole field into a private and a public sector is somewhat misleading. As R. C. Cornuelle has forcefully argued,[8] it is most important for a healthy society that we preserve between the commercial and the governmental a third, *independent sector* which often can and ought to provide more effectively much that we now believe must be provided by government. Indeed, such an independent sector could to a great extent, in direct competition with government for public service, mitigate the gravest danger of governmental action, namely the creation of a monopoly with all the powers and inefficiency of a monopoly. It just is not true that, as J. K. Galbraith tells us, 'there is no alternative to public management'.[9] There often is, and at least

50

in the USA people owe to it much more than they are aware of. To develop this independent sector and its capacities is in many fields the only way to ward off the danger of complete domination of social life by government. R. C. Cornuelle has shown the way; and his optimism regarding what the independent sector could achieve if deliberately cultivated and developed, though it may at first seem illusionary, does not appear excessive. His small book on the subject seems to me to be one of the most promising developments of political ideas in recent years.

Though the actual and potential achievements of this independent sector would constitute a very good illustration of one of the basic contentions of the present book, we can, since our aim is chiefly to devise effective limits to governmental powers, give only passing attention to them. I wish I could write about the subject at length, even if it were only to drive home the point that public spirit need not always mean demand for or support of government action. I must, however, not stray too far from the proper subject of this chapter, which is the service functions which government might usefully perform, not those which it need not take upon itself.

Taxation and the size of the public sector

The degrees of interest of different individuals in the various services provided by government differ a great deal; true agreement between them is likely to be achieved only on the volume of such services to be rendered, provided that each may expect that he will get approximately as much in services as he pays in taxes. This, as we have seen, ought to be interpreted not as each agreeing to pay the costs of all government services, but rather as each consenting to pay according to the same uniform principle for the services which he receives at the expense of the common pool. It ought therefore to be the decision on the level of taxation that should determine the total size of the public sector.

But if it is only through agreement on the total volume of government services, that is, agreement on the total of resources to be entrusted to government, that a rational decision regarding the services which government is to render can be achieved, this presupposes that every citizen voting for a particular expenditure should know that he will have to bear his predetermined share in the cost. Yet the whole practice of public finance has been developed in an endeavour to outwit the taxpayer and to induce him to pay more than he is aware of, and to make him agree to expenditure in the belief that somebody else will be made to pay for it. Even in the theory of public finance all possible considerations have been advanced for determining the principles of taxation, except the one that seems to be the most important in a democracy: that the decision procedure should lead to a rational limitation of the volume of public expenditure. This would seem to require that the principles on which the burden is to be shared by the individuals be determined in advance, and that whoever votes in favour of a particular expenditure knows that he will have to contribute to it at a predetermined rate and thus be able to balance advantages against costs.

The main concern of public finance, however, has from the beginning been to raise the largest sums with the least resistance; and what should have been the main consideration, namely that the method of raising the means should operate as a check on total expenditure, has been little considered. But a method of taxation that encourages the belief that 'the other fellow will pay for it', together with the admission of the principle that any majority has the right to tax minorities in accordance with rules which do not apply to the former (as in any overall progression of the tax burden), must produce a continuous growth of public expenditure beyond what the individual really desires. A rational and responsible decision on the volume of public expenditure by democratic vote presupposes that in each decision the individual voters are aware that they will have to pay for the expenditure determined. Where those who consent to an item of expenditure do not know that they will have to pay for it, and the question that is considered is rather to whom the burden can be shifted, and where the majority in consequence feel that their decisions refer to expenditure to be paid for from other people's pockets, the result is that it is not expenditure which is adjusted to available means, but that means will be found to meet an expenditure which is determined without regard to costs. This process leads in the end to a general attitude which regards political pressure, and the compulsion of others, as the cheap way of paying for most services one desires.

A rational decision on the volume of public expenditure is to be expected only if the principles by which the contribution of each is assessed assures that in voting on any expenditure he will take the costs into account, and therefore only if each voter knows that he will have to contribute to all expenditure he approves in accordance with a predetermined rule, but cannot command anything to be done at somebody else's expense. The prevailing system provides instead a built-in inducement to irresponsible and wasteful expenditure.

The tendency of the public sector to grow progressively and indefinitely led, almost a hundred years ago, to the formulation of a 'law of growing government expenditure'.[10] In some countries such as Great Britain the growth has now reached the point where the share of national income controlled by government amounts to more than 50 per cent. This is but a consequence of that built-in bias of the existing institutions towards the expansion of the machinery of government; and we can hardly expect it to be otherwise in a system in which the 'needs' are fixed first and the means then provided by the decision of people who are mostly under the illusion that they will not have to provide them.

While there is some reason to believe that with the increase in general wealth and of the density of population, the share of all needs that can be satisfied only by collective action will continue to grow, there is little reason to believe that the share which governments, and especially central governments, already control is conducive to an economic use of resources. What is generally overlooked by those who favour this development is that every step made in this direction means a transformation of more and more of the spontaneous order to society that serves the varying needs of the individuals, into an organization which can serve only a particular set of ends determined by the majority—or increasingly, since this organization is becoming far too complex to be understood by the voters, by the bureaucracy in whose hands the administration of those means is placed.

In recent times it has been seriously maintained that the existing political institutions lead to an insufficient provision for the public sector.[11] It is probably true that some of those services which the government ought to render are provided inadequately. But this does not mean that the aggregate of government expenditure is too small. It may well be true that having assumed too many tasks, government is neglecting some of the most important ones. Yet the present character of the procedure by which it is determined what share of the resources ought to be entrusted to government seems to make it more likely that the total is already much larger than most individuals approve or are even aware of. This seems to be more than confirmed by the results of the various opinion polls, the most recent one for Great Britain indicating that about 80 per cent of all the various classes and age groups desire a decrease and no more than 5 per cent of any age group favour an increase in the rate of the income tax—the only burden concerning the magnitude of which they seemed to have at least an approximately correct idea.[12]

Security

There is no need here to enlarge further on the second unquestioned task of government that it would have to perform even in a 'minimal state', that of defence against external enemies. Together with the whole field of external relations it has to be mentioned merely as a reminder of how big is the sphere of those government activities which cannot be strictly bound by general rules (or even effectively guided by a representative assembly), and where the executive must be given far-reaching discretionary powers. It may be useful to recall at this point that it has always been the desire to make central governments strong in their dealings with other countries that has led to their being entrusted also with other tasks which could probably be more efficiently performed by regional or local authorities. The main cause of the progressive centralization of government powers has always been the danger of war.

But the danger from foreign enemies (or possibly internal insurrection) is not the only danger to all members of society which can be effectively dealt with only by an organization with compulsory powers. Few people will question that only such an organization can deal with the effects of such natural disasters as storms, floods, earthquakes, epidemics and the like, and carry out measures to forestall or remedy them. This again is mentioned only to remind us of another reason why it is important that government be in control of material means which it is largely free to use at discretion.

There is, however, yet another class of common risks with regard to which the need for government action has until recently not been generally admitted and where as a result of the dissolution of the ties of the local community, and of the development of a highly mobile open society, an increasing number of people are no longer closely associated with particular groups whose help and support they can count upon in the case of misfortune. The problem here is chiefly the fate of those who for various reasons cannot make their living in the market, such as the sick, the old, the physically or

54

mentally defective, the widows and orphans—that is all people suffering from adverse conditions which may affect anyone and against which most individuals cannot alone make adequate provision but in which a society that has reached a certain level of wealth can afford to provide for all.

The assurance of a certain minimum income for everyone, or a sort of floor below which nobody need fall even when he is unable to provide for himself, appears not only to be a wholly legitimate protection against a risk common to all, but a necessary part of the Great Society in which the individual no longer has specific claims on the members of the particular small group into which he was born. A system which aims at tempting large numbers to leave the relative security which the membership in the small group has given would probably soon produce great discontent and violent reaction when those who have first enjoyed its benefits find themselves without help when, through no fault of their own, their capacity to earn a living ceases.[13]

It is unfortunate that the endeavour to secure a uniform minimum for all who cannot provide for themselves has become connected with the wholly different aims of securing a 'just' distribution of incomes, which, as we have seen, leads to the endeavour to ensure to the individuals the particular standard they have reached. Such assurance would clearly be a privilege that could not be granted to all and could be granted to some only at the expense of worsening the prospects of others. When the means needed for this purpose are raised by general taxation, it even produces the unintended effect of increasing inequality beyond the degree that is the necessary condition of a functioning market order; because, in contrast to the case in which such pensions to the old, disabled or dependents are provided either by the employer as part of the contract of service (i.e. as a sort of deferred payment) or by voluntary or compulsory insurance, there will be no corresponding reduction of the remuneration that is received while the more highly priced services are rendered, with the result that the continued payment of this higher income out of public funds after the services have ceased will constitute a net addition to the higher income that has been earned in the market.

Even the recognition of a claim by every citizen or inhabitant of a country to a certain minimum standard, dependent upon the average level of wealth of that country, involves, however, the recognition of a kind of collective ownership of the resources of the country which is not compatible with the idea of an open society and which raises serious problems. It is obvious that for a long time to come it will be wholly impossible to secure an adequate and uniform minimum standard for all human beings everywhere, or at least that the wealthier countries would not be content to secure for their citizens no higher standards than can be secured for all men. But to confine to the citizens of particular countries provisions for a minimum standard higher than that universally applied makes it a privilege and necessitates certain limitations on the free movement of men across frontiers. There exist, of course, other reasons why such restrictions appear unavoidable so long as certain differences in national or ethnic traditions (especially differences in the rate of propagation) exist—which in turn are not likely to disappear so long as restrictions on migration continue. We must face the fact that we here encounter a limit to the universal application of those liberal principles of policy which the existing facts of the present world make unavoidable. These limits do not constitute fatal flaws in the argument since they imply merely that, like tolerance in particular, liberal principles can be consistently applied only to those who themselves obey liberal principles, and cannot always be extended to those who do not. The same is true of some moral principles. Such necessary exceptions to the general rule do therefore provide no justification for similar exceptions within the sphere in which it is possible for government consistently to follow liberal principles.

We cannot attempt here to consider any of the technical details of the appropriate arrangement of an apparatus of 'social security' which will not destroy the market order or infringe on the basic principles of individual liberty. We have attempted to do so on another occasion.[14]

Government monopoly of services

There are two very important fields of services in which governments have for so long claimed a monopoly (or prerogative) that this has come to be regarded as a necessary and natural attribute of government, although these monopolies neither have been introduced for, nor have ever redounded to, the benefit of the public: the exclusive right of issuing money and of providing postal services. They were not established in order that people should be served better, but solely to enhance the powers of government; and as a result the public is not only much worse served than it would otherwise be, but, at least in the case of money, exposed to hazards and risks in their ordinary efforts of gaining a living which are inseparable from a political control of money and which they would soon have discovered a way of preventing if they had only been allowed to.

So far as the postal monopoly (in the USA only with respect to the delivery of letters) is concerned, all that need be said is that it owes its existence solely to, and has no other justification than, the government's desire to control communications between citizens.[15] It was not government which first created it but it took over what private enterprise had provided. Far from assuring better communications, or even revenue for the government, it has in recent times all over the world steadily deteriorated and is becoming not only an increasing burden on the taxpayer but a serious handicap to business. For having discovered that government is the most helpless of employers, the labour unions in public employments have achieved an increasing power to blackmail all and sundry by paralysing public life. But even apart from strikes and the like the increasing inefficiency of the governmental postal services is becoming a real obstacle to the efficient use of resources. There apply to it also all the other objections against the policy of running the various other 'public unitilities' in transport, communications and power supplies as government monopolies which we shall have to consider later.

The problem of proper monetary arrangements, on the other hand, is too big and difficult to deal with adequately in the present context.[16] To understand what is involved here requires freeing oneself of deeply ingrained habits, and a rethinking of much monetary theory. If the abolition of the government monopoly led to the general use of several competing currencies, that would in itself be an improvement on a governmental monetary monopoly which has without exception been abused in order to defraud and deceive the citizens; but its main purpose would be to impose a very necessary discipline upon the governmental issue of currency through the threat of its being displaced by a more reliable one. In that case the ordinary citizen would still be able in his daily transactions to use the kind of money with which he is now familiar but one which he could at last trust. Government would then be deprived not only of one of the main means of damaging the economy and subjecting individuals to restrictions of their freedom but also of one of the chief causes of its constant expansion. It is of course nonsense that government is ever needed to 'protect' the money used in a country against any threat (except counterfeiting which, like all fraud, the ordinary rules of law forbid) other than that which comes from government itself: it is against the state that money must primarily be protected. The exporters of money, or providers of another kind of money, and the like, against whom the responsible politicians skilfully direct the indignation of the public, are in fact the best watchdogs who, if they are allowed freely to practice their trade, will force government to provide honest money. Exchange control and the like merely serve government to continue with their nefarious practices of competing on the market with the citizen for resources by spending money manufactured for the purpose.

There is no justification for the assiduously fostered myth that there must be within a given territory a uniform sort of money or legal tender. Government may at one time have performed a useful function when it certified weight and fineness of coins, although even that was done at least as reliably and honestly by some respected merchants. But when the princes claimed the minting prerogative, it was for the gain from seignorage and in order to carry their image to the remotest corners of their territory and show the inhabitants to whom they were subject. They and their successors have shamelessly abused this prerogative as an instrument of power and fraud. Further, the blind transfer of rights relating to coinage to modern forms of money was claimed solely as an instrument of power and finance and not because of any belief that it would benefit the people. The British government gave the Bank of England in 1694 a (slightly limited) monopoly of the issue of bank notes because it was paid for it, not because it was for the common good. And though the illusion that government monopoly would secure for the countries a better money than the market has governed all the development of monetary institutions ever since, the fact is of course that wherever the exercise of this power was not limited by some such automatic mechanism as the gold standard, it was abused to defraud the people. A study of the history of money shows that no government that had direct control of the quantity of money can be trusted for any length of time not to abuse it. We shall not get a decent money until others are free to offer us a better one than the government in charge does. So long as the defalcating practices are not prevented by the prompt desertion of the official currency by the people, governments will again and again be driven to such practices by the false belief that they can, and therefore must, ensure full employment by monetary manipulation—which has even been adduced as the reason why we are irrevocably committed to a 'planned', 'directed', 'guided', or 'steered' economy. Of course experience has once more confirmed that it is the very inflationary policies to which governments resort which cause the malady they seek to cure; for though they may reduce unemployment for the moment, they do so only at the price of much greater unemployment later on.

Similar considerations apply to the monopolies of rendering other services which government, mostly local government, can usefully render but which any monopolist is likely to abuse, indeed will probably be forced to abuse. The most harmful abuse here is not that which the public most fears, namely demanding extortionate prices, but on the contrary the political coercion to make uneconomic use of resources. The monopolies in transport, communications, and energy supply which not only prevent competition but make politically determined tariffs necessary, which are determined by supposed considerations of equity, are chiefly responsible for such phenomena as the sprawling of the cities. This is of course the inevitable result if anybody, at however a remote and inaccessible place he chooses to live, is supposed to have a just claim to be served, in disregard of costs, at the same prices as those who live in the centre of a densely occupied city.

On the other hand, it is merely common sense that government, as the biggest spender and investor whose activities cannot be guided wholly by profitability, and which for finance is in a great measure independent of the state of the capital market, should so far as practicable distribute its expenditure over time in such a manner that it will step in when private investment flags, and thereby employ resources for public investment at the least cost and with the greatest benefit to society. The reason why this old prescription has in fact been so little acted upon, hardly any more effectively since it has become fashionable than when it was supported by only a few economists, are of a political and administrative kind. To bring about the required changes in the rate of governmental investment promptly enough to act as a stabilizer, and not, as is usually the case, with such delays that they do more harm than good, would require that the whole investment programme of government be so designed that the speed of its execution could be accelerated or delayed at short notice. To achieve this it would be necessary that all capital expenditure of government be fixed at a certain average rate for as long a period ahead as five or seven years, with the provision that this was to be only the average speed. If we call this 'speed 3' it would then on central direction have to be temporarily increased by all departments by 20 or 40 per cent to 'speed 4' or 'speed 5' or reduced by 20 or 40 per cent to 'speeds 2' or '1'. Each department or section would know that it would later have to make up for this increase or reduction and to endeavour to let the brunt of these changes fall on those activities where the costs of such variations was least, and particularly where it would gain most from adapting to the temporary abundance or scarcity of labour and other resources. It need hardly be pointed out how difficult an effective execution of such a programme would be, or how far we still are from possessing the kind of governmental machinery required for such a task.

Information and education

This, also, is a field which we can only briefly touch on here. The reader will find a fuller treatment of it in my earlier discussion of the subject.[17]

Information and education of course shade into each other. The argument for the provision at public expense is similar in the two cases, but not quite the same as that in the case of public goods. Though information and education can be sold to particular people, those who do not possess either often will not know that it would be to their advantage to acquire them; yet it may be to the advantage of others that they should possess them. This is evident so far as the knowledge is concerned which the individuals must possess if they are to obey the law and take part in the democratic procedures of government. But the market process, though one of the most efficient instruments for conveying information, will also function more effectively if the access to certain kinds of information is free. Also useful knowledge that could assist the individuals in their efforts accrues incidentally in the process of government, or can be obtained only by government, such as that contained in statistics, land registers, etc. Again, much knowledge once acquired is in its nature no longer a scarce commodity and could be made generally available at a fraction of the costs of first acquiring it. This is not necessarily a valid argument for entrusting its distribution to government: we certainly would not wish government to acquire a dominating position in the distribution of news; and the conferment in some countries of a monopoly of wireless broadcasting to governments is probably one of the most hazardous political decisions made in modern times.

But even though it is often very doubtful whether government is the most effective agency for distributing any particular kind of information, and though there is the danger that by preempting this task it may prevent others from performing it better, it would be difficult to maintain that government should not enter this field at all. The real problem is in what form and to what extent government should provide such services.

With regard to education the primary argument in support of its being assisted by government is that children are not yet responsible citizens and cannot be assumed to know what they need, and do not control resources which they can devote to the acquisition of knowledge; and that parents are not always able or prepared to invest in the children's education as much as would make the returns on this intangible capital correspond to those on material capital. This argument applies to children and minors only. But it is supplemented by a further consideration which applies also to adults, namely that education may awaken in those who receive it capacities they did not know they possessed. Here, too, it may often be the case that only if the individual is assisted during the first stages will he be able to develop his potentialities further by his own initiative.

The strong case for a government finance of at least general education does not however imply that this education should also be managed by government, and still less that government should acquire a monopoly of it. At least so far as general education rather than advanced training for the professions is concerned, Professor Milton Friedmann's proposal mentioned before[18] for giving the parents vouchers with which they can pay for their children's education at schools of their own choosing seems to have great advantages over the prevailing system. Though the choice of the parents would have to be limited to a range of schools meeting certain minimum standards, and the vouchers would cover fully the fees of only some of these schools, the system would have the great advantage over schools managed by authority that it would allow parents to pay for the additional costs of a special preferred form of education. In the special training for the professions, etc., where the problems arise after the students have reached the age of discretion, a system of students' loans repayable out of the higher earnings to

61

which such training leads, such as developed by Mr Richard Cornuelle's United Student Aid Fund, Inc., offer alternative and probably preferable possibilities.[19]

Other critical issues

Several other important issues which would need consideration even in a cursory survey of the field of legitimate government policy can however be barely mentioned here. One is that of the problem of *certification* by government or others of the quality of some goods and services which may include a kind of *licensing* of particular activities by government. It can hardly be denied that the choice of the consumer will be greatly facilitated, and the working of the market improved, if the possession of certain qualities of things or capacities by those who offer services is made recognizable for the inexpert though it is by no means obvious that only the government will command the confidence required. Building regulations, pure food laws, the certification of certain professions, the restrictions on the sale of certain dangerous goods (such as arms, explosives, poisons and drugs), as well as some safety and health regulations for the processes of production and the provision of such public institutions as theatres, sports grounds, etc., certainly assists intelligent choice and sometimes may be indispensable for it. That the goods offered for human consumption satisfy certain minimum standards of hygiene, as for example that pork is not trichinuous or milk not tuberculous, or that somebody who describes himself by a term generally understood to imply a certain competence, such as a physician, really possesses that competence, will be most effectively assured by some general rules applying to all who supply such goods or services. It is probably merely a question of expediency whether it will be sufficient to have a generally understood manner in which such goods and services can be described, or whether to permit the sale of such goods only if they are thus certified. All that is required for the preservation of the rule of law and of a functioning market order is that everybody who satisfies the prescribed standards has a legal claim to the required certification, which means that the control of admissions authorities must *not* be used to regulate supply.

A problem which raises particular difficulties is that of the regulation of *expropriation* or *compulsory purchase,* a right which seems to be needed by government for some of its desirable functions. At least for the purpose of providing an adequate system of communications such a right seems to be indispensable and under the name of 'eminent domain' it appears indeed to have been granted to government at all times.[20] So long as the grant of such powers is strictly limited to instances that can be defined by general rules of law, payment of compensation at full value is required, and the decisions of the administrative authorities subject to the control of independent courts, such powers need not seriously interfere with the working of the market process or with the principles of the rule of law. It is not to be denied, however, that in this connection a *prima facie* conflict arises between the basic principles of a libertarian order and what appear to be unquestioned necessities of governmental policy, and that we still lack adequate theoretical principles for a satisfactory solution of some of the problems which arise in this field.

There are also probably several fields in which government has not yet given the private individual the protection he needs if he is to pursue his ends most effectively and to the greatest benefit of the community. One of the most important of these seems to be the *protection of privacy and secrecy* which only the modern increase of the density of population has raised in acute form and with respect to which government has so far clearly failed to provide appropriate rules or to enforce them.[21] The delimitation of some such fields in which the individual is protected against the inquisitiveness of his neighbours or even the representatives of the public at large, such as the press, seems to me an important requirement of full liberty.

Finally we must once more remind the reader that to reduce the discussion of these problems to manageable dimensions it was necessary to discuss them in terms of a unitary, central government. Yet one of the most important conclusions to be derived from our general approach is the desirability of devolving many of these functions of government to regional or local authorities. Indeed, much is to be said in favour of limiting the task of whatever is the supreme authority to the essentially limited one of enforcing law and order on all the individuals, organizations and sectional government bodies, and leaving all rendering of positive services to smaller governmental organizations. Most of the service functions of government would probably be much more effectively performed and controlled if those local authorities had, under a law they could not alter, to compete for residents. It has been the unfortunate necessity of making central governments strong for the task of defence against external enemies that has produced the situation in which the laying down of general rules and the rendering of particular services have been placed into the same hands, with the result that they have become increasingly confused.

FIFTEEN

GOVERNMENT POLICY AND THE MARKET

The pure market economy assumes that government, the social apparatus of compulsion and coercion, is intent upon preserving the operation of the market system, abstains from hindering its functioning, and protects it against encroachment on the part of other people.

Ludwig von Mises*

The advantages of competition do not depend on it being 'perfect' [1]

In certain conditions competition will bring about an allocation of the resources for the production of the different commodities and services which leads to an output of that particular combination of products as large as that which could be brought about by a single mind who knew all those facts actually known only to all the people taken together, and who was fully capable of utilizing this knowledge in the most efficient manner. The special case in which these results follow from the competitive market process has been found intellectually so satisfying by economic theorists that they have tended to treat it as paradigmatic. The case for the competition has in consequence regularly been stated as if competition were desirable because as a rule it achieves these results, or even as if it were desirable only when in fact it does so. From basing the argument for the market on this special case of 'perfect' competition it is, however, not far to the realization that it is an exceptional case approached in only a few instances, and that, in consequence, if the case for competition rested on what it achieves under those special conditions, the case for it as a general principle would be very weak indeed. The setting of a wholly unrealistic, over-high standard of what competition should achieve thus often leads to an erroneously low estimate of what in fact it does achieve.

This model of perfect competition rests on assumptions of facts which do not exist except in a few sectors of economic life and which in many sectors it is not in our power to create and would sometimes not even be desirable to create if we could. The crucial assumption on which that model is based is that any commodity of service that differs significantly from others can be supplied to most consumers at the same cost by a large number of producers, with the result that none of the latter can deliberately determine the price because, if he tried to change more than his marginal costs, it would be in the interests of others to undersell him. This ideal case, in which for each competitor the price is given, and where his interests will induce him to increase his production until the marginal costs are equal to price, came to be regarded as the model and was used as a standard by which the achievement of competition in the real world was judged.

It is true that, if we could bring about such a state, it would be desirable that the production of each article should be extended to the point where prices equalled marginal costs because, so long as this was not so, a further increase of production of the commodity in question would mean that the factors of production required would be used more productively than elsewhere. This, however, does not mean that where we have to use the process of competition to find out what the different people want and are able to do, we are also in a position to bring about the ideal state, or that the results even of 'imperfect' competition will not be preferable to any condition we can bring about by any other known method such as direction by government.

It is evidently neither desirable nor possible that every commodity or service that is significantly different from others should be produced by a large number of producers, or that there should always be a large number of producers capable of producing any particular thing at the same cost. As a rule there will exist at any one time not only an optimum size of the productive unit, below and above which costs will rise, but also special advantages of skill, location, traditions, etc. which only some but not all enterprises will possess. Frequently a few enterprises or perhaps only a single one will be able to supply as much of a particular commodity as can be sold at prices covering its costs which may be cheaper than those of any other firm. In this case a few firms (or the single firm) will not be under the necessity of bringing their prices down to the marginal costs, or of producing such a quantity of their product that they can be sold only at prices just covering its marginal costs. All that their interests will induce the firm to do will be to keep prices below the figure at which new producers would be tempted to enter the market. Within this range such firms (or such a firm) would indeed be free to act as monopolists or obligopolists and to fix their prices (or the quantities of goods produced) at the level which would bring them the highest profits, limited only by the consideration that they must be low enough to keep out others.

In all such instances an omniscient dictator could indeed improve the use of the available resources by requiring the firms to expand production until prices only just covered marginal costs. On this standard, habitually applied by some theorists, most of the markets in the existing world are undoubtedly very imperfect. For all practical problems, however, this standard is wholly irrelevant, because it rests on a comparison, not with some other state that could be achieved by some known procedure, but with one that might have been achieved if certain facts which we cannot alter were other that they in fact are. To use as a standard by which we measure the actual achievement of competition the hypothetical arrangements made by an omniscient dictator comes naturally to the economist whose analysis must proceed on the fictitious assumption that *he* knows all the facts which determine the order of the market. But it does not provide us with a valid test which can meaningfully be applied to the achievements of practical policy. The test should not be the degree of approach towards an unachievable result, but should be whether the results of a given policy exceed or fall short of the results of other available procedures. The real problem is how far we can raise efficiency above the pre-existing level, *not* how close we can come to what would be desirable if the fact were different.

That standard for judging the performance of competition, in other words, must not be the arrangements which would be made by somebody who had complete knowledge of all the facts, but the probability which only competition can secure that the different things will be done by those who thereby produce more of what the others want than they would do otherwise.

Competition as a discovery procedure

Quite generally outside as well as inside the economic sphere, competition is a sensible procedure to employ only if we do not know beforehand who will do best. In examinations or in sport meetings as well as on the market, it will tell us, however, only who did best on the particular occasion, and not necessarily that each did as well as he could have done—though it also provides one of the most effective spurs to achievement. It will produce an inducement to do better than the next best, but if this next best is far behind, the range within which the better one will be free to decide how much to exert himself may be very wide. Only if the next best is pressing on his heels and he himself does not know how much better he really is, will he find it necessary to exert himself to the full. And only if there is a more or less continuous graduation of capacities, and each anxious to achieve as good a place as he can, will each be kept on tiptoe and be looking over his shoulder to see whether the next best is catching up with him.

Competition is thus, like experimentation in science, first and foremost a discovery procedure. No theory can do justice to it which starts from the assumption that the facts to be discovered are already known.[2] There is no pre-determined range of known or 'given' facts which will ever all be taken into account. All we can hope to secure is a procedure that is on the whole likely to bring about a situation where more of the potentially useful objective facts will be taken into account than would be done in any other procedure which we know. It is the circumstances which makes so irrelevant for the choice of a desirable policy all evaluation of the results of competition that starts from the assumption that all the relevant facts are known to some single mind. The real issue is how we can best assist the optimum utilization of the knowledge, skills and opportunities to acquire knowledge, that are dispersed among hundreds of thousands of people, but given to nobody in their entirety. Competition must be seen as a process in which people acquire and communicate knowledge; to treat it as if all this knowledge were available to any one person at the outset is to make nonsense of it. And it is as nonsensical to judge the concrete results of competition by some preconception of the products it 'ought' to bring forth as it would be to judge the results of scientific experimentation by their correspondence with what had been expected. As is true of the results of scientific experimentation, we can judge the value of the results only by the conditions under which it was conducted, not by the results. It therefore cannot be said of competition any more than of any other sort of experimentation that it leads to a maximization of any measurable results. It merely leads, under favourable conditions, to the use of more skill and knowledge than any other known procedure. Though every successful use of skill and knowledge can be regarded as a gain, and therefore each additional act of exchange in which both parties prefer what they get for what they give can be regarded as an advantage, we can never say by what aggregate amount the net benefits available to the people have increased. We have not to deal with measurable or additive magnitudes, but must accept as the possible optimum the results of those general conditions which are most likely to lead to the discovery of the largest number of opportunities.

How any individual will act under the pressure of competition, what particular circumstance he will encounter in such conditions, is not known before even to him and must be still more unknown to anyone else. It is therefore literally meaningless to require him to act 'as if ' competition existed, or as if it were more complete than it is. We shall see in particular that one of the chief sources of error in this field is the conception derived from the fictitious assumption that the individual's 'cost curves' are an objectively given fact ascertainable by inspection, and not something which can be determined only on the basis of his knowledge and judgment—a knowledge which will be wholly different when he acts in a highly competitive market from what it would be if he were the sole producer or one of a very few.

Though to explain the results of competition is one of the chief aims of economic theory (or catallactics), the facts we have considered greatly restrict the extent to which this theory can predict the particular results of competition in the kind of situation in which we are practically interested. Indeed, competition is of value precisely because it constitutes a discovery procedure which we would not need if we could predict its results. Economic theory can elucidate the operation of this discovery procedure by constructing models in which it is assumed that the theoretician possesses all the knowledge which guides all the several individuals whose interaction his model represents. We are interested in such a model only because it tells how a system of this sort will work. But we have to apply it to actual situations in which we do not possess that knowledge of the particulars. What the economist alone can do is to derive from mental models in which he assumes that, as it were, he can look into the cards of all the individual players, certain conclusions about the general character of the result, conclusions which he may perhaps be able to test on artificially constructed models, but which are interesting only in the instances where he cannot test them because he does not possess that knowledge which he would need.

If the factual requirements of 'perfect' competition are absent, it is not possible to make firms act 'as if' it existed

Competition as a discovery procedure must rely on the self-interest of the producers, that is it must allow them to use their knowledge for their purposes, because nobody else possesses the information on which they must base their decision. Where the conditions of 'perfect' competition are absent, some will find it profitable to sell their products at prices above their marginal costs, though they could still make an adequate profit by selling at lower prices. It is this that those object to who regard the condition of perfect competition as the standard. They contend that producers in such conditions ought to be made to act as if perfect competition existed, although their self-interest will not lead them to do so. But we rely on self-interest because only through it can we induce producers to use knowledge which we do not possess, and to take actions the effects of which only they can determine. We cannot at the same time rely on their self-interest to find the most economical method of production and not allow them to produce the kinds and quantities of goods by the methods which best serve their interest. The inducement to improve the manner of production will often consist in the fact that whoever does so first will thereby gain a temporary profit. Many of the improvements of production are due to each striving for such profits even though he knows that they will only be temporary and last only so long as he leads.

If the future costs of production of any producer (and particularly his marginal costs of any additional quantity produced) were an objectively ascertainable magnitude which could unambiguously be determined by a supervising authority, it might be meaningful to demand that producers should be made to sell at marginal costs. But, though we are in the habit of arguing in theory as if costs were a 'datum', that is, given knowledge, the lowest costs at which a thing can be produced are exactly what we want competition to discover. They are not necessarily known to anyone but to him who has succeeded in discovering them—and even he will often not be aware what it is that enables him to produce more cheaply than others can.

It is, therefore, generally also not possible for an outsider to establish objectively whether a large excess of price over costs, manifesting itself in high profits and due to some improvement in technique or organization, is merely an 'adequate' return on investment. 'Adequate' in this connection must mean a return the expectation of which was sufficient to justify the risk incurred. In technologically advanced production the cost of a particular product will quite generally not be an objectively ascertainable fact, but will in a large measure depend on the opinion of the producer about probable future developments. The success of the individual enterprise and its long-run efficiency will depend on the degree of correctness of the expectations which are reflected in the entrepreneur's estimate of costs.

Whether a firm that has made large investments in improving its plant should at once extend production to the point where prices will fall to its new marginal costs will thus depend on judgment about the probability of future developments. It clearly is desirable that some investment in new and more efficient plant should be undertaken that will be profitable only if for some time after they come into operation prices will remain above the cost of operating the already existing plant. The construction of a new plant will only be justified if it is expected that the prices at which the product can be sold will remain sufficiently above marginal costs to provide not only amortization of the capital sunk in it but also to compensate for the risk of creating it. Who can say how great this risk did appear, or ought to have appeared, to those who in the first instance made the decision to build the plant? It would clearly make the running of such risks impossible if, after the venture had proved successful, the firm were required to reduce prices to what would then appear as its long-run marginal costs. Competitive improvement of productive techniques rests largely on the endeavour of each to gain temporary monopolistic profits so long as he leads; and it is in a great measure out of such profits that the successful obtain the capital for further improvements.

Nor is it unreasonable that in such situations some of the benefits which the producers could offer to the consumers will still be served better by the producer with the new equipment than by anybody else, and that is all we can demand so long as we rely on his use of his knowledge. Not to do as well as one could cannot be treated as an offence in a free society in which each is allowed to choose the manner of employing his person and property.

Quite apart from the practical difficulty of ascertaining whether

71

such a *de facto* monopolist does extend his production to the point at which prices will only just cover marginal costs, it is by no means clear that to require him to do so could be reconciled with the general principles of just conduct on which the market order rests. So far as his monopoly is a result of his superior skill or of the possession of some factor of production uniquely suitable for the product in question, this would hardly be equitable. At least so long as we allow persons possessing special skills or unique objects not to use them at all, it would be paradoxical that as soon as they use them for commercial purposes, they should be required to use them to the greatest possible extent. We have no more justification for prescribing how intensively anyone must use his skill or his possessions than we have for prohibiting him from using his skill for solving crossword puzzles or his capital for acquiring a collection of postage stamps. Where the source of a monopoly position is a unique skill, it would be absurd to punish the possessor for doing better than anyone else by insisting that he should do as well as he can. And even where the monopoly position is the result of the possession of some object conferring a unique advantage, such as a particular site, it would seem hardly any less absurd to allow somebody to use for his private swimming pool a spring of water which would provide unique advantages for a brewery or whisky distillery, and then, once he turns it to such purpose, insist that he must not make a monopoly profit from it.

The power to determine the price or the quality of a product at the figure most profitable to the owner of such a rare resource used in its production is a necessary consequence of the recognition of private property in particular things, and cannot be eliminated without abandoning the institution of private property. There is in this respect no difference between a manufacturer or merchant who has built up a unique organization, or acquired a uniquely suitable site, and a painter who limits his output to what will bring him the largest income. There exists no more an argument in justice, or a moral case, against such a monopolist making a monopoly profit than there is against anyone who decides that he will work no more than he finds worth his while.

We shall see that the situation is wholly different where 'market power' consists in a power of preventing others from serving the customers better. In certain circumstances it is true that even the power over prices, etc. may confer upon a monopolist the power of influencing the market behaviour of others in a manner which protects him against unwelcome competition. We shall see that in such cases there is indeed a strong argument for preventing him from doing so.

Sometimes, however, the appearance of a monopoly (or of an obligopoly) may even be a desirable result of competition, that is, competition will have done its best when, for the time being, it has led to a monopoly. Although, except in a special case which we shall consider later, production is not likely to be more efficient *because* it is conducted by a monopoly, it will often be conducted most effectively by one particular enterprise that for some special reason is more efficient than other existing ones.[3] While this does not provide a justification for protecting monopolistic positions or assisting their preservation, it makes it desirable not only to tolerate monopolies but even to allow them to exploit their monopolistic positions—so long as they maintain them solely by serving their customers better than anyone else, and not by preventing those who think they could do still better from trying to do so. So long as any producer is in a monopoly position because he can produce at costs lower than anybody else can, and sells at prices which are lower than those which anybody else can sell, that is all we can hope to achieve—even though we can in theory conceive of a better use of resources which, however, we have no way of realizing.

If such a position appears objectionable to many people this is chiefly due to the false suggestion of the word monopoly that it constitutes a privilege. But the bare fact that one producer (or a few producers) can meet the demand at prices which nobody else can match, does not constitute a privilege so long as the inability of others to do the same is not due to their being prevented from trying. The term privilege is used legitimately only to describe a right conferred by special decree (*privi-legium*) which others do not have, and not for an objective possibility which circumstances offer to some but not others.

So far as monopoly does not rest on privilege in the strict sense, it is indeed always objectionable when it depends on people being prevented from trying to do better than others. But those monopolies or obligopolies of which we have spoken in this section do not rest upon any such discrimination. They rest on the fact that men and things are not perfectly alike and that often a few or even only one of them will possess certain advantages over all others. We know how to induce such individuals or organizations to serve their fellows better than anyone else can do. But we have no means of always making them serve the public as well as they could.

The achievements of the free market

What, then, is it that we want competition to bring about and which it normally does bring about if it is not prevented from doing so? It is a result so simple and obvious that most of us are inclined to take it for granted; and we are wholly unaware that it is a remarkable thing which is brought about and which never could be achieved by any authority telling the individual producer what to do. Competition, if not prevented, tends to bring about a state of affairs in which: *first*, everything will be produced which somebody knows how to produce and which he can sell profitably at a price at which buyers will prefer it to the available alternatives; *second*, everything that is being produced is produced by persons who can do so at least as cheaply as anybody else who in fact is not producing it;[4] and *third*, that everything will be sold at prices lower than, or at least as low as, those at which it could be sold by anybody who in fact does not do so.

There are three points which have to be considered if one wants to see the significance of such a state in its proper light: first, that this is a state of affairs which no central direction could ever bring about; second, that this state is approached remarkably closely in all fields where competition is not prevented by government or where governments do not tolerate such prevention by private persons or organizations; third, that in very large sectors of economic activity this state has never been closely approached because governments have restricted competition or allowed and often assisted private persons or organizations to restrict competition.

Modest as these accomplishments of competition may at first appear, the fact is that we do not know of any other method that would bring about better results; and wherever competition is prevented or impeded the conditions for their achievement are usually very far from being satisfied. Considering that competition has always been prevented in many fields by the deliberate policies of government from achieving this, while the result is very closely approximated wherever competition is allowed to operate, we should certainly be more concerned to make it generally possible than to make it operate in accordance with an unachievable standard of 'perfection'.

To what a great extent in a normally functioning society the result described is in fact achieved in all sectors where competition is not prevented is demonstrated by the difficulty of discovering opportunities for making a living by serving the customers better than is already being done. We know only too well how difficult this in fact is and how much ingenuity is needed in a functioning catallaxy to discover such opportunities.[5] It is also instructive to compare in this respect the situation in a country which possesses a large commercially alert class, where most of the existing opportunities will have been taken advantage of, and in a country where people are less versatile or enterprising and which in consequence will often offer to one with a different outlook great opportunities for rapid gain.[6] The important point here is that a highly developed commercial spirit is itself as much the product as the condition of effective competition, and that we know of no other method of producing it than to throw competition open to all who want to take advantage of the opportunities it offers.

Competition and rationality

Competition is not merely the only method which we know for utilizing the knowledge and skills that other people may possess, but it is also the method by which we all have been led to acquire much of the knowledge and skills we do possess. This is not understood by those who maintain that the argument for competition rests on the assumption of rational behaviour of those who take part in it. But rational behaviour is not a premise of economic theory, though it is often presented as such. The basic contention of theory is rather that competition will make it necessary for people to act rationally in order to maintain themselves. It is based not on the assumption that most or all the participants in the market process are rational, but, on the contrary, on the assumption that it will in general be through competition that a few relatively more rational individuals will make it necessary for the rest to emulate them in order to prevail.[7] In a society in which rational behaviour confers an advantage on the individual, rational methods will progressively be developed and be spread by imitation. It is no use being more rational than the rest if one is not allowed to derive benefits from being so. And it is therefore in general not rationality which is required to make competition work, but competition, or traditions which allow competition, which will produce rational behaviour.[8] The endeavour to do better than can be done in the customary manner is the process in which that capacity for thinking is developed which will later manifest itself in argument and criticism. No society which has not first developed a commercial group within which the improvement of the tools of thought has brought advantage to the individual has ever gained the capacity of systematic rational thinking.

This should be remembered particularly by those who are inclined to argue that competition will not work among people who lack the spirit of enterprise: let merely a few rise and be esteemed and powerful because they have successfully tried new ways, even if they may be in the first instance foreign intruders, and let those tempted to imitate them be free to do so, however few they may be in the first instance, and that spirit of enterprise will emerge by the only method which can produce it. Competition is as much a method for breeding certain types of mind as anything else: the very cast of thinking of the great entrepreneurs would not exist but for the environment in which they developed their gifts. The same innate capacity to think will take a wholly different turn according to the task it is set.

Such a development will be possible only if the traditionalist majority does not have power to make compulsory for everyone those traditional manners and mores which would prevent the experimentation with new ways inherent in competition. This means that the powers of the majority must be limited to the enforcement of such general rules as will prevent the individuals from encroaching on the protected domains of their fellows, and should not extend to positive prescriptions of what the individuals must do. If the majority view, or any *one* view, is made generally to prevail concerning how things must be done, such developments as we have sketched by which the more rational procedures gradually replace the less rational ones become impossible. The intellectual growth of a community rests on the views of a few gradually spreading, even to the disadvantage of those who are reluctant to accept them; and though nobody should have the power to force upon them new views because he thinks they are better, if success proves that they are more effective, those who stick to their old ways must not be protected against a relative or even absolute decline in their position. Competition is, after all, always a process in which a small number makes it necessary for larger numbers to do what they do not like, be it to work harder, to change habits, or to devote a degree of attention, continuous application, or regularity to their work which without competition would not be needed.

If in a society in which the spirit of enterprise has not yet spread, the majority has power to prohibit whatever it dislikes, it is most unlikely that it will allow competition to arise. I doubt whether a functioning market has ever newly arisen under an unlimited democracy, and it seems at least likely that unlimited democracy will destroy it where it has grown up. To those with whom others compete, the fact that they have competitors is always a nuisance that prevents a quiet life; and such direct effects of competition are always much more visible than the indirect benefits which we derive from it. In particular, the direct effects will be felt by the members of the same trade who see how competition is operating, while the consumer will generally have little idea to whose actions the reduction of prices or the improvement of quality is due.

Size, concentration and power

The misleading emphasis on the influence of the individual firm on prices, in combination with the popular prejudice against bigness as such, with various 'social' considerations supposed to make it desirable to preserve the middle class, the independent entrepreneur, the small craftsman or shopkeeper, or quite generally the existing structure of society, has acted against changes caused by economic and technological development. The 'power' which large corporations can exercise is represented as in itself dangerous and as making necessary special governmental measures to restrict it. This concern about size and power of individual corporations more often than perhaps any other consideration produces essentially .antiliberal conclusions drawn from liberal premises.

We shall presently see that there are two important respects in which monopoly may confer on its possessor harmful power. But neither size in itself, nor ability to determine the prices at which all can buy their product is a measure of their harmful power. More important still, there is no possible measure or standard by which we can decide whether a particular enterprise is too large. Certainly the bare fact that one big firm in a particular industry 'dominates' the market because the other firms of the industry will follow its price leadership, is no proof that this position can in fact be improved upon in any way other than by the appearance of an effective competitor—an event which we may hope for, but which we cannot bring about so long as nobody is available who does enjoy the same (or other compensating) special advantages as the firm that is now dominant.

The most effective size of the individual firm is as much one of the unknowns to be discovered by the market process as the prices, quantities or qualities of the goods to be produced and sold. There can be no general rule about what is the desirable size since this will depend on the ever-changing technological and economic conditions; and there will always be many changes which will give advantages to enterprises of what on past standards will appear to be an excessive size. It is not to be denied that the advantages of the size will not always rest on facts which we cannot alter, such as the scarcity of certain kinds of talents or resources (including such accidental and yet unavoidable facts as that somebody has been earlier in the field and therefore has had more time to acquire experience and special knowledge); they will often be determined by institutional arrangements which happen to give an advantage to size which is artificial in the sense that it does not secure smaller social costs of the unit of output. In so far as tax legislation, the law of corporations, or the greater influence on the administrative machinery of government, give to the larger unit differential advantages which are not based on genuine superiority of performance, there is indeed every reason for so altering the framework as to remove such artificial advantages of bigness. But there is as little justification for discrimination by policy against large size as such as there is for assisting it.

The argument that mere size confers harmful power over the market behaviour of competitors possesses a degree of plausibility when we think in terms of one 'industry' within which there may indeed sometimes be room only for one specialised big firm. But the growth of the giant corporation has made largely meaningless the conception of separate industries which one corporation, because of the magnitude of its resources, can dominate. One of the unforeseen results of the increase of size of the individual corporations which the theorists have not yet quite digested is that large size has brought diversification far beyond the bounds of any definable industry. In consequence, the size of the corporations in other industries has become the main check on the power which size might give a single large corporation in one industry. It may well be that, say in the electrical industry of one country, no other corporation has the strength or staying power to 'take on' an established giant intent upon defending its *de facto* monopoly of some of the products. But as the development of the great automobile or chemical concerns in the USA shows, they have no compunction about encroaching on such fields in which the backing of large resources is essential to make the prospects of entry promising. Size has thus become the most effective antidote to the power of size: what will control the power of large aggregations of capital are other large aggregations of capital, and such control will be much more effective than any supervision by government, whose permission of an act carries its authorization, if not outright protection. As I cannot repeat too often, government-supervised monopoly always tends to become government-protected monopoly; and the fight against bigness only too often results in preventing those very developments through which size becomes the antidote of size.

I do not intend to deny that there are real social and political (as distinct from merely economic) considerations which make a large number of small enterprises appear as more desirable or 'healthy' structures than a smaller number of large ones. We have already had occasion to refer to the danger arising from the fact that constantly increasing numbers of the population work in ever larger corporations, and as a result are familiar with the organizational type of order but strangers to the working of the market which co-ordinates the activities of the several corporations. Considerations like this are often advanced in justification of measures designed to curb the growth of individual enterprise or to protect the less efficient smaller firms against their displacement or absorption into a big one.

Yet, even granting that such measures might in some sense be desirable, it is one of those things which, even though in themselves desirable, cannot be achieved without conferring a discretionary and arbitrary power on some authority, and which therefore must give way to the higher consideration that no authority should be given such power. We have already stressed that such a limitation on all power may make impossible the achievement of some particular aims which may be desired by a majority of the people, and that generally, to avoid greater evils, a free society must deny itself certain kinds of power even if the foreseeable consequences of its exercise appear only beneficial and constitute perhaps the only available method of achieving that particular result.

The political aspects of economic power

The argument that the great size of an individual corporation confers great power on its management, and that such power of a few men is politically dangerous and morally objectionable, certainly deserves serious consideration. Its persuasiveness derives, however, in a great measure from a confusion of the different meanings of the word 'power', and from a constant shifting from one of the senses in which the possession of great power is desirable to another in which it is objectionable: power over material things and power over the conduct of other men. These two kinds of power are not necessarily connected and can to a large extent be separated. It is one of the ironies of history that socialism, which gained influence by promising the substitution of the administration of things for the power over men, inevitably leads to an unbounded increase of the power exercised by men over other men.

So long as large aggregations of material resources make it possible to achieve better results in terms of improved or cheaper products or more desirable services than smaller organizations provide, every extension of this kind of power must be regarded as in itself beneficial. The fact that large aggregations of resources under a single direction often increase power of this kind more than in proportion to size is often the reason for the development of very large enterprises. Although size is not an advantage in every respect, and though there will always be a limit to the increase of size which still brings an increase of productivity, there will at all times exist fields in which technological change gives an advantage to units larger than those which have existed before. From the replacement of the cottage weaver by the factory to the growth of the continuous process in steel production and to the supermarket, advances in technological knowledge have again and again made larger units more efficient. But if such increase in size leads to more effective use of resources, it does not necessarily increase the power over the conduct of the people, except the limited power which the head of an enterprise wields over those who join it for their benefit. Even though a mail-order house like Sears Roebuck & Co. has grown to be one of the 100 largest corporations in the world and far exceeds in size any comparable enterprise, and although its activities have profoundly affected the standards and habits of millions, it cannot be said to exercise power in any sense other than that of offering services which people prefer when they become available. Nor would a single corporation gain power over the conduct of other men if it were so efficient in the production of a piece of mechanical equipment as universally employed as, say, ball bearings, that it would drive out all competition: so long as it stood ready to supply everyone awaiting its product on the same terms, even though it thereby made a huge profit, not only would all its customers be better off for its existence, but they could also not be said to be dependent on its power.

In modern society it is not the size of the aggregate of resources controlled by an enterprise which gives it power over the conduct of other people, so much as its capacity to withhold services on which people are dependent. As we shall see in the next section, it is therefore also not only simply power over the price of their products but the power to exact different terms from different customers which confers power over conduct. This power, however, is not directly dependent on size and not even an inevitable product of monopoly—although it will be possessed by the monopolist of any essential product, whether he be big or small, so long as he is free to make a sale dependent on terms not exacted from all customers alike. We shall see that it is not only the power of the monopolist to discriminate, together with the influence he may exercise on government possessing similar powers, which is truly harmful and ought to be curbed. But this power, although often associated with large size, is neither a necessary consequence of size nor confined to large organizations. The same problem arises when some small enterprise, or a labour union, which controls an essential service can hold the community to ransom by refusing to supply it.

Before we consider further the problem of checking these harmful actions of monopolists we must, however, consider some other reasons why size as such is often regarded as harmful.

The fact that the welfare of many more people is affected by the decisions of a big enterprise rather than by those of a small one does not mean that other considerations should enter into those decisions, or that it is desirable or possible in the case of the former to safeguard against mistakes by some sort of public supervision. Much of the resentment against the big corporations is due to the

81

belief that they do not take consequences into account which we think that they could because they are big, although a smaller firm admittedly could not do so: if a large concern closes down an unprofitable local plant, there will be an outcry because it 'could have afforded' to run it at a loss in order to preserve the jobs, while if the same plant had been an independent enterprise everybody would accept its closing down as inevitable. It is, however, no less desirable that an uneconomical plant be closed down if it belongs to a large concern, although it could be kept going out of the profits of the rest of the concern, than if it is an enterprise which cannot draw on such other sources of revenue.

There exists a widespread feeling that a big corporation, because it is big, should take more account of the indirect consequences of its decisions, and that it should be required to assume responsibilities not imposed upon smaller ones. But it is precisely here that there lies the danger of a big enterprise acquiring objectionably large powers. So long as the management has the one overriding duty of administering the resources under its control as trustees for the shareholders and for their benefit, its hands are largely tied; and it will have no arbitrary power to benefit this or that particular interest. But once the management of a big enterprise is regarded as not only entitled but even obliged to consider in its decisions whatever is regarded as the public or social interest, or to support good causes and generally to act for the public benefit, it gains indeed an uncontrollable power—a power which could not long be left in the hands of private managers but would inevitably be made the subject of increasing public control.[9]

In so far as corporations have power to benefit groups of individuals, mere size will also become a source of influencing government, and thus beget power of a very objectionable kind. We shall see presently that such influence, much more serious when it is exerted by the organized interests of groups than when exerted by the largest single enterprise, can be guarded against only by depriving government of the power of benefiting particular groups.

We must finally mention another instance in which it is undeniable that the mere fact of bigness creates a highly undesirable position: namely where, because of the consequences of what happens to a big enterprise, government cannot afford to let such an enterprise fail. At least in so far as the expectation that it will thus be protected makes investment in very big corporations appear less risky than investment in smaller ones, this will produce one of the 'artificial' advantages of bigness which are not based on better performance and which policy ought to eliminate. It seems clear that this can be done only by effectively depriving government of the power of providing such protection, for as long as it has such power it is vulnerable to pressure.

The chief point to remember, which is often obscured by the current talk about monopoly, is that it is not monopoly as such but only the prevention of competition which is harmful. These are so very far from being the same thing that it ought to be repeated that a monopoly that rests entirely on superior performance is wholly praiseworthy—even if such a monopolist keeps prices at a level at which he makes large profits and only just low enough to make it impossible for others to compete with him successfully, because he still uses a smaller amount of resources than others would do if they produced the same quantity of the product. Nor can there be a legitimate claim that such a monopolist is under a moral obligation to sell his product as cheaply as he still could while making a 'normal' profit—as little as we are under a moral obligation to work as hard as possible, or to sell a rare object at a moderate gain. Just as nobody dreams of attacking the 'monopoly' price of the unique skill of an artist or surgeon, so there is no wrong in the 'monopoly' profit of an enterprise capable of producing more cheaply than anybody else.

That it is not monopoly but only the prevention of competition (and all prevention of competition, whether it leads to monopoly or not) which is morally wrong should be specially remembered by those 'neo-liberals' who believe that they must show their impartiality by thundering against all enterprise monopoly as much as against labour monopolies, forgetting that much enterprise monopoly is the result of better performance, while all labour monopoly is due to the coercive suppression of competition. Where enterprise monopoly is based on a similar prevention of competition, it is as reprehensible and in as much need of prevention as those of labour and ought to be severely dealt with. But neither the existence of monopoly nor size as such are on economic or moral grounds undesirable or comparable with any acts aiming at the prevention of competition.

When monopoly becomes harmful

We leave out here deliberately one model case in which it must be admitted that monopolies are likely to arise—the case of scarce and exhaustible resources such as the deposits of certain ores and the like. The reason for the omission is that the problems which arise in this connection are much too complex for any brief discussion to be useful. We need merely note that this one case in which the development of a monopoly may be inevitable is also a case in which it is by no means clear that a monopoly is harmful, since such a monopoly is likely only to spread over a longer period the exploitation of the resource in question, but not to lead to any permanent withholding of goods or services at the expense of the total output.

Quite generally it can probably be said that what is harmful is not the existence of monopolies that are due to greater efficiency or to the control of particular limited resources, but the ability of some monopolies to protect and preserve their monopolistic position after the original cause of their superiority has disappeared. The main reason for this is that such monopolies will be able to use their power, not only over the prices which they charge uniformly to all, but over the prices which it can charge to particular customers. This power over the prices they will charge particular customers, or the power to discriminate, can in many ways be used to influence the market behaviour of these others, and particularly to deter or otherwise influence potential competitors.

It is probably not much of an exaggeration to say that almost all really harmful power of non-privileged monopolies rests on this power of discrimination because it alone, short of violence, gives them power over potential competitors. So long as a monopolist enjoys a monopolistic position because he offers to all better terms than anybody else can, even if these terms are not as favourable as those he could offer, everybody is better off for his existence. But if, because he can supply most people at better terms than anyone else, no other firm is ready to supply the product in question, anyone to whom he refuses to supply at those terms will have no alternative opportunity to satisfy his needs. Though the majority of the people may still be better off for the existence of such a monopolist, anyone may be at his mercy in so far as the nature of the product or service makes aimed discrimination possible and the monopolist chooses to practice it in order to make the buyer behave in some respect in a manner that suits the monopolist. He can, in particular, use this power to keep out a potential competitor by offering specially favourable terms to customers only in that limited region in which a newcomer at first will be able to compete.

The task of preventing such use of discrimination is especially difficult because certain kinds of discrimination by a monopolist will often be desirable. We have already mentioned that there is one case in which a monopolist may render better services *because* he is a monopolist. This is the case where his power to discriminate between different users of his product enables him to cover most of his fixed costs from those who can pay a relatively higher price and then to supply others at little more than variable costs. In such fields as transport and public utilities it is at least possible that some services could not be supplied at all at a profit if it were not for the possibility of discrimination such as monopoly confers.

The problem can therefore not be solved by imposing upon all monopolists the obligation to serve all customers alike. Yet since the power of the monopolist to discriminate can be used to coerce particular individuals or firms, and is likely to be used to restrict competition in an undesirable manner, it clearly ought to be curbed by appropriate rules of conduct. Though it would not be desirable to make all discrimination illegal, aimed discrimination intended to enforce a certain market conduct should clearly be prohibited. It is doubtful, however, whether it would be effectively achieved by making it a punishable offence rather than merely the basis of a claim for damages. The knowledge required here in order to prosecute successfully is not the kind of knowledge that any authority is likely to possess.

The problem of anti-monopoly legislation

It would seem more promising to give potential competitors a claim to equal treatment where discrimination cannot be justified on grounds other than the desire to enforce a particular market conduct, and to hold out an inducement for enforcing such claims in the form of multiple damages to all who feel they have been unreasonably discriminated against. Thus to set potential competitors as watchdogs over the monopolist and to give them a remedy against the use of price discrimination would seem a more promising check on such practices than to place enforcement in the hands of a supervising authority. Particularly if the law explicitly authorized that a part of the damages awarded might be collected by the lawyers conducting such cases, in lieu of fees and expenses, highly specialized legal consultants would probably soon grow up who, since they would owe the whole of their business to such suits, would not be inhibited through fear of offending the big corporations.

The same applies largely to the case where not a single monopolist but small groups of firms acting in concert to control the market are concerned. It is generally thought necessary to prohibit such monopolistic combinations or cartels by prohibiting them under penalties. The example set in the USA by Section One of the Sherman Act 1890 has been widely imitated. It seems also that this provision of the Act has been remarkably successful in creating in the business world a climate of opinion which regards as improper such explicit agreements to restrict competition. I have no doubt that such a general prohibition of all cartels, if it were consistently carried through, would be preferable to any discretionary power given to authorities for the purpose of merely preventing 'abuses'. The latter leads to a distinction between good and bad monopolies and usually to governments becoming more concerned with protecting the good monopolies than with combating the bad ones. There is no reason to believe that any monopolistic organization deserves protection against threatening competition, and much reason to believe that some wholly voluntary organizations of firms that do not rely on compulsion are not only not harmful but actually beneficial. It would seem that prohibition under penalties cannot be carried out without a discretionary power of granting exemptions, or of imposing upon courts the difficult task of deciding whether a particular agreement is, or is not, in the public interest. Even in the USA, under the Sherman Act and its various amendments and supplements, a situation has in consequence arisen of which it could be said that 'the law tells some businessmen that they must not cut prices, others that they must not raise prices, and still others that there is something evil in similar prices'.[10] It seems to me; therefore, that a third possibility, less far-reaching than prohibition under penalties, but more general than discretionary surveillance to prevent abuses, would be both more effective and more in conformity with the rule of law than either. This would be to declare invalid and legally unenforceable all agreement in restraint of trade, without any exceptions, and to prevent all attempts to enforce them by aimed discrimination or the like by giving those upon whom such pressures were brought a claim for multiple damages as suggested above.

We need not here again consider the misconception that this would be contrary to the principle of freedom of contract. Freedom of contract, like any other freedom, means merely that what kind of contract is enforceable in the courts depends only on the general rules of law and not on the previous approval by authority of the particular contents of the contract. Many kinds of contracts, such as gambling contracts, or contracts for immoral purposes, or contracts for life-long service, have long been held invalid and unenforceable. There is no reason why the same should not also apply to all contracts in restraint of trade, and no reason why all attempts to make someone, by the threat of withholding usual services, conform to certain rules of conduct should not be treated as unwarranted interference in this private domain which entitles him to damages. The practical solution of our problem may be much facilitated by the necessity which, as we shall see later, will arise of imposing special limitations upon the power of 'legal persons' (corporations and all other formal or informal organizations) which do not apply to private individuals.

The reason why such a modest aim of the law seems to me to promise greater results is that it can be applied universally without exceptions, while all the more ambitious attempts are generally emasculated by so many exceptions that they become not nearly so effective than the general application of a less far-reaching rule would be—not to mention the wholly undesirable discretionary power which, under the first system confers on government the power of determining the character of economic activity.

There is probably no better illustration of the failure of the more ambitious attempt than the German Federal Republic's law against restriction of competition.[11] It begins with a sweeping provision which, wholly in the sense of what has been suggested, declares as invalid all agreements in restraint of competition. But after it has also made such agreements a punishable offence, it ends up by perforating the general rule with so many exceptions, which wholly exempt various kinds of contracts, or confer upon authorities discretionary powers to permit them, and finally confines the application of the law to such a limited sector of the economy, that it deprives the whole of most of its effectiveness. There would have been no need for most of if not for all of these exceptions if the law had confined itself to what it provided in the first paragraph and had not added to the declaration of the invalidity of agreements in restraint of trade a prohibition under penalties.

As there exist undoubtedly all kinds of understandings on standards and the like which are to apply unless other terms are explicitly agreed upon in the particular instances, and which are wholly beneficial so long as adherence to them is purely voluntary and no pressure can be brought on those who find it in their interest to divert from them, any outright prohibition of such agreements would be harmful. Both as regards types of products and terms of the contract the establishment of such norms as it would be in the interest of most to observe in ordinary instances would produce considerable economies. In such instances it will, however, be not so much that the norm is obligatory as that it pays the individual to adhere to an established standard practice which will bring about his conformity. The necessary check on such agreements on standards becoming obstructive will be provided by any individual firms being free explicitly to deviate from the norm in making a contract whenever this is to the interest of both parties to the contract.

Before leaving this particular subject a few words may be added on the curiously contradictory attitude of most governments towards monopoly. While in recent times they have generally endeavoured to control monopolies in the production and distribution of manufactured goods, and have in this field often applied overly rigorous standards, they have at the same time in much larger fields—in transport, public utilities, labour, agriculture, and, in many countries, also finance—deliberately assisted monopoly or used it as an instrument of policy. Also, the anti-cartel or anti-trust legislation has mostly been aimed at the combination of a few big firms and has rarely effectively touched the restrictive practices of the large groups of smaller firms organized in trade associations and the like. If we add to this the extent to which monopolies have been assisted by tariffs, industrial patents, some features of the law of corporations and the principles of taxation, one may well ask whether, if government had merely refrained from favouring monopolies, monopoly would ever have been a serious problem. Though I do believe that it should be one of the aims of the development of law to reduce private power over the market conduct of others, and that some beneficial results would follow from this, it does not appear to me that this compares in importance with what could be achieved by government refraining from assisting monopoly by discriminatory rules or measures of policy.

Not individual but group selfishness is the chief threat

While public indignation and in consequence also legislation has been directed almost entirely against the selfish actions of single monopolists, or of a few conspicuous enterprises acting in concert, what is chiefly threatening to destroy the market order is not the selfish action of individual firms but the selfishness of organized groups. These have gained their power largely through the assistance government has given them to suppress those manifestations of individual selfishness which would have kept their action in check. The extent to which the functioning of the market order has already been impeded, and threatens to become progressively more inoperative, is a result not so much of the rise of large productive units as of the deliberately furthered organization of the units for collective interests. What is increasingly suspending the working of the spontaneous forces of the market is not what the public has in mind when it complains about monopolies, but the ubiquitous associations and unions of the different 'trades'. They operate largely through the pressure they can bring on government to 'regulate' the market in their interest.

It was a misfortune that these problems became acute for the first time in connection with labour unions when widespread sympathy with their aims led to the toleration of methods which certainly could not be generally permitted, and which even in the field of labour will have to be curbed, though most workers have come to regard them as their hard-earned and sacred rights. One need merely ask what the results would be if the same techniques were generally used for political instead of economic purposes (as indeed they sometimes already are) in order to see that they are irreconcilable with the preservation of what we know as a free society.

The very term 'freedom of organization', hallowed by its use as a battle cry not only by labour but also by those political organizations which are indispensable for democratic government, carries overtones which are not in accord but in conflict with the reign of law on which a free society rests. Certainly any control of these activities through a discretionary supervision by government would be incompatible with a free order. But 'freedom of organization' should no more than 'freedom of contract' be interpreted to mean that the activities of organizations must not be subject to rules restricting their methods, or even that the collective

89

action of organizations should not be restricted by rules which do not apply to individuals. The new powers created by the perfection of organizational techniques, and by the right conceded to them by existing laws, will probably require limitations by general rules of law far more narrow than those it has been found necessary to impose by law on the actions of private individuals.

It is easy to see why the weak individual will often derive comfort from the knowledge that he is a member of an organized group comprising individuals with common aims and which, as an organized group, is stronger than the strongest individual. It is an illusion, however, to believe that he would benefit, or that generally the many will benefit at the expense of the few, if all interests were so organized. The effect of such organization on society as a whole would be to make power not less but more oppressive. Though groups may then count for more than individuals, small groups may still be more powerful than large ones, simply because the former are more organizable, or the whole of their produce more indispensable than the whole of the produce of larger groups. And even though to the individual his single most important interest may be enhanced by joining an organization, this single most important interest that is organizable may still be less important to him than the sum of all his other interests which will be encroached upon by other organizations and which he himself cannot defend by joining a corresponding number of other organizations.

The importance attached and the respect paid to the collective bodies is a result of an understandable though erroneous belief that the larger the group becomes the more its interests will correspond to the interest of all. The term 'collective' has become invested with much the same aura of approval which the term 'social' commands. But far from the collective interests of the various groups being nearer to the interests of society as a whole, the exact opposite is true. While as a rough approximation it can legitimately be said that individual selfishness will in most instances lead the individual to act in a manner conducive to the preservation of the spontaneous order of society, the selfishness of a closed group, or the desire of its members to become a closed group, will always be in opposition to the true common interest of the members of a Great Society.[12]

That is what classical economics had already clearly brought out and modern marginal analysis has put into a more satisfying form. The importance of any particular service which any individual renders to the members of society is always only that of the last (or marginal) additions he makes to all the services of that kind; and if, whatever any member of society takes out of the pool of products and services is to leave as much as possible to the others, this requires that not the groups as such but the separate individuals composing them, by their free movement between the groups, strive to make their respective incomes as large as possible. The common interest of the members of any organized group will, however, be to make the value of their services correspond, not to the importance of the last increment, but to the importance which the aggregate of the services rendered by the group has for the users. The producers of food or electrical energy, of transport or medical services, etc., will therefore aim to use their joint power of determining the volume of such services to achieve a price that will be much higher than that which the consumers would be prepared to pay for the last increment. There exists no necessary relationship between the importance of a kind of commodity or service as a whole and the importance of the last addition that is still provided. If to have some food is essential for survival, this does not mean that the last addition to the supply of food is also more important than the production of an additional quantity of some frivolity, or that the production of food should be better remunerated than the production of things whose existence is certainly much less import-ant than the availability of food as such.

The special interest of the producers of food, or electricity, or transport, or medical services will be, however, to be remunerated not merely according to the marginal value of the kind of services they render, but according to the value that the total supply of the services in question has to the users. Public opinion, which still sees the problem in terms of the importance of this kind of service as such, therefore tends to give some support to such demands because it is felt that remuneration should be appropriate to the absolute importance of the commodity in question. It is only through the efforts of the marginal producers who can earn a living by rendering their services much below the value which the consumers would be prepared to pay if the total supply were smaller, that we are assured of plenty and that the chances of all are improved. The collective interests of the organized groups, on the other hand, will always be opposed to this general interest and aim at preventing those marginal individuals from adding to the total supply.

Any control wielded by the members of a trade or profession over the total amount of goods or services to be supplied will therefore always be opposed to the true general interest of society, while the selfish interests of the individual will normally drive them to make those marginal contributions which will cost approximately as much as the price at which they can be sold.

It is a wholly mistaken conception that a bargaining between groups in which the producers and the consumers of each of the different commodities or services respectively are combined would lead to a state of affairs which secures either efficiency in production or a kind of distribution which from any point of view would appear to be just. Even if all the separate interests (or even all 'important' interests) could be organized (which, as we shall see, they cannot), the sort of balance between the strengths of different organized groups which some people expect as the necessary or even desirable outcome of the developments which have been going on for some time, would in fact produce a structure which would be demonstrably irrational and inefficient, and unjust to the extreme in the light of any test of justice which requires a treatment of all according to the same rules.

The decisive reason for this is that in negotiations between existing organized groups the interests of those who bring about the required adjustments to changes, namely those who could improve their position by moving from one group to another, are systematically disregarded. So far as the group to which they wish to move is concerned, it will be its chief aim to keep them out. And the groups they wish to leave will have no incentive to assist their entry into what will often be a great variety of other groups. Thus, in a system in which the organizations of the existing producers of the various commodities and services determine prices and quantities to be produced, those who would bring about the continuous adjustment to change would be deprived of influence on events. It is not true, as the argument in support of the various syndicalist or corporativist systems assumes, that anybody's interest is bound up with the interest of all others who produce the same goods. It may be much more important to some to be able to shift to another group, and these movements are certainly most important for the preservation of the overall order. Yet it is these changes which, possible in a free market, agreements between organized groups will aim to prevent.

The organized producers of particular commodities or services will in general attempt to justify the exclusive policies by pleading that they can still meet the whole demand, and that, if and when they are not able to do so, they will be fully prepared to let others enter the trade. What they do not say is that this means merely that they can meet the demand at prevailing prices which give them what they regard as adequate profits. What is desirable, however, is that the demand be satisfied at the lower prices at which others might be able to supply—leaving those now in the trade perhaps only an income reflecting the fact that their particular skill is no longer scarce, or their equipment no longer up-to-date. In particular, though it should be as profitable for those in possession to introduce improvements in technique as it is for any newcomers, this will involve for the former risks and often the necessity of raising outside capital which will disturb their comfortable established position and seem not worth while unless their position is threatened by those not content with theirs. To allow the established producers to decide when new entrants are to be permitted would normally lead simply to the *status quo* being preserved.

Even in a society in which all the different interests were organized as separate closed groups, this would therefore lead merely to a freezing of the existing structure and as a result, to a gradual decline of the economy as it became progressively less adjusted to the changed conditions. It is therefore not true that such a system is unsatisfactory and unjust only so long as not all groups are equally organized. The belief of such authors as G. Myrdal and J. K. Galbraith[13] that the defects of the existing order are only those of a transitory kind which will be remedied when the process of organization is completed, is therefore erroneous. What makes most Western economies still viable is that the organization of interests is yet only partial and incomplete. If it were complete, we would have a deadlock between these organized interests, producing a wholly rigid economic structure which no agreement between the established interests and only the force of some dictatorial power could break.

The consequences of a political determination of the incomes of the different groups

The interest which is common to all members of a society is not the sum of the interests which are common to the members of the existing groups of producers, but only the interest in the continuous adaptation to changing conditions which some particular groups will always find it in their interests to prevent. The interest of the organized producers is therefore always contrary to the one permanent interest of all the individual members of society, namely the interest in the continuous adaptation to unpredictable changes, an adaptation necessary even if only the existing level of production is to be maintained (cf. chapters 8 and 10). The interest of organized producers is always to prevent the influx of others who want to share their prosperity or to avoid being driven out from a group by the more efficient producers when demand should decline. By this all strictly economic decisions, that is all new adjustments to unforeseen changes, will be impeded. The viability of a society, however, depends on the smooth and continuous execution of such gradual changes and their not being blocked by obstacles which can only be broken down when sufficient pressure accumulates. All the benefits we receive from the spontaneous order of the market are the results of such changes, and will be maintained only if the changes are allowed to continue. But every change of this kind will hurt some organized interests; and the preservation of the market order will therefore depend on those interests not being allowed to prevent what they dislike. All the time it is thus the interest of most that some be placed under the necessity of doing something they dislike (such as changing their jobs or accepting a lower income), and this general interest will be satisfied only if the principle is recognized that each has to submit to changes when circumstances nobody can control determine that he is the one who is placed under such a necessity. This risk itself is inseparable from the occurrence of unforeseen changes; and the only choice we have is either to allow the effects of such changes to fall, through the impersonal mechanism of the market, on the individuals whom the market will require to make the change or to accept a reduction of income, or to decide, arbitrarily or by a power struggle, who are to be those who must bear the burden which in this case will necessarily be greater than it would have been if we had let the market bring about the necessary change.

The deadlock to which the political determination of prices and wages by organized interests has already led has produced in some countries the demand for an 'incomes policy' which is to substitute an authoritative fixing of the remuneration of the different factors of production for their determination by the market. The demand is based on the recognition that if wages and other incomes are no longer determined by the market but by the political force of the organized groups, some deliberate co-ordination becomes necessary—and particularly that, if such political determination is to be effected with regard to wages, where the political determination had become most conspicuous, this would be possible to achieve only if a similar control was applied to all other incomes also.

The immediate danger which led to the demand for an 'incomes policy' was, however, the process of inflation which the competitive pressure for an increase of all incomes produced. As a means of curbing this upward movement of all money incomes, these 'incomes policies' were bound to fail. And the inflationary policies by which we are at present attempting to overcome those 'rigidities' are no more than palliatives that in the long run will not solve the problem but merely make it worse: because the temporary escape which they provide from the difficulties only allows the rigidities to grow stronger and stronger. No wage and price stop can alter the basic malaise, and every attempt to bring about the necessary alterations in relative prices by authoritative decision must fail, not only because no authority can know which prices are appropriate, but even more because such authority must, in whatever it does, endeavour to appear to be just, though the changes that will be required will have nothing whatever to do with justice. In consequence, all the measures of 'incomes policy' that have been taken have not even come near to solving the really central problem, that of restoring the process by which the relative incomes of the different groups are adjusted to changing conditions; and by treating this as a matter of political decisions they have, if anything, made matters only worse. As we have seen, the only definite content that can be given to the concept of 'social justice' is the preservation of the relative positions of the different groups; but these are what must be altered if adjustment to changed conditions is to be achieved. If change can be brought about only by political decision, the effect can only be, since there exists no basis for real agreement, an increasing rigidity of the whole economic structure.

Since Great Britain was the only big country which, at a time when a thorough readaptation of the deployment of her resources was required, found itself in the grip of extreme rigidity produced by an essentially politically determined wage structure, the resulting difficulties have come to be known as the 'English disease'. But in many other countries, where the situation is not very different, similar methods are now being tried in vain to solve the same kind of difficulties.

What is not yet generally recognized is that the real exploiters in our present society are not egotistic capitalists or entrepreneurs, and in fact not separate individuals, but organizations which derive their power from the moral support of collective action and the feeling of group loyalty. It is the built-in bias of our existing institutions in favour of organized interests which gives these organizations an artificial preponderance over the market forces and which is the main cause of real injustice in our society and of distortion of its economic structure. More real injustice is probably done in the name of group loyalty than from any selfish individual motives. Once we recognize that the degree of organizability of an interest has no relation to its importance from any social point of view, and that interests can be effectively organized only if they are in a position to exercise anti-social powers of coercion, the naive conception that, if the power of organized interests is checked by 'countervailing power',[14] this will produce a viable social order, appears as an absurdity. If by 'regulatory mechanism', of which the chief expounder of these ideas speaks, is meant a mechanism conducive to the establishment of an advantageous or rational order, 'countervailing powers' certainly produces no such mechanism. The whole conception that the power of organized interests can or will be made innocuous by 'countervailing power' constitutes a relapse into the methods of settling conflicts which once prevailed among individuals and from which the development and enforcement of rules of just conduct has gradually freed us. The problem of developing similar rules of just conduct for organized groups is still largely a problem for the future, and the main concern in the efforts to solve it will have to be the protection of the individuals against group pressure.

Organizable and non-organizable interests

During the last half century or so the dominant opinion which has guided policy has been that the growth of organized interests for the purpose of bringing pressure on government is inevitable, and that its obviously harmful effects are due to the fact that only some interests are yet so organized; this defect, it is thought, will disappear as soon as all important interests are equally organized so as to balance each other. Both views are demonstrably false. In the first instance, it is worth bringing pressure on government only if government has the power to benefit particular interests and this power exists only if it has authority to lay down and enforce aimed and discriminatory rules. In the second instance, as has been shown in an important study by M. Olson,[15] except in the case of relatively small groups, the existence of common interests will normally *not* lead to the spontaneous formation of a comprehensive organization of such interests, and has in fact done so only when government either positively assisted the efforts to organize all members of such groups, or has at least tolerated the use of coercion or discrimination to bring about such organization. It can be shown that these methods, however, can never bring about a comprehensive organization of all important interests but will always produce a condition in which the non-organizable interests will be sacrificed to and exploited by the organizable interests.

Olson's demonstration that, *first*, only relatively small groups will in general spontaneously form an organization, *second*, that the organizations of the great economic interests which today dominate government to a large extent have come about only with the help of the power of that government, and, *third*, that it is impossible in principle to organize all interests and that in consequence the organization of certain large groups assisted by government leads to a persistent exploitation of unorganized and unorganizable groups is here of fundamental importance. To the latter seem to belong such important groups as the consumers in general, the taxpayers, the women, the aged, and many others who together constitute a very substantial part of the population. All these groups are bound to suffer from the power of organized group interests.

SIXTEEN

THE MISCARRIAGE OF THE DEMOCRATIC IDEAL: A RECAPITULATION

An nescis, mi fili, quantilla prudentia regitur orbis?

Axel Oxenstjerna (1648)

The miscarriage of the democratic ideal

It is no longer possible to ignore that more and more thoughtful and well-meaning people are slowly losing their faith in what was to them once the inspiring ideal of democracy.

This is happening at the same time as, and in part perhaps in consequence of, a constant extension of the field to which the principle of democracy is being applied. But the growing doubts are clearly not confined to these obvious abuses of a political ideal: they concern its true core. Most of those who are disturbed by their loss of trust in a hope which has long guided them, wisely keep their mouths shut. But my alarm about this state makes me speak out.

It seems to me that the disillusionment which so many experience is not due to a failure of the principle of democracy as such but to our having tried it the wrong way. It is because I am anxious to rescue the true ideal from the miscredit into which it is falling that I am trying to find out the mistake we made and how we can prevent the bad consequences of the democratic procedure we have observed.

To avoid disappointment, of course, any ideal has to be approached in a sober spirit. In the case of democracy in particular we must not forget that the word refers solely to a particular method of government. It meant orginally no more than a certain procedure for arriving at political decisions, and tells us nothing about what the aims of government ought to be. Yet as the only method of peaceful change of government which men have yet discovered it is nevertheless precious and worth fighting for.

A 'bargaining' democracy

Yet it is not difficult to see why the outcome of the democratic process in its present form must bitterly disappoint those who believed in the principle that government should be guided by the opinion of the majority.

Though some claim this is now the case, it is too obviously not true to deceive observant persons. Never, indeed, in the whole of history were governments so much under the necessity of satisfying the particular wishes of numerous special interests as is true of government today. Critics of present democracy like to speak of 'mass-democracy'. But if democratic government were really bound to what the masses agree upon there would be little to object to. The cause of complaints is not that the governments serve an agreed opinion of the majority, but that they are bound to serve the several interests of a conglomerate of numerous groups. It is at least conceivable, though unlikely, that an autocratic government will exercise self-restraint; but an omnipotent democratic government simply cannot do so. If its powers are not limited, it simply cannot confine itself to serving the agreed views of the majority of the electorate. It will be forced to bring together and keep together a majority by satisfying the demands of a multitude of special interests, each of which will consent to the special benefits granted to other groups only at the price of their own special interests being equally considered. Such a bargaining democracy has nothing to do with the conceptions used to justify the principle of democracy.

The playball of group interests

When I speak here of the necessity of democratic government being limited, or more briefly of limited democracy, I do not, of course, mean that the part of government conducted democratically should be limited, but that *all* government, specially if democratic, should be limited. The reason is that democratic government, if nominally omnipotent, becomes as a result of unlimited powers exceedingly weak, the playball of all the separate interests it has to satisfy to secure majority support.

How has the situation come about?

For two centuries, from the end of absolute monarchy to the rise of unlimited democracy the great aim of constitutional government had been to limit all governmental powers. The chief principles gradually established to prevent all arbitrary exercise of power were the separation of powers, the rule or sovereignty of law, government under the law, the distinction between private and public law, and the rules of judicial procedure. They all served to define and limit the conditions under which any coercion of individuals was admissible. Coercion was thought to be justified only in the general interest. And only coercion according to uniform rules equally applicable to all was thought to be in the general interest.

All these great liberal principles were given second rank and were half forgotten when it came to be believed that democratic control of government made unnecessary any other safeguards against the arbitrary use of power. The old principles were not so much forgotten as their traditional verbal expression deprived of meaning by a gradual change of the key words used in them. The most important of the crucial terms on which the meaning of the classical formulae of liberal constitution turned was the term 'Law'; and all the old principles lost their significance as the content of this term was changed.

Laws versus directions

To the founders of constitutionalism the term 'Law' had had a very precise narrow meaning. Only from limiting government by law in this sense was the protection of individual liberty expected. The philosophers of law in the nineteenth century finally defined it as rules regulating the conduct of persons towards others, applicable to an unknown number of future instances and containing prohibitions delimiting (but of course not specifying) the boundaries of the protected domain of all persons and organized groups. After long discussions, in which the German jurisprudents in particular had at last elaborated this definition of what they called 'law in the material sense', it was in the end suddenly abandoned for what now must seem an almost comic objection. Under this definition the rules of a constitution would not be law in the material sense.

They are, of course, not rules of conduct but rules for the organization of government, and like all public law are apt to change frequently while private (and criminal) law can last.

Law was meant to prevent unjust conduct. Justice referred to principles equally applicable to all and was contrasted to all specific commands or privileges referring to particular individuals and groups. But who still believes today, as James Madison could two hundred years ago, that the House of Representatives would be unable to make 'law which will not have its full operation on themselves and their friends, as well as the great mass of society'?

What happened with the apparent victory of the democratic ideal was that the power of laying down laws and the governmental power of issuing directions were placed into the hands of the same assemblies. The effect of this was necessarily that the supreme governmental authority became free to give itself currently whatever laws helped it best to achieve the particular purposes of the moment. But it necessarily meant the end of the principle of government *under* the law. While it was reasonable enough to demand that not only legislation proper but also governmental measures should be determined by democratic procedure, placing both powers into the hands of the same assembly (or assemblies) meant in effect return to unlimited government.

It also invalidated the original belief that a democracy, because it had to obey the majority, could only do what was in the general interest. This would have been true of a body which could give only *general* laws or decide on issues of truly *general* interest. But this is not only *not* true but outright *impossible* for a body which has unlimited powers and must use them to buy the votes of particular interests, including those of some small groups or even powerful individuals. Such a body, which does not owe its authority to demonstrating its belief in the justice of its decisions by committing itself to general rules, is constantly under the necessity of rewarding the support by the different groups by conceding special advantages. The 'political necessities' of contemporary democracy are far from all being demanded by the majority!

Laws and arbitrary government

The result of this development was not merely that government was no longer under the law. It also brought it about that the concept of law itself lost its meaning. The so-called legislature was no longer (as John Locke had thought it should be) confined to giving laws in the sense of general rules. *Everything* the 'legislature' resolved came to be called 'law', and it was no longer called legislature because it gave laws, but 'laws' became the name for everything which emanated from the 'legislature'. The hallowed term 'law' thus lost all its old meaning, and it became the name for the commands of what the fathers of constitutionalism would have called arbitrary government. Government became the main business of the 'legislature' and legislation subsidiary to it.

The term 'arbitrary' no less lost its classical meaning. The word had meant 'rule-less' or determined by particular will rather than according to recognized rules. In this true sense even the decision of an autocratic ruler may be lawful, and the decision of a democratic majority entirely arbitrary. Even Rousseau, who is chiefly responsible for bringing into political usage the unfortunate conception of 'will', understood at least occasionally that, to be just, this will must be *general in intent*. But the decision of the majorities in contemporary legislative assemblies need, of course, not have that attribute. Anything goes, so long as it increases the number of votes supporting governmental measures.

An omnipotent sovereign parliament, not confined to laying down general rules, means that we have an arbitrary government. What is worse, a government which cannot, even if it wished, obey any principles, but must maintain itself by handing out special favours to particular groups. It must buy its authority by discrimination. Unfortunately the British Parliament which had been the model for most representative institutions also introduced the idea of the sovereignty (i.e. omnipotence) of Parliament. But the sovereignty of the *law* and the sovereignty of an unlimited *Parliament* are irreconcilable. Yet today, when Mr Enoch Powell claims that 'a Bill of Rights is incompatible with the free constitution of this country', Mr Gallagher hastens to assure him that he understands that and agrees with Mr Powell.[1]

It turns out that the Americans two hundred years ago were right and an almighty Parliament means the death of the freedom of the individual. Apparently a free constitution no longer means the freedom of the individual but a *licence to the majority in Parliament to act as arbitrarily as it pleases*. We can either have a free Parliament or a free people. Personal freedom requires that all authority is restrained by long-run principles which the opinion of the people approves.

From unequal treatment to arbitrariness

It took some time for those consequences of unlimited democracy to show themselves.

For a while the traditions developed during the period in which liberal constitutionalism operated as a restraint on the extent of governmental power. Wherever these forms of democracy were imitated in parts of the world where no such tradition existed, they invariably, of course, soon broke down. But in the countries with longer experience with representative government the traditional barriers to arbitrary use of power were at first penetrated from entirely benevolent motives. Discrimination to assist the least fortunate did not seem to be discrimination. (More recently we even invented the nonsense word 'under-privileged' to conceal this.) But in order to put into a more equal material position people who are inevitably very different in many of the conditions on which their wordly success depends it is necessary to treat them unequally.

Yet to break the principle of *equal treatment under the law* even for charity's sake inevitably opened the floodgates to arbitrariness. To disguise it the pretence of the formula of 'social justice' was resorted to; nobody knows precisely what it means, but for that very reason it served as the magic wand which broke down all barriers to partial measures. Dispensing gratuities at the expense of somebody else *who cannot be readily identified* became the most attractive way of buying majority support. But a parliament or government which becomes a charitable institution thereby becomes exposed to irresistible blackmail. And it soon ceases to be the 'deserts' but becomes exclusively the 'political necessity' which determines which groups are to be favoured at general expense.

This legalized corruption is not the fault of the politicians; they cannot avoid it if they are to gain positions in which they can do any good. It becomes a built-in feature of any system in which majority support authorizes a special measure assuaging particular discontent. Both a legislature confined to laying down general rules and a governmental agency which can use coercion only to enforce general rules which it cannot change can resist such pressure; an omnipotent assembly cannot. Deprived of all power of discretionary coercion, government might, of course, still discriminate in rendering services - but this would be less harmful and could be more easily prevented. But once central government possesses no power of discriminatory coercion, most services could be and probably should be delegated to regional or local corporations competing for inhabitants by providing better services at lower costs.

Separation of powers to prevent unlimited government

It seems clear that a nominally unlimited ('sovereign') representative assembly must be progressively driven into a steady and unlimited extension of the powers of government. It appears equally clear that this can be prevented only by dividing the supreme power between two distinct democratically elected assemblies, i.e. by applying the principle of the separation of powers on the highest level.

Two such distinct assemblies would, of course, have to be differently composed if the *legislative* one is to represent the *opinion* of the people about which sorts of government actions are just and which are not, and the other *governmental* assembly were to be guided by the *will* of the people on the particular measures to be taken within the frame of rules laid down by the first. For this second task - which has been the main occupation of existing parliaments - the practices and organization of parliaments have become well adapted, especially with their organization on party lines which is indeed indispensable for conducting government.

But it was not without reason that the great political thinkers of the eighteenth century were without exception deeply distrustful of party divisions in a true legislature. It can hardly be denied that the existing parliaments are largely unfit for legislation proper. They have neither the time nor the right frame of mind to do it well.

SEVENTEEN

A MODEL CONSTITUTION

In all cases it must be advantageous to know what is the most perfect in the kind, that we may be able to bring any real constitution or form of government as near it as possible, by such gentle alterations and innovations as may not give too great a disturbance to society.

David Hume*

The wrong turn taken by the development of representative institutions

What can we do today, in the light of the experience gained, to accomplish the aims which, nearly two hundred years ago, the fathers of the Constitution of the United States of America for the first time attempted to secure by a deliberate construction? Though our aims may still be the same, there is much that we ought to have learnt from the great experiment and its numerous imitations. We know now why the hope of the authors of those documents, that through them they could effectively limit the powers of government, has been disappointed. They had hoped by a separation of the legislative from executive as well as the judicial powers to subject government and the individuals to rules of just conduct. They could hardly have forseen that, because the legislature was also entrusted with the direction of government, the task of stating rules of just conduct and the task of directing particular activities of government to specific ends would come to be hopelessly confounded, and that law would cease to mean only such universal and uniform rules of just conduct as would limit all arbitrary coercion. In consequence, they never really achieved that separation of powers at which they had aimed. Instead they produced in the USA a system under which, often to the detriment of the efficiency of government, the power of organizing and directing government was divided between

105

the chief executive and a representative assembly elected at different times and on different principles and therefore frequently at loggerheads with each other.

We have already seen that the desire to have the laying down of rules of just conduct as well as the direction of current government in the hands of representative bodies need not mean that both these powers should be entrusted to the same body. The possibility of a different solution of the problem[1] is in fact suggested by an earlier phase of the development of representative institutions. The control of the conduct of government was, at least at first, brought about mainly through the control of revenue. By an evolution which started in Britain as early as the end of the fourteenth century the power of the purse had progressively devolved upon the House of Commons. When at last at the end of the seventeenth century the exclusive right of the Commons over 'money bills' was definitely conceded by the House of Lords, the latter, as the highest court in the country, still retained ultimate control of the development of the rules of common law. What would have been more natural than that, in conceding to the Commons sole control of the current conduct of government, the second chamber should have in return claimed the exclusive right to alter by statute the enforceable rules of just conduct?

Such a development was not really possible so long as the upper house represented a small privileged class. But in principle a division by functions instead of a division according to the different classes represented might have led to a situation in which the Commons would have obtained full power over the apparatus of government and all the material means put at its disposal, but would have been able to employ coercion only within the limits of the rules laid down by the House of Lords. In organizing and directing what was properly the task of government they would have been entirely free. To guide the actions of the officers of government concerning what was the property of the state they could have laid down any rules they agreed upon. But neither they nor their servants could have coerced private citizens except to make them obey the rules recognized or laid down by the Upper House. It would then have been entirely logical if the current affairs of government were conducted by a committee of the Lower House, or rather of its majority. Such a government would then in its powers over citizens have been entirely under a law which it would have had no power to alter in order to make it suit its particular purposes.

106

Such a separation of tasks would have required and gradually produced a sharp distinction between rules of just conduct and instructions to government. It would soon have shown the need for a superior judicial authority, capable of deciding conflicts between the two representative bodies, and by doing so, gradually building up an ever more precise distinction between the two kind of rules; the private (including criminal) and the public law, which are now confused because they are described by the same term, 'law'.

Instead of such a progressive clarification of the fundamental distinction the combination of wholly different tasks in the hands of one and the same body has led to an increasing vagueness of the concept of law. We have seen that the distinction is not an easy one to draw and that the task presents even modern legal thought with some hard problems. But it is not an impossible task. Though a wholly satisfactory solution may require further advance of our understanding. It is through such advance that all law has grown.

The value of a model of an ideal constitution

Assuming that a distinction between the two kinds of rules which we now call laws can be drawn clearly, its significance will be put into sharper focus if we sketch in some detail the sort of constitutional arrangements which would secure a real separation of powers between two distinct representative bodies whereby law-making in the narrow sense as well as government proper would be conducted democratically, but by different and mutually independent agencies. My purpose in presenting such a sketch is not to propose a constitutional scheme for present application. I certainly do not wish to suggest that any country with a firmly established constitutional tradition should replace its constitution by a new one drawn up on the lines suggested. But apart from the fact that the general principles discussed in the preceding pages will obtain more definite shape if I outline here a constitution embodying them, there are two further reasons which appear to make such a sketch worth while.

In the first instance, very few countries in the world are in the fortunate position of possessing a strong constitutional tradition. Indeed, outside the English-speaking world probably only the smaller countries of Northern Europe and Switzerland have such traditions. Most of the other countries have never preserved a constitution long enough to make it become a deeply entrenched tradition; and in many of them there is also lacking the background of traditions and beliefs which in the more fortunate countries have made constitutions work which did not explicitly state all that they presupposed, or which did not even exist in written form. This is even more true of those new countries which, without a tradition even remotely similar to the ideal of the Rule of Law which the nations of Europe have long held, have adopted from the latter the institutions of democracy without the foundations of beliefs and convictions presupposed by those institutions.

If such attempts to transplant democracy are not to fail, much of that background of unwritten traditions and beliefs, which in the successful democracies had for a long time restrained the abuse of the majority power, will have to be spelled out in such instruments of government for the new democracies. That most of such attempts have so far failed does not prove that the basic conceptions of democracy are inapplicable, but only that the particular institutions which for a time worked tolerably well in the West presuppose the tacit acceptance of certain other principles which were in some measure observed there but which, where they are not yet recognized, must be made as much a part of the written constitution as the rest. We have no right to assume that the particular forms of democracy which have worked with us must also work elsewhere. Experience seems to show that they do not. There is, therefore, every reason to ask how those conceptions which our kind of representative institutions tacitly presupposed can be explicitly put into such constitutions.

In the second instance, the principles embodied in the scheme to be outlined may be of relevance in connection with the contemporary endeavours to create new supra-national institutions. There seems to be a growing feeling that we may hope to achieve some sort of international law but that it is doubtful whether we can, or even whether we should, create a supra-national government beyond some pure service agencies. Yet if anything should be clear it is that, if these endeavours are not to fail, or even not to do more harm than good, these new supra-national institutions will for a long time have to be limited to restraining national governments from actions harmful to other countries, but possess no powers to order them to do particular things. Many of the objections which people understandably have to entrusting an international authority with the power of issuing orders to the several national governments might well be met if such a new authority were to be restricted to the establishment of general rules which merely prohibited certain kinds of actions of the member states or their citizens. But to achieve this we have yet to discover how the power of legislation, in the sense in which it was understood by those who believed in the separation of powers, can be effectively separated from the powers of government.

The basic principles

The basic clause of such a constitution would have to state that in normal times, and apart from certain clearly defined emergency situations, men could be restrained from doing what they wished, or coerced to do particular things, only in accordance with the recognized rules of just conduct designed to define and protect the individual domain of each; and that the accepted set of rules of this kind could be deliberately altered only by what we shall call the Legislative Assembly. This in general would have power only in so far as it proved its intention to be just by committing itself to universal rules intended to be applied in an unknown number of future instances and over the application of which to particular cases it had no further power. The basic clause would have to contain a definition of what can be law in this narrow sense of *nomos* which would enable a court to decide whether any particular resolution of the Legislative Assembly possessed the formal properties to make it law in this sense.

We have seen that such a definition could not rely only on purely logical criteria but would have to require that the rules should be intended to apply to an indefinite number of unknown future instances, to serve the formation and preservation of an abstract order whose concrete contents were unforeseeable, but not the achievement of particular concrete purposes, and finally to exclude all provisions intended or known to affect principally particular identifiable individuals or groups. It would also have to recognize that, though alterations of the recognized body of existing rules of just conduct were the exclusive right of the Legislative Assembly, the initial body of such rules would include not only the products of past legislation but also those not yet articulated conceptions implicit in past decisions by which the courts should be bound and which it would be their task to make explicit.

The basic clause would of course not be intended to define the functions of government but merely to define the limits of its coercive powers. Though it would restrict the means that government could employ in rendering services to the citizens, it would place no direct limit on the content of the services government might render. We shall have to return to this matter when we turn to the functions of the second representative body, the Governmental Assembly.

Such a clause would by itself achieve all and more than the traditional Bills of Rights were meant to secure; and it would therefore make any separate enumeration of a list of special protected fundamental rights unnecessary. This will be clear when it is remembered that none of the traditional Rights of Man, such as the freedom of speech, of the press, of religion, of assembly and association, or of the inviolability of the home or of letters, etc., can be, or ever have been, absolute rights that may not be limited by general rules of law. Freedom of speech does of course not mean that we are free to slander, libel, deceive, incite to crime or cause a panic by false alarm, etc., etc. All these rights are either tacitly or explicitly protected against restrictions only 'save in accordance with the law'. But this limitation, as has become only too clear in modern times, is meaningful and does not deprive the protection of those rights of all efficacy against the 'legislature', only if by 'law' is not meant every properly passed resolution of a representative assembly but only such rules as can be described as laws in the narrow sense here defined.

Nor are the fundamental rights, traditionally protected by Bills of Rights, the only ones that must be protected if arbitrary power is to be prevented, nor can all such essential rights which constitute individual liberty ever be exhaustively enumerated. Though, as has been shown before, the efforts to extend the concept to what are now called social and economic rights were misguided (see appendix to chapter 9), there are many unforeseeable exercises of individual freedom which are no less deserving of protection other than those enumerated by various Bills of Rights. Those which are commonly explicitly named are those which at particular times were specially threatened, and particularly those which seemed to need safeguarding if democratic government was to work. But to single them out as being specially protected suggests that in other fields government may use coercion without being bound by general rules of law.

This, indeed, has been the reason why the original framers of the American Constitution did not at first wish to include in it a Bill of

Rights, and why, when it was added, the ineffective and all but forgotten Ninth Amendment provided that 'the enumeration in the Constitution, of certain rights, shall not be construed to deny or disparage others retained by the people'. The enumeration of particular rights as being protected against infringements 'save in accordance with the law' indeed might seem to imply that in other respects the legislature is free to restrain or coerce people without committing itself to a general rule. And the extension of the term 'law' to almost any resolution of the legislature has lately made even this protection meaningless. The purpose of a constitution, however, is precisely to prevent even the legislature from all arbitrary restraints and coercion. And, as has been forcefully pointed out by a distinguished Swiss jurist,[2] the new possibilities which technological developments create may in the future make other liberties even more important than those protected by the traditional fundamental rights.

What the fundamental rights are intended to protect is simply individual liberty in the sense of the absence of arbitrary coercion. This requires that coercion be used only to enforce the universal rules of just conduct protecting the individual domains and to raise means to support the services rendered by government; and since what is implied here is that the individual can be restrained only in such conduct as may encroach upon the protected domain of others, he would under such a provision be wholly unrestricted in all actions which affected only his personal domain or that of other consenting responsible persons, and thus be assured all freedom that can be secured by political action. That this freedom may have to be temporarily suspended when those institutions are threatened which are intended to preserve it in the long run, and when it becomes necessary to join in common action for the supreme end of defending them, or to avert some other common danger to the whole society, is another matter which we shall take up later.

The two representative bodies with distinctive functions

The idea of entrusting the task of stating the general rules of just conduct to a representative body distinct from the body which is entrusted with the task of government is not entirely new. Something like this was attempted by the ancient Athenians when they allowed only the *nomothetae,* a distinct body, to change the fundamental *nomos.*[3] As *nomos* is about the only term which has

111

preserved at least approximately the meaning of general rules of just conduct, and as the term *nomothetae* was revived in a somewhat similar context in seventeenth century England[4] and again by J.S. Mill,[5] it will be convenient occasionally to use it as a name for that purely legislative body which the advocates of the separation of powers and the theorists of the Rule of Law had in mind, whenever it is necessary emphatically to distinguish it from the second representative body which we shall call the Governmental Assembly.

Such a distinctive legislative assembly would evidently provide an effective check on the decisions of an equally representative governmental body only if its membership were not composed in the same way; this would in practice appear to require that the two assemblies must not be chosen in the same manner, or for the same period. If the two assemblies were merely charged with different tasks but composed of approximately the same proportions of representatives of the same groups and especially parties, the legislature would probably simply provide those laws which the governmental body wanted for its purposes as much as if they were one body.

The different tasks also require that the different assemblies should represent the views of the electors in different respects. For the purpose of government proper it seems desirable that the concrete wishes of the citizens for particular results should find expression, or, in other words, that their particular interests should be represented; for the conduct of government a majority committed to a programme of action and 'capable of governing' is thus clearly needed. Legislation proper, on the other hand, should not be governed by interests but by opinion, i.e. by views about what *kind* of action is right or wrong – not as an instrument for the achievement of particular ends but as a permanent rule and irrespective of the effect on particular individuals or groups. In choosing somebody most likely to look effectively after their particular interests and in choosing persons whom they can trust to uphold justice impartially the people would probably elect very different persons: effectiveness in the first kind of task demands qualities very different from the probity, wisdom, and judgment which are of prime importance in the second.

The system of periodic election of the whole body of representatives is well designed not only to make them responsive to the fluctuating wishes of the electorate, but also to make them organize into parties and to render them dependent on the agreed aims of parties committed to support particular interests and particular programmes of actions. But it also in effect compels the individual member to submit to party discipline to get the support of the party for re-election.

To expect from an assembly of representatives charged with looking after particular interests the qualities which were expected by the classical theorists of democracy from a representative sample of the people at large is unreasonable. But this does not mean that if the people were asked to elect representatives who had no power to grant them particular favours they could not be induced to respond by designating those whose judgment they have learnt most to respect, especially if they had to choose among persons who already had made their reputation in the ordinary pursuits of life.

What would thus appear to be needed for the purposes of legislation proper is an assembly of men and women elected at a relatively mature age for fairly long periods, such as fifteen years, so that they would not have to be concerned about being re-elected, after which period, to make them wholly independent of party discipline, they should not be re-eligible nor forced to return to earning a living in the market but be assured of continued public employment in such honorific but neutral positions as lay judges, so that during their tenure as legislators they would be neither dependent on party support nor concerned about their personal future. To assure this only people who have already proved themselves in the ordinary business of life should be elected and at the same time to prevent the assembly's containing too high a proportion of old persons, it would seem wise to rely on the old experience that a man's contemporaries are his fairest judges and to ask each group of people of the same age once in their lives, say in the calendar year in which they reached the age of 45, to select from their midst representatives to serve for fifteen years.

The result would be a legislative assembly of men and women between their 45th and 60th years, one-fifteenth of whom would be replaced every year. The whole would thus mirror that part of the population which had already gained experience and had had an opportunity to make their reputation, but who would still be in their best years. It should be specially noted that, although the under 45s would not be represented in such an assembly, the average age of the members - 52½ years - would be less than that of most existing representative bodies, even if the strength of the older part were kept constant by replacement of those dropping out through death and disease, which in the normal course of events would seem unnecessary and would only increase the proportion of those with little experience in the business of legislating.

Various additional safeguards might be employed to secure the entire independence of these *nomothetae* from the pressure of particular interests or organized parties. Persons who had already served in the Governmental Assembly or in party organizations might be made ineligible for the Legislative Assembly. And even if many members might have closer attachment to certain parties, there would be little inducement for them to obey instructions of the party leadership or the government in power.

Members would be removable only for gross misconduct or neglect of duty by some group of their present or former peers on the principles which today apply to judges. The assurance after the end of their tenure and up to the age of retirement with a pension (that is for the time from their 60th to their 70th year) of a dignified position such as that of lay members of judicial courts would be an important factor contributing to their independence; indeed, their salary might be fixed by the Constitution at a certain percentage of the average of, say, the twenty most highly paid posts in the gift of government.

It could be expected that such a position would come to be regarded by each age class as a sort of prize to be awarded to the most highly respected of their contemporaries. As the Legislative Assembly should not be very numerous, comparatively few individuals would have to be elected every year. This might well make it advisable to employ an indirect method of election, with regionally appointed delegates electing the representative from their midst. Thus a further inducement would be provided for each district to appoint as delegates persons of such standing as would have the best chance of being chosen in the second poll.

It might at first seem as if such a purely legislative assembly would have very little work to do. If we think exclusively of those tasks which we have so far stressed, namely the revision of the body of private (including commercial and criminal) law, they would indeed appear to require action only at long intervals, and hardly provide adequate continuous occupation for a select group of highly competent persons. Yet this first impression is misleading. Though we have used private and criminal law as our chief illustrations, it must be remembered that all enforceable rules of conduct would have to have the sanction of this assembly. While, within the compass of this book, we have had little opportunity to go into detail on these matters we have repeatedly pointed out that those tasks include not only the principles of taxation but also all those regulations of safety and health, including regulations of production or construction, that have to be enforced in the general interest and should be stated in the form of general rules. These comprise not only what used to be called safety legislation but also all the difficult problems of creating an adequate framework for a functioning competitive market and the law of corporations which we have mentioned in the last chapter.

Such matters have in the past had to be largely delegated by the legislature which had no time for careful consideration of the often highly technical issues involved, and have in consequence been placed in the hands of the bureaucracy or special agencies created for the purpose. Indeed, a 'legislature' chiefly concerned with the pressing matters of current government is bound to find it difficult to give such matters the attention they require. They are nevertheless matters not of administration but of legislation proper, and the danger that the bureaucracy, if the tasks are delegated to it, will assume discretionary and essentially arbitrary powers is considerable. There are no intrinsic reasons why the regulation of these matters should not take the form of general rules (as was still the rule in Britain before 1914), if it were seriously attempted by a legislature, instead of being considered from the point of view of the convenience of administrators ambitious of acquiring power. Probably most of the powers which bureaucracy has acquired, and which are in effect uncontrollable, are the result of delegation by legislatures.

Yet, though I am not really concerned about the members of the legislature lacking adequate occupation, I will add that I should regard it as by no means unfortunate but rather as desirable if a selected group of men and women, who had already made a reputation in the ordinary business of life, were then freed for part of their lives from the necessity or duty of devoting themselves to tasks imposed on them by circumstances so that they would be able to reflect on the principles of government or might take up whatever cause they thought important. A certain sprinkling of people who have leisure is essential if public spirit is to express itself in those voluntary activities where new ideals can manifest themselves. Such was the function of the man of independent means, and though I believe it to be a strong argument for his preservation, there is no

115

reason why people who have acquired property should be the only ones given such an opportunity. If those who have been entrusted by their contemporaries with the highest confidence they can show were to be free to devote a substantial part of their time to tasks of their own choice, they may contribute much to the development of that 'voluntary sector' which is so necessary if government is not to assume overwhelming power. And if the position of a member of the legislature should not prove to be a very onerous one, it ought nevertheless to be made one of great honour and dignity so that in some respects the members of this democratically elected body would be able to play the role of what Max Weber has called the *honoratiores*, independent public figures who, apart from their functions as legislators, and without party ties, could take a leading part in various voluntary efforts.

So far as the chief task of these *nomothetae* is concerned, it may be felt that the main problem would probably not be whether they had enough work to do, but rather whether there would be a sufficient inducement for them to do it. It might be feared that the very degree of independence which they enjoyed might tempt them to become lazy. Though it seems to me not very likely that persons who had earlier made their mark in active life, and whose position would henceforth rest on public reputation should, once they were elected for fifteen years to a position in which they were practically irremovable, in such a manner neglect their duties, yet provisions might be made similar to those applying in the case of judges. Though they must be wholly independent of the governmental organization there might well be some supervision by some senate of former members of the body who in the case of neglect of duties might even be entitled to remove representatives. It would also be such a body which at the end of the tenure of membership of the Legislative Assembly would have to assign positions to each retiring member, ranging from that of a president of the Constitutional Court to that of a lay assessor of some minor judicial body.

The Constitution should, however, also guard against the eventuality of the Legislative Assembly becoming wholly inactive by providing that, while it should have exclusive powers to lay down general rules of just conduct, this power might devolve temporarily to the Governmental Assembly if the former did not respond within a reasonable period to a notice given by government that some rules should be laid down on a particular question. Such a constitutional provision would probably by its mere existence make it unnecessary that it should ever have to be invoked. The jealousy of the Legislative Assembly would probably operate strongly enough to assure that it would within a reasonable time answer any question of rules of just conduct which was raised.

Further observations on representation by age groups

Although only the general principle of the suggested model constitution is relevant to the main theme of this book, the method of representation by generations proposed for the Legislative Assembly offers so many interesting possibilities for the development of democratic institutions that it seems worthwhile to elaborate on it a little further. The fact that the members of each age class would know that some day they would have an important common task to perform might well lead to the early formation of local clubs of contemporaries, and since this would contribute towards the proper education of suitable candidates, such a tendency would seem to deserve public support, at least through the provision of regular meeting places and facilities for contacts between the groups of different localities. The existence in each locality of only one such publically assisted and recognised group for every age class might also help to prevent a splitting of groups on party lines.

Clubs of contemporaries might well be formed either at school-leaving age or at least when each class entered public life, say at the age of 18. They would possibly be more attractive if men of one age group were brought together with women two years or so younger. This might be achieved, without any objectionable legal discrimination, by allowing men and women at the age of eighteen to join either the then newly formed club or one of those formed in one of the preceding two or three years, in which case probably most men would prefer to join their own new club, while women would seem more likely to join one of those started in the preceding years. Such a choice would of course imply that those opting for the higher age class would permanently belong to it and vote for the delegate and be eligible as delegates and representatives earlier than would otherwise be the case.

The clubs would, by bringing together the contemporaries of all social classes, and preserving contacts between those who were together at school (and perhaps national service), but now go entirely different ways, provide a truly democratic link by serving to provide contacts cutting across all other stratifications and providing an education in, and an incentive for, interest in public institutions as well as training in parliamentry procedures. They would also provide a regular channel for the expression of dissent of those not yet represented in a Legislative Assembly. If they should occasionally also become platforms for party debates, their advantage would be that those leaning towards different parties would be induced to discuss the issues together, and would become conscious that they had the common task of representing the outlook of their generation and to qualify for possible later public service.

Though individual membership ought to be primarily in the local group, it should confer on a member the right to take part as visitors in the clubs of one's age class at places other than that of one's permanent residence; and if it were known that in each locality a particular age class met regularly at a particular time and place (as it is the case with Rotarians and similar organizations), this might become an important means of inter-local contacts. In many other respects such clubs would probably introduce an important element of social coherence, especially to the structure of urban society, and do much to reduce the existing occupational and class distinctions.

The rotating chairmanship of these clubs would provide the members with an opportunity to become acquainted with the suitability of potential candidates for election as delegates or representatives; in the case of indirect elections they might therefore be based on personal knowledge even in the second round and the delegates ultimately selected might thereafter act not only as chairmen but also as voluntary but officially recognized spokesmen of their respective age groups, a sort of special honorary 'ombudsmen', who would protect the interests of their age groups against authorities. The advantage of their performing such functions would be that in voting for them the members would be more likely to elect somebody whose integrity they trusted.

Though after the election of the representatives these clubs would have few further formal tasks they would probably continue as means of social contact which might in fact also be called upon in case of need to restore the number of representatives if by some unusual accidents it had been depleted much below normal strength – perhaps not to the full original number but at

118

least so that the numerical strength of their age group was adequately represented.

The governmental assembly

We need say little here about the second or Governmental Assembly because for it the existing parliamentary bodies, which have developed mainly to serve governmental tasks, could serve as model. There is no reason why it should not be formed by periodic re-elections of the whole body on party lines,[6] and why its chief business should not be conducted by an executive committee of the majority. This would constitute the government proper and operate subject to the control and criticism of an organized opposition ready to offer an alternative government. Concerning the various possible arrangements with regard to methods of election, periods for which the representatives are elected, etc., the arguments to be considered would be more or less the same as those currently discussed and need not detain us here. Perhaps the case for securing an effective majority capable of conducting government would under this scheme even more strongly than it does now outweigh the case for an exact mirroring of the proportional distribution of the different interests in the population at large, and the case against proportional representation would therefore, in my opinion, become even stronger.

The one important difference between the position of such a representative Governmental Assembly and the existing parliamentary bodies would of course be that in all that it decided it would be bound by the rules of just conduct laid down by the Legislative Assembly, and that, in particular, it could not issue any orders to private citizens which did not follow directly and necessarily from the rules laid down by the latter. Within the limits of these rules the government would, however, be complete master in organizing the apparatus of government and deciding about the use of material and personal resources entrusted to the government.

A question which should be reconsidered is whether, with regard to the right to elect representatives to this Governmental Assembly, the old argument does not assume new strength that employees of government and all who received pensions or other support from government should have no vote. The argument was clearly not conclusive so long as it concerned the vote for a representative assembly whose primary task was conceived to be the laying down

119

of universal rules of just conduct. Undoubtedly the civil servant or government pensioner is as competent to form an opinion on what is just as anybody else, and it would have appeared as invidious for such persons to be excluded from a right granted to many who are less informed and less educated. But it is an altogether different matter when what is at issue is not an opinion but frankly interest in seeing particular results achieved. Here neither the instruments of policy nor those who, without contributing to the means, merely share in the results, seem to have the same claim as the private citizen. That civil servants, old age pensioners, the unemployed, etc., should have a vote on how they should be paid out of the pocket of the rest, and their vote be solicited by a promise of a rise in their pay, is hardly a reasonable arrangement. Nor would it seem reasonable that, in addition to formulating projects for action, the government employees should also have a say on whether their projects should be adopted or not, or that those who are subject to orders by the Governmental Assembly should have a part in deciding what these orders ought to be.

The task of the governmental machinery, though it would have to operate within the framework of a law it could not alter, would still be very considerable. Though it would be under an obligation not to discriminate in the services it renders, the choice, organization, and aims of these services would still give it great power, limited only so far as coercion or other discriminatory treatment of the citizens was excluded. And though the manner in which it could raise funds would thus be restricted, the amount or the general purposes for which they are spent would not be, except indirectly.

The constitutional court

The whole arrangement rests on the possibility of drawing a sharp distinction between the enforceable rules of just conduct to be developed by the Legislative Assembly and binding the government and citizens alike, and all those rules of the organization and conduct of government proper which, within the limits of the law, it would be the task of the Governmental Assembly to determine. Though we have endeavoured to make the principle of the distinction clear, and the basic clause of the constitution would have to attempt to define what is to be considered law in the relevant sense of rules of just conduct, in practice the application of the distinction would undoubtedly raise many difficult problems, and all its implications could be worked out only through the continuous efforts of a special court. The problems would arise chiefly in the form of a conflict of competence between the two assemblies, generally through the questioning by one of the validity of the resolution passed by the other.

To give the court of last instance in these matters the required authority, and in view of the special qualification needed by its members, it would probably be desirable to establish it as a separate Constitutional Court. It would seem appropriate that in addition to professional judges its membership should include former members of the Legislative and perhaps also of the Governmental Assembly. In the course of gradually building up a body of doctrine it should probably be bound by its own former decisions, while whatever reversal of such decisions might seem necessary had best been left to an amending procedure provided by the constitution.

The only other point about this Constitutional Court that needs to be stressed here is that its decisions often would have to be, not that either of the two Assemblies were competent rather than the other to take certain kinds of action, but that nobody at all was entitled to take certain kinds of coercive measures. This would in particular apply, except in periods of emergency to be considered later, to all coercive measures not provided for by general rules of just conduct which were either traditionally recognized or explicitly laid down by the Legislative Assembly.

The scheme proposed also raises all kinds of problems concerning the organization of the administration of justice in general. To organize the judicial machinery would clearly seem an organizational and therefore governmental task, yet to place it into the hands of government might threaten the complete independence of the courts. So far as the appointment and promotion of judges is concerned, this might well be placed into the hands of that committee of former members of the Legislative Assembly which we suggested should decide about the employment of their fellows as lay judges and the like. And the independence of the individual judge might be secured by his salary being determined in the same manner as that which we have proposed for the determination of the salaries of the members of the Legislative Assembly, namely as a certain percentage of the average salary of a fixed number of the highest positions in the gift of government.

Quite a different problem is that of the technical organization of the courts, their non-judicial personnel and their material needs. To organize these might seem more clearly a matter of government proper, yet there are good reasons why in the Anglo-Saxon tradition the conception of a Ministry of Justice responsible for such matters has long been suspect. It might at least be considered whether such a task, which clearly should not be performed by the Legislative Assembly, might not be entrusted to that committee selected from its former members which we have already mentioned, and which thereby would become the permanent organizational body for the third, the judicial power, commanding for its purposes a block grant of financial means assigned to it by government.

All this is closely connected with another important and difficult issue which we have not yet considered and that even here we can barely touch upon. It is the whole question of competence for laying down the law of procedure as against substantive law. In general this, as all rules subsidiary to the enforcement of justice, should be a matter for the Legislative Assembly, though some points of a more organizational character that today are also regulated in the codes of procedure might well seem matters to be decided either by the special body suggested or by the Governmental Assembly. These are, however, technical questions which we cannot further consider here.

The general structure of authority

The function of the Legislative Assembly must not be confused with that of a body set up to enact or amend the Constitution. The functions of these two bodies would indeed be entirely different. Strictly speaking, a Constitution ought to consist wholly of organizational rules, and need touch on substantive law in the sense of universal rules of just conduct only by stating the general attributes such laws must possess in order to entitle government to use coercion for their enforcement.

But though the Constitution must define what can be substantive law in order to allocate and limit powers among the parts of the organization it sets up, it leaves the content of this law to be developed by the legislature and judiciary. It represents a protective superstructure designed to regulate the continuous process of developing an existing body of law and to prevent any confusion of the powers of government in enforcing the rules on which the spontaneous order of society rests, and those of using the material means entrusted to its administration for the rendering of services to the individuals and groups.

There is no need here to enter into a discussion of the appropriate procedure for establishing and amending the Constitution. But perhaps the relation between the body called upon for this task and those established *by* the Constitution can be further elucidated by our saying that the proposed scheme replaces the existing two-tiered arrangement with a three-tiered one: while the Constitution allocates and restricts powers, it should not prescribe positively how these powers are to be used. The substantive law in the sense of rules of just conduct would be developed by the Legislative Assembly which would be limited in its powers only by the provision of the Constitution defining the general attributes which enforceable rules of just conduct must possess. The Governmental Assembly and its government as its executive organ on the other hand would be restricted both by the rules of the Constitution and by the rules of just conduct laid down or recognized by the Legislative Assembly. This is what government under the law means. The government, the executive organ of the Governmental Assembly, would of course also be bound by the decision of that Assembly and might thus be regarded as the fourth tier of the whole structure, with the administrative bureaucratic apparatus as the fifth.

If it be asked where under such an arrangement 'sovereignty' rests, the answer is nowhere – unless it temporally resides in the hands of the constitution-making or constitution-amending body. Since constitutional government is limited government there can be no room in it for a sovereign body if sovereignty is defined as unlimited power. We have seen before that the belief that there must always be an unlimited ultimate power is a superstition deriving from the erroneous belief that all law derives from the deliberate decision of a legislative agency. But government never starts from a lawless state; it rests on and derives its support from the expectation that it will enforce the prevailing opinions concerning what is right.

It might be noticed that the hierarchy of tiers of authority is related to the periods for which the different agencies have to make provision. Ideally the Constitution ought to be intended for all time, though of course, as is true of any product of the human mind, defects will be discovered which will need correction by amendment. Substantive law, though also intended for an indefinite period, will need continual development and revision as new and unforeseen problems arise with which the judiciary cannot deal adequately. The administration of the resources entrusted to government for the purpose of rendering services to the citizens is in its nature concerned with short-term problems and has to provide satisfaction of particular needs as they arise, and commanding as means for this task not the private citizen but only the resources explicity placed under its control.

Emergency powers

The basic principle of a free society, that the coercive powers of government are restricted to the enforcement of universal rules of just conduct, and cannot be used for the achievement of particular purposes, though essential to the normal working of such a society, may yet have to be temporarily suspended when the long-run preservation of that order is itself threatened. Though normally the individuals need be concerned only with their own concrete aims, and in pursuing them will best serve the common welfare, there may temporarily arise circumstances when the preservation of the overall order becomes the overruling common purpose, and when in consequence the spontaneous order, on a local or national scale, must for a time be converted into an organization. When an external enemy threatens, when rebellion or lawless violence has broken out, or a natural catastrophe requires quick action by whatever means can be secured, powers of compulsory organization, which normally nobody possesses, must be granted to somebody. Like an animal in flight from mortal danger society may in such situations have to suspend temporarily even vital functions on which in the long run its existence depends if it is to escape destruction.

The conditions under which such emergency powers may be granted without creating the danger that they will be retained when the absolute necessity has passed are among the most difficult and important points a constitution must decide on. 'Emergencies' have always been the pretext on which the safeguards of individual liberty have been eroded – and once they are suspended it is not difficult for anyone who has assumed such emergency powers to see to it that the emergency will persist. Indeed if all needs felt by important groups that can be satisfied only by the exercise of dictatorial powers constitute an emergency, every situation is an emergency situation. It has been contended with some plausibility that whoever has the power to proclaim an emergency and on this ground to suspend any part of the constitution is the true sovereign.[7] This would seem to be true enough if any person or body were able to arrogate to itself such emergency powers by declaring a state of emergency.

It is by no means necessary, however, that one and the same agency should possess the power to declare an emergency and to assume emergency powers. The best precaution against the abuse of emergency powers would seem to be that the authority that can declare a state of emergency is made thereby to renounce the powers it normally possesses and to retain only the right of revoking at any time the emergency powers it has conferred on another body. In the scheme suggested it would evidently be the Legislative Assembly which would not only have to delegate some of its powers to the government, but also to confer upon this government powers which in normal circumstances nobody possesses. For this purpose an emergency committee of the Legislative Assembly would have to be in permanent existence and quickly accessible at all times. The committee would have to be entitled to grant limited emergency powers until the Assembly as a whole could be convened which itself then would have to determine both the extent and duration of the emergency powers granted to government. So long as it confirmed the existence of an emergency, any measures taken by government within the powers granted to it would have full force, including such specific commands to particular persons as in normal times nobody would have the power to issue. The Legislative Assembly, however, would at all times be free to revoke or restrict the powers granted, and after the end of the emergency to confirm or to revoke any measures proclaimed by the government, and to provide for compensation to those who in the general interest were made to submit to such extraordinary powers.

Another kind of emergency for which every constitution should provide is the possible discovery of a gap in its provisions, such as the appearance of questions of authority to which the constitutional rules do not give an answer. The possibility of a discovery of such lacunae in any scheme, however carefully thought out, can never be excluded: and there may well arise questions which require a prompt authoritative answer if the whole machinery of government is not to be paralysed. Yet though somebody should have the power to provide a temporary answer to such questions by *ad hoc* decisions, these decisions should remain in effect only until the Legislative Assembly, the Constitutional Court, or the normal apparatus for amending the Constitution has filled the gap by an appropriate regulation. Until then a normally purely ceremonial Head of State might well be given power to fill such gaps by provisional decisions.

The division of financial powers

The field in which the constitutional arrangements here sketched would produce the most far-reaching changes would be that of finance. It is also the field in which the nature of these consequences can be best illustrated in such a condensed outline as is attempted here.

The central problem arises from the fact that the levying of contributions is necessarily an act of coercion and must therefore be done in accordance with general rules laid down by the Legislative Assembly, while the determination of both the volume and the direction of expenditure is clearly a governmental matter. Our scheme would therefore require that the uniform rules according to which the total means to be raised are apportioned among the citizens be laid down by the Legislative Assembly, while the total amount of expenditure and its direction would have to be decided by the Governmental Assembly.

Nothing would probably provide a more salutary discipline of expenditure than such a condition in which everybody voting for a particular outlay would know that the costs would have to be borne by him and his constituents in accordance with a predetermined rule which he could not alter. Except in those cases where the beneficiaries of a particular outlay could be clearly identified (although, once the service was provided for all it could not be withheld from those not voluntarily paying for it and the costs would therefore have to be raised by compulsion) as is the case with a motor tax for the provision of roads, or a wireless tax, or the various local and communal taxes for the finance of particular services, all expenditure decided upon would automatically lead to a corresponding increase of the general burden of taxes for all under the general scheme determined by the Legislative Assembly. There could then be no support for any expenditure based on the expectation that the burden could afterwards be shifted on to other shoulders: everyone would know that of all that would be spent he had to bear a fixed share.

Current methods of taxation have been shaped largely by the endeavour to raise funds in such a manner as to cause the least resistance or resentment on the part of the majority who had to approve the expenditure. They certainly were not designed to assure responsible decisions on expenditure, but on the contrary to produce the feeling that somebody else would pay for it. It is regarded as obvious that the methods of taxation should be adjusted to the amount to be raised, since in the past the need for additional revenue regularly led to a search for new sources of taxation. Additional expenditure thus always raised the question of who should pay for it. The theory and practice of public finance has been shaped almost entirely by the endeavour to disguise as far as possible the burden imposed, and to make those who will ultimately have to bear it as little aware of it as possible. It is probable that the whole complexity of the tax structure we have built up is largely the result of the efforts to persuade citizens to give the government more than they would knowingly consent to do.

To distinguish effectively the legislation on the general rules by which the tax burden is to be apportioned among the individuals from the determination of the total sums to be raised, would require such a complete re-thinking of all the principles of public finance that the first reaction of those familiar with the existing institutions will probably be to regard such a scheme as wholly impracticable. Yet nothing short of such a complete reconsideration of the institutional setting of financial legislation can probably stop that trend towards a continuing and progressive rise of that share of the income of society which is controlled by government. This trend, if allowed to continue, would before long swallow up the whole of society in the organization of government.

It is evident that taxation in accordance with a uniform rule can have no place for any overall progression of the total tax burden, although, as I have discussed elsewhere,[8] some progression of the direct taxes may not only be permissible but necessary to offset the tendency of indirect taxes to be regressive. I have in the same place also suggested some general principles by which we might so limit taxation as to prevent the shifting of the burden by a majority to the shoulders of a minority, but at the same time leave open the unobjectionable possibility of a majority conceding to a weak minority certain advantages.

EIGHTEEN

THE CONTAINMENT OF POWER AND THE DETHRONEMENT OF POLITICS

We are living at a time when justice has vanished. Our parliaments light-heartedly produce statutes which are contrary to justice. States deal with their subjects arbitrarily without attempting to preserve a sense of justice. Men who fall under the power of another nation find themselves to all intents and purposes outlawed. There is no longer any respect for their natural right to their homeland or their dwelling place or property, their right to earn a living or to sustenance, or to anything whatever. Our trust in justice has been wholly destroyed.

Albert Schweitzer

Limited and unlimited power

The effective limitation of power is the most important problem of social order. Government is indispensable for the formation of such an order only to protect all against coercion and violence from others. But as soon as, to achieve this, government successfully claims the monopoly of coercion and violence, it becomes also the chief threat to individual freedom. To limit this power was the great aim of the founders of constitutional government in the seventeenth and eighteenth centuries. But the endeavour to contain the powers of government was almost inadvertently abandoned when it came to be mistakenly believed that democratic control of the exercise of power provided a sufficient safeguard against its excessive growth.[1]

We have since learnt that the very omnipotence conferred on democratic representative assemblies exposes them to irresistible pressure to use their power for the benefit of special interests, a pressure a majority with unlimited powers cannot resist if it is to remain a majority. This development can be prevented only by depriving the governing majority of the power to grant discriminat-

THE CONTAINMENT OF POWER

ory benefits to groups or individuals. This has generally been believed to be impossible in a democracy because it appears to require that another will be placed above that of the elected representatives of a majority. In fact democracy needs even more severe restraints on the discretionary powers government can exercise than other forms of government, because it is much more subject to effective pressure from special interests, perhaps of small numbers, on which its majority depends.

The problem seemed insoluble, however, only because an older ideal had been forgotten, namely that the power of all authorities exercising governmental functions ought to be limited by long run rules which nobody has the power to alter or abrogate in the service of particular ends: principles which are the terms of association of the community that recognizes an authority because this authority is committed to such long-term rules. It was the constructivistic-positivist superstition which led to the belief that there must be some single unlimited supreme power from which all other power is derived, while in fact the supreme authority owes its respect to restraint by limiting general rules.

What today we call democratic government serves, as a result of its construction, not the opinion of the majority but the varied interests of a conglomerate of pressure groups whose support the government must buy by the grant of special benefits, simply because it cannot retain its supporters when it refuses to give them something it has the power to give. The resulting progressive increase of discriminating coercion now threatens to strangle the growth of a civilization which rests on individual freedom. An erroneous constructivistic interpretation of the order of society, combined with mistaken understanding of the meaning of justice, has indeed become the chief danger to the future not only of wealth, but of morals and peace. Nobody with open eyes can any longer doubt that the danger to personal freedom comes chiefly from the left, not because of any particular ideals it pursues, but because the various socialist movements are the only large organized bodies which, for aims which appeal to many, want to impose upon society a preconceived design. This must lead to the extinction of all moral responsibility of the individual and has already progressively removed, one after the other, most of those safeguards of individual freedom which had been built up through centuries of the evolution of law.

To regain certain fundamental truths which generations of

demagoguery have obliterated, it is necessary to learn again to understand why the basic values of a great or open society must be negative, assuring the individual of the right within a known domain to pursue his own aims on the basis of his own knowledge. Only such negative rules make possible the formation of a self-generating order, utilizing the knowledge, and serving the desires, of the individuals. We shall have to reconcile ourselves to the still strange fact that in a society of free men the highest authority must in normal times have no power of positive commands whatever. Its sole power should be that of prohibition according to rule, so that it would owe its supreme position to its commitment with every act to a general principle.

Peace, freedom and justice: the three great negatives

The fundamental reason why the best that a government can give a great society of free men is negative is the unalterable ignorance of any single mind, or any organization that can direct human action, of the immeasurable multitude of particular facts which must determine the order of its activities. Only fools believe that they know all, but there are many. This ignorance is the cause why government can only assist (or perhaps make possible) the formation of an abstract pattern or structure in which the several expectations of the members approximately match each other, through making these members observe certain negative rules or prohibitions which are independent of particular purposes. It can only assure the abstract character and not the positive content of the order that will arise from the individuals' use of their knowledge for their purpose by delimiting their domains against each other by abstract and negative rules. Yet this very fact that in order to make most effective the use by the individuals of the information they possess for their own purposes, the chief benefit government can offer them must be 'merely' negative, most people find difficult to accept. In consequence all constructivists try to chisel on the original conception of these ideals.

Perhaps the only one of the great ideals with regard to which people are generally prepared to accept its negative character and would at once reject any attempt at chiselling its peace. I hope, at least, that if, say, a Krushchev had used the popular socialist gambit to agree to peace provided it was 'positive peace', everybody would have understood that this simply meant peace only if he could do what he liked. But few seem to recognize that if the intellectual chisellers demand that liberty, or justice, or law be made 'positive', this is a similar attempt to pervert and abuse the basic ideals. As in the case of many other good things, such as quiet, health, leisure, peace of mind, or a good conscience, it is the absence of certain evils rather than the presence of positive goods which is the pre-condition of the success of individual endeavours.

Current usage, which has come to employ 'positive' and 'negative' almost as equivalent to 'good' and 'bad', and makes people feel that a 'negative value' is the opposite of a value, a dis-value or a harm, blinds many people to the crucial character of the greatest benefits our society can offer to us.

The three great negatives of Peace, Freedom and Justice are in fact the sole indispensable foundations of civilization which government must provide. They are necessarily absent in the 'natural' condition of primitive man, and man's innate instincts do not provide them for his fellows. They are, as we shall see in the postscript, the most important yet still only imperfectly assured products of the rules of civilization.

Coercion can assist free men in the pursuit of their ends only by the enforcement of a framework of universal rules which do not direct them to particular ends, but, by enabling them to create for themselves a domain protected against unpredictable disturbance caused by other men – including agents of government – to pursue their own ends. And if the greatest need is security against infringement of such a protected sphere by others, including government, the highest authority needed is one who can merely say 'no' to others but has itself no 'positive' powers.

The conception of a highest authority which cannot issue any commands sounds strange and even contradictory to us because it has come to be believed that a highest authority must be an all-comprehensive, omnipotent authority which comprises all the powers of the subordinate authorities. But there is no justification at all for this 'positivist' belief. Except when as a result of external human or natural forces the self-generating order is disturbed and emergency measures are required to restore the conditions for its operation, there is no need for such 'positive' powers of the supreme authority. Indeed, there is every reason to desire as the highest authority such a one that all its powers rest on its committing itself to the kind of abstract rules which, independently of the particular consequences, require it to prevent interference with the

131

acquired rights of the individuals by government or private agencies. Such an authority which normally is committed to certain recognized principles and then can order enforcement of such general rules, but so long as society is not threatened by outside forces has no other coercive powers whatever, may still be above all governmental powers – even be the only common power over a whole territory, while all the properly governmental powers might be separate for the different regions.

Centralization and decentralization

The amount of centralization which we take for granted and in which the supreme legislature and the supreme governmental power are part of the same unitary organization of what we call a nation or a state (and which is little reduced even in federal states), is essentially the effect of the need of making this organization strong for war. But now, when at least in Western Europe and North America we believe we have excluded the possibility of war between the associated nations and are relying for defence (we hope effectively) on a supranational organization, we ought gradually to discover that we can reduce the centralization and cease to entrust so many tasks to the national government, merely to make that government strong against external enemies.

It was necessary, in the interest of clarity, in the context of this book to discuss the changes in the constitutional structure, required if individual freedom is to be preserved, with reference to the most familiar type of a unitary state. But they are in fact even more suitable for a decentralized hierarchic structure on federal lines. We can here mention only a few major aspects of this.

The bicameral system, usually regarded as essential for a federal constitution, has under the scheme proposed here been preempted for another purpose; but its function in a federation could be achieved by other means, such as a system of double counting of votes, at least in the governmental assembly: once according to heads and once according to the number of states represented in the central assembly. It would probably be desirable to restrict federal arrangements to government proper and to have a single legislative assembly for the whole federation. But it is not really necessary always to have both legislative assemblies and governmental assemblies on the same level of the hierarchy, provided that the governmental power, whether extending to a smaller or a larger territory than the legislative power, is always limited by the latter.

132

This would seem to make it desirable that the legislative power should extend over a larger territory than the governmental one; but there exist of course several instances (Great Britain with a different system of private law in England and Scotland, the USA with the common law in most states and the Code Napoleon in one) with a central governmental executive ruling over territories with different law, and a few (the British Commonwealth of Nations to some extent and for a period) where the highest power determining the law (the court of last instance) was common to a number of otherwise wholly independent governments.

More important for our purposes are, however, the desirable devolutions which would become possible once the power of a supranational authority to say 'no' to actions harmful to associated states had reduced the necessity of a strong central national government for defence purposes. Most service activities of government might then indeed with advantage be delegated to regional or local authorities, wholly limited in their coercive powers by the rules laid down by a higher legislative authority.

There exists, of course, neither on the national nor on the international level, a moral ground why poorer regions should be entitled to tap for their purposes the wealth of richer regions. Yet centralization advances, not because the majority of the people in the large region are anxious to supply the means for assistance to the poorer regions, but because the majority, to be a majority, needs the additional votes from the regions which benefit from sharing in the wealth of the larger unit. And what is happening in the existing nations is beginning to happen on an international scale, where, by a silly competition with Russia, the capitalist nations, instead of lending capital to enterprise in countries which pursue economic policies which they regard as promising, are actually subsidizing on a large scale the socialist experiments of underdeveloped countries where they know that the funds that they supply will be largely wasted.

The rule of the majority versus *the rule of laws approved by the majority*

Not only peace, justice and liberty, but also democracy is basically a negative value, a procedural rule which serves as protection against despotism and tyranny, and certainly no more but not much less important than the first Three Great Negatives – or, to put it differently, a convention which mainly serves to prevent harm. But,

133

like liberty and justice, it is now being destroyed by endeavours to give it a 'positive' content. I am fairly certain that the days of unlimited democracy are numbered. We will, if we are to pre-serve the basic values of democracy, have to adopt a different form of it, or sooner or later lose altogether the power of getting rid of an oppressive government.

As we have seen (chapters 12, 13 and 16), under the pre-vailing system it is not the common opinion of a majority that decides on common issues, but a majority that owes its existence and power to the gratifying of the special interests of numerous small groups, which the representatives cannot refuse to grant if they are to remain a majority. But while agreement of the maj-ority of a great society on general rules is possible, the so-called approval by the majority of a conglomerate of measures serving particular interests is a farce. Buying majority support by deals with special interests, though this is what contemporary democ-racy has come to mean, has nothing to do with the original ideal of democracy, and is certainly contrary to the more fundamental moral conception that all use of force ought to be guided and limited by the opinion of the majority. The vote-buying process which we have come to accept as a necessary part of the demo-cracy we know, and which indeed is inevitable in a representative assembly which has the power both to pass general laws and to issue commands, is morally indefensible and produces all that which to the outsider appears as contemptible in politics. It is certainly not a necessary consequence of the ideal that the opin-ion of the majority should rule, but is in conflict with it.

This error is closely connected with the misconception that the majority must be free to do what it likes. A majority of the representatives of the people based on bargaining over group demands can never represent the opinion of the majority of the people. Such 'freedom of Parliament' means the oppression of the people. It is wholly in conflict with the conception of a con-stitutional limitation of governmental power, and irreconcilable with the ideal of a society of free men. The exercise of the power of a representative democracy beyond the range where voters can comprehend the significance of its decisions can cor-respond to (or be controlled by) the opinion of the majority of the people only if in all its coercive measures government is con-fined to rules which apply equally to all members of the community.

So long as the present form of democracy persists, decent government cannot exist, even if the politicians are angels or profoundly
convinced of the supreme value of personal freedom. We have no
right to blame them for what they do, because it is we who, by
maintaining the present institutions, place them in a position in
which they can obtain power to do any good only if they commit
themselves to secure special benefits for various groups. This has
led to the attempt to justify these measures by the construction of a
pseudo-ethics, called 'social justice', which fails every test which a
system of moral rules must satisfy in order to secure a peace and
voluntary co-operation of free men.

It is the crucial contention of this book that what in a society of
free men can alone justify coercion is a predominant opinion on the
principles which ought to govern and restrain individual conduct. It
is obvious that a peaceful and prosperous society can exist only if
some such rules are generally obeyed and, when necessary, enforced. This has nothing to do with any 'will' aiming at a particular
objective.

What to most people still seems strange and even incomprehensible is that in such a society the supreme power must be a
limited power, not all-comprehensive but confined to restraining
both organized government and private persons and organizations
by the enforcement of general rules of conduct. Yet it can be the
condition of submission which creates the state that the only authorization for coercion by the supreme authority refers to the
enforcement of general rules of conduct equally applicable to all.
Such a supreme power ought to owe the allegiance and respect
which it claims to its commitment to the general principles, to secure
obedience to which is the sole task for which it may use coercion. It
is to make these principles conform to general opinion that the
supreme legislature is made representative of the views of the
majority of the people.

Moral confusion and the decay of language

Under the influence of socialist agitation in the course of the last
hundred years the very sense in which many of the key words
describing political ideals are used has so changed meaning that one
must today hesitate to use even words like 'liberty', 'justice', 'democracy' or 'law', because they no longer convey the meaning they
once did. But, as Confucius is reported to have said, 'when words

135

lose their meaning, people will lose their liberty'. It was, unfortunately, not only ignorant propagandists but often grave social philosophers who contributed to this decay of language by twisting well established words to seduce people to serve what they imagined to be good purposes. When a John Dewey defines liberty as 'the effective power to do specific things'[2] this might seem a devious trick to delude innocents. But if another social philosopher argues in discussing democracy that 'the most promising line of approach is to say that democracy . . . is considered good because on the whole it is the best device for securing certain elements of social justice',[3] it is evidently just incredible naivety.

The younger generation of social philosophers apparently do not even know what the basic concepts once meant. Only thus can it be explained when we find a young scholar seriously asserting that the usage of speaking of a 'just state of affairs . . . must be regarded as the primary one, for when we describe a man as just we mean that he usually attempts to act in such a way that a just state of affairs results'[4] and even adding a few pages later that 'there appears [!] to be a category of "private justice" which concerns the dealing of a man with his fellows where he is not acting as a participant in one of the major social institutions.'[5] This may perhaps be accounted for by the fact that today a young man will first encounter the term 'justice' in some such connection, but it is of course a travesty of the evolution of the concept. As we have seen, a state of affairs which has not been deliberately brought about by men can possess neither intelligence nor virtue, nor justice, nor any other attribute of human values – not even if it is the unpredictable result of a game which people have consented to play by entering in their own interest into exchange relations with others. Justice is, of course, not a question of the aims of an action but of its obedience to rules which it obeys.

These instances, culled almost at random, of the current abuse of political terms in which those who have skill with words, by shifting the meaning of concepts they have perhaps never quite understood, have gradually emptied them of all clear content, could be increased indefinitely. It is difficult to know what to do when the enemies of liberty describe themselves as liberals, as is today common practice in the USA – except calling them persistently, as we ought to do, pseudo-liberals – or when they appeal to democracy when they mean egalitarianism. It is all part of that 'Treason of the Intellectuals' which Julien Benda castigated forty years ago, but which has since succeeded in creating a reign of untruthfulness which has become habitual in discussing issues of 'social' policy, and in the current language of politicians who habitually employ this make-believe without themselves knowing it as such.

But it is not merely the confessed socialists who drive us along that road. Socialist ideas have so deeply penetrated general thought that it is not even only those pseudo-liberals who merely disguise their socialism by the name they have assumed, but also many conservatives who have assumed socialist ideas and language and constantly employ them in the belief that they are an established part of current thought. Nor is it only people who have strong views on, or take an active part in public affairs.[7] Indeed the most active spreading of socialist conceptions still takes place through what David Hume called the fiction of poets,[8] the ignorant literati who are sure that the appealing words they employ have definite meaning. Only because we are so habituated to this can it be explained that, for instance, hundreds of thousands of business men all over the world still allow over their doorsteps journals which in their literary part will resort even to obscene language (such as 'the excremental abundance of capitalist production' in *Time* magazine of 27 June 1977) to ridicule capitalism.[9] Though the principle of freedom requires that we tolerate such scandalous scurrilities, one might have hoped that the good sense of the readers would soon learn what publications they can trust.[10]

Democratic procedure and egalitarian objectives

Perhaps the worst sufferer in this process of the emptying of the meaning of words has in recent times been the word 'democracy' itself. Its chief abuse is to apply it not to a procedure of arriving at agreement on common action, but to give it a substantive content prescribing what the aim of those activities ought to be. However absurd this clearly is, many of the current invocations of democracy amount to telling democratic legislatures what they ought to do. Except so far as organization of government is concerned, the term 'democratic' says nothing about the particular aims people ought to vote for.

The true value of democracy is to serve as a sanitary precaution protecting us against an abuse of power. It enables us to get rid of a government and try to replace it by a better one. Or, to put it differently, it is the only convention we have yet discovered to make peaceful change possible. As such it is a high value well worth

137

fighting for, since any government the people cannot get rid of by such an agreed procedure is bound to fall sooner or later into bad hands. But it is far from being the highest political value, and an unlimited democracy may well be worse than limited governments of a different kind.

In its present unlimited form democracy has today largely lost the capacity of serving as a protection against arbitrary power. It has ceased to be a safeguard of personal liberty, a restraint on the abuse of governmental power which it was hoped it would prove to be when it was naively believed that, when all power was made subject to democratic control, all the other restraints on governmental power could be dispensed with. It has, on the contrary, become the main cause of a progressive and accelerating increase of the power and weight of the administrative machine.

The omnipotent and omnicompetent single democratic assembly, in which a majority capable of governing can maintain itself only by trying to remove all sources of discontent of any supporter of that majority, is thereby driven to take control of all spheres of life. It is forced to develop and impose, in justification of the measures it must take to retain majority support, a non-existing and in the strict sense of the word inconceivable code of distributive justice. In such a society, to have political pull becomes much more rewarding than adding to the means of satisfying the needs of one's fellows. As everything tends to become a political issue for which the inter-ference of the coercive powers of government can be invoked, an ever larger part of human activity is diverted from productive into political efforts – not only of the political machinery itself but, worse, of that rapidly expanding apparatus of para-government designed to bring pressure on government to favour particular interests.

What is still not understood is that the majority of a representa-tive assembly with unlimited powers is neither able, nor constrain-ed, to confine its activities to aims which all the members of the majority desire, or even approve of.[11] If such an assembly has the power to grant special benefits, a majority can regularly be kept together only by paying off each of the special groups by which it is composed. In other words, we have under the false name of demo-cracy created a machinery in which not the majority decides, but each member of the majority has to consent to many bribes to get majority support for his own special demands. However admirable the principle of majority decisions may be with respect to matters which necessarily concern all, so vicious must be the result of an application of this procedure to distributing the booty which can be extracted from a dissident minority.

It seems to be inevitable that if we retain democracy in its present form, the concept itself is bound to become discredited to such an extent that even the legitimate case for majority decisions on questions of principle will go by default. Democracy is in danger because the particular institutions by which we have tried to realize it have produced effects which we mistake for those of the genuine article. As I have myself suggested before, I am even no longer certain that the name democracy can still be freed from the distaste with which increasing numbers of people for good reasons have come to regard it, even though few yet dare publicly to express their disillusionment.[12]

The root of the trouble is, of course, to sum up, that in an unlimited democracy the holders of discretionary powers are forced to use them, whether they wish it or not, to favour particular groups on whose swing-vote their powers depend. This applies as much to government as to such democratically organized institutions as trades unions. Even if, in the case of government, some of these powers may serve to enable it to do much that might be desirable in itself, we must renounce conferring them since such discretionary powers inevitably and necessarily place the authority into a position in which it will be forced to do even more that is harmful.

'State' and 'society'

If democracy is to maintain a society of free men, the majority of a political body must certainly not have the power to 'shape' a society, or make its members serve particular ends – i.e. ends other than the abstract order which it can secure only by enforcing equally abstract rules of conduct. The task of government is to create a framework within which individuals and groups can successfully pursue their respective aims, and sometimes to use its coercive powers of raising revenue to provide services which for one reason or other the market cannot supply. But coercion is justified only in order to provide such a framework within which all can use their abilities and knowledge for their own ends so long as they do not interfere with the equally protected individual domains of others. Except when 'Acts of God or the King's enemies' make it necessary to confer temporary emergency powers on an authority which can at any time

139

be revoked by the agency which has conferred them, nobody need possess power of discriminating coercion. (Where such powers may have to be used to prevent suspected crime, the person to whom it has been erroneously applied ought to be entitled to full compensation for all injury suffered.)

Much confusion of this issue is due to a tendency (particularly strong in the Continental tradition, but with the spreading of socialist ideas growing rapidly also in the Anglo-Saxon world) to identify 'state' and 'society'. The state, the organization of the people of a territory under a single government, although an indispensible condition for the development of an advanced society, is yet very far from being identical with society, or rather with the multiplicity of grown and self-generating structures of men who have any freedom that alone deserves the name of society. In a free society the state is one of many organizations – the one which is required to provide an effective external framework within which self-generating orders can form, but an organization which is confined to the government apparatus and which does not determine the activities of the free individuals. And while this organization of the state will contain many voluntary organizations, it is the spontaneously grown network of relationships between the individuals and the various organizations they create that constitutes societies. Societies form but states are made. This is why so far as they can produce the needed services, or self-generating structures, societies are infinitely preferable, while the organizations based on the power of coercion tend to become a straitjacket that proves to be harmful as soon as it uses its powers beyond the enforcement of the indispensibly abstract rules of conduct.

It is in fact very misleading to single out the inhabitants or citizens of a particular political unit as the prototype of a society. There exists, under modern conditions, no single society to which an individual normally belongs, and it is highly desirable that this should not be so. Each of us is fortunately a member of many different overlapping and interlacing societies to which he may belong more or less strongly or lastingly. Society is a network of voluntary relationships between individuals and organized groups, and strictly speaking there is hardly ever merely one society to which any person exclusively belongs. For practical purposes it may be innocuous to single out, in a particular context, some part of the complex order of often hierarchically related networks as specially relevant for the topic discussed, and to assume that it will be understood to which part of this complex the speaker or writer refers as 'the society'. But it should never be forgotten that today many persons and organizations belong to networks which extend over national boundaries as well as that within any nation any one may be an element in many different structures of this kind.

Indeed, the operation of the spontaneous ordering forces, and of the rules of conduct making possible the formations of such orderly structures which we describe as societies, becomes fully intelligible (and at the same time our inability to comprehend their functioning in detail evident) only if we are aware of the multiplicity of such overlapping structures.

Anyone aware of the complex nature of this net of relationships determining the processes of society should also readily recognize the erroneous anthropomorphism of conceiving of society as 'acting' or 'willing' anything. Originally it was of course an attempt of socialists to disguise the fact that their proposals amounted to an endeavour to enhance the coercive powers of government when they prefered to speak of 'socialization' rather than 'nationalization' or 'politicalization' of the means of production, etc. But this led them deeper and deeper into the anthropomorphic interpretation of society – that tendency of interpreting the results of spontaneous processes as being directed by some 'will', or being produced or producible by design, which is so deeply engrained in the structure of primitive human thinking.

Not only do most processes of social evolution take place without anybody willing or foreseeing them – it is only because of this that they lead to cultural evolution. Out of a directed process nothing greater can emerge than the directing mind can foresee. He will be the only one who would be allowed to profit from experience. A developing society does not advance by government impressing new ideas on it, but by new ways and methods constantly being tried in a process of trial and error. It is, to repeat once more, the favourable general conditions that will assist unknown persons in unknown circumstances which produce the improvement which no supreme authority could bring about.

A game according to rules can never know justice of treatment

It was in effect the discovery that playing a game according to rules improved the *chances* of all, even at the risk that the outcome for some might be worse than it would be otherwise, which made

141

classical liberalism aim at the complete elimination of power in determining relative incomes earned in the market. Combined with the provision of cushioning the risk by providing *outside* the market a uniform minimum income for all those who for some reason are unable to earn at least that much in the market, it leaves no moral justification for a use of force to determine relative incomes by government or any other organized group. Indeed, it becomes the clear moral duty of government not only itself to refrain from any such interference in the game, but also to prevent the arrogation of such power by any organized group.

In such an order in which the use of force to determine relative or absolute material positions is on principle excluded, it can be as little a matter of justice what at any given moment a person ought to be induced to do in the general interest, as how much he ought to be offered in remuneration. The relative social usefulness of the different activities of any one person, and even of the various activities which different persons may pursue, is unfortunately not a matter of justice but the result of events which cannot be foreseen or controlled. What the public, and, I am afraid, even many reputed economists, fail to understand is that the prices offered for services in this process serve not as remunerations of the different people for what they have done, but as signals telling them what they ought to do, in their own as well as in the general interest.

It is simply silly to represent the different prizes which different persons will draw in the game that we have learnt to play because it secures the fullest utilization of dispersed knowledge and skills, as if the participants were 'treated' differently by society – even if the initial position is determined by the accidental circumstances of previous history, during which the game may not always have been played honestly, if the aim is to provide maximum opportunity to men as they are, without any arbitrary coercion, we can achieve our ends only by treating them according to the same rules irrespective of their factual differences, leaving the outcome to be decided by those constant restructurings of the economic order which are determined by circumstances nobody can foresee.

The basic conception of classical liberalism, which alone can make decent and impartial government possible, is that government must *regard* all people as equal, however unequal they may in fact be, and that in whatever manner the government restrains (or assists) the action of one, so it must, under the same abstract rules, restrain (or assist) the actions of all others. Nobody has special

142

claims on government because he is either rich or poor, beyond the assurance of protection against all violence from anybody and the assurance of a certain flat minimum income if things go wholly wrong. Even to take notice of the factual inequality of individuals, and to make this the excuse of any discriminating coercion, is a breach of the basic terms on which free man submits to government.

This game serves not only the winner, because his gain from having served the others best is always only part of what he has added to the social product; and it is only by playing according to the rules of this game that we can assure that high degree of utilization of resources which no other known method can achieve.

The para-government of organized interests and the hypertrophy of government

Many of the gravest defects of contemporary government, widely recognized and deplored but believed to be inevitable consequences of democracy, are in fact the consequences only of the unlimited character of present democracy. The basic fact is still not clearly seen that under this form of government whatever the government has constitutional power to do it can be forced to do, even against its better judgment, if those benefiting by the measure are 'swing groups' on whose support the majority of the government depends. The consequence is that the apparatus of organized particular interests designed solely to bring pressure on government is becoming the worst incubus forcing government to be harmful.

The pretence can hardly be taken seriously that all these features of incipient corporativism which make up the para-government are necessary to advise government on the probable effects of its decisions. I will not attempt here to estimate how large a proportion of the ablest and best informed members of society are already absorbed into these essentially anti-social activities beyond emphasizing that both sides of what are now euphemistically called 'social partners' (*Sozialpartner*) are frequently forced to divert some of their best people from supplying what the public needs to the task of stultifying each other's efforts. I have little to add to the masterly description of the mechanism of this process of government by coalitions of organized interests which Professor Mancur Olson, Jr, has given in his book on *The Logic of Collective Action*, [13] and will merely recapitulate a few points.

Of course, all pressure on government to make it use its coercive

143

powers to benefit particular groups is harmful to the generality. But it is inexcusable to pretend that in this respect the position is the same on all sides and that in particular the pressure which can be brought by the large firms or corporations is comparable to that of the organization of labour which in most countries have been authorized by law or jurisdiction to use coercion to gain support for their policies. By conferring, for supposedly 'social' reasons, on the trades unions unique privileges, which hardly government itself enjoys, organizations of workers have been enabled to exploit other workers by altogether depriving them of the opportunity of good employment. Though this fact is conventionally still ignored, the chief powers of the trades unions rests today entirely on their being allowed to use power to prevent other workers from doing work they would wish to do.

But quite apart from the fact that by the exercise of this power particular trade unions can achieve only a relative improvement of the wages of their members, at the price of reducing the general productivity of labour and thus the general level of real wages, combined with the necessity in which they can place a government that controls the quantity of money to inflate, this system is rapidly destroying the economic order. Trades unions can now put governments in a position in which the only choice they have is to inflate or to be blamed for the unemployment which is caused by the wage policy of the trades unions (especially their policy of keeping relations between wages of different unions constant). This position must before long destroy the whole market order, probably through the price controls which accelerating inflation will force governments to impose.

As little as the whole role of the growing para-government can I at this stage begin to discuss the threat created by the incessant growth of the government machinery, i.e. the bureaucracy. Democracy, at the same time at which it seems to become all-engulfing, becomes on the governmental level an impossibility. It is an illusion to believe that the people, or their elected representatives, can govern a complex society in detail. Government relying on the general support from a majority will of course still determine the major steps, so far as it is not merely driven to these by the momentum of its previous proceedings. But Government is already becoming so complex that is is inevitable that its members, as heads of the various departments, are increasingly becoming puppets of the bureaucracy, to which they will still give 'general directions', but on the operation of which the execution of all the detail depends. It is not without reason that socialist governments want to politicize this bureaucracy, because it is by it and not in any democratic body that more and more of the crucial decisions are made. No totalitarian power can be achieved without this.

Unlimited democracy and centralization

Nowhere are the effects of unlimited democracy more clearly shown than in the general increase of the power of central government by the assumption of functions formerly performed by regional or local authorities. Probably with the sole exception of Switzerland, central government has almost everywhere not only become *the* government *par excellence,* but it is steadily drawing more and more activities into its exclusive competence. That a nation is governed chiefly from its national capital and that this central power not only gives it a common structure of law (or at least secures that there is a determinable law regulating the relations between all its inhabitants), but that also more and more of the services which government renders to the people are directed from a single centre of command, has come to be regarded as inevitable and natural – even though recently in many parts of the world tendencies to secessionism show an increasingly resentment of this situation.

Recently the growth of the powers of central government has also been much assisted by those central planners who, when their schemes failed on a local or regional level, regularly claimed that in order to be effective they must be applied on a larger scale. The failure to master even the problems of a moderate range was often made the excuse for attempting still more ambitious schemes still less suitable for the central direction or control by authority.

But the decisive ground of the growing preponderance of central government in modern times is that only on that level, at least in unitary states, the legislation possessed the unlimited power which no legislation ought to possess and which enabled it so to fashion its 'laws' as to empower the administration to use the discretionary and discriminatory measures which are necessary to achieve the desired control of the economic process. If the central government can order many things which a local government cannot, it becomes the easiest way to meet group demands to push the decision up to the authority that possesses these powers. To deprive the national (and

145

in federations the state) legislatures of the power to use legislation for conferring discretionary powers on the administration would therefore remove the chief cause of the progressive centralization of all government.

The devolution of internal policy to local government [14]

Without those arbitrary powers inadvertently conferred on 'legislatures', the whole structure of governments would undoubtedly have developed on very different lines. If all administration were under a uniform law it could not alter, and which nobody could change to make it serve specific administrative purposes, the abuse of legislation in the service of special interests would cease. Most service activities now rendered by central government could be devolved to regional or local authorities which would possess the power to raise taxes at a rate they could determine but which they could levy or apportion only according to general rules laid down by a central legislature.

I believe the result would be the transformation of local and even regional governments into quasi-commercial corporations competing for citizens. They would have to offer a combination of advantages and costs which made life within their territory at least as attractive as elsewhere within the reach of its potential citizens. Assuming their powers to be so limited by law as not to restrict free migration, and that they could not discriminate in taxation, their interest would be wholly to attract those who in their particular condition could make the greatest contribution to the common product.

To re-entrust the management of most service activities of government to smaller units would probably lead to the revival of a communal spirit which has been largely suffocated by centralization. The widely felt inhumanity of the modern society is not so much the result of the impersonal character of the economic process, in which modern man of necessity works largely for aims of which he is ignorant, but of the fact that political centralization has largely deprived him of the chance to have a say in shaping the environment which he knows. The Great Society can only be an abstract society – an economic order from which the individual profits by obtaining the means for all his ends, and to which he must make his anonymous contribution. This does not satisfy his emotional, personal needs. To the ordinary individual it is much more

146

important to take part in the direction of his local affairs that are now taken largely out of the hands of men he knows and can learn to trust, and transferred to a remoter bureaucracy which to him is an inhuman machine. And while within the sphere which the individual knows, it can only be beneficial to rouse his interest and induce him to contribute his knowledge and opinion, it can produce only disdain for all politics if he is mostly called upon to express views on matters which do not recognizably concern him.[15]

The abolition of the government monopoly of services

There is of course no need for central government to decide who should be entitled to render the different services, and it is highly undesirable that it should possess mandatory powers to do so. Indeed, though it may in some instances for the time being be true that only governmental agencies with compulsory powers of levying contributions can render certain services, there is no justification for any governmental agency possessing the exclusive right of supplying any particular service. Though it might turn out that the established supplier of some services is in so much better a position to render it than any possible competitor from private enterprise, and thus will achieve a *de facto* monopoly, there is no social interest in giving him a legal monopoly of any kind of activity. This means of course that any governmental agency allowed to use its taxing power to finance such services ought to be required to refund any taxes raised for these purposes to all those who prefer to get the services in some other way. This applies without exception to all those services of which today government possesses or aspires to a legal monopoly, with the only exception of maintaining and enforcing the law and maintaining for this purpose (including defence against external enemies) an armed force, i.e. all those from education to transport and communications, including post, telegraph, telephone and broadcasting services, all the so-called 'public' utilities', the various 'social' insurances and, above all, the issue of money. Some of these services may well for the time being most efficiently be performed by a *de facto* monopoly; but we can neither insure improvement nor protect ourselves against extortion unless the possibility exists of somebody else offering better services of any of these kinds.

As with most of the topics touched upon in this final chapter, I cannot enter here into any more detailed discussion of the service activities which are today rendered by government; but in some of these cases the question whether the government ought to possess an exclusive right to them is of decisive importance, not merely a question of efficiency but of crucial significance of the preservation of a free society. In these cases the objection against any monopoly powers of government must preponderate, even if such a monopoly should promise services of higher quality. We may still discover for example, that a government broadcasting monopoly may prove as great a threat to political freedom as an abolition of the freedom of the press would be. The postal system is another instance where the prevailing government monopoly is the result solely of the striving of government for control over private activity and has in most parts of the world produced a steadily deteriorating service.

Above all, however, I am bound to stress that in the course of the work on this book I have been, by the confluence of political and economic considerations, led to the firm conviction that a free economic system will never again work satisfactorily and we shall never remove its most serious defects or stop the steady growth of government, unless the monopoly of the issue of money is taken from government. I have found it necessary to develop this argument in a separate book,[16] indeed I fear now that all the safeguards against oppression and other abuses of governmental power which the restructuring of government on the lines suggested in this volume are intended to achieve, would be of little help unless at the same time the control of government over the supply of money is removed. Since I am convinced that there are now no longer any rigid rules possible which would secure a supply of money by government by which at the same time the legitimate demands for money are satisfied and the value of that money kept stable, there appears to me to exist no other way of achieving this than to replace the present national moneys by competing different moneys offered by private enterprise, from which the public would be free to choose that which serves best for their transactions.

This seems to me so important that it would be essential for the constitution of a free people to entrench this principle by some special clause such as: 'Parliament shall make no law abridging the right of anybody to hold, buy, sell or lend, make and enforce contracts, calculate and keep their accounts in any kind of money they choose.' Although this is in fact implied in the basic principle that government can enforce or prohibit kinds of action only by general abstract rules, applying equally to everyone, including government itself, this particular application of the principle is still too unfamiliar to expect courts to comprehend that the age-old prerogative of government is no longer to be recognized, unless this is explicitly spelled out in the constitution.

The dethronement of politics

Though I had wished at the end of this work to give some indication of the implications of the principles developed for international affairs, I find it impossible to do so without letting the exposition grow to undue length. It would also require further investigations which I am loath to undertake at this stage. I believe the reader will have no difficulty in seeing in what manner the dismantling of the monolithic state, and the principle that all supreme power must be confined to essentially negative tasks – powers to say no – and that all positive powers must be confined to agencies which have to operate under rules they cannot alter, must have far-reaching applications to international organization. As I have suggested earlier,[17] it seems to me that in this century our attempts to create an international government capable of assuring peace have generally approached the task from the wrong end: creating large numbers of specialized authorities aiming at particular regulations rather than aiming at a true international law which would limit the powers of national governments to harm each other. If the highest common values are negative, not only the highest common rules but also the highest authority should essentially be limited to prohibitions.

It can scarcely be doubted that quite generally politics has become much too important, much too costly and harmful, absorbing much too much mental energy and material resources, and that at the same time it is losing more and more the respect and sympathetic support of the public at large who have come to regard it increasingly as a necessary but incurable evil that must be borne. Yet the present magnitude and remoteness and still all-pervasiveness of the whole apparatus of politics is not something men have chosen, but the outcome of a self-willed mechanism they have set up without foreseeing its effects. Government is now of course not a human being one can trust, as the inherited ideal of the good ruler still suggests to the naive mind. Nor is it the result of the joint wisdom of trusted representatives the majority of whom can agree on what is best. It is a machinery directed by 'political necessities' which are only remotely affected by the opinions of the majority.

While legislation proper is a matter of long-run principles and not particular interests, all particular measures which government may take must become issues of day-to-day politics. It is an illusion to believe that such specific measures are normally determined by objective necessities on which all reasonable people ought to be able to agree. There are always costs to be balanced against the objectives aimed at, and there is no objective tests of the relative importance of what may be achieved and what will have to be sacrificed. It is the great difference between general laws which aim at improving the chances of all by securing an order in which there are good prospects of finding a partner for a transaction favourable to both sides, and coercive measures aiming at benefiting particular people or groups. So long as it is legitimate for government to use force to effect a redistribution of material benefits – and this is the heart of socialism – there can be no curb on the rapacious instincts of all groups who want more for themselves. Once politics becomes a tug-of-war for shares in the income pie, decent government is impossible. This requires that all use of coercion to assure a certain income to particular groups (beyond a flat minimum for all who cannot earn more in the market) be outlawed as immoral and strictly anti-social.

Today the only holders of power unbridled by any law which binds them and who are driven by the political necessities of a self-willed machine are the so-called legislators. But this prevailing form of democracy is ultimately self-destructive, because it imposes upon governments tasks on which an agreed opinion of the majority does not and cannot exist. It is therefore necessary to restrain these powers in order to protect democracy against itself.

A constitution like the one here proposed would of course make all socialist measures for redistribution impossible. This is no less justified than any other constitutional limitations of power intended to make impossible the destruction of democracy and the rise of totalitarian powers. At least at the time, which I believe is not far off, when the traditional beliefs of socialism will be recognized as an illusion, it will be necessary to make provision against the ever-recurring infection with such illusions that is bound again and again to cause an inadvertent slide into socialism.

For this it will not be sufficient to stop those who desire to destroy democracy in order to achieve socialism, or even only those wholly committed to a socialist programme. The strongest support of the trend towards socialism comes today from those who claim that they want neither capitalism nor socialism but a 'middle way', or a 'third world'. To follow them is a certain path to socialism, because once we give licence to the politicians to interfere in the spontaneous order of the market for the benefit of particular groups, they cannot deny such concessions to any group on which their support depends. They thus initiate that cumulative process which by inner necessity leads, if not to what the socialists imagine, then to an ever-growing domination over the economic process by politics.

There exists no third principle for the organization of the economics process which can be rationally chosen to achieve any desirable ends, in addition to either a functioning market in which nobody can conclusively determine how well-off particular groups or individuals will be, or a central direction where a group organized for power determines it. The two principles are irreconcilable, since any combination prevents the achievement of the aims of either. And while we can never reach what the socialists imagine, the general licence to politicians to grant special benefits to those whose support they need still must destroy that self-forming order of the market which serves the general good, and replace it by a forcibly imposed order determined by some arbitrary human wills. We face an inescapable choice between two irreconcilable principles, and however far we may always remain from fully realizing either, there can be no stable compromise. Whichever principle we make the foundation of our proceedings, it will drive us on, no doubt always to something imperfect, but more and more closely resembling one of the two extremes.

Once it is clearly recognized that socialism as much as fascism or communism inevitably leads into the totalitarian state and the destruction of the democratic order, it is clearly legitimate to provide against our inadvertently sliding into a socialist system by constitutional provisions which deprive government of the discriminating powers of coercion even for what at the moment may generally be regarded as good purposes.

However little it may often appear to be true, the social world is governed in the long run by certain moral principles on which the people at large believe. The only moral principle which has ever made the growth of an advanced civilization possible was the principle of individual freedom, which means that the individual is guided in his decisions by rules of just conduct and not by specific commands. No principles of collective conduct which bind the individual can exist in a society of free men. What we have achieved we owe to securing to the individuals the chance of creating for themselves a protected domain (their 'property') within which they can use their abilities for their own purposes. Socialism lacks any principles of individual conduct yet dreams of a state of affairs which no moral action of free individuals can bring about.

The last battle against arbitrary power is still ahead of us – the fight against socialism and for the abolition of all coercive power to direct individual efforts and deliberately to distribute its results. I am looking forward to a time when this totalitarian and essentially arbitrary character of all socialism will be as generally understood as that of communism and of fascism and therefore constitutional barriers against any attempt to acquire such totalitarian powers on any pretext will be generally approved.

What I have been trying to sketch in these volumes (and the separate study of the role of money in a free society) has been a guide out of the process of degeneration of the existing form of government, and to construct an intellectual emergency equipment which will be available when we have no choice but to replace the tottering structure by some better edifice rather than resort in despair to some sort of dictatorial regime. Government is of necessity the product of intellectual design. If we can give it a shape in which it provides a beneficial framework for the free growth of society, without giving to any one power to control this growth in the particular, we may well hope to see the growth of civilization continue.

We ought to have learnt enough to avoid destroying our civilization by smothering the spontaneous process of the interaction of the individuals by placing its direction in the hands of any authority. But to avoid this we must shed the illusion that we can deliberately 'create the future of mankind', as the characteristic hubris of a socialist sociologist has recently expressed it.[18] This is the final conclusion of the forty years which I have now devoted to the study of these problems since I became aware of the process of the Abuse and Decline of Reason which has continued throughout that period.[19]

THE THREE SOURCES OF
HUMAN VALUES

Prophete rechts, Prophete links,
Das Weltkind in der Mitten

J. W. Goethe**

The errors of sociobiology

The challenge which made me re-order my thoughts on the present subject was an unusually explicit statement of what I now recognize as a widespread error implicit in much current discussion. I met it in an interesting new work of what is regarded as the new American science of social biology, Dr. G. E. Pugh's *The Biological Origin of Human Values*,[1] a book which has received great praise from the recognized head of this school, Professor Edward O. Wilson of Harvard University.[2] The startling point about it is that its whole argument is based on the express assumption that there are only two kinds of human values which Dr Pugh designates as 'primary' and 'secondary', meaning by the first term those which are genetically determined and therefore innate, while he defines the secondary ones as 'products of rational thought'.[3]

Social biology is, of course, the outcome of what is now already a fairly long development. Older members of the London School of Economics will remember that more than forty years ago a chair of sociobiology was established there. We have since had the great development of the fascinating study of ethology, founded by Sir Julian Huxley,[4] Konrad Lorenz,[5] and Niko Tinbergen,[6] now rapidly developed by their many gifted followers,[7] as well as a large number of American students. I must admit that even in the work of my Viennese friend Lorenz, which I have been following closely for fifty years, I have occasionally felt uneasy about an all-too-rapid application of conclusions drawn from the observation of animals to the explanation of human conduct. But none of these has done me

153

the favour to state as a basic assumption and to proceed consistently on what with the others seemed occasional careless formulations, namely that those two kinds of values are the only kinds of human values.

What is so surprising about this view occurring so frequently among biologists,[8] is that one might rather have expected that they would be sympathetic to that analogous yet in important respects different process of selective evolution to which is due the formation of complex cultural structures. Indeed, the idea of cultural evolution is undoubtedly older than the biological concept of evolution. It is even probable that its application by Charles Darwin to biology was, through his grandfather Erasmus, derived from the cultural evolution concept of Bernard Mandeville and David Hume, if not more directly from the contemporary historical schools of law and language.[9] It is true that, after Darwin, those 'social Darwinists' who had needed Darwin to learn what was an older tradition in their own subjects, had somewhat spoiled the case by concentrating on the selection of congenitally more fit individuals, the slowness of which makes it comparatively unimportant for cultural evolution, and at the same time neglecting the decisively important selective evolution of rules and practices. But there was certainly no justification for some biologists treating evolution as solely a genetic process,[10] and completely forgetting about the similar but much faster process of cultural evolution that now dominates the human scene and presents to our intelligence problems it has not yet learnt to master.

What I had not foreseen, however, was that a close examination of this mistake, common among some specialists, would lead right to the heart of some of the most burning moral and political issues of our time. What at first may seem a question of concern only to specialists, turns out to be a paradigm of some of the gravest ruling misconceptions. Though I rather hope that most of what I shall have to say is somewhat familiar to cultural anthropologists – and the concept of cultural evolution has of course been stressed not only by L. T. Hobhouse and his followers[11] and more recently particularly by Sir Julian Huxley,[12] Sir Alexander Carr-Saunders[13] and C. H. Waddington[14] in Britain and even more by G. G. Simpson, Theodosius Dobzhansky[15] and Donald T. Campbell[16] in the USA, it seems to me that the attention of moral philosophers, political scientists and economists still needs to be emphatically drawn to its importance. What has yet to be more widely recognized is that the present order of society has largely arisen, not by design, but by the prevailing of the more effective institutions in a process of competition.

Culture is neither natural nor artificial, neither genetically trans-mitted nor rationally designed. It is a tradition of learnt rules of conduct which have never been 'invented' and whose functions the acting individuals usually do not understand. There is surely as much justification to speak of the wisdom of culture as of the wisdom of nature – except, perhaps, that, because of the powers of government, errors of the former are less easily corrected.

It is here that the constructivistic Cartesian approach[17] has made thinkers accept as 'good' for a long time only what were either innate or deliberately chosen rules, and to regard all merely grown formations as mere products of accident or caprice. Indeed, 'merely cultural' has now to many the connotation of changeable at will, arbitrary, superficial, or dispensable. Actually, however, civilization has largely been made possible by subjugating the innate animal instincts to the non-rational customs which made possible the formation of larger orderly groups of gradually increasing size.

The process of cultural evolution

That cultural evolution is not the result of human reason con-sciously building institutions, but of a process in which culture and reason developed concurrently is, perhaps, beginning to be more widely understood. *It is probably no more justified to claim that thinking man has created his culture than that culture created his reason*[18] As I have repeatedly had occasion to point out, the mis-taken view has become deeply embedded in our thinking through the false dichotomy between what is 'natural' and what is 'artificial' which we have inherited from the ancient Greeks.[19] The structures formed by traditional human practices are neither natural in the sense of being genetically determined, nor artificial in the sense of being the product of intelligent design, but the result of a process of winnowing or sifting,[20] directed by the differential advantages gained by groups from practices adopted for some unknown and perhaps purely accidental reasons. We know now that not only among animals such as birds and particularly apes, learnt habits are transmitted by imitation, and even that different 'cultures' may develop among different groups of them,[21] but also that such acquired cultural traits may affect physiological evolution – as is obvious in the case of language: its rudimentary appearance undoubtedly made the physical capacity of clear articulation a great advantage, favouring genetic selection of a suitable speech apparatus.[22]

Nearly all writings on this topic stress that what we call cultural evolution took place during the last 1 per cent of the time during which *Homo sapiens* existed. With respect to what we mean by cultural evolution in a narrower sense, that is, the fast and accelerating development of civilization, this is true enough. Since it differs from genetic evolution by relying on the transmission of acquired properties, it is very fast, and once it dominates, it swamps genetic evolution. But this does not justify the misconception that it was the developed mind which in turn directed cultural evolution. This took place not merely after the appearance of *Homo sapiens*, but also during the much longer earlier existence of the genus *Homo* and its hominid ancestors. To repeat: *mind and culture developed concurrently and not successively*. Once we recognize this, we find that we know so little about precisely how this development took place, of which we have so few recognizable fossils, that we are reduced to reconstruct it as a sort of conjectural history in the sense of the Scottish moral philosophers of the eighteenth century. The facts about which we know almost nothing are the evolution of those rules of conduct which governed the structure and functioning of the various small groups of men in which the race developed. On this the study of still surviving primitive people can tell us little. Though the conception of conjectural history is somewhat suspect today, when we cannot say precisely how things did happen, to understand how they could have come about may be an important insight. The evolution of society and of language and the evolution of mind raise in this respect the same difficulty: the most important part of cultural evolution, the taming of the savage, was completed long before recorded history begins. It is this cultural evolution which man alone has undergone that now distinguishes him from the other animals. As Sir Ernest Gombrich put it somewhere: 'The history of civilization and of culture was the history of man's rise from a near animal state to polite society, the cultivation of arts, the adoption of civilized values and the free exercise of reason.[23]

To understand this development we must completely discard the conception that man was able to develop culture because he was endowed with reason. What apparently distinguished him was the capacity to imitate and to pass on what he had learned. Man probably began with a superior capacity to learn what to do – or even more, what not to do – in different circumstances. And much if not most of what he learnt about what to do he probably learnt by learning the meaning of words.[24] Rules for his conduct which made him adapt what he did to his environment were certainly more important to him than 'knowledge' about how other things behaved. In other words: man has certainly more often learnt to do the right thing without comprehending why it was the right thing, and he still is often served better by custom than by understanding. Other objects were primarily defined for him by the appropriate way of conduct towards them. It was a repertoire of learnt rules which told him what was the right and what was the wrong way of acting in different circumstances that gave him his increasing capacity to adapt to changing conditions – and particularly to co-operate with the other members of his group. Thus a tradition of rules of conduct, existing apart from any one individual who had learnt them, began to govern human life.[25] It was when these learnt rules, involving classifications of different kinds of objects, began to include a sort of model of the environment that enabled man to predict and anticipate in action external events, that what we call reason appeared.[26] There *was then probably much more 'intelligence' incorporated in the system of rules of conduct than in man's thoughts about his surroundings.*

It is therefore misleading to represent the individual brain or mind as the capping stone of the hierarchy of complex structures produced by evolution, which then designed what we call culture. The mind is embedded in a traditional impersonal structure of learnt rules, and its capacity to order experience is an acquired replica of cultural patterns which every individual mind finds given. *The brain is an organ enabling us to absorb, but not to design culture.* This 'world 3', as Sir Karl Popper has called it,[27] though at all times kept in existence by millions of separate brains participating in it, is the outcome of a process of evolution distinct from the biological evolution of the brain, the elaborate structure of which became useful when there was a cultural tradition to absorb. Or, to put it differently, mind can exist only as part of another independently existing distinct structure or order, though that order persists and can develop only because millions of minds constantly absorb and modify parts of it. If we are to understand it, we must direct our attention to that process of sifting of practices which sociobiology systematically neglects. This is the third and most important source of what in the title of this lecture I have called human values and about which we necessarily know little, but to which I still want to devote most of what I have to say. Before I turn, however, to the specific questions of how such social structures evolved, it may be helpful if I briefly consider some of the methodological issues which arise in all attempts to analyse such grown complex structures.

The evolution of self-maintaining complex structures

We understand now that *all* enduring structures above the level of the simplest atoms, and up to the brain and society, are the results of, and can be explained only in terms of, processes of selective evolution,[28] and that the more complex ones maintain themselves by constant adaptation of their internal states to changes in the environment. 'Wherever we look, we discover evolutionary processes leading to diversification and increasing complexity' (Nicolis and Prigogine; see n. 33). These changes in structure are brought about by their elements possessing such regularities of conduct, or such capacities to follow rules, that the result of their individual actions will be to restore the order of the whole if it is disturbed by external influences. Hence what on an earlier occasion I have called the twin concepts of evolution and spontaneous order[29] enables us to account for the persistence of these complex structures, not by a simple conception of one-directional laws of cause and effect, but by a complex interaction of patterns which Professor Donald Campbell described as 'downward causation'.[30]

This insight has greatly altered our approach to the explanation of, and our views about the achievable scope of our endeavours to explain, such complex phenomena. There is now, in particular, no justification for believing that the search for quantitative relationships, which proved so effective for accounting for the interdependence of two or three different variables, can be of much help in the explanation of the self-maintaining structures that exist only because of their self-maintaining attributes.[31] One of the most important of these self-generating orders is the wide-ranging division of labour which implies the mutual adjustment of activities of people who do not know each other. This foundation of modern civilization was first understood by Adam Smith in terms of the operation of feedback mechanism by which he anticipated what we now know as cybernetics.[32] The once popular organismic interpretations of social phenomena, that tried to account for one unexplained order by the analogy with another equally unexplained, has now been replaced by system theory, originally developed by yet another Viennese friend, Ludwig von Bertalanffy, and his numerous followers.[33] This has brought out the common features of those diverse complex orders which are also discussed by information and communication theory and semiotics.[34]

In particular, in order to explain the economic aspects of large social systems, we have to account for the course of a flowing stream, constantly adapting itself as a whole to changes in circumstances of which each participant can know only a small fraction, and not for a hypothetical state of equilibrium determined by a set of ascertainable data. And the numerical measurements with which the majority of economists are still occupied today may be of interest as historical facts; but for the theoretical explanation of those patterns which restore themselves, the quantitative data are about as significant as it would be for human biology if it concentrated on explaining the different sizes and shapes of such human organs as stomachs and livers of different individuals which happen to appear in the dissecting room very different from, and to resemble only rarely, the standard size or shapes in the textbooks.[35] With the functions of the system these magnitudes have evidently very little to do.

The stratification of rules of conduct[36]

But, to return to my central theme: the differences between the rules which have developed by each of the three distinct processes has led to a *super-imposition of not merely three layers of rules, but of many more,* according as traditions have been preserved from the successive stages through which cultural evolution has passed. The consequence is that modern man is torn by conflicts which torment him and force him into ever-accelerating further changes. There is, of course, in the first instance, the solid, i.e. little changing foundation of genetically inherited, 'instinctive' drives which are determined by his physiological structure. There are then all the remains of the traditions acquired in the successive types of social structures through which he has passed – rules which he did not deliberately choose but which have spread because some practices enhanced the prosperity of certain groups and led to their expansion, perhaps less by more rapid procreation than by the attraction of outsiders. And there is, third, on top of all

159

this, the thin layer of rules, deliberately adopted or modified to serve known purposes.

The transition from the small band to the settled community and finally to the open society and with it to civilization was due to men learning to obey the same abstract rules instead of being guided by innate instincts to pursue common perceived goals. The innate natural longings were appropriate to the condition of life of the small band during which man had developed the neural structure which is still characteristic of *Homo sapiens*. These innate structures built into man's organization in the course of perhaps 50,000 generations were adapted to a wholly different life from that which he has made for himself during the last 500, or for most of us only 100, generations or so. It would probably be more correct to equate these 'natural' instincts with 'animal' rather than with characteristically human or good instincts. Indeed, the general use of 'natural' as a term of praise is becoming very misleading, because one of the main functions of the rules learned later was to restrain the innate or natural instincts in the manner that was required to make the Great Society possible. We are still inclined to assume that what is natural must be good; but it may be very far from good in the Great Society. What has made men good is neither nature nor reason but tradition. There is not much common humanity in the biological endowment of the species. But most groups had to acquire certain similar traits to form into larger societies; or, more probably, those who did not were exterminated by those who did. And though we still share most of the emotional traits of primitive man, he does not share all ours, or the restraints which made civilization possible. Instead of the direct pursuit of felt needs or perceived objects, the obedience to learnt rules has become necessary to restrain those natural instincts which do not fit into the order of the open society. It is this 'discipline' (one of the lexical meanings of this word is 'systems of rules of conduct') against which man still revolts.

The morals which maintain the open society do not serve to gratify human emotions – which never was an aim of evolution – but they served only as the signals that told the individual what he ought to do in the kind of society in which he had lived in the dim past. What is still only imperfectly appreciated is that the cultural selection of new learnt rules became necessary chiefly in order to repress some of the innate rules which were adapted to the hunting and gathering life of the small bands of fifteen to forty persons, led by a headman and defending a territory against all outsiders. From that stage practically all advance had to be achieved by infringing or repressing some of the innate rules and replacing them by new ones which made the co-ordination of activities of larger groups possible. Most of these steps in the evolution of culture were made possible by some individuals breaking some traditional rules and practising new forms of conduct – not because they understood them to be better, but because the groups which acted on them prospered more than others and grew.[37] We must not be surprised that these rules often took the form of magic or ritual. The conditions of admission to the group was to accept all its rules, though few understood what depended on the observance of any particular one. There was just in each group only one acceptable way of doing things, with little attempt to distinguish between effectiveness and moral desirability.

Customary rules and economic order

It would be interesting, but I cannot attempt here, to account for the succession of the different economic orders through which civilization has passed in terms of changes in the rules of conduct. They made that evolution possible mostly by relaxations of prohibitions: an evolution of individual freedom and a development of rules which protected the individual rather than commanded it to do particular things. There can be little doubt that from the toleration of bartering with the outsider, the recognition of delimited private property, especially in land, the enforcement of contractual obligations, the competition with fellow craftsmen in the same trade, the variability of initially customary prices, the lending of money, particularly at interest, were all initially infringements of customary rules – so many falls from grace. And the law-breakers, who were to be path-breakers, certainly did not introduce the new rules because they recognized that they were beneficial to the community, but they simply started some practices advantageous to them which then did prove beneficial to the group in which they prevailed. There can, for instance, be little doubt that Dr Pugh is right when he observes,

> within primitive human society 'sharing' is a way of life. . . . The sharing is not limited to food, but extends to all kinds of resources. The practical result is that scarce resources are shared within the society approximately in proportion to

need. This behaviour may reflect some innate and uniquely human values that evolved during the transition to a hunting economy.[38]

That was probably true enough in that stage of development. But these habits had to be shed again to make the transition to the market economy and the open society possible. The steps of this transition were all breaches of that 'solidarity' which governed the small group and which are still resented. Yet they were the steps towards almost all that we now call civilization. The greatest change which man has still only partially digested came with the transition from the face-to-face society[39] to what Sir Karl Popper has appropriately called the abstract society:[40] a society in which no longer the known needs of known people but only abstract rules and impersonal signals guide action towards strangers. This made a specialization possible far beyond the range any one man can survey.

Even today the overwhelming majority of people, including, I am afraid, a good many supposed economists, do not yet understand that this extensive social division of labour, based on widely dispersed information, has been made possible entirely by the use of those impersonal signals which emerge from the market process and tell people what to do in order to adapt their activities to events of which they have no direct knowledge. That in an economic order involving a far-ranging division of labour it can no longer be the pursuit of perceived common ends but only abstract rules of conduct – and the whole relationship between such rules of individual conduct and the formation of an order which I have tried to make clear in earlier volumes of this work – is an insight which most people still refuse to accept. That neither what is instinctively recognized as right, nor what is rationally recognized as serving specific purposes, but inherited traditional rules, or that what is neither instinct nor reason, should often be most beneficial to the functioning of society is a truth which the dominant constructivistic outlook of our times refuses to accept. If modern man finds that his inborn instincts do not always lead him in the right direction, he at least flatters himself that it was his reason which made him recognize that a different kind of conduct will serve his innate values better. The conception that man has, in the service of his innate desires, consciously constructed an order of society is, however, erroneous, because without the cultural evolution which lies between instinct and the capacity of rational design he would not have possessed the reason which now makes him try to do so.

Man did not adopt new rules of conduct because he was intelligent. He became intelligent by submitting to new rules of conduct. The most important insight which so many rationalists still resist and are even inclined to brand as a superstition, namely that man has not only never invented his most beneficial institutions, from language to morals and law, and even today does not yet understand why he should preserve them when they satisfy neither his instincts nor his reason, still needs to be emphasized. The basic tools of civilization – language, morals, law and money – are all the result of spontaneous growth and not of design, and of the last two organized power has got hold and thoroughly corrupted them.

Although the Left is still inclined to brand all such efforts as apologetics, it may still be one of the most important tasks of our intelligence to discover the significance of rules we never deliberately made, and the obedience to which builds more complex orders than we can understand. I have already pointed out that the pleasure which man is led to strive for is of course not the end which evolution serves but merely the signal that in primitive conditions made the individual do what was usually required for the preservation of the group, but which under present conditions may no longer do so. The constructivistic theories of utilitarianism that derive the now valid rules from their serving individual pleasure are therefore completely mistaken. The rules which contemporary man has learnt to obey have indeed made possible an immense proliferation of the human race. I am not so certain that this has also increased the pleasure of the several individuals.

The discipline of freedom

Man has not developed in freedom. The member of the little band to which he had had to stick in order to survive was anything but free. *Freedom is an artefact of civilization* that released man from the trammels of the small group, the momentary moods of which even the leader had to obey. Freedom was made possible by the gradual evolution of *the discipline of civilization which is at the same time the discipline of freedom.* It protects him by impersonal abstract rules against arbitrary violence of others and enables each individual to try to build for himself a protected domain with which nobody else is allowed to interfere and within which he can use his own knowledge for his own purposes. We owe our freedom to restraints of freedom. 'For', Locke wrote, 'who could be free when every other man's humour might domineer over him?' (2nd Treatise, sect. 57.)

163

The great change which produced an order of society which became increasingly incomprehensible to man, and for the preservation of which he had to submit to learnt rules which were often contrary to his innate instincts, was the transition from the face-to-face society, or at least of groups consisting of known and recognizable members, to the open abstract society that was no longer held together by common concrete ends but only by the obedience to the same abstract rules.[41] What man probably found most difficult to comprehend was that the only common values of an open and free society were not concrete objects to be achieved, but only those common abstract rules of conduct that secured the constant maintenance of an equally abstract order which merely assured to the individual better prospects of achieving his individual ends but gave him no claims to particular things.[42]

The conduct required for the preservation of a small band of hunters and gatherers, and that presupposed by an open society based on exchange, are very different. But while mankind had hundreds of thousands of years to acquire and genetically to embody the responses needed for the former, it was necessary for the rise of the latter that he not only learned to acquire new rules, but that some of the new rules served precisely to repress the instinctive reactions no longer appropriate to the Great Society. These new rules were not supported by the awareness that they were more effective. *We have never designed our economic system. We were not intelligent enough for that.* We have stumbled into it and it has carried us to unforeseen heights and given rise to ambitions which may yet lead us to destroy it.

This development must be wholly unintelligible to all those who recognize only innate drives on the one hand and deliberately designed systems of rules on the other. But if anything is certain it is that no person who was not already familiar with the market could have designed the economic order which is capable of maintaining the present numbers of mankind.

This exchange society and the guidance of the co-ordination of a far-ranging division of labour by variable market prices was made possible by the spreading of certain gradually evolved moral beliefs which, after they had spread, most men in the Western world learned to accept. These rules were inevitably learned by all the members of a population consisting chiefly of independent farmers, artisans and merchants and their servants and apprentices who shared the daily experiences of their masters. They held an ethos

that esteemed the prudent man, the good husbandman and provider who looked after the future of his family and his business by
building up capital, guided less by the desire to be able to consume
much than by the wish to be regarded as successful by his fellows
who pursued similar aims.[43] It was the thousands of individuals who
practised the new routine more than the occasional successful
innovators whom they would imitate that maintained the market
order. Its mores involved withholding from the known needy
neighbours what they might require in order to serve the unknown
needs of thousands of unknown others. Financial gain rather than
the pursuit of a known common good became not only the basis of
approval but also the cause of the increase of general wealth.

The re-emergence of suppressed primordial instincts

At present, however, an ever increasing part of the population of
the Western World grow up as members of large organizations and
thus as strangers to those rules of the market which have made the
great open society possible. To them the market economy is largely
incomprehensible; they have never practised the rules on which it
rests, and its results seem to them irrational and immoral. They
often see in it merely an arbitrary structure maintained by some
sinister power. In consequence, the long-submerged innate instincts have again surged to the top. Their demand for a just distribution in which organized power is to be used to allocate to each
what he deserves, is thus strictly an *atavism,* based on primordial
emotions. And it is these widely prevalent feelings to which prophets, moral philosophers and constructivists appeal by their plan
for the deliberate creation of a new type society.[44]

But, though they all appeal to the same emotions, their arguments take very different and in some respects almost contradictory forms. A first group proposes a return to the older rules of
conduct which have prevailed in the distant past and are still dear to
men's sentiments. A second wants to construct new rules which will
better serve the innate desires of the individuals. Religious prophets
and ethical philosophers have of course at all times been mostly
reactionaries, defending the old against the new principles. Indeed,
in most parts of the world the development of an open market
economy has long been prevented by those very morals preached by
prophets and philosophers, even before governmental measures

165

did the same. *We must admit that modern civilization has become largely possible by the disregard of the injunctions of those indignant moralists.* As has been well said by the French historian Jean Baechler, '*the expansion of capitalism owes its origins and raison d'être to political anarchy*'.[45] That is true enough of the Middle Ages, which, however, could draw on the teaching of the ancient Greeks who – in some measure also as a result of political anarchy – had not only discovered individual liberty and private property,[46] but also the inseparability of the two,[47] and thereby created the first civilization of free men.

When the prophets and philosophers, from Moses to Plato and St Augustine, from Rousseau to Marx and Freud, protested against the prevailing morals, clearly none of them had any grasp of the extent to which the practices which they condemned had made possible the civilization of which they were part. They had no conception that the system of competitive prices and remunerations signalling to the individual what to do, had made possible that extensive specialization by informing the individuals how best to serve others of whose existence they might not know – and to use in this opportunities of the availability of which they also had no direct knowledge. Nor did they understand that those condemned moral beliefs were less the effect than the cause of the evolution of the market economy.

But the gravest deficiency of the older prophets was their belief that the intuitively perceived ethical values, divined out of the depth of man's breast, were immutable and eternal. This prevented them from recognizing that all rules of conduct served a particular kind of order to society, and that, though such a society will find it necessary to enforce its rules of conduct in order to protect itself against disruption, it is not society with a given structure that creates the rules appropriate to it, but the rules which have been practised by a few and then imitated by many which created a social order of a particular kind. Tradition is not something constant but the product of a process of selection guided not by reason but by success. It changes but can rarely be deliberately changed. Cultural selection is not a rational process; it is not guided by but it creates reason.

The belief in the immutability and permanence of our moral rules receives of course some support from the recognition that as little as we have designed our whole moral system, is it in our power to change it as a whole.[48] We do not really understand how it maintains the order of actions on which the co-ordination of the activities of

166

many millions depends.[49] And since we owe the order of our society to a tradition of rules which we only imperfectly understand, *all progress must be based on tradition.* We must build on tradition and can only tinker with its products.[50] It is only by recognizing the conflict between a given rule and the rest of our moral beliefs that we can justify our rejection of an established rule. Even the success of an innovation by a rule-breaker, and the trust of those who follow him, has to be bought by the esteem he has earned by the scrupulous observation of most of the existing rules. To become legitimized, the new rules have to obtain the approval of society at large – not by a formal vote, but by gradually spreading acceptance. And though we must constantly re-examine our rules and be prepared to question every single one of them, we can always do so only in terms of their consistency or compatibility with the rest of the system from the angle of their effectiveness in contributing to the formation of the same kind of overall order of actions which all the other rules serve.[51] There is thus certainly room for improvement, but we cannot redesign but only further evolve what we do not fully comprehend.

The successive changes in morals were therefore not a moral decline, even though they often offended inherited sentiments, but a necessary condition to the rise of the open society of free men. The confusion prevailing in this respect is most clearly shown by the common identification of the terms 'altruistic' and 'moral',[52] and the constant abuse of the former, especially by the sociobiologists,[53] to describe any action which is unpleasant or harmful to the doer but beneficial to society. Ethics is not a matter of choice. We have not designed it and cannot design it. And perhaps all that is innate is the fear of the frown and other signs of disapproval of our fellows. The rules which we learn to observe are the result of cultural evolution. We can endeavour to improve the system of rules by seeking to reconcile its internal conflicts or its conflicts with our emotions. But instinct or intuition do not entitle us to reject a particular demand of the prevailing moral code, and only a responsible effort to judge it as part of the system of other requirements may make it morally legitimate to infringe a particular rule.

There is, however, so far as present society is concerned, no 'natural goodness', because with his innate instincts man could never have built the civilization on which the numbers of present mankind depend for their lives. To be able to do so, he had to

167

shed many sentiments that were good for the small band, and to submit to the sacrifices which the discipline of freedom demands but which he hates. The abstract society rests on learnt rules and not on pursuing perceived desirable common objects: and wanting to do good to known people will not achieve the most for the community, but only the observation of its abstract and seemingly purposeless rules. Yet this little satisfies our deeply engrained feelings, or only so long as it brings us the esteem of our fellows.[54]

Evolution, tradition and progress

I have so far carefully avoided saying that evolution is identical with progress, but when it becomes clear that it was the evolution of a tradition which made civilization possible, we may at least say that spontaneous evolution is a necessary if not a sufficient condition of progress. And though it clearly produces also much that we did not foresee and do not like when we see it, it does bring to ever-increasing numbers what they have been mainly striving for. We often do not like it because the new possibilities always also bring a new discipline. *Man has been civilized very much against his wishes.* It was the price he had to pay for being able to raise a larger number of children. We especially dislike the economic disciplines and economists are often accused of over-rating the importance of the economic aspects of the process. The indispensable rules of the free society require from us much that is unpleasant, such as suffering competition from others, seeing others being richer than ourselves, etc., etc. But it is a misunderstanding when it is suggested that the economists want everything to serve economic goals. Strictly speaking, no final ends are economic, and the so-called economic goals which we pursue are at most intermediate goals which tell us how to serve others for ends which are ultimately non-economic.[55] And it is the discipline of the market which forces us to calculate, that is, to be responsible for the means we use up in the pursuit of our ends.

Unfortunately social usefulness is not distributed according to any principles of justice – and could be so distributed only by some authority assigning specific tasks to particular individuals, and rewarding them for how industriously and faithfully they have carried out orders, but depriving them at the same time of the use of their own knowledge for their own values. Any attempt to make the remuneration of the different services correspond to our atavistic conception of distributive justice must destroy the effective utilization of the dispersed individual knowledge, and what we know as a pluralistic society.

That progress may be faster than we like, and that we might be better able to digest it if it were slower, I will not deny. But, unfortunately, *progress cannot be dosed*, (nor, for that matter, economic growth!) All we can do is to create conditions favourable to it and then hope for the best.[56] It may be stimulated or damped by policy, but nobody can predict the precise effects of such measures; to pretend to know the desirable direction of progress seems to me to be the extreme of hubris. Guided progress would not be progress. But civilization has fortunately outstripped the possibility of collective control, otherwise we would probably smother it.

I can already hear our modern intellectuals hurling against such an emphasis on tradition their deadly thunderbolt of 'conservative thinking'. But to me there can be no doubt that it were favourable moral traditions which made particular groups strong rather than intellectual design that made the progress of the past possible and will do so also in the future. To confine evolution to what we can foresee would be to stop progress; and it is due to the favourable framework which is provided by a free market but which I cannot further describe here that the new which is better has a chance to emerge.

The construction of new morals to serve old instincts: Marx

The real leaders among the reactionary social philosophers are of course all the socialists. Indeed the whole of socialism is a result of that revival of primordial instincts, though most of its theorists are too sophisticated to deceive themselves that in the great society those old instincts could be satisfied by re-instating the rules of conduct that governed primitive man. So these recidivists join the opposite wing and endeavour to construe new morals serving the instinctive yearnings.

The extent to which particularly Karl Marx was completely unaware of the manner in which appropriate rules of individual conduct induce the formation of an order in the Great Society is best

169

seen when we inquire what made him speak of the 'chaos' of capitalist production. What prevented him from appreciating the signal-function of prices through which people are informed what they ought to do was, of course, his labour theory of value. His vain search for a physical cause of value made him regard prices as determined by labour costs, that is, by what people had done in the past rather than as the signal telling them what they must do in order to be able to sell their products. In consequence, any Marxist is to the present day wholly incapable of understanding that self-generating order, or to see how a selective evolution that knows no laws that determine its direction can produce a self-directing order. Apart from the impossibility of bringing about by central direction an efficient social division of labour by inducing the constant adaptation to the ever-changing awareness of events possessed by millions of people, his whole scheme suffers from the illusion that in a society of free individuals in which the remuneration offered tells the people what to do, the products could be distributed by some principles of justice.

But if the illusion of social justice must be sooner or later disappointed,[57] the most destructive of the constructivistic morals is egalitarianism – for which Karl Marx can certainly *not* be blamed. It is wholly destructive because it not only deprives the individuals of the signals which alone can offer to them the opportunity of a choice of the direction of their efforts, but even more through eliminating the one inducement by which free men can be made to observe any moral rules: the differentiating esteem by their fellows. I have no time to analyse here the dreadful confusion which leads from the fundamental presupposition of a free society, that all must be judged and treated by others according to the same rules (the equality before the law), to the demand that government should treat different people differently in order to place them in the same material position. This might indeed be the only 'just' rule for any socialist system in which the power of coercion must be used to determine both the assignment to kinds of work and the distribution of incomes. An egalitarian distribution would necessarily remove all basis for the individual's decision how they are to fit themselves into the pattern of general activities and leave only outright command as the foundation of all order.

But as moral views create institutions, so institutions create moral views; and under the prevailing form of unlimited democracy in which the power to do so creates the necessity of benefiting par-

170

ticular groups, government is led to concede claims the satisfaction of which destroys all morals. While the realization of socialism would make the scope of private moral conduct dwindle, the political necessity of gratifying all demands of large groups must lead to the degeneration and destruction of all morals.

All morals rest on the different esteem in which different persons are held by their fellows according to their conforming to accepted moral standards. It is this which makes moral conduct a social value. Like all rules of conduct prevailing in a society, and the observance of which makes an individual a member of the society, their acceptance demands equal application to all. This involves that morals are preserved by discriminating between people who observe them and those who do not, irrespective of why particular people may infringe them. *Morals presuppose a striving for excellence and the recognition that in this some succeed better than others*, without inquiring for the reasons which we can never know. Those who observe the rules are regarded as better in the sense of being of superior value compared with those who do not, and whom in consequence the others may not be willing to admit into their company. Without this morals would not persist.

I doubt whether any moral rule could be preserved without the exclusion of those who regularly infringe it from decent company – or even without people not allowing their children to mix with those who have bad manners. It is by the separation of groups and their distinctive principles of admission to them that sanctions of moral behaviour operate. Democratic morals may demand a presumption that a person will conduct himself honestly and decently until he proves the contrary – but they cannot require us to suspend that essential discipline without destroying moral beliefs.

The conscientious and courageous may on rare occasions decide to brave general opinion and to disregard a particular rule which he regards as wrong, if he proves his general respect for the prevailing moral rules by carefully observing the others. But there can be no excuse or pardon for a systematic disregard of accepted moral rules because they have no understood justification. The only base for judging particular rules is their reconcilability or conflict with the majority of other rules which are generally accepted.

It is certainly sad that men can be made bad by their environment, but this does not alter the fact that they are bad and must be treated as such. The repentant sinner may earn absolution, but so long as he continues breaking the rules of morals he must remain a less valued member of society. Crime is not necessarily the result of poverty and not excused by environment. There are many poor people much more honest than many rich, and middle-class morals are probably in general better than those of the rich. But morally a person breaking the rules must be counted bad even if he knows no better. And that often people will have much to learn in order to be accepted by another group is much to the good. Even moral praise is not based on intention but on performance and must be so.

In a culture formed by group selection, the imposition of egalitarianism must stop further evolution. Egalitarianism is of course not a majority view but a product of the necessity under unlimited democracy to solicit the support even of the worst. And while it is one of the indispensable principles of a free society that we value people differently according to the morality of their manifest conduct, irrespective of the, never fully known, reasons of their failures, egalitarianism preaches that nobody is better than anybody else. The argument is that it is nobody's fault that he is as he is, but that all is the responsibility of 'society'. It is by the slogan that 'it is not your fault' that the demagoguery of unlimited democracy, assisted by a scientistic psychology, has come to the support of those who claim a share in the wealth of our society without submitting to the discipline to which it is due. It is not by conceding 'a right to equal concern and respect'[58] to those who break the code that civilization is maintained. Nor can we, for the purpose of maintaining our society, accept all moral beliefs which are held with equal conviction as equally legitimate, and recognize a right to blood feud or infanticide or even theft, or any other moral beliefs contrary to those on which the working of our society rests. What makes an individual a member of society and gives him claims is that he obeys its rules. Wholly contradictory views may give him rights in other societies but not in ours. For the science of anthropology all cultures or morals may be equally good, but we maintain our society by treating others as less so.

Our civilization advances by making the fullest use of the infinite variety of the individuals of the human species, apparently greater than that of any wild animal species,[59] which had generally to adapt to one particular ecological niche. Culture has provided a great variety of cultural niches in which that great diversity of men's innate or acquired gifts can be used. And if we are to make use of the distinct factual knowledge of the individuals

172

inhabiting different locations on this world, we must allow them to be told by the impersonal signals of the market how they had best use them in their own as well as in the general interest.

It would indeed be a tragic joke of history if man, who owes his rapid advance to nothing so much as to the exceptional variety of individual gifts, were to terminate his evolution by imposing a compulsory egalitarian scheme on all.

The destruction of indispensable values by scientific error: Freud

I come finally to what for many years has increasingly become one of my main concerns and causes of apprehension: the progressive destruction of irreplaceable values by scientific error.[60] The attacks do not all come from socialism, although the errors I shall have to consider mostly lead to socialism. It finds support from purely intellectual errors in the associated fields of philosophy, sociology, law and psychology. In the first three fields these errors derive mostly from the Cartesian scientism and constructivism as developed by Auguste Comte.[61] Logical positivism has been trying to show that all moral values are 'devoid of meaning', purely 'emotive'; it is wholly contemptuous of the conception that even emotional responses selected by biological *or* cultural evolution may be of the greatest importance for the coherence of an advanced society. The sociology of knowledge, deriving from the same source, similarly attempts to discredit all moral views by the alleged interested motifs of their defenders.

I must confess here that, however grateful we all must be for some of the descriptive work of the sociologists, for which, however, perhaps anthropologists and historians would have been equally qualified, there seems to me still to exist no more justification for a theoretical discipline of sociology than there would be for a theoretical discipline of naturology apart from the theoretical disciplines dealing with particular classes of natural or social phenomena. I am quite certain, however, that the sociology of knowledge with its desire that mankind should pull itself up by its own bootstraps (a belief characteristically re-asserted now in these very words by the behaviourist B. F. Skinner) has wholly misconceived the process of the growth of knowledge. I have earlier in this work attempted to show why legal positivism, with its belief that every legal rule must be derivable from a conscious act of legislation, and that all conceptions of justice are

173

the product of particular interests, is conceptually as much mistaken as historically.[62]

But the culturally most devastating effects have come from the endeavour of psychiatrists to cure people by releasing their innate instincts. After having lauded earlier my Viennese friends Popper, Lorenz, Gombrich and Bertalanffy, I am afraid I must now concede that the logical positivism of Carnap and the legal positivism of Kelsen are far from the worst things that have come out of Vienna. Through his profound effects on education, Sigmund Freud has probably become the greatest destroyer of culture. Although in his old age, in his *Civilisation and its Discontents*,[63] he seems himself to have become not a little disturbed by some of the effects of his teaching, his basic aim of undoing the culturally acquired repressions and freeing the natural drives, has opened the most fatal attack on the basis of all civilization. The movement culminated about thirty years ago and the generation grown up since has been largely brought up on its theories. I will give you from that date only one particular crass expression of the fundamental ideas by an influential Canadian psychiatrist who later became the first Secretary General of the World Health Organization. In 1946 the late Dr G. B. Chisholm in a work praised by high American legal authority, advocated

> the eradication of the concept of right and wrong which has been the basis of child training, the substitution of intelligent and rational thinking for the faith in the certainties of old people [. . . since] most psychiatrists and psychologists and many other respectable people have escaped from these moral chains and are able to observe and think freely.

In his opinion it was the task of the psychiatrists to free the human race from 'the crippling burden of good and evil' and the 'perverse concepts of right and wrong' and thereby to decide its immediate future.[64]

It is the harvest of these seeds which we are now gathering. Those non-domesticated savages who represent themselves as alienated from something they have never learnt, and even undertake to construct a 'counter-culture', are the necessary product of the permissive education which fails to pass on the burden of culture, and trusts to the *natural instincts which are the instincts of the savage*. It did not surprise me in the least when, according to a report in *The Times*, a recent international con-

174

ference of senior police officers and other experts acknowledged that a noticeable proportion of today's terrorists have studied sociology or political and educational sciences.[65] What can we expect from a generation who grew up during the fifty years during which the English intellectual scene was dominated by a figure who had publicly pronounced that he always had been and would remain an immoralist?

We must be grateful that before this flood has finally destroyed civilization, a revulsion is taking place even within the field in which it originated. Three years ago Professor Donald Campbell of Northwestern University, in his presidential address to the American Psychological Association on 'The Conflicts between Biological and Social Evolution', said that

> if, as I assert, there is in psychology today a general background assumption that the human impulses provided by biological evolution are right and optimal, both individually and socially, and that repressive or inhibitory moral traditions are wrong, then in my judgment this assumption may now be regarded as scientifically wrong from the enlarged scientific perspective that comes from the joint consideration of population genetics and social system evolution. . . . Psychology may be contributing to the undermining of the retention of what may be extremely valuable, social-evolutionary inhibitory systems which we do not yet fully understand.[66]

And he added a little later: 'the recruitment of scholars into psychology and psychiatry may be such as to select persons unusually eager to challenge the cultural orthodoxy'.[67] From the furore this lecture caused[68] we can judge how deeply embedded these ideas still are in contemporary psychological theory. There are similar salutary efforts by Professor Thomas Szasz of Syracuse University[69] and by Professor H. J. Eysenck in this country.[70] So all hope is not yet lost.

The tables turned

If our civilization survives, which it will do only if it renounces those errors, I believe men will look back on our age as an age of superstition, chiefly connected with the names of Karl Marx and Sigmund

Freud. I believe people will discover that the most widely held ideas which dominated the twentieth century, those of a planned economy with a just distribution, a freeing ourselves from repressions and conventional morals, of permissive education as a way to freedom, and the replacement of the market by a rational arrangement of a body with coercive powers, were all based on superstitions in the strict sense of the word. An age of superstitions is a time when people imagine that they know more than they do. In this sense the twentieth century was certainly an outstanding age of superstition, and the cause of this is an overestimation of what science has achieved – not in the field of the comparatively simple phenomena, where it has of course been extraordinarily successful, but in the field of complex phenomena, where the application of the techniques which proved so helpful with essentially simple phenomena has proved to be very misleading.

Ironically, these superstitions are largely an effect of our inheritance from the Age of Reason, that great enemy of all that *it* regarded as superstitions. If the Enlightenment has discovered that the role assigned to human reason in intelligent construction had been too small in the past, we are discovering that the task which our age is assigning to the rational construction of new institutions is far too big. What the age of rationalism – and modern positivism – has taught us to regard as senseless and meaningless formations due to accident or human caprice, turn out in many instances to be the foundations on which our capacity for rational thought rests. *Man is not and never will be the master of his fate: his very reason always progresses by leading him into the unknown and unforeseen where he learns new things.*

In concluding this epilogue I am becoming increasingly aware that it ought not to be that but rather a new beginning. But I hardly dare hope that for me it can be so.

NOTES

* Xenophon, *Helenica,* I, vii, 12–16. A German translation of an earlier version of what have now become chapters 12 and 13 has appeared under the title 'Anschauungen der Mehrheit und zeitgenössische Demokratie' as long ago as 1965 in *Ordo* XV/ XVI (Düsseldorf and Munich, 1965) and was reprinted in my *Freiburger Studien* (Tübingen, 1969).

1 A significant symptom was an article by Cecil King in *The Times* (London) of 16 September 1968, entitled 'The Declining Reputation of Parliamentary Democracy' in which he argued:

> What is to my mind most disturbing is the world-wide decline in authority and in respect for democratic institutions. A century ago it was generally agreed in the advanced countries of the world that parliamentary government was the best form of government. But today dissatisfaction with parliamentary government is widespread. Nobody can seriously argue that in Europe or America parliaments are adding to their prestige. . . . So low has the reputation of parliamentary government sunk that it is now defended on the grounds that bad as it is, other forms of government are worse.

Of the ever-increasing literature on this topic, some of the more recent books are: Robert Moss, *The Collapse of Democracy* (London, 1975); K. Sontheimer, G. A. Ritter *et al., Der Über-druss an der Demokratie* (Cologne, 1970); C. Julien, *La Suicide de la democratie* (Paris, 1972); and Lord Hailsham, *The Dilemma of Democracy* (London, 1978).

2 Harold D. Lasswell, *Politics–Who get What, When, How* (New York, 1936).
3 J. A. Schumpeter, *Capitalism, Socialism and Democracy* (New York, 1942; 3rd edn., 1950).
4 Demosthenes, *Against Leptines,* 92, Loeb Classical Library edn., trs. J. H. Vince. pp. 552–3. Cf. also on the episode to which the passage from Xenophon at the head of this chapter refers, Lord Acton, *History of Freedom* (London, 1907), p. 12:

> On a memorable occasion the assembled Athenians declared it monstrous that they should be prevented from doing whatever they chose; no force that existed could restrain them; they resolved that no duty should restrain them, and that they would be bound by no laws that were not of their own making. In this way the emancipated people of Athens became a tyrant.

5 Aristotle, *Politics,* IV, iv, 7, Loeb Classical Library edn., trs. H. Rackham (Cambridge, Mass. and London, 1932), pp. 304–5.
6 Giovanni Sartori, *Democratic Theory* (New York), 1965), p. 312. The whole section 7 of chapter 13; pp. 306–14, of this book is highly relevant to the present theme.
7 Richard Wollheim, 'A Paradox in the Theory of Democracy', in Peter Laslett and W. G. Runciman (eds), *Philosophy, Politics and Society*, 2nd series (Oxford, 1962), p. 72.
8 George Burdeau as quoted before in vol. 1, p. 1, note 4.
9 It would seem, and is confirmed by M. J. C. Vile, *Constitutionalism and the Separation of Powers* (Oxford, 1967), p. 217, that James Mill was in this respect the main culprit, though it is difficult to find in his *Essay on Government* a precise statement to that effect. But we can trace his influence clearly in his son when, for instance, J. S. Mill argues in *On Liberty* that 'the nation did not need to be protected against its own will' (Everyman edn., p. 67).
10 The Americans at the time of the revolution fully understood this defect of the British Constitution and one of their most acute thinkers on constitutional questions, James Wilson (as M. J. C. Vile, *op. cit.,* p. 158 reports)

> rejected Blackstone's doctrine of parliamentary sovereignty as outmoded. The British do not understand the idea of a constitution [he argued] which limits and superintends the

operations of legislature. This was an improvement in the science of government reserved to the Americans.

Cf. also the article 'An Enviable Freedom' in *The Economist*, 2 April 1977, p. 38:

> The American system may thus represent what might have developed if Britain had not turned to the doctrine of absolute parliamentary sovereignty – with its corollary, now largely mythical, that the abused citizen can look to parliament for vindication of his rights.

But I doubt whether they succeeded in solving the problem more successfully. Closely examined in fact both the two paradigms of democratic government, Britain and the USA, are really two monstrosities and caricatures of the ideal of the separation of powers, since in the first the governing body incidentally also legislates as it suits its momentary aims but regards as its chief task the supervision of the current conduct of government, while in the second the administration is not responsible to, and the President as the chief executive for the whole of his tenure of office may lack the support of, the majority of the representative assembly largely concerned with governmental problems. For a long time these defects could be overlooked on the ground that the systems 'worked', but they hardly do so any longer.

The power of the British Parliament may be illustrated by the fact that so far as I know Parliament could, if it regarded me as important enough, for the statement in the text order me for contempt of Parliament to be confined in the Tower!

11 Cf. J. L. Talmon, *The Origins of Totalitarian Democracy* (London, 1952) and R. R. Palmer, *The Age of Democratic Revolution* (Princeton, 1959).

12 E. Heimann, 'Rationalism, Christianity and Democracy', *Festgabe für Alfred Weber* (Heidelberg, 1949), p. 175.

13 Cf. Wilhelm Hennis, *Demokratisierung: Zur Problematik eines Begriffs* (Cologne, 1970); also J. A. Schumpeter, *op. cit.*, p. 242.

14 Cf. Ludwig von Mises, *Human Action* (Yale University Press, 1949; 3rd rev. edn., Chicago, 1966), p. 150: Democracy 'provides a method for the peaceful adjustment of government to the will of the majority'; also K. R. Popper, *The Open Society and its Enemies* (London, 1945; 4th edn., Princeton, 1963), vol. 1, p. 124: 'I suggest the term "democracy" as a short handy label for

... governments of which we can get rid without bloodshed – for example, by way of general elections; that is to say, the social institutions provide the means by which the rulers may be dismissed by the ruled'; also J. A. Schumpeter, *op. cit., passim*; also the references in my *The Constitution of Liberty* (London and Chicago, 1960), p. 444, note 9. I rather regret that in that book (p. 108), carried away by de Tocqueville, I described the third of the three arguments in support of democracy which I mentioned, namely that it is the only effective method of educating the majority in political matters, as the 'most powerful' argument. It is very important but of course less important than what I had then mentioned as the first: its function as an instrument of peaceful change.

15 These dangers of democratic government were remarkably well understood by the Old Whigs. See, for instance, the discussion in the very important *Cato's Letters* by John Trenchard and Thomas Gordon which appeared in the London press between 1720 and 1722 and then were reprinted many times as a collection (now most conveniently available in the volume *The English Libertarian Heritage,* ed. David L. Jacobson, Indianapolis, 1965), where the letter of 13 January 1721 (p. 124 of edition quoted) argues that 'when the weight of infamy is divided among many, no one sinks under his own burthen'. It is also true that, while a task which is regarded as a distinction is commonly also felt to impose an obligation, one which is everybody's right is easily regarded as legitimately governed by one's personal caprice.

16 Cf. J. A. Schumpeter, *op. cit.,* p. 258: about

the little field which the individual citizen's mind can encompass with a full sense of its reality. Roughly, it consists of the things that directly concern himself, his family, his business dealings, his hobbies, his friends and enemies, his township or ward, his class, church, trade union or any other social group of which he is an active member – the things under his personal observation, the things which are familiar to him independently of what his newspapers tell him, which he can directly influence or manage, and for which he develops the kind of responsibility that is induced by a direct relation to the favourable or unfavourable effects of a course of action.

17 Cf. *Cato's Letters*, letter no. 60 of 6 January 1721, *op. cit.*, p. 121. Cf. the quotation from William Paley on p. 21 above. On the influence of *Cato's Letters* on the development of American political ideals Clinton Rossiter writes in *Seedtime of the Republic* (New York, 1953) p. 141:

> No one can spend any time in the newspapers, library inventories, and pamphlets of colonial America without realising that *Cato's Letters* rather than Locke's *Civil Government* was the most popular, quotable, esteemed source of political ideas in the colonial period.

18 See *Cato's Letters*, letter no. 62 of 20 January 1721, p. 128:

> It is a mistaken notion in government, that the interest of the majority is only to be consulted, since in society every man has a right to every man's assistance in the enjoyment and defence of his private property; otherwise the greater number may sell the lesser, and divide their estates among themselves; and so, instead of a society where all peaceable men are protected, become a conspiracy of the many against the majority. With as much equity may one man wantonly dispose of all, and violence may be sanctified by mere power.

19 On these matters see particuarly R. A. Dahl, *A Preface to Democratic Theory* (Chicago, 1950) and R. A. Dahl and C. E. Lindblom, *Politics, Economics, and Welfare* (New York, 1953).

20 For the full text and reference of this quotation from Immanuel Kant see the quotation at the head of chapter 9 of volume 2 and note.

21 Or in Austria, where the head of the association of trade unions is the undisputed most powerful man in the country and only his general good sense makes, for the time being, the position tolerable.

22 C. A. R. Crossland, *The Future of Socialism* (London, 1956), p. 205.

23 See E. E. Schattschneider, *Politics, Pressure, and the Tariff* (New York, 1935) and *The Semi-Sovereign People* (New York, 1960).

24 Cf. Mancur Olson Jr, *The Logic of Collective Action* (Harvard, 1965).

25 The most consistent expounder of this view is Lady Wootton (Mrs Barbara Wootton). See her latest book on the subject, *Incomes Policy* (London, 1974).

26 There is in English an appropriate word lacking for describing those growths which can at least approximately be referred to by the German term *Bildungen*, i.e. structures which have emerged from a process of spontaneous evolution. 'Institutions', which one is often tempted to use instead, is misleading because it suggests that these structures have been 'instituted' or deliberately established.

27 See the passage by C. R. A. Crossland quoted at note 22 above.

28 See in this connection the very relevant discussion of the abstract character of society in K. R. Popper, *op. cit.*, p. 175.

CHAPTER THIRTEEN THE DIVISION OF DEMOCRATIC POWERS

* W. H. Hutt, *Politically Impossible . . .?* (London, 1971), p. 43; cf. also H. Schoeck, *Was heisst politisch unmöglich?* (Zürich, 1959), and R. A. Dahl and C. E. Lindblom, *Politics, Economics and Welfare* (New York, 1953), p. 325: 'perhaps the most fateful limit of American capacity for rational action in economic affairs is the enormous extent to which bargaining shapes all our governmental decisions.'

1 M. J. C. Vile, *Constitutionalism and the Separation of Powers* (Oxford, 1967), p. 43. See also the important conclusion, *op. cit.*, p. 347: 'It is the concern with social justice which above all else has disrupted the earlier triad of government functions and agencies, and has added a new dimension to modern government.'

2 *Ibid.*, p. 63.

3 John Trenchard and Thomas Gordon, *Cato's Letters* (1720–2), reprinted in D. L. Jacobsen (ed.), *The English Libertarian Heritage* (Indianapolis, 1965), p. 121.

4 William Paley, *The Principles of Moral and Political Philosophy* (1785: London edn., 1824), pp. 348 ff. Cf. also Thomas Day, 'Speech at the general meeting of the freeholders of the county of Cambridge' 20 March 1782 (quoted Diana Spearman, *Democracy in England*, London 1957, p. 12): 'With us no discriminatory power which can affect the life, the property or the liberty of an individual, is permitted to the sovereign itself.'

5 M. J. C. Vile, *op. cit.*, p. 158. Cf. also the interesting arguments by James Iredell in an article of 1786 quoted in Gerald Stourzh, *Vom Widerstandsrecht zur Verfassungsgerichtsbarkeit: Zum*

NOTES TO PAGE 21

Problem der Verfassungswidrigkeit im 18. Jahrhundert (Graz, 1974), p. 31. In the article of 1786, reprinted in Griffith J. McRee, *Life and Correspondence of James Iredell*, vol. II (New York, 1857; reprinted New York, 1949), of which Professor Stourzh has kindly supplied me with a copy, Iredell pleads (pp. 145–8) for the 'subordination of the Legislature to the authority of the Constitution'. He protests against all 'abuse of unlimited power, which was not to be trusted' and particularly against 'the omnipotent power of the British Parliament . . . the theory *of the necessity of the legislature being absolute in all cases*, because it was the great ground of the British pretensions'. He speaks later of 'the principle of *unbounded legislative power* . . . that our Constitution reprobates. In England they are in this condition. In England, therefore, they are less free than we are.' And he concludes: 'It will not be denied, I suppose, that the constitution is a *law of the state*, as well as an *act of Assembly*, with this difference only, that it is *the fundamental law*, and unalterable by the legislature, which derives all its power from it.'

These ideas survived very long among American radicals and were finally used by them as arguments against the restrictions of democracy. Indeed, the manner in which the American Constitution was designed was still correctly, though with a half-critical intention, expounded in the posthumous *Growth and Decadence of Constitutional Government* (New York, 1931; re-edited Seattle, 1972) by Professor J. Allen Smith. In his Introduction to that book Vernon Louis Parrington refers to the earlier work of J. A. Smith on *The Spirit of American Government* (New York, 1907) of which 'to the liberalism of 1907, the most suggestive contribution was the demonstration from the speeches and writings of the time [when the Constitution was written] that the system was devised deliberately for undemocratic ends.' It is not surprising that the concluding chapter of the later book in which the danger to individual liberty of the removal of these barriers to democratic omnipotence are clearly pointed out was much less popular with the American pseudo-liberals. Smith's exposition of how 'The effectiveness of our constitutional guaranties of individual liberty was greatly impaired when the government, and especially the branch of it which was furthest removed from popular influence, the Supreme Court, acquired the recognized right to interpret them' (p. 279), and how 'individual liberty is not necessarily secure where the majority are in control' (p. 282), and his description how 'individual liberty in the United States to-day not only lacks the support of an active, intelligent public opinion, but often encounters a degree of public hostility which renders constitutional guarantees wholly ineffective' (p. 284) reads much like a criticism of the effects of the ideas he once advocated and is still well worth reading.

6 On the recognition of this fact by some earlier German authors such as the philosopher G. W. F. Hegel and the historian of political institutions W. Hasbach see vol. 1, p. 176, notes 17 and 18.

7 On the systematic support of this development by legal positivism see vol. 3, chapter 8.

8 Cf. G. Sartori, *Democratic Theory* (New York, 1965), p. 312:

> Whereas law, as it was formerly understood, effectively served as a solid dam against arbitrary power, legislation, as it is now understood, may be, or may become, no guarantee at all. . . . When the rule of law resolves itself into the rule of the legislators, the way is open, at least in principle, to an oppression 'in the name of law' that has no precedent in the history of mankind.

9 Edmund Burke could still describe a party as a principled union of men 'united for promoting by their joint endeavours the national interest upon some principle in which they are all agreed' (*Thoughts on the Causes of the Present Discontents* (London, 1779)).

10 See above, vol. 2, p. 126.

11 Courtenay Ilbert, *Legislative Methods and Forms* (Oxford, 1901), p. 210.

12 In *Cato's Letters*, 9 February 1722, in the edition of D. L. Jacobson quoted in note 3 above, p. 256.

13 See Gerald Abrahams, *Trade Unions and the Law* (London, 1968).

14 Robert Moss, *The Collapse of Democracy* (London, 1975), p. 102: 'So the Liberals who blithely passed a bill drawn up by the first generation of Labour MPs in keeping of an electoral promise quite literally had no idea what they were doing.'

15 Cf. the quotation from P. Vinogradoff above, vol. 1, p. 179, note 7, and the passage from A. V. Dicey, Lord McDermot and J. A.

Schumpeter quoted in my *The Constitution of Liberty* (London and Chicago, 1960), p. 506, note 3.

16 Cf. the last section of chapter 1 in volume 1 and chapter 8 in volume 2 of the present work as well as K. R. Popper, *The Open Society and its Enemies* (London, 1945; sixth edn., 1966), vol. 1, p. 121.

17 Quoted by C. H. McIlwain, *The High Court of Parliament* (Yale University Press, 1910).

18 See on this Wilhelm Hennis, *Demokratisierung: Zur Problematik eines Begriffs* (Cologne, 1970).

19 Since I first suggested the term 'demarchy' (in a pamphlet on *The Confusion of Language in Political Thought*, Occasional Paper 20 of the Institute of Economic Affairs (London, 1968)) I have noted that the terminological problem has been examined in some detail in the German literature. See particularly the studies by Christian Meier: 'Drei Bemerkungen zur Vor- und Frühgeschichte des Begriffes Demokratie' in *Discordia Concors, Festschrift für Edgar Bonjour* (Basel, 1968); *Die Entstehung des Begriffes 'Demokratie'* (Frankfurt a.M., 1970); and his contribution to the article *'Demokratie'* in O. Brunner, W. Conze and R. Kosselek (eds), *Geschichtliche Grundbegriffe, Historisches Lexikon zur politisch-sozialen Sprache in Deutschland* (Stuttgart, vol. I, 1972), in each of which further references to the discussion will be found.

CHAPTER FOURTEEN THE PUBLIC SECTOR AND THE PRIVATE SECTOR

* The quotation at the head of the chapter is taken from a speech of William Pitt to the House of Commons on 14 January 1766, *Parliamentary History of England* (London, 1813), vol. 16. It deserves notice that to Pitt at that time it appears to have been only measures of taxation which among the subjects coming before Parliament involved coercion of private persons, since the rest of the obligatory rules of just conduct consisted mainly of common and not statute law and therefore appeared to be outside the normal concern of a body occupied chiefly with government rather than with the making of law.

1 Mancur Olson Jr, *The Logic of Collective Action* (Harvard University Press, 1965).

2 On the important recent discussion of the 'minimal state' in

Robert Nozik, *Anarchy, State, and Utopia* (New York, 1974) see the Preface to the present volume.

3 See Mancur Olson Jr, *op. cit.*, and the various important studies by R. H. Coase on this subject.

4 Milton Friedman, *Capitalism and Freedom* (Chicago, 1962).

5 *Ibid.*

6 In Japan, however, museums and the like are to a remarkable extent provided by private enterprise.

7 Cf. Martin Anderson, *The Federal Bulldozer* (Cambridge, Mass., 1964); Jane Jacobs, *The Economy of Cities* (New York, 1969); and Edward C. Banfield, *The Unheavenly City* (Boston, 1970) and *Unheavenly City Revisited* (Boston, 1974).

8 Richard C. Cornuelle, *Reclaiming the American Dream* (New York, 1965). Cornuelle concludes (p. 40):

> If fully mobilized the independent sector could, I believe:
> (1) Put to work everyone who is willing and able to work.
> (2) Wipe out poverty. (3) Find and solve the farm problem.
> (4) Give everyone good medical care. (5) Stop juvenile crime. (6) Renew our towns and cities, and turn anonymous slums into human communities. (7) Pay reasonable retirement benefits to all. (8) Replace hundreds of governmental regulations with more effective codes of conduct, vigorously enforced by each profession and an alert press. (9) Handle the nation's total research effort. (10) Turn our foreign policy into a world crusade for human welfare and personal dignity. (11) Lever a wider distribution of stock ownership. (12) Stop air and water pollution. (13) Give every person the education he needs, wants, and can profit by. (14) Provide cultural and educational outlets for everyone who wants them. (15) Wipe out racial segregation. The independent sector has power to do these formidable things. But, curiously, as its strength has increased we have given it less and less to do, and assigned more and more common tasks to government.

I reproduce this remarkable claim to tempt as many readers as possible to consult this unduly neglected book.

9 J. K. Galbraith, *The Affluent Society* (Boston, 1969).

10 Adolf Wagner, *Finanzwissenschaft* (1873; 3rd edn. Leipzig, 1883), Part I, p. 67, and cf. H. Timm, 'Das Gesetz der wachsenden Staatsaufgaben', *Finanzarchiv*, N.F. 21, 1961, as well as H.

Timm and R. Haller (eds), *Beiträge zur Theorie der öffentlichen Ausgaben. Schriften des Vereins für Sozialpolitik,* N. F. 47, 1967. While so far as the coercive activities of government are concerned it has been justly said that we ought to be grateful that we do not get as much government as we pay for, with regard to the services which it renders the opposite is probably true. The size of government expenditure is, of course, no measure whatever of the value of the services actually provided by government. The technical necessity of valuing in all national income statistics government services at costs probably gives a wholly misleading picture of the actual size of the contribution it makes to the stream of services provided for the people.

11 J. K. Galbraith, *op. cit.,* and cf. also Anthony Downs, 'Why Government Budget is too Small in a Democracy', *World Politics,* vol. 12, 1966.

12 See Arthur Seldon, *Taxation and Welfare,* I.E.A. Research Monograph No. 14 (London, 1967), especially the table on p. 18.

13 About the fact that in all advanced European states even at the height of the so-called *laissez faire* period there existed provisions for the maintenance of the poor cf. above, vol. 2, p. 190, note 8.

14 See my *The Constitution of Liberty* (London and Chicago, 1960), chapter 19.

15 Cf. R. H. Coase, 'The British Post Office and the Messenger Companies', *Journal of Law and Economics,* vol. IV, 1961, and the statement of the General Secretary of the British Union of Post Office Workers made at Bournemouth, on 24 May 1976 and reported on the next day in *The Times,* London, that 'Government of both political complexions had reduced a once great public service to the level of a music hall joke'.

16 See my *Denationalization of Money* (Institute of Economic Affairs, 2nd edn., London, 1978).

17 See *The Constitution of Liberty* (London, 1960), chapter 24.

18 See note 4 above.

19 See the book by R. C. Cornuelle quote in note 8 above.

20 Cf. F. A. Mann, 'Outlines of a History of Expropriation', *Law Quarterly Review,* 75, 1958.

21 Cf. Alan F. Westin, *Privacy and Freedom* (New York, 1968). How well founded were the apprehensions which I expressed in *The Constitution of Liberty* (p. 300) concerning the effect of a

universal national health service on the liberty of the private individual has been depressingly confirmed by an article by D. Gould, 'To Hell with Medical Secrecy' in the *New Statesman* of 3 March 1967 in which it is argued that

> ideally, our medical cards ought to be sent to the Ministry of Health, say once a year, and all the information on them should be fed into a computer. Moreover, these cards . . . should list our jobs, past and present, our travels, our relatives, whether and what we smoke and drink, what we eat and do not eat, how much we earn, what sort of exercise we take, how much we weigh, how tall we are, even perhaps the results of regular psychological tests, and a lot of other intimate details. . . .
>
> Proper records, analysed by computer . . . could even reveal the people who ought not to be allowed to drive a motor car, or have a seat in the Cabinet! Ah! What about the sacred freedom of the individual? Freedom, my foot. We survive as a community or not at all, and doctors today are as much servants of the state as their patients. Away with the humbug, and let us admit that all secrets are bad secrets.

CHAPTER FIFTEEN GOVERNMENT POLICY AND THE MARKET

* Ludwig von Mises, *Human Action: A Treatise on Economics* (Yale University Press, 1949), p.239.

1 This chapter, written in more or less the present form about ten years ago and partly published, after having been used for public lectures at Chicago and Kiel, as 'Der Wettbewerb als Entdeckungsverfahren' in *'Kieler Vorträge'*, No. 56 (Kiel, 1969) and in English more recently in my *New Studies in Philosophy, Politics, Economics and the History of Ideas* (London and Chicago, 1977), I have let stand largely unchanged since it already occupies an undue amount of space in the present context and any attempt to deal with more recent developments would in this place have been inappropriate. I should, however, refer here at least to some of the works which have substantially developed the conceptions here sketched, such as Murray Rothbart, *Power and Market* (Menlo Park, 1970), John S. MacGee, *In Defence of Industrial Concentration* (New York, 1971), D. T. Armentano,

The Myth of Antitrust (New Rochelle, N.Y., 1972), and particularly Israel Kirzner, *Competition and Entrepreneurship* (Chicago, 1973) and a number of German essays by Erich Hoppmann, especially 'Missbrauch der Missbrauchaufsicht', *Mitteilungen der List Gesellschaft*, May 1976, and 'Preisunelastizität der Nachfrage als Quelle von Marktbeherrschung', in H. Gutzler and J. H. Kaiser (eds), *Wettbewerb im Wandel* (Baden-Baden, 1976).

2 Among the few who have seen this is the sociologist Leopold von Wiese. See his lecture on 'Die Konkurrenz, vorwiegend in soziologisch-systematischer Betrachtung', *Verhandlungen des 6. Deutschen Soziologentages*, 1929.

3 This seems to have been confused by J. A. Schumpeter, *Capitalism, Socialism, and Democracy* (New York, 1942), p. 101 where he contends that:

> there are superior methods available to the monopolist which either are not available to a crowd of competitors or are not available to them so readily: for their advantages which, though not strictly available on the competitive level of enterprise, are as a matter of fact secured only on the monopoly level, for instance, because monopolization may increase the share of influence of the better, and decrease the share of influence of the inferior brains.

Such a situation may indeed lead to monopoly, but it would not be monopoly but perhaps size which would give the better brains greater influence.

4 Where in both cases we must count as part of these costs of production the alternative products which the particular person or firm could produce instead. It would therefore be compatible with these conditions that somebody who could produce some commodity more cheaply than anybody else will in fact not do so and produce something else instead with respect to which his comparative advantage over other producers is even greater.

5 It may be instructive if I illustrate the kind of obstacles into which one who believes he has discovered a possibility of improving upon existing routines is likely to encounter in modern conditions. The instance of such a frustration which many years I had the opportunity to watch in detail was the case of an American building contractor who, after looking at the prices and rents of houses, the wages and the prices of building materials in a

European city, felt convinced that he could provide better houses at a considerably lower price and still make a substantial profit. What made him in the end give up his plan was that building regulations, trade union rules, cartellized prices of special building equipment and the cost of the bureaucratic procedure of obtaining all the required permissions and approvals precluded the economies in production on which he had based his calculations. I cannot say now whether the obstacles raised directly by government or those due to its toleration of restrictive practices or producers and trade unions were more decisive. What was obvious was that the reason why well-tried possibilities of reducing the costs of houses could not be applied were that those who knew how to use them were not allowed to do so.

6 It deserves observation that an economy in which it is easy to make large profits rapidly, although it is one in which there exist possibilities of rapid growth because there is much that can be quickly remedied, is one which almost certainly has been in a very unsatisfactory state and where the aim of exploiting the obvious opportunities will soon be achieved. This shows, incidentally, how absurd it is to judge relative performance by rate of growth, which is as often as not evidence of past neglect rather than of present achievement. In many respects it is easier and not more difficult for an undeveloped country to grow rapidly once an appropriate framework has been secured.

7 Even the statement of the problem as one of utilizing knowledge dispersed among hundreds of thousands of individuals still over-simplifies its character. It is not merely a task of utilizing information about particular concrete facts which the individuals already possess, but one of using their abilities of discovering such facts as will be relevant to their purposes in the particular situation. This is the reason why all the information accessible to (rather than already possessed by) the individuals can never be put at the disposal of some other agency but can be used only if those who know where the relevant information is to be found are called upon to make the decisions. Every person will discover what he knows or can find out only when faced with a problem where this will help, but can never pass on all the knowledge he commands and still less all the knowledge he knows how to acquire if needed by somebody else.

8 Cf. W. Mieth, 'Unsicherheitsbereiche beim wirtschafts-

politischen Sachurteil als Quelle volkswirtschaftlicher Vorurteile' in W. Strzelewicz (ed.), *Das Vorurteil als Bildungsbarriere* (Göttingen, 1965), p. 192.

9 This has been repeatedly emphasized by Milton Friedman, see, for example, his *Capitalism and Freedom* (Chicago, 1962).

10 W. L. Letwin, *Law and Economic Policy in America* (New York, 1965), p. 281.

11 The *Gesetz gegen Wettbewerbsbeschränkungen* of 27 July 1957.

12 On all this and the issues discussed in the following paragraphs see Mancur Olson Jr, *The Logic of Collective Action* (Harvard University Press, 1933).

13 Gunnar Myrdal, *An International Economy* (New York, 1956), and J. K. Galbraith, *The Affluent Society* (Boston, 1969).

14 J. K. Galbraith, *op. cit.*

15 Mancur Olson Jr, *op. cit.*

CHAPTER SIXTEEN THE MISCARRIAGE OF THE DEMOCRATIC IDEAL: A RECAPITULATION

* Count Axel Oxenstjerna (1583–1654) in a letter to his son, 1648: 'Dost thou not know, my son, with how little wisdom the world is governed?' Since much of the argument leading to the proposal offered in the next chapter was written, and in part also published, and therefore seen by many readers, a long time ago, I insert here a brief summary in which I believe I have succeeded quite recently in restating the chief points more succinctly. It is an only slightly revised version of an outline published in *Encounter* for March 1978.

1 House of Commons, 17 May 1977. There would in fact be no need for a catalogue of protected rights but merely of a single restriction of all governmental powers that no coercion was permissible except to enforce obedience to laws as defined before. That would include all the recognized fundamental rights and more.

CHAPTER SEVENTEEN A MODEL CONSTITUTION

* David Hume, *Essays*, Part II, Essay XVI, 'The Idea of a Perfect Commonwealth'.

1 The suggestion for the reconstruction of the representative

assemblies has by now occupied me over a long period and I have sketched it in writing on numerous earlier occasions. The first, I believe, was a talk on 'New Nations and the Problem of Power' in the *Listener*, no. 64, London, 10 November 1960. See also 'Libertad bayo la Ley' in *Orientacion Economica*, Caracas, April 1962; 'Recht, Gesetz und Wirtschaftsfreiheit', *Hundert Jahre Industrie – und Handelskammer zu Dortmund 1863–1963* (Dortmund, 1963; reprinted in the *Frankfurter Allgemeine Zeitung* 1/2 May 1963, and in my *Freiburger Studien* (Tübingen, 1969)); 'The Principles of a Liberal Social Order', *Il Politico*, December 1966, and reprinted in *Studies in Philosophy, Politics and Economics* (London and Chicago, 1967); 'Die Anschauungen der Mehrheit und die zeitgenössische Demokratie', *Ordo* 15/16 (Düsseldorf, 1963); 'The Constitution of a Liberal State', *Il Politico* 31, 1967; *The Confusion of Language in Political Thought* (Institute of Economic Affairs, London, 1968); and *Economic Freedom and Representative Government* (Institute of Economic Affairs, London, 1973). Most of the later ones are reprinted in my *New Studies in Philosophy, Politics, Economics and the History of Ideas* (London and Chicago, 1977). The latest statement is in *Three Lectures on Democracy, Justice and Socialism* (Sydney, 1977), also available in German, Spanish and Portuguese translations.

2 Z. Giacommetti, *Der Freiheitskatalog als Kodifikation der Freiheit* (Zürich, 1955).

3 Cf. A. R. W. Harris, 'Law Making at Athens at the End of the Fifth Century B.C.', *Journal of Hellenic Studies*, 1955, and further references given there.

4 E. G. Philip Hunton, *A Treatise on Monarchy* (London, 1643), p. 5.

5 J. S. Mill, *Considerations on Representative Government* (London, 1861), ch. 5.

6 While for the purposes of legislation a division of the assembly on party lines is altogether undesirable, for the purpose of government a two-party system is obviously desirable. There is, therefore, in neither instance a case for proportional representation, the general arguments against which have been powerfully marshalled in a work which, because of the date of its publication, has not received the attention it deserves: F. A. Hermens, *Democracy or Anarchy* (Notre Dame, Ind., 1941).

7 Carl Schmitt, 'Soziologie des Souverainitätsbegriffes und

politische Theologie' in M Palyi (ed.), *Hauptprobleme der Soziologie, Erinnerungsgabe für Max Weber*, (Munich, 1923), II, p. 5.

8 See my *The Constitution of Liberty* (London and Chicago, 1960), chapter 20.

CHAPTER EIGHTEEN THE CONTAINMENT OF POWER
AND THE DETHRONMENT OF POLITICS

* The quotation at the head of the chapter is translated from the original German version of Albert Schweitzer, *Kultur und Ethik, Kulturphilosophie*, vol. 2 (Bern, 1923), p. xix. In the English translation, published under the title *Civilization and Ethics* (London, 1923), the corresponding passage will be found on p. xviii.

1 Cf. K. R. Popper, *The Open Society and its Enemies* (5th edn., London, 1974), vol. I, p. 124:

> For we may distinguish two main types of government. The first type consists of governments of which we can get rid without bloodshed – for example, by way of general elections; that is to say, the social institutions provide means by which the rulers may be dismissed by the ruled, and the social traditions ensure that these institutions will not easily be destroyed by those who are in power. The second type consists of governments which the ruled cannot get rid of except by way of a successful revolution – that is to say, in most cases not at all. I suggest the term 'democracy' as a short-hand label for a government of the first type, and the term 'tyranny' or 'dictatorship' for the second. This, I believe, corresponds to traditional usage.

In connection with what follows concerning the negative character of the highest political values compare also K. R. Popper's *Conjectures and Refutations* (2nd edn., London, 1965), p. 230.

2 John Dewey, 'Liberty and social control', *Social Frontier*, November 1935, and cf. the fuller comments in my *The Constitution of Liberty*, note 21 to chapter 1.

3 Morris Ginsberg in W. Ebenstein (ed.), *Modern Political Thought: The Great Issues* (New York, 1960).

4 David Miller, *Social Justice* (Oxford, 1976), p. 17. Cf. also M. Duverger, *The Idea of Politics* (Indianapolis, 1966), p 171: 'The definition of justice . . . nearly always centers on the dis-

tribution of wealth and social advantages.' One begins to wonder whether these writers have ever heard of John Locke or David Hume or even of Aristotle. See, e.g., John Locke, *Essays Concerning Human Understanding*, IV, iii, 18:

> Where there is no property there is no injustice, is a proposition as certain as any demonstration in Euclid: for the idea of property being a right to anything, and the idea to which the name of 'injustice' is given being the invasion or violation of that right, it is evident that these ideas, being thus established, and these names annexed to them, I can as certainly know the proposition to be true, as that a triangle has three angles equal to two right ones.

5 D. Miller, *op. cit.*, p. 23.

6 J. A. Schumpeter, *History of Economic Analysis* (New York, 1954), p. 394: 'As a supreme, if unintended compliment, the enemies of the system of private enterprise have thought it wise to appropriate its label.'

7 As a friend recently observed to me, if we count all persons who believe in what they call 'social justice' socialists, as we ought, because what they mean by it could be achieved only by the use of governmental power, we must admit that probably something like 90 per cent of the population of the Western democracies are today socialists.

8 David Hume, *A Treatise of Human Nature*, book III, section 2, ed. L. A. Selby-Bigge (Oxford, 1958), p. 495.

9 The literary part of that magazine is full of constant erroneous references to the supposed injustice of our economic order. What, for instance, is supposed to be the causal connection when a little earlier (16 May 1977) a television reviewer speaks about 'how much misery it cost to maintain those ducal shrubs in such well shaved elegance'.

10 In connection with the preceding section see generally my brochure on *The Confusion of Language in Political Thought* (Occasional Paper 20 of the Institute of Economic Affairs, London, 1968).

11 This weakness of the government of an omnipotent democracy was very clearly seen by the extraordinary German student of politics, Carl Schmitt, who in the 1920s probably understood the character of the developing form of government better than most people and then regularly came down on what to me

appears both morally and intellectually the wrong side. Cf. e.g., in his essay on 'Legalität und Legitimität' of 1932 (reprinted in his *Verfassungsrechtliche Aufsätze*, Berlin, 1958, p. 342):

Ein pluralistischer Parteienstaat wird nicht aus Stärke und Kraft, sondern aus Schwäche 'total'; er interveniert in alle Lebensgebiete, weil er die Ansprüche aller Interessenten erfüllen muss. Insbesondere muss er sich in das Gebiet der bisher staatsfreien Wirtschaft begeben, auch wenn er dort auf jede Leitung und politischen Einfluss verzichtet.

Many of these important conclusions were already stated in 1926 in his *Die geistesgeschichtliche Lage des Parlamentarismus*.

12 See above, p. 38.

13 Harvard University Press, 1965. Cf. also my introduction to the German translation of this book produced by the members of my Freiburg seminar and published as *Die Logik des kollektiven Handelns* (Tübingen, 1968).

14 There are of course many problems arising out of such situations which were intensively discussed by nineteenth-century English liberals in connection with their struggle against the laws of settlement. Much wisdom on these matters will still be found in Edwin Cannan, *The History of Local Rates in England* (2nd edn, London, 1912).

One of the most difficult problems here is perhaps how the desire to attract or retain residents should and can be combined with a freedom of choice whom to accept and whom to reject as a member of a particular community. Freedom of migration is one of the widely accepted and wholly admirable principles of liberalism. But should this generally give the stranger a right to settle down in a community in which he is not welcome? Has he a claim to be given a job or be sold a house if no resident is willing to do so? He clearly should be entitled to accept a job or buy a house if offered to him. But have the individual inhabitants a duty to offer either to him? Or ought it to be an offence if they voluntarily agree not to do so? Swiss and Tyrolese villages have a way of keeping out strangers which neither infringe nor rely on any law. Is this anti-liberal or morally justified? For established old communities I have no certain answers to these questions. But future developments, as I have suggested in *The Constitution of Liberty*, pp. 349–53, seem to me possible on the lines of estate developments with a division of property rights between a freehold ownership of the estate by a corporation and very long leases of the plot owners assuring them of a certain protection against undesirable developments of the neighbourhood. Such a corporation should of course be free to decide to whom it is willing to lease plots.

15 Cf. the passage from J. A. Schumpeter quoted above, chapter 12, note 16.

16 *Denationalization of Money – The Argument Refined* (2nd extended edn, Institute of Economic Affairs, London, 1978).

17 See above pp. 133 ff.

18 Torgny F. Segerstedt, 'Wandel der Gesellschaft', *Bild der Wissenschaft*, VI/5, May 1969.

19 This was the title I had intended to give to a work I had planned in 1939, in which a part on the 'Hubris of Reason' was to be followed by one on 'The Nemesis of the Planned Society'. Only a fragment of this plan was ever carried out and the parts written published first in *Economica* 1941–5 and then reprinted in a volume entitled *The Counter-Revolution of Science* (Chicago, 1952), to the German translation of which I later gave the title *Missbrauch und Verfall der Vernunft* (Frankfurt, 1959) when it became clear that I would never complete it according to the original plan. *The Road to Serfdom* (London and Chicago, 1944) was an advance sketch of what I had intended to make the second part. But it has taken me forty years to think through the original idea.

EPILOGUE: THE THREE SOURCES OF HUMAN VALUES

* Although originally conceived as a Postscript to this volume, I found it easier to write the following pages out as a lecture that was delivered as the Hobhouse Lecture at the London School of Economics on 17 May 1978. In order not further to delay publication of the last volume of this work, I then decided to include it here in the form it was given as a lecture. The lecture has also been published separately by the London School of Economics in 1978.

** J. W. Goethe, *Dichtung und Wahrheit*, book XIV. The date of this passage is 1774.

1 New York, 1977 and London, 1978.

2 See his monumental *Sociobiology, A New Synthesis* (Cambridge, Mass., 1975 and London, 1976) and for a more popular

exposition David P. Barash, *Sociobiology and Behavior* (New York etc., 1977).

3 G. E. Pugh, *op. cit.*, pp. 33 and 341; cf. also on the former page the statement: 'primary values determine what types of secondary criteria the individual will be motivated to adopt.'

4 Huxley's path-breaking work on *The Courtship of the Great Crested Grebe* of 1914 was reprinted (London, 1968) with a foreword by Desmond Morris.

5 Best known of K. Z. Lorenz's works is *King Solomon's Ring* (London, 1952).

6 N. Tinbergen *The Study of Instinct* (Oxford, 1951).

7 See especially I. Eibl-Eibesfeld, *Ethology* (2nd edn, New York, 1975) and particularly Wolfgang Wickler, and Uta Seibt, *Das Prinzip Eigennutz* (Hamburg, 1977), not yet known to me when the text of this book was completed. The original and not sufficiently appreciated works of Robert Ardrey, especially the more recent ones, *The Territorial Imperative*, (London and New York, 1966), and *The Social Contract* (London and New York, 1970) should also be mentioned.

8 See, e.g., also Desmond Morris, *The Naked Ape* (London, 1967), Introduction: '[Man's] old impulses have been with him for millions of years, his new ones only a few thousand at the most.' The transmission of learnt rules probably goes back some hundred thousand years!

9 See my essay 'Dr Bernard Mandeville', *Proceedings of the British Academy*, LII, 1967 and reprinted in *New Studies in Philosophy, Politics, Economics and the History of Ideas* (London and Chicago, 1978).

10 As I had occasion to point out with reference to C. D. Darlington, *The Evolution of Man and Society* (London, 1969), in *Encounter*, February 1971, reprinted in *New Studies*, etc. as note 9 above.

11 L. T. Hobhouse, *Morals in Evolution* (London, 1906) and M. Ginsberg, *On the Diversity of Morals* (London, 1956).

12 J. S. Huxley, *Evolutionary Ethics* (London, 1943).

13 A. M. Carr Saunders, *The Population Problem, A Study in Human Evolution* (Oxford, 1922).

14 C. H. Waddington, *The Ethical Animal* (London, 1960).

15 G. G. Simpson, *The Meaning of Evolution* (Yale University Press, 1949) and T. H. Dobzhansky, *Mankind Evolving: The Evolution of the Human Species* (Yale University Press, 1962)

and 'Ethics and values in biological and cultural evolution', *Zygon*, 8, 1973. See also Stephen C. Pepper, *The Sources of Value* (University of California Press, 1953), pp. 640–56.

16 D. T. Campbell, 'Variation and selective retention in socio-cultural evolution' in H. R. Barringer, G. I. Blankstein and R. W. Mack (eds), *Social Change in Developing Areas: A reinterpretation of Evolutionary Theory* (Cambridge, Mass., 1965); 'Social attitudes and other acquired behavior dispositions' in S. Koch (ed.), *Psychology: A Study of a Science*, vol. 6, *Investigations of Man as Socius* (New York, 1963).

17 My long-growing conviction that it was Cartesian influence which has been the chief obstacle to a better understanding of the self-ordering processes of enduring complex structures has been unexpectedly confirmed by the report of a French biologist that it was Cartesian rationalism which produced a 'persistent opposition' to Darwinian evolution in France. See Ernest Boesiger, 'Evolutionary theory after Lamarck', in F. J. Ayala and T. Dobzhansky (eds), *Studies in the Philosophy of Biology* (London, 1974), p. 21.

18 The thesis that culture created man has been first stated by L. A. White in his *The Science of Culture* (New York, 1949) and *The Evolution of Culture* (New York, 1959), but spoilt by his belief in 'laws of evolution'. A belief in selective evolution has, however, nothing to do with a belief in laws of evolution. It postulates merely the operation of a mechanism the results of which depend wholly on the unknown marginal conditions in which it operates. I do not believe there are any laws of evolution. Laws make prediction possible, but the effect of the process of selection depends always on unforeseeable circumstances.

19 See my lecture on 'Dr Bernard Mandeville' quoted in note 9 above, p. 253–4 of the reprint, and *Law, Legislation and Liberty*, vol. 1, p. 20.

20 Cf. Richard Thurnwald (a well known anthropologist and a former student of the economist Carl Menger), 'Zur Kritik der Gesellschaftsbiologie', *Archiv für Sozialwissenschaften*, 52, 1924, and 'Die Gesaltung der Wirtschaftsentwicklung aus ihren Anfängen heraus' in *Die Hauptprobleme der Soziologie, Erinnerungsgabe für Max Weber* (Tübingen, 1923), who speaks of *Siebung*, in contrast to biological selection, though he applies it only to the selection of individuals, not of institutions.

21 See the reference given in *Law, Legislation and Liberty*, vol. 1, p. 163, note 7.

22 I find it difficult to believe, as is usually said, that Sir Alister Hardy in his illuminating book *The Living Stream* (London, 1966) was the first to point out this reverse effect of cultural on biological evolution. But if this should be correct, it would represent a major breakthrough of decisive importance.

23 E. H. Gombrich, *In Search of Cultural History* (Oxford, 1969), p. 4, and cf. Clifford Geertz, *The Interpretation of Cultures* (New York, 1973), p. 44: 'Man is precisely the animal most desperately dependent on much extra-genetic, outside-the-skin control mechanisms, such cultural programs, for organizing behavior'; and *ibid.*, p. 49: 'there is no such thing as a human nature independent of culture. . . . our central nervous system . . . grew up in great part in interaction with culture. . . . We are, in sum, incomplete or unfinished animal who complete or finish ourselves through culture.'

24 See B. J. Whorf, *Language, Truth, and Reality, Selected Writings*, ed. J. B. Carroll (Cambridge, Mass., 1956), and E. Sapir, *Language: an Introduction to the Study of Speech* (New York, 1921); and *Selected writings in Language, Culture and Personality*, ed. D. Mandelbaum (Berkeley and Los Angeles, 1949); as well as F. B. Lenneberg, *Biological Foundations of Language* (New York, 1967).

25 The genetic primacy of rules of conduct of course does not mean, as behaviourists seem to believe, that *we* can still reduce the pattern of the world which now guide our behaviour to rules of conduct. If the guides to conduct are hierarchies of classification of complexes of stimuli which affect our ongoing mental processes so as to put a particular behaviour pattern into effect, we would still have to explain most of what we call mental processes before we could predict behavioural reactions.

26 My colleagues in the social sciences generally find my study on *The Sensory Order. An inquiry into the Foundations of Theoretical Psychology* (London and Chicago, 1952) uninteresting or indigestible. But the work on it has helped me greatly to clear my mind on much that is very relevant to social theory. My conception of evolution, of a spontaneous order and of the methods and limits of our endeavours to explain complex phenomena have been formed largely in the course of the work on that book. As I was using the work I had done in my student days on

theoretical psychology in forming my views on the methodology of the social science, so the working out of my earlier ideas on psychology with the help of what I had learnt in the social science helped me greatly in all my later scientific development. It involved the sort of radical departure from received thinking of which one is more capable at the age of 21 than later, but which, even, though years later, when I published them they received a respectful but not very comprehending welcome by the psychologists. Another 25 years later psychologists seem to discover the book (see W. B. Weimer and D. S. Palermo (eds), *Cognition and Symbolic Processes*, vol. II (New York, 1978)), but I certainly least expected to be discovered by the behaviourists. But see now Rosemary Agonito, 'Hayek revisited: Mind as a process of classification' in *Behaviorism. A Forum for Critical Discussion*, III/2 (University of Nevada, 1975).

27 See most recently Karl R. Popper and John C. Eccles, *The Self and Its Brain. An Argument for Interactionism* (Berlin, New York and London, 1977).

28 Cf. particularly Carsten Bresch, *Zwischenstufe Leben. Evolution ohne Ziel?* (Munich, 1977) and M. Eigen and R. Winkler, *Das Spiel, Naturgesetze steuern den Zufall*, (Munich, 1975).

29 See my lecture on 'Dr Bernard Mandeville' quoted in note 9 above, p. 250 of the reprint.

30 Donald T. Campbell, 'Downward Causation in Hierarchically Organised Biological Systems' in F. J. Ayala and T. Dobzhansky as quoted in note 17 above. See also Karl Popper and John C. Eccles as quoted in note 27 above.

31 On the limited applicability of the concept of law in the explanation of complex self-maintaining structures see the postscript to my article on 'The Theory of Complex Phenomena' in my *Studies in Philosophy, Politics and Economics* (London and Chicago, 1967), pp. 40 ff.

32 *Cf.* Garret Hardin, 'The cybernetics of competition', in P. Shepard and D. McKinley, *The Subversive Science: Essays towards an Ecology of Man* (Boston, 1969).

33 Ludwig von Bertalanffy, *General System Theory: Foundations, Development, Applications* (New York, 1969) and cf. H. von Foerster, and G. W. Zopf Jr (eds), *Principles of Self-Organization* (New York, 1962); G. J. Klir (ed.), *Trends in General System Theory* (New York, 1972); and G. Nicolis and I. Prigogine, *Self-organization in Nonequilibrium Systems* (New York, 1977).

34 See Colin Cherry, *On Human Communication* (New York, 1961), and Noam Chomsky, *Syntactic Structures* (The Hague, 1957).

35 Roger Williams, *You are Extraordinary* (New York, 1967), pp. 26 and 37. People who study statistics, even such very important statistical subjects as demography, do not study society. Society is a structure, not a mass phenomenon, and all its characteristic attributes are those of a constantly changing order or system, and of these orders or system we do not have a sufficient number of specimens to treat the behaviour of the wholes statistically. The belief that within these structures constant quantitative relationships can be discovered by observing the behaviour of particular aggregates or averages is today the worst obstacle to a real understanding of those complex phenomena of which we can study only a few instances. The problems with which the explanation of these structures have to deal have nothing to do with the law of large numbers.

Real masters of the subject have often seen this. See, e.g., G. Udney Yule, *British Journal of Psychology*, XII, 1921/2, p. 107: 'Failing the possibility of measuring that which you desire, the lust for measurement may, for instance, merely result in your measuring something else – and perhaps forgetting the difference – or in ignoring some things merely because they cannot be measured.'

Unfortunately, techniques of research can be readily learnt, and the facility with them lead to teaching positions, by men who understand little of the subject investigated, and their work is then often mistaken for science. But without a clear conception of the problems the state of theory raises, empirical work is usually a waste of time and resources.

The childish attempts to provide a basis for 'just' action by measuring the relative utilities or satisfactions of different persons simply cannot be taken seriously. To show that these efforts are just so much nonsense would require entering into somewhat abstruse argument for which this is not the place. But most economists seem to begin to see that the whole of the so-called 'welfare economics', which pretends to base its arguments on inter-personal comparisons of ascertainable utilities, lacks all scientific foundation. The fact that most of us believe that they can judge which of the several needs of two or more known persons are more important, does not prove either that there is

any objective basis for this, nor that we can form such a conceptions about people whom we do not know individually. The
idea of basing coercive actions by government on such fantasies
is clearly an absurdity.

36 D. S. Shwayder, *The Stratification of Behaviour* (London, 1965)
ought to contain much helpful information on this subject of
which I have not yet been able to make use.

37 Although the conception of group selection may now not appear
as important as it had been thought after its introduction by
Sewall Wright in 'Tempo and Mode in Evolution: A Critical
Review', *Ecology*, 26, 1945, and V. C. Wynne-Edwards, *Animal
Dispersion in Relation to Social Behaviour* (Edinburgh, 1966) –
cf. E. O. Wilson, *op. cit.* pp. 106–12, 309–16, and George C.
Williams, *Adaptation and Natural Selection, A Critique of Some
Current Evolutionary Thought* (Princeton, 1966) and, edited by
the same, *Group Selection* (Chicago/New York, 1976), – there
can be no doubt that it is of the greatest importance for cultural
evolution.

38 G. E. Pugh, *op. cit.*, p. 267, and see now Glynn Isaac, 'The
Food-sharing Behaviour of Protohuman Hominids', *Scientific
American*, April 1978.

39 This was, of course, not always a peaceful process. It is very
likely that in the course of this development a wealthier urban
and commercial population often imposed upon larger rural
populations a law which was still contrary to the mores of the
latter, just as after the conquest by a military band a military
land-owning aristocracy imposed in feudal ages upon the urban
population a law which had survived from a more primitive stage
of economic evolution. This is also one form of the process by
which the more powerfully structured society, which can attract
individuals by the lures it has to offer in the form of spoils, may
displace a more highly civilized one.

40 K. R. Popper, *The Open Society and its Enemies* (5th edn,
London, 1966), vol. I, pp. 174–6.

41 The nostalgic character of these longings has been particularly
well described by Bertrand de Jouvenel in the passage quoted
from his *Sovereignty* (Chicago, 1957, p. 136), *Law, Legislation
and Liberty*, vol. 2, p. 182.

42 In view of the latest trick of the Left to turn the old liberal
tradition of human rights in the sense of limits to the powers both
of government and of other persons over the individual into

positive claims for particular benefits (like the 'freedom from want' invented by the greatest of modern demagogues) it should be stressed here that in a society of free men the goals of collective action can always only aim to provide opportunities for unknown people, means of which anyone can avail himself for his purposes, but no concrete national goals which anyone is obliged to serve. The aim of policy should be to give all a better chance to find a position which in turn gives each a good chance of achieving his ends than they would otherwise have.

43 *Cf.* David Hume, *A Treatise of Human Nature*, III, ii, ed. L. A. Selby-Bigge, p. 501: 'There is nothing which touches us more nearly than our reputation, and nothing on which our reputation more depends than our conduct with relation to the property of others.' This is perhaps as good a place as any other to point out that our present understanding of the evolutionary deter-mination of the economic order is in a great measure due to a seminal study of Armen Alchian, 'Uncertainty, Evolution and Economics Theory', *Journal of Political Economy*, 58, 1950 and since reprinted in an improved form in the author's *Economic Forces at Work* (Indianapolis, 1977). The conception has now widely spread beyond the circle in which it was initiated and a good survey of the further discussion of these problems and a very full bibliography will be found in the important and scho-larly work by Jochem Roepke, *Die Strategie der Innovation* (Tübingen, 1977), which I have not yet been able fully to digest.

44 Long before Calvin the Italian and Dutch commercial towns had practised and later the Spanish schoolmen codified the rules which made the modern market economy possible. See in this connection particularly H. M. Robertson, *Aspects of the Rise of Economic Individualism* (Cambridge, 1933), a book which, if it had not appeared at a time when it practically remained unknown in Germany, should have disposed once and for all of the Weberian myth of the Protestant source of capitalist ethics. He shows that if any religious influences were at work, it was much more the Jesuits than the Calvinists who assisted the rise of the 'capitalist spirit'.

45 Jean Baechler, *The Origin of Capitalism*, trans. Barry Cooper (Oxford, 1975), p. 77 (italics in original).

46 Cf. M. I. Finley, *The Ancient Economy* (London, 1975), pp. 28–9, and 'Between Slavery and Freedom', *Comparative Studies in Society and History*, 6, 1964.

47 See the provision of the ancient Cretan constitution quoted as a motto at the head of chapter 5 of vol. 1 of *Law, Legislation and Liberty*.

48 If rules are adopted, not because their specific effects are understood, but because those groups who practice them are successful, it is not surprising that in primitive society magic and ritual dominate. The condition of admission to the group was to accept all its rules, though few understood what depended on the observation of any particular one. There was merely one accepted way of doing things with little effort to distinguish between effectiveness and moral desirability. If there is anything in which history has almost wholly failed it is in explaining the changes of causes of morals, among which preaching was probably the least important, and which may have been one of the most important factors determining the course of human evolution. Though present morals evolved by selection, this evolution was not made possible by a licence to experiment but on the contrary by strict restraints which made changes of the whole system impossible and granted tolerance to the breaker of accepted rules, who may have turned out a pioneer, only when he did so at his own risk and had earned such licence by his strict observation of most rules which alone could gain him the esteem which legitimized experimentation in a particular direction. The supreme superstition that the social order is created by government is of course just a flagrant manifestation of the constructivistic error.

49 See my lecture on 'Rechtsordnung und Handelnsordnung' in *Zur Einheit der Rechts- und Staatswissenschaften*, ed. E. Streissler, (Karlsruhe, 1967) and reprinted in my *Freiburger Studien* (Tübingen, 1969).

50 The idea is of course the same as what Karl Popper calls 'piecemeal social engineering' (*The Open Society*, etc., as quoted in note 40 above, vol. 2, p. 222), on which I wholly agree, though I still dislike the particular expression.

51 Cf. Ludwig von Mises, *Theory and History* (Yale University Press, 1957) p. 54:

> The ultimate yardstick of justice is conduciveness to the preservation of social co-operation. Conduct suited to preserve social co-operation is just, conduct detrimental to the preservation of society is unjust. There cannot be any

question of organizing society according to the postulate of an arbitrary preconceived idea of justice. The problem is to organize society for the best possible realization of those ends which men want to attain by social co-operation. Social utility is the only standard of justice. It is the sole guide of legislation.

Though this is more rationalistically formulated than I would care to do, it clearly expresses an essential idea. But Mises was of course a rationalist utilitarian in which direction, for reasons given, I cannot follow him.

52 This confusion stems in modern times at least from Emile Durkheim, whose celebrated work *The Division of Labour in Society* (trans. George Simpson, London, 1933, see especially p. 228) shows no comprehension of the manner in which rules of conduct bring about a division of labour and who tends, like the sociobiologist, to call all action 'altruistic' which benefits others, whether the acting person intends or even knows this. But compare the sensible position in the textbook *Evolution* by T. Dobzhansky, F. J. Ayala, G. L. Stebbins and J. W. Valentine (San Francisco, 1977), pp. 456 ff.:

Certain kinds of behavior found in animals would be ethical or altruistic, and others unethical and egotistic, *if these behaviors were exhibited by men.* . . . unlike any other species, every human generation inherits and also transmits a body of knowledge, customs, and beliefs that are not coded in the genes. . . . the mode of transmission is quite unlike that of biological heredity. . . . For perhaps as long as two million years cultural changes were increasingly preponderant over genetic ones;

also the passage quoted by them in this context from G. G. Simpson, *This View of Life* (New York, 1964):

It is nonsensical to speak of ethics in connection with any animal other than man. . . . There is really no point in discussing ethics, indeed one might say that the concept of ethics is meaningless, unless the following conditions exist: (a) There are alternative modes of action; (b) man is capable of judging the alternatives in ethical terms; and (c) he is free to choose what he judges to be ethically good. Beyond that, it bears repeating that the evolutionary functioning of ethics depends on man's capacity, unique at least in degree, of predicting the results of his actions.

53 See E. O. Wilson, *op. cit.*, p. 117:

> When a person (or animal) increases the fitness of another of the species at the expense of his own fitness, he can be said to have performed an act of *altruism*. Self-sacrifice for the benefit of offspring is altruism in the conventional but not in the strict genetic sense, because individual fitness is measured by the number of surviving offspring. But self-sacrifice on behalf of second cousins is true altruism on both levels, and when directed at total strangers such abnegating behaviour is so surprising (that is, 'noble') as to demand some kind of theoretical explanation.

Cf. also D. P. Barash, *op. cit.*, who discovers even 'altruistic viruses' (p. 77) and R. Trivers, 'The evolution of reciprocal altruism', *Q. Rev. Biol*, 46, 1971.

54 If today the preservation of the present order of the market economy depends, as Daniel Bell and Irving Kristol (eds), *Capitalism Today* (New York, 1970) in effect argue, that the people rationally understand that certain rules are indispensible to preserve the social division of labour, it may well be doomed. It will always be only a small part of the population who will take the trouble to do so, and the only persons who could teach the people, the intellectuals who write and teach for the general public, certainly rarely make an attempt to do so.

55 See Lionel C. Robbins, *An Essay on the Nature and Significance of Economic Science* (London, 1932).

56 It is perhaps sad that culture is inseparable from progress, but the same forces which maintain culture also drive us into progress. What is true of economics is also true of culture generally: it cannot remain stationary and when it stagnates it soon declines.

57 See particularly H. B. Acton, *The Morals of the Market* (London, 1971).

58 Ronald Dworkin, *Taking Rights Seriously* (London, 1977), p. 180

59 See Roger J. Williams, *Free and Unequal: The Biological Basis of Individual Liberty* (University of Texas Press, 1953), pp. 23 and 70; also J. B. S. Haldane, *The Inequality of Men* (London, 1932), P. B. Medawar, *The Uniqueness of the Individual* (Lon-

don, 1957), and H. J. Eysenck, *The Inequality of Man* (London, 1973).

60 The problem had certainly occupied me for some time before I first used the phrase in print in the lecture on 'The Moral Element in Free Enterprise' (1961), reprinted in my *Studies in Philosophy, etc.* (London and Chicago, 1967), p. 232.

61 On the nineteenth-century history of scientism and the associated views which I now prefer to call constructivism see my *The Counter-Revolution of Science. Studies in the Abuse of Reason* (Chicago, 1952).

62 See vol. 2, chapter 8, of *Law, Legislation and Liberty*. The contrast between legal positivism and its opposite, 'the classical theories of Natural law' which, in the definition of H. L. A. Hart (*The Concept of Law*, Oxford University Press, 1961, p. 182), hold 'that there are certain principles of human conduct, *awaiting discovery by human reason,* with which man-made law must conform to be valid' (italics added), is indeed one of the clearest instances of the false dichotomy between 'natural' and 'artificial'. Law is, of course, neither an unalterable fact of nature, nor a product of intellectual design, but the result of a process of evolution in which a system of rules developed in constant interaction with a changing order of human actions which is distinct from it.

63 Sigmund Freud, *Civilisation and its Discontents* (London, 1957), and cf. Richard La Pierre, *The Freudian Ethic* (New York, 1959). If for a life-long student of the theory of money who had fought his intellectual struggles with Marxism and Freudianism in the Vienna of the 1920s and had later dabbled in psychology, any evidence had still been necessary that eminent psychologists, including Sigmund Freud, could talk utter nonsense on social phenomena, it has been provided for me by the selection of some of their essays, edited by Ernest Borneman, under the title *The Psychoanalysis of Money* (New York, 1976, a translation of *Die Psychoanalyse des Geldes*, Frankfurt, 1973), which also in a great measure accounts for the close association of psychoanalysis with socialism and especially Marxism.

64 G. B. Chisholm, 'The re-establishment of a peace-time society', *Psychiatry*, vol. 6, 1946. Characteristic for the literary views of that time is also a title like Herbert Read, *To Hell with Culture. Democratic Values are New Values* (London, 1941).

65 *The Times*, 13 April 1978.

66 Donald T. Campbell, 'On the conflicts between biological and social evolution', *American Psychologist*, 30 December 1975, p. 1120.

67 *Ibid.*, p. 1121.

68 The *American Psychologist* of May 1975 carried forty pages of mostly critical reactions to Professor Campbell's lecture.

69 Apart from Thomas Szasz, *The Myth of Mental Illness* (New York, 1961), see particularly his *Law, Liberty and Psychiatry*, (New York, 1971).

70 H. J. Eysenck, *Uses and Abuses of Psychology* (London, 1953).

INDEX OF AUTHORS CITED
IN VOLUMES 1-3

Note: In this index the roman numerals indicate the volume number; the arabic number refers to the pages in the volume.

211

Lugo, J. de, I: 157; II: 179
Lykurgus, I: 81, 165
Lyons, D., II: 156

Mabbott, J. D., II: 156
McCloskey, H. J., II: 156
MacDermot, Lord, I: 179; III: 183
MacGee, J. S., III: 188
Machiavelli, N., I: 160
McIlwain, C. H., I: 145, 174; II: 154; III: 185
McNair, A. D., I: 166
Madison, J., III: 100
Maine, H. S., I: 22, 74, 107, 172; II: 168
Maitland, F. W., I: 90, 167–8
Malinowski, B., I: 173
Mandeville, B., I: 20, 22, 29, 146, 156; II: 155, 185; III: 154, 197
Mann, F. A., III: 187
Mannheim, K., II: 181
Mansfield, Lord, I: 86
Marx, K., I: 24, 57; III: 165, 170
Maupertuis, P. L. M. de, II: 155
Mayer, O., I: 164
Mayer-Maly, T. I: 157
Mayo, B., II: 164
Mazzini, G., I: 161
Medawar, P. B., III: 207
Meggers, B. J., I. 152
Meier, C., III: 185
Menger, C., I: 22, 147, 157, 161, 163, 169; II: 184; III: 198
Merk, W., II: 153
Messner, J., II: 176
Michel, H., I: 147
Mieth, W., III: 190
Mill, J., I: 129, 176; III: 178
Mill, J. S., I: 161; II: 63–4, 98, 162, 176, 183, 186, III: 112, 178, 192
Millar, J., I: 150; II: 162
Miller, D., III: 193–4
Mises, L. von, II: 175, 178, 185, 188; III: 65, 179, 188–9, 204–5
Mohl, M., II: 190
Molina, L., I: 21, 150; II: 178–9

Mommsen, T., I: 166
Montesquieu, C. de S. de, I: v, 1, 85, 107, 128–30, 147, 153, 172; II: 185
Moore, G. E., II: 19, 156
Morgenthau, H. J., I: 179
Morris, D., III: 197
Moses, III: 166
Moss, R., III: 177, 184
Müller, M., I: 153
Mumford, L., I: 148
Myrdal, G., II: 186; III: 93, 191

Napoleon, I., I: 57, 130, 175
Nawiaski, H., I: 177
Needham, J., I: 154
Needham, M., I: 175
Newman, F. W., II: 176
Nicolis, G., III: 200
Nozik, R., III: xii, 186

Oakeshott, M., II: 15; III: xii
Olbrechts-Tyteca, L., I: 171
Olson, M., III: 97, 143, 180, 184–5, 188
Osborn, H. F., I: 152
Ortega y Gasset, J., I: 156; II: 133, 146, 189
Oxenstjerna, A., III: 150

Palermo, D. S., III: 200
Paley, W., II: 19, 156, 159; III: 21, 181–2
Palmer, R. A., I: 129, 147, 154, 176; III: 179
Pantaleoni, M., II: 175, 179
Pareto, V., II: 44, 119, 168
Parrington, V. L., III: 183
Paschukanis, E., II: 181
Pasquier, C. de, II: 176
Paulus, J., I: 72, 162
Peirce, C. S., I: 153
Pepper, S. C., III: 191
Perelman, C., I: 171; II: 190
Peter, H., II: 187
Peters, R. S., I: 147
Philo of Alexandria, I: 157
Piaget, J., I: 154

213

215

Subject Index to Volumes 1–3

Prepared by Vernelia A. Crawford

Note: This index includes the titles of chapters and sections, each listed under the appropriate subject classification. The Roman numeral indicates the volume number; the Arabic number refers to the pages in the volume.

England—*contd.*
  opinion poll in, III: 54
  Parliament of, I: 85, 124–6, 168
    n.36, 173–4 n.1
  political opinion in, I: 128
  principles of, I: 60
  separation of power in, I: 85;
    III: 179 n.10
  sovereignty in, III: 2–3, 179
    n.10
  trade in, I: 65, 142, 179 n.32
  wages in, III: 95
  see also Common law
Enthropy, I: 44
Entrepreneurs, III: 76; *see
  also* Market economy
Environment
  adaptations to, I: 12; II: 4–5
  changes in, I: 103
  choice-making and, II: 132
  conditions of, II: 24
  importance of, I: 43; II: 132,
    189 n.25; III: 172
  response to, I: 18, 43–6
  use of, II: 9–11
Equality
  arbitrariness and, III: 102–3
  benefit of, I: 139–40
  change and, II: 107
  claim to, II: 63–4, 176 n.6; II:
    83, 181 n.30
  discrimination and, II: 141–2
  Great Society and, II: 180 n.28
  judgment of, II: 107
  liberty and, I: 101, 170 n.11; II:
    83, 181 n.30
  material, II: 81–4
  opportunity and, II: 129–31,
    179 n.16
  regard for, III: 142–3
  slavery and, II: 83, 181 n.30
  social justice and, II: 63,
    80–4
  standard of, II: 63–5
Essentialism, methodological, II:
  171–2 n.55
Ethics, III: 205 n.52
Ethology, I: 74–6
Eunomia, I: 156 n.9

Evolution
  abstract, I: 69
  approach to, I: 22–4, 152–3
    nn.33–4; II: 60
  biological, I: 22–4, 152–3
    nn.33–4; II: 21–2
  complex structures and, III:
    158–9
  construction and, I: 8–9
  cultural, III: 154–8, 160–2, 202
    n.37
  Darwinian, III: 198 n.17; *see
    also* Darwinians laws and, I:
    22–4, 74; II: 60
  morality and, III: 204 n.48
  political, I: 65–7
  reason and, I: 8–34, 146–54
  rules of, I: 74–6
  social theory of, I: 22–4, 152–3
    nn.33–4; II: 21–2, 30; III:
    175
Exchange. *See* Trade
Expectations
  disappointments of, I: 86–7,
    106; II: 26, 93
  fulfillment of, I: 97, 169 n.5
  group, I: 99
  judicial decisions and, I: 15–18
  legitimate, I: 98; II: 37, 93–6
  protection of, I: 101–10; II: 37,
    124–5
  reasonable, I: 102, 170 n.12; II:
    37, 170 n.12
  rules of conduct, I: 106–10
Expediency principles, I: 55–71,
  160–2; II: 44, 167 n.28
Experience
  learning from, I: 18, 115–16
  legal, I: 170–1, n.14
  result of, II: 4–5
  value in, I: 60; II: 24

Family, I: 164 n.8; II: 9–10, 36,
  131–2, 134–5, 188 n.25
Federation, function of, III: 132
Finances, I: 136–7; III: 51–4,
  60–2, 126–7, 189–90 nn.4–5
First Agreement of the People of
  1647, I: 128

223

SUBJECT INDEX—VOLUMES 1–3

Particularism—*contd.*
  individual rights, II: 101–6
  language and, I: 76–7
  means and ends, II: 14–17, 109–
    11, 114–15
  measures required, II: 65
  order and, I: 40–1, 114–15
  reason and, I: 33
  response to, I: 44
  result of action, II: 129–30
  technique of, I: 64, 108
Past, II: 120–2
Patterns, I: 30, 35–7, 40, 155 n.4
Peace
  chance for, II: 91
  conditions of, II: 109–11
  negativism and, III: 132–3
  preservation of, I: 72, 98
  price of, II: 36, 165 n.12
Pensions, III: 55, 119
Perfection, I: 163 n.3; II: 146, 191
    n.15; III: 65–75
Performing arts, II: 76–7
Physics, order in, I: 39–40, 44
Pleasure and pain, II: 18–19, 23,
    155–6 n.15
Police power, I: 135, 137–9, 178
    n.22
Policy, measure of, I: 59–65, 139–
    40
Politics
  American development of, III:
    181 n.17
  arguments in, II: 65
  bargaining in, II: 142
  economics of, III: 80–3
  education for, III: 117–19
  friend-enemy, II: 149
  power in, II: 99; III: 128–52,
    193–6
  problems in, I: 10, 147 n.6; II: 13,
    154 n.9
  realism and, I: 58–9
  social justice in, II: 65–8
  support of, II: 7, 102
  view of, III: 27
Population, I: 75, 164 n.8; II: 9–11,
    131, 188 n.24; III: 202 n.39,
    202–3 n.39

Positivism. *See* Legal positivism
Possessions, I: 167–8 n.34; II: 1,
    37–8, 155 n.14, 165–6 n.18
Post office, III: 56, 187 n.15
Poverty, II: 139–42, 177 n.8; III:
    187 n.13
Power
  arbitrary, III: 138, 146–7
  bigness and, III: 77–80
  coercive, III: 5–6
  democratic, III: 20–40, 182–5
  derivation of, III: 3–4
  division of, III: 35–8
  economic aspects of, III: 80–3
  emergency, III: 124–6, 139
  financial, III: 126–7
  kinds of, III: 80
  law-making and, III: 25–7
  limited, III: 128–30, 135, 150
  majority in, III: 76–7
  monopoly, III: 77–80
  parliamentary, III: 20–2, 183 n.5
  political, II: 99; III: 128–52,
    193–6
  representative bodies and, III:
    35–8
  separation of, III: 104
  source of, III: 33–5
  unlimited, III: 3–4, 8–13, 128–30
  see also Separation of power
Pragmatism, I: 10, 18, 147 n.5; II:
    44, 167 n.28
Predictions
  basis of, I: 106
  dangers of, I: 61–3
  elements and, I: 42
  future and, I: 24, 42, 60–5, 106,
    115–18
  judicial decisions and, I: 115–18
  particular events and, I: 16
  result of, II: 4
Prejudice, II: 160 n.3, II: 77, 145,
    191 n.13; III: 77–8
Pressure groups, III: 13–17, 93–7,
    128–9, 143–5
Price mechanism
  competitive, III: 66–7
  conflicts of, II: 80, 116–20, 181
    n.29

Price mechanism—*contd.*
  determination of, I: 21, 141; II: 71-8, 125; III: 94-5
  discrimination, III: 85-6
  effect of, II: 71, 73-4
  function of, III: 169
  future, II: 121-2, 125
  justice and, I: 141; II: 73, 178 n.15
  marginal costs and, III: 70-4
  market economy and, III: 71-3
  monopoly and, III: 83
  natural, I: 21
  services and, II: 75-8
Principles
  application of, I: 119-20, 144
  constant, II: 159 n.4
  expediency and, I: 55-71, 160-2; II: 44, 167 n.28
  income, II: 131, 188 n.24
  legal, I: 65-7
  morals and legislation, II: 14, 154 n.10, 175*
  remunerative, II: 63, 76, 175 n.5, 179 n.21
  social justice, II: 62-5, 176 n.6
  subsidiarity, II: 153 n.6
  welfare, II: 62
Privacy and public sector, III: 41-64, 184-7
Private law
  basis of, II: 31
  displacement of, II: 87
  enforcement of, II: 34-5
  influence on, II: 46-7
  nomos, II: 31
  public and, I: 131-4, 141-3, 174-5 nn.2, 6, 177 n.19
  systems of, I: 168 n.35; II: 40
Probabilities, II: 118-19, 130
Production and consumption
  cost of, III: 74-5, 189 n.4
  factors of, II: 115-20, 141
  influence of, II: 80-5
  marginal costs and, III: 66-7, 90-3
  market economy and, II: 115-20, 141
  organization of, III: 93-4

Production/consumption—*contd.*
  self-interest in, III: 70-4
Profit and loss, II: 122, 145; III: 70-4, 83, 190 n.6
Progress, II: 146, 191 n.15; III: 168-9, 205 n.56
Prohibitions, I: 8, 146 n.1
Property
  attacks on (socialistic), I: 121
  competition for, I: 75, 164 n.8
  defence of, III: 181 n.18
  division of, III: 195 n.14
  freedom and, I: 107-8, 172 n.24
  housing and, III: 189-90 n.5, 195 n.14
  idea of, III: 194 n.4
  importance of, I: 106-8, 172 nn.22-5
  law and, I: 108, 167-8 n.34, 172 nn.22-5; II: 38, 165-6 n.18
  ownership of, I: 37, 94, 165 n.14
  private v. public, II: 47, 169 n.42
  protection of, I: 106-10; II: 35-8, 123-4, 163-4 n.9
  regulation of, I: 87, 167-8 n.34; II: 38, 165-6 n.18
  respect for, I: 106-12
  socialism and, I: 108, 121
Protectionism
  corporate, III: 82-3
  domains and, I: 106-10; II: 35-8, 123-4, 162 n.9
  expectations and, I: 101-10; II: 124-5
  freedom and, II: 101-2, 157 n.11
  fundamentals of, III: 110-11
  government, III: 48-9, 62-4, 82-3
  individual, I: 55, 101
  job status and, II: 93-6
  legal, I: 157 n.11
  monopoly and, III: 79-80, 85-6
  possessions and, II: 37-8
  property, I: 106-10; II: 35-8, 123-4, 163-4 n.9
  rules of just conduct, II: 34-42, 123-4
  vested interests in, II: 139-42
Psychiatry, III: 174-5

Valuation—*contd.*
lawyer's, I: 65–7
marginal return and, II: 118;
III: 66–7, 70–4, 90–3
market, II: 123–5
means and ends, II: 15–17
model constitution, III: 107–9
moral, II: 66–7
services, II: 76, 92–3, 179 n.20
socialist, II: 136
societal, II: 75–8
sources of, III: 153–6, 196–208
system of, II: 4–5
test of, II: 28
Vested interests, I: 3; II: 139–42
Virtue
award for, II: 175*
importance of, I: 21, 151 n.25
nature of, II: 22, 157 n.23
negative, II: 36, 162–4 n.9
Voting. *See* Elections
Vouchers, educational, III: 61

Wages, I: 141; II: 75–8, 116–17,
182 n.40; III: 95, 144; *see
also* Remunerations
Want-satisfaction, I: 108, 173*; II:
70–3, 117, 144
War
family placement and, II: 189
n.25
French, I: 53, 166 n.25
Russian, II: 103
view of, III: 132
see also Tyranny
Wealth
accumulation of, I: 167–8 n.34;
II: 165–6 n.18
claim to, II: 93–6, 98
creation of, II: 115–20
distribution of, II: 86, 114, 142,
188 nn.23–4; III: 55–6

Wealth—*contd.*
growth of, II: 131, 139
increase in, III: 53
shared, II: 89; III: 133
theory of, III: 56–8, 147–8, 207
n.63
see also Capitalism; Income
Welfare
benefits of, II: 110, 185 n.7
claims on, II: 101–6, 183–4
economics, III: 201 n.35
general, II: 1–30, 153–7
government, II: 101–6, 183–4;
III: 11
labour, III: 82
principle of, II: 62
responsibility for, II: 79
Western civilization
democracy in, I: 2–3; *see also*
Democracy
disadvantages in, I: 1
liberty in, I: 52, 157 n.11
norms of conduct in, I: 83, 166
n.25
perspective of, II: 135
rationalism in, I: 57, 161 n.9
Whigs, III: 20, 180 n.15
Will
control of, II: 41
general, II: 143, 191 n.10
influence of, II: 45–8, 51–2, 61
law and, I: 10, 82, 147 n.6; II:
13, 154 n.9
legislator, I: 91–2; II: 46, 168
n.38
limitations of, II: 157–8*, 168
n.38
opinions and, II: 13–14
power of, I: 82–5
rule and, I: 52, 157 n.13
term of, II: 13, 154 n.9
use of, I: 56, 160 n.2
World, I: 3; III: 157